Title 15
Commerce and Foreign Trade

Parts 0 to 299

Revised as of January 1, 2014

Containing a codification of documents of general applicability and future effect

As of January 1, 2014

Published by the Office of the Federal Register
National Archives and Records Administration
as a Special Edition of the Federal Register

U.S. GOVERNMENT OFFICIAL EDITION NOTICE

Legal Status and Use of Seals and Logos

The seal of the National Archives and Records Administration (NARA) authenticates the Code of Federal Regulations (CFR) as the official codification of Federal regulations established under the Federal Register Act. Under the provisions of 44 U.S.C. 1507, the contents of the CFR, a special edition of the Federal Register, shall be judicially noticed. The CFR is prima facie evidence of the original documents published in the Federal Register (44 U.S.C. 1510).

It is prohibited to use NARA's official seal and the stylized Code of Federal Regulations logo on any republication of material without the express, written permission of the Archivist of the United States or the Archivist's designee. Any person using NARA's official seals and logos in a manner inconsistent with the provisions of 36 CFR part 1200 is subject to the penalties specified in 18 U.S.C. 506, 701, and 1017.

Use of ISBN Prefix

This is the Official U.S. Government edition of this publication and is herein identified to certify its authenticity. Use of the 0–16 ISBN prefix is for U.S. Government Printing Office Official Editions only. The Superintendent of Documents of the U.S. Government Printing Office requests that any reprinted edition clearly be labeled as a copy of the authentic work with a new ISBN.

U.S. GOVERNMENT PRINTING OFFICE

U.S. Superintendent of Documents • Washington, DC 20402–0001

http://bookstore.gpo.gov

Phone: toll-free (866) 512-1800; DC area (202) 512-1800

Table of Contents

Cite this Code: CFR

To cite the regulations in this volume use title, part and section number. Thus, 15 CFR 0.735–1 *refers to title 15, part 0, section 735–1.*

Explanation

The Code of Federal Regulations is a codification of the general and permanent rules published in the Federal Register by the Executive departments and agencies of the Federal Government. The Code is divided into 50 titles which represent broad areas subject to Federal regulation. Each title is divided into chapters which usually bear the name of the issuing agency. Each chapter is further subdivided into parts covering specific regulatory areas.

Each volume of the Code is revised at least once each calendar year and issued on a quarterly basis approximately as follows:

Title 1 through Title 16 .... as of January 1
Title 17 through Title 27 .... as of April 1
Title 28 through Title 41 .... as of July 1
Title 42 through Title 50 .... as of October 1

The appropriate revision date is printed on the cover of each volume.

LEGAL STATUS

The contents of the Federal Register are required to be judicially noticed (44 U.S.C. 1507). The Code of Federal Regulations is prima facie evidence of the text of the original documents (44 U.S.C. 1510).

HOW TO USE THE CODE OF FEDERAL REGULATIONS

The Code of Federal Regulations is kept up to date by the individual issues of the Federal Register. These two publications must be used together to determine the latest version of any given rule.

To determine whether a Code volume has been amended since its revision date (in this case, January 1, 2014), consult the "List of CFR Sections Affected (LSA)," which is issued monthly, and the "Cumulative List of Parts Affected," which appears in the Reader Aids section of the daily Federal Register. These two lists will identify the Federal Register page number of the latest amendment of any given rule.

EFFECTIVE AND EXPIRATION DATES

Each volume of the Code contains amendments published in the Federal Register since the last revision of that volume of the Code. Source citations for the regulations are referred to by volume number and page number of the Federal Register and date of publication. Publication dates and effective dates are usually not the same and care must be exercised by the user in determining the actual effective date. In instances where the effective date is beyond the cut-off date for the Code a note has been inserted to reflect the future effective date. In those instances where a regulation published in the Federal Register states a date certain for expiration, an appropriate note will be inserted following the text.

OMB CONTROL NUMBERS

The Paperwork Reduction Act of 1980 (Pub. L. 96–511) requires Federal agencies to display an OMB control number with their information collection request.

Many agencies have begun publishing numerous OMB control numbers as amendments to existing regulations in the CFR. These OMB numbers are placed as close as possible to the applicable recordkeeping or reporting requirements.

PAST PROVISIONS OF THE CODE

Provisions of the Code that are no longer in force and effect as of the revision date stated on the cover of each volume are not carried. Code users may find the text of provisions in effect on any given date in the past by using the appropriate List of CFR Sections Affected (LSA). For the convenience of the reader, a "List of CFR Sections Affected" is published at the end of each CFR volume. For changes to the Code prior to the LSA listings at the end of the volume, consult previous annual editions of the LSA. For changes to the Code prior to 2001, consult the List of CFR Sections Affected compilations, published for 1949-1963, 1964-1972, 1973-1985, and 1986-2000.

"[RESERVED]" TERMINOLOGY

The term "[Reserved]" is used as a place holder within the Code of Federal Regulations. An agency may add regulatory information at a "[Reserved]" location at any time. Occasionally "[Reserved]" is used editorially to indicate that a portion of the CFR was left vacant and not accidentally dropped due to a printing or computer error.

INCORPORATION BY REFERENCE

What is incorporation by reference? Incorporation by reference was established by statute and allows Federal agencies to meet the requirement to publish regulations in the Federal Register by referring to materials already published elsewhere. For an incorporation to be valid, the Director of the Federal Register must approve it. The legal effect of incorporation by reference is that the material is treated as if it were published in full in the Federal Register (5 U.S.C. 552(a)). This material, like any other properly issued regulation, has the force of law.

What is a proper incorporation by reference? The Director of the Federal Register will approve an incorporation by reference only when the requirements of 1 CFR part 51 are met. Some of the elements on which approval is based are:

(a) The incorporation will substantially reduce the volume of material published in the Federal Register.

(b) The matter incorporated is in fact available to the extent necessary to afford fairness and uniformity in the administrative process.

(c) The incorporating document is drafted and submitted for publication in accordance with 1 CFR part 51.

What if the material incorporated by reference cannot be found? If you have any problem locating or obtaining a copy of material listed as an approved incorporation by reference, please contact the agency that issued the regulation containing that incorporation. If, after contacting the agency, you find the material is not available, please notify the Director of the Federal Register, National Archives and Records Administration, 8601 Adelphi Road, College Park, MD 20740-6001, or call 202-741-6010.

CFR INDEXES AND TABULAR GUIDES

A subject index to the Code of Federal Regulations is contained in a separate volume, revised annually as of January 1, entitled CFR INDEX AND FINDING AIDS. This volume contains the Parallel Table of Authorities and Rules. A list of CFR titles, chapters, subchapters, and parts and an alphabetical list of agencies publishing in the CFR are also included in this volume.

An index to the text of "Title 3—The President" is carried within that volume.

The Federal Register Index is issued monthly in cumulative form. This index is based on a consolidation of the "Contents" entries in the daily Federal Register.

A List of CFR Sections Affected (LSA) is published monthly, keyed to the revision dates of the 50 CFR titles.

REPUBLICATION OF MATERIAL

There are no restrictions on the republication of material appearing in the Code of Federal Regulations.

INQUIRIES

For a legal interpretation or explanation of any regulation in this volume, contact the issuing agency. The issuing agency's name appears at the top of odd-numbered pages.

For inquiries concerning CFR reference assistance, call 202–741–6000 or write to the Director, Office of the Federal Register, National Archives and Records Administration, 8601 Adelphi Road, College Park, MD 20740-6001 or e-mail *fedreg.info@nara.gov*.

SALES

The Government Printing Office (GPO) processes all sales and distribution of the CFR. For payment by credit card, call toll-free, 866-512-1800, or DC area, 202-512-1800, M-F 8 a.m. to 4 p.m. e.s.t. or fax your order to 202-512-2104, 24 hours a day. For payment by check, write to: US Government Printing Office – New Orders, P.O. Box 979050, St. Louis, MO 63197-9000.

ELECTRONIC SERVICES

The full text of the Code of Federal Regulations, the LSA (List of CFR Sections Affected), The United States Government Manual, the Federal Register, Public Laws, Public Papers of the Presidents of the United States, Compilation of Presidential Documents and the Privacy Act Compilation are available in electronic format via *www.ofr.gov*. For more information, contact the GPO Customer Contact Center, U.S. Government Printing Office. Phone 202-512-1800, or 866-512-1800 (toll-free). E-mail, *ContactCenter@gpo.gov*.

The Office of the Federal Register also offers a free service on the National Archives and Records Administration's (NARA) World Wide Web site for public law numbers, Federal Register finding aids, and related information. Connect to NARA's web site at *www.archives.gov/federal-register*.

The e-CFR is a regularly updated, unofficial editorial compilation of CFR material and Federal Register amendments, produced by the Office of the Federal Register and the Government Printing Office. It is available at *www.ecfr.gov*.

CHARLES A. BARTH,
Director,
Office of the Federal Register.
January 1, 2014.

THIS TITLE

Title 15—Commerce and Foreign Trade is composed of three volumes. The parts in these volumes are arranged in the following order: Parts 0–299, 300–799, and part 800–End. The first volume containing parts 0–299 is comprised of Subtitle A—Office of the Secretary of Commerce, Subtitle B, chapter I—Bureau of the Census, Department of Commerce, and chapter II—National Institute of Standards and Technology, Department of Commerce. The second volume containing parts 300–799 is comprised of chapter III—International Trade Administration, Department of Commerce, chapter IV—Foreign-Trade Zones Board, and chapter VII—Bureau of Industry and Security, Department of Commerce. The third volume containing part 800–End is comprised of chapter VIII—Bureau of Economic Analysis, Department of Commerce, chapter IX—National Oceanic and Atmospheric Administration, Department of Commerce, chapter XI—Technology Administration, Department of Commerce, chapter XIII—East-West Foreign Trade Board, chapter XIV—Minority Business Development Agency, chapter XX—Office of the United States Trade Representative, and chapter XXIII—National Telecommunications and Information Administration, Department of Commerce. The contents of these volumes represent all current regulations codified under this title of the CFR as of January 1, 2014.

For this volume, Cheryl E. Sirofchuck was Chief Editor. The Code of Federal Regulations publication program is under the direction of the Managing Editor, assisted by Ann Worley.

Title 15—Commerce and Foreign Trade

(This book contains parts 0 to 299)

Subtitle A—Office of the Secretary of Commerce

PART 0—EMPLOYEE RESPONSIBILITIES AND CONDUCT

AUTHORITY: 5 U.S.C. 301, 7301, 7353; 5 U.S.C. App. (Ethics in Government Act of 1978); 26 U.S.C. 7214(b); E.O. 12674, 54 FR 15159, 3 CFR 1989 Comp., p. 215, as modified by E.O. 12731, 55 FR 42547, 3 CFR 1990 Comp., p. 306; 5 CFR part 2635.

SOURCE: 32 FR 15222, Nov. 2, 1967, unless otherwise noted.

Subpart A—General Provisions

§ 0.735–1 Purpose.

The purpose of this part is to set forth Department of Commerce policy and procedure relating to employee responsibilities and conduct.

§ 0.735–2 Cross-references to ethical conduct, financial disclosure, and other applicable regulations.

Employees of the Department of Commerce should refer to the executive branch-wide Standards of Ethical Conduct at 5 CFR part 2635 and the executive branch-wide financial disclosure regulations at 5 CFR part 2634.

[68 FR 24879, May 9, 2003]

§ 0.735–3 Applicability.

This part applies to all persons included within the term "employee" as defined in § 0.735–4, except as otherwise provided in this part.

§ 0.735–4 Definitions.

For purposes of this part, except as otherwise indicated in this part:

(a) *Employee.* (1) Shall include: (i) Every officer and employee of the Department of Commerce (regardless of location), including commissioned officers of the Environmental Science Services Administration; and

(ii) Every other person who is retained, designated, appointed, or employed by a Federal officer or employee, who is engaged in the performance of a function of the Department under authority of law or an Executive act, and who is subject to the supervision of a Federal officer or employee while engaged in the performance of the duties of his position not only as to what he does but also as to how he performs his duties, regardless of whether the relationship to the Department is created by assignment, detail, contract, agreement or otherwise.

(2) Shall not include: (i) Members of the Executive Reserve except when they are serving as employees of the

Department under the circumstances described in paragraph (a)(1) of this section;

(ii) Members of crews of vessels owned or chartered to the Government and operated by or for the Maritime Administration under a General Agency Agreement; or

(iii) Any other person who is determined legally not to be an officer or employee of the United States.

(b) *Special Government employee* shall mean an employee as defined in paragraph (a) of this section who is retained, designated, appointed, or employed to perform with or without compensation, for not to exceed 130 days during any period of 365 consecutive days, temporary duties on either a full-time or intermittent basis.

(c) *Personnel officer* means a personnel official to whom the power of appointment is redelegated under Administrative Order 202–250.

(d) *Operating unit* means, for purposes of this part, primary and constituent operating units designated as such in the Department Order Series of the Department of Commerce and, in addition, the Office of the Secretary.

(e) *Head of an operating unit*, for the purposes of this part, includes the Assistant Secretary for Administration with respect to the performance of functions under this part for the Office of the Secretary.

Subparts B–C [Reserved]

Subpart D—Regulatory Limitations Upon Employee Conduct

§0.735–10 Administrative extension of statutory limitations.

The provisions of the statutes identified in this part which relate to the ethical and other conduct of Federal employees are adopted and will be enforced as administrative regulations, violations of which may in appropriate cases be the basis for disciplinary action, including removal. The fact that a statute which may relate to employee conduct is not identified in this part does not mean that it may not be the basis for disciplinary action against an employee.

§§0.735–10a—0.735–15 [Reserved]

§0.735–16 Indebtedness.

(a) An employee shall pay each just financial obligation in a proper and timely manner, especially one imposed by law such as Federal, State, or local taxes. For purposes of this section, "a just financial obligation" means one acknowledged by the employee or reduced to judgment by a court, and "in a proper and timely manner" means in a manner which, in the view of the Department, does not, under the circumstances, reflect adversely on the Government as his employer.

(b) In the event of dispute between an employee and an alleged creditor, this section does not require the Department to determine the validity or amount of the disputed debt.

§0.735–17 Gambling, betting, and lotteries.

An employee shall not participate while on Government-owned or leased property or while on duty for the Government, in any gambling activity including the operation of a gambling device, in conducting a lottery or pool, in a game for money or property or in selling or purchasing a numbers slip or ticket. However, this section does not preclude activities

(a) Necessitated by an employee's law enforcement duties, or

(b) Under section 3 of Executive Order 10927 (relating to solicitations conducted by organizations composed of civilian employees or members of the armed forces among their own members for organizational support or for benefit or welfare funds for their own members) and similar agency-approved activities.

§0.735–18 General conduct prejudicial to the Government.

(a) *General policy*. Officers and employees of the Federal Government are servants of the people. Because of this, their conduct must, in many instances, be subject to more restrictions and to higher standards than may be the case in certain private employments. They are expected to conduct themselves in a manner which will reflect favorably upon their employer. Although the

Government is not particularly interested in the private lives of its employees, it does expect them to be honest, reliable, trustworthy, and of good character and reputation. They are expected to be loyal to the Government, and to the department or agency in which they are employed.

(b) *Specific policy*. An employee shall not engage in criminal, infamous, dishonest, immoral, or notoriously disgraceful conduct, or other conduct prejudicial to the Government.

(c) *Regulations applicable to public buildings and grounds*. Each employee is responsible for knowing and complying with regulations of the General Services Administration and of the Department of Commerce applicable to public buildings and grounds.

§0.735–19 Reporting undue influence to superiors.

Each employee shall report to his superior any instance in which another person inside or outside the Federal Government uses or attempts to use undue influence to induce, by reason of his official Government position, former Government employment, family relationship, political position, or otherwise, the employee to do or omit to do any official act in derogation of his official duty.

Subpart E [Reserved]

Subpart F—Supplementary Regulations

§0.735–32 Departmental.

The Assistant Secretary for Administration may prescribe supplementary instructions consistent with this part.

§0.735–33 Operating units.

Each operating unit is hereby authorized and directed to prescribe, after approval by the Assistant Secretary for Administration, such additional regulations not inconsistent with this part as may be necessary to effectuate the general purpose of this part in the light of its individual operating requirements, including but not limited to pertinent statutory provisions, such as:

(a) 35 U.S.C. 4, 122 (Patent Office);

(b) 46 U.S.C. 1111(b) (Maritime Administration);

(c) Certain provisions of the Defense Production Act of 1950, e.g., 50 U.S.C. App. 2160(b)(2) (avoidance of conflicts of interest), 50 U.S.C. App. 2160(b)(6) (financial statements), and 50 U.S.C. App. 2160(f) (prohibition of use of confidential information for purposes of speculation) (Business and Defense Services Administration and any other primary operating unit affected); and

(d) Certain provisions of Pub. L. 89–136, the Public Works and Economic Development Act of 1965, e.g., section 711 (restriction on employing certain EDA employees by applicants for financial assistance), and section 710(b) (embezzlement), false book entries, sharing in loans, etc., and giving out unauthorized information for speculation).

§0.735–34 Effective date of supplementary regulations.

Supplementary regulations prescribed pursuant to §0.735 33, shall become effective upon approval by the issuing officer unless a different date is required by law or a later date is specified therein.

Subpart G—Administration

§0.735–35 Responsibilities of employees.

It is the responsibility of each employee:

(a) To assure, at the outset of his employment, that each of his interests and activities is consistent with the requirements established by or pursuant to this part;

(b) To submit a statement of employment and financial interests at such times and in such form as may be specified in or pursuant to this part;

(c) To certify, upon entering on duty in the Department, that he has read this part and applicable regulations supplementary thereto;

(d) To obtain prior written authorization of any interest or activity about the propriety of which any doubt exists in the employee's mind, as provided in §0.735–39;

(e) To confine each of his interests and activities at all times within the requirements established by or pursuant to this part, including any authorizations granted pursuant to this part; and

(f) To obtain a further written authorization whenever circumstances change, or the nature or extent of the interest or activity changes, in such a manner as to involve the possibility of a violation or appearance of a violation of a limitation or requirement prescribed in or pursuant to this part.

§ 0.735–36 Responsibilities of operating units.

The head of each operating unit, or his designee, shall:

(a) Furnish or make available to each employee a copy of this part (or a comprehensive summary thereof) within 90 days after approval of this part by the Office of Personnel Management, and, upon their issuance, a copy of any regulations supplementary thereto (or a comprehensive summary thereof);

(b) Furnish or make available to each new employee at the time of his entrance on duty a copy of this part as it may be amended and any supplementary regulations (or a comprehensive summary thereof);

(c) Bring this part (or as it may be amended and any supplementary regulations thereto) to the attention of each employee annually, and at such other times as circumstances may warrant as may be determined by the Assistant Secretary for Administration;

(d) Have available for review by employees, as appropriate, copies of laws, Executive orders, this part, supplementary regulations, and pertinent Office of Personnel Management regulations and instructions relating to ethical and other conduct of Government employees;

(e) Advise each employee who is a special Government employee of his status for purposes of 18 U.S.C. 203 and 205;

(f) Require each employee specified in § 0.735–22 to submit a statement of employment and financial interests, as provided by or pursuant to this part;

(g) Develop an appropriate form, with the approval of the counselor of the Department, on which the employee may certify that he has read this part and applicable regulations supplementary thereto, in accordance with § 0.735–35(c), and on which he may, if he so desires, indicate that he has a private activity or interest about which he requests advice and guidance as provided by § 0.735–38.

(h) Require each employee upon entering on duty and at such other times as may be specified, to execute the certification required by § 0.735–35(c);

(i) Report to the program Secretarial Officer concerned and to the Assistant Secretary for Administration promptly any instance in which an employee, after notice, fails to submit the certification required under § 0.735–35(c) or a statement of employment or financial interests required under this part within 14 calendar days following the prescribed time limit for doing so; and

(j) Take action to impress upon each employee required to submit a statement of employment and financial interests, upon his supervisor, and upon employees with whom the employee works, their responsibility as follows:

(1) The employee's supervisor is responsible (i) for excluding from the range of duties of the employee any contracts or other transactions between the Government and his outside employer, clients, or entities in which he has an interest within the purview of this part, and (ii) for overseeing the employee's activities in order to insure that the public interest is protected from improper conduct on his part and that he will not, through ignorance or inadvertence, embarrass the Government or himself.

(2) The employee's supervisor and employees with whom he works are responsible for avoiding the use of the employee's services in any situation in which a violation of law, regulation, or ethical standards is likely to occur or to appear to occur.

(3) The supervisor of an employee is responsible for initiating prompt and proper disciplinary or remedial action when a violation, intentional or innocent, is detected.

(4) Employees shall avoid divulging to a special Government employee privileged Government information which is not necessary to the performance of his governmental responsibility or information which directly involves

the financial interests of his non-Government employer.

(5) An employee shall make every effort in his private work to avoid any personal contact with respect to negotiations with the Department for contracts, grants, or loans, if the subject matter is related to the subject matter of his Government employment. When this is not possible, he may participate if not otherwise prohibited by law (e.g., 18 U.S.C. 203 and 205) in the negotiations for his private employer only with the prior approval of the head of the operating unit concerned.

[32 FR 15222, Nov. 2, 1967, as amended at 55 FR 53489, Dec. 31, 1990]

§0.735-37 Procedure.

The review of statements of employment and financial interests shall include the following basic measures, among others:

(a) Statements shall be submitted to the designated officer, who will review each employee's statement of employment and financial interests to ascertain whether they are consistent with the requirements established by or pursuant to this part. (See §0.735-24(b).)

(b) Where the statement raises any question of compliance with the requirements of this part, it shall be submitted to a deputy counselor for the organization unit concerned. The deputy counselor may, in his discretion, utilize the advice and services of others (including departmental facilities) to obtain further information needed to resolve the questions.

(c) The designated officer shall maintain the statements of employment and financial interests in a file apart from the official personnel files and shall take every measure practicable to insure their confidentiality. Statements of employment and financial interests shall be preserved for 5 years following the separation of an employee from the Department or following termination of any other relationship under which the individual rendered service to the Department, except as may be otherwise authorized by the Assistant Secretary for Administration or as required by law.

§0.735-38 Availability for counseling.

(a) The General Counsel of the Department shall:

(1) Serve as the counselor for the Department of Commerce with respect to matters covered by the basic provisions cited in §0.735-2(a) and otherwise by or pursuant to this part;

(2) Serve as the Department of Commerce designee to the Office of Personnel Management on matters covered by this part; and

(3) Coordinate the counseling services provided under this part and assure that counseling and interpretations on questions of conflicts of interest and other matters covered by this part are available to deputy counselors designated under paragraph (b) of this section.

(b) The counselor shall designate employees who shall serve as deputy counselors for employees of the Department of Commerce with respect to matters covered by or pursuant to this part and shall give authoritative advice and guidance to each employee who seeks advice and guidance on questions of conflict of interests and other matters covered by or pursuant to this part.

(c) Each operating unit shall notify its employees of the availability of counseling services and of how and where these services are available. This notification shall be given within 90 days after approval of this part by the Office of Personnel Management and periodically thereafter. In the case of a new employee appointed after the foregoing notification, notification shall be made at the time of his entrance on duty.

(d) In each operating unit a deputy counselor shall advise and counsel each employee concerning any adjustments necessary in his financial interests or activities, or in any contemplated interests or activities, in order to meet the requirements established by or pursuant to this part.

[32 FR 15222, Nov. 2, 1967, as amended at 55 FR 53489, Dec. 31, 1990]

§0.735-39 Authorizations.

All requests for authorizations required under this part shall be addressed to the head of the operating unit concerned. In the Office of the

Secretary such requests shall be addressed to the Secretary or such person as he may designate. When granted, authorizations will be in writing, and a copy of each authorization will be filed in the employees' official personnel file.

(a) In case of doubt, or upon the request of the employee concerned, cases or questions will be forwarded to the counselor or a deputy counselor. (See § 0.735–38.)

(b) Where an activity requested to be authorized can be conducted as official business, it shall not be authorized as a private activity, but shall be conducted as official business.

(c) Where authorizations involve speaking, writing, or teaching, use of the official title of the employee for identification purposes may be authorized, provided the employee makes it clear that his statements and actions are not of an official nature.

(d) If an authorization has been granted for a specific activity or interest, and the activity or interest is subsequently deemed to constitute a violation of the limitations or requirements prescribed in or pursuant to this part, the employee concerned shall be notified in writing of the cancellation of the authorization and shall modify or stop the activity or interest involved, as requested.

§ 0.735–40 Disciplinary and other remedial action.

(a) Violation of a requirement established in or pursuant to this part shall be cause for appropriate disciplinary action, which may be in addition to any penalty prescribed by law.

(b) When, after consideration of the explanation of the employee provided by § 0.735–20(c), the reviewing officer, in cooperation with the responsible supervisory official, decides that remedial action is required, he will take or cause to be taken immediate action to end the conflict or appearance of conflict of interest. Remedial action may include, but is not limited to:

(1) Changes in assigned duties;

(2) Divestment by the employee of his conflicting interest;

(3) Disciplinary action (including removal from the service); or

(4) Disqualification for a particular assignment.

Remedial action, whether disciplinary or otherwise, shall be effected in accordance with applicable laws, Executive orders, and regulations.

(c) No disciplinary or remedial action may be taken under this section against an employee of another Federal department or agency on detail to the Department of Commerce other than through and with the concurrence of the detailed employee's employing agency.

§ 0.735–41 Inquiries and exceptions.

(a) Inquiries relating to legal aspects of the limitations set forth in or cited in or pursuant to this part should be submitted to the appropriate deputy counselor. Inquiries relating to other aspects of this part or regulations supplementary thereto should be referred to the appropriate personnel office.

(b) Within the limits of administrative discretion permitted to the Department, exceptions to the requirements of this part may be granted from time to time in unusual cases by the head of the operating unit, whenever the facts indicate that such an exception would promote the efficiency of the service. Each request for such an exception should be submitted in writing to the head of the operating unit concerned, and shall contain a full statement of the justification for the request. Reports concerning such requests, if approved, shall be forwarded to the program Secretarial Officer concerned and to the Assistant Secretary for Administration by the head of the operating unit concerned.

Subpart H—Disciplinary Actions Concerning Post-Employment Conflict of Interest Violations

AUTHORITY: 18 U.S.C. 207(j); 5 CFR 737.27.

SOURCE: 49 FR 32057, Aug. 10, 1984; 50 FR 928, Jan. 8, 1985, unless otherwise noted.

§ 0.735–42 Scope.

(a) These regulations establish procedures for imposing sanctions against a former employee for violating the post-employment restrictions of the conflict of interest laws and regulations set forth in 18 U.S.C. 207 and 5 CFR Part 737. These procedures are established pursuant to the requirement in 18 U.S.C. 207(j). The General Counsel is responsible for resolving questions on the legal interpretation of 18 U.S.C. 207 or regulations issued thereunder and for advising employees on these provisions.

(b) For purposes of this subpart, (1) "Former employee" means a former Government employee as defined in 5 CFR 737.3(a)(4) who had served in the Department;

(2) "Lesser included sanctions" means sanctions of the same type but more limited scope as the proposed sanction; thus a bar on communication with an operating unit is a lesser included sanction of a proposed bar on communication with the Department and a bar on communication for one year is a lesser included sanction of a proposed five year bar;

(3) "Assistant Secretary" means the Assistant Secretary for Administration or designee;

(4) "Director" means the Director for Personnel and Civil Rights, Office of the Secretary, or designee;

(5) "Inspector General" and "General Counsel" include any persons designated by them to perform their functions under this subpart; and

(6) "Days" means calendar days except that a dead line which falls on a weekend or holiday shall be extended to the next working day.

§0.735-43 Report of violations and investigation.

(a) If an employee has information which indicates that a former employee has violated any provisions of 18 U.S.C. 207 or regulations thereunder, that employee shall report such information to the Inspector General.

(b) Upon receiving information as set forth in paragraph (a) of this section from an employee or any other person, the Inspector General, upon a determination that it is nonfrivolous, shall expeditiously provide the information to the Director, Office of Government Ethics, and to the Criminal Division, Department of Justice. The Inspector General shall coordinate any investigation under this subpart with the Department of Justice, unless the Department of Justice informs the Inspector General that it does not intend to initiate criminal prosecution.

(c) All investigations under this subpart shall be conducted in such a way as to protect the privacy of former employees. To ensure this, to the extent reasonable and practical, any information received as a result of an investigation shall remain confidential except as necessary to carry out the purposes of this subpart, including the conduct of an investigation, hearing, or judicial proceeding arising thereunder, or as may be required to be released by law.

(d) The Inspector General shall report the findings of the investigation to the Director.

§0.735-44 Initiation of proceedings.

If the Director determines, after an investigation by the Inspector General, that there is reasonable cause to believe that a former employee has violated post-employment statutes or regulations, the Director shall initiate administrative proceedings under this subpart by proposing sanctions against the former employee and by providing notice to the former employee as set forth in §0.735-45.

§0.735-45 Notice.

(a) The Director shall notify the former employee of the proposed disciplinary action in writing by registered or certified mail, return receipt requested, or by any means which gives actual notice or is reasonably calculated to give actual notice. Notice shall be considered received if sent to the last known address of the former employee.

(b) The notice shall include:

(1) A statement of allegations and the basis thereof sufficiently detailed to enable the former employee to prepare a defense;

(2) A statement that the former employee is entitled to a hearing if requested within 20 days from date of notice;

(3) An explanation of the method by which the former employee may request a hearing under this subpart including the name, address, and telephone number of the person to contact if there are further questions;

(4) A statement that the former employee has the right to submit documentary evidence to the Director if a hearing is not requested and an explanation of the method of submitting such evidence and the date by which it must be received; and

(5) A statement of the sanctions which have been proposed.

§0.735–46 Hearing.

(a) *Examiner*. (1) Upon timely receipt of a request for a hearing, the Director shall refer the matter to the Assistant Secretary who shall appoint an examiner to conduct the hearing and render an initial decision.

(2) The examiner shall be impartial, shall not be an individual who has participated in any manner in the decision to initiate the proceedings, and shall not have been employed under the immediate supervision of the former employee or have been employed under a common immediate supervisor. The examiner shall be admitted to practice law and have suitable experience and training to conduct the hearing, reach a determination and render an initial decision in an equitable manner.

(b) *Time, date, and place*. The hearing shall be conducted at a reasonable time, date, and place as set by the examiner. In setting the date, the examiner shall give due regard to the need for both parties to adequately prepare for the hearing and the importance of expeditiously resolving allegations that may be damaging to the former employee's reputation.

(c) *Former employee's rights*. At a hearing, the former employee shall have the right:

(1) To represent himself or herself or to be represented by counsel,

(2) To introduce and examine witnesses and to submit physical evidence,

(3) To confront and cross-examine adverse witnesses,

(4) To present oral argument, and

(5) To receive a transcript or recording of the proceedings, on request.

(d) *Procedure and evidence*. In a hearing under this subpart, the Federal Rules of Evidence and Civil Procedure do not apply but the examiner shall exclude irrelevant or unduly repetitious evidence and all testimony shall be taken under oath or affirmation. The examiner may make such orders and determinations regarding the admissibility of evidence, conduct of examination and cross-examination, and similar matters which the examiner deems necessary or appropriate to ensure orderliness in the proceedings and fundamental fairness to the parties. There shall be no discovery unless agreed to by the parties and ordered by the examiner. The hearing shall not be open to the public unless the former employee or the former employee's representative waives the right to a closed hearing, in which case the examiner shall determine whether the hearing will be open to the public.

(e) *Ex-parte communications*. The former employee, the former employee's representative, and the agency representative shall not make any exparte communications to the examiner concerning the merits of the allegations against the former employee prior to the issuance of the initial decision.

(f) *Initial decision*. (1) The proposed sanctions shall be sustained in an initial decision upon a determination by the examiner that the preponderance of the evidence indicated a violation of post-employment statutes or regulations.

(2) The examiner shall issue an initial decision which is based exclusively on the transcript of testimony and exhibits together with all papers and requests filed in connection with the proceeding and which sets forth all findings of fact and conclusions of law relevant to the matter at issue.

(3) The initial decision shall become final thirty days after issuance if there has been no appeal filed under §0.735–48.

§0.735–47 Decision absent a hearing.

(a) If the former employee does not request a hearing in a timely manner, the Director shall make an initial decision on the basis of information compiled in the investigation, and any submissions made by the former employee.

(b) The proposed sanction or a lesser included sanction shall be imposed if the record indicates a violation of post-employment statutes or regulations by a preponderance of the evidence.

(c) The initial decision shall become final thirty days after issuance if there has been no appeal filed under § 0.735-48.

§ 0.735-48 Administrative appeal.

(a) Within 30 days after issuance of the initial decision, either party may appeal the initial decision or any portion thereof to the Assistant Secretary. The opposing party shall have 20 days to respond.

(b) If an appeal is filed, the Assistant Secretary shall issue a final decision which shall be based solely on the record, or portions thereof cited by the parties to limit issues, and the appeal and response. The Assistant Secretary shall also decide whether to impose the proposed sanction or a lesser included sanction.

(c) If the final decision modifies or reverses the initial decision, it shall state findings of fact and conclusions of law which differ from the initial decision.

§ 0.735-49 Sanctions.

(a) If there has been a final determination that the former employee has violated post-employment statutes or regulations, the Director shall impose, subject to the authority of the Assistant Secretary under § 0.735-48(b), the sanction which was proposed in the notice to the former employee or a lesser included sanction.

(b) Sanctions which may be imposed include:

(1) Prohibiting the former employee from making, on behalf of any other person except the United States, any formal or informal appearance before or, with the intent to influence, any oral or written communication to the Department or any organizational subunit thereof on any matter of business for a period not to exceed five years; and

(2) Other appropriate disciplinary action.

(c) The Director may enforce the sanctions of paragraph (b)(1) of this section by directing any or all employees to refuse to participate in any such appearance or to accept any such communication. As a method of enforcement, the Director may establish a list of former employees against whom sanctions have been imposed.

§ 0.735-50 Judicial review.

Any former employee found to have violated 18 U.S.C. 207, or regulations issued thereunder, by a final administrative decision under this subpart may seek judicial review of the administrative determination.

APPENDIX A TO PART 0—STATUTES GOVERNING CONDUCT OF FEDERAL EMPLOYEES

There are numerous statutes pertaining to the ethical and other conduct of Federal employees, far too many to attempt to list them all. Consequently, only the more important ones of general applicability are referred to in this appendix.

A. BRIBERY AND GRAFT

.01 Title 18, U.S.C., section 201, prohibits anyone from bribing or attempting to bribe a public official by corruptly giving, offering, or promising him or any person selected by him, anything of value with intent (a) to influence any official act by him, (b) to influence him to commit or allow any fraud on the United States, or (c) to induce him to do or omit to do any act in violation of his lawful duty. As used in section 201, "Public officials" is broadly defined to include officers, employees, and other persons carrying on activities for or on behalf of the Government.

.02 Section 201 also prohibits a public official's solicitation or acceptance of, or agreement to take, a bribe. In addition, it forbids offers or payments to, and solicitations or receipt by, a public official of anything of value "for or because of" any official act performed or to be performed by him.

.03 Section 201 further prohibits the offering to or the acceptance by a witness of anything of value involving intent to influence his testimony at a trial, Congressional hearing, or agency proceeding. A similar provision applies to witnesses "for or because of" testimony given or to be given. The provisions summarized in this section do not preclude lawful witness fees, travel and subsistence expenses, or reasonable compensation for expert testimony.

B. COMPENSATION TO OFFICERS AND EMPLOYEES IN MATTERS AFFECTING THE GOVERNMENT

.01 Title 18, U.S.C., section 203, prohibits an officer or employee from receiving compensation for services rendered for others before a Federal department or agency in matters in which the Government is a party or is interested.

.02 Section 203 applies to a special Government employee as follows:

a. If the special Government employee has served in the Department of Commerce more than 60 days during the preceding period of 365 days, section 203 applies to him only in relation to a particular matter involving a specific party or parties (1) in which he has at any time participated personally and substantially in his governmental capacity, or (2) which is pending in the Department of Commerce; or

b. If the special Government employee has served in the Department no more than 60 days during the preceding period of 365 days, section 203 applies to him only in relation to a particular matter involving a specific party or parties in which he has at any time participated personally and substantially in his governmental capacity.

.03 Section 203 does not apply to a retired officer of the uniformed services while not on active duty and not otherwise an officer or employee of the United States.

C. ACTIVITIES OF OFFICERS AND EMPLOYEES IN CLAIMS AGAINST AND OTHER MATTERS AFFECTING THE GOVERNMENT

.01 Title 18, U.S.C., section 205, prohibits an officer or employee, otherwise than in the performance of his official duties, from:

a. Acting as agent or attorney for prosecuting any claim against the United States, or receiving any gratuity, or any share of or interest in any such claim in consideration of assistance in the prosecution of such claims; or

b. Acting as agent or attorney for anyone before any Government agency, court, or officer in connection with any matter in which the United States is a party or has a direct and substantial interest.

.02 Section 205 applies to a special Government employee as follows:

a. If the special Government employee has served in the Department more than 60 days during the preceding period of 365 days, section 205 applies to him only in relation to a particular matter involving a specific party or parties (1) in which he has at any time participated personally and substantially in his governmental capacity, or (2) which is pending in the Department of Commerce; or

b. If the special Government employee has served in the Department no more than 60 days during the preceding period of 365 days, section 205 applies to him only in relation to a particular matter involving a specific party or parties in which he has at any time participated personally and substantially in his governmental capacity.

.03 Section 205 does not preclude:

a. An employee, if not inconsistent with faithful performance of his duties, from acting without compensation as agent or attorney for any person who is the subject of disciplinary, loyalty, or other personnel administration proceedings, in connection with those proceedings; or

b. An employee from giving testimony under oath or from making statements required to be made under penalty for perjury or contempt.

.04 Sections 203 and 205 do not preclude:

a. An employee from acting as agent or attorney for his parents, spouse, child, or any person for whom, or for any estate for which, he is serving as guardian, executor, administrator, trustee, or other personal fiduciary, except in those matters in which he has participated personally and substantially as a Government employee or which are the subject of his official responsibility, provided the head of the operating unit concerned approves; or

b. A special Government employee from acting as agent or attorney for another person in the performance of work under a grant by, or a contract with, or for the benefit of, the United States, provided the head of the operating unit concerned, with the approval of the appropriate program Secretarial Officer, shall certify in writing that the national interest so requires, and such certification shall be published in the FEDERAL REGISTER.

.05 Section 205 does not apply to a retired officer of the uniformed services while not on active duty and not otherwise an officer or employee of the United States.

D. DISQUALIFICATION OF FORMER OFFICERS AND EMPLOYEES IN MATTERS CONNECTED WITH FORMER DUTIES OR OFFICIAL RESPONSIBILITIES; DISQUALIFICATION OF PARTNERS

.01 Title 18 U.S.C., section 207:

a. Provides that a former Government officer or employee, including a former special Government employee, shall be permanently barred from acting as agent or attorney for anyone other than the United States in any matter in which the United States is a party or is interested and in which he participated personally and substantially in a governmental capacity;

b. Bars a former Government officer or employee, including a special Government employee, of an agency, for a period of 1 year after his employment with it has ceased, from appearing personally as agent or attorney for another person before any court or agency in connection with a matter in which the Government has an interest and which was under his official responsibility at the employing agency (e.g., Department of Commerce) at any time within 1 year prior to the end of such responsibility; and

c. Prohibits a partner of a person employed by the Government, including a special Government employee, from acting as agent or attorney for anyone other than the United States in matters in which the employee participates or has participated personally and substantially for the Government or which are the subject of his official responsibility.

.02 Subparagraphs .01a. and .01b. of this section do not prevent a former officer or employee or special Government employee who has outstanding scientific or technical qualifications from acting as attorney or agent or appearing personally before the Department of Commerce in connection with a particular matter in a scientific or technological field if the Assistant Secretary of Commerce for Science and Technology shall make a certification in writing, published in the FEDERAL REGISTER, that the national interest would be served by such action or appearance by the former officer or employee.

E. ACTS AFFECTING A PERSONAL FINANCIAL INTEREST

.01 Title 18, U.S.C., section 208 prohibits an officer or employee, including a special Government employee, from participating personally and substantially in a governmental capacity in any matter in which, to his knowledge, he, his spouse, minor child, partner, organization in which he is serving as officer, director, trustee, partner, or employee, or any person or organization with whom he is negotiating or has any arrangement concerning prospective employment, has a financial interest.

.02 Section 208 does not apply:

a. If the officer or employee first advises the head of the operating unit concerned of the nature and circumstances of the matter involved, makes full disclosure of the financial interest, and receives in advance a written determination made by such official, with the approval of the appropriate program Secretarial Officer, that the interest is not so substantial as to be deemed likely to affect the integrity of the services which the Government may expect from the officer or employee; or

b. If, by general rule or regulation published in the FEDERAL REGISTER, the financial interest has been exempted from the requirements of section 208 as being too remote or too inconsequential to affect the integrity of Government officers' or employees' services.

F. SALARY OF GOVERNMENT OFFICIALS AND EMPLOYEES

.01 Title 18, U.S.C., section 209, prohibits:

a. An officer or employee from receiving any salary, or any contribution to or supplementation of salary, as compensation for his services as an officer or employee of the United States from any source other than the Government of the United States, except as may be contributed out of the treasury of a State, county, or municipality; and

b. Any person or organization from paying, contributing to, or supplementing the salary of an officer or employee under circumstances which would make its receipt a violation of subparagraph .01a. of this section.

.02 Section 209:

a. Does not prevent a Government employee from continuing to participate in a bona fide pension or other welfare plan maintained by a former employer;

b. Exempts special Government employees and employees serving the Government without compensation, and grants a corresponding exemption to any outside person paying compensation to such individuals; and

c. Does not prohibit the payment or acceptance of sums under the terms of the Government Employees Training Act.

G. CODE OF ETHICS FOR GOVERNMENT SERVICE

"Code of Ethics for Government Service," House Concurrent Resolution 175, 85th Congress, 2d Session, 72 Stat. B12 of July 11, 1958, which reads as follows:

"Any Person in Government Service Should:

"Put loyalty to the highest moral principles and to country above loyalty to persons, party, or Government department.

"UPHOLD the Constitution, laws, and legal regulations of the United States and all governments therein and never be a party to their evasion.

"GIVE a full day's labor for a full day's pay; giving to the performance of his duties his earnest effort and best thought.

"SEEK to find and employ more efficient and economical ways of getting tasks accomplished.

"NEVER discriminate unfairly by the dispensing of special favors or privileges to anyone, whether for remuneration or not; and never accept for himself or his family, favors or benefits under circumstances which might be construed by reasonable persons as influencing the performance of his governmental duties.

"MAKE no private promises of any kind binding upon the duties of office, since a Government employee has no private word which can be binding on public duty.

"ENGAGE in no business with the Government, either directly or indirectly, which is inconsistent with the conscientious performance of his governmental duties.

"NEVER use any information coming to him confidentially in the performance of governmental duties as a means for making private profit.

"EXPOSE corruption wherever discovered.

"UPHOLD these principles, ever conscious that public office is a public trust."

H. PROHIBITIONS

.01 The prohibition against lobbying with appropriated funds (18 U.S.C. 1913) reads as follows:

"No part of the money appropriated by any enactment of Congress shall, in the absence of express authorization by Congress, be used directly or indirectly to pay for any personal service, advertisement, telegram, telephone, letter, printed or written matter, or other device, intended or designed to influence in any manner a Member of Congress, to favor or oppose, by vote or otherwise, any legislation or appropriation by Congress, whether before or after the introduction of any bill or resolution proposing such legislation or appropriation, but this shall not prevent officers or employees of the United States or of its departments or agencies from communicating to Members of Congress on the request of any Member or to Congress, through the proper official channels, requests for legislation or appropriations which they deem necessary for the efficient conduct of the public business.

"Whoever, being an officer or employee of the United States or of any department or agency thereof, violates or attempts to violate this section, shall be fined not more than $500 or imprisoned not more than 1 year, or both; and after notice and hearing by the superior officer vested with the power of removing him, shall be removed from office or employment."

.02 The prohibitions against disloyalty and striking (5 U.S.C. 7311, 18 U.S.C. 1918). An individual may not accept or hold a position in the Government of the United States if he:

a. Advocates the overthrow of our constitutional form of government;

b. Is a member of an organization that he knows advocates the overthrow of our constitutional form of government;

c. Participates in a strike, or asserts the right to strike, against the Government of the United States or the government of the District of Columbia; or

d. Is a member of an organization of employees of the Government of the United States or of individuals employed by the government of the District of Columbia that he knows asserts the right to strike against the Government of the United States or the government of the District of Columbia.

.03 The prohibition against employment of a member of a Communist organization (50 U.S.C. 784).

.04 The prohibitions against (a) the disclosure of classified information (18 U.S.C. 798, 50 U.S.C. 788); and (b) the disclosure of confidential information (18 U.S.C. 1905). Each employee who has access to classified information, e.g., confidential, secret, or top secret, or to a restricted area is responsible for knowing and for complying strictly with the security regulations of the Department of Commerce. (See Administrative Order 207–2.)

.05 The prohibition against employment in the competitive civil service of any person who habitually uses intoxicating beverages to excess (5 U.S.C. 7352).

.06 The prohibition against the misuse of a Government vehicle (31 U.S.C. 638a(c)). No employee may willfully use or authorize the use of a Government-owned or Government-leased passenger motor vehicle or aircraft for other than official purposes.

.07 The prohibition against the use of the franking privilege to avoid payment of postage on private mail (18 U.S.C. 1719).

.08 The prohibition against the use of deceit in an examination or personnel action in connection with Government employment (18 U.S.C. 1917).

.09 The prohibition against fraud or false statements in a Government matter (18 U.S.C. 1001). An employee in connection with an official matter shall not knowingly and willfully conceal or cover up a material fact or falsify official papers or documents.

.10 The prohibition against mutilating or destroying a public record (18 U.S.C. 2071). No employee may conceal, remove, mutilate, or destroy Government documents or records except for the disposition of records in accordance with law or regulation.

.11 The prohibition against counterfeiting and forging transportation requests (18 U.S.C. 508). Falsely making, altering or forging, in whole or in part, any form of transportation request is prohibited.

.12 The prohibitions against:

a. Embezzlement of Government money or property (18 U.S.C. 641). No employee may convert any Government money or Government property to his own use or the use of another person.

b. Failure to account for public money (18 U.S.C. 643). Any employee, who, having received public money which he is not authorized to retain, fails to render his accounts for same as provided by law, is guilty of embezzlement.

c. Embezzlement of the money or property of another person in the possession of the employee by reason of his employment (18 U.S.C. 654). An employee is prohibited from embezzling or wrongfully converting for his own use the money or property of another which comes under his control as the result of his employment.

.13 The prohibition against unauthorized removal or use of documents relating to claims from or by the Government (18 U.S.C. 285). No employee, without authority, may remove from the place where it was kept by authority of the United States any document, record, file, or paper intended to be used to procure the payment of money from or by the United States or the allowance or payment of any claim against the United States, regardless of whether the document or paper has already been used or the claim has already been allowed or paid; and no employee may use or attempt to use any such document, record, file, or paper to procure the payment of any money from or by the United States or the allowance or payment of any claim against the United States.

.14 The prohibition against proscribed political activities, including the following, among others:

a. Using official authority or influence for the purpose of interfering with or influencing the result of an election, except as authorized by law (5 U.S.C. 7324);

b. Taking an active part in political management or in political campaigns, except as authorized by law (5 U.S.C. 7324);

c. Offering or promising to pay anything of value in consideration of the use of, or promise to use, any influence to procure any appointive office or place under the United States for any person (18 U.S.C. 210);

d. Soliciting or receiving, either as a political contribution or for personal emolument, anything of value in consideration of a promise of support or use of influence in obtaining for any person any appointive office or place under the United States (18 U.S.C. 211);

e. Using official authority to interfere with a Federal election (18 U.S.C. 595);

f. Promising any employment compensation, or other benefit made possible by Act of Congress in consideration of political activity or support (18 U.S.C. 600);

g. Action by a Federal officer or employee to solicit or receive, or to be in any manner concerned with soliciting or receiving, any contribution for any political purpose whatever from any other Federal officer or employee or from any person receiving compensation for services from money derived from the Treasury of the United States (18 U.S.C. 602);

h. Soliciting or receiving (by any person) anything of value for any political purpose whatever on any Government premises (18 U.S.C. 603);

i. Soliciting or receiving contributions for political purposes from anyone on Federal relief or work relief (18 U.S.C. 604);

j. Payment of a contribution for political purposes by any Federal officer or employee to another Federal officer or employee (18 U.S.C. 607); and

k. Payment of a political contribution in excess of statutory limitations and purchase of goods, commodities, advertising, or articles the proceeds of which inure to the benefit of certain political candidates or organizations (18 U.S.C. 608).

.15 The prohibition against an employee acting as the agent of a foreign principal registered under the Foreign Agents Registration Act (18 U.S.C. 219).

PART 1—THE SEAL OF THE DEPARTMENT OF COMMERCE

AUTHORITY: Sec. 1, 32 Stat. 825, as amended, 15 U.S.C. 1501.

SOURCE: 33 FR 9337, June 26, 1968, unless otherwise noted.

§1.1 Purpose.

The purpose of this part is to describe the seal of the Department of Commerce and to delegate authority to affix the seal to certifications and documents of the Department.

§1.2 Description and design.

(a) The Act of February 14, 1903 (32 Stat. 825, as amended) (15 U.S.C. 1501), which established the Department of Commerce, provided that "The said Secretary shall cause a seal of office to be made for the said department of such device as the President shall approve, and judicial notice shall be taken of the said seal." On April 4, 1913, the President approved and declared to be the seal of the Department of Commerce the device which he described as follows:

Arms: Per fesse azure and or, a ship in full sail on waves of the sea, in chief proper; and in base a lighthouse illumined proper.

Crest: The American Eagle displayed. Around the Arms, between two concentric circles, are the words:

DEPARTMENT OF COMMERCE

UNITED STATES OF AMERICA

(b) The design of the approved seal is as shown below. Where necessitated by requirements of legibility, immediate comprehension, or clean reproduction, the concentric circles may be eliminated from the seal on publications and exhibits, and in slides, motion pictures, and television. In more formal uses of the seal, such as on letterheads, the full, proper rendition of the seal shall be used.

(c) The official symbolism of the seal shall be the following: The ship is a symbol of commerce; the blue denotes uprightness and constancy; the lighthouse is a well-known symbol representing guidance from the darkness which is translated to commercial enlightenment; and the gold denotes purity. The crest is the American bald eagle denoting the national scope of the Department's activities. (The above is a modification of the original symbolism issued with the President's approval of the seal, made necessary by changes in the functions of the Department.)

§ 1.3 Delegation of authority.

(a) Pursuant to authority vested in the Secretary of Commerce by law, (1) the Chief Administrative Officer of each operating unit, and (2) the Director, Office of Administrative Services in the Office of the Secretary, are hereby authorized to sign as Certifying Officers certifications as to the official nature of copies of correspondence and records from the files, publications and other documents of the Department and to affix the seal of the Department of Commerce to such certifications or documents for all purposes, including the purpose authorized by 28 U.S.C. 1733(b).

(b) Delegations of authority to persons other than those named in paragraph (a) of this section may be made by the Assistant Secretary for Administration.

(c) This delegation shall not affect or prejudice the use of properly authorized office or bureau seals in appropriate cases.

PART 2—PROCEDURES FOR HANDLING AND SETTLEMENT OF CLAIMS UNDER THE FEDERAL TORT CLAIMS ACT

AUTHORITY: 28 U.S.C. 2672.

§ 2.1 Purpose.

(a) The purpose of this part is to delegate authority to settle or deny claims under the Federal Tort Claims Act (in part, 28 U.S.C. 2671–2680) as amended by Pub. L. 89–506, 80 Stat. 306, and to establish procedures for the administrative adjudication of such claims accruing on or after January 18, 1967.

[32 FR 3769, Mar. 7, 1967, as amended at 48 FR 31636, July 11, 1983]

§ 2.2 Provisions of law and regulations thereunder.

(a) Section 2672 of Title 28, U.S. Code, as above amended, provides that:

The head of each Federal agency or his designee, in accordance with regulations prescribed by the Attorney General, may consider, ascertain, adjust, determine, compromise, and settle any claim for money damages against the United States for injury or loss of property or personal injury or death caused by the negligent or wrongful act or omission of any employee of the agency while acting within the scope of his office or employment, under circumstances where the United States, if a private person, would be liable to the claimant in accordance with the law of the place where the act or omission occurred: *Provided*, that any award, compromise, or settlement in excess of $25,000 shall be effected only with the prior written approval of the Attorney General or his designee.

Subject to the provisions of this title relating to civil actions on tort claims against the United States, any such award, compromise, settlement, or determination shall be final and conclusive on all officers of the Government, except when procured by means of fraud.

Any award, compromise, or settlement in an amount of $2,500 or less made pursuant to this section shall be paid by the head of the Federal agency concerned out of appropriations available to that agency. Payment of any award, compromise, or settlement in an amount in excess of $2,500 made pursuant to this section or made by the Attorney General in any amount pursuant to section 2677 of this title shall be paid in a manner similar to judgments and compromises in like causes and appropriations or funds available for the payment of such judgments and compromises are hereby made available for the payment of awards, compromises, or settlements under this chapter.

The acceptance by the claimant of any such award, compromise, or settlement shall be final and conclusive on the claimant, and shall constitute a complete release of any claim against the United States and against the employee of the Government whose act or omission gave rise to the claim, by reason of the same subject matter.

(b) Subsection (a) section 2675 of said Title 28 provides that:

An action shall not be instituted upon a claim against the United States for money damages for injury or loss of property or personal injury or death caused by the negligent or wrongful act or omission of any employee of the Government while acting within the scope of his office or employment, unless the claimant shall have first presented the claim to the appropriate Federal agency and his claim shall have been finally denied by the agency in writing and sent by certified or registered mail. The failure of an agency to make final disposition of a claim within 6 months after it is filed shall, at the option of the claimant any time thereafter, be deemed a final denial of the claim for purposes of this section. The provisions of this subsection shall not apply to such claims as may be asserted under the Federal Rules of Civil Procedure by third party complaint, crossclaim, or counterclaim.

(c) Section 2678 of said Title 28 provides that no attorney shall charge fees in excess of 25 percent of a judgment or settlement after litigation, or over 20 percent of administrative settlements.

(d) Section 2401(b) of said Title 28 provides that:

A tort claim against the United States shall be forever barred unless it is presented in writing to the appropriate Federal agency within 2 years after such claim accrues or unless action is begun within 6 months after the date of mailing, by certified or registered mail, of notice of final denial of the claim by the agency to which it was presented.

(e) Pursuant to section 2672 as amended, the Attorney General has issued regulations (herein referred to as "the Regulations"; 28 CFR Part 14) prescribing standards and procedures for settlement of tort claims (31 FR 16616). Persons delegated authority under this part shall follow and be guided by such Regulations (28 CFR Part 14).

[32 FR 3769, Mar. 7, 1967, as amended at 63 FR 29945, June 2, 1998]

§2.3 Delegation of authority.

(a) The General Counsel is hereby named as the designee of the Secretary ofCommerce with respect to tort claims filed under section 2672 of Title 28, U.S. Code, as described in §2.2, with authority to act on such claims as provided in said section 2672, including denial thereof.

(b) Authority delegated under this section may, with the approval of the General Counsel, be redelegated to other designees.

(c) Settlement or denial of any claim under this part is final for the Department of Commerce.

[48 FR 31636, July 11, 1983]

§2.4 Procedure for filing claims.

(a) The procedure for filing and the contents of claims shall be pursuant to §§14.2, 14.3, and 14.4 of the Regulations (28 CFR Part 14).

(b) Claims shall be filed with the Assistant General Counsel for Finance and Litigation, Department of Commerce, Washington, D.C. 20230.

(c) If a claim is filed elsewhere in the Department, it shall immediately be recorded and transmitted to the Assistant General Counsel for Finance and Litigation.

[32 FR 3769, Mar. 7, 1967, as amended at 48 FR 31636, July 11, 1983; 63 FR 29945, June 2, 1998]

§2.5 Adjudication and settlement of claims.

(a) Upon receipt of a claim by the Assistant General Counsel for Finance and Litigation, the time and date of receipt shall be recorded. The Assistant General Counsel may, after recording the claim, transmit it to the Departmental office or primary operating unit involved in the claim and request that an investigation be conducted. The appropriate Departmental office or primary operating unit shall designate an official to conduct the investigation, who shall prepare a file, obtain additional information as necessary, and prepare for the Assistant General Counsel's signature a proposed award or denial of the claim. If the investigation capabilities of the office or unit are insufficient for a proper and complete investigation, the office or unit shall consult with the Departmental Office of Investigations and Security to:

(1) Have that Office conduct the investigation or

(2) Request another Federal agency to conduct the investigation as necessary, pursuant to § 14.8 of the regulations (28 CFR Part 14), all on a reimbursable basis.

(b) If the amount of the proposed award exceeds $25,000 (in which case, approval by the Attorney General is required), or if consultation with the Department of Justice is desired or required pursuant to § 14.6 of the regulations, the Assistant General Counsel for Finance and Litigation will prepare and compile the material required by the Department of Justice under § 14.7 of the Regulations.

(c) Denial of a claim shall be communicated as provided by § 14.9 of the regulations (28 CFR Part 14).

(d) Designees hereunder are responsible for the control over and expeditious handling of claims, bearing in mind the applicable statutory time limitations for adjudications of claims.

[32 FR 3769, Mar. 7, 1967, as amended at 48 FR 31636, July 11, 1983; 63 FR 29945, June 2, 1998]

§ 2.6 Payment of claims.

When an award is made, the file on the case shall be transmitted to the appropriate fiscal office for payment by the Department or for transmittal for payment as prescribed by § 14.10 of the Regulations (28 CFR Part 14). Prior to payment appropriate releases shall be obtained, as provided in said section.

[32 FR 3769, Mar. 7, 1967]

§ 2.7 Supplementary regulations.

(a) The Assistant General Counsel for Finance and Litigation may from time to time issue such supplementary regulations or instructions as he/she deems appropriate to carry out the purpose of this part.

(b) Any designee mentioned in paragraph (a) of § 2.3 may issue regulations or instructions covering his/her area of responsibility hereunder which are consistent with this part and with those issued under paragraph (a) of this section, such regulations and instructions to be approved by the Assistant General Counsel for Finance and Litigation.

[32 FR 3769, Mar. 7, 1967, as amended at 48 FR 31636, July 11, 1983. Redesignated and amended at 63 FR 29945, June 2, 1998]

PART 3 [RESERVED]

PART 4—DISCLOSURE OF GOVERNMENT INFORMATION

Subpart A—Freedom of Information Act

Sec.

Subpart B—Privacy Act

APPENDIX A TO PART 4—FREEDOM OF INFORMATION PUBLIC INSPECTION FACILITIES, AND ADDRESSES FOR REQUESTS FOR RECORDS UNDER THE FREEDOM OF INFORMATION ACT AND PRIVACY ACT, AND REQUESTS FOR CORRECTION OR AMENDMENT UNDER THE PRIVACY ACT.

APPENDIX B TO PART 4—OFFICIALS AUTHORIZED TO DENY REQUESTS FOR RECORDS UNDER THE FREEDOM OF INFORMATION ACT, AND REQUESTS FOR RECORDS AND REQUESTS FOR CORRECTION OR AMENDMENT UNDER THE PRIVACY ACT.

APPENDIX C TO PART 4—SYSTEMS OF RECORDS NOTICED BY OTHER FEDERAL AGENCIES AND APPLICABLE TO RECORDS OF THE DEPARTMENT, AND APPLICABILITY OF THIS PART THERETO.

AUTHORITY: 5 U.S.C. 301; 5 U.S.C. 552; 5 U.S.C. 552a; 5 U.S.C. 553; 31 U.S.C. 3717; 44 U.S.C. 3101; Reorganization Plan No. 5 of 1950.

SOURCE: 66 FR 65632, Dec. 20, 2001, unless otherwise noted.

Subpart A—Freedom of Information Act

§4.1 General.

(a) The information in this part is furnished for the guidance of the public and in compliance with the requirements of the Freedom of Information Act (FOIA), as amended (5 U.S.C. 552). This part sets forth the procedures the Department of Commerce (Department) and its components follow to make publicly available the materials and indices specified in 5 U.S.C. 552(a)(2) and records requested under 5 U.S.C. 552(a)(3). Information routinely provided to the public as part of a regular Department activity (for example, press releases issued by the Office of Public Affairs) may be provided to the public without following this part.

(b) As used in this subpart, *component* means any office, division, bureau or other unit of the Department listed in Appendix A to this part (except that a regional office of a larger office or other unit does not constitute a separate component).

§4.2 Public reference facilities.

(a) The Department maintains public reference facilities (listed in Appendix A to this part) that contain the records the FOIA requires to be made regularly available for public inspection and copying; furnishes information; receives and processes requests for records under the FOIA; and otherwise assists the public concerning Department operations under the FOIA.

(b) Each component of the Department shall determine which of its records are required to be made available for public inspection and copying, and make those records available either in its own public reference facility or in the Department's Central Reference and Records Inspection Facility. Each component shall maintain and make available for public inspection and copying a current subject-matter index of its public inspection facility records. Each index shall be updated regularly, at least quarterly, with respect to newly included records. In accordance with 5 U.S.C. 552(a)(2), the Department has determined that it is unnecessary and impracticable to publish quarterly or more frequently and distribute copies of the index and supplements thereto.

(c) Each component shall make public inspection facility records created on or after November 1, 1996 available electronically through the Department's "FOIA Home Page" link found at the Department's World Wide Web site (*http://www.doc.gov*). Information available at the site shall include:

(1) Each component's index of its public inspection facility records, which indicates which records are available electronically; and

(2) The general index referred to in paragraph (d)(3) of this section.

(d) The Department shall maintain and make available for public inspection and copying:

(1) A current index providing identifying information for the public as to any matter that is issued, adopted, or promulgated after July 4, 1997, and that is retained as a record and is required to be made available or published. Copies of the index are available upon request after payment of the direct cost of duplication;

(2) Copies of records that have been released and that the component that maintains them determines, because of their subject matter, have become or are likely to become the subject of subsequent requests for substantially the same records;

(3) A general index of the records described in paragraph (d)(2) of this section;

(4) Final opinions and orders, including concurring and dissenting opinions made in the adjudication of cases;

(5) Those statements of policy and interpretations that have been adopted by a component and are not published in the FEDERAL REGISTER; and

(6) Administrative staff manuals and instructions to staff that affect a member of the public.

§ 4.3 Records under the FOIA.

(a) Records under the FOIA include all Government records, regardless of format, medium or physical characteristics, and include electronic records and information, audiotapes, videotapes, and photographs.

(b) Under the FOIA, the Department has no obligation to create, compile, or obtain from outside the Department a record to satisfy a request. In complying with a request for electronic data, whether the Department creates or compiles records (as by undertaking significant programming work) or merely extracts them from an existing database may be unclear. The Department shall in any case undertake reasonable efforts to search for the information in electronic format.

(c) Department officials may, upon request, create and provide new records pursuant to user fee statutes, such as the first paragraph of 15 U.S.C. 1525, or in accordance with authority otherwise provided by law. Such creation and provision of records is outside the scope of the FOIA.

(d) Components shall preserve all correspondence pertaining to the requests they receive under this subpart, as well as copies of all requested records, until disposition or destruction is authorized by Title 44 of the United States Code or the National Archives and Records Administration's General Records Schedule 14. Components shall not dispose of records while they are the subject of a pending request, appeal, or lawsuit under the FOIA.

§ 4.4 Requirements for making requests.

(a) A request for records of the Department which are not customarily made available to the public as part of the Department's regular informational services must be in writing (and may be sent by mail, facsimile, or E-mail), and shall be processed under the FOIA, regardless whether the FOIA is mentioned in the request. Requests should be mailed to the Department component identified in Appendix A to this part that maintains those records, or may be sent by facsimile or E-mail to the numbers or addresses, respectively, listed at the Department's "FOIA Home Page" link found at the Department's World Wide Web site (*http://www.doc.gov*).[1] If the proper component cannot be determined, the request should be sent to the central facility identified in Appendix A to this part. The central facility will forward the request to the component(s) it believes most likely to have the requested records. For the quickest handling, the request (and envelope, if the request is mailed) should be marked "Freedom of Information Act Request."

(b) For requests for records about oneself, § 4.24 contains additional requirements. For requests for records about another individual, either a written authorization signed by the individual permitting disclosure of his or her records to the requester or proof that the individual is deceased (for example, a copy of a death certificate or an obituary) facilitates processing the request.

(c) The records requested must be described in enough detail to enable Department personnel to locate them with a reasonable amount of effort. If possible, a request should include specific information about each record sought, such as the date, title or name, author, recipient, and subject matter

[1] The United States Patent and Trademark Office (USPTO), which is established as an agency of the United States within the Department of Commerce, operates under its own FOIA regulations at 37 CFR part 102, subpart A. Accordingly, requests for USPTO records should be sent directly to the USPTO.

of the record, and the name and location of the office where the record is located. Also, if records about a court case are sought, the title of the case, the court in which the case was filed, and the nature of the case should be included. If known, any file designations or descriptions of the requested records should be included. In general, the more specifically the request describes the records sought, the greater the likelihood that the Department will be able to locate those records. If a component determines that a request does not reasonably describe records, it shall inform the requester what additional information is needed or how the request is otherwise insufficient, to enable the requester to modify the request to meet the requirements of this section.

§4.5 Responsibility for responding to requests.

(a) *In general.* Except as stated in paragraph (b) of this section, the proper component of the Department to respond to a request for records is the component that first receives the request and has responsive records, or the component to which the Departmental Freedom of Information Officer assigns lead responsibility for responding to the request. Records responsive to a request shall include those records within the Department's possession and control as of the date the Department begins its search for them.

(b) *Consultations and referrals.* If a component receives a request for a record in its possession in which another Federal agency subject to the FOIA has the primary interest, the component shall refer the record to that agency for direct response to the requester. Ordinarily, the agency that originated a record will be presumed to have the primary interest in it. A component shall consult with another Federal agency before responding to a requester if the component receives a request for a record in which another Federal agency subject to the FOIA has a significant interest, but not the primary interest; or another Federal agency not subject to the FOIA has the primary interest or a significant interest (see §4.8 for additional information about referrals of classified information).

(c) *Notice of referral.* Whenever a component refers a document to another Federal agency for direct response to the requester, it ordinarily shall notify the requester in writing of the referral and inform the requester of the name of the agency to which the document was referred.

(d) *Timing of responses to consultations and referrals.* All consultations and referrals shall be handled in chronological order, based on when the FOIA request was received by the first Federal agency.

(e) *Agreements regarding consultations and referrals.* Components may make agreements with other Federal agencies to eliminate the need for consultations or referrals for particular types of records.

[66 FR 65632, Dec. 20, 2001, as amended at 71 FR 31073, June 1, 2006]

§4.6 Time limits and expedited processing.

(a) *In general.* Components ordinarily shall respond to requests according to their order of receipt.

(b) *Initial response and appeal.* Subject to paragraph (c)(1) of this section, an initial response shall be made within 20 working days (*i.e.*, excluding Saturdays, Sundays, and legal public holidays) of the receipt of a request for a record under this part by the proper component identified in accordance with §4.5(a), and an appeal shall be decided within 20 working days of its receipt by the Office of the General Counsel.

(c) *Unusual circumstances.* (1) In unusual circumstances as specified in paragraph (c)(2) of this section, an official listed in Appendix B to this part may extend the time limits in paragraph (b) of this section by notifying the requester in writing as soon as practicable of the unusual circumstances and of the date by which processing of the request is expected to be completed. If the extension is for more than ten working days, the component shall provide the requester an opportunity either to modify the request so that it may be processed within the applicable time limit, or to arrange an alternative time frame for processing the request or a modified request.

(2) As used in this section, *unusual circumstances* means, but only to the extent reasonably necessary to properly process the particular request:

(i) The need to search for and collect the requested records from field facilities or other establishments separate from the office processing the request;

(ii) The need to search for, collect, and appropriately examine a voluminous amount of separate and distinct records that are the subject of a single request; or

(iii) The need for consultation, which shall be conducted with all practicable speed, with another component or Federal agency having a substantial interest in the determination of the request.

(3) If a component reasonably believes that multiple requests submitted by a requester, or by a group of requesters acting in concert, constitute a single request that would otherwise involve unusual circumstances, and the requests involve clearly related matters, the component may aggregate them. Multiple requests involving unrelated matters will not be aggregated.

(d) *Multitrack processing.* (1) A component may use two or more processing tracks by distinguishing between simple and more complex requests based on the number of pages involved, or some other measure of the amount of work and/or time needed to process the request, and whether the request qualifies for expedited processing as described in paragraph (e) of this section.

(2) A component using multitrack processing may provide requesters in its slower track(s) with an opportunity to limit the scope of their requests in order to qualify for faster processing. A component doing so shall contact the requester by telephone, E-mail, or letter, whichever is most efficient in each case.

(e) *Expedited processing.* (1) Requests and appeals shall be taken out of order and given expedited treatment whenever it is determined that they involve:

(i) Circumstances in which the lack of expedited treatment could reasonably be expected to pose an imminent threat to the life or physical safety of an individual;

(ii) The loss of substantial due process rights;

(iii) A matter of widespread and exceptional media interest involving questions about the Government's integrity which affect public confidence; or

(iv) An urgency to inform the public about an actual or alleged Federal Government activity, if made by a person primarily engaged in disseminating information.

(2) A request for expedited processing may be made at the time of the initial request for records or at any later time. For a prompt determination, a request for expedited processing should be sent to the component listed in Appendix A to this part that maintains the records requested.

(3) A requester who seeks expedited processing must submit a statement, certified to be true and correct to the best of that person's knowledge and belief, explaining in detail the basis for requesting expedited processing. For example, a requester within the category described in paragraph (e)(1)(iv) of this section, if not a full-time member of the news media, must establish that he or she is a person whose main professional activity or occupation is information dissemination, though it need not be his or her sole occupation. A requester within the category described in paragraph (e)(1)(iv) of this section must also establish a particular urgency to inform the public about the Government activity involved in the request, beyond the public's right to know about Government activity generally.

(4) Within ten calendar days of its receipt of a request for expedited processing, the proper component shall decide whether to grant it and shall notify the requester of the decision. Solely for purposes of calculating the foregoing time limit, any request for expedited processing shall always be considered received on the actual date of receipt by the proper component. If a request for expedited processing is granted, the request shall be given priority and processed as soon as practicable, subject to §4.11(i). If a request for expedited processing is denied, any appeal of that decision shall be acted on expeditiously.

§4.7 Responses to requests.

(a) *Grants of requests.* If a component makes a determination to grant a request in whole or in part, it shall notify the requester in writing. The component shall inform the requester in the notice of any fee to be charged under §4.11 and disclose records to the requester promptly upon payment of any applicable fee. Records disclosed in part shall be marked or annotated to show the applicable FOIA exemption(s) and the amount of information deleted, unless doing so would harm an interest protected by an applicable exemption. The location of the information deleted shall also be indicated on the record, if feasible.

(b) *Adverse determinations of requests.* If a component makes an adverse determination regarding a request, it shall notify the requester of that determination in writing. An adverse determination is a denial of a request in any respect, namely: a determination to withhold any requested record in whole or in part; a determination that a requested record does not exist or cannot be located; a determination that a record is not readily reproducible in the form or format sought by the requester; a determination that what has been requested is not a record subject to the FOIA (except that a determination under §4.11(j) that records are to be made available under a fee statute other than the FOIA is not an adverse determination); a determination against the requester on any disputed fee matter, including a denial of a request for a reduction or waiver of fees; or a denial of a request for expedited processing. Each denial letter shall be signed by an official listed in Appendix B to this part, and shall include:

(1) The name and title or position of the denying official;

(2) A brief statement of the reason(s) for the denial, including applicable FOIA exemption(s);

(3) An estimate of the volume of records or information withheld, in number of pages or some other reasonable form of estimation. This estimate need not be provided if the volume is otherwise indicated through deletions on records disclosed in part, or if providing an estimate would harm an interest protected by an applicable FOIA exemption; and

(4) A statement that the denial may be appealed, and a list of the requirements for filing an appeal under §4.10(b).

§4.8 Classified Information.

In processing a request for information classified under Executive Order 12958 or any other executive order concerning the classification of records, the information shall be reviewed to determine whether it should remain classified. Ordinarily the component or other Federal agency that classified the information should conduct the review, except that if a record contains information that has been derivatively classified by a component because it contains information classified by another component or agency, the component shall refer the responsibility for responding to the request to the component or agency that classified the underlying information. Information determined to no longer require classification shall not be withheld on the basis of FOIA exemption (b)(1) (5 U.S.C. 552(b)(1)), but should be reviewed to assess whether any other FOIA exemptions should be invoked. Appeals involving classified information shall be processed in accordance with §4.10(c).

§4.9 Business Information.

(a) *In general.* Business information obtained by the Department from a submitter will be disclosed under the FOIA only under this section.

(b) *Definitions.* For the purposes of this section:

(1) *Business information* means commercial or financial information, obtained by the Department from a submitter, which may be protected from disclosure under FOIA exemption (b)(4) (5 U.S.C. 552(b)(4)).

(2) *Submitter* means any person or entity outside the Federal Government from which the Department obtains business information, directly or indirectly. The term includes corporations; state, local and tribal governments; and foreign governments.

(c) *Designation of business information.* A submitter of business information should designate by appropriate markings, either at the time of submission or at a reasonable time thereafter, any portions of its submission that it considers protected from disclosure under FOIA exemption (b)(4). These designations will expire ten years after the date of the submission unless the submitter requests, and provides justification for, a longer period.

(d) *Notice to submitters.* A component shall provide a submitter with prompt written notice of a FOIA request or administrative appeal that seeks its business information whenever required under paragraph (e) of this section, except as provided in paragraph (h) of this section, in order to give the submitter an opportunity under paragraph (f) of this section to object to disclosure of any specified portion of that information. Such written notice shall be sent via certified mail, return receipt requested, or similar means. The notice shall either describe the business information requested or include copies of the requested records containing the information. If notification of a large number of submitters is required, notification may be made by posting or publishing the notice in a place reasonably likely to accomplish notification.

(e) *When notice is required.* Notice shall be given to the submitter whenever:

(1) The submitter has designated the information in good faith as protected from disclosure under FOIA exemption (b)(4); or

(2) The component has reason to believe that the information may be protected from disclosure under FOIA exemption (b)(4).

(f) *Opportunity to object to disclosure.* A component shall allow a submitter seven working days (*i.e.*, excluding Saturdays, Sundays, and legal public holidays) from the date of receipt of the written notice described in paragraph (d) of this section to provide the component with a statement of any objection to disclosure. The statement must identify any portions of the information the submitter requests to be withheld under FOIA exemption (b)(4), and describe how each qualifies for protection under the exemption: that is, why the information is a trade secret, or commercial or financial information that is privileged or confidential. If a submitter fails to respond to the notice within the time specified, the submitter will be considered to have no objection to disclosure of the information. Information a submitter provides under this paragraph may itself be subject to disclosure under the FOIA.

(g) *Notice of intent to disclose.* A component shall consider a submitter's objections and specific grounds under the FOIA for nondisclosure in deciding whether to disclose business information. If a component decides to disclose business information over a submitter's objection, the component shall give the submitter written notice via certified mail, return receipt requested, or similar means, which shall include:

(1) A statement of reason(s) why the submitter's objections to disclosure were not sustained;

(2) A description of the business information to be disclosed; and

(3) A statement that the component intends to disclose the information seven working days from the date the submitter receives the notice.

(h) *Exceptions to notice requirements.* The notice requirements of paragraphs (d) and (g) of this section shall not apply if:

(1) The component determines that the information should not be disclosed;

(2) The information has been lawfully published or has been officially made available to the public;

(3) Disclosure of the information is required by statute (other than the FOIA) or by a regulation issued in accordance with Executive Order 12600; or

(4) The designation made by the submitter under paragraph (c) of this section appears obviously frivolous, in which case the component shall provide the submitter written notice of any final decision to disclose the information seven working days from the date the submitter receives the notice.

(i) *Notice to submitter of FOIA lawsuit.* Whenever a requester files a lawsuit seeking to compel the disclosure of business information, the component shall promptly notify the submitter.

(j) *Corresponding notice to requester.* Whenever a component provides a submitter with notice and an opportunity to object to disclosure under paragraph (d) of this section, the component shall also notify the requester. Whenever a submitter files a lawsuit seeking to prevent the disclosure of business information, the component shall notify the requester.

§4.10 Appeals from initial determinations or untimely delays.

(a) If a request for records is initially denied in whole or in part, or has not been timely determined, or if a requester receives an adverse initial determination regarding any other matter under this subpart (as described in §4.7(b)), the requester may file a written appeal or an electronic appeal, which must be received by the Office of General Counsel during normal business hours (8:30 a.m. to 5 p.m., Eastern Time, Monday through Friday) within thirty calendar days of the date of the written denial or, if there has been no determination, may be submitted anytime after the due date, including the last extension under §4.6(c), of the determination. Written or electronic appeals arriving after normal business hours will be deemed received on the next normal business day.

(b) Appeals shall be decided by the Assistant General Counsel for Administration (AGC-Admin), except that appeals for records which were initially denied by the AGC-Admin shall be decided by the General Counsel. Written appeals should be addressed to the AGC-Admin, or the General Counsel if the records were initially denied by the AGC-Admin. The address of both is: U.S. Department of Commerce, Office of General Counsel, Room 5875, 14th and Constitution Avenue NW., Washington, DC 20230. An appeal may also be sent via facsimile at 202–482–2552. For a written appeal, both the letter and the appeal envelope should be clearly marked "Freedom of Information Appeal". The address for electronic appeals is *FOIAAppeals@doc.gov*. The appeal (written or electronic) must include a copy of the original request and the initial denial, if any, and a statement of the reasons why the records requested should be made available and why the initial denial, if any, was in error. No opportunity for personal appearance, oral argument or hearing on appeal is provided.

(c) Upon receipt of an appeal involving records initially denied on the basis of FOIA exemption (b)(1), the records shall be forwarded to the Deputy Assistant Secretary for Security (DAS) for a declassification review. The DAS may overrule previous classification determinations in whole or in part if continued protection in the interest of national security is no longer required, or no longer required at the same level. The DAS shall advise the AGC-Admin, or the General Counsel, as appropriate, of his or her decision.

(d) If an appeal is granted, the person who filed the appeal shall be immediately notified and copies of the releasable documents shall be made available promptly thereafter upon receipt of appropriate fees determined in accordance with §4.11.

(e) If no determination on an appeal has been sent to the requester within the twenty working day period specified in §4.6(b) or the last extension thereof, the requester is deemed to have exhausted all administrative remedies with respect to the request, giving rise to a right of judicial review under 5 U.S.C. 552(a)(6)(C). If the requester initiates a court action against the Department based on the provision in this paragraph, the administrative appeal process may continue.

(f) The determination on an appeal shall be in writing and, when it denies records in whole or in part, the letter to the requester shall include:

(1) A brief explanation of the basis for the denial, including a list of the applicable FOIA exemptions and a description of how they apply;

(2) A statement that the decision is final for the Department;

(3) Notification that judicial review of the denial is available in the district court of the United States in the district in which the requester resides, or has his or her principal place of business, or in which the agency records are located, or in the District of Columbia; and

(4) The name and title or position of the official responsible for denying the appeal.

[66 FR 65632, Dec. 20, 2001, as amended at 69 FR 49784, Aug. 12, 2004]

§4.11 Fees.

(a) *In general.* Components shall charge for processing requests under the FOIA in accordance with paragraph (c) of this section, except when fees are limited under paragraph (d) of this section or when a waiver or reduction of fees is granted under paragraph (k) of this section. A component shall collect all applicable fees before sending copies of requested records to a requester. Requesters must pay fees by check or money order made payable to the Treasury of the United States.

(b) *Definitions.* For purposes of this section:

(1) *Commercial use request* means a request from or on behalf of a person who seeks information for a use or purpose that furthers his or her commercial, trade, or profit interests, which can include furthering those interests through litigation. Components shall determine, whenever reasonably possible, the use to which a requester will put the requested records. If it appears that the requester will put the records to a commercial use, or if a component has reasonable cause to doubt a requester's asserted non-commercial use, the component shall provide the requester a reasonable opportunity to submit further clarification.

(2) *Direct costs* means those expenses a component incurs in providing a particular service. Such expenses would include, for example, the labor costs of the employee performing the service (the basic rate of pay for the employee, plus 16 percent of that rate to cover benefits). Not included in direct costs are overhead expenses such as the costs of space, heating, or lighting of the facility in which the service is performed.

(3) *Duplication* means the making of a copy of a record, or of the information contained in it, necessary to respond to a FOIA request. Copies may take the form of paper, microform, audiovisual materials, or electronic records (for example, magnetic tape or disk), among others. A component shall honor a requester's specified preference of form or format of disclosure if the component can reproduce the record in the requested form or format with reasonable effort.

(4) *Educational institution* means a preschool, a public or private elementary or secondary school, an institution of undergraduate higher education, an institution of graduate higher education, an institution of professional education, or an institution of vocational education, that operates a program of scholarly research. To be in this category, a requester must show that the request is authorized by and is made under the auspices of a qualifying institution, and that the records are sought to further scholarly research rather than for a commercial use.

(5) *Noncommercial scientific institution* means an institution that is not operated on a "commercial" basis, as that term is defined in paragraph (b)(1) of this section, and that is operated solely for the purpose of conducting scientific research, the results of which are not intended to promote any particular product or industry. To be in this category, a requester must show that the request is authorized by and is made under the auspices of a qualifying institution and that the records are sought to further scientific research rather than for a commercial use.

(6) *Representative of the news media, or news media requester* means any person actively gathering news for an entity that is organized and operated to publish or broadcast news to the public. The term "news" means information that is about current events or that would be of current interest to the public. Examples of news media entities include television or radio stations broadcasting to the public at large and publishers of periodicals (but only if they can qualify as disseminators of "news") that make their products available for purchase or subscription by the general public. For "freelance" journalists to be regarded as working for a news organization, they must demonstrate a solid basis for expecting publication through that organization. A publication contract would be the clearest proof, but components shall also look to the past publication record of a requester in making this determination. To be in this category, a requester must not be seeking the requested records for a commercial use.

However, a request for records supporting the news-dissemination function of the requester shall not be considered to be for a commercial use.

(7) *Review* means the examination of a record located in response to a request in order to determine whether any portion of it is exempt from disclosure. It also includes processing any record for disclosure, for example, redacting it and marking any applicable exemptions. Review costs are recoverable even if a record ultimately is not disclosed. Review time does not include time spent resolving general legal or policy issues regarding the application of exemptions.

(8) *Search* means the process of looking for and retrieving records or information responsive to a request. It includes page-by-page or line-by-line identification of information within records and also includes reasonable efforts to locate and retrieve information from records maintained in electronic form or format. Components shall ensure that searches are done in the most efficient and least expensive manner reasonably possible.

(c) *Fees.* In responding to FOIA requests, components shall charge the fees summarized in chart form in paragraphs (c)(1) and (c)(2) of this section and explained in paragraphs (c)(3) through (c)(5) of this section, unless a waiver or reduction of fees has been granted under paragraph (k) of this section.

(1) The four categories and chargeable fees are:

Category	Chargeable fees
(i) Commercial Use Requesters	Search, Review, and Duplication.
(ii) Educational and Non-commercial Scientific Institution Requesters.	Duplication (excluding the cost of the first 100 pages).
(iii) Representatives of the News Media	Duplication (excluding the cost of the first 100 pages).
(iv) All Other Requesters	Search and Duplication (excluding the cost of the first 2 hours of search and 100 pages).

(2) Uniform fee schedule.

Service	Rate
(i) Manual search	Actual salary rate of employee involved, plus 16 percent of salary rate.
(ii) Computerized search	Actual direct cost, including operator time.
(iii) Duplication of records:	
(A) Paper copy reproduction	$.16 per page
(B) Other reproduction (e.g., computer disk or printout, microfilm, microfiche, or microform).	Actual direct cost, including operator time.
(iv) Review of records (including redaction)	Actual salary rate of employee conducting review, plus 16 percent of salary rate.

(3) *Search.* (i) Search fees shall be charged for all requests—other than requests made by educational institutions, noncommercial scientific institutions, or representatives of the news media—subject to the limitations of paragraph (d) of this section. Components shall charge for time spent searching even if they do not locate any responsive records or if they withhold any records located as entirely exempt from disclosure. Search fees shall be the direct costs of conducting the search by the involved employees.

(ii) For computer searches of records, requesters will be charged the direct costs of conducting the search, although certain requesters (as provided in paragraph (d)(1) of this section) will be charged no search fee and certain other requesters (as provided in paragraph (d)(3) of this section) are entitled to the cost equivalent of two hours of manual search time without charge.

(4) *Duplication.* Duplication fees shall be charged to all requesters, subject to the limitations of paragraph (d) of this section. For a paper photocopy of a record (no more than one copy of which need be supplied), the fee shall be $.16 cents per page. For copies produced by computer, such as tapes or printouts, components shall charge the direct

costs, including operator time, of producing the copy. For other forms of duplication, components shall charge the direct costs of that duplication.

(5) *Review.* Review fees shall be charged to requesters who make a commercial use request. Review fees shall be charged only for the initial record review, in which a component determines whether an exemption applies to a particular record at the initial request level. No charge shall be imposed for review at the administrative appeal level for an exemption already applied. However, records withheld under an exemption that is subsequently determined not to apply may be reviewed again to determine whether any other exemption not previously considered applies, and the costs of that review are chargeable. Review fees shall be the direct costs of conducting the review by the involved employees.

(d) *Limitations on charging fees.* (1) No search fee shall be charged for requests from educational institutions, noncommercial scientific institutions, or representatives of the news media.

(2) No search fee or review fee shall be charged for a quarter-hour period unless more than half of that period is required for search or review.

(3) Except for requesters seeking records for a commercial use, components shall provide without charge:

(i) The first 100 pages of duplication (or the cost equivalent); and

(ii) The first two hours of search (or the cost equivalent).

(4) If a total fee calculated under paragraph (c) of this section is $20.00 or less for any request, no fee shall be charged. If such total fee is more than $20.00, the full amount of such fee shall be charged.

(5) The provisions of paragraphs (d)(3) and (4) of this section work together. This means that for requesters other than those seeking records for a commercial use, no fee shall be charged unless the cost of search in excess of two hours plus the cost of duplication in excess of 100 pages totals more than $20.00.

(e) *Notice of anticipated fees over $20.00.* If a component determines or estimates that the total fee to be charged under this section will be more than $20.00, the component shall notify the requester of the actual or estimated fee, unless the requester has stated in writing a willingness to pay a fee as high as that anticipated. If only a portion of the fee can be estimated readily, the component shall advise the requester that the estimated fee may be only a portion of the total fee. If the component has notified a requester that the actual or estimated fee is more than $20.00, the component shall not consider the request received for purposes of calculating the time limit in §4.6(b) to respond to a request, or process it further, until the requester agrees to pay the anticipated total fee. Any agreement to pay should be memorialized in writing. A notice under this paragraph shall offer the requester an opportunity to contact Departmental personnel to discuss modifying the request to meet the requester's needs at a lower cost.

(f) *Charges for other services.* Apart from the other provisions of this section, if a component decides, as a matter of administrative discretion, to comply with a request for special services, the component shall charge the direct cost of providing them. Such services could include certifying that records are true copies or sending records by other than ordinary mail.

(g) *Charging interest.* Components shall charge interest on any unpaid bill starting on the 31st calendar day following the date of billing the requester. Interest charges shall be assessed at the rate provided in 31 U.S.C. 3717 and accrue from the date of the billing until the component receives payment. Components shall take all steps authorized by the Debt Collection Act of 1982, as amended by the Debt Collection Improvement Act of 1996, to effect payment, including offset, disclosure to consumer reporting agencies, and use of collection agencies.

(h) *Aggregating requests.* If a component reasonably believes that a requester or a group of requesters acting together is attempting to divide a request into a series of requests for the purpose of avoiding fees, the component may aggregate those requests and charge accordingly. Among the factors a component shall consider in deciding whether to aggregate are the closeness in time between the component's receipt of the requests, and the relatedness of the matters about which the requests are made. A component may generally presume that multiple requests that involve related matters made by the same requester or a closely related group of requesters within a 30 calendar day period have been made in order to avoid fees. If requests are separated by a longer period, a component shall aggregate them only if a solid basis exists for determining that aggregation is warranted under all the circumstances involved. Multiple requests involving unrelated matters shall not be aggregated.

(i) *Advance payments.* (1) For requests other than those described in paragraphs (i)(2) and (3) of this section, a component shall not require the requester to make an advance payment: a payment made before work is begun or continued on a request. Payment owed for work already completed (*i.e.*, a payment before copies are sent to a requester) is not an advance payment.

(2) If a component determines or estimates that a total fee to be charged under this section will be more than $250.00, the component shall not consider the request received for purposes of calculating the time limit in §4.6(b) to respond to a request, or process it further, until it receives payment from the requester of the entire anticipated fee.

(3) If a requester has previously failed to pay a properly charged FOIA fee to any component or other Federal agency within 30 calendar days of the date of billing, a component shall require the requester to pay the full amount due, plus any applicable interest, and to make an advance payment of the full amount of any anticipated fee, before the component begins to process a new request or continues to process a pending request from that requester. For purposes of calculating the time limit in §4.6(b) to respond to a request, the component shall not consider the request received until it receives full payment of all applicable fees and interest in this paragraph.

(4) Upon the completion of processing of a request, if a specific fee is determined to be payable and appropriate notice has been given to the requester, a component shall make records available to the requester only upon receipt of full payment of the fee.

(j) *Other statutes specifically providing for fees.* The fee schedule of this section does not apply to fees charged under any statute (except for the FOIA) that specifically requires an agency to set and collect fees for particular types of records. If records responsive to requests are maintained for distribution by agencies operating such statutorily based fee schedule programs, components shall inform requesters how to obtain records from those sources. Provision of such records is not handled under the FOIA.

(k) *Requirements for waiver or reduction of fees.* (1) Records responsive to a request will be furnished without charge, or at a charge reduced below that established under paragraph (c) of this section, if the requester asks for such a waiver in writing and the responsible component determines, after consideration of information provided by the requester, that the requester has demonstrated that:

(i) Disclosure of the requested information is in the public interest because it is likely to contribute significantly to public understanding of the operations or activities of the Government; and

(ii) Disclosure of the information is not primarily in the commercial interest of the requester.

(2) To determine whether the first fee waiver requirement is met, components shall consider the following factors:

(i) *The subject of the request:* whether the subject of the requested records concerns the operations or activities of the Government. The subject of the requested records must concern identifiable operations or activities of the Federal Government, with a connection that is direct and clear, not remote or attenuated.

(ii) *The informative value of the information to be disclosed:* whether the disclosure is "likely to contribute" to an understanding of Government operations or activities. The disclosable portions of the requested records must be meaningfully informative about Government operations or activities in order to be "likely to contribute" to an increased public understanding of those operations or activities. The disclosure of information that already is in the public domain, in either a duplicative or a substantially identical form, would not be likely to contribute to such understanding.

(iii) *The contribution to an understanding of the subject by the public likely to result from disclosure:* whether disclosure of the requested information will contribute to the understanding of a reasonably broad audience of persons interested in the subject, as opposed to the individual understanding of the requester. A requester's expertise in the subject area and ability and intention to effectively convey information to the public shall be considered. It shall be presumed that a representative of the news media satisfies this consideration. Merely providing information to media sources is insufficient to satisfy this consideration.

(iv) *The significance of the contribution to public understanding:* whether the disclosure is likely to contribute "significantly" to public understanding of Government operations or activities. The public's understanding of the subject in question prior to the disclosure must be significantly enhanced by the disclosure.

(3) To determine whether the second fee waiver requirement (*i.e.*, that disclosure is not primarily in the commercial interest of the requester) is met, components shall consider the following factors:

(i) *The existence and magnitude of a commercial interest:* whether the requester has a commercial interest that would be furthered by the requested disclosure. Components shall consider any commercial interest of the requester (with reference to the definition of "commercial use request" in paragraph (b)(1) of this section), or of any person on whose behalf the requester may be acting, that would be furthered by the requested disclosure. Requesters shall be given an opportunity to provide explanatory information regarding this consideration.

(ii) *The primary interest in disclosure:* whether any identified commercial interest of the requester is sufficiently great, in comparison with the public interest in disclosure, that disclosure is "primarily in the commercial interest of the requester." A fee waiver or reduction is justified if the public interest standard (paragraph (k)(1)(i) of this section) is satisfied and the public interest is greater than any identified commercial interest in disclosure. Components ordinarily shall presume that if a news media requester has satisfied the public interest standard, the public interest is the primary interest served by disclosure to that requester. Disclosure to data brokers or others who merely compile and market Government information for direct economic return shall not be presumed to primarily serve the public interest.

(4) If only some of the records to be released satisfy the requirements for a fee waiver, a waiver shall be granted for those records.

(5) Requests for the waiver or reduction of fees should address the factors listed in paragraphs (k)(2) and (3) of this section, insofar as they apply to each request.

Subpart B—Privacy Act

§4.21 Purpose and scope.

(a) This subpart establishes policies and procedures for implementing the Privacy Act of 1974, as amended (5 U.S.C. 552a). The main objectives of the subpart are to facilitate full exercise of rights conferred on individuals under the Act, and to protect the privacy of individuals on whom the Department maintains records in systems of records under the Act.

(b) The Department shall act promptly and in accordance with the Act upon receipt of any inquiry, request or appeal from a citizen of the United States or an alien lawfully admitted for permanent residence into the United States, regardless of the individual's age. Further, the Department shall maintain only such information on individuals as is relevant and necessary to the performance of its lawful functions; maintain that information with such accuracy, relevancy, timeliness, and completeness as is reasonably necessary to assure fairness in determinations made by the Department about the individual; obtain information from the individual to the extent practicable; and take every reasonable step to protect that information from unwarranted disclosure. The Department shall maintain no record describing how an individual exercises rights guaranteed by the First Amendment unless expressly authorized to do so by statute or by the individual about whom the record is maintained, or unless to do so is pertinent to and within the scope of an authorized law enforcement activity. An individual's name and address shall not be sold or rented by the Department unless such action is specifically authorized by law.

(c) This subpart applies to all components of the Department. Components may promulgate supplementary orders and rules not inconsistent with this subpart.

(d) The Assistant Secretary for Administration is delegated responsibility for maintaining this subpart, for issuing such orders and directives internal to the Department as are necessary for full compliance with the Act, and for publishing all required notices concerning systems of records.

(e) Matters outside the scope of this subpart include:

(1) Requests for records that do not pertain to the requester, or to the individual about whom the request is made if the requester is the parent or guardian of the individual;

(2) Requests involving information pertaining to an individual that is in a record or file but not within the scope of a system of records notice published in the FEDERAL REGISTER;

(3) Requests to correct a record if a grievance procedure is available to the individual either by regulation or through a provision in a collective bargaining agreement with the Department or a component of the Department, and the individual has initiated, or expressed in writing the intention of initiating, such a grievance procedure; and

(4) Requests for employee-employer services and counseling that were routinely granted prior to enactment of the Act, including, but not limited to, test calculations of retirement benefits, explanations of health and life insurance programs, and explanations of tax withholding options.

(f) Any request for records that pertains to the requester, or to the individual about whom the request is made if the requester is the parent or guardian of the individual, shall be processed under the Act and this subpart and under the Freedom of Information Act and the Department's implementing regulations at subpart A of this part, regardless whether the Act or the Freedom of Information Act is mentioned in the request.

§4.22 Definitions.

(a) All terms used in this subpart which are defined in 5 U.S.C. 552a shall have the same meaning herein.

(b) As used in this subpart:

(1) *Act* means the "Privacy Act of 1974, as amended (5 U.S.C. 552a)".

(2) *Appeal* means a request by an individual to review and reverse an initial denial of a request from that individual for correction or amendment.

(3) *Component* means any office, division, bureau or other unit of the Department listed in Appendix A to this part (except that a regional office of a larger office or other unit does not constitute a separate component).

(4) *Department* means the Department of Commerce.

(5) *Inquiry* means either a request for general information regarding the Act and this subpart or a request from an individual (or that individual's parent or guardian) that the Department determine whether it has any record in a system of records that pertains to that individual.

(6) *Person* means any human being and also shall include, but is not limited to, corporations, associations, partnerships, trustees, receivers, personal representatives, and public or private organizations.

(7) *Privacy Officer* means those officials, identified in Appendix B to this part, who are authorized to receive and act upon inquiries, requests for access, and requests for correction or amendment.

(8) *Request for access* means a request from an individual or an individual's parent or guardian to see a record pertaining to that individual in a particular system of records.

(9) *Request for correction or amendment* means a request from an individual or an individual's parent or guardian that the Department change (by correction,

amendment, addition or deletion) a particular record pertaining to that individual in a system of records.

§4.23 Procedures for making inquiries.

(a) Any individual, regardless of age, who is a citizen of the United States or an alien lawfully admitted for permanent residence into the United States may submit an inquiry to the Department. The inquiry should be made either in person or by mail addressed to the appropriate component identified in Appendix A to this part or to the official identified in the notification procedures paragraph of the systems of records notice published in the FEDERAL REGISTER.[2] If an individual believes the Department maintains a record pertaining to him or her but does not know which system of records might contain such a record and/or which component of the Department maintains the system of records, assistance in person or by mail will be provided at the first address listed in Appendix A to this part.

(b) Inquiries submitted by mail should include the words "PRIVACY ACT INQUIRY" in capital letters at the top of the letter and on the face of the envelope. If the inquiry is for general information regarding the Act and this subpart, no particular information is required. The Department reserves the right to require compliance with the identification procedures appearing at §4.24(d). If the inquiry is a request that the Department determine whether it has a record pertaining to the individual, the following information should be submitted:

(1) Name of individual whose record is sought;

(2) Statement that individual whose record is sought is either a U.S. citizen or an alien lawfully admitted for permanent residence;

(3) Identifying data that will help locate the record (for example, maiden name, occupational license number, period or place of employment, etc.);

(4) Record sought, by description and by record system name, if known;

(5) Action requested (that is, sending information on how to exercise rights under the Act; determining whether requested record exists; gaining access to requested record; or obtaining copy of requested record);

(6) Copy of court guardianship order or minor's birth certificate, as provided in §4.24(d)(3), but only if requester is guardian or parent of individual whose record is sought;

(7) Requester's name (printed), signature, address, and (optional) telephone number;

(8) Date; and,

(9) Certification of request by notary or other official, but only if

(i) Request is for notification that requested record exists, for access to requested record, or for copy of requested record;

(ii) Record is not available to any person under 5 U.S.C. 552; and

(iii) Requester does not appear before an employee of the Department for verification of identity.

(c) Any inquiry which is not addressed as specified in paragraph (a) of this section or which is not marked as specified in paragraph (b) of this section will be so addressed and marked by Department personnel and forwarded immediately to the responsible Privacy Officer. An inquiry which is not properly addressed by the individual will not be deemed to have been "received" for purposes of measuring the time period for response until actual receipt by the Privacy Officer. In each instance when an inquiry so forwarded is received, the Privacy Officer shall notify the individual that his or her inquiry was improperly addressed and the date the inquiry was received at the proper address.

(d)(1) Each inquiry received shall be acted upon promptly by the responsible Privacy Officer. Every effort will be made to respond within ten working days (*i.e.*, excluding Saturdays, Sundays and legal public holidays) of the date of receipt at the proper address. If a response cannot be made within ten working days, the Privacy Officer shall send an acknowledgment during that

[2] The United States Patent and Trademark Office (USPTO), which is established as an agency of the United States within the Department of Commerce, operates under its own PA regulations at 37 CFR part 102, subpart B. Accordingly, requests concerning records maintained by the USPTO should be sent directly to the USPTO.

period providing information on the status of the inquiry and asking for such further information as may be necessary to process the inquiry. The first correspondence sent by the Privacy Officer to the requester shall contain the Department's control number assigned to the request, as well as a statement that the requester should use that number in all future contacts with the Department. The Department shall use that control number in all subsequent correspondence.

(2) If the Privacy Officer fails to send an acknowledgment within ten working days, as provided in paragraph (d)(1) of this section, the requester may ask the Assistant General Counsel for Administration to take corrective action. No failure of a Privacy Officer to send an acknowledgment shall confer administrative finality for purposes of judicial review.

(e) An individual shall not be required to state a reason for or otherwise justify his or her inquiry.

(f) Special note should be taken that certain agencies are responsible for publishing notices of systems of records having Government-wide application to other agencies, including the Department. The agencies known to be publishing these general notices and the types of records covered therein appear in Appendix C to this part. These general notices do not identify the Privacy Officers in the Department to whom inquiries should be presented or mailed. The provisions of this section, and particularly paragraph (a) of this section, should be followed in making inquiries with respect to such records. Such records in the Department are subject to the provisions of this part to the extent indicated in Appendix C to this part. The exemptions, if any, determined by the agency publishing a general notice shall be invoked and applied by the Department after consultation, as necessary, with that other agency.

§4.24 Procedures for making requests for records.

(a) Any individual, regardless of age, who is a citizen of the United States or an alien lawfully admitted for permanent residence into the United States may submit a request to the Department for access to records. The request should be made either in person or by mail addressed to the appropriate office listed in Appendix A to this part.

(b) Requests submitted by mail should include the words "PRIVACY ACT REQUEST" in capital letters at the top of the letter and on the face of the envelope. Any request which is not addressed as specified in paragraph (a) of this section or which is not marked as specified in this paragraph will be so addressed and marked by Department personnel and forwarded immediately to the responsible Privacy Officer. A request which is not properly addressed by the individual will not be deemed to have been "received" for purposes of measuring time periods for response until actual receipt by the Privacy Officer. In each instance when a request so forwarded is received, the Privacy Officer shall notify the individual that his or her request was improperly addressed and the date the request was received at the proper address.

(c) If the request follows an inquiry under §4.23 in connection with which the individual's identity was established by the Department, the individual need only indicate the record to which access is sought, provide the Department control number assigned to the request, and sign and date the request. If the request is not preceded by an inquiry under §4.23, the procedures of this section should be followed.

(d) The requirements for identification of individuals seeking access to records are:

(1) *In person.* Each individual making a request in person shall be required to present satisfactory proof of identity. The means of proof, in the order of preference and priority, are:

(i) A document bearing the individual's photograph (for example, driver's license, passport or military or civilian identification card);

(ii) A document, preferably issued for participation in a Federally-sponsored program, bearing the individual's signature (for example, unemployment insurance book, employer's identification card, national credit card, and professional, craft or union membership card); and,

(iii) A document bearing neither the photograph nor the signature of the individual, preferably issued for participation in a Federally-sponsored program (for example, Medicaid card). If the individual can provide no suitable documentation of identity, the Department will require a signed statement asserting the individual's identity and stipulating that the individual understands the penalty provision of 5 U.S.C. 552a(i)(3) recited in §4.32(a). In order to avoid any unwarranted disclosure of an individual's records, the Department reserves the right to determine the adequacy of proof of identity offered by any individual, particularly if the request involves a sensitive record.

(2) *Not in person.* If the individual making a request does not appear in person before a Privacy Officer or other employee authorized to determine identity, then identity must be determined by:

(i) A certification of a notary public or equivalent officer empowered to administer oaths must accompany the request under the circumstances prescribed in §4.23(b)(9). The certification in or attached to the letter must be substantially in accordance with the following text:

City of ______ County of ______. (Name of individual), who affixed (his) (her) signature below in my presence, came before me, a (title), in and for the aforesaid County and State, this ___ day of ___, 20__, and established (his) (her) identity to my satisfaction. My commission expires ______.

Signature: _________.; or

(ii) Statement of identity made under 28 U.S.C. 1746, a law that permits statements to be made under penalty of perjury as a substitute for notarization.

(3) *Parents of minors and legal guardians.* An individual acting as the parent of a minor or the legal guardian of the individual to whom a record pertains shall establish his or her personal identity in the same manner prescribed in either paragraph (d)(1) or (d)(2) of this section. In addition, such other individual shall establish his or her identity in the representative capacity of parent or legal guardian. In the case of the parent of a minor, the proof of identity shall be a certified or authenticated copy of the minor's birth certificate. In the case of a legal guardian of an individual who has been declared incompetent due to physical or mental incapacity or age by a court of competent jurisdiction, the proof of identity shall be a certified or authenticated copy of the court's order. For purposes of the Act, a parent or legal guardian may represent only a living individual, not a decedent. A parent or legal guardian may be accompanied during personal access to a record by another individual, provided the provisions of §4.25(f) are satisfied.

(e) If the provisions of this subpart are alleged to impede an individual in exercising his or her right to access, the Department will consider, from an individual making a request, alternative suggestions regarding proof of identity and access to records.

(f) An individual shall not be required to state a reason for or otherwise justify his or her request for access to a record.

[66 FR 65632, Dec. 20, 2001, as amended at 73 FR 10381, Feb. 27, 2008]

§4.25 Disclosure of requested records to individuals.

(a)(1) The responsible Privacy Officer shall act promptly upon each request. Every effort will be made to respond within ten working days (*i.e.*, excluding Saturdays, Sundays and legal public holidays) of the date of receipt. If a response cannot be made within ten working days due to unusual circumstances, the Privacy Officer shall send an acknowledgment during that period providing information on the status of the request and asking for any further information that may be necessary to process the request. "Unusual circumstances" shall include circumstances in which:

(i) A search for and collection of requested records from inactive storage, field facilities or other establishments is required;

(ii) A voluminous amount of data is involved;

(iii) Information on other individuals must be separated or expunged from the particular record; or

(iv) Consultations with other agencies having a substantial interest in the determination of the request are necessary.

(2) If the Privacy Officer fails to send an acknowledgment within ten working days, as provided in paragraph (a)(1) of this section, the requester may ask the Assistant General Counsel for Administration to take corrective action. No failure of a Privacy Officer to send an acknowledgment shall confer administrative finality for purposes of judicial review.

(b) Grant of access: (1) *Notification.* An individual shall be granted access to a record pertaining to him or her, unless the provisions of paragraph (g)(1) of this section apply. The Privacy Officer shall notify the individual of a determination to grant access, and provide the following information:

(i) The methods of access, as set forth in paragraph (b)(2) of this section;

(ii) The place at which the record may be inspected;

(iii) The earliest date on which the record may be inspected and the period of time that the records will remain available for inspection. In no event shall the earliest date be later than thirty calendar days from the date of notification;

(iv) The estimated date by which a copy of the record will be mailed and the fee estimate pursuant to §4.31. In no event shall the estimated date be later than thirty calendar days from the date of notification;

(v) The fact that the individual, if he or she wishes, may be accompanied by another individual during personal access, subject to the procedures set forth in paragraph (f) of this section; and,

(vi) Any additional prerequisites for granting access to a specific record.

(2) *Methods of access.* The following methods of access to records by an individual may be available depending on the circumstances of a given situation:

(i) Inspection in person may be had in the office specified by the Privacy Officer granting access, during the hours indicated in Appendix A to this part;

(ii) Transfer of records to a Federal facility more convenient to the individual may be arranged, but only if the Privacy Officer determines that a suitable facility is available, that the individual's access can be properly supervised at that facility, and that transmittal of the records to that facility will not unduly interfere with operations of the Department or involve unreasonable costs, in terms of both money and manpower; and,

(iii) Copies may be mailed at the request of the individual, subject to payment of the fees prescribed in §4.31. The Department, at its own initiative, may elect to provide a copy by mail, in which case no fee will be charged the individual.

(c) Access to medical records is governed by the provisions of §4.26.

(d) The Department shall supply such other information and assistance at the time of access as to make the record intelligible to the individual.

(e) The Department reserves the right to limit access to copies and abstracts of original records, rather than the original records. This election would be appropriate, for example, when the record is in an automated data medium such as tape or disc, when the record contains information on other individuals, and when deletion of information is permissible under exemptions (for example, 5 U.S.C. 552a(k)(2)). In no event shall original records of the Department be made available to the individual except under the immediate supervision of the Privacy Officer or his or her designee.

(f) Any individual who requests access to a record pertaining to that individual may be accompanied by another individual of his or her choice. "Accompanied" includes discussing the record in the presence of the other individual. The individual to whom the record pertains shall authorize the presence of the other individual in writing. The authorization shall include the name of the other individual, a specific description of the record to which access is sought, the Department control number assigned to the request, the date, and the signature of the individual to whom the record pertains. The other individual shall sign the authorization in the presence of the Privacy Officer. An individual shall not be required to state a reason or otherwise justify his or her decision to be accompanied by another individual during personal access to a record.

(g) Initial denial of access: (1) *Grounds.* Access by an individual to a record that pertains to that individual will be denied only upon a determination by the Privacy Officer that:

(i) The record is exempt under §4.33 or 4.34, or exempt by determination of another agency publishing notice of the system of records, as described in §4.23(f);

(ii) The record is information compiled in reasonable anticipation of a civil action or proceeding;

(iii) The provisions of §4.26 pertaining to medical records temporarily have been invoked; or,

(iv) The individual unreasonably has failed to comply with the procedural requirements of this part.

(2) *Notification.* The Privacy Officer shall give notice of denial of access to records to the individual in writing, and the notice shall include the following information:

(i) The Privacy Officer's name and title or position;

(ii) The date of the denial;

(iii) The reasons for the denial, including citation to the appropriate section of the Act and this part;

(iv) The individual's opportunities, if any, for further administrative consideration, including the identity and address of the responsible official. If no further administrative consideration within the Department is available, the notice shall state that the denial is administratively final; and,

(v) If stated to be administratively final within the Department, the individual's right to judicial review provided under 5 U.S.C.552a(g)(1), as limited by 5 U.S.C. 552a(g)(5).

(3) *Administrative review.* If a Privacy Officer issues an initial denial of a request, the individual's opportunities for further consideration shall be as follows:

(i) As to denial under paragraph (g)(1)(i) of this section, two opportunities for further consideration are available in the alternative:

(A) If the individual contests the application of an exemption to the records, the review procedures in §4.25(g)(3)(ii) shall apply; or,

(B) If the individual challenges the validity of the exemption itself, the individual must file a petition for the issuance, amendment, or repeal of a rule under 5 U.S.C. 553(e). If the exemption was determined by the Department, such petition shall be filed with the Assistant Secretary for Administration. If the exemption was determined by another agency (as described in §4.23(f)), the Department will provide the individual with the name and address of the other agency and any relief sought by the individual shall be that provided by the regulations of the other agency. Within the Department, no such denial is administratively final until such a petition has been filed by the individual and disposed of on the merits by the Assistant Secretary for Administration.

(ii) As to denial under paragraphs (g)(1)(ii) of this section, (g)(1)(iv) of this section or (to the limited extent provided in paragraph (g)(3)(i)(A) of this section) paragraph (g)(1)(i) of this section, the individual may file for review with the Assistant General Counsel for Administration, as indicated in the Privacy Officer's initial denial notification. The individual and the Department shall follow the procedures in §4.28 to the maximum extent practicable.

(iii) As to denial under paragraph (g)(1)(iii) of this section, no further administrative consideration within the Department is available because the denial is not administratively final until expiration of the time period indicated in §4.26(a).

(h) If a request is partially granted and partially denied, the Privacy Officer shall follow the appropriate procedures of this section as to the records within the grant and the records within the denial.

§4.26 Special procedures: Medical records.

(a) No response to any request for access to medical records from an individual will be issued by the Privacy Officer for a period of seven working days (*i.e.*, excluding Saturdays, Sundays and legal public holidays) from the date of receipt.

(b) For every request from an individual for access to medical records, the Privacy Officer shall:

(1) Inform the individual of the waiting period prescribed in paragraph (a) of this section;

(2) Seek from the individual the name and address of the individual's physician and/or psychologist;

(3) Seek from the individual written consent for the Department to consult the individual's physician and/or psychologist, if the Department believes such consultation is advisable;

(4) Seek written consent from the individual for the Department to provide the medical records to the individual's physician or psychologist, if the Department believes access to the record by the individual is best effected under the guidance of the individual's physician or psychologist; and,

(5) Forward the individual's medical record to the Department's medical officer for review and a determination on whether consultation with or transmittal of the medical records to the individual's physician or psychologist is warranted. If consultation with or transmittal of such records to the individual's physician or psychologist is determined to be warranted, the Department's medical officer shall so consult or transmit. Whether or not such a consultation or transmittal occurs, the Department's medical officer shall provide instruction to the Privacy Officer regarding the conditions of access by the individual to his or her medical records.

(c) If an individual refuses in writing to give the names and consents set forth in paragraphs (c)(2) through (c)(4) of this section, the Department shall give the individual access to said records by means of a copy, provided without cost to the requester, sent registered mail, return receipt requested.

§ 4.27 Procedures for making requests for correction or amendment.

(a) Any individual, regardless of age, who is a citizen of the United States or an alien lawfully admitted for permanent residence into the United States may submit a request for correction or amendment to the Department. The request should be made either in person or by mail addressed to the Privacy Officer who processed the individual's request for access to the record, and to whom is delegated authority to make initial determinations on requests for correction or amendment. The offices of Privacy Officers are open to the public between the hours of 9 a.m. and 4 p.m. Monday through Friday (excluding Saturdays, Sundays, and legal public holidays).

(b) Requests submitted by mail should include the words "PRIVACY ACT REQUEST" in capital letters at the top of the letter and on the face of the envelope. Any request that is not addressed as specified in paragraph (a) of this section or that is not marked as specified in this paragraph will be so addressed and marked by Department personnel and forwarded immediately to the responsible Privacy Officer. A request that is not properly addressed by the individual will not be deemed to have been "received" for purposes of measuring the time period for response until actual receipt by the Privacy Officer. In each instance when a request so forwarded is received, the Privacy Officer shall notify the individual that his or her request was improperly addressed and the date the request was received at the proper address.

(c) Since the request, in all cases, will follow a request for access under § 4.25, the individual's identity will be established by his or her signature on the request and use of the Department control number assigned to the request.

(d) A request for correction or amendment should include the following:

(1) Specific identification of the record sought to be corrected or amended (for example, description, title, date, paragraph, sentence, line and words);

(2) The specific wording to be deleted, if any;

(3) The specific wording to be inserted or added, if any, and the exact place at which it is to be inserted or added; and,

(4) A statement of the basis for the requested correction or amendment, with all available supporting documents and materials that substantiate the statement. The statement should identify the criterion of the Act being invoked, that is, whether the information in the record is unnecessary, inaccurate, irrelevant, untimely or incomplete.

§4.28 Agency review of requests for correction or amendment.

(a)(1)(i) Not later than ten working days (*i.e.*, excluding Saturdays, Sundays and legal public holidays) after receipt of a request to correct or amend a record, the Privacy Officer shall send an acknowledgment providing an estimate of time within which action will be taken on the request and asking for such further information as may be necessary to process the request. The estimate of time may take into account unusual circumstances as described in §4.25(a). No acknowledgment will be sent if the request can be reviewed, processed and the individual notified of the results of review (either compliance or denial) within the ten working days. Requests filed in person will be acknowledged in writing at the time submitted.

(ii) If the Privacy Officer fails to send the acknowledgment within ten working days, as provided in paragraph (a)(1)(i) of this section, the requester may ask the Assistant General Counsel for Administration to take corrective action. No failure of a Privacy Officer to send an acknowledgment shall confer administrative finality for purposes of judicial review.

(2) Promptly after acknowledging receipt of a request, or after receiving such further information as might have been requested, or after arriving at a decision within the ten working days, the Privacy Officer shall either:

(i) Make the requested correction or amendment and advise the individual in writing of such action, providing either a copy of the corrected or amended record or, in cases in which a copy cannot be provided (for example, erasure of information from a record maintained only in magnetically-recorded computer files), a statement as to the means by which the correction or amendment was effected; or,

(ii) Inform the individual in writing that his or her request is denied and provide the following information:

(A) The Privacy Officer's name and title or position;

(B) The date of the denial;

(C) The reasons for the denial, including citation to the appropriate sections of the Act and this subpart; and,

(D) The procedures for appeal of the denial as set forth in §4.29, including the address of the Assistant General Counsel for Administration.

(3) The term *promptly* in this section means within thirty working days (*i.e.*, excluding Saturdays, Sundays and legal public holidays). If the Privacy Officer cannot make the determination within thirty working days, the individual will be advised in writing of the reason for the delay and of the estimated date by which the determination will be made.

(b) Whenever an individual's record is corrected or amended pursuant to a request from that individual, the Privacy Officer shall notify all persons and agencies to which the corrected or amended portion of the record had been disclosed prior to its correction or amendment, if an accounting of such disclosure required by the Act was made. The notification shall require a recipient agency maintaining the record to acknowledge receipt of the notification, to correct or amend the record, and to apprise any agency or person to which it had disclosed the record of the substance of the correction or amendment.

(c) The following criteria will be considered by the Privacy Officer in reviewing a request for correction or amendment:

(1) The sufficiency of the evidence submitted by the individual;

(2) The factual accuracy of the information to be corrected or amended;

(3) The relevance and necessity of the information in terms of the purpose for which it was collected;

(4) The timeliness and currency of the information in light of the purpose for which it was collected;

(5) The completeness of the information in terms of the purpose for which it was collected;

(6) The degree of risk that denial of the request could unfairly result in determinations adverse to the individual;

(7) The character of the record sought to be corrected or amended; and,

(8) The propriety and feasibility of complying with the specific means of correction or amendment requested by the individual.

(d) The Department will not undertake to gather evidence for the individual, but does reserve the right to verify the evidence the individual submits.

(e) Correction or amendment of a record requested by an individual will be denied only upon a determination by the Privacy Officer that:

(1) The individual has failed to establish, by a preponderance of the evidence, the propriety of the correction or amendment in light of the criteria set forth in paragraph (c) of this section;

(2) The record sought to be corrected or amended is part of the official record in a terminated judicial, quasi-judicial or quasi-legislative proceeding to which the individual was a party or participant;

(3) The information in the record sought to be corrected or amended, or the record sought to be corrected or amended, is the subject of a pending judicial, quasi-judicial or quasi-legislative proceeding to which the individual is a party or participant;

(4) The correction or amendment would violate a duly enacted statute or promulgated regulation; or,

(5) The individual unreasonably has failed to comply with the procedural requirements of this part.

(f) If a request is partially granted and partially denied, the Privacy Officer shall follow the appropriate procedures of this section as to the records within the grant and the records within the denial.

§4.29 Appeal of initial adverse agency determination on correction or amendment.

(a) If a request for correction or amendment is denied initially under §4.28, the individual may submit a written appeal within thirty working days (*i.e.*, excluding Saturdays, Sundays and legal public holidays) of the date of the initial denial. If an appeal is submitted by mail, the postmark is conclusive as to timeliness.

(b) An appeal should be addressed to the Assistant General Counsel for Administration, U.S. Department of Commerce, Room 5875, 14th and Constitution Avenue, NW., Washington, DC 20230. An appeal should include the words "PRIVACY APPEAL" in capital letters at the top of the letter and on the face of the envelope. An appeal not addressed and marked as provided herein will be so marked by Department personnel when it is so identified, and will be forwarded immediately to the Assistant General Counsel for Administration. An appeal which is not properly addressed by the individual will not be deemed to have been "received" for purposes of measuring the time periods in this section until actual receipt by the Assistant General Counsel for Administration. In each instance when an appeal so forwarded is received, the Assistant General Counsel for Administration shall notify the individual that his or her appeal was improperly addressed and the date on which the appeal was received at the proper address.

(c) The individual's appeal shall be signed by the individual, and shall include a statement of the reasons why the initial denial is believed to be in error, and the Department's control number assigned to the request. The Privacy Officer who issued the initial denial shall furnish to the Assistant General Counsel for Administration the record the individual requests to be corrected or amended, and all correspondence between the Privacy Officer and the requester. Although the foregoing normally will comprise the entire record on appeal, the Assistant General Counsel for Administration may seek any additional information necessary to ensure that the final determination is fair and equitable and, in such instances, disclose the additional information to the individual to the greatest extent possible, and provide an opportunity for comment thereon.

(d) No personal appearance or hearing on appeal will be allowed.

(e) The Assistant General Counsel for Administration shall act upon the appeal and issue a final determination in writing not later than thirty working days (*i.e.*, excluding Saturdays, Sundays and legal public holidays) from the date on which the appeal is received, except that the Assistant General Counsel for Administration may extend the thirty days upon deciding that a fair and equitable review cannot be made within that period, but only if the individual is advised in writing of the reason for the extension and the estimated date by which a final determination will issue. The estimated date should not be later than the sixtieth working day after receipt of the appeal unless unusual circumstances, as described in §4.25(a), are met.

(f) If the appeal is determined in favor of the individual, the final determination shall include the specific corrections or amendments to be made and a copy thereof shall be transmitted promptly to the individual and to the Privacy Officer who issued the initial denial. Upon receipt of such final determination, the Privacy Officer shall promptly take the actions set forth in §4.28(a)(2)(i) and (b).

(g) If the appeal is denied, the final determination shall be transmitted promptly to the individual and state the reasons for the denial. The notice of final determination also shall inform the individual that:

(1) The individual has a right under the Act to file with the Assistant General Counsel for Administration a concise statement of reasons for disagreeing with the final determination. The statement ordinarily should not exceed one page and the Department reserves the right to reject an excessively lengthy statement. It should provide the Department control number assigned to the request, indicate the date of the final determination and be signed by the individual. The Assistant General Counsel for Administration shall acknowledge receipt of such statement and inform the individual of the date on which it was received;

(2) Any such disagreement statement submitted by the individual would be noted in the disputed record, and filed with it;

(3) The purposes and uses to which the statement would be put are those applicable to the record in which it is noted, and that a copy of the statement would be provided to persons and agencies to which the record is disclosed subsequent to the date of receipt of such statement;

(4) The Department would append to any such disagreement statement a copy of the final determination or summary thereof, which also would be provided to persons and agencies to which the disagreement statement is disclosed; and

(5) The individual has a right to judicial review of the final determination under 5 U.S.C. 552a(g)(1)(A), as limited by 5 U.S.C. 552a(g)(5).

(h) In making the final determination, the Assistant General Counsel for Administration shall employ the criteria set forth in §4.28(c) and shall deny an appeal only on the grounds set forth in §4.28(e).

(i) If an appeal is partially granted and partially denied, the Assistant General Counsel for Administration shall follow the appropriate procedures of this section as to the records within the grant and the records within the denial.

(j) Although a copy of the final determination or a summary thereof will be treated as part of the individual's record for purposes of disclosure in instances where the individual has filed a disagreement statement, it will not be subject to correction or amendment by the individual.

(k) The provisions of paragraphs (g)(1) through (g)(3) of this section satisfy the requirements of 5 U.S.C. 552a(e)(3).

§4.30 Disclosure of record to person other than the individual to whom it pertains.

(a) The Department may disclose a record pertaining to an individual to a person other than the individual to whom it pertains only in the following instances:

(1) Upon written request by the individual, including authorization under §4.25(f);

(2) With the prior written consent of the individual;

(3) To a parent or legal guardian under 5 U.S.C. 552a(h);

(4) When required by the Act and not covered explicitly by the provisions of 5 U.S.C. 552a(b); and

(5) When permitted under 5 U.S.C. 552a(b)(1) through (12), as follows:[3]

(i) To those officers and employees of the agency that maintains the record

[3] 5 U.S.C. 552a(b)(4) has no application within the Department.

who have a need for the record in the performance of their duties;

(ii) Required under 5 U.S.C. 552;

(iii) For a routine use as defined in 5 U.S.C. 552a(a)(7);

(iv) To the Bureau of the Census for purposes of planning or carrying out a census or survey or related activity pursuant to the provisions of Title 13 of the U.S. Code;

(v) To a requester who has provided the agency with advance adequate written assurance that the record will be used solely as a statistical research or reporting record, and the record is to be transferred in a form that is not individually identifiable;

(vi) To the National Archives and Records Administration as a record that has sufficient historical or other value to warrant its continued preservation by the United States Government, or for evaluation by the Archivist of the United States, or the designee of the Archivist, to determine whether the record has such value;

(vii) To another agency or to an instrumentality of any governmental jurisdiction within or under the control of the United States for a civil or criminal law enforcement activity if the activity is authorized by law, and if the head of the agency or instrumentality has made a written request to the agency which maintains the record, specifying the particular portion desired and the law enforcement activity for which the record is sought;

(viii) To a person pursuant to a showing of compelling circumstances affecting the health or safety of an individual if upon such disclosure notification is transmitted to the last known address of such individual;

(ix) To either House of Congress, or, to the extent of matter within its jurisdiction, any committee or subcommittee thereof, any joint committee of Congress or subcommittee of any such joint committee;

(x) To the Comptroller General, or any of his or her authorized representatives, in the course of the performance of the duties of the General Accounting Office;

(xi) Pursuant to the order of a court of competent jurisdiction; or

(xii) To a consumer reporting agency in accordance with 31 U.S.C. 3711(e).

(b) The situations referred to in paragraph (a)(4) of this section include the following:

(1) 5 U.S.C. 552a(c)(4) requires dissemination of a corrected or amended record or notation of a disagreement statement by the Department in certain circumstances;

(2) 5 U.S.C. 552a(d) requires disclosure of records to the individual to whom they pertain, upon request; and

(3) 5 U.S.C. 552a(g) authorizes civil action by an individual and requires disclosure by the Department to the court.

(c) The Privacy Officer shall make an accounting of each disclosure by him of any record contained in a system of records in accordance with 5 U.S.C. 552a(c)(1) and (2). Except for a disclosure made under 5 U.S.C. 552a(b)(7), the Privacy Officer shall make such accounting available to any individual, insofar as it pertains to that individual, upon any request submitted in accordance with §4.24. The Privacy Officer shall make reasonable efforts to notify any individual when any record in a system of records is disclosed to any person under compulsory legal process, promptly upon being informed that such process has become a matter of public record.

[66 FR 65632, Dec. 20, 2001, as amended at 67 FR 60282, Sept. 25, 2002]

§4.31 Fees.

(a) The only fee to be charged to an individual under this part is for duplication of records at the request of the individual. Components shall charge a fee for duplication of records under the Act in the same way in which they charge a duplication fee under §4.11, except as provided in this section. Accordingly, no fee shall be charged or collected for: search, retrieval, or review of records; copying at the initiative of the Department without a request from the individual; transportation of records; or first-class postage.

(b) The Department shall provide an individual one copy of each record corrected or amended pursuant to the individual's request without charge as evidence of the correction or amendment.

(c) As required by the United States Office of Personnel Management in its published regulations implementing the Act, the Department shall charge no fee for a single copy of a personnel record covered by that agency's Government-wide published notice of systems of records.

§ 4.32 Penalties.

(a) The Act provides, in pertinent part:

Any person who knowingly and willfully requests or obtains any record concerning an individual from an agency under false pretenses shall be guilty of a misdemeanor and fined not more than $5,000. (5 U.S.C. 552a(i)(3)).

(b) A person who falsely or fraudulently attempts to obtain records under the Act also may be subject to prosecution under such other criminal statutes as 18 U.S.C. 494, 495 and 1001.

§ 4.33 General exemptions.

(a) Individuals may not have access to records maintained by the Department but which were provided by another agency which has determined by regulation that such information is subject to general exemption under 5 U.S.C. 552a(j). If such exempt records are within a request for access, the Department will advise the individual of their existence and of the name and address of the source agency. For any further information concerning the record and the exemption, the individual must contact that source agency.

(b) The general exemptions determined to be necessary and proper with respect to systems of records maintained by the Department, including the parts of each system to be exempted, the provisions of the Act from which they are exempted, and the justification for the exemption, are as follows:

(1) *Individuals identified in Export Transactions*—COMMERCE/ITA–1. Pursuant to 5 U.S.C. 552a(j)(2), these records are hereby determined to be exempt from all provisions of the Act, except 5 U.S.C. 552a(b), (c)(1) and (2), (e)(4) (A) through (F), (e) (6), (7), (9), (10), and (11), and (i). These exemptions are necessary to ensure the proper functioning of the law enforcement activity, to protect confidential sources of information, to fulfill promises of confidentiality, to maintain the integrity of the law enforcement process, to avoid premature disclosure of the knowledge of criminal activity and the evidentiary bases of possible enforcement actions, to prevent interference with law enforcement proceedings, to avoid disclosure of investigative techniques, and to avoid endangering law enforcement personnel. Section 12(c) of the Export Administration Act of 1979, as amended, also protects this information from disclosure.

(2) *Fisheries Law Enforcement Case Files—COMMERCE/NOAA–5*. Pursuant to 5 U.S.C. 552a(j)(2), these records are hereby determined to be exempt from all provisions of the Act, except 5 U.S.C. 552a (b), (c) (1) and (2), (e) (4) (A) through (F), (e) (6), (7), (9), (10), and (11), and (i). These exemptions are necessary to ensure the proper functioning of the law enforcement activity, to protect confidential sources of information, to fulfill promises of confidentiality, to prevent interference with law enforcement proceedings, to avoid the disclosure of investigative techniques, to avoid the endangering of law enforcement personnel, to avoid premature disclosure of the knowledge of criminal activity and the evidentiary bases of possible enforcement actions, and to maintain the integrity of the law enforcement process.

(3) *Investigative and Inspection Records—COMMERCE/DEPT–12*. Pursuant to 5 U.S.C. 552a(j)(2), these records are hereby determined to be exempt from all provisions of the Act, except 5 U.S.C. 552a (b), (c) (1) and (2), (e)(4) (A) through (F), (e) (6), (7), (9), (10), and (11), and (i). These exemptions are necessary to ensure the proper operation of the law enforcement activity, to protect confidential sources of information, to fulfill promises of confidentiality, to prevent interference with law enforcement proceedings, to avoid the disclosure of investigative techniques, to avoid the endangering of law enforcement personnel, to avoid premature disclosure of the knowledge of criminal activity and the evidentiary bases of possible enforcement actions, and to maintain the integrity of the law enforcement process.

§4.34 Specific exemptions.

(a)(1) Certain systems of records under the Act that are maintained by the Department may occasionally contain material subject to 5 U.S.C. 552a(k)(1), relating to national defense and foreign policy materials. The systems of records published in the FEDERAL REGISTER by the Department that are within this exemption are:

COMMERCE/ITA-1, COMMERCE/ITA-2, COMMERCE/ITA-3, COMMERCE/NOAA-11, COMMERCE/PAT-TM-4, COMMERCE/DEPT-12, COMMERCE/DEPT-13, and COMMERCE/DEPT-14.

(2) The Department hereby asserts a claim to exemption of such materials wherever they might appear in such systems of records, or any systems of records, at present or in the future. The materials would be exempt from 5 U.S.C. 552a (c)(3), (d), (e)(1), (e)(4) (G), (H), and (I), and (f), because the materials are required by Executive order to be kept secret in the interest of the national defense and foreign policy.

(b) The specific exemptions determined to be necessary and proper with respect to systems of records maintained by the Department, including the parts of each system to be exempted, the provisions of the Act from which they are exempted, and the justification for the exemption, are as follows:

(1) Exempt under 5 U.S.C. 552a(k)(1). The systems of records exempt hereunder appear in paragraph (a) of this section. The claims for exemption of COMMERCE/DEPT–12, COMMERCE/ITA–1, and COMMERCE/NOAA–11 under this paragraph are subject to the condition that the general exemption claimed in §4.33(b)(3) is held to be invalid.

(2)(i) Exempt under 5 U.S.C. 552a(k)(2). The systems of records exempt (some only conditionally), the sections of the Act from which exempted, and the reasons therefor are as follows:

(A) Individuals identified in Export Administration compliance proceedings or investigations—COMMERCE/ITA–1, but only on condition that the general exemption claimed in §4.33(b)(1) is held to be invalid;

(B) Individuals involved in export transactions—COMMERCE/ITA–2;

(C) Fisheries Law Enforcement Case Files—COMMERCE/NOAA–11, but only on condition that the general exemption claimed in §4.33(b)(2) is held to be invalid;

(D) Investigative and Inspection Records—COMMERCE/DEPT–12, but only on condition that the general exemption claimed in §4.33(b)(3) is held to be invalid;

(E) Investigative Records—Persons Within the Investigative Jurisdiction of the Department—COMMERCE/DEPT–13;

(F) Litigation, Claims and Administrative Proceeding Records—COMMERCE/DEPT–14; and

(ii) The foregoing are exempted from 5 U.S.C. 552a (c)(3), (d), (e)(1), (e)(4)(G), (H), and (I), and (f). The reasons for asserting the exemption are to prevent subjects of investigation from frustrating the investigatory process; to ensure the proper functioning and integrity of law enforcement activities; to prevent disclosure of investigative techniques; to maintain the ability to obtain necessary information; to fulfill commitments made to sources to protect their identities and the confidentiality of information; and to avoid endangering these sources and law enforcement personnel. Special note is taken that the proviso clause in this exemption imports due process and procedural protections for the individual. The existence and general character of the information exempted shall be made known to the individual to whom it pertains.

(3)(i) Exempt under 5 U.S.C. 552a(k)(4). The systems of records exempt, the sections of the Act from which exempted, and the reasons therefor are as follows:

(A) Agriculture Census Records for 1974 and 1978—COMMERCE/CENSUS–1;

(B) Individual and Household Statistical Surveys and Special Census Studies Records—COMMERCE/CENSUS–3;

(C) Minority-Owned Business Enterprises Survey Records—COMMERCE/CENSUS–4;

(D) Population and Housing Census Records of the 1960 and Subsequent Censuses—COMMERCE/ CENSUS–5;

(E) Population Census Personal Service Records for 1900 and All Subsequent Decennial Censuses—COMMERCE/CENSUS–6; and

(F) Special Censuses of Population Conducted for State and Local Government—COMMERCE/CENSUS–7.

(G) Statistical Administrative Records System—COMMERCE/CENSUS–8.

(ii) The foregoing are exempted from 5 U.S.C. 552a(c)(3), (d), (e)(1), (e)(4)(G) (H), and (I), and (f). The reasons for asserting the exemption are to comply with the prescription of Title 13 of the United States Code, especially sections 8 and 9 relating to prohibitions against disclosure, and to avoid needless consideration of these records whose sole statistical use comports fully with a basic purpose of the Act, namely, that no adverse determinations are made from these records as to any identifiable individual.

(4)(i) Exempt under 5 U.S.C. 552a(k)(5). The systems of records exempt (some only conditionally), the sections of the Act from which exempted, and the reasons therefor are as follows:

(A) Applications to U.S. Merchant Marine Academy (USMMA)—COMMERCE/MA–1;

(B) USMMA Midshipman Medical Files—COMMERCE/MA–17;

(C) USMMA Midshipman Personnel Files—COMMERCE/MA–18;

(D) USMMA Non-Appropriated fund Employees—COMMERCE/MA–19;

(E) Applicants for the NOAA Corps—COMMERCE/NOAA–4;

(F) Commissioned Officer Official Personnel Folders—COMMERCE/NOAA–7;

(G) Conflict of Interest Records, Appointed Officials—COMMERCE/DEPT–3;

(H) Investigative and Inspection Records—COMMERCE/DEPT–12, but only on condition that the general exemption claimed in §4.33(b)(3) is held to be invalid;

(I) Investigative Records—Persons Within the Investigative Jurisdiction of the Department—COMMERCE/DEPT–13; and

(J) Litigation, Claims, and Administrative Proceeding Records—COMMERCE/DEPT–14.

(ii) The foregoing are exempted from 5 U.S.C. 552a (c)(3), (d), (e)(1), (e)(4) (G), (H), and (I), and (f). The reasons for asserting the exemption are to maintain the ability to obtain candid and necessary information, to fulfill commitments made to sources to protect the confidentiality of information, to avoid endangering these sources and, ultimately, to facilitate proper selection or continuance of the best applicants or persons for a given position or contract. Special note is made of the limitation on the extent to which this exemption may be asserted. The existence and general character of the information exempted will be made known to the individual to whom it pertains.

(c) At the present time, the Department claims no exemption under 5 U.S.C. 552a(k) (3), (6) and (7).

APPENDIX A TO PART 4—FREEDOM OF INFORMATION PUBLIC INSPECTION FACILITIES, AND ADDRESSES FOR REQUESTS FOR RECORDS UNDER THE FREEDOM OF INFORMATION ACT AND PRIVACY ACT, AND REQUESTS FOR CORRECTION OR AMENDMENT UNDER THE PRIVACY ACT

Each address listed below is the respective component's mailing address for receipt and processing of requests for records under the Freedom of Information Act and Privacy Act, for requests for correction or amendment under the Privacy Act and, unless otherwise noted, its public inspection facility for records available to the public under the Freedom of Information Act. Requests should be addressed to the component the requester knows or has reason to believe has possession of, control over, or primary concern with the records sought. Otherwise, requests should be addressed to the Central Reference and Records Inspection Facility. The telephone number for each component is included after its address. Public inspection facilities are open to the public Monday through Friday (excluding Saturdays, Sundays, and legal public holidays) between 9 a.m. and 4 p.m. local time of the facility at issue. Certain public inspection facility records of components are also available electronically through the Department's "FOIA Home Page" link found at the Department's World Wide Web site (*http://www.doc.gov*)), as described in §4.2(b). The Departmental Freedom of Information Officer is authorized to revise this appendix to reflect changes in the information contained in it. Any such revisions shall be posted at the Department's "FOIA Home Page" link found at the Department's World Wide Web site (*http://www.doc.gov*).

(1) Department of Commerce Freedom of Information Central Reference and Records Inspection Facility, U.S. Department of Commerce, Room 6022, 14th and Constitution Avenue, NW, Washington, DC 20230; (202) 482–4115. This facility serves the Office of the Secretary, all other components of the Department not identified below, and those components identified below that do not have separate public inspection facilities.

(2) Bureau of the Census, Policy Office, U.S. Department of Commerce, Federal Building 3, Room 2430, Suitland, Maryland 20233; (301) 457–2520. This agency maintains a separate public inspection facility in Room 2455, Federal Building 3, Suitland, Maryland 20233.

(3) Bureau of Economic Analysis/Economics and Statistics Administration, Office of the Under Secretary for Economic Affairs, Department of Commerce, Room 4836, 14th and Constitution Avenue, NW, Washington, DC 20230; (202) 482–3308. This component does not maintain a separate public inspection facility.

(4) Bureau of Export Administration, Office of Administration, U.S. Department of Commerce, Room 6883, 14th and Constitution Avenue, NW, Washington, DC 20230; (202) 482–0500. This component does not maintain a separate public inspection facility.

(5) Economic Development Administration, Office of the Chief Counsel, U.S. Department of Commerce, Room 7005, 14th and Constitution Avenue, NW, Washington, DC 20230; (202) 482–4687. Regional EDA offices (none of the following regional EDA offices maintains a separate public inspection facility):

(i) Philadelphia Regional Office, EDA, U.S. Department of Commerce, Curtis Center, Suite 140 South, Independence Square West, Philadelphia, Pennsylvania 19106; (215) 597–7896.

(ii) Atlanta Regional Office, EDA, U.S. Department of Commerce, 401 West Peachtree Street, NW, Suite 1820, Atlanta, GA 30308; (404) 730–3006.

(iii) Denver Regional Office, EDA, U.S. Department of Commerce, Room 670, 1244 Speer Boulevard, Denver, Colorado 80204; (303) 844–4716.

(iv) Chicago Regional Office, EDA, U.S. Department of Commerce, 111 North Canal Street, Suite 855, Chicago, IL 60606; (312) 353–8580.

(v) Seattle Regional Office, EDA, U.S. Department of Commerce, Jackson Federal Building, Room 1856, 915 Second Avenue, Seattle WA 98174; (206) 220–7701.

(vi) Austin Regional Office, EDA, U.S. Department of Commerce, 327 Congress Avenue, Suite 200, Austin, Texas 78701; (512) 381–8169.

(6) International Trade Administration, Office of Organization and Management Support, U.S. Department of Commerce, Room 4001, 14th and Constitution Avenue, NW, Washington, DC 20230; (202) 482–3032.

(7) Minority Business Development Agency, Data Resources Division, U.S. Department of Commerce, Room 5084, 14th and Constitution Avenue, NW, Washington, DC 20230; (202) 482–2025. This agency does not maintain a separate public inspection facility.

(8) National Institute of Standards and Technology, Management and Organization Division, Administration Building, Room A525, 100 Bureau Drive, Gaithersburg, Maryland 20899; (301) 975–4054. This agency maintains a separate public inspection facility in Room E–106, Administration Building, Gaithersburg, Maryland.

(9) National Oceanic and Atmospheric Administration, Public Reference Facility (OFAx2) 1315 East West Highway (SSMC3), Room 10730, Silver Spring, Maryland 20910; (301) 713–3540.

(10) National Technical Information Service, Office of Administration, 5285 Port Royal Road, Springfield, Virginia 22161; (703) 605–6449. This agency does not maintain a separate public inspection facility.

(11) National Telecommunications and Information Administration, Office of the Chief Counsel, U.S. Department of Commerce, Room 4713, 14th and Constitution Avenue, NW, Washington, DC 20230; (202) 482–1816. This component does not maintain a separate public inspection facility.

(12) Office of Inspector General, Counsel to the Inspector General, U.S. Department of Commerce, Room 7892, 14th and Constitution Avenue, NW, Washington, DC 20230; (202) 482–5992. This component does not maintain a separate public inspection facility.

(13) Technology Administration, Office of the Under Secretary, U.S. Department of Commerce, Room 4835, 14th and Constitution Avenue, NW, Washington, DC 20230; (202) 482–1984. This component does not maintain a separate public inspection facility.

APPENDIX B TO PART 4—OFFICIALS AUTHORIZED TO DENY REQUESTS FOR RECORDS UNDER THE FREEDOM OF INFORMATION ACT, AND REQUESTS FOR RECORDS AND REQUESTS FOR CORRECTION OR AMENDMENT UNDER THE PRIVACY ACT

The officials of the Department listed below and their superiors have authority, with respect to the records for which each is responsible, to deny requests for records under the FOIA,[1] and requests for records and requests for correction or amendment under the PA. In addition, the Departmental

[1] The foregoing officials have sole authority under §4.7(b) to deny requests for records in any respect, including, for example, denying requests for reduction or waiver of fees.

Freedom of Information Officer and the Freedom of Information Officer for the Office of the Secretary have the foregoing FOIA and PA denial authority for all records of the Department, and the Departmental Freedom of Information officer is authorized to assign that authority, on a case-by-case basis only, to any of the officials listed below, if the records responsive to a request include records for which more than one official listed below is responsible. The Departmental Freedom of Information Officer is authorized to revise this appendix to reflect changes in designation of denial officials. Any such revisions shall be posted at the Department's "FOIA Home Page" link found at the Department's World Wide Web site (*http://www.doc.gov*).

OFFICE OF THE SECRETARY

Office of the Secretary: Executive Secretary; Freedom of Information Officer
Office of Business Liaison: Director
Office of Public Affairs: Director; Deputy Director; Press Secretary; Deputy Press Secretary
Assistant Secretary for Legislative and Intergovernmental Affairs; Deputy Assistant Secretary for Legislative and Intergovernmental Affairs
Office of the Inspector General: FOIA Officer; Senior Associate Counsel to the Inspector General.
Office of the General Counsel: Deputy General Counsel; Assistant General Counsel for Administration
Office of Executive Support: Director

ASSISTANT SECRETARY FOR ADMINISTRATION

Office of Civil Rights: Director
Office of Budget: Director
Office of Management and Organization: Director
Office of Chief Information Officer: Director
Office of Executive Budgeting and Assistance Management: Director
Office of Executive Assistance Management: Director; Grants Officer
Departmental Freedom of Information Officer.
Office of Financial Management: Director
Office of Human Resources Management: Director; Deputy Director.
Office of Administrative Services: Director
Office of Security: Director, Deputy Director
Office of Acquisition Management: Director
Office of Acquisition Services: Director
Office of Small and Disadvantaged Business Utilization: Director

BUREAU OF EXPORT ADMINISTRATION

Under Secretary
Deputy Under Secretary
Director, Office of Administration
Director, Office of Planning, Evaluation and Management
Assistant Secretary for Export Administration
Deputy Assistant Secretary for Export Administration
Director, Office of Strategic Industries and Economic Security
Director, Office of Nonproliferation Controls and Treaty Compliance
Director, Office of Strategic Trade and Foreign Policy Controls
Director, Office of Exporter Services
Assistant Secretary for Export Enforcement
Deputy Assistant Secretary for Export Enforcement
Director, Office of Export Enforcement
Director, Office of Enforcement Analysis
Director, Office of Antiboycott Compliance

ECONOMICS AND STATISTICS ADMINISTRATION

Office of Administration: Director
Bureau of Economic Analysis: Director
Bureau of the Census: Freedom of Information Act Officer

ECONOMIC DEVELOPMENT ADMINISTRATION

Freedom of Information Officer

INTERNATIONAL TRADE ADMINISTRATION

Under Secretary for International Trade
Deputy Under Secretary for International Trade
Counselor to the Department
Director, Trade Promotion Coordinating Committee Secretariat
Director, Office of Public Affairs
Director, Office of Legislative and Intergovernmental Affairs

Administration

Chief Financial Officer and Director of Administration
Director, Office of Organization and Management Support
Director, Office of Human Resources Management
Director, Office of Information Resources Management
ITA Freedom of Information Officer

Import Administration

Assistant Secretary for Import Administration
Deputy Assistant Secretary for Antidumping and Countervailing Duty Enforcement I
Deputy Assistant Secretary for Antidumping and Countervailing Duty Enforcement II
Deputy Assistant Secretary for Antidumping and Countervailing Duty Enforcement III
Director for Policy and Analysis
Director, Office of Policy
Director, Office of Accounting
Director, Central Records Unit
Director, Foreign Trade Zones Staff
Director, Statutory Import Programs Staff
Director, Office of Antidumping Countervailing Duty Enforcement I

Director, Office of Antidumping Countervailing Duty Enforcement II
Director, Office of Antidumping Countervailing Duty Enforcement III
Director, Office of Antidumping Countervailing Duty Enforcement IV
Director, Office of Antidumping Countervailing Duty Enforcement V
Director, Office of Antidumping Countervailing Duty Enforcement VI
Director, Office of Antidumping Countervailing Duty Enforcement VII
Director, Office of Antidumping Countervailing Duty Enforcement VIII
Director, Office of Antidumping Countervailing Duty Enforcement IX

Market Access and Compliance

Assistant Secretary for Market Access and Compliance
Deputy Assistant Secretary for Agreements Compliance
Deputy Assistant Secretary for the Middle East and North Africa
Deputy Assistant Secretary for Europe
Deputy Assistant Secretary for the Western Hemisphere
Deputy Assistant Secretary for Asia and the Pacific
Deputy Assistant Secretary for Africa
Director, Office of Policy Coordination
Director, Office of Multilateral Affairs
Director, Trade Compliance Center
Director, Office of the Middle East and North Africa
Director, Office of European Union and Regional Affairs
Director, Office of Eastern Europe, Russia and Independent States
Director, Office of Latin America and the Caribbean
Director, Office of NAFTA and Inter-American Affairs
Director, Office of China Economic Area
Director, Office of the Pacific Basin
Director, Office of South Asia and Oceania
Director, Office of Japan
Director, Office of Africa

Trade Development

Assistant Secretary for Trade Development
Deputy Assistant Secretary for Transportation and Technology Industries
Deputy Assistant Secretary for Textiles, Apparel and Consumer Goods Industries
Deputy Assistant Secretary for Service Industries and Finance
Deputy Assistant Secretary for Basic Industries
Deputy Assistant Secretary for Information Technology Industries
Deputy Assistant Secretary for Environmental Technologies Industries
Deputy Assistant Secretary for Tourism Industries
Director, Office of Export Promotion Coordination
Director, Trade Information Center
Director, Office of Trade and Economic Analysis
Director, Advocacy Center
Director, Office of Planning, Coordination and Resource Management
Director, Office of Aerospace
Director, Office of Automotive Affairs
Director, Office of Microelectronics, Medical Equipment and Instrumentation
Director, Office of Textiles and Apparel
Director, Office of Consumer Goods
Director, Office of Environmental Technologies
Director, Office of Export Trading Company Affairs
Director, Office of Finance
Director, Office of Service Industries
Director, Office of Metals, Materials and Chemicals
Director, Office of Energy, Infrastructure and Machinery
Director, Office of Electronic Commerce
Director, Office of Information Technologies
Director, Office of Telecommunications Technologies

U.S. and Foreign Commercial Service

Assistant Secretary and Director General
Deputy Director General
Deputy Assistant Secretary for International Operations
Deputy Assistant Secretary for Export Promotion Services
Deputy Assistant Secretary for Domestic Operations
Director, Office of Information Systems
Director, Office of Planning
Director, Office of Foreign Service Human Resources
Director for Europe
Director for Western Hemisphere
Director for East Asia and the Pacific
Director, Multilateral Development Bank Operations
Director, Office of Public/Private Initiatives
Director, Office of Export Information and Marketing Services
Director, Office of Operations

MINORITY BUSINESS DEVELOPMENT ADMINISTRATION

Freedom of Information Officer

NATIONAL OCEANIC AND ATMOSPHERIC ADMINISTRATION

Under Secretary
Assistant Secretary
Director, Office of Public and Constituent Affairs
Director, Office of Marine and Aviation Operations
General Counsel
Assistant Administrator for Ocean Services and Coastal Zone Management
Assistant Administrator for Fisheries

Assistant Administrator for Weather Services
Assistant Administrator for Satellite and Information Services
Assistant Administrator for Oceanic and Atmospheric Research
Office of Finance and Administration: Chief Financial Officer/Chief Administrative Officer
Director, Acquisition and Grants Office
Director, Systems Acquisition Office
Director, Human Resources Management Office
Director, Office of Finance
Director, Budget Office
Director, Facilities Office
Director, Information Systems Management Office
Director, Eastern Administrative Support Center
Director, Central Administrative Support Center
Director, Mountain Administrative Support Center
Director, Western Administrative Support Center
Freedom of Information Officer

NATIONAL TELECOMMUNICATIONS AND INFORMATION ADMINISTRATION

Deputy Assistant Secretary
Chief Counsel
Deputy Chief Counsel

TECHNOLOGY ADMINISTRATION

Under Secretary for Technology
Deputy Under Secretary for Technology
Assistant Secretary for Technology Policy
Deputy Assistant Secretary for Technology Policy
Chief Counsel
Deputy Chief Counsel
Senior Counsel for Internet Technology
National Institute of Standards and Technology: Director for Administration and Chief Financial Officer; Chief, Management and Organization Division; NIST Counsel.
National Technical Information Service: Director; Deputy Director; Chief Financial Officer/Associate Director for Finance and Administration.

[66 FR 65632, Dec. 20, 2001, as amended at 70 FR 47725, Aug. 15, 2005; 70 FR 75730, Dec. 21, 2005; 72 FR 36595, July 5, 2007; 76 FR 39769, July 7, 2011]

APPENDIX C TO PART 4—SYSTEMS OF RECORDS NOTICED BY OTHER FEDERAL AGENCIES AND APPLICABLE TO RECORDS OF THE DEPARTMENT AND APPLICABILITY OF THIS PART THERETO

Category of records	Other Federal Agency
Federal Personnel Records	Office of Personnel Management. [1]
Federal Employee Compensation Act Program Program	Department of Labor. [2]
Equal Employment Opportunity Appeal Complaints	Equal Employment Opportunity Commission. [3]
Formal Complaints/Appeals of Adverse Personnel Actions	Merit Systems Protection Board. [4]

[1] The provisions of this part do not apply to these records covered by notices of systems of records published by the Office of Personnel Management for all agencies. The regulations of OPM alone apply.
[2] The provisions of this part apply only initially to these records covered by notices of systems of records published by the U.S. Department of Labor for all agencies. The regulations of that Department attach at the point of any denial for access or for correction or amendment.
[3] The provisions of this part do not apply to these records covered by notices of systems of records published by the Equal Employment Opportunity Commission for all agencies. The regulations of the Commission alone apply.
[4] The provisions of this part do not apply to these records covered by notices of systems of records published by the Merit Systems Protection Board for all agencies. The regulations of the Board alone apply.

PART 4a—CLASSIFICATION, DECLASSIFICATION, AND PUBLIC AVAILABILITY OF NATIONAL SECURITY INFORMATION

Sec.

AUTHORITY: E.O. 12958; 47 FR 14874, April 6, 1982; 47 FR 15557, April 12, 1982.

SOURCE: 66 FR 65650, Dec. 20, 2001, unless otherwise noted.

§ 4a.1 General.

Executive Order 12958 provides the only basis for classifying information within the Department of Commerce (Department), except as provided in the Atomic Energy Act of 1954, as amended. The Department's policy is to make information concerning its activities available to the public, consistent with the need to protect the national defense and foreign relations of the United States. Accordingly, security classification shall be applied only to protect the national security.

§4a.2 Deputy Assistant Secretary for Security.

The Deputy Assistant Secretary for Security (DAS) is responsible for implementing E.O. 12958 and this part.

§4a.3 Classification levels.

Information may be classified as national security information by a designated original classifier of the Department if it is determined that the information concerns one or more of the categories described in §1.5 of E.O. 12958. The levels established by E.O. 12958 (Top Secret, Secret, and Confidential) are the only terms that may be applied to national security information. Except as provided by statute, no other terms shall be used within the Department for the three classification levels.

§4a.4 Classification authority.

Authority to originally classify information as Secret or Confidential may be exercised only by the Secretary of Commerce and by officials to whom such authority is specifically delegated. No official of the Department is authorized to originally classify information as Top Secret.

§4a.5 Duration of classification.

(a) Information shall remain classified no longer than ten years from the date of its original classification, except as provided in §1.6(d) of E.O. 12958. Under E.O. 12958, information may be exempted from declassification within ten years if the unauthorized disclosure of such information could reasonably be expected to cause damage to the national security for more than ten years and meets one of the eight criteria listed in §1.6 (d).

(b) Department of Commerce originally classified information marked for an indefinite duration of classification under predecessor orders to E.O. 12958 shall be declassified after twenty years. Classified information contained in archive records determined to have permanent historical value under Title 44 of the United States Code shall be automatically declassified no longer than 25 years from the date of its original classification, except as provided in §3.4(d) of E.O. 12958.

§4a.6 General.

National security information over which the Department exercises final classification jurisdiction shall be declassified or downgraded as soon as national security considerations permit. If information is declassified, it may continue to be exempt from public disclosure by the Freedom of Information Act (5 U.S.C. 552) or other applicable law.

§4a.7 Mandatory review for declassification.

(a) *Requests.* Classified information under the jurisdiction of the Department is subject to review for declassification upon receipt of a written request that describes the information with sufficient specificity to locate it with a reasonable amount of effort. Requests must be submitted to the Deputy Assistant Secretary for Security, U.S. Department of Commerce, Room 1069, 14th and Constitution Avenue, NW., Washington, DC 20230.

(b) *Exemptions.* The following are exempt from mandatory review for declassification:

(1) Information that has been reviewed for declassification within the past two years;

(2) Information that is the subject of pending litigation;

(3) Information originated by the incumbent President, the incumbent President's White House Staff, committees, commissions, or boards appointed by the incumbent President, or other entities within the Executive Office of the President that solely advise and assist the incumbent President; and

(4) Information specifically exempt from such review by law.

(c) *Processing requirements.* (1) The DAS shall acknowledge receipt of the request directly to the requester. If a request does not adequately describe the information sought in accordance with paragraph (a) of this section, the requester shall be notified that unless additional information is provided, no further action will be taken. The request shall be forwarded to the component that originated the information or that has primary interest in the subject matter. The component assigned action shall review the information in accordance with § 4a.7(c)(2) through (4) within twenty working days.

(2) The component assigned action shall determine whether, under the declassification provisions of the U.S. Department of Commerce Security Manual, the entire document or portions thereof may be declassified. Declassification of the information shall be accomplished by a designated declassification authority. Upon declassification the information shall be remarked. If the information is not partially or entirely declassified, the reviewing official shall provide the reasons for denial by citing the applicable provisions of E.O. 12958. If the classification is a derivative decision based on classified source material of another Federal agency, the component shall provide the information to the originator for review.

(3) If information is declassified, the component shall also determine whether it is releasable under the Freedom of Information Act. If the information is not releasable, the component shall advise the DAS that the information has been declassified but that it is exempt from disclosure, citing the appropriate exemption of the Freedom of Information Act.

(4) If the request for declassification is denied in whole or in part, the requester shall be notified of the right to appeal the determination within sixty calendar days and of the procedures for such an appeal. If declassified information remains exempt from disclosure under the Freedom of Information Act, the requester shall be advised of the appellate procedures under that law.

(d) *Fees.* If the request requires services for which fees are chargeable, the component assigned action shall calculate the anticipated fees to be charged, and may be required to ascertain the requester's willingness to pay the allowable charges as a precondition to taking further action on the request, in accordance with § 4.11 of the Department of Commerce Freedom of Information Act rules and § 4.31 of the Department's Privacy Act rules.

(e) *Right of appeal.* (1) A requester may appeal to the DAS when information requested under this section is not completely declassified and released after expiration of the applicable time limits. Within thirty working days (*i.e.*, excluding Saturdays, Sundays, and legal public holidays) of receipt of a written appeal:

(i) The DAS shall determine whether continued classification of the requested information is required in whole or in part;

(ii) If information is declassified, determine whether it is releasable under the Freedom of Information Act; and

(iii) Notify the requester of his or her determination, making available any information determined to be releasable. If continued classification is required under the provisions of the Department of Commerce National Security Manual, the DAS shall notify the requester of his or her determination, including the reasons for denial based on applicable provisions of E.O. 12958, and of the right of final appeal to the Interagency Security Classification Appeals Panel.

(2) During the declassification review of information under appeal the DAS may overrule previous determinations in whole or in part if continued protection in the interest of national security is no longer required. If the DAS determines that the information no longer requires classification, it shall be declassified and, unless it is otherwise exempt from disclosure under the Freedom of Information Act, released to the requester. The DAS shall advise the original reviewing component of his or her decision.

§ 4a.8 Access to classified information by individuals outside the Government.

(a) *Industrial, Educational, and Commercial Entities.* Certain bidders, contractors, grantees, educational, scientific, or industrial organizations may receive classified information under the procedures prescribed by the National Industrial Security Program Operating Manual.

(b) *Access by historical researchers and former Presidential appointees.* An individual engaged in historical research projects or who has previously occupied a policy-making position to which he or she was appointed by the President may be authorized access to classified information for a limited period, provided that the head of the component with jurisdiction over the information:

(1) Determines in writing that:

(i) Access is consistent with national security;

(ii) The individual has a compelling need for access; and

(iii) The Department's best interest is served by providing access;

(2) Obtains in writing from the individual:

(i) Consent to a review by the Department of any resultant notes and manuscripts for the purpose of determining that no classified information is contained in them; and

(ii) Agreement to safeguard classified information in accordance with applicable requirements; and

(iii) A detailed description of the individual's research;

(3) Ensures that custody of classified information is maintained at a Department facility;

(4) Limits access granted to former Presidential appointees to items that the individual originated, reviewed, signed, or received while serving as a Presidential appointee; and

(5) Receives from the DAS:

(i) A determination that the individual is trustworthy; and

(ii) Approval to grant access to the individual.

(c) An individual seeking access should describe the information with sufficient specificity to locate and compile it with a reasonable amount of effort. If the access requested by a historical researcher or former Presidential appointee requires services for which fees are chargeable, the responsible component shall notify the individual in advance.

(d) This section applies only to classified information originated by the Department, or to information in the sole custody of the Department. Otherwise, the individual shall be referred to the classifying agency.

PART 5—OPERATION OF VENDING STANDS

Sec.

AUTHORITY: Sec. 4, 68 Stat. 663; 20 U.S.C. 107.

SOURCE: 28 FR 7772, July 31, 1963, unless otherwise noted.

§5.1 Purpose.

This part prescribes regulations to assure the granting of preference to blind persons licensed under the provisions of the Randolph-Sheppard Vending Stand Act (49 Stat. 1559, as amended by the act of August 3, 1954, 68 Stat. 663; 20 U.S.C. 107) for the operation of vending stands (which term as used in this order includes vending machines).

§5.2 Policy.

(a) The Department adopts the Federal policy announced in the Randolph-Sheppard Vending Stand Act, as amended, to provide blind persons with remunerative employment to enlarge the economic opportunities of the blind and to stimulate the blind to greater efforts in striving to make themselves self-supporting.

(b) It shall be the policy of the Department to authorize blind persons licensed under the provisions of the Randolph-Sheppard Vending Stand Act, as amended to operate vending stands without any charge for space or necessary utilities on properties owned and occupied by the Department or on which the Department controls maintenance, operation, and protection.

(c) The Department will cooperate with the Department of Education and State licensing agencies in making surveys to determine whether and where vending stands may be properly and profitably operated by licensed blind persons.

(d) The application of a State licensing agency for a permit may be denied or revoked if it is determined that the interests of the United States would be adversely affected or the Department would be unduly inconvenienced by the issuance of a permit or its continuance.

(e) Disagreements concerning the denial, revocation, or modification of a permit may be appealed by the State licensing agency as set forth in § 5.6.

[28 FR 7772, July 31, 1963, as amended at 55 FR 53489, Dec. 31, 1990]

§ 5.3 Assignment of functions and authorities.

(a) The Director, Office of Administrative Services, shall carry out the Department's responsibility to provide, in accordance with applicable law and regulation, the maximum opportunity for qualified blind persons to operate vending stands.

(b) Subject to instructions issued by the Director, Office of Administrative Services, the head of each primary organization unit shall be responsible for implementing this program within his area.

(c) The Director, Office of Administrative Services for the primary organization units located in the main Commerce building and the head of each other primary organization unit will make determinations with respect to the terms of permits including the location and operation of vending stands and machines in their respective areas.

(d) Unresolved differences and significant violations of the terms of permits shall be reported to the State licensing agency. Where no corrective action is forthcoming, the matter shall be referred to the Office of Vocational Rehabilitation, Department of Education for consideration prior to further action.

[28 FR 7772, July 31, 1963, as amended at 55 FR 53489, Dec. 31, 1990]

§ 5.4 Permits.

(a) No permit, lease, or other arrangement for the operation of a vending stand on property under control of the Department shall be entered into or renewed without first consulting the State licensing agency or equivalent authority.

(b) The permit shall be conditioned upon the vending stand meeting specified standards, including standards relating to appearance, safety, sanitation, maintenance, and efficiency of operation. Due regard shall be given to laws and regulations for the public welfare which are applicable, or would be applicable, if the property involved was not owned or controlled by the Federal Government.

(c) The permit shall specify the types of articles specified in section 2(a)(4) of the Act as amended (newspapers, periodicals, confections, tobacco products, articles dispensed automatically or in containers or wrappings in which they are placed before delivery to the vending stand). Such other related articles as the State licensing agency asks to be included shall be permitted to be sold, unless such factors as inadequacy of available facilities, safety, health, public welfare, or legal requirements demand otherwise.

(d) The permit shall contain a provision that alterations made by other than the United States shall be approved by and conducted under the supervision of an appropriate official of the Department or the primary organization unit concerned.

(e) The permit may contain other reasonable conditions necessary for the protection of the Government and prospective patrons of the stand.

(f) The permit shall describe the location of the stand proper and the location of any vending machines which are operated in conjunction with it.

§ 5.5 Vending machines.

(a) The income from any vending machines which are located within reasonable proximity to and are in direct competition with a vending stand for which a permit has been issued under these regulations shall be assigned to the operator of such stand.

(b) If a vending machine vends articles of a type authorized by the permit and is so located that it attracts customers who would otherwise patronize the vending stand, such machine shall be deemed to be in reasonable proximity to and direct competition with the stand.

§ 5.6 Appeals.

(a) In any instance where the Department of Commerce official as provided in §5.3(c) and the State licensing agency fail to reach agreement concerning the granting, revocation, or modification of a permit, the location, method of operation, assignment of proceeds, or other terms of a permit (including articles which may be sold), the State licensing agency shall be notified in writing by the Commerce official concerned that it has the right to appeal such disagreements, within 30 days of the notice, to the Assistant Secretary for Administration for investigation and final decision.

(b) Upon receipt of a timely appeal the Assistant Secretary for Administration will cause a full investigation to be made. The State licensing agency shall be given an opportunity to present information pertinent to the facts and circumstances of the case. The complete investigation report including the recommendations of the investigating officer shall be submitted to the Assistant Secretary for Administration within 60 days from the date of the appeal.

(c) The Assistant Secretary for Administration will render a final decision on the appeal within 90 days of the date of appeal.

(d) The State licensing agency will be informed of the final decision on its appeal. Copies of the decision will be forwarded to the Department of Commerce official concerned and the Department of Education.

[28 FR 7772, July 31, 1963, as amended at 55 FR 53489, Dec. 31, 1990]

§5.7 Reports.

No later than fifteen days following the end of each fiscal year the responsible officials set forth in §5.3(c) shall forward to the Director, Office of Administrative Services a report on activities under this order. The report shall include:

(a) The number of applications, including requests for installations initiated by the Department, for vending stands received from State licensing agencies;

(b) The number of such requests accepted or approved;

(c) The number denied, on which no appeal was made and the number denied on which an appeal was made; and

(d) The number and status of any requests still pending.

§5.8 Approval of regulations.

The provisions of this part have been approved by the Director, Bureau of the Budget, pursuant to Executive Order 10604, of April 22, 1955.

PART 6—CIVIL MONETARY PENALTY INFLATION ADJUSTMENTS

Sec.

AUTHORITY: Sec. 4, as amended, and sec. 5, Pub. L. 101–410, 104 Stat. 890 (28 U.S.C. 2461 note); Pub. L. 104–134, 110 Stat. 1321, 28 U.S.C. 2461 note.

SOURCE: 61 FR 55093, Oct. 24, 1996, unless otherwise noted.

§6.1 Definitions.

As used in this part:

(a) *Inflation Adjustment Act* means the Federal Civil Penalties Inflation Adjustment Act of 1990 (Pub. L. 101–410, October 5, 1990, 104 Stat. 890, 28 U.S.C. 2461 note).

(b) *Improvement Act* means the Debt Collection Improvement Act of 1996 (Public Law 104–134, April 26, 1996).

(c) *Amended Section Four* means section 4 of the *Inflation Adjustment Act*, as amended by the *Improvement Act*.

(d) *Section Five* means section 5 of the *Inflation Adjustment Act*.

(e) *Department* means the Department of Commerce.

(f) *Secretary* means the Secretary of the Department of Commerce.

(g) *First Adjustments* means the inflation adjustments made by §6.4 of this part which, as provided in §6.5 of this part, are effective on October 23, 1996.

§6.2 Purpose and scope.

The purpose of this part is to make the inflation adjustment, described in *Section Five* and required by *Amended Section Four*, of each minimum and maximum civil monetary penalty provided by law within the jurisdiction of the *Department*.

§ 6.3 Limitation on *First Adjustments*.

Each of the *First Adjustments* may not exceed ten percent (10%) of the respective penalty being adjusted.

§ 6.4 Adjustments to penalties.

The civil monetary penalties provided by law within the jurisdiction of the respective agencies or bureaus of the Department, as set forth below in this section, are hereby adjusted in accordance with the inflation adjustment procedures prescribed in Section 5, Pub. L. 101–410, from the amounts of such penalties in effect prior to December 7, 2012, to the amounts of such penalties, as thus adjusted, except for the penalties that are being adjusted for the first time, stated in paragraphs, (a)(1), which became effective on October 21, 1986; (a)(2), which became effective on March 2, 1863; (b)(5), which became effective on December 18, 2006; and (f)(1) and (f)(2), which became effective on December 18, 2010.

(a) *Department of Commerce*. (1) 31 U.S.C. 3802(a)(1)(D), Program Fraud Civil Remedies Act of 1986, from $5,000 to $5,500.

(2) 31 U.S.C. 3729(a)(1)(G), False Claims Act; minimum from $5,000 to $5,500; maximum from $10,000 to $11,000.

(b) *Bureau of Industry and Security*. (1) 15 U.S.C. 5408(b)(1), Fastener Quality Act—Violation, from $32,500 to $32,500.

(2) 22 U.S.C. 6761(a)(1)(A), Chemical Weapons Convention Implementation Act—Inspection Violation, from $25,000 to $25,000.

(3) 22 U.S.C. 6761(a)(l)(B), Chemical Weapons Convention Implementation Act—Record Keeping Violation, from $5,000 to $5,000.

(4) 50 U.S.C. 1705(a), International Emergency Economic Powers Act (2007)—Violation, from $250,000 to $250,000.

(5) 22 U.S.C. 8142(a), United States Additional Protocol Implementation Act (2006)— Violation, from $25,000 to $27,500.

(c) *Bureau of the Census*. (1) 13 U.S.C. 304, Collection of Foreign Trade Statistics—Delinquency on Delayed Filing of Export Documentation; maximum penalty for each day's delinquency, from $1,000 to $1,000; maximum per violation, from $10,000 to $10,000.

(2) 13 U.S.C. 305(b), Collection of Foreign Trade Statistics—Violations, from $10,000 to $10,000.

(d) Economics and Statistics Administration. 22 U.S.C. 3105(a), International Investment and Trade in Services Act—Failure to Furnish Information; minimum, from $2,500 to $2,500; maximum, from $32,500 to $32,500.

(e) *International Trade Administration*. (1) 19 U.S.C. 81s, Foreign Trade Zone—Violation, from $1,100 to $1,100.

(2) 19 U.S.C. 1677f(f)(4), U.S.-Canada FTA Protective Order—Violation, from $130,000 to $130,000.

(f) *National Oceanic and Atmospheric Administration*. (1) 51 U.S.C. 60123(a)(3), Land Remote Sensing Policy Act of 2010; new penalty $10,000.

(2) 51 U.S.C. 60148(c), Land Remote Sensing Policy Act of 2010, new penalty $10,000.

(3) 16 U.S.C. 773f(a), Northern Pacific Halibut Act of 1982 (2007), from $200,000 to $200,000.

(4) 16 U.S.C. 783, Sponge Act (1914), from $650 to $650.

(5) 16 U.S.C. 957, Tuna Conventions Act of 1950 (1962);

(i) Violation/Subsection (a), from $32,500 to $32,500.

(ii) Subsequent Violation/Subsection (a), from $70,000 to $70,000.

(iii) Violation/Subsection (b), from $1,100 to $1,100.

(iv) Subsequent Violation/Subsection (b), from $6,500 to $6,500.

(v) Violation/Subsection (c), from $140,000 to $140,000.

(6) 16 U.S.C. 971e(e), Atlantic Tunas Convention Act of 1975 (1995), from $140,000 to $140,000.

(7) 16 U.S.C. 972f(b), Eastern Pacific Tuna Licensing Act of 1984;

(i) Violation/Subsections (a)(1)–(3), from $32,500 to $32,500.

(ii) Subsequent Violation/Subsections (a)(1)–(3), from $65,000 to $65,000.

(iii) Violation/Subsections (a)(4)–(5), from $6,500 to $6,500.

(iv) Subsequent Violation/Subsections (a)(4)–(5), from $6,500 to $6,500.

(v) Violation/Subsection (a)(6), from $140,000 to $140,000.

(8) 16 U.S.C. 973f(a), South Pacific Tuna Act of 1988, from $350,000 to $350,000.

(9) 16 U.S.C. 1174(b), Fur Seal Act Amendments of 1983, from $11,000 to $11,000.

(10) 16 U.S.C. 1375(a) (1), Marine Mammal Protection Act of 1972 (1981), from $11,000 to $11,000.

(11) 16 U.S.C. 1385(e), Dolphin Protection Consumer Information Act (1990), from $130,000 to $130,000.

(12) 16 U.S.C. 1437(d)(1), National Marine Sanctuaries Act (1992), from $140,000 to $140,000.

(13) 16 U.S.C. 1540(a)(1), Endangered Species Act of 1973;

(i) Knowing Violation of Section 1538 (1988), from $32,500 to $32,500.

(ii) Other Knowing Violation (1988), from $13,200 to $13,200.

(iii) Otherwise Violation (1978), from $650 to $650.

(14) 16 U.S.C. 1858(a), Magnuson-Stevens Fishery Conservation and Management Act (1990), from $140,000 to $140,000.

(15) 16 U.S.C. 2437(a)(1), Antarctic Marine Living Resources Convention Act of 1984;

(i) Violation, from $6,500 to $6,500.

(ii) Knowing Violation, from $11,000 to $11,000.

(16) 16 U.S.C. 2465(a), Antarctic Protection Act of 1990;

(i) Violation, from $6,500 to $6,500.

(ii) Knowing Violation, from $11,000 to $11,000.

(17) 16 U.S.C. 3373(a), Lacey Act Amendments of 1981;

(i) Sale and Purchase Violation, from $11,000 to $11,000.

(ii) Marking Violation, from $275 to $275.

(iii) False Labeling Violation, from $11,000 to $11,000.

(iv) Other than Marking Violation, from $11,000 to $11,000.

(18) 16 U.S.C. 3606(b)(1), Atlantic Salmon Convention Act of 1982 (1990), from $140,000 to $140,000.

(19) 16 U.S.C. 3637(b), Pacific Salmon Treaty Act of 1985 (1990), from $140,000 to $140,000.

(20) 16 U.S.C. 4016(b)(1)(B), Fish and Seafood Promotion Act of 1986; minimum from $500 to $500; maximum from $6,500 to $6,500.

(21) 16 U.S.C. 5010(a)(1), North Pacific Anadromous Stocks Act of 1992, from $130,000 to $130,000.

(22) 16 U.S.C. 5103(b)(2), Atlantic Coastal Fisheries Cooperative Management Act (1993), from $140,000 to $140,000.

(23) 16 U.S.C. 5154(c)(1), Atlantic Striped Bass Conservation Act (1990), from $140,000 to $140,000.

(24) 16 U.S.C. 5507(a)(1), High Seas Fishing Compliance Act of 1995, from $130,000 to $130,000.

(25) 16 U.S.C. 5606(b), Northwest Atlantic Fisheries Convention Act of 1995, from $140,000 to $140,000.

(26) 16 U.S.C. 6905(c), Western and Central Pacific Fisheries Convention Implementation Act (2007), from $140,000 to $140,000.

(27) 16 U.S.C. 7009(c), Pacific Whiting Act of 2006 (2007); from $140,000 to $140,000.

(28) 22 U.S.C. 1978(e), Fishermen's Protective Act of 1967 (1971);

(i) Violation, from $11,000 to $11,000.

(ii) Subsequent Violation, from $32,500 to $32,500.

(29) 30 U.S.C. 1462(a), Deep Seabed Hard Mineral Resources Act (1980), from $32,500 to $32,500.

(30) 42 U.S.C. 9152(c)(1), Ocean Thermal Energy Conversion Act of 1980, from $32,500 to $32,500.

[77 FR 72916, Dec. 7, 2012]

§6.5 Effective date of adjustments.

The adjustments made by §6.4 of this part, of the penalties there specified, are effective on December 7, 2012, and said penalties, as thus adjusted by the adjustments made by §6.4 of this part, shall apply only to violations occurring after December 7, 2012, and before the effective date of any future inflation adjustment thereto made subsequent to December 7, 2012 as provided in §6.6 of this part.

[77 FR 72917, Dec. 7, 2012]

§6.6 Subsequent adjustments.

The *Secretary or his or her designee* by regulation shall, at least once every four years after October 23, 1996, make the inflation adjustment, described in *Section Five* and required by *Amended Section Four*, of each civil monetary penalty provided by law and within the jurisdiction of the *Department*.

PART 7 [RESERVED]

PART 8—NONDISCRIMINATION IN FEDERALLY ASSISTED PROGRAMS OF THE DEPARTMENT OF COMMERCE—EFFECTUATION OF TITLE VI OF THE CIVIL RIGHTS ACT OF 1964

Subpart A—General Provisions; Prohibitions: Nondiscrimination Clause; Applicability to Programs

Subpart B—General Compliance

AUTHORITY: Sec. 602, Civil Rights Act of 1964 (42 U.S.C. 2000d–1).

SOURCE: 38 FR 17938, July 5, 1973, unless otherwise noted.

EDITORIAL NOTE: Nomenclature changes to part 8 appear at 68 FR 51352, Aug. 26, 2003.

Subpart A—General Provisions; Prohibitions: Nondiscrimination Clause; Applicability to Programs

§ 8.1 Purpose.

The purpose of this part is to effectuate the provisions of title VI of the Civil Rights Act of 1964 (hereafter referred to as the "Act") to the end that no person in the United States shall, on the ground of race, color, or national origin, be excluded from participation in, be denied the benefits of, or be otherwise subjected to discrimination under any program receiving Federal financial assistance from the Department of Commerce. This part is consistent with achievement of the objectives of the statutes authorizing the financial assistance given by the Department of Commerce as provided in section 602 of the Act.

§ 8.2 Application of this part.

(a) This part applies to any program for which Federal financial assistance is authorized under a law administered by the Department, including the types of Federal financial assistance listed in Appendix A to this part and as said Appendix may be amended. It applies to money paid, property transferred, or other Federal financial assistance extended after January 9, 1965, pursuant to an application approved prior to such effective date.

(b) This part does not apply to (1) any Federal financial assistance by way of insurance or guaranty contracts, (2) money paid, property transferred, or other assistance extended before January 9, 1965, except where such assistance was subject to the title VI regulations of this Department or of any other agency whose responsibilities are now exercised by this Department, (3) any assistance to any individual who is the ultimate beneficiary under any such program, or (4) any employment practice, under any such program, of any employer, employment agency, or labor organization except to the extent described in § 8.4(c). The fact that a type of Federal financial assistance is not listed in Appendix A shall not mean, if title VI of the Act is otherwise applicable, that a program is not covered. Other types of Federal financial assistance under statutes now in force or hereinafter enacted may be added to the list by notice published in the FEDERAL REGISTER.

§ 8.3 Definitions.

(a) *Department* means the Department of Commerce, and includes each and all of its operating and equivalent other units.

(b) *Secretary* means the Secretary of Commerce.

(c) *United States* means the States of the United States, the District of Columbia, Puerto Rico, the Virgin Islands, American Samoa, Guam, Wake

Island, the Canal Zone, and the territories and possessions of the United States, and the term *State* means anyone of the foregoing.

(d) *Person* means an individual in the United States who is or is eligible to be a participant in or an ultimate beneficiary of any program which receives Federal financial assistance, and includes an individual who is an owner or member of a firm, corporation, or other business or organization which is or is eligible to be a participant in or an ultimate beneficiary of such a program. Where a primary objective of the Federal financial assistance to a program is to provide employment, "person" includes employees or applicants for employment of a recipient or other party subject to this part under such program.

(e) *Responsible department official* with respect to any program receiving Federal financial assistance means the Secretary or other official of the Department who by law or by delegation has the principal authority within the Department for the administration of a law extending such assistance. It also means any officials so designated by due delegation of authority within the Department to act in such capacity with regard to any program under this part.

(f) *Federal financial assistance* includes

(1) Grants, loans, or agreements for participation in loans, of Federal funds,

(2) The grant or donation of Federal property or interests in property,

(3) The sale or lease of, or the permission to use (on other than a casual or transient basis), Federal property or any interest in such property or in property in which the Federal Government has an interest, without consideration, or at a nominal consideration, or at a consideration which is reduced, for the purpose of assisting the recipient, or in recognition of the public interest to be served by such sale or lease to or use by the recipient,

(4) Waiver of charges which would normally be made for the furnishing of Government services,

(5) The detail of Federal personnel,

(6) Technical assistance, and

(7) Any Federal agreement, arrangement, contract, or other instrument which has as one of its purposes the provision of assistance.

(g) *Program or activity* and *program* mean all of the operations of any entity described in paragraphs (g)(1) through (4) of this section, any part of which is extended Federal financial assistance:

(1)(i) A department, agency, special purpose district, or other instrumentality of a State or of a local government; or

(ii) The entity of such State or local government that distributes such assistance and each such department or agency (and each other State or local government entity) to which the assistance is extended, in the case of assistance to a State or local government;

(2)(i) A college, university, or other postsecondary institution, or a public system of higher education; or

(ii) A local educational agency (as defined in 20 U.S.C. 7801), system of vocational education, or other school system;

(3)(i) An entire corporation, partnership, or other private organization, or an entire sole proprietorship—

(A) If assistance is extended to such corporation, partnership, private organization, or sole proprietorship as a whole; or

(B) Which is principally engaged in the business of providing education, health care, housing, social services, or parks and recreation; or

(ii) The entire plant or other comparable, geographically separate facility to which Federal financial assistance is extended, in the case of any other corporation, partnership, private organization, or sole proprietorship; or

(4) Any other entity which is established by two or more of the entities described in paragraph (g)(1), (2), or (3) of this section.

(h) *Facility* includes all or any portion of structures, equipment, vessels, or other real or personal property or interests therein, and the provision of facilities includes the construction, expansion, renovation, remodeling, alteration, contract for use, or acquisition of facilities.

(i) *Recipient* means any governmental, public or private agency, institution, organization, or other entity, or any individual, who or which is an applicant for Federal financial assistance, or to whom Federal financial assistance is extended directly or through another recipient. Recipient further includes a subgrantee, an entity which leases or operates a facility for or on behalf of a recipient, and any successors, assignees, or transferees of any kind of the recipient, but does not include any person who is an ultimate beneficiary.

(j) *Primary recipient* means any recipient which is authorized or required to extend or distribute Federal financial assistance to another recipient.

(k) *Applicant* means one who submits an application, request, or plan required to be approved by a responsible Department official, or by a primary recipient, as a condition to eligibility for Federal financial assistance, and "application" means such an application, request, or plan.

(l) *Other parties subject to this part* includes any governmental, public or private agency, institution, organization, or other entity, or any individual, who or which, like a recipient, is not to engage in discriminatory acts with respect to applicable persons covered by this part, because of his or its direct or substantial participation in any program, such as a contractor, subcontractor, provider of employment, or user of facilities or services provided under any program.

[38 FR 17938, July 5, 1973, as amended at 68 FR 51352, Aug. 26, 2003]

§ 8.4 Discrimination prohibited.

(a) *General.* No person in the United States shall, on the ground of race, color, or national origin be excluded from participation in, be denied the benefits of, or be otherwise subjected to discrimination under, any program to which this part applies.

(b) *Specific discriminatory acts prohibited.* (1) A recipient of Federal financial assistance, or other party subject to this part, shall not participate, directly or through contractual or other arrangements, in any act or course of conduct which, on the ground of race, color, or national origin:

(i) Denies to a person any service, financial aid, or other benefit provided under the program;

(ii) Provides any service, financial aid, or other benefit, to a person which is different, or is provided in a different manner, from that provided to others under the program;

(iii) Subjects a person to segregation or separate or other discriminatory treatment in any matter related to his receipt (or nonreceipt) of any such service, financial aid, property, or other benefit under the program.

(iv) Restricts a person in any way in the enjoyment of services, facilities, or any other advantage, privilege, property, or benefit provided to others under the programs;

(v) Treats a person differently from others in determining whether he satisfies any admission, enrollment, quota, eligibility, membership, or other requirement or condition which persons must meet in order to be provided any service, financial aid, or other benefit provided under the program;

(vi) Denies a person an opportunity to participate in the program through the provision of property or services or otherwise, or affords him an opportunity to do so which is different from that afforded others under the program (including the opportunity to participate in the program as an employee but only to the extent set forth in paragraph (c) of this section);

(vii) Denies a person the same opportunity or consideration given others to be selected or retained or otherwise to participate as a contractor, subcontractor, or subgrantee;

(viii) Denies a person the opportunity to participate as a member of a planning or advisory body which is an integral part of the program.

(2) A recipient, or other party subject to this part, in determining the types of services, financial aid, or other benefits, or facilities which will be provided under any program, or the class of persons to whom, or the situations in which, such services, financial aid, other benefits, or facilities will be provided under any such program, or the class of persons to be afforded an opportunity to participate in any such program, shall not, directly or through contractual or other arrangements,

utilize criteria or methods of administration which have the effect of subjecting persons to discrimination because of their race, color, or national origin, or have the effect of defeating or substantially impairing accomplishment of the objectives of the program as respect any persons of a particular race, color, or national origin.

(3) In determining the site or location of facilities, a recipient or other party subject to this part may not make selections with the purpose or effect of excluding persons from, denying them the benefits of, or subjecting them to discrimination under any program to which this part applies, on the grounds of race, color or national origin; or with the purpose or effect of defeating or substantially impairing the accomplishment of the objectives of the Act or this part.

(4) As used in this section, the services, financial aid, or other benefits provided under a program receiving Federal financial assistance shall be deemed to include any service, financial aid, or other benefit provided or made available in or through or utilizing a facility provided with the aid of Federal financial assistance.

(5) The enumeration of specific forms of prohibited discrimination in this paragraph and paragraph (c) of this section does not limit the generality of the prohibition in paragraph (a) of this section.

(6)(i) In administering a program regarding which the recipient has previously discriminated against persons on the ground of race, color, or national origin, the recipient must take affirmative action to overcome the effects of prior discrimination.

(ii) Even in the absence of such prior discrimination, a recipient in administering a program may take affirmative action to overcome the effects of conditions which resulted in limiting participation by persons of a particular race, color or national origin.

(c) *Employment practices.* (1) Where a primary objective of the Federal financial assistance to a program to which this part applies is to provide employment, a recipient or other party subject to this part shall not, directly or through contractual or other arrangements, subject a person to discrimination on the ground of race, color, or national origin in its employment practices under such program (including recruitment or recruitment advertising, hiring, firing, upgrading, promotion, demotion, transfer, layoff, termination, rates of pay or other forms of compensation or benefits, selection for training or apprenticeship, use of facilities, and treatment of employees). Such recipients and other parties subject to this part shall take affirmative action to ensure that applicants are employed, and employees are treated during employment without regard to their race, color, or national origin. Such recipients and other parties subject to this part shall, as may be required by supplemental regulations, develop a written affirmative action plan. The requirements applicable to construction employment under any such program shall be in addition to those specified in or pursuant to Part III of Executive Order 11246 or any Executive order which supersedes it. Federal financial assistance to programs under laws funded or administered by the Department which has as a primary objective the providing of employment include those set forth in Appendix A II of this part.

(2) Where a primary objective of the Federal financial assistance to a program to which this part applies is not to provide employment, but discrimination on the grounds of race, color, or national origin, in the employment practices of the recipient or other party subject to this part, tends, on the grounds of race, color, or national origin, to exclude persons from participating in, to deny them the benefits of, or to subject them to discrimination under any such program, the provisions of paragraph (c)(1) of this section shall apply to the employment practices of the recipient or other party subject to this part, to the extent necessary to assure equality of opportunity to, and nondiscriminatory treatment of such persons.

[38 FR 17938, July 5, 1973; 38 FR 23777, Sept. 4, 1973]

§ 8.5 Nondiscrimination clause.

(a) *Applicability.* Every application for, and every grant, loan, or contract authorizing approval of, Federal financial assistance and to provide a facility subject to this part, and every modification or amendment thereof, shall, as a condition to its approval and to the extension of any Federal financial assistance pursuant thereto, contain or be accompanied by an assurance that the program will be conducted in compliance with all requirements imposed by or pursuant to this part. The assurances shall be set forth in a nondiscrimination clause. The responsible Department official shall specify the form and contents of the nondiscrimination clause for each program as appropriate.

(b) *Contents.* Without limiting its scope or language in any way, a nondiscrimination clause shall contain, where determined to be appropriate, and in an appropriate form, reference to the following assurances, undertakings, and other provisions:

(1) That the recipient or other party subject to this part will not participate directly or indirectly in the discrimination prohibited by §8.4, including employment practices when a program covering such is involved.

(2) That when employment practices are covered, the recipient or other party subject to this part will (i) in all solicitations or advertisements for employees placed by or for the recipient, state that qualified applicants will receive consideration for employment without regard to race, color, or national origin; (ii) notify each labor union or representative of workers with which it has a collective bargaining agreement or other contract or understanding of the recipient's commitments under this section; (iii) post the nondiscrimination clause and the notice to labor unions in conspicuous places available to employees and applicants for employment; and (iv) otherwise comply with the requirements of §8.4(c).

(3) When continuing Federal financial assistance is involved, the recipient thereunder (i) will state that the program is (or, in the case of a new program, will be) conducted in compliance with all requirements imposed by or pursuant to this part, and (ii) will provide for such methods of administration for the program as are found by the responsible Department official to give reasonable assurance that all recipients of Federal financial assistance under such program and any other parties connected therewith subject to this part will comply with all requirements imposed by or pursuant to this part.

(4) That the recipient agrees to secure the compliance or to cooperate actively with the Department to secure the compliance by others with this part and the nondiscrimination clause as may be directed under an applicable program. For instance, the recipient may be requested by the responsible Department official to undertake and agree (i) to obtain or enforce or to assist and cooperate actively with the responsible Department official in obtaining or enforcing, the compliance of other recipients or of other parties subject to this part with the nondiscrimination required by this part; (ii) to insert appropriate nondiscrimination clauses in the respective contracts with or grants to such parties; (iii) to obtain and to furnish to the responsible Department official such information as he may require for the supervision or securing of such compliance; (iv) to carry out sanctions for noncompliance with the obligations imposed upon recipients and other parties subject to this part; and (v) to comply with such additional provisions as the responsible Department official deems appropriate to establish and protect the interests of the United States in the enforcement of these obligations. In the event that the cooperating recipient becomes involved in litigation with a noncomplying party as a result of such departmental direction, the cooperating recipient may request the Department to enter into such litigation to protect the interests of the United States.

(5) In the case of real property, structures or improvements thereon, or interests therein, which are acquired for a program receiving Federal financial assistance, or in the case where Federal financial assistance is provided in the form of a transfer of real property or interest therein from the Federal Government, the instrument effecting or recording the transfer shall contain

a covenant running with the land assuring nondiscrimination for the period during which the real property is used for a purpose for which the Federal financial assistance is extended or for another purpose involving the provision of similar services or benefits, or for as long as the recipient retains ownership or possession of the property, whichever, is longer. Where no transfer of property is involved, but property is improved with Federal financial assistance, the recipient shall agree to include such a covenant in any subsequent transfer of such property. Where the property is obtained from the Federal Government, such covenant may also include a condition coupled with a right to be reserved by the Department to revert title to the property in the event of a breach of the covenant where, in the discretion of the responsible Department official, such a condition and right of reverter is appropriate to the statute under which the real property is obtained and to the nature of the grant and the grantee. In such event if a transferee of real property proposes to mortgage or otherwise encumber the real property as security for financing construction of new, or improvement of existing facilities on such property for the purposes for which the property was transferred, the responsible Department official may agree, upon request of the transferee and if necessary to accomplish such financing, and upon such conditions as he deems appropriate to forebear the exercise of such right to revert title for so long as the lien of such mortgage or other encumbrance remains effective.

(6) In programs receiving Federal financial assistance in the form, or for the acquisition, of real property or an interest in real property to the extent that rights to space on, over, or under any such property are included as part of the program receiving such assistance the nondiscrimination requirements of this part shall extend to any facility located wholly or in part in such space.

(7) That a recipient shall not take action that is calculated to bring about indirectly what this part forbids it to accomplish directly.

(8) Provisions specifying the extent to which like assurances will be required of subgrantees, contractors and subcontractors, lessees, transferees, successors in interest, and other participants in the program.

(9) Provisions which give the United States a right to seek judicial enforcement of the assurances.

(10) In the case where any assurances are required from an academic, a medical care, detention or correctional, or any other institution or facility, insofar as the assurances relate to the institution's practices with respect to the admission, care, or other treatment of persons by the institution or with respect to the opportunity of persons to participate in the receiving or providing of services, treatment, or benefits, such assurances shall be applicable to the entire institution or facility.

(11) In the case where the Federal financial assistance is in the form of or to aid in the acquisition of personal property, or real property or interest therein or structures thereon, the assurance shall obligate the recipients, or, in the case of a subsequent transfer, the transferee, for the period during which the property is used for a purpose for which the Federal financial assistance is extended or for another purpose involving the provision of similar services and benefits, or for as long as the recipient or transferee retains ownership or possession of the property, whichever is longer. In the case of any other type or form of assistance, the assurances shall be in effect for the duration of the period during which Federal financial assistance is extended to the program.

[38 FR 17938, July 5, 1973; 38 FR 23777, Sept. 4, 1973, as amended at 68 FR 51352, Aug. 26, 2003]

§8.6 Applicability of this part to Department assisted programs.

The following examples illustrate the applicability of this part to programs which receive or may receive Federal financial assistance administered by the Department. The fact that a particular type of Federal financial assistance is not listed does not indicate that it is not covered by this part, The discrimination referred to is that described in §8.4 against persons on the ground of race, color, or national origin.

(a) *Assistance to support economic development.* Discrimination in which recipients and other parties subject to this part shall not engage, directly or indirectly, includes discrimination in

(1) The letting of contracts or other arrangements for the planning, designing, engineering, acquisition, construction, rehabilitation, conversion, enlargement, installation, occupancy, use, maintenance, leasing, subleasing, sales, or other utilization or disposition of property or facilities purchased or financed in whole or in part with the aid of Federal financial assistance;

(2) The acquisition of goods or services, or the production, preparation, manufacture, marketing, transportation, or distribution of goods or services in connection with a program or its operations;

(3) The onsite operation of the project or facilities;

(4) Services or accommodations offered to the public in connection with the program; and

(5) In employment practices in connection with or which affect the program (as defined in § 8.4(c)); in the following programs:

(i) Any program receiving Federal financial assistance for the purchase or development of land and facilities (including machinery and equipment) for industrial or commercial usage.

(ii) Any program receiving Federal financial assistance in the form of loans or direct or supplementary grants for the acquisition or development of land and improvements for public works, public service or development facility usage, and the acquisition, construction, rehabilitation, alteration, expansion, or improvement of such facilities, including related machinery and equipment.

(iii) In any program receiving any form of technical assistance designed to alleviate or prevent conditions of excessive employment or underemployment.

(iv) In any program receiving Federal financial assistance in the form of administrative expense grants.

(b) *Assistance to support the training of students.* A current example of such assistance is that received by State maritime academies or colleges, by contract, of facilities (vessels), related equipment and funds to train merchant marine officers. In this and other instances of student training, discrimination which is prohibited by recipients and other parties subject to this part includes discrimination in the selection of persons to be trained and in their treatment by the recipients in any aspect of the educational process and discipline during their training, or in the availability or use of any academic, housing, eating, recreational, or other facilities and services, or in financial assistance to students furnished or controlled by the recipients or incidental to the program. In any case where selection of trainees is made from a predetermined group, such as the students in an institution or area, the group must be selected without discrimination.

(c) *Assistance to support mobile or other trade fairs.* In programs in which operators of mobile trade fairs using U.S. flag vessels and aircraft and designed to exhibit and sell U.S. products abroad, or in which other trade fairs or exhibitions, receive technical and financial assistance, discrimination which is prohibited by recipients and other parties subject to this part includes discrimination in the selection or retention of any actual or potential exhibitors, or in access to or use of the services or accommodations by, or otherwise with respect to treatment of, exhibitors or their owners, officers, employees, or agents.

(d) *Assistance to support business entities eligible for trade adjustment assistance.* In programs in which eligible business entities receive any measure or kind of technical, financial or tax adjustment assistance because of or in connection with the impact of U.S. international trade upon such business, discrimination which is prohibited by recipients and other parties subject to this part includes discrimination in their employment practices as defined in § 8.4(c).

(e) *Assistance to support research and development and related activities.* In programs in which individuals, educational or other institutions, public governmental or business entities receive Federal financial assistance in order to encourage or foster research or development activities as such, or to obtain, promote, develop, or protect thereby technical, scientific, environmental, or other information, products, facilities, resources, or services which are to be made available to or used by others; but where such programs do not constitute Government procurement of property or services, discrimination which is prohibited by recipients and other parties subject to this part includes discrimination with respect to (1) the choice, retention or treatment of contractors, subcontractors, subgrantees or of any other person; (2) the provision of services, facilities, or financial aid; (3) the participation of any party in the research activities; (4) the dissemination to or use by any person of the results or benefits of the research or development, whether in the form of information, products, services, facilities, resources, or otherwise. If research is performed within an educational institution under which it is expected that students or others will participate in the research as a part of their experience or training, on a compensated or uncompensated basis, there shall be no discrimination in admission of students to, or in their treatment by, that part of the school from which such students are drawn or in the selection otherwise of trainees or participants. The recipient educational institutions will be required to give the assurances provided in §8.5(b)(10).

(f) *Assistance to aid in the operations of vessels engaged in U.S. foreign commerce.* In programs in which the operators of American-flag vessels used to furnish shipping services in the foreign commerce of the United States receive Federal financial assistance in the form of operating differential subsidies, discrimination which is prohibited by recipients and other parties subject to this part includes discrimination in soliciting, accepting or serving in any way passengers or shippers of cargo entitled to protection in the United States under the Act.

[38 FR 17938, July 5, 1973, as amended at 68 FR 51352, Aug. 26, 2003]

Subpart B—General Compliance

§8.7 Cooperation, compliance reports and reviews and access to records.

(a) *Cooperation and assistance.* Each responsible Department official shall to the fullest extent practicable seek the cooperation of recipients and other parties subject to this part in obtaining compliance with this part and shall provide assistance and guidance to recipients and other parties to help them comply voluntarily with this part.

(b) *Compliance reports.* Each recipient and other party subject to this part shall keep such records and submit to the responsible Department official timely, complete, and accurate compliance reports at such times and in such form and containing such information as the responsible Department official may determine to be necessary to enable him to ascertain whether the recipient or such other party has complied or is complying with this part. In general, recipients should have available for the department racial and ethnic data showing the extent to which members of minority groups are beneficiaries of federally assisted programs. In the case in which a primary recipient extends Federal financial assistance to any other recipient, or under which a recipient is obligated to obtain or to cooperate in obtaining the compliance of other parties subject to this part, such other recipients or other parties shall also submit such compliance reports to the primary recipient or recipients as may be necessary to enable them to carry out their obligations under this part.

(c) *Access to sources of information.* Each recipient or other party subject to this part shall permit access by the responsible Department official or his designee during normal business hours to such of its books, records, accounts, and other sources of information, and its facilities, as may be pertinent to ascertain compliance with this part. Where any information required of a recipient or other party is in the exclusive possession of another who fails or refuses to furnish this information, the recipient or other party shall so certify in its report and shall set forth what efforts it has made to obtain the information.

(d) *Information to beneficiaries and participants.* Each recipient or other party subject to this part shall make available to participants, beneficiaries, and other interested persons such information regarding the provisions of this part and its applicability to the program for which the recipient receives Federal financial assistance, and make such information available to them in such manner as this part and the responsible Department official finds necessary to apprise such persons of the protections against discrimination assured them by the Act and this part.

(e) *Compliance review.* The responsible Department official or his designee shall from time to time review the practices of recipients and other parties subject to this part to determine whether they are complying with this part.

§ 8.8 Complaints.

(a) *Filing complaints.* Any person who believes himself or any specific class of persons to be subjected to discrimination prohibited by this part may by himself or by a representative file with the responsible Department official a written complaint. A complaint shall be filed not later than 180 days from the date of the alleged discrimination, unless the time for filing is extended by the responsible Department official.

(b) [Reserved]

§ 8.9 Intimidatory or retaliatory acts prohibited.

(a) No recipient or other party subject to this part shall intimidate, threaten, coerce, or discriminate against, any person for the purpose of interfering with any right or privilege secured by section 601 of the Act of this part, or because the person has made a complaint, testified, assisted, or participated in any manner in an investigation, proceeding, or hearing under this part.

(b) The identity of complainants shall be kept confidential except to the extent necessary to carry out the purposes of this part, including the conduct of any investigation, hearing, or judicial or other proceeding arising thereunder.

§ 8.10 Investigations.

(a) *Making the investigation.* The responsible Department official or his designee will make a prompt investigation whenever a compliance review, report, complaint, or any other information indicates a possible failure to comply with this part. The investigation shall include, where appropriate, a review of the pertinent practices and policies of the recipient or other party subject to this part, the circumstances under which the possible noncompliance with this part occurred, and other factors relevant to a determination as to whether there has been a failure to comply with this part.

(b) *Resolution of matters.* (1) If an investigation pursuant to paragraph (a) of this section indicates a failure to comply with this part, the responsible Department official will so inform the recipient or other party subject to this part and the matter will be resolved by informal means whenever possible. If it has been determined that the matter cannot be resolved by informal means, action will be taken as provided for in § 8.11.

(2) If an investigation does not warrant action pursuant to paragraph (b)(1) of this section, the responsible Department official will so inform the recipient or other party subject to this part and the complainant, if any, in writing.

§ 8.11 Procedures for effecting compliance.

(a) *General.* If there appears to be a failure or threatened failure to comply with this part, and if the noncompliance or threatened noncompliance cannot be corrected by informal means, compliance with this part may be effected by the suspension or termination of or refusal to grant or to continue Federal financial assistance or by any other means authorized by law. Such other means may include, but are not limited to, (1) a reference to the Department of Justice with a recommendation that appropriate proceedings be brought to enforce any rights of the United States under any law of the United States (including other titles of the Act), or any assurance or other contractual undertaking, and (2) any applicable proceeding under State or local law.

(b) *Noncompliance with §8.5.* If a recipient or other party subject to this part fails or refuses to furnish an assurance required under §8.5 or otherwise fails or refuses to comply with a requirement imposed by or pursuant to that section, Federal financial assistance may be refused in accordance with the procedures of paragraph (c) of this section. The Department shall not be required to provide assistance in such a case during the pendency of the administrative proceedings under said paragraph except that the Department shall continue assistance during the pendency of such proceedings where such assistance is due and payable pursuant to an application or contract therefor approved prior to the effective date of this part.

(c) *Termination of or refusal to grant or to continue Federal financial assistance.* No order suspending, terminating, or refusing to grant or continue Federal financial assistance shall become effective until (1) the responsible Department official has advised the recipient or other party subject to this part of his failure to comply and has determined that compliance cannot be secured by voluntary means, (2) there has been an express finding on the record, after opportunity for hearing, of a failure by such recipient or other party to comply with a requirement imposed by or pursuant to this part, (3) the action has been approved by the Secretary pursuant to §8.13(e), and (4) the expiration of 30 days after the Secretary has filed with the committee of the House and the committee of the Senate having legislative jurisdiction over the program involved, a full written report of the circumstances and the grounds for such action. Any action to suspend or terminate or to refuse to grant or to continue Federal financial assistance shall be limited to the particular political entity, or part thereof, or other recipient or other party as to whom such a finding has been made and shall be limited in its effect to the particular program, or part thereof, in which such noncompliance has been so found.

(d) *Other means authorized by law.* No action to effect compliance by any other means authorized by law shall be taken until (1) the responsible Department official has determined that compliance cannot be secured by voluntary means, (2) the recipient or other party has been notified of its failure to comply and of the action to be taken to effect compliance, and (3) the expiration of at least 10 days from the mailing of such notice to the recipient or other party. During this period of at least 10 days additional efforts shall be made to persuade the recipient or other party to comply with this part and to take such corrective action as may be appropriate.

§8.12 Hearings.

(a) *Opportunity for hearing.* Whenever an opportunity for a hearing is required by §8.11(c), reasonable notice shall be given by registered or certified mail, return receipt requested, to the affected recipient or other party subject to this part. This notice shall advise the recipient or other party of the action proposed to be taken, the specific provision under which the proposed action against it is to be taken, and the matters of fact or law asserted as the basis for this action, and either (1) fix a date not less than 20 days after the date of such notice within which the recipient or other party may request of the responsible Department official that the matter be scheduled for hearing, or (2) advise the recipient or other party that the matter in question has been set down for hearing at a stated place and time. The time and place so fixed shall be reasonable and shall be subject to change for cause. The complainant, if any, shall be advised of the time and place of the hearing. A recipient or other party may waive a hearing and submit written information and argument for the record. The failure of a recipient or other party to request a hearing under this paragraph of this section or to appear at a hearing for which a date has been set shall be deemed to be a waiver of the right to a hearing under section 602 of the Act and §8.11(c) and consent to the making of a decision on the basis of such information as is available.

(b) *Time and place of hearing.* Hearings shall be held at the offices of the Department in Washington, D.C., at a time fixed by the responsible Department official or hearing officer unless he determines that the convenience of the recipient or other party or of the Department requires that another place be selected. Hearings shall be held before the responsible Department official, or at his discretion, before a hearing officer.

(c) *Right to counsel.* In all proceedings under this section, the recipient or other party and the Department shall have the right to be represented by counsel.

(d) *Procedures, evidence, and record.* (1) The hearing, decision, and any administrative review thereof shall be conducted in conformity with 5 U.S.C. 554–557 (sections 5–8 of the Administrative Procedures Act), and in accordance with such rules of procedure as are proper (and not inconsistent with this section) relating to the conduct of the hearing, giving of notices subsequent to those provided for in paragraph (a) of this section, taking of testimony, exhibits, arguments and briefs, requests for findings, and other related matters. Both the Department and the recipient or other party shall be entitled to introduce all relevant evidence on the issues as stated in the notice for hearing or as determined by the officer conducting the hearing at the outset of or during the hearing.

(2) Technical rules of evidence shall not apply to hearings conducted pursuant to this part, but rules or principles designed to assure production of the most credible evidence available and to subject testimony to test by cross-examination shall be applied where reasonably necessary by the officer conducting the hearing. The hearing officer may exclude irrelevant, immaterial, or unduly repetitious evidence. All documents and other evidence offered or taken for the record shall be open to examination by the parties and opportunity shall be given to refute facts and arguments advanced on either side of the issues. A transcript shall be made of the oral evidence except to the extent the substance thereof is stipulated for the record. All decisions shall be based upon the hearing record and written findings shall be made.

(e) *Consolidated or joint hearings.* In cases in which the same or related facts are asserted to constitute noncompliance with this part with respect to two or more Federal statutes, authorities, or other means by which Federal financial assistance is extended and to which this part applies, or noncompliance with this part and the regulations of one or more other Federal departments or agencies issued under Title VI of the Act, the Secretary may, by agreement with such other departments or agencies where applicable, provide for the conduct of consolidated or joint hearings and for the application to such hearings of rules of procedures not inconsistent with this part. Final decisions in such cases, insofar as this part is concerned, shall be made in accordance with § 8.13.

§ 8.13 Decisions and notices.

(a) *Decision by person other than the responsible Department official.* If the hearing is held by a hearing officer such hearing officer shall either make an initial decision, if so authorized, or certify the entire record including his recommended findings and proposed decision to the responsible Department official for a final decision, and a copy of such initial decision or certification shall be mailed to the recipient or other party subject to this part. Where the initial decision is made by the hearing officer, the recipient or other party may within 30 days of the mailing of such notice of initial decision file with the responsible Department official his exceptions to the initial decision, with his reasons therefor. In the absence of exceptions, the responsible Department official may on his own motion within 45 days after the initial decision serve on the recipient or other party a notice that he will review the decision. Upon the filing of such exceptions or of such notice of review, the responsible Department official shall review the initial decision and issue his own decision thereon including the reasons therefor. In the absence of either exceptions or a notice of review the initial decision shall constitute the final decision of the responsible Department official.

(b) *Decisions on record or review by the responsible Department official.* Whenever a record is certified to the responsible Department official for decision or he reviews the decision of a hearing officer pursuant to paragraph (a) of this section, or whenever the responsible Department official conducts the hearing, the recipient or other party shall be given reasonable opportunity to file with him briefs or other written statements of its contentions, and a copy of the final decision of the responsible Department official shall be given in writing to the recipient or other party and to the complainant, if any.

(c) *Decisions on record where a hearing is waived.* Whenever a hearing is waived pursuant to §8.12(a) a decision shall be made by the responsible departmental official on the record and a copy of such decision shall be given in writing to the recipient or other party, and to the complainant, if any.

(d) *Ruling required.* Each decision of a hearing officer or responsible Department official shall set forth his ruling on each finding, conclusion, or exception presented, and shall identify the requirement or requirements imposed by or pursuant to this part with which it is found that the recipient or other party has failed to comply.

(e) *Approval by Secretary.* Any final decision of a responsible Department official (other than the Secretary) which provides for the suspension or termination of, or the refusal to grant or continue, Federal financial assistance, or the imposition of any other sanction available under this part of the Act, shall promptly be transmitted to the Secretary, who may approve such decision, may vacate it, or remit or mitigate any sanction imposed.

(f) *Content of orders.* The final decision may provide for suspension or termination of, or refusal to grant or continue, Federal financial assistance, in whole or in part, to which this regulation applies, and may contain such terms, conditions, and other provisions as are consistent with and will effectuate the purposes of the Act and this part, including provisions designed to assure that no Federal financial assistance to which this regulation applies will thereafter be extended to the recipient or other party determined by such decision to be in default in its performance of an assurance given by it pursuant to this part, or to have otherwise failed to comply with this part, unless and until it corrects its noncompliance and satisfies the responsible Department official that it will fully comply with this part.

(g) *Posttermination proceedings.* (1) Any recipient or other party which is adversely affected by an order issued under paragraph (f) of this section shall be restored to full eligibility to receive Federal financial assistance if it satisfies the terms and conditions of that order for such eligibility or if it brings itself into compliance with this part and provides reasonable assurance that it will fully comply with this part.

(2) Any recipient or other party adversely affected by an order entered pursuant to paragraph (f) of this section may at any time request the responsible Department official to restore fully its eligibility to receive Federal financial assistance. Any such request shall be supported by information showing that the recipient or other party has met the requirements of paragraph (g)(1) of this section. If the responsible Department official determines that those requirements have been satisfied, he shall restore such eligibility.

(3) If the responsible Department official denies any such request, the recipient or other party may submit a request for a hearing in writing, specifying why it believes such official to have been in error. It shall thereupon be given an expeditious hearing, with a decision on the record in accordance with rules of procedure issued by the responsible Department official. The recipient or other party will be restored to such eligibility if it proves at such a hearing that it satisfied the requirements of paragraph (g)(1) of this section. While proceedings under this paragraph are pending, the sanctions imposed by the order issued under paragraph (f) of this section shall remain in effect.

§8.14 Judicial review.

Action taken pursuant to section 602 of the Act is subject to judicial review as provided in section 603 of the Act.

§ 8.15 Effect on other laws; supplementary instructions; coordination.

(a) *Effect on other laws.* All regulations, orders, or like directions heretofore issued by any officer of the Department which impose requirements designed to prohibit any discrimination against individuals on the ground of race, color, or national origin under any program to which this part applies, and which authorizes the suspension or termination of or refusal to grant or to continue Federal financial assistance to any recipient or other party subject to this part of such assistance for failure to comply with such requirements, are hereby superseded to the extent that such discrimination is prohibited by this part, except that nothing in this part shall be deemed to relieve any one of any obligations assumed or imposed under any such superseded regulation, order, instruction, or like direction prior to January 9, 1965. Nothing in this part, however, shall be deemed to supersede any of the following (including future amendments thereof):

(1) Executive Order 11246 and regulations issued thereunder, or

(2) Executive Order 11063 and regulations issued thereunder, or any other regulations or instructions, insofar as such order, regulations, or instructions prohibit discrimination on the ground of race, color, or national origin in any program or situation to which this part is inapplicable, or prohibit discrimination on any other ground.

(b) *Forms and instructions.* Each responsible Department official shall issue and promptly make available to interested parties forms and detailed instructions and procedures for effectuating this part as applied to programs to which this part applies and for which he is responsible.

(c) *Supervision and coordination.* The Secretary may from time to time assign to officials of the Department, or to officials of other departments or agencies of the Government with the consent of such departments or agencies, responsibilities in connection with the effectuation of the purposes of title VI of the Act and this part (other than responsibility for final decision as provided in § 8.13), including the achievement of effective coordination and maximum uniformity within the Department and within the executive branch of the government in the application of title VI and this part to similar programs and in similar situations. Any action taken, determination made, or requirement imposed by an official of another Department or agency acting pursuant to an assignment of responsibility under this paragraph shall have the same effect as though such action had been taken by the responsible official of this Department.

APPENDIX A TO PART 8—FEDERAL FINANCIAL ASSISTANCE COVERED BY TITLE VI

I. FEDERAL FINANCIAL ASSISTANCE TO WHICH TITLE 15, SUBTITLE A, PART 8 APPLIES

Economic Development Administration

1. Loans, grants, technical and other assistance for public works and development facilities, for supplementing Federal grants-in-aid, for private businesses, and for other purposes, including assistance in connection with designated economic development districts and regions (Public Works and Economic Development Act of 1965, as amended, 42 U.S.C. 3121 *et seq.*).

2. Financial and technical assistance to firms to aid economic adjustment to the effects of increased imports in direct competition with firm products (Trade Act of 1974, 19 U.S.C. 2341–2354).

3. Assistance to communities adversely affected by increased imports in direct competition with products manufactured in the community area (Trade Act of 1974, 19 U.S.C. 2371–2374).

4. Assistance to projects involving construction of local and State public facilities in order to reduce unemployment and provide State and local governments with badly needed public facilities (Local Public Works Capital Development and Assistance Act of 1976, 42 U.S.C. 6701–6710).

5. Trade adjustment assistance: Loans, dissemination of technical information (title II of the Trade Act of 1974, 19 U.S.C. 2341–2374).

Maritime Administration

1. Operating differential subsidy assistance to operators of U.S. flag vessels engaged in U.S. foreign commerce (46 U.S.C. 1171 *et seq.*).

2. Assistance to operate State maritime academies and colleges to train merchant marine officers (46 U.S.C. 1381–1388).

3. Ship construction differential subsidies, direct payments (Merchant Marine Act of 1936, as amended, 46 U.S.C. 1151–1161).

National Bureau of Standards

1. Grants to universities and other research organizations for fire research and safety programs (15 U.S.C. 278f).

National Fire Prevention and Control Administration

1. Academy planning assistance: To assist States in the development of training and education in the fire prevention and control area (15 U.S.C. 2201–2219).

2. State fire incident reporting assistance: To assist States in the establishment and operation of a statewide fire incident and casualty reporting system (15 U.S.C. 2201–2219).

3. Public education assistance planning: Publications, audiovisual presentations and demonstrations, research, testing, and experimentation to determine the most effective means for such public education (15 U.S.C. 2205c).

4. Policy development assistance: Studies of the operations and management aspects of fire services (15 U.S.C. 2207c).

National Oceanic and Atmospheric Administration

1. Assistance to States, educational institutions, and the commercial fishing industry for the development of tuna and other latent fisheries (16 U.S.C. 758e).

2. Assistance to States for the development and implementation of programs to protect and study certain species of marine mammals (16 U.S.C. 1379b).

3. Financial assistance to States with agencies which have entered into a cooperative agreement to assist in the preservation of threatened and endangered species (16 U.S.C. 1535).

4. Assistance to coastal States for the development of estuarine sanctuaries to serve as field laboratories and for acquiring access to public beaches (16 U.S.C. 1461).

5. Assistance to coastal States for the development, implementation, and administration of coastal zone management programs (16 U.S.C. 1454–1455).

6. Assistance to coastal States to help communities in dealing with the economic, social, and environmental consequences resulting from expanded coastal energy activity (16 U.S.C. 1456).

7. Authority to enter into cooperative agreements with "colleges and universities, with game and fish departments of the several States, and with nonprofit organizations relating to cooperative research units." Assistance limited to assignment of personnel, supplies, and incidental expenses (16 U.S.C. 753 a and b).

8. Grants for education and training of personnel in the field of commercial fishing, "to public and nonprofit private universities and colleges * * *" (16 U.S.C. 760d).

9. Grants for "office and any other necessary space" for the Northern Pacific Halibut Commission (16 U.S.C. 772).

10. The "Dingell Johnson Act": Apportionment of dollars to States for restoration and management of sport or recreational species (16 U.S.C. 777–777i; 777k).

11. Authority to cooperate with and provide assistance to States in controlling jellyfish, etc. (16 U.S.C. 1201, 1202).

12. Authority to cooperate with and provide assistance to certain States and territories in the study and control of "Crown of Thorns" starfish (16 U.S.C. 1211–1213).

13. Technical assistance to fishing cooperatives regarding catching and marketing aquatic products (15 U.S.C. 521–522).

14. Fish research and experimentation program cooperation with other agencies in acquisition of lands, construction of buildings, employment of personnel in establishing and maintaining research stations (16 U.S.C. 778a).

15. Assistance to upgrade commercial fishing vessels and gear (16 U.S.C. 742c).

16. Assistance to State projects designed for the research and development of commercial fisheries resources of the nation (16 U.S.C. 779a–779f).

17. Assistance to State and other non-Federal interests under cooperative agreements to conserve, develop, and enhance anadromous and Great Lakes Fisheries (16 U.S.C. 757a *et seq.*).

18. Grants and other assistance under the National Sea Grant College and Program Act of 1966: To support establishment of major university centers for marine research, education, training, and advisory services (33 U.S.C. 1121–1124).

19. Geodetic surveys and services; advisory services; dissemination of technical information (33 U.S.C. 883a).

20. Nautical charts assistance; advisory services; dissemination of technical information (33 U.S.C. 883a).

21. River and flood forecast and warning services; advisory services (15 U.S.C. 313).

22. Weather forecast and warning services (15 U.S.C. 311 and 313, 49 U.S.C. 1351 and 1463).

23. Commercial fisheries disaster assistance (16 U.S.C. 779b).

24. Provision for the Weather Service to assist in joint projects "of mutual interest" (15 U.S.C. 1525).

National Telecommunications and Information Administration

1. Grants for the planning and construction of public telecommunications facilities for the production and distribution of noncommercial educational and cultural radio and television programming and related instructional and informational materials. (Public Telecommunications Financing Act of 1978, 47 U.S.C. Sections 390–394).

Office of Minority Business Enterprise

1. Assistance to minority business enterprises: Grants, contracts, advisory service, technical information (15 U.S.C. 1512; title III of the Public Works and Economic Development Act of 1965, as amended, 42 U.S.C. 3151; Executive Order 11625, Oct. 13, 1971).

Regional Action Planning Commissions

1. Supplemental grants to Federal grant-in-aid programs and technical assistance funds for planning, investigations, studies, training programs, and demonstration projects, including demonstrations in energy, transportation, health and nutrition, education and indigenous arts and crafts (title V of the Public Works and Economic Development Act of 1965, as amended, 42 U.S.C. 3181–3196).

United States Travel Service

1. Assistance to strengthen the domestic and foreign commerce of the United States, and to promote friendly understanding and appreciation of the United States by encouraging foreign residents to visit the United States (22 U.S.C. 2121 *et seq.*).

Departmentwide

1. Authority to make basis scientific research grants (42 U.S.C. 1891–1893; to be superseded no later than Feb. 3, 1979, by the Federal Grant and Cooperative Agreement Act of 1977, Pub. L. 95–224).

II. A PRIMARY OBJECTIVE OF THE FINANCIAL ASSISTANCE AUTHORIZED BY THE FOLLOWING STATUTES, ALREADY LISTED ABOVE IN APPENDIX AI, IS TO PROVIDE EMPLOYMENT

1. Public Works and Economic Development Act of 1965, as amended (42 U.S.C. 3121 *et seq.*).

2. Trade Act of 1974 (19 U.S.C. 2341–2354).

3. Local Public Works Capital Development and Assistance Act of 1976 (42 U.S.C. 6701–6710)

[43 FR 49303, Oct. 23, 1978, as amended at 44 FR 12642, Mar. 8, 1979]

PART 8a—NONDISCRIMINATION ON THE BASIS OF SEX IN EDUCATION PROGRAMS OR ACTIVITIES RECEIVING FEDERAL FINANCIAL ASSISTANCE

Subpart A—Introduction

Subpart B—Coverage

Subpart C—Discrimination on the Basis of Sex in Admission and Recruitment Prohibited

Subpart D—Discrimination on the Basis of Sex in Education Programs or Activities Prohibited

Subpart E—Discrimination on the Basis of Sex in Employment in Education Programs or Activities Prohibited

Subpart F—Procedures

AUTHORITY: 20 U.S.C. 1681, 1682, 1683, 1685, 1686, 1687, 1688.

SOURCE: 65 FR 52865, 52877, Aug. 30, 2000, unless otherwise noted.

Subpart A—Introduction

§8a.100 Purpose and effective date.

The purpose of these Title IX regulations is to effectuate Title IX of the Education Amendments of 1972, as amended (except sections 904 and 906 of those Amendments) (20 U.S.C. 1681, 1682, 1683, 1685, 1686, 1687, 1688), which is designed to eliminate (with certain exceptions) discrimination on the basis of sex in any education program or activity receiving Federal financial assistance, whether or not such program or activity is offered or sponsored by an educational institution as defined in these Title IX regulations. The effective date of these Title IX regulations shall be September 29, 2000.

§8a.105 Definitions.

As used in these Title IX regulations, the term:

Administratively separate unit means a school, department, or college of an educational institution (other than a local educational agency) admission to which is independent of admission to any other component of such institution.

Admission means selection for part-time, full-time, special, associate, transfer, exchange, or any other enrollment, membership, or matriculation in or at an education program or activity operated by a recipient.

Applicant means one who submits an application, request, or plan required to be approved by an official of the Federal agency that awards Federal financial assistance, or by a recipient, as a condition to becoming a recipient.

Designated agency official means with respect to any program receiving Federal financial assistance, the Secretary or other official of the Department who by law or by delegation has the principal authority within the Department for the administration of a law extending such assistance. *Designated agency official* also means any officials so designated by due delegation of authority within the Department to act in such capacity with regard to any program under these Title IX regulations.

Educational institution means a local educational agency (LEA) as defined by 20 U.S.C. 8801(18), a preschool, a private elementary or secondary school, or an applicant or recipient that is an institution of graduate higher education, an institution of undergraduate higher education, an institution of professional education, or an institution of vocational education, as defined in this section.

Federal financial assistance means any of the following, when authorized or extended under a law administered by the Federal agency that awards such assistance:

(1) A grant or loan of Federal financial assistance, including funds made available for:

(i) The acquisition, construction, renovation, restoration, or repair of a building or facility or any portion thereof; and

(ii) Scholarships, loans, grants, wages, or other funds extended to any entity for payment to or on behalf of students admitted to that entity, or extended directly to such students for payment to that entity.

(2) A grant of Federal real or personal property or any interest therein, including surplus property, and the proceeds of the sale or transfer of such property, if the Federal share of the fair market value of the property is not, upon such sale or transfer, properly accounted for to the Federal Government.

(3) Provision of the services of Federal personnel.

(4) Sale or lease of Federal property or any interest therein at nominal consideration, or at consideration reduced for the purpose of assisting the recipient or in recognition of public interest to be served thereby, or permission to use Federal property or any interest therein without consideration.

(5) Any other contract, agreement, or arrangement that has as one of its purposes the provision of assistance to any education program or activity, except a contract of insurance or guaranty.

Institution of graduate higher education means an institution that:

(1) Offers academic study beyond the bachelor of arts or bachelor of science degree, whether or not leading to a certificate of any higher degree in the liberal arts and sciences;

(2) Awards any degree in a professional field beyond the first professional degree (regardless of whether the first professional degree in such field is awarded by an institution of undergraduate higher education or professional education); or

(3) Awards no degree and offers no further academic study, but operates ordinarily for the purpose of facilitating research by persons who have received the highest graduate degree in any field of study.

Institution of professional education means an institution (except any institution of undergraduate higher education) that offers a program of academic study that leads to a first professional degree in a field for which there is a national specialized accrediting agency recognized by the Secretary of Education.

Institution of undergraduate higher education means:

(1) An institution offering at least two but less than four years of college-level study beyond the high school level, leading to a diploma or an associate degree, or wholly or principally creditable toward a baccalaureate degree; or

(2) An institution offering academic study leading to a baccalaureate degree; or

(3) An agency or body that certifies credentials or offers degrees, but that may or may not offer academic study.

Institution of vocational education means a school or institution (except an institution of professional or graduate or undergraduate higher education) that has as its primary purpose preparation of students to pursue a technical, skilled, or semiskilled occupation or trade, or to pursue study in a technical field, whether or not the school or institution offers certificates, diplomas, or degrees and whether or not it offers full-time study.

Recipient means any State or political subdivision thereof, or any instrumentality of a State or political subdivision thereof, any public or private agency, institution, or organization, or other entity, or any person, to whom Federal financial assistance is extended directly or through another recipient and that operates an education program or activity that receives such assistance, including any subunit, successor, assignee, or transferee thereof.

Student means a person who has gained admission.

Title IX means Title IX of the Education Amendments of 1972, Public Law 92–318, 86 Stat. 235, 373 (codified as amended at 20 U.S.C. 1681–1688) (except sections 904 and 906 thereof), as amended by section 3 of Public Law 93–568, 88 Stat. 1855, by section 412 of the Education Amendments of 1976, Public Law 94–482, 90 Stat. 2234, and by Section 3 of Public Law 100–259, 102 Stat. 28, 28–29 (20 U.S.C. 1681, 1682, 1683, 1685, 1686, 1687, 1688).

Title IX regulations means the provisions set forth at §§ 8a.100 through 8a.605.

Transition plan means a plan subject to the approval of the Secretary of Education pursuant to section 901(a)(2) of the Education Amendments of 1972, 20 U.S.C. 1681(a)(2), under which an educational institution operates in making the transition from being an educational institution that admits only students of one sex to being one that admits students of both sexes without discrimination.

§ 8a.110 Remedial and affirmative action and self-evaluation.

(a) *Remedial action.* If the designated agency official finds that a recipient has discriminated against persons on the basis of sex in an education program or activity, such recipient shall take such remedial action as the designated agency official deems necessary to overcome the effects of such discrimination.

(b) *Affirmative action.* In the absence of a finding of discrimination on the basis of sex in an education program or activity, a recipient may take affirmative action consistent with law to overcome the effects of conditions that resulted in limited participation therein by persons of a particular sex. Nothing in these Title IX regulations shall be interpreted to alter any affirmative action obligations that a recipient may have under Executive Order 11246, 3 CFR, 1964–1965 Comp., p. 339; as amended by Executive Order 11375, 3 CFR, 1966–1970 Comp., p. 684; as amended by Executive Order 11478, 3 CFR, 1966–1970 Comp., p. 803; as amended by Executive Order 12086, 3 CFR, 1978 Comp., p. 230; as amended by Executive Order 12107, 3 CFR, 1978 Comp., p. 264.

(c) *Self-evaluation.* Each recipient education institution shall, within one year of September 29, 2000:

(1) Evaluate, in terms of the requirements of these Title IX regulations, its current policies and practices and the effects thereof concerning admission of students, treatment of students, and employment of both academic and non-academic personnel working in connection with the recipient's education program or activity;

(2) Modify any of these policies and practices that do not or may not meet the requirements of these Title IX regulations; and

(3) Take appropriate remedial steps to eliminate the effects of any discrimination that resulted or may have resulted from adherence to these policies and practices.

(d) *Availability of self-evaluation and related materials.* Recipients shall maintain on file for at least three years following completion of the evaluation required under paragraph (c) of this section, and shall provide to the designated agency official upon request, a description of any modifications made pursuant to paragraph (c)(2) of this section and of any remedial steps taken pursuant to paragraph (c)(3) of this section.

§ 8a.115 Assurance required.

(a) *General.* Either at the application stage or the award stage, Federal agencies must ensure that applications for Federal financial assistance or awards of Federal financial assistance contain, be accompanied by, or be covered by a specifically identified assurance from the applicant or recipient, satisfactory to the designated agency official, that each education program or activity operated by the applicant or recipient and to which these Title IX regulations apply will be operated in compliance with these Title IX regulations. An assurance of compliance with these Title IX regulations shall not be satisfactory to the designated agency official if the applicant or recipient to whom such assurance applies fails to commit itself to take whatever remedial action is necessary in accordance with § 8a.110(a) to eliminate existing discrimination on the basis of sex or to eliminate the effects of past discrimination whether occurring prior to or subsequent to the submission to the designated agency official of such assurance.

(b) *Duration of obligation.* (1) In the case of Federal financial assistance extended to provide real property or structures thereon, such assurance shall obligate the recipient or, in the case of a subsequent transfer, the transferee, for the period during which the real property or structures are used to provide an education program or activity.

(2) In the case of Federal financial assistance extended to provide personal property, such assurance shall obligate the recipient for the period during which it retains ownership or possession of the property.

(3) In all other cases such assurance shall obligate the recipient for the period during which Federal financial assistance is extended.

(c) *Form.* (1) The assurances required by paragraph (a) of this section, which may be included as part of a document that addresses other assurances or obligations, shall include that the applicant or recipient will comply with all applicable Federal statutes relating to nondiscrimination. These include but are not limited to: Title IX of the Education Amendments of 1972, as amended (20 U.S.C. 1681–1683, 1685–1688).

(2) The designated agency official will specify the extent to which such assurances will be required of the applicant's or recipient's subgrantees, contractors, subcontractors, transferees, or successors in interest.

§ 8a.120 Transfers of property.

If a recipient sells or otherwise transfers property financed in whole or in part with Federal financial assistance to a transferee that operates any education program or activity, and the Federal share of the fair market value of the property is not upon such sale or transfer properly accounted for to the Federal Government, both the transferor and the transferee shall be deemed to be recipients, subject to the provisions of §§ 8a.205 through 8a.235(a).

§ 8a.125 Effect of other requirements.

(a) *Effect of other Federal provisions.* The obligations imposed by these Title IX regulations are independent of, and do not alter, obligations not to discriminate on the basis of sex imposed by Executive Order 11246, 3 CFR, 1964–1965 Comp., p. 339; as amended by Executive Order 11375, 3 CFR, 1966–1970 Comp., p. 684; as amended by Executive Order 11478, 3 CFR, 1966–1970 Comp., p. 803; as amended by Executive Order 12087, 3 CFR, 1978 Comp., p. 230; as amended by Executive Order 12107, 3 CFR, 1978 Comp., p. 264; sections 704 and 855 of the Public Health Service Act (42 U.S.C. 295m, 298b-2); Title VII of the Civil Rights Act of 1964 (42 U.S.C. 2000e *et seq.*); the Equal Pay Act of 1963 (29 U.S.C. 206); and any other Act of Congress or Federal regulation.

(b) *Effect of State or local law or other requirements.* The obligation to comply with these Title IX regulations is not obviated or alleviated by any State or local law or other requirement that would render any applicant or student ineligible, or limit the eligibility of any applicant or student, on the basis of sex, to practice any occupation or profession.

(c) *Effect of rules or regulations of private organizations.* The obligation to comply with these Title IX regulations is not obviated or alleviated by any rule or regulation of any organization, club, athletic or other league, or association that would render any applicant or student ineligible to participate or limit the eligibility or participation of any applicant or student, on the basis of sex, in any education program or activity operated by a recipient and that receives Federal financial assistance.

§ 8a.130 Effect of employment opportunities.

The obligation to comply with these Title IX regulations is not obviated or alleviated because employment opportunities in any occupation or profession are or may be more limited for members of one sex than for members of the other sex.

§ 8a.135 Designation of responsible employee and adoption of grievance procedures.

(a) *Designation of responsible employee.* Each recipient shall designate at least one employee to coordinate its efforts to comply with and carry out its responsibilities under these Title IX regulations, including any investigation of any complaint communicated to such recipient alleging its noncompliance with these Title IX regulations or alleging any actions that would be prohibited by these Title IX regulations. The recipient shall notify all its students and employees of the name, office address, and telephone number of the employee or employees appointed pursuant to this paragraph.

(b) *Complaint procedure of recipient.* A recipient shall adopt and publish grievance procedures providing for prompt and equitable resolution of student and employee complaints alleging any action that would be prohibited by these Title IX regulations.

§ 8a.140 Dissemination of policy.

(a) *Notification of policy.* (1) Each recipient shall implement specific and continuing steps to notify applicants for admission and employment, students and parents of elementary and secondary school students, employees, sources of referral of applicants for admission and employment, and all unions or professional organizations holding collective bargaining or professional agreements with the recipient, that it does not discriminate on the basis of sex in the educational programs or activities that it operates, and that it is required by Title IX and these Title IX regulations not to discriminate in such a manner. Such notification shall contain such information, and be made in such manner, as the designated agency official finds necessary to apprise such persons of the protections against discrimination assured them by Title IX and these Title IX regulations, but shall state at least that the requirement not to discriminate in education programs or activities extends to employment therein, and to admission thereto unless §§8a.300 through 8a.310 do not apply to the recipient, and that inquiries concerning the application of Title IX and these Title IX regulations to such recipient may be referred to the employee designated pursuant to §8a.135, or to the designated agency official.

(2) Each recipient shall make the initial notification required by paragraph (a)(1) of this section within 90 days of September 29, 2000 or of the date these Title IX regulations first apply to such recipient, whichever comes later, which notification shall include publication in:

(i) Newspapers and magazines operated by such recipient or by student, alumnae, or alumni groups for or in connection with such recipient; and

(ii) Memoranda or other written communications distributed to every student and employee of such recipient.

(b) *Publications.* (1) Each recipient shall prominently include a statement of the policy described in paragraph (a) of this section in each announcement, bulletin, catalog, or application form that it makes available to any person of a type, described in paragraph (a) of this section, or which is otherwise used in connection with the recruitment of students or employees.

(2) A recipient shall not use or distribute a publication of the type described in paragraph (b)(1) of this section that suggests, by text or illustration, that such recipient treats applicants, students, or employees differently on the basis of sex except as such treatment is permitted by these Title IX regulations.

(c) *Distribution.* Each recipient shall distribute without discrimination on the basis of sex each publication described in paragraph (b)(1) of this section, and shall apprise each of its admission and employment recruitment representatives of the policy of nondiscrimination described in paragraph (a) of this section, and shall require such representatives to adhere to such policy.

Subpart B—Coverage

§8a.200 Application.

Except as provided in §§8a.205 through 8a.235(a), these Title IX regulations apply to every recipient and to each education program or activity operated by such recipient that receives Federal financial assistance.

§8a.205 Educational institutions and other entities controlled by religious organizations.

(a) *Exemption.* These Title IX regulations do not apply to any operation of an educational institution or other entity that is controlled by a religious organization to the extent that application of these Title IX regulations would not be consistent with the religious tenets of such organization.

(b) *Exemption claims.* An educational institution or other entity that wishes to claim the exemption set forth in paragraph (a) of this section shall do so by submitting in writing to the designated agency official a statement by the highest-ranking official of the institution, identifying the provisions of these Title IX regulations that conflict with a specific tenet of the religious organization.

§8a.210 Military and merchant marine educational institutions.

These Title IX regulations do not apply to an educational institution whose primary purpose is the training of individuals for a military service of the United States or for the merchant marine.

§8a.215 Membership practices of certain organizations.

(a) *Social fraternities and sororities.* These Title IX regulations do not apply to the membership practices of social fraternities and sororities that are exempt from taxation under section 501(a) of the Internal Revenue Code of 1954, 26 U.S.C. 501(a), the active membership of which consists primarily of students in attendance at institutions of higher education.

(b) *YMCA, YWCA, Girl Scouts, Boy Scouts, and Camp Fire Girls.* These Title IX regulations do not apply to the membership practices of the Young Men's Christian Association (YMCA), the Young Women's Christian Association (YWCA), the Girl Scouts, the Boy Scouts, and Camp Fire Girls.

(c) *Voluntary youth service organizations.* These Title IX regulations do not apply to the membership practices of a voluntary youth service organization that is exempt from taxation under section 501(a) of the Internal Revenue Code of 1954, 26 U.S.C. 501(a), and the membership of which has been traditionally limited to members of one sex and principally to persons of less than nineteen years of age.

§ 8a.220 Admissions.

(a) Admissions to educational institutions prior to June 24, 1973, are not covered by these Title IX regulations.

(b) *Administratively separate units.* For the purposes only of this section, §§ 8a.225 and 8a.230, and §§ 8a.300 through 8a.310, each administratively separate unit shall be deemed to be an educational institution.

(c) *Application of §§ 8a.300 through .310.* Except as provided in paragraphs (d) and (e) of this section, §§ 8a.300 through 8a.310 apply to each recipient. A recipient to which §§ 8a.300 through 8a.310 apply shall not discriminate on the basis of sex in admission or recruitment in violation of §§ 8a.300 through 8a.310.

(d) *Educational institutions.* Except as provided in paragraph (e) of this section as to recipients that are educational institutions, §§ 8a.300 through 8a.310 apply only to institutions of vocational education, professional education, graduate higher education, and public institutions of undergraduate higher education.

(e) *Public institutions of undergraduate higher education.* §§ 8a.300 through 8a.310 do not apply to any public institution of undergraduate higher education that traditionally and continually from its establishment has had a policy of admitting students of only one sex.

§ 8a.225 Educational institutions eligible to submit transition plans.

(a) *Application.* This section applies to each educational institution to which §§ 8a.300 through 8a.310 apply that:

(1) Admitted students of only one sex as regular students as of June 23, 1972; or

(2) Admitted students of only one sex as regular students as of June 23, 1965, but thereafter admitted, as regular students, students of the sex not admitted prior to June 23, 1965.

(b) *Provision for transition plans.* An educational institution to which this section applies shall not discriminate on the basis of sex in admission or recruitment in violation of §§ 8a.300 through 8a.310.

§ 8a.230 Transition plans.

(a) *Submission of plans.* An institution to which § 8a.225 applies and that is composed of more than one administratively separate unit may submit either a single transition plan applicable to all such units, or a separate transition plan applicable to each such unit.

(b) *Content of plans.* In order to be approved by the Secretary of Education, a transition plan shall:

(1) State the name, address, and Federal Interagency Committee on Education Code of the educational institution submitting such plan, the administratively separate units to which the plan is applicable, and the name, address, and telephone number of the person to whom questions concerning the plan may be addressed. The person who submits the plan shall be the chief administrator or president of the institution, or another individual legally authorized to bind the institution to all actions set forth in the plan.

(2) State whether the educational institution or administratively separate unit admits students of both sexes as regular students and, if so, when it began to do so.

(3) Identify and describe with respect to the educational institution or administratively separate unit any obstacles to admitting students without discrimination on the basis of sex.

(4) Describe in detail the steps necessary to eliminate as soon as practicable each obstacle so identified and indicate the schedule for taking these steps and the individual directly responsible for their implementation.

(5) Include estimates of the number of students, by sex, expected to apply for, be admitted to, and enter each

class during the period covered by the plan.

(c) *Nondiscrimination.* No policy or practice of a recipient to which § 8a.225 applies shall result in treatment of applicants to or students of such recipient in violation of §§ 8a.300 through 8a.310 unless such treatment is necessitated by an obstacle identified in paragraph (b)(3) of this section and a schedule for eliminating that obstacle has been provided as required by paragraph (b)(4) of this section.

(d) *Effects of past exclusion.* To overcome the effects of past exclusion of students on the basis of sex, each educational institution to which § 8a.225 applies shall include in its transition plan, and shall implement, specific steps designed to encourage individuals of the previously excluded sex to apply for admission to such institution. Such steps shall include instituting recruitment programs that emphasize the institution's commitment to enrolling students of the sex previously excluded.

§ 8a.235 Statutory amendments.

(a) This section, which applies to all provisions of these Title IX regulations, addresses statutory amendments to Title IX.

(b) These Title IX regulations shall not apply to or preclude:

(1) Any program or activity of the American Legion undertaken in connection with the organization or operation of any Boys State conference, Boys Nation conference, Girls State conference, or Girls Nation conference;

(2) Any program or activity of a secondary school or educational institution specifically for:

(i) The promotion of any Boys State conference, Boys Nation conference, Girls State conference, or Girls Nation conference; or

(ii) The selection of students to attend any such conference;

(3) Father-son or mother-daughter activities at an educational institution or in an education program or activity, but if such activities are provided for students of one sex, opportunities for reasonably comparable activities shall be provided to students of the other sex;

(4) Any scholarship or other financial assistance awarded by an institution of higher education to an individual because such individual has received such award in a single-sex pageant based upon a combination of factors related to the individual's personal appearance, poise, and talent. The pageant, however, must comply with other nondiscrimination provisions of Federal law.

(c) *Program or activity* or *program* means:

(1) All of the operations of any entity described in paragraphs (c)(1)(i) through (iv) of this section, any part of which is extended Federal financial assistance:

(i)(A) A department, agency, special purpose district, or other instrumentality of a State or of a local government; or

(B) The entity of such State or local government that distributes such assistance and each such department or agency (and each other State or local government entity) to which the assistance is extended, in the case of assistance to a State or local government;

(ii)(A) A college, university, or other postsecondary institution, or a public system of higher education; or

(B) A local educational agency (as defined in section 8801 of title 20), system of vocational education, or other school system;

(iii)(A) An entire corporation, partnership, or other private organization, or an entire sole proprietorship—

(*1*) If assistance is extended to such corporation, partnership, private organization, or sole proprietorship as a whole; or

(*2*) Which is principally engaged in the business of providing education, health care, housing, social services, or parks and recreation; or

(B) The entire plant or other comparable, geographically separate facility to which Federal financial assistance is extended, in the case of any other corporation, partnership, private organization, or sole proprietorship; or

(iv) Any other entity that is established by two or more of the entities described in paragraphs (c)(1)(i), (ii), or (iii) of this section.

(2)(i) *Program or activity* does not include any operation of an entity that is controlled by a religious organization if the application of 20 U.S.C. 1681 to such operation would not be consistent with the religious tenets of such organization.

(ii) For example, all of the operations of a college, university, or other postsecondary institution, including but not limited to traditional educational operations, faculty and student housing, campus shuttle bus service, campus restaurants, the bookstore, and other commercial activities are part of a "program or activity" subject to these Title IX regulations if the college, university, or other institution receives Federal financial assistance.

(d)(1) Nothing in these Title IX regulations shall be construed to require or prohibit any person, or public or private entity, to provide or pay for any benefit or service, including the use of facilities, related to an abortion. Medical procedures, benefits, services, and the use of facilities, necessary to save the life of a pregnant woman or to address complications related to an abortion are not subject to this section.

(2) Nothing in this section shall be construed to permit a penalty to be imposed on any person or individual because such person or individual is seeking or has received any benefit or service related to a legal abortion. Accordingly, subject to paragraph (d)(1) of this section, no person shall be excluded from participation in, be denied the benefits of, or be subjected to discrimination under any academic, extracurricular, research, occupational training, employment, or other educational program or activity operated by a recipient that receives Federal financial assistance because such individual has sought or received, or is seeking, a legal abortion, or any benefit or service related to a legal abortion.

Subpart C—Discrimination on the Basis of Sex in Admission and Recruitment Prohibited

§ 8a.300 Admission.

(a) *General.* No person shall, on the basis of sex, be denied admission, or be subjected to discrimination in admission, by any recipient to which §§ 8a.300 through §§ 8a.310 apply, except as provided in §§ 8a.225 and §§ 8a.230.

(b) *Specific prohibitions.* (1) In determining whether a person satisfies any policy or criterion for admission, or in making any offer of admission, a recipient to which §§ 8a.300 through 8a.310 apply shall not:

(i) Give preference to one person over another on the basis of sex, by ranking applicants separately on such basis, or otherwise;

(ii) Apply numerical limitations upon the number or proportion of persons of either sex who may be admitted; or

(iii) Otherwise treat one individual differently from another on the basis of sex.

(2) A recipient shall not administer or operate any test or other criterion for admission that has a disproportionately adverse effect on persons on the basis of sex unless the use of such test or criterion is shown to predict validly success in the education program or activity in question and alternative tests or criteria that do not have such a disproportionately adverse effect are shown to be unavailable.

(c) *Prohibitions relating to marital or parental status.* In determining whether a person satisfies any policy or criterion for admission, or in making any offer of admission, a recipient to which §§ 8a.300 through 8a.310 apply:

(1) Shall not apply any rule concerning the actual or potential parental, family, or marital status of a student or applicant that treats persons differently on the basis of sex;

(2) Shall not discriminate against or exclude any person on the basis of pregnancy, childbirth, termination of pregnancy, or recovery therefrom, or establish or follow any rule or practice that so discriminates or excludes;

(3) Subject to § 8a.235(d), shall treat disabilities related to pregnancy, childbirth, termination of pregnancy, or recovery therefrom in the same manner and under the same policies as any other temporary disability or physical condition; and

(4) Shall not make pre-admission inquiry as to the marital status of an applicant for admission, including whether such applicant is "Miss" or "Mrs." A recipient may make pre-admission

inquiry as to the sex of an applicant for admission, but only if such inquiry is made equally of such applicants of both sexes and if the results of such inquiry are not used in connection with discrimination prohibited by these Title IX regulations.

§ 8a.305 Preference in admission.

A recipient to which §§ 8a.300 through 8a.310 apply shall not give preference to applicants for admission, on the basis of attendance at any educational institution or other school or entity that admits as students only or predominantly members of one sex, if the giving of such preference has the effect of discriminating on the basis of sex in violation of §§ 8a.300 through 8a.310.

§ 8a.310 Recruitment.

(a) *Nondiscriminatory recruitment.* A recipient to which §§ 8a.300 through 8a.310 apply shall not discriminate on the basis of sex in the recruitment and admission of students. A recipient may be required to undertake additional recruitment efforts for one sex as remedial action pursuant to § 8a.110(a), and may choose to undertake such efforts as affirmative action pursuant to § 8a.110(b).

(b) *Recruitment at certain institutions.* A recipient to which §§ 8a.300 through 8a.310 apply shall not recruit primarily or exclusively at educational institutions, schools, or entities that admit as students only or predominantly members of one sex, if such actions have the effect of discriminating on the basis of sex in violation of §§ 8a.300 through 8a.310.

Subpart D—Discrimination on the Basis of Sex in Education Programs or Activities Prohibited

§ 8a.400 Education programs or activities.

(a) *General.* Except as provided elsewhere in these Title IX regulations, no person shall, on the basis of sex, be excluded from participation in, be denied the benefits of, or be subjected to discrimination under any academic, extracurricular, research, occupational training, or other education program or activity operated by a recipient that receives Federal financial assistance. Sections 8a.400 through 8a.455 do not apply to actions of a recipient in connection with admission of its students to an education program or activity of a recipient to which §§ 8a.300 through 8a.310 do not apply, or an entity, not a recipient, to which §§ 8a.300 through 8a.310 would not apply if the entity were a recipient.

(b) *Specific prohibitions.* Except as provided in §§ 8a.400 through 8a.455, in providing any aid, benefit, or service to a student, a recipient shall not, on the basis of sex:

(1) Treat one person differently from another in determining whether such person satisfies any requirement or condition for the provision of such aid, benefit, or service;

(2) Provide different aid, benefits, or services or provide aid, benefits, or services in a different manner;

(3) Deny any person any such aid, benefit, or service;

(4) Subject any person to separate or different rules of behavior, sanctions, or other treatment;

(5) Apply any rule concerning the domicile or residence of a student or applicant, including eligibility for in-state fees and tuition;

(6) Aid or perpetuate discrimination against any person by providing significant assistance to any agency, organization, or person that discriminates on the basis of sex in providing any aid, benefit, or service to students or employees;

(7) Otherwise limit any person in the enjoyment of any right, privilege, advantage, or opportunity.

(c) *Assistance administered by a recipient educational institution to study at a foreign institution.* A recipient educational institution may administer or assist in the administration of scholarships, fellowships, or other awards established by foreign or domestic wills, trusts, or similar legal instruments, or by acts of foreign governments and restricted to members of one sex, that are designed to provide opportunities to study abroad, and that are awarded to students who are already matriculating at or who are graduates of the recipient institution; *Provided,* that a recipient educational institution that administers or assists in the administration of such scholarships, fellowships, or other awards that are restricted to members of one sex provides, or otherwise makes available, reasonable opportunities for similar studies for members of the other sex. Such opportunities may be derived from either domestic or foreign sources.

(d) *Aids, benefits or services not provided by recipient.* (1) This paragraph (d) applies to any recipient that requires participation by any applicant, student, or employee in any education program or activity not operated wholly by such recipient, or that facilitates, permits, or considers such participation as part of or equivalent to an education program or activity operated by such recipient, including participation in educational consortia and cooperative employment and student-teaching assignments.

(2) Such recipient:

(i) Shall develop and implement a procedure designed to assure itself that the operator or sponsor of such other education program or activity takes no action affecting any applicant, student, or employee of such recipient that these Title IX regulations would prohibit such recipient from taking; and

(ii) Shall not facilitate, require, permit, or consider such participation if such action occurs.

§ 8a.405 Housing.

(a) *Generally.* A recipient shall not, on the basis of sex, apply different rules or regulations, impose different fees or requirements, or offer different services or benefits related to housing, except as provided in this section (including housing provided only to married students).

(b) *Housing provided by recipient.* (1) A recipient may provide separate housing on the basis of sex.

(2) Housing provided by a recipient to students of one sex, when compared to that provided to students of the other sex, shall be as a whole:

(i) Proportionate in quantity to the number of students of that sex applying for such housing; and

(ii) Comparable in quality and cost to the student.

(c) *Other housing.* (1) A recipient shall not, on the basis of sex, administer different policies or practices concerning occupancy by its students of housing other than that provided by such recipient.

(2)(i) A recipient which, through solicitation, listing, approval of housing, or otherwise, assists any agency, organization, or person in making housing available to any of its students, shall take such reasonable action as may be necessary to assure itself that such housing as is provided to students of one sex, when compared to that provided to students of the other sex, is as a whole:

(A) Proportionate in quantity; and

(B) Comparable in quality and cost to the student.

(ii) A recipient may render such assistance to any agency, organization, or person that provides all or part of such housing to students of only one sex.

§ 8a.410 Comparable facilities.

A recipient may provide separate toilet, locker room, and shower facilities on the basis of sex, but such facilities provided for students of one sex shall be comparable to such facilities provided for students of the other sex.

§ 8a.415 Access to course offerings.

(a) A recipient shall not provide any course or otherwise carry out any of its education program or activity separately on the basis of sex, or require or refuse participation therein by any of its students on such basis, including health, physical education, industrial, business, vocational, technical, home economics, music, and adult education courses.

(b)(1) With respect to classes and activities in physical education at the elementary school level, the recipient shall comply fully with this section as expeditiously as possible but in no event later than one year from September 29, 2000. With respect to physical education classes and activities at the secondary and post-secondary levels, the recipient shall comply fully with this section as expeditiously as possible but in no event later than three years from September 29, 2000.

(2) This section does not prohibit grouping of students in physical education classes and activities by ability as assessed by objective standards of individual performance developed and applied without regard to sex.

(3) This section does not prohibit separation of students by sex within physical education classes or activities during participation in wrestling, boxing, rugby, ice hockey, football, basketball, and other sports the purpose or major activity of which involves bodily contact.

(4) Where use of a single standard of measuring skill or progress in a physical education class has an adverse effect on members of one sex, the recipient shall use appropriate standards that do not have such effect.

(5) Portions of classes in elementary and secondary schools, or portions of education programs or activities, that deal exclusively with human sexuality may be conducted in separate sessions for boys and girls.

(6) Recipients may make requirements based on vocal range or quality that may result in a chorus or choruses of one or predominantly one sex.

§8a.420 Access to schools operated by LEAs.

A recipient that is a local educational agency shall not, on the basis of sex, exclude any person from admission to:

(a) Any institution of vocational education operated by such recipient; or

(b) Any other school or educational unit operated by such recipient, unless such recipient otherwise makes available to such person, pursuant to the same policies and criteria of admission, courses, services, and facilities comparable to each course, service, and facility offered in or through such schools.

§8a.425 Counseling and use of appraisal and counseling materials.

(a) *Counseling.* A recipient shall not discriminate against any person on the basis of sex in the counseling or guidance of students or applicants for admission.

(b) *Use of appraisal and counseling materials.* A recipient that uses testing or other materials for appraising or counseling students shall not use different materials for students on the basis of their sex or use materials that permit or require different treatment of students on such basis unless such different materials cover the same occupations and interest areas and the use of such different materials is shown to be essential to eliminate sex bias. Recipients shall develop and use internal procedures for ensuring that such materials do not discriminate on the basis of sex. Where the use of a counseling test or other instrument results in a substantially disproportionate number of members of one sex in any particular course of study or classification, the recipient shall take such action as is necessary to assure itself that such disproportion is not the result of discrimination in the instrument or its application.

(c) *Disproportion in classes.* Where a recipient finds that a particular class contains a substantially disproportionate number of individuals of one sex, the recipient shall take such action as is necessary to assure itself that such disproportion is not the result of discrimination on the basis of sex in counseling or appraisal materials or by counselors.

§8a.430 Financial assistance.

(a) *General.* Except as provided in paragraphs (b) and (c) of this section, in providing financial assistance to any of its students, a recipient shall not:

(1) On the basis of sex, provide different amounts or types of such assistance, limit eligibility for such assistance that is of any particular type or source, apply different criteria, or otherwise discriminate;

(2) Through solicitation, listing, approval, provision of facilities, or other services, assist any foundation, trust, agency, organization, or person that provides assistance to any of such recipient's students in a manner that discriminates on the basis of sex; or

(3) Apply any rule or assist in application of any rule concerning eligibility for such assistance that treats persons of one sex differently from persons of the other sex with regard to marital or parental status.

(b) *Financial aid established by certain legal instruments.* (1) A recipient may administer or assist in the administration of scholarships, fellowships, or other forms of financial assistance established pursuant to domestic or foreign wills, trusts, bequests, or similar legal instruments or by acts of a foreign government that require that awards be made to members of a particular sex specified therein; *Provided*, that the overall effect of the award of such sex-restricted scholarships, fellowships, and other forms of financial assistance does not discriminate on the basis of sex.

(2) To ensure nondiscriminatory awards of assistance as required in paragraph (b)(1) of this section, recipients shall develop and use procedures under which:

(i) Students are selected for award of financial assistance on the basis of nondiscriminatory criteria and not on the basis of availability of funds restricted to members of a particular sex;

(ii) An appropriate sex-restricted scholarship, fellowship, or other form of financial assistance is allocated to each student selected under paragraph (b)(2)(i) of this section; and

(iii) No student is denied the award for which he or she was selected under paragraph (b)(2)(i) of this section because of the absence of a scholarship, fellowship, or other form of financial assistance designated for a member of that student's sex.

(c) *Athletic scholarships*. (1) To the extent that a recipient awards athletic scholarships or grants-in-aid, it must provide reasonable opportunities for such awards for members of each sex in proportion to the number of students of each sex participating in interscholastic or intercollegiate athletics.

(2) A recipient may provide separate athletic scholarships or grants-in-aid for members of each sex as part of separate athletic teams for members of each sex to the extent consistent with this paragraph (c) and § 8a.450.

§ 8a.435 Employment assistance to students.

(a) *Assistance by recipient in making available outside employment*. A recipient that assists any agency, organization, or person in making employment available to any of its students:

(1) Shall assure itself that such employment is made available without discrimination on the basis of sex; and

(2) Shall not render such services to any agency, organization, or person that discriminates on the basis of sex in its employment practices.

(b) *Employment of students by recipients*. A recipient that employs any of its students shall not do so in a manner that violates §§ 8a.500 through 8a.550.

§ 8a.440 Health and insurance benefits and services.

Subject to § 8a.235(d), in providing a medical, hospital, accident, or life insurance benefit, service, policy, or plan to any of its students, a recipient shall not discriminate on the basis of sex, or provide such benefit, service, policy, or plan in a manner that would violate §§ 8a.500 through 8a.550 if it were provided to employees of the recipient. This section shall not prohibit a recipient from providing any benefit or service that may be used by a different proportion of students of one sex than of the other, including family planning services. However, any recipient that provides full coverage health service shall provide gynecological care.

§ 8a.445 Marital or parental status.

(a) *Status generally*. A recipient shall not apply any rule concerning a student's actual or potential parental, family, or marital status that treats students differently on the basis of sex.

(b) *Pregnancy and related conditions*. (1) A recipient shall not discriminate against any student, or exclude any student from its education program or activity, including any class or extracurricular activity, on the basis of such student's pregnancy, childbirth, false pregnancy, termination of pregnancy, or recovery therefrom, unless the student requests voluntarily to participate in a separate portion of the program or activity of the recipient.

(2) A recipient may require such a student to obtain the certification of a physician that the student is physically and emotionally able to continue participation as long as such a certification is required of all students for other physical or emotional conditions requiring the attention of a physician.

(3) A recipient that operates a portion of its education program or activity separately for pregnant students, admittance to which is completely voluntary on the part of the student as provided in paragraph (b)(1) of this section, shall ensure that the separate portion is comparable to that offered to non-pregnant students.

(4) Subject to § 8a.235(d), a recipient shall treat pregnancy, childbirth, false pregnancy, termination of pregnancy and recovery therefrom in the same manner and under the same policies as any other temporary disability with respect to any medical or hospital benefit, service, plan, or policy that such recipient administers, operates, offers, or participates in with respect to students admitted to the recipient's educational program or activity.

(5) In the case of a recipient that does not maintain a leave policy for its students, or in the case of a student who does not otherwise qualify for leave under such a policy, a recipient shall treat pregnancy, childbirth, false pregnancy, termination of pregnancy, and recovery therefrom as a justification for a leave of absence for as long a period of time as is deemed medically necessary by the student's physician, at the conclusion of which the student shall be reinstated to the status that she held when the leave began.

§ 8a.450 Athletics.

(a) *General.* No person shall, on the basis of sex, be excluded from participation in, be denied the benefits of, be treated differently from another person, or otherwise be discriminated against in any interscholastic, intercollegiate, club, or intramural athletics offered by a recipient, and no recipient shall provide any such athletics separately on such basis.

(b) *Separate teams.* Notwithstanding the requirements of paragraph (a) of this section, a recipient may operate or sponsor separate teams for members of each sex where selection for such teams is based upon competitive skill or the activity involved is a contact sport. However, where a recipient operates or sponsors a team in a particular sport for members of one sex but operates or sponsors no such team for members of the other sex, and athletic opportunities for members of that sex have previously been limited, members of the excluded sex must be allowed to try out for the team offered unless the sport involved is a contact sport. For the purposes of these Title IX regulations, contact sports include boxing, wrestling, rugby, ice hockey, football, basketball, and other sports the purpose or major activity of which involves bodily contact.

(c) *Equal opportunity.* (1) A recipient that operates or sponsors interscholastic, intercollegiate, club, or intramural athletics shall provide equal athletic opportunity for members of both sexes. In determining whether equal opportunities are available, the designated agency official will consider, among other factors:

(i) Whether the selection of sports and levels of competition effectively accommodate the interests and abilities of members of both sexes;

(ii) The provision of equipment and supplies;

(iii) Scheduling of games and practice time;

(iv) Travel and per diem allowance;

(v) Opportunity to receive coaching and academic tutoring;

(vi) Assignment and compensation of coaches and tutors;

(vii) Provision of locker rooms, practice, and competitive facilities;

(viii) Provision of medical and training facilities and services;

(ix) Provision of housing and dining facilities and services;

(x) Publicity.

(2) For purposes of paragraph (c)(1) of this section, unequal aggregate expenditures for members of each sex or unequal expenditures for male and female teams if a recipient operates or sponsors separate teams will not constitute noncompliance with this section, but the designated agency official may consider the failure to provide necessary funds for teams for one sex in assessing equality of opportunity for members of each sex.

(d) *Adjustment period.* A recipient that operates or sponsors interscholastic, intercollegiate, club, or intramural athletics at the elementary school level shall comply fully with this section as expeditiously as possible but in no event later than one year from September 29, 2000. A recipient that operates or sponsors interscholastic, intercollegiate, club, or intramural athletics at the secondary or postsecondary school level shall comply fully with this section as expeditiously as possible but in no event later than three years from September 29, 2000.

§ 8a.455 Textbooks and curricular material.

Nothing in these Title IX regulations shall be interpreted as requiring or prohibiting or abridging in any way the use of particular textbooks or curricular materials.

Subpart E—Discrimination on the Basis of Sex in Employment in Education Programs or Activities Prohibited

§ 8a.500 Employment.

(a) *General.* (1) No person shall, on the basis of sex, be excluded from participation in, be denied the benefits of, or be subjected to discrimination in employment, or recruitment, consideration, or selection therefor, whether full-time or part-time, under any education program or activity operated by a recipient that receives Federal financial assistance.

(2) A recipient shall make all employment decisions in any education program or activity operated by such recipient in a nondiscriminatory manner and shall not limit, segregate, or classify applicants or employees in any way that could adversely affect any applicant's or employee's employment opportunities or status because of sex.

(3) A recipient shall not enter into any contractual or other relationship which directly or indirectly has the effect of subjecting employees or students to discrimination prohibited by §§ 8a.500 through 8a.550, including relationships with employment and referral agencies, with labor unions, and with organizations providing or administering fringe benefits to employees of the recipient.

(4) A recipient shall not grant preferences to applicants for employment on the basis of attendance at any educational institution or entity that admits as students only or predominantly members of one sex, if the giving of such preferences has the effect of discriminating on the basis of sex in violation of these Title IX regulations.

(b) *Application.* The provisions of §§ 8a.500 through 8a.550 apply to:

(1) Recruitment, advertising, and the process of application for employment;

(2) Hiring, upgrading, promotion, consideration for and award of tenure, demotion, transfer, layoff, termination, application of nepotism policies, right of return from layoff, and rehiring;

(3) Rates of pay or any other form of compensation, and changes in compensation;

(4) Job assignments, classifications, and structure, including position descriptions, lines of progression, and seniority lists;

(5) The terms of any collective bargaining agreement;

(6) Granting and return from leaves of absence, leave for pregnancy, childbirth, false pregnancy, termination of pregnancy, leave for persons of either sex to care for children or dependents, or any other leave;

(7) Fringe benefits available by virtue of employment, whether or not administered by the recipient;

(8) Selection and financial support for training, including apprenticeship, professional meetings, conferences, and other related activities, selection for tuition assistance, selection for sabbaticals and leaves of absence to pursue training;

(9) Employer-sponsored activities, including social or recreational programs; and

(10) Any other term, condition, or privilege of employment.

§ 8a.505 Employment criteria.

A recipient shall not administer or operate any test or other criterion for any employment opportunity that has a disproportionately adverse effect on persons on the basis of sex unless:

(a) Use of such test or other criterion is shown to predict validly successful performance in the position in question; and

(b) Alternative tests or criteria for such purpose, which do not have such disproportionately adverse effect, are shown to be unavailable.

§8a.510 Recruitment.

(a) *Nondiscriminatory recruitment and hiring.* A recipient shall not discriminate on the basis of sex in the recruitment and hiring of employees. Where a recipient has been found to be presently discriminating on the basis of sex in the recruitment or hiring of employees, or has been found to have so discriminated in the past, the recipient shall recruit members of the sex so discriminated against so as to overcome the effects of such past or present discrimination.

(b) *Recruitment patterns.* A recipient shall not recruit primarily or exclusively at entities that furnish as applicants only or predominantly members of one sex if such actions have the effect of discriminating on the basis of sex in violation of §§8a.500 through 8a.550.

§8a.515 Compensation.

A recipient shall not make or enforce any policy or practice that, on the basis of sex:

(a) Makes distinctions in rates of pay or other compensation;

(b) Results in the payment of wages to employees of one sex at a rate less than that paid to employees of the opposite sex for equal work on jobs the performance of which requires equal skill, effort, and responsibility, and that are performed under similar working conditions.

§8a.520 Job classification and structure.

A recipient shall not:

(a) Classify a job as being for males or for females;

(b) Maintain or establish separate lines of progression, seniority lists, career ladders, or tenure systems based on sex; or

(c) Maintain or establish separate lines of progression, seniority systems, career ladders, or tenure systems for similar jobs, position descriptions, or job requirements that classify persons on the basis of sex, unless sex is a bona fide occupational qualification for the positions in question as set forth in §8a.550.

§8a.525 Fringe benefits.

(a) *"Fringe benefits" defined.* For purposes of these Title IX regulations, *fringe benefits* means: Any medical, hospital, accident, life insurance, or retirement benefit, service, policy or plan, any profit-sharing or bonus plan, leave, and any other benefit or service of employment not subject to the provision of §8a.515.

(b) *Prohibitions.* A recipient shall not:

(1) Discriminate on the basis of sex with regard to making fringe benefits available to employees or make fringe benefits available to spouses, families, or dependents of employees differently upon the basis of the employee's sex;

(2) Administer, operate, offer, or participate in a fringe benefit plan that does not provide for equal periodic benefits for members of each sex and for equal contributions to the plan by such recipient for members of each sex; or

(3) Administer, operate, offer, or participate in a pension or retirement plan that establishes different optional or compulsory retirement ages based on sex or that otherwise discriminates in benefits on the basis of sex.

§8a.530 Marital or parental status.

(a) *General.* A recipient shall not apply any policy or take any employment action:

(1) Concerning the potential marital, parental, or family status of an employee or applicant for employment that treats persons differently on the basis of sex; or

(2) Which is based upon whether an employee or applicant for employment is the head of household or principal wage earner in such employee's or applicant's family unit.

(b) *Pregnancy.* A recipient shall not discriminate against or exclude from employment any employee or applicant for employment on the basis of pregnancy, childbirth, false pregnancy, termination of pregnancy, or recovery therefrom.

(c) *Pregnancy as a temporary disability.* Subject to §8a.235(d), a recipient shall treat pregnancy, childbirth, false pregnancy, termination of pregnancy, recovery therefrom, and any temporary disability resulting therefrom as any other temporary disability for all job-related purposes, including commencement, duration, and extensions of leave, payment of disability income, accrual of seniority and any other benefit or service, and reinstatement, and under any fringe benefit offered to employees by virtue of employment.

(d) *Pregnancy leave.* In the case of a recipient that does not maintain a leave policy for its employees, or in the case of an employee with insufficient leave or accrued employment time to qualify for leave under such a policy, a recipient shall treat pregnancy, childbirth, false pregnancy, termination of pregnancy, and recovery therefrom as a justification for a leave of absence without pay for a reasonable period of time, at the conclusion of which the employee shall be reinstated to the status that she held when the leave began or to a comparable position, without decrease in rate of compensation or loss of promotional opportunities, or any other right or privilege of employment.

§ 8a.535 Effect of state or local law or other requirements.

(a) *Prohibitory requirements.* The obligation to comply with §§ 8a.500 through 8a.550 is not obviated or alleviated by the existence of any State or local law or other requirement that imposes prohibitions or limits upon employment of members of one sex that are not imposed upon members of the other sex.

(b) *Benefits.* A recipient that provides any compensation, service, or benefit to members of one sex pursuant to a State or local law or other requirement shall provide the same compensation, service, or benefit to members of the other sex.

§ 8a.540 Advertising.

A recipient shall not in any advertising related to employment indicate preference, limitation, specification, or discrimination based on sex unless sex is a bona fide occupational qualification for the particular job in question.

§ 8a.545 Pre-employment inquiries.

(a) *Marital status.* A recipient shall not make pre-employment inquiry as to the marital status of an applicant for employment, including whether such applicant is ''Miss'' or ''Mrs.''

(b) *Sex.* A recipient may make pre-employment inquiry as to the sex of an applicant for employment, but only if such inquiry is made equally of such applicants of both sexes and if the results of such inquiry are not used in connection with discrimination prohibited by these Title IX regulations.

§ 8a.550 Sex as a bona fide occupational qualification.

A recipient may take action otherwise prohibited by §§ 8a.500 through 8a.550 provided it is shown that sex is a bona fide occupational qualification for that action, such that consideration of sex with regard to such action is essential to successful operation of the employment function concerned. A recipient shall not take action pursuant to this section that is based upon alleged comparative employment characteristics or stereotyped characterizations of one or the other sex, or upon preference based on sex of the recipient, employees, students, or other persons, but nothing contained in this section shall prevent a recipient from considering an employee's sex in relation to employment in a locker room or toilet facility used only by members of one sex.

Subpart F—Procedures

§ 8a.600 Notice of covered programs.

Within 60 days of September 29, 2000, each Federal agency that awards Federal financial assistance shall publish in the FEDERAL REGISTER a notice of the programs covered by these Title IX regulations. Each such Federal agency shall periodically republish the notice of covered programs to reflect changes in covered programs. Copies of this notice also shall be made available upon request to the Federal agency's office that enforces Title IX.

§ 8a.605 Enforcement procedures.

The investigative, compliance, and enforcement procedural provisions of Title VI of the Civil Rights Act of 1964 (42 U.S.C. 2000d) (''Title VI'') are hereby adopted and applied to these Title IX regulations. These procedures may be found at 15 CFR 8.7 through 8.15, and 13 CFR part 317.

[65 FR 52877, Aug. 30, 2000]

PART 8b—PROHIBITION OF DISCRIMINATION AGAINST THE HANDICAPPED IN FEDERALLY ASSISTED PROGRAMS OPERATED BY THE DEPARTMENT OF COMMERCE

AUTHORITY: 29 U.S.C. 794.

SOURCE: 47 FR 17746, Apr. 23, 1982, unless otherwise noted.

EDITORIAL NOTE: Nomenclature changes to part 8b appear at 68 FR 51353, Aug. 26, 2003.

Subpart A—General Provisions

§8b.1 Purpose.

Section 504 of the Rehabilitation Act of 1973, as amended, prohibits discrimination on the basis of handicap in any program or activity receiving Federal financial assistance. The purpose of this part is to implement section 504 with respect to programs or activities receiving Federal financial assistance from the Department of Commerce.

§8b.2 Application.

This part applies to each recipient of Federal financial assistance from the Department of Commerce and to each program or activity receiving such assistance. The requirements of this part do not apply to the ultimate beneficiaries of Federal financial assistance in the program or activity receiving Federal financial assistance.

§8b.3 Definitions.

As used in this part, the term:

(a) *The Act* means the Rehabilitation Act of 1973, Pub. L. 93–112, as amended by the Rehabilitation Act Amendments of 1974, Pub. L. 93–516, and by the Rehabilitation, Comprehensive Services, and Developmental Disabilities Amendments of 1978, Pub. L. 95–602 (codified at 29 U.S.C. 794 (1976 & Supp. II 1978)).

(b) *Applicant for assistance* means one who submits an application, request, or plan required to be approved by a Department official or by a recipient as a condition to becoming a recipient.

(c) *Department* means the Department of Commerce and any of its constituent units authorized to provide Federal financial assistance.

(d) *Facility* means all or any portion of buildings, ships, structures, equipment, roads, walks, parking lots, industrial parks, or other real or personal property or interest in such property.

(e) *Federal financial assistance* means any grant, loan, contract (other than a procurement contract or a contract of insurance or guarantee), or any other arrangement by which the Department provides or otherwise makes available assistance in the form of:

(1) Funds;

(2) Services of Federal personnel; or

(3) Real and personal property or any interest in or use of such property, including:

(i) Transfers or leases of such property for less than fair market value or for reduced consideration; and

(ii) Proceeds from a subsequent transfer or lease of such property if the Federal share of its fair market value is not returned to the Federal Government.

(f) *Handicap* means any condition or characteristic that renders a person a handicapped person as defined in paragraph (g) of this section.

(g) *Handicapped person*—(1) *Handicapped person* means any person who:

(i) Has a physical or mental impairment which substantially limits one or more major life activities;

(ii) Has a record of such an impairment; or

(iii) Is regarded as having such an impairment.

(2) For purposes of employment, the term "handicapped person" does not include any person who is an alcoholic or drug abuser whose current use of alcohol or drugs prevents that individual from performing the duties of the job in question, or whose employment, because of current alcohol or drug abuse, would constitute a direct threat to property or to the safety of others.

(3) As used in paragraph (g)(1) of this section, the phrase:

(i) *Physical or mental impairment* means:

(A) Any physiological disorder or condition, cosmetic disfigurement, or anatomical loss affecting one or more of the following body systems: Neurological; musculoskeletal; special sense organs; respiratory, including speech organs; cardiovascular; reproductive; digestive; genito-urinary; hemic and lymphatic; skin; and endocrine; or

(B) Any mental or psychological disorder, such as mental retardation, organic brain syndrome, emotional or mental illness, and specific learning disabilities;

(C) The term "physical or mental impairment" includes, but is not limited to, such diseases and conditions as orthopedic, visual speech and hearing impairments, cerebral palsy, epilepsy, muscular dystrophy, multiple sclerosis, cancer, heart disease, diabetes, mental retardation, emotional illness, drug addiction and alcoholism.

(ii) *Major life activities* means functions such as caring for one's self, performing manual tasks, walking, seeing, hearing, speaking, breathing, learning, working, and receiving education or vocational training.

(iii) *Has a record of such an impairment* means that the individual has a history of, or has been misclassified as having, a mental or physical impairment that substantially limits one or more major life activities.

(iv) *Is regarded as having an impairment* means that the individual:

(A) Has a physical or mental impairment that does not substantially limit major life activities, but that is treated by a recipient as constituting such a limitation;

(B) Has a physical or mental impairment that substantially limits major life activities only as a result of the attitudes of others toward such impairment; or

(C) Has none of the impairments defined in paragraph (g)(3)(i) of this section, but is treated by a recipient as having such an impairment.

(h) *Program or activity* means all of the operations of any entity described in paragraphs (h)(1) through (4) of this section, any part of which is extended Federal financial assistance:

(1)(i) A department, agency, special purpose district, or other instrumentality of a State or of a local government; or

(ii) The entity of such State or local government that distributes such assistance and each such department or agency (and each other State or local government entity) to which the assistance is extended, in the case of assistance to a State or local government;

(2)(i) A college, university, or other postsecondary institution, or a public system of higher education; or

(ii) A local educational agency (as defined in 20 U.S.C. 7801), system of vocational education, or other school system;

(3)(i) An entire corporation, partnership, or other private organization, or an entire sole proprietorship—

(A) If assistance is extended to such corporation, partnership, private organization, or sole proprietorship as a whole; or

(B) Which is principally engaged in the business of providing education, health care, housing, social services, or parks and recreation; or

(ii) The entire plant or other comparable, geographically separate facility to which Federal financial assistance is extended, in the case of any other corporation, partnership, private organization, or sole proprietorship; or

(4) Any other entity which is established by two or more of the entities described in paragraph (h)(1), (2), or (3) of this section.

(i) *Qualified handicapped person* means:

(1) With respect to employment, a handicapped person who, with reasonable accommodation, can perform the essential functions of the job in question;

(2) With respect to post secondary and vocational education services, a handicapped person who meets the academic and technical standards requisite to admission or participation in the recipient's education program or activity;

(3) With respect to other services, a handicapped person who meets the essential eligibility requirements for the receipt of such services.

(j) *Recipient* means any State or its political subdivisions, any instrumentality of a State or its political subdivisions, any public or private agency, institution, organization, or other entity, or any person to which Federal financial assistance is extended directly or indirectly through another recipient, or including any successor, assignee, or transferee of a recipient, but excluding the ultimate beneficiary of the assistance.

(k) *Secretary* means the Secretary of Commerce, U.S. Department of Commerce.

(l) *Section 504* means section 504 of the Act.

(m) *Small recipient* means a recipient who serves fewer than 15 beneficiaries and who employs fewer than 15 employees at all times during a grant year.

[47 FR 17746, Apr. 23, 1982, as amended at 68 FR 51353, Aug. 26, 2003]

§ 8b.4 Discrimination prohibited.

(a) *General.* No qualified handicapped individual shall, on the basis of handicap, be excluded from participation in, be denied the benefits of, or otherwise be subjected to discrimination under any program or activity that receives Federal financial assistance.

(b) *Discriminatory actions prohibited.* (1) A recipient, in providing any aid, benefit, or service, may not, directly or through contractual, licensing, or other arrangements, on the basis of handicap:

(i) Deny a qualified handicapped individual the opportunity to participate in or benefit from the aid, benefit, or service;

(ii) Afford a qualified handicapped individual an opportunity to participate in or benefit from the aid, benefit, or service that is not equal to that afforded others;

(iii) Provide a qualified handicapped individual with any aid, benefit, or service that is not as effective as that provided to others;

(iv) Provide different or separate aid, benefits, or services to handicapped individuals or to any class of handicapped individuals, unless such action is necessary to provide qualified handicapped individuals with aid, benefits, or services that are as effective as those provided to others;

(v) Aid or perpetuate discrimination against a qualified handicapped individual by providing significant assistance to an agency, organization, or person that discriminates on the basis of handicap in providing any aid, benefit, or service to beneficiaries of the recipient's program or activity;

(vi) Deny a qualified handicapped individual the opportunity to participate as a member of planning or advisory boards; or

(vii) Otherwise limit a qualified handicapped individual in the enjoyment of any right, privilege, advantage, or opportunity enjoyed by others receiving any aid, benefits, or services.

(2) For purposes of this part, aid, benefits, and services must afford handicapped individuals an equal opportunity to obtain the same result, to gain the same benefit, or to reach the same level of achievement as afforded

to others, in the most integrated setting appropriate to the individual's needs. However, aid, benefits and services, to be equally effective, need not produce the identical result or level of achievement for handicapped and nonhandicapped individuals.

(3) A recipient may not deny a qualified handicapped individual the opportunity to participate in its regular aid, benefits, or services, despite the existence of separate or different aid, benefits, or services which are established in accordance with this part.

(4) A recipient may not, directly or through contractual or other arrangements, use criteria or methods of administration:

(i) That have the effect of subjecting qualified handicapped individuals to discrimination on the basis of handicap;

(ii) That have the purpose or effect of defeating or substantially impairing accomplishment of the objectives of the recipient's program or activity with respect to handicapped individuals; or

(iii) That perpetuate the discrimination of another recipient if both recipients are subject to common administrative control or are agencies of the same state.

(5) In determining the geographic site or location of a facility, an applicant for assistance or a recipient may not make selections:

(i) That have the effect of excluding handicapped individuals from, denying them the benefit of, or otherwise subjecting them to discrimination under any program or activity that receives Federal financial assistance; or

(ii) That have the purpose or effect of defeating or substantially impairing the accomplishment of the objectives of the program or activity with respect to handicapped individuals.

(6) As used in this section, the aid, benefit, or service provided under a program or activity receiving Federal financial assistance includes any aid, benefit, or service provided in or through a facility that has been constructed, expanded, altered, leased, rented or otherwise acquired, in whole or in part, with Federal financial assistance.

(7)(i) In providing services, recipients to which this subpart applies, except small recipients, shall ensure that no handicapped participant is denied the benefits of, excluded from participation in, or otherwise subjected to discrimination under the program or activity operated by the recipient because of the absence of auxiliary aids for participants with impaired sensory, manual or speaking skills. A recipient shall operate each program or activity to which this subpart applies so that, when viewed in its entirety, auxiliary aids are readily available. The Secretary may require small recipients to provide auxiliary aids in order to ensure that no handicapped participant is denied the benefits of, excluded from participation in, or otherwise subjected to discrimination under the program or activity operated by small recipients, when this would not significantly impair the ability of the small recipient to provide benefits or services.

(ii) Auxiliary aids may include brailled and taped materials, interpreters, telecommunications devices, or other equally effective methods of making orally delivered information available to persons with hearing impairments, readers for persons with visual impairments, equipment adapted for use by persons with manual impairments, and other similar devices and actions. Recipients need not provide attendants, individually prescribed devices, readers for personal use or study, or other devices or services of a personal nature.

(c) *Aid, benefits, or services limited by Federal law.* The exclusion of nonhandicapped persons from aid, benefits, or services limited by Federal statute or Executive order to handicapped individuals, or the exclusion of a specific class of handicapped individuals from aid, benefits, or services limited by Federal statute or Executive order to a different class of handicapped individuals is not prohibited by this part.

(d) *Integrated setting.* Recipients shall administer programs or activities in the most integrated setting appropriate to the needs of qualified handicapped individuals.

(e) *Communications with individuals with impaired vision and hearing.* Recipients shall ensure that communications with their applicants, employees and beneficiaries are available to persons with impaired vision or hearing. Appropriate modes of communication may include braille, enlarged type, sign language and telecommunications devices.

[47 FR 17746, Apr. 23, 1982, as amended at 68 FR 51353, Aug. 26, 2003]

§8b.5 Assurances required.

(a) *Assurances.* An applicant for Federal financial assistance to which this part applies shall submit an assurance, on a form specified by the Secretary, that the program or activity will be operated in compliance with this part. An applicant may incorporate these assurances by reference in subsequent applications to the Department.

(b) *Duration of obligation.* (1) In the case of Federal financial assistance extended in the form of real property or structures on the property, the assurance will obligate the recipient or, in the case of a subsequent transfer, the transferee, for the period during which the real property or structures are used for the purpose for which Federal financial assistance is extended, or for another purpose involving the provision of similar services or benefits.

(2) In case of Federal financial assistance extended to provide personal property, the assurance will obligate the recipient for the period during which it retains ownership or possession of the property.

(3) In all other cases, the assurance will obligate the recipient for the period during which Federal financial assistance is extended or the federally-funded program or activity is operated, whichever is longer.

(c) *Covenants.* (1) Where Federal financial assistance is provided in the form of real property or interest in the property from the Department, the instrument effecting or recording this transfer shall contain a covenant running with the land to assure nondiscrimination for the period during which the real property is used for a purpose for which the Federal financial assistance is extended or for another purpose involving the provision of similar services or benefits.

(2) Where no transfer or property is involved but property is purchased or improved with Federal financial assistance, the recipient shall agree to include the covenant described in paragraph (c)(1) of this section in the instrument effecting or recording any subsequent transferee of the property.

(3) Where Federal financial assistance is provided in the form of real property or interest in the property from the Department, the covenant shall also include a condition coupled with a right to be reserved by the Department to revert title to the property in the event of a breach of the covenant. If a transferee of real property proposed to mortgage or otherwise encumber the real property as security to finance construction of new, or improvement of existing, facilities on the property for the purposes for which the property was transferred, the Secretary may agree to forbear the exercise of such right to revert title for so long as the lien of such mortgage or other encumbrance remains effective. Such an agreement by the Secretary may be entered into only upon the request of the transferee (recipient) if it is necessary to accomplish such financing and upon such terms and conditions as the Secretary deems appropriate.

(d) *Interagency agreements.* Where funds are granted by the Department to another Federal agency to carry out the objectives of Federal financial assistance under a law administered by the Department, and where the grant obligates the recipient agency to comply with the rules and regulations of the Department applicable to that grant the provisions of this part shall apply to programs or activities operated with such funds.

§8b.6 Remedial action, voluntary action, and self-evaluation.

(a) *Remedial action.* (1) If the Secretary finds that a recipient has discriminated against persons on the basis of handicap in violation of section 504 or this part, the recipient shall take such remedial action as the Secretary deems necessary to overcome the effects of the discrimination.

(2) Where a recipient is found to have discriminated against persons on the basis of handicap in violation of section 504 or this part and where another

recipient exercises control over the recipient that has discriminated, the Secretary, where appropriate, may require either or both recipients to take remedial action.

(3) The Secretary may, where necessary to overcome the effects of discrimination in violation of section 504 or this part, require a recipient to take remedial action:

(i) With respect to handicapped individuals who would have been participants in the program or activity had the discrimination not occurred; and

(ii) With respect to handicapped persons who are no longer participants in the recipient's program or activity, but who were participants in the program or activity when the discrimination occurred; and

(iii) with respect to employees and applicants for employment.

(b) *Voluntary action.* A recipient may take steps, in addition to any action that is required by this part, to overcome the effects of conditions that resulted in limited participation in the recipient's program or activity by qualified handicapped individuals.

(c) *Self-evaluation.* (1) A recipient shall, within one year of the effective date of this part:

(i) Evaluate, with the assistance of interested persons, including handicapped individuals or organizations representing handicapped individuals, its current policies and practices and the effects thereof that do not or may not meet the requirements of this part;

(ii) Modify, after consultation with interested persons, including handicapped individuals or organizations representing handicapped individuals, any policies and practices that do not meet the requirements of this part; and

(iii) Take, after consultation with interested persons, including handicapped individuals or organizations representing handicapped individuals, appropriate remedial steps to eliminate the effects of any discrimination that resulted from adherence to these policies and practices.

(2) A recipient, other than a small recipient, shall for at least three years following completion of the evaluation required under paragraph (c)(1) of this section, maintain on file, make available for public inspection, and provide to the Secretary upon request:

(i) A list of the interested persons consulted;

(ii) A description of areas examined and any problems identified; and

(iii) A description of any modifications made and of any remedial steps taken.

(3) The Secretary may, as he or she deems necessary, direct recipients to conduct additional self-evaluations, in accordance with the requirements of paragraph (c)(1) of this section.

(Approved by the Office of Management and Budget under control number 0605–0006)

[47 FR 17746, Apr. 23, 1982, as amended at 47 FR 35472, Aug. 16, 1982]

§ 8b.7 Designation of responsible employee and adoption of grievance procedures.

(a) *Designation of responsible employee.* A recipient, other than a small recipient, shall designate at least one person to coordinate its efforts to comply with this part.

(b) *Adoption of grievance procedures.* A recipient, other than a small recipient, shall adopt grievance procedures that incorporate appropriate due process standards and that provide for the prompt and equitable resolution of complaints alleging any action prohibited by this part. Such procedures need not be established with respect to complaints from applicants for employment or from applicants for admission to post secondary educational institutions.

§ 8b.8 Notice.

(a) A recipient, other than a small recipient, shall take appropriate initial and continuing steps to notify participants, beneficiaries, applicants and employees, including those with impaired vision or hearing, and unions or professional organizations holding collective bargaining or professional agreements with the recipient, that it does not discriminate on the basis of handicap in violation of Section 504 and of this part. The notification shall state, where appropriate, that the recipient does not discriminate in the admission or access to, or treatment or employment in, its programs or activities. The notification shall also include an identification of the responsible employee designated pursuant to §8b.7(a). A recipient shall make the initial notification required by this paragraph within 90 days of the effective date of this part. Methods of initial and continuing notification may include the posting of notices, publications in newspapers and magazines, placement of notices in recipient's publications, and distribution of memoranda or other written communication. A recipient shall take appropriate steps to ensure that notice is available to persons with impaired vision or hearing.

(b) If a recipient publishes or uses recruitment materials or publications containing general information made available to participants, beneficiaries, applicants, or employees, it shall include in those materials or publications a statement of the policy described in paragraph (a) of this section. A recipient may meet the requirement of this paragraph either by including appropriate inserts in existing materials and publications, or by revising and reprinting the materials and publications.

§8b.9 Administrative requirements for small recipients.

The Secretary may require small recipients to comply with §§8b.7 and 8b.8, in whole or in part, when the Secretary finds a violation of this part or finds that such compliance will not significantly impair the ability of the small recipient to provide benefits or services.

§8b.10 Effect of state or local law or other requirements and effect of employment opportunities.

(a) The obligation to comply with this part is not obviated or alleviated by the existence of any state or local law or other requirement that, on the basis of handicap, imposes prohibitions or limits upon the eligibility of qualified handicapped individuals to receive services, participate in programs or activities, or practice any occupation or profession.

(b) The obligation to comply with this part is not obviated or alleviated because employment opportunities in any occupation or profession are or may be more limited for handicapped individuals than for nonhandicapped persons.

Subpart B—Employment Practices

§8b.11 Discrimination prohibited.

(a) *General.* (1) No qualified handicapped individual shall, on the basis of handicap, be subjected to discrimination in employment under any program or activity that receives Federal financial assistance.

(2) A recipient shall make all decisions concerning employment under any program or activity to which this part applies in a manner which ensures that discrimination on the basis of handicap does not occur and may not limit, segregate, or classify applicants or employees in any way that adversely affects their opportunities or status because of handicap.

(3) A recipient may not participate in a contractual or other relationship that has the effect of subjecting qualified handicapped applicants or employees to discrimination prohibited by this subpart. The relationships referred to in this subparagraph include relationships with employment and referral agencies, with labor unions, with organizations providing or administering fringe benefits to employees of the recipient, and with organizations providing training and apprenticeships.

(b) *Specific activities.* The prohibition against discrimination in employment applies to the following activities:

(1) Recruitment, advertising and the processing of applicants for employment;

(2) Hiring, upgrading, promotion, award of tenure, demotion, transfer, layoff, termination, right of return from layoff and rehiring;

(3) Rates of pay or any other form of compensation and changes in compensation; pension or other benefit the applicant or employee receives from any other source.

§8b.12 Reasonable accommodation.

(a) A recipient shall make reasonable accommodation to the known physical or metal limitations of an otherwise qualified handicapped applicant or employee unless the recipient can demonstrate that the accommodation would impose an undue hardship on the operation of its program or activity.

(b) Reasonable accommodation may include:

(1) Making the facilities used by the employees in the area where the program or activity is conducted, including common areas used by all employees such as hallways, restrooms, cafeterias and lounges, readily accessible to and usable by handicapped persons; and

(2) Job restructuring, part-time or modified work schedules, acquisition or modification of equipment or devices, the provision of readers or interpreters, and other similar actions.

(c) In determining pursuant to paragraph (a) of this section whether an accommodation would impose an undue hardship on the operation of a recipient's program or activity, factors to be considered include:

(1) The overall size of the recipient's program or activity with respect to number of employees, number of participants, number and type of facilities, and size of budget;

(2) The type of the recipient's operation, including the composition and structure of the recipient's workforce; and

(3) The nature and cost of the accommodation needed.

(d) A recipient may not deny any employment opportunity to a qualified handicapped employee or applicant if the basis for the denial is the need to make reasonable accommodation to the physical or mental limitations of the employee or applicant.

(e) Nothing in this paragraph shall relieve a recipient of its obligation to make its program or activity accessible as required in subpart C of this part, or to provide auxiliary aids, as required by § 8b.4(b)(7).

§ 8b.13 Employment criteria.

(a) A recipient may not make use of any employment test or other selection criterion that screens out or tends to screen out handicapped individuals or any class of handicapped individuals unless;

(1) The test score or other selection criterion, as used by the recipient, is shown to be job-related for the position in question; and

(2) Alternative job-related tests or criteria that do not screen out or tend to screen out as many handicapped individuals are not shown by the Secretary to be available.

(b) A recipient shall select and administer tests concerning employment so as best to ensure that, when administered to an applicant or employee who has a handicap that impairs sensory, manual, or speaking skills, the test results accurately to reflect the applicant's or employee's job skills aptitude, or whatever factor the test purports to measure, rather than reflecting the applicant's or employee's impaired sensory, manual, or speaking skills (except where those skills are the factors that the test purports to measure).

§ 8b.14 Preemployment inquiries.

(a) Except as provided in paragraphs (b) and (c) of this section, a recipient may not conduct preemployment inquiry of an applicant for employment as to whether the applicant is a handicapped individual, or as to the nature or severity of a handicap. A recipient may, however, make preemployment inquiry into an applicant's ability to perform job-related functions.

(b) When a recipient is taking remedial action to correct the effects of past discrimination pursuant to § 8b.6(a), when a recipient is taking voluntary action to overcome the effects of conditions that resulted in limited participation in this federally assisted program or activity pursuant to § 8b.6(b), or when a recipient is taking affirmative action pursuant to section 503 of the Act, the recipient may invite applicants for employment to indicate whether and to what extent they are handicapped, *Provided*, That:

(1) The recipient states clearly on any written questionnaire used for this purpose or makes clear orally, if no written questionnaire is used, that the information requested is intended for use solely in connection with its remedial action obligations or its voluntary or affirmative action efforts; and

(2) The recipient states clearly that the information is being requested on a voluntary basis, that it will be kept confidential as provided in paragraph

(d) of this section, that refusal to provide it will not subject the applicant or employee to any adverse treatment, and that it will be used only in accordance with this part.

(c) Nothing in this section shall prohibit a recipient from conditioning an offer of employment on the results of a medical examination conducted prior to the employee's entrance on duty, *Provided*, That:

(1) All employees are subject to such an examination regardless of handicap, and

(2) The results of such an examination are used only in accordance with the requirements of this part.

(d) Information obtained in accordance with this section as to the medical condition or history of the applicant shall be collected and maintained on separate forms that shall be accorded confidentiality as medical records, except:

(1) Employing officials may obtain the information after making a conditional decision to make a job offer to the applicant or the applicant was placed conditionally in a job pool or placed conditionally on an eligibility list;

(2) Supervisors and managers may be informed regarding restrictions on the work or duties of qualified handicapped individuals and regarding necessary accommodations;

(3) First aid and safety personnel may be informed, where appropriate, if the condition might require emergency treatment; and

(4) Government officials investigating compliance with the Act shall be provided information upon request.

§8b.15 Employment on ships.

No qualified handicapped individual possessing an appropriate license or certificate obtained from the United States Coast Guard pursuant to the requirements of 46 CFR 10.01–1 *et seq.* and 12.01–1 *et seq.* shall, on the basis of handicap, be subjected to discrimination in employment on ships under any program or activity to which this part applies.

Subpart C—Accessibility

§8b.16 Discrimination prohibited.

No qualified handicapped individual shall, because a recipient's facilities are inaccessible to or unusable by handicapped individuals, be denied the benefits of, be excluded from participation in, or otherwise be subjected to discrimination under any program or activity to which this part applies.

§8b.17 Existing facilities.

(a) *Accessibility.* A recipient shall operate each program or activity to which this part applies so that when each part is viewed in its entirety it is readily accessible to qualified handicapped individuals. This paragraph does not require a recipient to make each of its existing facilities or every part of a facility accessible to and usable by qualified handicapped individuals. However, if a particular program is available in only one location, that site must be made accessible or the aid, benefit, or service must be made available at an alternative accessible site or sites. Accessibility requires nonpersonal aids to make the aid, benefit, or service accessible to mobility impaired persons.

(b) *Methods.* A recipient may comply with the requirements of paragraph (a) of this section through such means as redesign of equipment, reassignment of classes or other services to accessible buildings, assignment of aides to beneficiaries, home visits, delivery of services at alternate accessible sites, alteration of existing facilities and construction of new facilities in conformance with the requirement of §8b.19, or any other method that results in making its program or activity accessible to handicapped individuals. A recipient is not required to make structural changes in existing facilities where other methods are effective in achieving compliance with paragraph (a) of this section. In choosing among available methods for meeting the requirement of paragraph (a) of this section, a recipient shall give priority to those methods that serve handicapped individuals in the most integrated setting appropriate.

(c) If a small recipient finds, after consultation with a qualified handicapped individual seeking its services, that there is no method of complying with paragraph (a) of this section other than making a significant alteration in its existing facilities or facility, the small recipient may, as an alternative, refer the qualified handicapped individual to other providers of those services that are accessible at no additional cost to the handicapped.

(d) *Time period.* A recipient shall comply with the requirement of paragraph (a) of this section within 60 days of the effective date of this part. Where structural changes in facilities are necessary, such changes shall be made within three years of the effective date of this part, but in any event as expeditiously as possible.

(e) *Transition plan.* In the event that structural changes to facilities are necessary to meet the requirement of paragraph (a) of this section, a recipient shall develop, within six months of the effective date of this part, a transition plan setting forth the steps necessary to complete such changes. The plan shall be developed with the assistance of interested persons, including handicapped persons or organizations representing handicapped persons. A copy of the transition plan shall be made available for public inspection. The plan shall, at a minimum:

(1) Identify physical obstacles in the recipient's facilities that limit the accessibility of its program or activity to qualified handicapped individuals;

(2) Describe in detail the methods that will be used to make the facilities accessible;

(3) Specify the schedule for taking the steps necessary to achieve full accessibility under § 8b.17(a) and, if the time period of the transition plan is longer than one year, identify the steps that will be taken during each year of the transition period; and

(4) Indicate the person responsible for implementation of the plan.

(f) *Notice.* The recipient shall adopt and implement procedures to ensure that interested persons, including persons with impaired vision or hearing, can obtain information as to the existence and location of services, activities and facilities that are accessible to and usable by qualified handicapped individuals.

(Approved by the Office of Management and Budget under control number 0605–0006)

[47 FR 17746, Apr. 23, 1982, as amended at 47 FR 35472, Aug. 16, 1982; 68 FR 51353, Aug. 26, 2003]

§ 8b.18 New construction.

(a) *Design and construction.* Each facility or part of a facility constructed by, on behalf of, or for the use of a recipient shall be designed and constructed in such manner that the facility or part of the facility is readily accessible to and usable by qualified handicapped individuals, if the construction was commenced after the effective date of this part.

(b) *Alteration.* Each facility or part of a facility which is altered by, on behalf of, or for the use of a recipient after the effective date of this part of the facility shall, to the maximum extent feasible, be altered in such manner that the altered portion of the facility is readily accessible to and usable by qualified handicapped individuals.

(c) *Conformance with Uniform Federal Accessibility Standards.* (1) Effective as of August 17, 1990, design, construction, or alteration of buildings in conformance with sections 3–8 of the Uniform Federal Accessibility Standards (UFAS) (Appendix A to 41 CFR subpart 101–19.6) shall be deemed to comply with the requirements of this section with respect to those buildings. Departures from particular technical and scoping requirements of UFAS by the use of other methods are permitted where substantially equivalent or greater access to and usability of the building is provided.

(2) For purposes of this section, section 4.1.6(1)(g) of UFAS shall be interpreted to exempt from the requirements of UFAS only mechanical rooms and other spaces that, because of their intended use, will not require accessibility to the public or beneficiaries or result in the employment or residence therein of persons with physical handicaps.

(3) This section does not require recipients to make building alterations

that have little likelihood of being accomplished without removing or altering a load-bearing structural member.

[47 FR 17746, Apr. 23, 1982, as amended at 55 FR 29320, July 18, 1990]

Subpart D—Post Secondary Education

§8b.19 Application of this subpart.

Subpart D applies to post secondary education programs or activities, including post secondary vocational education programs or activities, that receive Federal financial assistance for the operation of, such programs or activities.

§8b.20 Admission and recruitment.

(a) *General.* Qualified handicapped may not, on the basis of handicap, be denied admission or be subjected to discrimination in admission or recruitment by a recipient to which this subpart applies.

(b) *Admissions.* In administering its admission policies, a recipient to which this subpart applies:

(1) May not apply limitations upon the number or proportion of handicapped individuals who may be admitted; and

(2) May not make use of any test or criterion for admission that has a disproportionate, adverse effect on handicapped individuals or any class of handicapped individuals unless:

(i) The test or criterion, as used by the recipient, has been validated as a predictor of success in the education program or activity in question; and

(ii) Alternate tests or criteria that have a less disproportionate, adverse effect are not shown by the Secretary to be available.

(3) Shall assure itself that (i) admissions tests are selected and administered so as best to ensure that, when a test is administered to an applicant who has a handicap that impairs sensory, manual, or speaking skills, the test results accurately reflect the applicant's aptitude or achievement level of whatever other factor the test purports to measure, rather than reflecting the applicant's impaired sensory, manual, or speaking skills (except where those skills are the factors that the test purports to measure); (ii) admissions tests that are designed for persons with impaired sensory, manual, or speaking skills are offered as often and in as timely a manner as are other admissions tests; and (iii) admissions tests are administered in facilities that, on the whole, are accessible to handicapped individuals; and

(4) Except as provided in paragraph (c) of this section, may not make preadmission inquiry as to whether an applicant for admission is a handicapped individual but, after admission, may make inquiries on a confidential basis as to handicaps that may require accommodation.

(c) *Pre-admission inquiry exception.* When a recipient is taking remedial action to correct the effects of past discrimination pursuant to §8b.6(a) or when a recipient is taking voluntary action to overcome the effects of conditions that resulted in limited participation in its federally assisted program or activity pursuant to §8b.6(b), the recipient may invite applicants for admission to indicate whether and to what extent they are handicapped, *Provided,* That:

(1) The recipient states clearly on any written questionnaire used for this purpose or makes clear orally, if no written questionnaire is used, that the information requested is intended for use solely in connection with its remedial action obligations or its voluntary action efforts; and

(2) The recipient states clearly that the information is being requested on a voluntary basis, that it will be kept confidential, that refusal to provide it will not subject the applicant to any adverse treatment, and that it will be used only in accordance with this part.

(d) *Validity studies.* For the purpose of paragraph (b)(2) of this section, a recipient may base prediction equations on first year grades, but shall conduct periodic validity studies against the criterion of overall success in the education program or activity in question in order to monitor the general validity of the test scores.

§8b.21 Treatment of students.

(a) *General.* No qualified handicapped student shall, on the basis of handicap, be excluded from participation in, be denied the benefits of, or otherwise be subjected to discrimination under any academic research, occupational training, housing, health insurance, counseling, financial aid, physical education, athletics, recreation, transportation, other extracurricular, or other post secondary education aid, benefits, or services to which this subpart applies.

(b) A recipient to which this subpart applies that considers participation by students in education programs or activities not operated wholly by the recipient as part of, or equivalent to, education programs or activities operated by the recipient shall assure itself that the other education program or activity, as a whole, provides an equal opportunity for the participation of qualified handicapped persons.

(c) A recipient to which this subpart applies may not, on the basis of handicap exclude any qualified handicapped student from any course or study, or other part of its education program or activity.

(d) A recipient to which this subpart applies shall operate its program or activity in the most integrated setting appropriate.

§ 8b.22 Academic adjustments.

(a) *Academic requirements.* A recipient to which this subpart applies shall make such modifications to its academic requirements as are necessary to ensure that such requirements do not discriminate or have the effect of discriminating, on the basis of handicap, against a qualified handicapped applicant or student. Academic requirements that the recipient can demonstrate are essential to the instruction being pursued by such student or to any directly related licensing requirement will not be regarded as discriminatory within the meaning of this section. Modifications may include changes in the length of time permitted for the completion of degree requirements, substitution of specific courses required for the completion of degree requirements, and adaptation of the manner in which specific courses are conducted.

(b) *Other rules.* A recipient to which this subpart applies may not impose upon handicapped students other rules, such as the prohibition of tape recorders in classrooms or of dog guides in campus buildings, that have the effect of limiting the participation of handicapped students in the recipient's education program or activity.

(c) *Course examinations.* In its course examinations or other procedures for evaluating student's academic achievement, a recipient to which this subpart applies shall provide such methods for evaluating the achievement of students who have a handicap that impairs sensory, manual, or speaking skills as will best ensure that the results of the evaluation represents the student's achievement in the course, rather than reflecting the student's impaired sensory, manual, or speaking skills (except where such skills are the factors that the test purports to measure).

(d) *Auxiliary aids.* (1) A recipient to which this subpart applies shall ensure that no handicapped student is denied the benefits of, excluded from participation in, or otherwise subjected to discrimination because of the absence of educational auxiliary aids for students with impaired sensory, manual, or speaking skills. A recipient shall operate each program or activity to which this subpart applies so that, when viewed in its entirety, auxiliary aids are readily available.

(2) Auxiliary aids may include taped text, interpreters or other effective methods of making orally delivered materials available to students with hearing impairments, readers in libraries for students with visual impairments, classroom equipment adapted for use by students with manual impairments, and other similar services and actions. Recipients need not provide attendants, individually prescribed devices, readers for personal use or study, or other devices or services of a personal nature.

§ 8b.23 Housing provided by the recipient.

(a) A recipient that provides housing to its nonhandicapped students shall provide comparable, convenient, and accessible housing to handicapped students at the same cost as to others. At the end of transition period provided for in subpart C, such housing shall be available in sufficient quantity and variety so that the scope of handicapped students choice of living accommodations is, as a whole, comparable to that of nonhandicapped students.

(b) *Other housing.* A recipient that assists any agency, organization, or person in making housing available to any of its students shall take such action as may be necessary to assure itself that such housing is, as a whole, made available in a manner that does not result in discrimination on the basis of handicap.

§8b.24 Financial and employment assistance to students.

(a) *Provision of financial assistance.* (1) In providing financial assistance to qualified handicapped individuals, a recipient to which this subpart applies may not (i) on the basis of handicap, provide less assistance than is provided to nonhandicapped persons, limit eligibility for assistance, or otherwise discriminate or (ii) assist any entity or person that provides assistance to any of the recipient's students in a manner that discriminates against qualified handicapped individuals on the basis of handicap.

(2) A recipient may administer or assist in the administration of scholarships, fellowships, or other forms of financial assistance established under wills, trust, bequest, or similar legal instruments that require awards to be made on the basis of factors that discriminate or have the effect of discriminating on the basis of handicap only if the overall effect of the award of scholarships, fellowships, and other forms of financial assistance is not discriminatory on the basis of handicap.

(b) *Assistance in making available outside employment.* A recipient that assists any agency, organization, or person in providing employment opportunities to any of its students shall assure itself that such employment opportunities, as a whole, are made available in a manner that would not violate subpart B if they were provided by the recipient.

(c) *Employment of student by recipients.* A recipient that employs any of its students may not do so in a manner that violates subpart B.

§8b.25 Nonacademic services.

(a) *Physical education and athletics.* (1) In providing physical education courses and athletics and similar aid, benefits, or services to any of its students, a recipient to which this subpart applies may not discriminate on the basis of handicap. A recipient that offers physical education courses or that operates or sponsors intercollegiate, club, or intramural athletics shall provide to qualified handicapped students an equal opportunity for participation in these activities.

(2) A recipient may offer to handicapped students physical education and athletic activities that are separate or different only if separation of differentiation is consistent with the requirements of §8b.22(d) and only if no qualified handicapped student is denied the opportunity to compete for teams or to participate in courses that are not separate or different.

(b) *Counseling and placement services.* A recipient to which this subpart applies that provides personal, academic, or vocational counseling guidance, or placement services to its students shall provide these services without discrimination on the basis of handicap. The recipient shall ensure that qualified handicapped students are not counseled toward more restrictive career objectives than are nonhandicapped students with similar interests and abilities. This requirement does not preclude a recipient from providing factual information about licensing and certification requirements that may present obstacles to handicapped persons in their pursuit of particular careers.

(c) *Social organizations.* A recipient that provides significant assistance to fraternities, sororities, or similar organizations shall assure itself that the membership practices of such organizations do not permit discrimination otherwise prohibited by this subpart.

Subpart E—Procedures

§8b.26 Procedures.

The enforcement provisions applicable to Title VI of the Civil Rights Act of 1964 found at §§8.7 through 8.15 of this subtitle shall apply to this part.

PART 8c—ENFORCEMENT OF NONDISCRIMINATION ON THE BASIS OF HANDICAP IN PROGRAMS OR ACTIVITIES CONDUCTED BY THE DEPARTMENT OF COMMERCE

AUTHORITY: 29 U.S.C 794.

SOURCE: 53 FR 19277, May 27, 1988, unless otherwise noted.

§ 8c.1 Purpose.

This part effectuates section 119 of the Rehabilitation, Comprehensive Services, and Developmental Disabilities Amendments of 1978, which amended section 504 of the Rehabilitation Act of 1973 to prohibit discrimination on the basis of handicap in programs or activities conducted by Executive agencies or the United States Postal Service.

§ 8c.2 Application.

This part applies to all programs or activities conducted by the agency except for programs or activities conducted outside the United States that do not involve individuals with handicaps in the United States.

§ 8c.3 Definitions.

For purposes of this part, the term—

Agency means the Department of Commerce.

Assistant Attorney General means the Assistant Attorney General, Civil Rights Division, United States Department of Justice.

Auxiliary aids means services or devices that enable persons with impaired sensory, manual, or speaking skills to have an equal opportunity to participate in, and enjoy the benefits of, programs or activities conducted by the agency. For example, auxiliary aids useful for persons with impaired vision include readers, Brailled materials, audio recordings, and other similar services and devices. Auxiliary aids useful for persons with impaired hearing include telephone handset amplifiers, telephones compatible with hearing aids, telecommunication devices for deaf persons (TDD's), interpreters, notetakers, written materials, and other similar services and devices.

Complete complaint means a written statement that contains the complainant's name and address and describes the agency's alleged discriminatory action in sufficient detail to inform the agency of the nature and date of the alleged violation of section 504. It shall be signed by the complainant or by someone authorized to do so on his or her behalf. Complaints filed on behalf of classes or third parties shall describe or identify (by name, if possible) the alleged victims of discrimination.

Facility means all or any portion of buildings, structures, equipment, roads, walks, parking lots, rolling stock or other conveyances, or other real or personal property.

Individual with handicaps means any person who has a physical or mental impairment that substantially limits one or more major life activities, has a record of such an impairment, or is regarded as having such an impairment. As used in this definition, the phrase:

(1) ''Physical or mental impairment'' includes—

(i) Any physiological disorder or condition, cosmetic disfigurement, or anatomical loss affecting one or more of the following body systems: Neurological; musculoskeletal; special sense organs; respiratory, including speech organs; cardiovascular; reproductive; digestive; genitourinary; hemic and lymphatic; skin; and endocrine; or

(ii) Any mental or psychological disorder, such as mental retardation, organic brain syndrome, emotional or mental illness, and specific learning disabilities. The term "physical or mental impairment" includes, but is not limited to, such diseases and conditions as orthopedic, visual, speech, and hearing impairments, cerebral palsy, epilepsy, muscular dystrophy, multiple sclerosis, cancer, heart disease, diabetes, mental retardation, emotional illness, and drug addiction and alcoholism

(2) "Major life activities" includes functions such as caring for one's self, performing manual tasks, walking, seeing, hearing, speaking, breathing, learning, and working.

(3) "Has a record of such an impairment" means has a history of, or has been misclassified as having, a mental or physical impairment that substantially limits one or more major life activities.

(4) "Is regarded as having an impairment" means—

(i) Has a physical or mental impairment that does not substantially limit major life activities but is treated by the agency as constituting such a limitation;

(ii) Has a physical or mental impairment that substantially limits major life activities only as a result of the attitudes of others towards such impairment; or

(iii) Has none of the impairments defined in subparagraph (1) of this definition but is treated by the agency as having such an impairment.

Qualified individual with handicaps means—

(1) With respect to any agency program or activity under which a person is required to perform services or to achieve a level of accomplishment, an individual with handicaps who meets the essential eligibility requirements and who can achieve the purpose of the program or activity without modifications in the program or activity that the agency can demonstrate would result in a fundamental alteration in its nature;

(2) With respect to any other program or activity, an individual with handicaps who meets the essential eligibility requirements for participation in, or receipt of benefits from, that program or activity; and

(3) "Qualified handicapped person" as that term is defined for purposes of employment in 29 CFR 1613.702(f), which is made applicable to this part by §8c.40.

Section 504 means section 504 of the Rehabilitation Act of 1973 (Pub. L. 93–112, 87 Stat. 394 (29 U.S.C. 794)), as amended by the Rehabilitation Act Amendments of 1974 (Pub. L. 93–516, 88 Stat. 1617); the Rehabilitation, Comprehensive Services, and Developmental Disabilities Amendments of 1978) Pub. L. 95–602, 92 Stat. 2955); and the Rehabilitation Act Amendments of 1986 (Pub. L. 99–506, 100 Stat. 1810). As used in this part, section 504 applies only to programs or activities conducted by Executive agencies and not to federally assisted programs.

[53 FR 19277, May 27, 1988; 53 FR 25722, July 8, 1988]

§§8c.4–8c.9 [Reserved]

§8c.10 Self-evaluation.

(a) The agency shall, by July 26, 1989, evaluate its current policies and practices, and the effects thereof, that do not or may not meet the requirements of this part, and, to the extent modification of any such policies and practices is required, the agency shall proceed to make the necessary modifications.

(b) The agency shall provide an opportunity to interested persons, including individuals with handicaps or organizations representing individuals with handicaps, to participate in the self-evaluation process by submitting comments (both oral and written).

(c) The agency shall, until three years following the completion of the self-evaluation, maintain on file and make available for public inspection:

(1) A description of areas examined and any problems identified, and

(2) A description of any modifications made.

§8c.11 Notice.

The agency shall make available to employees, applicants, participants, beneficiaries, and other interested persons such information regarding the provisions of this part and its applicability to the programs or activities conducted by the agency, and make such information available to them in such manner as the Secretary of Commerce or the Secretary's designee finds necessary to apprise such persons of the protections against discrimination assured them by section 504 and this regulation.

§§ 8c.12–8c.29 [Reserved]

§ 8c.30 General prohibitions against discrimination.

(a) No qualified individual with handicaps shall, on the basis of handicap, be excluded from participation in, be denied the benefits of, or otherwise be subjected to discrimination under any program or activity conducted by the agency.

(b)(1) The agency, in providing any aid, benefit, or service, may not, directly or through contractual, licensing, or other arrangements, on the basis of handicap—

(i) Deny a qualified individual with handicaps the opportunity to participate in or benefit from the aid, benefit, or service;

(ii) Afford a qualified individual with handicaps an opportunity to participate in or benefit from the aid, benefit, or service that is not equal to that afforded others;

(iii) Provide a qualified individual with handicaps with an aid, benefit, or service that is not as effective in affording equal opportunity to obtain the same result, to gain the same benefit, or to reach the same level of achievement as that provided to others;

(iv) Provide different or separate aid, benefits, or services to individuals with handicaps or to any class of individuals with handicaps than is provided to others unless such action is necessary to provide qualified individuals with handicaps with aid, benefits, or services that are as effective as those provided to others;

(v) Deny a qualified individual with handicaps the opportunity to participate as a member of a planning or advisory board; or

(vi) Otherwise limit a qualified individual with handicaps in the enjoyment of any right, privilege, advantage, or opportunity enjoyed by others receiving the aid, benefit, or service.

(2) The agency may not deny a qualified individual with handicaps the opportunity to participate in programs or activities that are not separate or different, despite the existence of permissibly separate or different programs or activities.

(3) The agency may not, directly or through contractual or other arrangements, utilize criteria or methods of administration the purpose or effect of which would—

(i) Subject qualified individuals with handicaps to discrimination on the basis of handicaps; or

(ii) Defeat or substantially impair accomplishment of the objectives of a program or activity with respect to individuals with handicaps.

(4) The agency may not, in determining the site or location of a facility, make selections the purpose or effect of which would—

(i) Exclude individuals with handicaps from, deny them the benefits of, or otherwise subject them to discrimination under any program or activity conducted by the agency; or

(ii) Defeat or substantially impair the accomplishment of the objectives of a program with respect to individuals with handicaps.

(5) The agency, in the selection of procurement contractors, may not use criteria that subject qualified individuals with handicaps to discrimination on the basis of handicap.

(6) The agency may not administer a licensing or certification program in a manner that subjects qualified individuals with handicaps to discrimination on the basis of handicap, nor may the agency establish requirements for the programs or activities of licensees or certified entities that subject qualified individuals with handicaps to discrimination on the basis of handicap. However, the programs or activities of entities that are licensed or certified by the agency are not, themselves, covered by this part.

(c) The exclusion of nonhandicapped persons from the benefits of a program limited by Federal statute or Executive order to individuals with handicaps or the exclusion of a specific class of individuals with handicaps from a program limited by Federal statute or Executive order to a different class of individuals with handicaps is not prohibited by this part.

(d) The agency shall administer programs and activities in the most integrated setting appropriate to the needs of qualified individuals with handicaps.

§§8c.31–8c.39 [Reserved]

§8c.40 Employment.

No qualified individual with handicaps shall, on the basis of handicap, be subjected to discrimination in employment under any program or activity conducted by the agency. The definitions, requirements, and procedures of section 501 of the Rehabilitation Act of 1973 (29 U.S.C. 791), as established by the Equal Employment Opportunity Commission in 29 CFR Part 1613, shall apply to employment in federally conducted programs or activities.

§§8c.41–8c.48 [Reserved]

§8c.49 Program accessibility: Discrimination prohibited.

Except as otherwise provided in §8c.50, no qualified individual with handicaps shall, because the agency's facilities are inaccessible to or unusable by individuals with handicaps, be denied the benefits of, be excluded from participation in, or otherwise be subjected to discrimination under any program or activity conducted by the agency.

§8c.50 Program accessibility: Existing facilities.

(a) *General.* The agency shall operate each program or activity so that the program or activity, when viewed in its entirety, is readily accessible to and usable by individuals with handicaps. This paragraph does not—

(1) Necessarily require the agency to make each of its existing facilities accessible to and usable by individuals with handicaps; or

(2) Require the agency to take any action that it can demonstrate would result in a fundamental alteration in the nature of a program or activity or in undue financial and administrative burdens. In those circumstances where agency personnel believe that the proposed action would fundamentally alter the program or activity or would result in undue financial and administrative burdens, the agency has the burden of proving that compliance with section §8c.50(a) would result in such alteration or burdens. The decision that compliance would result in such alteration or burdens must be made by the Secretary of Commerce or the Secretary's designee after considering all agency resources available for use in the funding and operation of the conducted program or activity, and must be accompanied by a written statement of the reasons for reaching that conclusion. If an action would result in such an alteration or such burdens, the agency shall take any other action that would not result in such an alteration or such burdens but would nevertheless ensure that individuals with handicaps receive the benefits and services of the program or activity.

(b) *Methods.* The agency may comply with the requirements of this section through such means as redesign of equipment, reassignment of services to accessible buildings, assignment of aides to beneficiaries, home visits, delivery of services at alternate accessible sites, alteration of existing facilities and construction of new facilities, use of accessible rolling stock, or any other methods that result in making its programs or activities readily accessible to and usable by individuals with handicaps. The agency is not required to make structural changes in existing facilities where other methods are effective in achieving compliance with this section. The agency, in making alterations to existing buildings, shall meet accessibility requirements to the extent compelled by the Architectural Barriers Act of 1968, as amended (42 U.S.C. 4151–4157), and any regulations implementing it. In choosing among available methods for meeting the requirements of this section, the agency shall give priority to those methods that offer programs and activities to qualified individuals with handicaps in the most integrated setting appropriate.

(c) *Time period for compliance.* The agency shall comply with the obligations established under this section by September 26, 1988, except that where structural changes in facilities are undertaken, such changes shall be made by July 26, 1991, but in any event as expeditiously as possible.

(d) *Transition plan.* In the event that structural changes to facilities will be undertaken to achieve program accessibility, the agency shall develop, by January 26, 1989, a transition plan setting forth the steps necessary to complete such changes. The agency shall provide an opportunity to interested persons, including individuals with handicaps or organizations representing individuals with handicaps, to participate in the development of the transition plan by submitting comments (both oral and written). A copy of the transition plan shall be made available for public inspection. The plan shall, at a minimum—

(1) Identify physical obstacles in the agency's facilities that limit the accessibility of its program or activities to individuals with handicaps;

(2) Describe in detail the methods that will be used to make the facilities accessible;

(3) Specify the schedule for taking the steps necessary to achieve compliance with this section and, if the time period of the transition plan is longer than one year, identify steps that will be taken during each year of the transition period; and

(4) Indicate the official responsible for implementation of the plan.

§ 8c.51 Program accessibility: New construction and alterations.

Each building or part of a building that is constructed or altered by, on behalf of, or for the use of the agency shall be designed, constructed, or altered so as to be readily accessible to and usable by individuals with handicaps. The definitions, requirements, and standards of the Architectural Barriers Act (42 U.S.C. 4151–4157), as established in 41 CFR 101–19.600 to 101–19.607, apply to buildings covered by this section.

§§ 8c.52–8c.59 [Reserved]

§ 8c.60 Communications.

(a) The agency shall take appropriate steps to ensure effective communication with applicants, participants, personnel of other Federal entities, and members of the public.

(1) The agency shall furnish appropriate auxiliary aids where necessary to afford an individual with handicaps an equal opportunity to participate in, and enjoy the benefits of, a program or activity conducted by the agency.

(i) In determining what type of auxiliary aid is necessary, the agency shall give primary consideration to the requests of the individual with handicaps.

(ii) The agency need not provide individually prescribed devices, readers for personal use or study, or other devices of a personal nature.

(2) Where the agency communicates with applications and beneficiaries by telephone, telecommunication devices for deaf persons (TDD's) or equally effective telecommunication systems shall be used.

(b) The agency shall ensure that interested persons, including persons with impaired vision or hearing, can obtain information as to the existence and location of accessible services, activities, and facilities.

(c) The agency shall provide signs at a primary entrance to each of its inaccessible facilities, directing users to a location at which they can obtain information about accessible facilities. The international symbol for accessibility shall be used at each primary entrance of an accessible facility.

(d) This section does not require the agency to take any action that it can demonstrate would result in a fundamental alteration in the nature of a program or activity or in undue financial and administrative burdens. In those circumstances where agency personnel believe that the proposed action would fundamentally alter the program or activity or would result in undue financial and administrative burdens, the agency has the burden of proving that compliance with § 8c.60 would result in such alteration or burdens. The decision that compliance would result in such alteration of burdens must be made by the Secretary of Commerce or the Secretary's designee after considering all agency resources available for use in the funding and operation of the conducted program or activity, and must be accompanied by a written statement of the reasons for reaching that conclusion. If an action required to comply with this section would result in such an alteration or such burdens, the agency shall take any other action that would not result in such an alteration or such burdens but would nevertheless ensure that, to the maximum extent possible, individuals with handicaps receive the benefits and services of the program or activity.

§§ 8c.61–8.69 [Reserved]

§ 8c.70 Compliance procedures

(a) Except as provided in paragraph (b) of this section, this section applies to all allegations of discrimination on the basis of handicap in programs or activities conducted by the agency.

(b) The agency shall process complaints alleging violations of section 504 with respect to employment according to the procedures established by the Equal Employment Opportunity Commission in 29 CFR Part 1613 pursuant to section 501 of the Rehabilitation Act of 1973 (29 U.S.C. 791).

(c) The Chief of the Compliance Divison shall be responsible for coordinating implemention of this section. Complaints may be sent to Chief, Compliance Division, Office of Civil Rights, Room 6012, Herbert C. Hoover Building, 14th and Constitution Avenue, Washington, DC, 20230.

(d) The agency shall accept and investigate all complete complaints for which it has jurisdiction. All complete complaints must be filed within 180 days of the alleged act of discrimination. The agency may extend this time period for good cause.

(e) If the agency receives a complaint over which it does not have jurisdiction, it shall promptly notify the complainant and shall make reasonable efforts to refer the complaint to the appropriate government entity.

(f) The agency shall notify the Architectural and Transportation Barriers Compliance Board upon receipt of any complaint alleging that a building or facility that is subject to the Architectural Barriers Act of 1968, as amended (42 U.S.C. 4151–4157), is not readily accessible to and usable by individuals with handicaps.

(g) Within 180 days of the receipt of a complete complaint for which it has jurisdiction, the agency shall notify the complainant of the results of the investigation in a letter containing—

(1) Findings of fact and conclusions of law;

(2) A description of a remedy for each violation found; and

(3) A notice of the right to appeal.

(h) Appeals of the findings of fact and conclusions of law or remedies must be filed by the complainant within 90 days of receipt from the agency of the letter required by § 8c.70(g). The agency may extend this time for good cause.

(i) Timely appeals shall be accepted and processed by the Assistant Secretary for Administration.

(j) The Assistant Secretary for Administration shall notify the complainant of the results of the appeal within 60 days of the receipt of the request. If the Assistant Secretary for Administration determines that additional information is needed from the complainant, he or she shall have 60 days from the date of receipt of the additonal information to make his or her determination on the appeal.

(k) The time limits cited in paragraphs (g) and (j) of the section may be extended with the permission of the Assistant Attorney General.

(l) The agency may delegate its authority for conducting complaint investigations to other Federal agencies, except that the authority for making the final determination may not be delegated to another agency.

[53 FR 19277, May 27, 1988; 53 FR 25722, July 8, 1988]

PART 9—PROCEDURES FOR A VOLUNTARY LABELING PROGRAM FOR HOUSEHOLD APPLIANCES AND EQUIPMENT TO EFFECT ENERGY CONSERVATION

Sec.

AUTHORITY: Sec. 2, 31 Stat. 1449, as amended, sec. 1, 64 Stat. 371; 15 U.S.C. 272, Reorganization Plan No. 3 of 1946, Part VI; Message from the President of the United States Concerning Energy Resources, April 18, 1973 (119 Cong. Rec. H2886).

SOURCE: 38 FR 29574, Oct. 26, 1973, unless otherwise noted.

§9.0 Purpose.

The purpose of this part is to establish procedures relating to the Department's voluntary labeling program for household appliances and equipment to promote and effect energy conservation.

§9.1 Goal of program.

(a) This program was initiated in response to the direction of President Nixon in his 1973 Energy Message that the Department of Commerce in cooperation with the Council on Environmental Quality and the Environmental Protection Agency develop a voluntary labeling program which would apply to energy-consuming home appliances.

(b) The goal of this program is to encourage manufacturers to provide consumers, at the point of sale, with information on the energy consumption and energy efficiency of household appliances and equipment. Such information, presented in a uniform manner readily understandable to consumers, would be displayed on labels attached to or otherwise provided with the appliances or equipment. The labels will include a system intended to make it possible for consumers to compare by cost or otherwise the energy consumption and energy efficiency characteristics when purchasing household appliances and equipment and to select those that can effect savings in energy consumption.

§9.2 Definitions.

(a) The term *Secretary* means the Secretary of Commerce.

(b) The term *manufacturer* means any person engaged in the manufacturing or assembling of new appliances or equipment in the United States, or in the importing of such products for sale or resale, or any person whose brand or trademark appears on such products who owns such brand or trademark and has authorized its use on such products, if the brand or trademark of the person actually manufacturing or assembling the products does not appear on the products.

(c) The term *energy consumption* means the energy resources used by appliances or equipment under conditions of use approximating actual operating conditions insofar as practical as determined through test procedures contained or identified in a final Voluntary Energy Conservation Specification published under §9.4(e).

(d) The term *energy efficiency* means the energy use of appliances or equipment relative to their output of services, as determined through test procedures contained or identified in a final Voluntary Energy Conservation Specification published under §9.4(e).

(e) The term *consumer* means the first person who purchases a new appliance or item of equipment for purposes other than resale.

(f) The term *class of appliance or equipment* means a group of appliances or equipment whose functions or features are similar, and whose functional output covers a range that may be of interest to consumers.

(g) The term *Specification* means a Voluntary Energy Conservation Specification developed under §9.4.

(h) The term *label* means printed matter affixed to or otherwise provided with appliances or equipment and meeting all the requirements called for in a Voluntary Energy Conservation Specification published under §9.4(e).

[38 FR 29574, Oct. 26, 1973, as amended at 40 FR 33966, Aug. 13, 1975]

§9.3 Appliances and equipment included in program.

The appliances and equipment included in this program are room and central air conditioners, household refrigerators, home freezers, clothes washers, dishwashers, clothes dryers, kitchen ranges and ovens, water heaters, comfort heating equipment, and television receivers. Additional appliances and equipment may be included in the program by the Secretary pursuant to rule making procedures as set out in 5 U.S.C. 553. Individual units of appliances and equipment manufactured for export are not included in this program.

[38 FR 29574, Oct. 26, 1973, as amended at 40 FR 33966, Aug. 13, 1975]

§ 9.4 Development of voluntary energy conservation specifications.

(a) The Secretary in cooperation with appropriate Federal agencies and in cooperation with affected manufacturers, distributors, retailers, consumers, environmentalists, and other interested parties shall develop proposed Specifications for the specific classes of appliances and equipment covered under § 9.3.

(b) Each Specification shall as a minimum include:

(1) A description of the class of appliance or equipment covered by the Specification, listing the distribution of energy efficiencies for that class of appliance or equipment.

(2) Listings or descriptions of test methods to be used in measuring the energy consumption and/or energy efficiency characteristics of the class of appliance or equipment.

(3) A prototype Label and directions for displaying the Label on or with appliances or equipment of that class. The Label shall be prominent, readable, and visible and shall include information that will assist the consumer in comparing by cost or otherwise the energy consumption and/or energy efficiency characteristics of a particular appliance or item of equipment with all others in its class. The Label shall also include the Department of Commerce Energy Conservation Mark specified in § 9.7.

(4) Conditions for the participation of manufacturers in the program.

(c) The test methods listed or described in the Specification pursuant to § 9.4(b)(2) shall be those described in existing nationally-recognized voluntary standards where such methods are appropriate. Where appropriate test methods do not so exist, they will be developed by the Department of Commerce in cooperation with interested parties.

(d) The Secretary upon development of a proposed Specification shall publish in the FEDERAL REGISTER a notice giving the complete text of the proposed Specification, and any other pertinent information, and inviting any interested person to submit written comments on the proposed Specification within 30 days after its publication in the FEDERAL REGISTER, unless another time limit is provided by the Secretary. Interested persons wanting to express their views in an informal hearing may do so if, within 15 days after the proposed Specification is published in the FEDERAL REGISTER, they request the Secretary to hold a hearing. Such informal hearings shall be held so as to give all interested persons opportunity for the oral presentation of data, views, or arguments in addition to the opportunity to make written submissions. Notice of such hearings shall be published in the FEDERAL REGISTER. A transcript shall be kept of any oral presentations.

(e) The Secretary, after consideration of all written and oral comments and other materials received in accordance with paragraph (d) of this section, shall publish in the FEDERAL REGISTER within 30 days after the final date for receipt of comments, or as soon as practicable thereafter, a notice either:

(1) Giving the complete text of a final Specification, including conditions of use, and stating that any manufacturer of appliances or equipment in the class concerned desiring voluntarily to use the Label and Energy Conservation Mark with such appliances or equipment must advise the Department of Commerce; or

(2) Stating that the proposed Specification will be further developed before final publication; or

(3) Withdrawing the proposed Specification from further consideration.

§ 9.5 Participation of manufacturers.

(a) Manufacturers desiring to participate in this program will so notify the Department of Commerce. The notification will identify the particular Specification to be used and the manufacturer's model numbers for the products to be labeled. The notification will also state that the manufacturer will abide by all conditions contained in the Specification and will desist from using the Label and Energy Conservation Mark if requested by the Department of Commerce under the provisions of § 9.6.

(b) The conditions for participation will be set out in the Specification and will include, but not be limited to, the following:

(1) Prior to the use of a Label the manufacturer will make or have made the measurements to obtain the information required for inclusion on the Label and, if requested, will forward within 30 days such measurement data to the Department of Commerce. Such measurement data will be kept on file by the manufacturer or his agent for two years after that model of appliance or equipment is no longer manufactured unless otherwise provided in the Specification. The use of independent test laboratories or national certification programs available to any manufacturer is acceptable for the purposes of this program.

(2) The manufacturer will describe the test results on the Label as prescribed in the Specification.

(3) The manufacturer will display or arrange to display, in accordance with the appropriate Specification, the Label on or with each individual unit of appliance or equipment within the subject class and with the same brand name manufactured by him except for units exported from the United States. All models with the same brand name that fall within the class must be included in the program unless they are for export only.

(4) The manufacturer agrees at his expense to comply with any reasonable request of the Department of Commerce to have appliances or equipment manufactured by him tested to determine that testing has been done according to the relevant Specification.

(5) Manufacturers may reproduce the Department of Commerce Labels and Energy Conservation Mark in advertising provided that the entire Label, complete with all information required to be displayed at the point of retail sale, is shown legibly.

§ 9.6 Termination of participation.

(a) The Department of Commerce upon finding that a manufacturer is not complying with the conditions of participation set out in these procedures or in a Specification may terminate upon 30 days notice the manufacturer's participation in the program: *Provided,* That the manufacturer shall first be given an opportunity to show cause why the participation should not be terminated. Upon receipt of a notice of termination, a manufacturer may request within 30 days a hearing under the provisions of 5 U.S.C. 558.

(b) A manufacturer may at any time terminate his participation and responsibilities under this program with regard to a specific class of products by giving written notice to the Secretary that he has discontinued use of the Label and Energy Conservation Mark for all appliances or equipment within that class.

§ 9.7 Department of Commerce energy conservation mark.

The Department of Commerce shall develop an Energy Conservation Mark which shall be registered in the U.S. Patent Office under 15 U.S.C. 1054 for use on each Label described in a Specification.

§ 9.8 Amendment or revision of voluntary energy conservation specifications.

The Secretary may by order amend or revise any Specification published under § 9.4. The procedure applicable to the establishment of a Specification under § 9.4 shall be followed in amending or revising such Specification. Such amendment or revision shall not apply to appliances or equipment manufactured prior to the effective date of the amendment or revision.

§ 9.9 Consumer education.

The Department of Commerce, in close cooperation and coordination with interested Government agencies, appropriate industry trade associations and industry members, and interested consumers and environmentalists shall carry out a program to educate consumers relative to the significance of the labeling program. Some elements of this program shall also be directed toward informing retailers and other interested groups about the program.

§ 9.10 Coordination with State and local programs.

The Department of Commerce will establish and maintain an active program of communication with appropriate state and local government offices and agencies and will furnish and make available information and assistance that will promote to the greatest practicable extent uniformity in State, local, and Federal programs for the labeling of household appliances and equipment to effect energy conservation.

§ 9.11 Annual report.

The Secretary will prepare an annual report of activities under the program, including an evaluation of the program and a list of participating manufacturers and classes of appliances and equipment.

PART 10—PROCEDURES FOR THE DEVELOPMENT OF VOLUNTARY PRODUCT STANDARDS

AUTHORITY: Sec. 2.31 Stat. 1449, as amended, sec. 1, .64 Stat 371; 15 U.S.C. 272, Reorganization Plan No. 3 of 1946, Part VI (3 CFR 1943–1948 Comp., p. 1065).

SOURCE: 51 FR 22497, June 20, 1986, unless otherwise noted.

§ 10.0 General.

(a) *Introduction.* The Department of Commerce (hereinafter referred to as the "Department") recognizes the importance, the advantages, and the benefits of voluntary standards and standardization activities. Such standards may cover, but are not limited to, terms, classes, sizes (including quantities of packaged consumer commodities), dimensions, capacities, quality levels, performance criteria, inspection requirements, marking requirements, testing equipment, test procedures and installation procedures. Economic growth is promoted through:

(1) Reduction of manufacturing costs, inventory costs, and distribution costs;

(2) Better understanding among manufacturers, producers, or packagers (hereinafter referred to as producers), distributors, users, and consumers; and

(3) Simplification of the purchase, installation, and use of the product being standardized.

(b) *Requirements for Department of Commerce sponsorship.* The Department may sponsor the development of a voluntary Product Standard if, upon receipt of a request, the Department determines that:

(1) The proposed standard is likely to have substantial public impact;

(2) The proposed standard reflects the broad interest of an industry group or an organization concerned with the manufacture, production, packaging, distribution, testing, consumption, or use of the product, or the interest of a Federal or State agency;

(3) The proposed standard would not duplicate a standard published by, or actively being developed or revised by, a private standards-writing organization to such an extent that it would contain similar requirements and test methods for identical types of products, unless such duplication was deemed by the Department to be in the public interest;

(4) Lack of government sponsorship would result in significant public disadvantage for legal reasons or reasons of domestic and international trade;

(5) The proposed standard is not appropriate for development and maintenance by a private standards-writing organization; and

(6) The proposed standard will be funded by a proponent organization or government agency to cover costs for administrative and technical support services provided by the Department.

(c) *Role of the Department.* The Department assists in the establishment of a Voluntary Product Standard as follows:

(1) Acts as an unbiased coordinator in the development of the standard;

(2) Provides editorial assistance in the preparation of the standard;

(3) Supplies such assistance and review as is required to assure the technical soundness of the standard;

(4) Seeks satisfactory adjustment of valid points of disagreement;

(5) Determines the compliance with the criteria established in these procedures for such voluntary standards;

(6) Provides secretarial functions for each committee appointed by the Department under these procedures;

(7) Publishes the standard as a public document;

(8) Administers the funds for administrative and technical support services; and

(9) Seeks listing for standards developed under these procedures as American National Standards through the American National Standards Institute, when deemed appropriate by the Department.

(d) *Role of producers, distributors, users, and consumers.* Producers, distributors, users, consumers, and other interested groups may contribute to the development of a Voluntary Product Standard as follows:

(1) Initiate and participate in the development of the standard;

(2) Provide technical or other relevant counsel, as appropriate, relating to the standard;

(3) Promote the use of, and support for, the standard; and

(4) Assist in keeping the standard current with respect to advancing technology and marketing practices.

(e) *Role of the National Institute of Standards & Technology.* The National Institute of Standards & Technology (NIST) administers these procedures for the Department. Any communications concerning these procedures (e.g., questions, clarifications, appeals) should be addressed to the Office of Product Standards Policy, National Institute of Standards & Technology, Gaithersburg, Maryland 20899.

[51 FR 22497, June 20, 1986, as amended at 55 FR 38315, Sept. 18, 1990]

§ 10.1 Initiating development of a new standard.

(a) Any group or association of producers, distributors, users, or consumers, or a testing laboratory, or a State or Federal agency, may request the Department to initiate the development and publication of a Voluntary Product Standard under these procedures. Requests shall be in writing, signed by a representative of the group or agency, and forwarded to the Department. The initial request may be accompanied by a copy of a draft of the suggested standard.

(b) The request shall include a commitment to provide sufficient funding to cover all costs associated with the development and maintenance of the proposed Voluntary Product Standard.

(c) The Department may require additional information such as technical, marketing, or other appropriate data essential to discussion and development of the proposed standard, including, but not limited to, physical, mechanical, chemical, or performance characteristics, and production figures.

(d) Upon receipt of an appropriate request and after a determination by the Department that the development of a Voluntary Product Standard is justified, the Department may initiate the development by requesting that a draft of the suggested standard be prepared by an appropriate committee, provided such a draft has not previously been submitted under paragraph (a) of this section.

(e) The Department may initiate the development of a Voluntary Product Standard, if such action is deemed by the Department to be in the public interest, notwithstanding the absence of a request from an outside source. A voluntary standard initiated by the Department shall be processed in accordance with all requirements of these procedures and shall be developed in the same manner as a voluntary standard initiated by any group referred to in paragraph (a) of this section.

(f) An agreement regarding funding procedures and receipt of a deposit estimated by the Department to be sufficient to cover the first year's costs shall occur prior to the initiation of any project.

§ 10.2 Funding.

Groups who represent producers, distributors, consumers or users, or others that wish to act or continue to act as proponent organizations for the development or maintenance of a Voluntary Product Standard will be required to pay for administrative and technical support services provided by the National Institute of Standards & Technology and such other direct or indirect costs associated with the development or maintenance of that standard as may be deemed appropriate by the Department, including costs to the Department in connection with the operation of the Standard Review Committee and the Standing Committee. Funds may also be provided by a government agency at the request of a proponent organization or when acting on its own behalf for the development or maintenance of a Voluntary Product Standard. Proponents of standards that meet sponsorship criteria established in these procedures shall furnish an initial deposit of funds sufficient to cover the first year's services and other costs. Estimated annual costs will be based on an hourly rate for salary and overhead established by the Department for the National Institute of Standards & Technology's administrative and technical support services plus estimates of direct costs to provide funds for such items as the travel of consumer representatives unable to otherwise attend committee meetings, travel for Department staff, and printing costs. Project funds will be reviewed annually. Excess funds may be refunded or applied to the next accounting period. Should funds from deposits be inadequate during an accounting period, work on the project will continue only if funds are restored to a level estimated adequate to complete the 12-month period.

[51 FR 22497, June 20, 1986, as amended at 55 FR 38315, Sept. 18, 1990]

§ 10.3 Development of a proposed standard.

(a) A proposed standard as submitted to the Department:

(1) Shall be based on adequate technical information, or, in the case of size standards (including standards covering the quantities for packaged consumer commodities), on adequate marketing information, or both, as determined to be appropriate by the Department;

(2) Shall not be contrary to the public interest;

(3) Shall be technically appropriate and such that conformance or nonconformance with the standard can be determined either during or after the manufacturing process by inspection or other procedures which may be utilized by either an individual or a testing facility competent in the particular field;

(4) Shall follow the format prescribed by the National Institute of Standards & Technology. (Copies of the recommended format may be obtained from the Office of Product Standards Policy, National Institute of Standards & Technology, Gaithersburg, Maryland 20899.);

(5) Shall include performance requirements if such are deemed by the Department to be technically sound, feasible, and practical, and the inclusion of such is deemed to be appropriate;

(6) May include dimensions, sizes, material specifications, product requirements, design stipulations, component requirements, test methods, testing equipment descriptions, and installation procedures. The appropriateness of the inclusion in a standard of any particular item listed in this subparagraph shall be determined by the Department; and

(7) Shall be accompanied by rational statements pertaining to the requirements and test methods contained in the standard, if deemed necessary by the Department.

(b) A proposed standard that is determined by the Department to meet the criteria set forth in paragraph (a) of this section may be subjected to further review by an appropriate individual, committee, organization, or agency (either government or nongovernment, but not associated with the proponent group).

(c) A proposed standard may be circulated by the Department to appropriate producers, distributors, users, consumers, and other interested groups for consideration and comment as well as to others requesting the opportunity to comment.

(d) The proponent group or appropriate committee which drafted the initial proposal under § 10.1(d) shall consider all comments and suggestions submitted by the reviewer designated under paragraph (b) of this section, and those received by the Department as a result of any circulation under paragraph (c) of this section, and may make such adjustments in the proposal as are technically sound and as are believed to cause the standard to be generally acceptable to producers, distributors, users, consumers, and other interested parties. The proposal will then be submitted to the Department for further processing.

[51 FR 22497, June 20, 1986, as amended at 55 FR 38315, Sept. 18, 1990]

§ 10.4 Establishment of the Standard Review Committee.

(a) The Department shall establish and appoint the members of a Standard Review Committee within a reasonable time after receiving a proposed standard. The committee shall consist of qualified representatives of producers, distributors, and users or consumers of product for which a standard is sought or any other appropriate general interest groups such as State and Federal agencies. When requested by the Standard Review Committee, the Department shall appoint one voting member from among the representatives of the Federal agencies, other than the Department of Commerce. All other representatives of Federal agencies on the Standard Review Committees shall be advisory nonvoting members. (Alternates to committee members may be designated by the Department.) When deemed appropriate by the Department, project funds under § 10.2 may be made available to assure participation by consumer interests on the committee at required meetings.

(b) A Standard Review Committee may remain in existence for a period necessary for the final development of the standard, or for 2 years, whichever is less.

(c) The Department shall be responsible for the organization of the committee. Any formal operating procedures developed by the committee shall be subject to approval by the Department. The committee may conduct business either in a meeting or through correspondence, but only if a quorum participates. A quorum shall consist of two-thirds of all voting members of the committee. A majority of the voting members of the committee participating shall be required to approve any actions taken by the committee except for the action of recommending a standard to the Department, the requirements for which are contained in § 10.5(b).

§ 10.5 Development of a recommended standard.

(a) The Standard Review Committee, with the guidance and assistance of the Department and, if appropriate, the reviewer designated under § 10.3(b), shall review a proposed standard promptly. If the committee finds that the proposal meets the requirements set forth in § 10.3(a), it may recommend to the Department that the proposal be circulated for acceptance under § 10.6. If, however, the committee finds that the proposal being reviewed does not meet the requirements set forth in § 10.3(a), the committee shall change the proposal, after consulting with the proponent group, so that these requirements are met, before recommending such proposal to the Department.

(b) The recommendation of a standard by the Standard Review Committee shall be approved by at least three-quarters, or rejected by more than one-quarter, of all of the members of the committee eligible to vote. The voting on the recommendation of a standard shall be conducted by the Department if conducted by letter ballot. If such voting is accomplished at a meeting of the committee, the balloting shall be either by roll call or by signed written ballot conducted by the Department or the chairman of this committee. If conducted by the chairman, a report of the vote shall be made to the Department within 15 days. If the balloting at the meeting does not result in either approval by at least three-quarters of all members (or alternates) eligible to vote (whether present or not), or rejection by more than one-quarter of the members (or alternates) or the committee eligible to vote, the balloting shall be disregarded and the Department shall subsequently conduct a letter ballot of all members of the committee.

(c) Any member of the committee casting a negative ballot shall have the right to support an objection by furnishing the chairman of the committee and the Department with a written statement setting forth the basis for the objection. The written statement of objection shall be filed within 15 days after the date of the meeting during which the voting on the standard was accomplished, or, in the case of a letter ballot, within the time limit established for the return of the ballot.

(d) At the time a recommended standard is submitted to the Department, the Chairman of the Standard Review Committee shall furnish a written report in support of the committee's recommendation. Such report shall include a statement with respect to compliance with the requirements as established by these procedures, a discussion of the manner in which any objections were resolved, and a discussion of any unresolved objections together with the committee's reasons for rejecting such unresolved objections.

§ 10.6 Procedures for acceptance of a recommended standard.

(a) Upon receipt from the Standard Review Committee of a recommended standard and report, the Department shall give appropriate public notice and distribute the recommended standard for acceptance unless:

(1) Upon a showing by any member of the committee who has voted to oppose the recommended standard on the basis of an unresolved objection, the Department determines that if such objection were not resolved, the recommended standard:

(i) Would be contrary to the public interest, if published;

(ii) Would be technically inadequate; or

(iii) Would be inconsistent with law or established public policy; or

(2) The Department determines that all criteria and procedures set forth herein have not been met satisfactorily or that there is a legal impediment to the recommended standard.

(b) Distribution for acceptance or rejection for the purpose of determining general concurrence will be made to a list compiled by the Department, which, in the judgment of the Department, shall be representative of producers, distributors, and users and consumers.

(c) Distribution for comment will be made to any party filing a written request with the Department, and to such other parties as the Department may deem appropriate, including testing laboratories and interested State and Federal agencies.

(d) The Department shall analyze the recommended standard and the responses received under paragraphs (b) and (c) of this section. If such analysis indicates that the recommended standard is supported by a consensus, it shall be published as a Voluntary Product Standard by the Department: *Provided*, That all other requirements listed in these procedures have been satisfied.

(e) The following definitions shall apply to the term used in this section:

(1) "Consensus" means general concurrence and, in addition, no substantive objection deemed valid by the Department.

(2) "General concurrence" means acceptance among those responding to the distribution made under paragraph (b) of this section in accordance with the conditions set forth in paragraph (f) of this section.

(3) "Substantive objection" means a documented objection based on grounds that one or more of the criteria set forth in these procedures has not been satisfied.

(4) "Average industry acceptance" means a percentage equal to the sum of the percentages of acceptance obtained from responses to distribution of the recommended standard in the producer segment, the distributor segment, and the user and consumer segment, divided by three. No consideration will be given to volume of production or volume of distribution in determining average industry acceptance.

(5) "Producer segment" means those persons who manufacture or produce the product covered by the standard.

(6) "Distributor segment" means those persons who distribute at wholesale or retail the product covered by the standard.

(7) "User and consumer segment" means those persons who use or consume the product covered by the standard.

(8) "Acceptance by volume of production" means the weighted percentage of acceptance of those responding to the distribution in the producer segment. The weighting of each response will be made in accordance with the volume of production represented by each respondent.

(9) "Acceptance by volume of distribution" means the weighted percentage of acceptance of those responding to the distribution in the distributor segment. The weighting of each response will be made in accordance with the volume of distribution represented by each respondent.

(f) A recommended standard shall be deemed to be supported by general concurrence whenever:

(1) An analysis of the responses to the distribution under paragraph (b) of this section indicates:

(i) An average industry acceptance of not less than 75 percent;

(ii) Acceptance of not less than 70 percent by the producer segment, the distributor segment, and the user and consumer segment, each segment being considered separately; and

(iii) Acceptance by volume of production and acceptance by volume of distribution of not less than 70 percent in each case: *Provided*, That the Department shall disregard acceptance by volume of production or acceptance by volume of distribution or both unless, in the judgment of the Department, accurate figures for the volume of production or distribution are reasonably available and an evaluation of either or both of such acceptances is deemed necessary by the Department; or

(2) The Department determines that publication of the standard is appropriate under the procedures set forth in paragraph (g) of this section and, in addition, an analysis of the responses to the distribution under paragraph (b) of this section indicates:

(i) An average industry acceptance of not less than 66⅔ percent;

(ii) Acceptance of not less than 60 percent by the producer segment, the distributor segment, and the user and consumer segment, each segment being considered separately; and

(iii) Acceptance by volume of production and acceptance by volume of distribution of not less than 60 percent in each case: *Provided*, That the Department shall disregard acceptance by volume of production or acceptance by volume of distribution or both unless, in the judgment of the Department, accurate figures for the volume of production or distribution are reasonably available and an evaluation of either or both of such acceptances is deemed necessary by the Department.

(g) A recommended standard which fails to achieve the acceptance requirements of paragraph (f)(1) of this section, but which satisfies the acceptance criteria of paragraph (f)(2) of this section, shall be returned to the Standard Review Committee for reconsideration. The committee, by the affirmative vote of not less than three-quarters of all members eligible to vote, may resubmit the recommended standard without change to the Department with a recommendation that the standard be published as a Voluntary Product Standard. The Department shall then conduct a public rulemaking hearing in accordance with the requirements of law as set forth in section 553 of Title 5, United States Code, to assist it in determining whether publication of the standard is in the public interest. If the Department determines that publication of the standard is in the public interest, the standard shall be published as a Voluntary Product Standard.

§ 10.7 Procedure when a recommended standard is not supported by a consensus.

If the Department determines that a recommended standard is not supported by a consensus, the Department may:

(a) Return the recommended standard to the Standard Review Committee for further action, with or without suggestions;

(b) Terminate the development of the recommended standard under these procedures; or

(c) Take such other action as it may deem necessary or appropriate under the circumstances.

§ 10.8 Standing Committee.

(a) The Department shall establish and appoint the members of a Standing Committee prior to the publication of a standard. The committee may include members from the Standard Review Committee, and shall consist of qualified representatives of producers, distributors, and users or consumers of the product covered by the standard, and representatives of appropriate general interest groups such as municipal, State, and Federal agencies. When requested by the Standing Committee, the Department shall appoint one voting member from among the representatives of the Federal agencies, other than the Department of Commerce. When requested by the Standing Committee for PS 20-70, "American Softwood Lumber Standard," the Department shall appoint two voting members from among the representatives of the Federal agencies, other than the Department of Commerce. All other representatives of Federal agencies shall be advisory nonvoting members of Standing Committees. (Alternates to committee members may be designated by the Department.) When deemed appropriate by the Department, project funds under § 10.2, may be made available to assure participation by consumer interests on the committee at required meetings.

(b) Appointments to a Standing Committee may not exceed a term of 5 years. However, the committee may be reconstituted by the Department whenever appropriate, and members may be reappointed by the Department to succeeding terms. Appointments to the committee will be terminated upon the withdrawal of the standard.

(c) The Department shall be responsible for the organization of the committee. Any formal operating procedures developed by the committee shall be subject to approval by the Department. The committee may conduct business either in a meeting or through correspondence, but only if a quorum participates. A quorum shall consist of two-thirds of all voting members of the committee. A majority of the voting members of the committee participating shall be required to approve any actions taken by the committee except for the approval of revisions of the standard which shall be governed by the provisions of § 10.5 (b), (c), and (d),

(d) The members of a Standing Committee should be knowledgeable about:

(1) The product or products covered by the standard;

(2) The standard itself; and

(3) Industry and trade practices relating to the standard.

(e) The committee shall:

(1) Keep itself informed of any advancing technology that might affect the standard;

(2) Provide the Department with interpretations of provisions of the standard upon request;

(3) Make recommendations to the Department concerning the desirability or necessity of revising or amending the standard;

(4) Receive and consider proposals to revise or amend the standard; and

(5) Recommend to the Department the revision or amendment of a standard.

§ 10.9 Publication of a standard.

A Voluntary Product Standard published by the department under these procedures shall be assigned an appropriate number for purposes of identification and reference. Public notice shall be given regarding the publication and identification of the standard. A voluntary standard by itself has no mandatory or legally binding effect. Any person may choose to use or not to use such a standard. Appropriate reference in contracts, codes, advertising, invoices, announcements, product labels, and the like may be made to a Voluntary Product Standard published under these procedures. Such reference shall be in accordance with such policies as the Department may establish, but no product may be advertised or represented in any manner which would imply or tend to imply approval or endorsement of that product by the Department or by the Federal Government.

§ 10.10 Review of published standards.

(a) Each standard published under these or previous procedures shall be reviewed regularly to determine the feasibility of transferring sponsorship to a private standards-writing organization. While the Department encourages the development of standards to replace Voluntary Product Standards by private standards-writing organizations, withdrawal of a Voluntary Product Standard, which meets the requirements of § 10.0(b), shall not be considered until a replacement standard is published.

(b) Each standard published under these or previous procedures shall be reviewed by the Department, with such assistance of the Standing Committee or others as may be deemed appropriate by the Department, within 5 years after initial issuance or last revision and at least every 5 years thereafter. The purpose of this review shall be to determine whether the standard has become obsolete, technically inadequate, no longer acceptable to or used by the industry, or inconsistent with law or established public policy.

(c) If any of the above conditions is found to exist, the Department shall initiate action to amend, revise, or withdraw the standard in accordance with § 10.11 or § 10.13. If none is found to exist, the standard shall be kept in effect provided adequate funding is maintained.

§ 10.11 Revision or amendment of a standard.

(a) A published standard shall be subject to revision or amendment when it is determined to be inadequate by its Standing Committee or by the Department of one or more of the following reasons or for any other appropriate reasons:

(1) Any portion of the standard is obsolete, technically inadequate, or no longer generally acceptable to or used by the industry;

(2) The standard or any part of it is inconsistent with law or established public policy; or

(3) The standard or any part of it is being used to mislead users or consumers or is determined to be against the interest of users, consumers, or the public in general.

(b) A revision of a standard shall be considered by the Department to include changes which are comprehensive in nature, which have a substantive effect on the standards, which change the level of performance or safety or the design characteristics of the product being standardized, or which cannot reasonably be injected into a standard without disturbing the general applicability of the standard. Each suggestion for revision shall be submitted by the Department to the Standing Committee for appropriate consideration. The Standing Committee shall serve the same functions in the revision of a standard as the Standard Review Committee serves in the development of a new standard. The processing of a revision of a standard shall be dependent upon the age of the standard as computed from its effective date and shall be accomplished as follows:

(1) A proposed revision of a standard older than 5 years at the time such proposed revision is submitted to the Standing Committee by the Department shall be processed as a new standard under these procedures and, when approved for publication, the standard shall be republished and reidentified to indicate the year in which the revision became effective. The revised standard shall supersede the previously published standard.

(2) A proposed revision of a standard less than 5 years at the time such proposed revision is submitted to the Standing Committee by the Department shall be processed as a new standard except that:

(i) Distribution for acceptance or rejection shall be made to an appropriate list of producers, distributors, and users and consumers compiled by the Department;

(ii) If the revision affects only one subsection of the requirement section and/or only one subsection of the test methods section, it may be circulated separately for determining consensus and subsequently published as an addendum to the standard with appropriate dissemination and public notice of the addendum; and

(iii) If the revision does not change the level of performance or safety or the design characteristics of the product being standardized, the standard need not be reidentified.

(c) An amendment to a standard shall be considered by the Department to be any non-editorial change which is not comprehensive in nature, which has no substantive effect on the standard, which does not change the level of performance or safety or the design characteristics of the product being standardized, and which reasonably can be injected into a standard without disturbing the general applicability of the standard. Each suggestion for amendment shall be submitted by the Department to the Standing Committee for appropriate consideration. An amendment to a standard recommended by not less than 90 percent of the members of the committee eligible to vote and found acceptable by the Department, shall be published as an addendum (until the standard is republished) and distributed to acceptors of record. Public notice of the amendment shall be given and copies of the amendment shall be distributed to those filing written requests.

§ 10.12 Editorial changes.

The Department may, without prior notice, make such editorial or other minor changes as it deems necessary to reduce ambiguity or to improve clarity in any proposed, recommended, or published standard, or revision or amendment thereof.

§ 10.13 Withdrawal of a published standard.

(a) Standards published under these and previous procedures may be withdrawn by the Director of the National Institute of Standards & Technology at any time. Such action will be taken if, after consultation with the Standing Committee as provided in paragraph (a)(1) of this section and after public notice, the Director determines that the standard is: Obsolete; technically inadequate; no longer generally acceptable to and used by the industry; inconsistent with law or established public policy; not in the public interest; or otherwise inappropriate; and revision or amendment is not feasible or would serve no useful purpose. Additionally, a standard may be withdrawn if it cannot be demonstrated that a particular standard has substantial public impact, that it does not duplicate a standard published by a private standards-writing organization, or that lack of government sponsorship would result in significant public disadvantage for legal reasons or for reasons of domestic and international trade. The Director may withdraw a standard if costs to maintain such a standard are not reimbursed by the proponent or other government agencies.

(1) Before withdrawing a standard published under these procedures, the Director will review the relative advantages and disadvantages of amendment, revision, development of a new standard, or withdrawal with the members of the Standing Committee, if such committee was appointed or reappointed within the previous five years.

(2) Public notice of intent to withdraw an existing standard published under these procedures shall be given and a 30-day period will be provided for the filing with the Director or written objections to the withdrawal. Such objections will be considered and analyzed by the Director before a determination is made to withdraw the standard. If the Director determines that a particular standard does not meet the criteria set out in § 10.0(b), the standard will be withdrawn.

(b) The filing under paragraph (a) of this section of a request to retain a standard or standards shall operate to stay the withdrawal of such standard or standards until the Director's determination has been made. If the Director determines that the requested standard or standards shall be withdrawn, the stay will remain in effect, if an appeal is filed in accordance with the requirements of § 10.14, until the decision of the Director is announced in the FEDERAL REGISTER. If, however, no appeal is received, the Director shall announce withdrawal of the particular standard or standards.

(c) Notice of the withdrawal action will be published in the FEDERAL REGISTER and such withdrawal will take effect 60 days from the date the withdrawal notice is published.

[51 FR 22497, June 20, 1986, as amended at 55 FR 38315, Sept. 18, 1990]

§ 10.14 Appeals.

(a) Any person directly affected by a procedural action taken by NIST or the Standard Review Committee under §§ 10.5, 10.6 or 10.7 regarding the development of a standard, by NIST or the Standing Committee under § 10.10 regarding the review of a published standard, or under § 10.11 regarding the revision of a standard, or under § 10.13 regarding the withdrawal of a standard, may appeal such action.

(b) Such appeal shall be filed in written form with the body taking the action complained of (NIST, the Standard Review Committee, or the Standing Committee) within 30 days after the date of announcement of the action.

(c) If appeal is filed with the Standard Review Committee or the Standing Committee, the Committee shall attempt to resolve the appeal informally. If the appeal is filed with NIST, NIST with the consultation and advice of the Standard Review Committee or the Standing Committee, whichever is appropriate, shall attempt to resolve the appeal informally.

(d) If the appeal is to the Standard Review Committee or the Standing Committee and the Committee is unable to resolve such an appeal informally, the Committee shall hold a hearing regarding the appeal. Announcement of the hearing shall be made to members of the Standard Review Committee or the Standing Committee and all the acceptors of record, when appropriate, as well as other known interests. Notice of the hearing shall be published in the FEDERAL REGISTER. The hearing will be an informal, nonadversary proceeding at which there will be no formal pleadings or adverse parties. Written statements will be furnished by witnesses prior to the hearing. A record of the hearing will be made. Copies of the written statements and the record of the hearing will be available at cost.

(e) Those members of the Committee hearing the appeal will develop a recommendation to the Committee concerning the resolution of the appeal. NIST will review the recommendation and if found acceptable will subject it to a letter ballot of the Committee. Approval by three-fourths of the members of the Committee eligible to vote will constitute acceptance by the Committee and by NIST. Notice of the Committee decision will be published in the FEDERAL REGISTER.

(f) If the appeal is to NIST and the attempt to resolve the appeal informally under paragraph (c) of this section is not successful, the Deputy Director of NIST will schedule a hearing with an appeals panel at an appropriate location. Announcement of the hearing shall be made to members of the Standard Review Committee or Standing Committee and all acceptors of record, when appropriate, as well as to other known interests. Notice of the hearing shall be published in the FEDERAL REGISTER.

(g) The Deputy Director of NIST will name two other persons, who have not been directly involved in the matter in dispute and who will not be directly or materially affected by any decision made or to be made in the dispute, to sit on the panel with the Deputy Director, who will act as presiding officer. The presiding officer will have the right to exercise such authority as necessary to ensure the equitable and efficient conduct of the hearing and to maintain an orderly proceeding.

(h) The hearing will be an informal, nonadversary proceeding at which there will be no formal pleadings or adverse parties. The hearing will be open to the public. Witnesses shall submit a written presentation for the record seven days prior to the hearing. A record will be made of the hearing. Copies of the written statements and the record of the hearing will be available at cost.

(i) The appeals panel will make a recommendation to the Director of NIST. The Director's decision on the appeal will be announced within 60 days following the hearing and will be communicated to the complainant and other interested parties by letter. Notice of the Director's decision shall be published in the FEDERAL REGISTER.

[51 FR 22497, June 20, 1986, as amended at 55 FR 38315, Sept. 18, 1990]

§ 10.15 Interpretations.

(a) An interpretation of a Voluntary Product Standard may be obtained through the submission of a written request. The request shall identify the specific section of the standard involved.

(b) In the case of PS 20–70, the "American Softwood Lumber Standard," interpretations shall be made by the American Lumber Standards Committee (ALSC) under the procedures developed by the ALSC and found acceptable to NIST.

(c) In the case of the other Voluntary Product Standards, interpretations shall be made by the appropriate Standing Committees under procedures developed by those committees and found acceptable to NIST.

[51 FR 22497, June 20, 1986, as amended at 55 FR 38315, Sept. 18, 1990]

§ 10.16 Effect of procedures.

Nothing contained in these procedures shall be deemed to apply to the development, publication, revision, amendment, or withdrawal of any standard which is not identified as a "Voluntary Product Standard" by the Department. The authority of the Department with respect to engineering standards activities generally, including the authority to publish appropriate recommendations not identified as "Voluntary Product Standards," is not limited in any way by these procedures.

PART 11—UNIFORM RELOCATION ASSISTANCE AND REAL PROPERTY ACQUISITION FOR FEDERAL AND FEDERALLY ASSISTED PROGRAMS

AUTHORITY: Section 213, Uniform Relocation Assistance and Real Property Acquisition Policies Act of 1970, Pub. L. 91–646, 84 Stat. 1894 (42 U.S.C. 4601) as amended by the Surface Transportation and Uniform Relocation Assistance Act of 1987, Title IV of Pub. L. 100–17, 101 Stat. 246–256 (42 U.S.C. 4601 note).

§ 11.1 Uniform relocation and real property acquisition.

Regulations and procedures for complying with the Uniform Relocation Assistance and Real Property Acquisition Policies Act of 1970 (Pub. L. 91–646, 84 Stat. 1894, 42 U.S.C. 4601), as amended by the Surface Transportation and Uniform Relocation Assistance Act of 1987 (Title IV of Pub. L. 100–17, 101 Stat. 246–255, 42 U.S.C. 4601 note) are set forth in 49 CFR Part 24.

[52 FR 48018, Dec. 17, 1987 and 54 FR 8912, 8913, Mar. 2, 1989]

PART 12—FAIR PACKAGING AND LABELING

AUTHORITY: Secs. 5(d), 5(e), 80 Stat. 1298, 15 U.S.C. 1454; sec. 3, Dept. Order 177 (31 FR 6746), as amended (32 FR 3110).

SOURCE: 32 FR 11074, July 29, 1967, unless otherwise noted.

§ 12.1 Introduction.

(a) These procedures apply to the discharge of the responsibility given to the Secretary of Commerce by sections 5(d) and 5(e) of the Fair Packaging and Labeling Act (Pub. L. 89–755, 80 Stat. 1299), hereinafter called the "Act". The word "Secretary", as used hereinafter, shall refer to the Secretary of Commerce or his authorized delegate.

(b) The Secretary does not have the responsibility or the authority under the Act to issue any regulations governing the packaging or labeling practices of private industry.

(c) The Secretary does have the responsibility and authority to:

(1) Determine whether the reasonable ability of consumers to make value comparisions with respect to any consumer commodity or reasonably comparable consumer commodities is impaired by undue proliferation of the weights, measures, or quantities in which such commodity or commodities are being distributed in packages for sale at retail.

(2) Request manufacturers, packers, and distributors, where a determination of undue proliferation has been made, to participate in the development of a voluntary product standard under the procedures governing the Department's voluntary standards program.

(3) Report to Congress with a recommendation as to whether legislation providing regulatory authority should

be enacted, when after 1 year following the date private industry has been requested to participate in the development of a voluntary product standard it is determined that such a standard will not be published, or when following the publication of such a standard it is determined that the standard has not been observed.

(d) The Act does not furnish a detailed, definitive explanation of "undue proliferation". It does, however, point out that the condition of "undue proliferation" must be one which "impairs the reasonable ability of consumers to make value comparisons" with respect to consumer commodities. Generally, therefore, the Department will determine "undue proliferation" on a case-by-case basis, and, accordingly, is establishing by these procedures an orderly process for such determinations.

(e) As used hereinafter the term "undue proliferation" shall refer to such undue proliferation—of the weights, measures or quantities in which any consumer commodity or reasonably comparable consumer commodities are being distributed for sale at retail—as impairs the reasonable ability of consumers to make value comparisons with respect to such consumer commodity or commodities, as set out in section 5(d) of the Act.

§ 12.2 Undue proliferation.

(a) *Information as to possible undue proliferation.* Any person or group, including a State or local governmental entity, is invited to communicate information to the Secretary concerning the possible existence of undue proliferation. Such communications should be in writing and include supporting information and explanations.

(b) *Initiation of inquiry as to undue proliferation.* Upon receipt of information regarding the possible existence of undue proliferation, the Secretary will determine whether there has been a showing of good cause warranting an inquiry. If the Secretary determines that good cause exists, he shall initiate an inquiry for the purpose of finding facts concerning the existence of undue proliferation.

(c) *Procedures for inquiry*—(1) *Cooperation with State and local officials.* Any inquiry initiated under paragraph (b) of this section may be conducted in cooperation with State and local weights and measures officials.

(2) *Participation by interested persons.* The Secretary may, during the course of the inquiry, afford interested persons or groups an opportunity to submit in writing comments, data, arguments, views, or other information relevant to the inquiry.

(d) *Proposed determination as to existence of undue proliferation.* (1) If, after consideration of all relevant information, the Secretary concludes that undue proliferation appears to exist, he shall publish a proposed determination to this effect. The proposed determination shall identify the particular consumer commodity or commodities involved and shall be accompanied by a concise statement of the facts upon which it is based.

(2) Within 60 days after publication of the proposed determination, any interested party may submit in writing comments, data, arguments, views, or other information relevant to the proposed determination. All written submissions shall be made a part of the public record.

(3) Within 30 days after the proposed determination has been published, any interested party may request in writing an oral hearing to present his views. The granting of such a hearing shall be at the discretion of the Secretary. Any such hearing shall be public and notice thereof shall be published at least 15 days in advance. A transcript of the hearing shall be made part of the public record.

(e) *Final determination as to undue proliferation.* As soon as practicable following the conclusion of the proceedings described in paragraph (d) of this section, the Secretary shall either publish a final determination of undue proliferation, or he shall publish a notice withdrawing his proposed determination of undue proliferation. In no event shall the withdrawal of a proposed determination operate to preclude the initiation of another inquiry regarding the same or similar subject matter under paragraph (b) of this section.

§ 12.3 Development of voluntary product standards.

(a) *Invitation to participate in the development of a voluntary product standard.* Whenever the Secretary publishes a final determination of undue proliferation under § 12.2(e), he shall invite manufacturers, packers, and distributors of the commodity or commodities involved to participate in the development of a voluntary product standard in accordance with the terms of the Act and the Department's published procedures for voluntary product standards. The term "Voluntary Product Standard" as used in this section means a standard for weights, measures or quantities in which the commodity or commodities are being distributed in packages for sale at retail.

(b) *Determination that voluntary product standard will not be published.* (1) If a voluntary product standard has not been developed within one year from the date on which participation was invited, the Secretary may conclude that a voluntary product standard will not likely be published. Upon reaching such a conclusion, the Secretary will publish a proposed determination that a voluntary product standard will not be published.

(2) Within 60 days after publication of the proposed determination, any interested party may submit in writing comments, data, arguments, views, or other information relevant to the proposed determination. All written submissions shall be made a part of the public record.

(3) Within 30 days after the proposed determination has been published, any interested party may request in writing an oral hearing to present his views. The granting of such a hearing shall be at the discretion of the Secretary. Any such hearing shall be public and notice thereof shall be published at least 15 days in advance. A transcript of the hearing shall be made part of the public record.

(4) As soon as practicable following the conclusion of the proceedings described in paragraphs (b)(2) and (3) of this section, the Secretary shall either publish a final determination that a voluntary product standard will not be published, or he shall publish a notice withdrawing his proposed determination under paragraph (b)(1) of this section. In no event shall the withdrawal of a proposed determination operate to preclude the publication of another proposed determination under paragraph (b)(1) of this section with respect to the same or similar subject matter.

(c) *Determination that a published voluntary product standard has not been observed.* (1) Whenever the Secretary has reason to believe that a voluntary product standard published under these procedures is not being observed he shall initiate an inquiry to determine such fact.

(2) If, on the basis of the information developed during the inquiry, the Secretary concludes that the voluntary product standard is not being observed, he shall publish a proposed determination to this effect. The proposed determination shall identify the particular standard involved and shall be accompanied by a concise statement of the facts upon which it is based.

(3) Within 60 days after publication of the proposed determination, any interested party may submit in writing comments, data, arguments, views, or other information relevant to the proposed determination. All written submissions shall be made a part of the public record.

(4) Within 30 days after the proposed determination has been published, any interested party may request in writing an oral hearing to present his views. The granting of such a hearing shall be at the discretion of the Secretary. Any such hearing shall be public and notice thereof shall be published at least 15 days in advance. A transcript of the hearing shall be made part of the public record.

(5) As soon as practicable following the conclusion of the proceedings described in paragraphs (c)(3) and (4) of this section, and upon consideration of all relevant information, the Secretary shall either publish a final determination that the voluntary product standard is not being observed, or he shall publish a notice withdrawing his proposed determination under paragraph (c)(2) of this section. In no event shall the withdrawal of a proposed determination operate to preclude the initiation of another inquiry regarding the

same standard under paragraph (c)(1) of this section.

§ 12.4 Report to the Congress.

Whenever the Secretary publishes a final determination under § 12.3(b)(4) or § 12.3(c)(5), he shall promptly report such determination to the Congress with a statement of the efforts that have been made under the voluntary standards program and his recommendation as to whether Congress should enact legislation providing regulatory authority to deal with the situation in question.

PART 13—INTERGOVERNMENTAL REVIEW OF DEPARTMENT OF COMMERCE PROGRAMS AND ACTIVITIES

AUTHORITY: Executive Order 12372, July 14, 1982, 47 FR 30959, as amended April 8, 1983, 48 FR 15587, sec. 401, Intergovernmental Cooperation Act of 1968, as amended (31 U.S.C. 6506); sec. 204, Demonstration Cities and Metropolitan Development Act of 1966 as amended (42 U.S.C. 3334).

SOURCE: 48 FR 29134, June 24, 1983, unless otherwise noted.

§ 13.1 Purpose.

(a) The regulations in this part implement Executive Order 12372, "Intergovernmental Review of Federal Programs," issued July 14, 1982 and amended on April 8, 1983. These regulations also implement applicable provisions of section 401 of the Intergovernmental Cooperation Act of 1968 and section 204 of the Demonstration Cities and Metropolitan Development Act of 1966.

(b) These regulations are intended to foster an intergovernmental partnership and a strengthened Federalism by relying on state processes and on state, areawide, regional and local coordination for review of proposed Federal financial assistance and direct Federal development.

(c) These regulations are intended to aid the internal management of the Department, and are not intended to create any right or benefit enforceable at law by a party against the Department or its officers.

§ 13.2 Definitions.

Department means the U.S. Department of Commerce.

Order means Executive Order 12372, issued July 14, 1982, and amended April 8, 1983 and titled "Intergovernmental Review of Federal Programs."

Secretary means the Secretary of the U.S. Department of Commerce or an official or employee of the Department acting for the Secretary under a delegation of authority.

State means any of the 50 states, the District of Columbia, the Commonwealth of Puerto Rico, the Commonwealth of the Northern Mariana Islands, Guam, American Samoa, the U.S. Virgin Islands, or the Trust Territory of the Pacific Islands.

§ 13.3 Programs and activities of the Department subject to the regulations.

The Secretary publishes in the FEDERAL REGISTER a list of the Department's programs and activities that are subject to these regulations and identifies which of these are subject to the requirements of section 204 of the Demonstration Cities and Metropolitan Development Act.

§ 13.4 General responsibilities under the Order.

(a) The Secretary provides opportunities for consultation by elected officials of those state and local governments that would provide the non-Federal funds for, or that would be directly affected by, proposed Federal financial assistance from, or direct Federal development by, the Department.

(b) If a state adopts a process under the Order to review and coordinate proposed Federal financial assistance and direct Federal development, the Secretary, to the extent permitted by law:

(1) Uses the state process to determine official views of state and local elected officials;

(2) Communicates with state and local elected officials as early in a program planning cycle as is reasonably feasible to explain specific plans and actions;

(3) Makes efforts to accommodate state and local elected officials' concerns with proposed Federal financial assistance and direct Federal development that are communicated through the state process;

(4) Allows the states to simplify and consolidate existing federally required state plan submissions;

(5) Where state planning and budgeting systems are sufficient and where permitted by law, encourages the substitution of state plans for federally required state plans;

(6) Seeks the coordination of views of affected state and local elected officials in one state with those of another state when proposed Federal financial assistance or direct Federal development has an impact on interstate metropolitan urban centers or other interstate areas; and

(7) Supports state and local governments by discouraging the reauthorization or creation of any planning organization which is federally-funded, which has a limited purpose, and which is not adequately representative of, or accountable to, state or local elected officials.

§13.5 Obligations with respect to Federal interagency coordination.

The Secretary, to the extent practicable, consults with and seeks advice from all other substantially affected Federal departments and agencies in an effort to assure full coordination between such agencies and the Department regarding programs and activities covered under these regulations.

§13.6 State selection of programs and activities.

(a) A state may select any program or activity published in the FEDERAL REGISTER in accordance with §13.3 of this part for intergovernmental review under these regulations. Each state, before selecting programs and activities, shall consult with local elected officials.

(b) Each state that adopts a process shall notify the Secretary of the Department's programs and activities selected for that process.

(c) A state may notify the Secretary of changes in its selections at any time. For each change, the state shall submit to the Secretary an assurance that the state has consulted with elected local elected officials regarding the change. The Department may establish deadlines by which states are required to inform the Secretary of changes in their program selections.

(d) The Secretary uses a state's process as soon as feasible, depending on individual programs and activities, after the Secretary is notified of its selections.

§13.7 Communication with state and local officials concerning the Department's programs and activities.

(a) For those programs and activities covered by a state process under §13.6, the Secretary, to the extent permitted by law:

(1) Uses the state process to determine views of state and local elected officials; and,

(2) Communicates with state and local elected officials, through the state process, as early in a program planning cycle as is reasonably feasible to explain specific plans and actions.

(b) The Secretary provides notice to directly affected state, areawide, regional, and local entities in a state of proposed Federal financial assistance or direct Federal development if:

(1) The state has not adopted a process under the Order; or

(2) The assistance or development involves a program or activity not selected for the state process. This notice may be made by publication in the FEDERAL REGISTER or other appropriate means, which the Department in its discretion deems appropriate.

§ 13.8 Opportunity to comment on proposed Federal financial assistance and direct Federal development.

(a) Except in unusual circumstances, the Secretary gives state processes or directly affected state, areawide, regional and local officials and entities at least:

(1) 30 days from the date established by the Secretary to comment on proposed Federal financial assistance in the form of noncompeting continuation awards; and

(2) 60 days from the date established by the Secretary to comment on proposed direct Federal development or Federal financial assistance other than noncompeting continuation awards.

(b) This section also applies to comments in cases in which the review, coordination, and communication with the Department have been delegated.

(c) Applicants for programs and activities subject to section 204 of the Demonstration Cities and Metropolitan Act shall allow areawide agencies a 60-day opportunity for review and comment.

§ 13.9 Receipt of and response to comments.

(a) The Secretary follows the procedures in § 13.10 if:

(1) A state office or official is designated to act as a single point of contact between a state process and all Federal agencies; and

(2) That office or official transmits a state process recommendation for a program selected under § 13.6.

(b)(1) The single point of contact is not obligated to transmit comments from state, areawide, regional or local officials and entities where there is no state process recommendation.

(2) If a state process recommendation is transmitted by a single point of contact, all comments from state, areawide, regional, and local officials and entities that differ from it must also be transmitted.

(c) If a state has not established a process, or is unable to submit a state process recommendation, state, areawide, regional and local officials and entities may submit comments either to the applicant or to the Department.

(d) If a program or activity is not selected for a state process, state, areawide, regional and local officials and entities may submit comments either to the applicant or to the Department. In addition, if a state process recommendation for a nonselected program or activity is transmitted to the Department by the single point of contact, the Secretary follows the procedures of § 13.10 of this part.

(e) The Secretary considers comments which do not constitute a state process recommendation submitted under these regulations and for which the Secretary is not required to apply the procedures of § 13.10 of this part, when such comments are provided by a single point of contact, by the applicant, or directly to the Department by a commenting party.

§ 13.10 Accommodation of intergovernmental concerns.

(a) If a state process provides a state process recommendation to the Department through its single point of contact, the Secretary either:

(1) Accepts the recommendation;

(2) Reaches a mutually agreeable solution with the state process; or

(3) Provides the single point of contact with a written explanation of the decision in such form as the Secretary in his or her discretion deems appropriate. The Secretary may also supplement the written explanation by providing the explanation to the single point of contact by telephone, other telecommunication, or other means.

(b) In any explanation under paragraph (a)(3) of this section, the Secretary informs the single point of contact that:

(1) The Department will not implement its decision for at least ten days after the single point of contact receives the explanation; or

(2) The Secretary has reviewed the decision and determined that, because of unusual circumstances, the waiting period of at least ten days is not feasible.

(c) For purposes of computing the waiting period under paragraph (b)(1) of this section, a single point of contact is presumed to have received written notification 5 days after the date of mailing of such notification.

§ 13.11 Obligations in interstate situations.

(a) The Secretary is responsible for:

(1) Identifying proposed Federal financial assistance and direct Federal development that have an impact on interstate areas;

(2) Notifying appropriate officials and entities in states which have adopted a process and which select the Department's program or activity.

(3) Making efforts to identify and notify the affected state, areawide, regional, and local officials and entities in those states that have not adopted a process under the Order or do not select the Department's program or activity;

(4) Responding pursuant to § 13.10 of this part if the Secretary receives a recommendation from a designated areawide agency transmitted by a single point of contact, in cases in which the review, coordination, and communication with the Department have been delegated.

(b) The Secretary uses the procedures in § 13.10 if a state process provides a state process recommendation to the Department through a single point of contact.

PART 14—UNIFORM ADMINISTRATIVE REQUIREMENTS FOR GRANTS AND AGREEMENTS WITH INSTITUTIONS OF HIGHER EDUCATION, HOSPITALS, OTHER NON-PROFIT, AND COMMERCIAL ORGANIZATIONS

Subpart A—General

Subpart B—Pre-Award Requirements

Subpart C—Post-Award Requirements

FINANCIAL AND PROGRAM MANAGEMENT

PROPERTY STANDARDS

PROCUREMENT STANDARDS

REPORTS AND RECORDS

TERMINATION AND ENFORCEMENT

Subpart D—After-the-Award Requirements

AUTHORITY: 5 U.S.C. 301; OMB Circular A–110 (64 FR 54926, October 8, 1999).

SOURCE: 63 FR 47156, Sept. 4, 1998, unless otherwise noted.

EDITORIAL NOTE: Nomenclature changes to part 14 appear at 66 FR 49828, Oct. 1, 2001.

Subpart A—General

§ 14.1 Purpose.

This part establishes uniform administrative requirements for Department of Commerce (DoC) grants and agreements awarded to institutions of higher education, hospitals, other non-profit, and commercial organizations. The Grants Officer shall incorporate this part by reference into financial assistance awards made to organizations to which it will be applied. The DoC shall not impose additional or inconsistent requirements, except as provided in §§ 14.4, and 14.14 or unless specifically required by Federal statute or executive order. This part applies to grants and agreements awarded to foreign governments, organizations under the jurisdiction of foreign governments, and international organizations unless otherwise determined by the Grants Officer after coordination with the appropriate program officials. Uniform requirements for State, local, and tribal governments are in 15 CFR part 24, Uniform Administrative Requirements for Grants and Cooperative Agreements to State and Local Governments. Nonprofit organizations that implement Federal programs for the States are also subject to State requirements.

§ 14.2 Definitions.

(a) *Accrued expenditures* means the charges incurred by the recipient during a given period requiring the provision of funds for:

(1) Goods and other tangible property received;

(2) Services performed by employees, contractors, subrecipients, and other payees; and

(3) Other amounts becoming owed under programs for which no current services or performance is required.

(b) *Accrued income* means the sum of:

(1) Earnings during a given period from services performed by the recipient, and goods and other tangible property delivered to purchasers; and

(2) Amounts becoming owed to the recipient for which no current services or performance is required by the recipient.

(c) *Acquisition cost of equipment* means the net invoice price of the equipment, including the cost of modifications, attachments, accessories, or auxiliary apparatus necessary to make the property usable for the purpose for which it was acquired. Other charges, such as the cost of installation, transportation, taxes, duty or protective in-transit insurance, shall be included or excluded from the unit acquisition cost in accordance with the recipient's regular accounting practices.

(d) *Advance* means a payment made by electronic funds transfer, Treasury check, or other appropriate payment mechanism to a recipient upon its request either before outlays are made by the recipient or through the use of predetermined payment schedules.

(e) *Assistant Secretary* means the DoC Chief Financial Officer and Assistant Secretary for Administration who has been delegated by the Secretary of Commerce the responsibility for developing and implementing policies, standards, and procedures for the administration of financial assistance programs of the DoC.

(f) *Award* means financial assistance that provides support or stimulation to accomplish a public purpose. Awards include grants and other agreements in the form of money or property in lieu of money, by the Federal Government to an eligible recipient. The term does not include: technical assistance, which provides services instead of money; other assistance in the form of loans, loan guarantees, interest subsidies, or insurance; direct payments of any kind to individuals; and, contracts which are required to be entered into and administered under procurement laws and regulations.

(g) *Cash contributions* means the recipient's cash outlay, including the outlay of money contributed to the recipient by third parties.

(h) *Closeout* means the process by which the Grants Officer determines that all applicable administrative actions and all required work of the award have been completed by the recipient and the DoC.

(i) *Contract* means a procurement contract under an award or subaward, and a procurement subcontract under a recipient's or subrecipient's contract.

(j) *Cost sharing or matching* means that portion of project or program costs not borne by the Federal Government.

(k) *Date of completion* means the date on which all work under an award is completed or the date on the award document, or any supplement or amendment thereto, on which Federal sponsorship ends.

(l) *Disallowed costs* means those charges to an award that the Grants Officer determines to be unallowable, in accordance with the applicable Federal cost principles or other terms and conditions contained in the award.

(m) *DoC operating unit* means an organizational unit of the Department that has the authority to fund financial assistance awards.

(n) *Equipment* means tangible nonexpendable personal property including exempt property charged directly to the award having a useful life of more than one year and an acquisition cost of $5000 or more per unit. However, consistent with recipient policy, lower limits may be established.

(o) *Excess property* means property under the control of the DoC that, as determined by the Grants Officer after coordination with the authorized property official, is no longer required for DoC needs or the discharge of its responsibilities.

(p) *Exempt property* means tangible personal property acquired in whole or in part with Federal funds, where the DoC has statutory authority to vest title in the recipient without further obligation to the Federal Government. An example of exempt property authority is contained in the Federal Grant and Cooperative Agreement Act (31 U.S.C. 6306), for property acquired under an award to conduct basic or applied research by a non-profit institution of higher education or non-profit organization whose principal purpose is conducting scientific research.

(q) *Federal awarding agency* means the Federal agency that provides an award to the recipient.

(r) *Federal funds authorized* means the total amount of Federal funds obligated by the Federal Government for use by the recipient. This amount may include any authorized carryover of unobligated funds from prior funding periods when permitted by agency regulations or agency implementing instructions.

(s) *Federal share of real property, equipment, or supplies* means that percentage of the property's acquisition costs and any improvement expenditures paid with Federal funds.

(t) *Funding period* means the period of time when Federal funding is available for obligation by the recipient.

(u) *Grants Officer* means the DoC official with the delegated authority to award, amend, administer, closeout, suspend, and/or terminate grants and cooperative agreements and make related determinations and findings.

(v) *Intangible property and debt instruments* means, but is not limited to, trademarks, copyrights, patents and patent applications and such property as loans, notes and other debt instruments, lease agreements, stock and other instruments of property ownership, whether considered tangible or intangible.

(w) *Obligations* means the amounts of orders placed, contracts and grants awarded, services received and similar transactions during a given period that require payment by the recipient during the same or a future period.

(x) *Outlays or expenditures* means charges made to the project or program. They may be reported on a cash or accrual basis. For reports prepared on a cash basis, outlays are the sum of cash disbursements for direct charges for goods and services, the amount of indirect expense charged, the value of third party in-kind contributions applied and the amount of cash advances and payments made to subrecipients. For reports prepared on an accrual basis, outlays are the sum of cash disbursements for direct charges for goods and services, the amount of indirect expense incurred, the value of in-kind contributions applied, and the net increase (or decrease) in the amounts owed by the recipient for goods and other property received, for services performed by employees, contractors, subrecipients and other payees and other amounts becoming owed under programs for which no current services or performance are required.

(y) *Personal property* means property of any kind except real property. It may be tangible, having physical existence, or intangible, having no physical existence, such as copyrights, patents, or securities.

(z) *Prior approval* means written approval by an authorized official evidencing prior consent.

(aa) *Program income* means gross income earned by the recipient that is directly generated by a supported activity or earned as a result of the award (see exclusions in § 14.24 (e) and (h)). Program income includes, but is not limited to, income from fees for services performed, the use or rental of real or personal property acquired under federally-funded projects, the sale of commodities or items fabricated under an award, license fees and royalties on patents and copyrights, and interest on loans made with award funds. Interest earned on advances of Federal funds is not program income. Except as otherwise provided in DoC regulations or the terms and conditions of the award, program income does not include the receipt of principal on loans, rebates, credits, discounts, etc., or interest earned on any of them.

(bb) *Project costs* means all allowable costs, as set forth in the applicable Federal cost principles, incurred by a recipient and the value of the contributions made by third parties in accomplishing the objectives of the award during the project period.

(cc) *Project period* means the period established in the award document during which Federal sponsorship begins and ends.

(dd) *Property* means, unless otherwise stated, real property, equipment, intangible property and debt instruments.

(ee) *Real property* means land, including land improvements, structures and appurtenances thereto, but excludes movable machinery and equipment.

(ff) *Recipient* means an organization receiving financial assistance directly from the DoC to carry out a project or program. The term includes public and private institutions of higher education, public and private hospitals, and other quasi-public and private nonprofit organizations such as, but not limited to, community action agencies, research institutes, educational associations, and health centers. The term may include commercial organizations, foreign or international organizations (such as agencies of the United Nations) which are recipients, subrecipients, or contractors or subcontractors of recipients or subrecipients at the discretion of the DoC. The term does not include government-owned contractor-operated facilities or research centers providing continued support for mission-oriented, large-scale programs that are government-owned or controlled, or are designated as federally-funded research and development centers.

(gg) *Research and development* means all research activities, both basic and applied, and all development activities that are supported at universities, colleges, other non-profit, and commercial institutions. "Research" is defined as a systematic study directed toward fuller scientific knowledge or understanding of the subject studied. "Development" is the systematic use of knowledge and understanding gained from research directed toward the production of useful materials, devices, systems, or methods, including design and development of prototypes and processes. The term research also includes activities involving the training of individuals in research techniques where such activities utilize the same facilities as other research and development activities and where such activities are not included in the instruction function.

(hh) *Small awards* means a grant or cooperative agreement not exceeding the simplified acquisition threshold fixed at 41 U.S.C. 403(11) (currently $100,000).

(ii) *Subaward* means an award of financial assistance in the form of money, or property in lieu of money, made under an award by a recipient to an eligible subrecipient or by a subrecipient to a lower tier subrecipient. The term includes financial assistance when provided by any legal agreement, even if the agreement is called a contract, but does not include procurement of goods and services nor does it include any form of assistance which is excluded from the definition of "award" in paragraph (f) of this section.

(jj) *Subrecipient* means the legal entity to which a subaward is made and which is accountable to the recipient for the use of the funds provided. The term may include foreign or international organizations (such as agencies of the United Nations) at the discretion of the DoC.

(kk) *Supplies* means all personal property excluding equipment, intangible property, and debt instruments as defined in this section, and inventions of a contractor conceived or first actually reduced to practice in the performance of work under a funding agreement ("subject inventions"), as defined in 37 CFR part 401, "Rights to Inventions Made by Nonprofit Organizations and Small Business Firms Under Government Grants, Contracts, and Cooperative Agreements."

(ll) *Suspension* means an action taken by the Grants Officer after coordination with the DoC operating unit that temporarily withdraws Federal sponsorship under an award, pending corrective action by the recipient or pending a decision to terminate the award by the Grants Officer. Suspension of an award is a separate action from suspension under DoC regulations at 15 CFR part 26 implementing E.O.s 12549 and 12689, "Debarment and Suspension."

(mm) *Termination* means the cancellation by the Grants Officer of Federal sponsorship, in whole or in part, under an agreement at any time prior to the date of completion.

(nn) *Third party in kind contributions* means the value of non-cash contributions provided by non-Federal third parties. Third party in-kind contributions may be in the form of real property, equipment, supplies and other expendable property, and the value of goods and services directly benefiting and specifically identifiable to the project or program.

(oo) *Unliquidated obligations*, for financial reports prepared on a cash basis, means the amount of obligations incurred by the recipient that have not been paid. For reports prepared on an accrued expenditure basis, they represent the amount of obligations incurred by the recipient for which an outlay has not been recorded.

(pp) *Unobligated balance* means the portion of the funds authorized by the DoC that has not been obligated by the recipient and is determined by deducting the cumulative obligations from the cumulative funds authorized.

(qq) *Unrecovered indirect cost* means the difference between the amount awarded and the amount which could have been awarded under the recipient's approved negotiated indirect cost rate.

(rr) *Working capital advance* means a procedure whereby funds are advanced to the recipient to cover its estimated disbursement needs for a given initial period.

§ 14.3 Effect on other issuances.

For awards subject to this part, all administrative requirements of codified program regulations, program manuals, handbooks and other nonregulatory materials which are inconsistent with the requirements of this part shall be superseded, except to the extent they are required by statute, or authorized in accordance with the deviations provision in § 14.4.

§ 14.4 Deviations.

The Office of Management and Budget (OMB) may grant exceptions for classes of grants or recipients subject to the requirements of this part when exceptions are not prohibited by statute. However, in the interest of maximum uniformity, exceptions from the requirements of this part shall be permitted only in unusual circumstances. The Assistant Secretary may apply more restrictive requirements to a class of recipients when approved by OMB. The Assistant Secretary may apply less restrictive requirements when awarding small awards, except for those requirements which are statutory. Exceptions on a case-by-case basis may also be made by the Assistant Secretary. An exception made on a case-by-case basis will apply to a single award.

§ 14.5 Subawards.

Unless sections of this part specifically exclude subrecipients from coverage, the provisions of this part shall be applied to subrecipients performing work under awards if such subrecipients are institutions of higher education, hospitals, other non-profit, or commercial organizations. This part also applies to subrecipients performing work under awards if the subrecipients are foreign governments, organizations under the jurisdiction of foreign governments, and international organizations unless otherwise determined by the Grants Officer. State and local government subrecipients are subject to the provisions of regulations implementing the grants management common rule, "Uniform Administrative Requirements for Grants and Cooperative Agreements to State and Local Governments," (15 CFR part 24).

§ 14.6 Availability of OMB circulars.

OMB circulars cited in this part are available from the Office of Management and Budget (OMB) by writing to the Executive Office of the President, Publications Service, 725 17th Street, NW, Suite 200, Washington DC 20503.

Subpart B—Pre-Award Requirements

§ 14.10 Purpose.

Sections 14.11 through 14.18 prescribe forms and instructions and other preaward matters to be used in applying for Federal awards.

§ 14.11 Pre-award policies.

(a) *Use of grants and cooperative agreements, and contracts.* In each instance, the Grants Officer after coordination with the DoC operating unit shall decide on the appropriate award instrument (*i.e.*, grant, cooperative agreement, or contract). The Federal Grant and Cooperative Agreement Act (31 U.S.C. 6301–08) governs the use of grants, cooperative agreements and contracts. A grant or cooperative agreement shall be used only when the principal purpose of a transaction is to accomplish a public purpose of support or stimulation authorized by Federal statute. The statutory criterion for choosing between grants and cooperative agreements is that for the latter, "substantial involvement is expected between the executive agency and the State, local government, or other recipient when carrying out the activity contemplated in the agreement." Contracts shall be used when the principal purpose is acquisition of property or services for the direct benefit or use of the Federal Government.

(b) *Public notice and priority setting.* The DoC operating units shall notify the public of their intended funding priorities for discretionary grant programs, unless funding priorities are established by Federal statute. At a minimum, public notices shall be published in the FEDERAL REGISTER.

§ 14.12 Forms for applying for Federal assistance.

(a) The DoC operating units shall comply with the applicable report clearance requirements of 5 CFR part 1320, "Controlling Paperwork Burdens on the Public," with regard to all forms used by the DoC operating units in place of or as a supplement to the Standard Form 424 (SF–424) series.

(b) Applicants shall use the SF–424 series or those forms and instructions prescribed by the DoC.

(c) For Federal programs covered by E.O. 12372, "Intergovernmental Review of Federal Programs," the applicant shall complete the appropriate sections of the SF–424 (Application for Federal Assistance) indicating whether the application was subject to review by the State Single Point of Contact (SPOC). The name and address of the SPOC for a particular State can be obtained from the DoC or the *Catalog of Federal Domestic Assistance.* The SPOC shall advise the applicant whether the program for which application is made has been selected by that State for review.

(d) DoC operating units that do not use the SF–424 form should indicate whether the application is subject to review by the State under E.O. 12372.

§ 14.13 Debarment and suspension.

The DoC and recipients shall comply with the nonprocurement debarment and suspension common rule implementing E.O.s 12549 and 12689, "Debarment and Suspension," which is implemented by DoC at 2 CFR part 1326. This common rule restricts subawards and contracts with certain parties that are debarred, suspended or otherwise excluded from or ineligible for participation in Federal assistance programs or activities.

[63 FR 47156, Sept. 4, 1998, as amended at 71 FR 76575, Dec. 21, 2006]

§ 14.14 High risk special award conditions.

If an applicant or recipient: has a history of poor performance, is not financially stable, has a management system that does not meet the standards prescribed in this part, has not conformed to the terms and conditions of a previous award, or is not otherwise responsible, the Grants Officer may impose additional requirements as needed, provided that such applicant or recipient is notified in writing as to: the nature of the additional requirements, the reason why the additional requirements are being imposed, the nature of the corrective action needed, the time allowed for completing the corrective actions, and the method for requesting reconsideration of the additional requirements imposed. Any special conditions shall be promptly removed once the conditions that prompted them have been corrected.

§ 14.15 Metric system of measurement.

The Metric Conversion Act, as amended by the Omnibus Trade and Competitiveness Act (15 U.S.C. 205) declares that the metric system is the preferred measurement system for U.S. trade and commerce. The Act requires each Federal agency to establish a date or dates in consultation with the Secretary of Commerce, when the metric system of measurement will be used in the agency's procurements, grants, and other business-related activities. Metric implementation may take longer where the use of the system is initially impractical or likely to cause significant inefficiencies in the accomplishment of federally-funded activities. The DoC shall follow the provisions of E.O. 12770, "Metric Usage in Federal Government Programs."

§ 14.16 Resource Conservation and Recovery Act (RCRA).

Under RCRA (Pub. L. 94–580, 42 U.S.C. 6962), any State agency or agency of a political subdivision of a State which is using appropriated Federal funds must comply with section 6002. Section 6002 requires that preference be given in procurement programs to the purchase of specific products containing recycled materials identified in guidelines developed by the Environmental Protection Agency (EPA) (40 CFR parts 247–254). Accordingly, State and local institutions of higher education, hospitals, non-profit, and commercial organizations that receive direct Federal awards or other Federal funds shall give preference in their procurement programs funded with Federal funds to the purchase of recycled products pursuant to the EPA guidelines.

§ 14.17 Certifications and representations.

Unless prohibited by statute or codified regulation, Grants Officers may allow recipients to submit certifications and representations required by statute, executive order, or regulation on an annual basis, if the recipients have ongoing and continuing relationships with the agency. When authorized, annual certifications and representations shall be signed by responsible officials with the authority to ensure recipients' compliance with the pertinent requirements.

§ 14.18 Taxpayer identification number.

In accordance with the provisions of the Debt Collection Improvement Act of 1996 (31 U.S.C. 7701), the taxpayer identifying number will be required from applicants for grants and cooperative agreements funded by the DoC. This number may be used for purposes of collecting and reporting on any delinquent amounts arising from awards made under this part.

Subpart C—Post-Award Requirements

FINANCIAL AND PROGRAM MANAGEMENT

§ 14.20 Purpose of financial and program management.

Sections 14.21 through 14.28 prescribe standards for financial management systems, methods for making payments and rules for: satisfying cost sharing and matching requirements, accounting for program income, budget revision approvals, conducting audits, determining allowability of cost, and establishing fund availability.

§ 14.21 Standards for financial management systems.

(a) The Grants Officer shall require recipients to relate financial data to performance data and develop unit cost information whenever practical.

(b) Recipients' financial management systems shall provide for the following:

(1) Accurate, current and complete disclosure of the financial results of each federally-sponsored project or program in accordance with the reporting requirements set forth in § 14.52. If the Grants Officer requires reporting on an accrual basis from a recipient that maintains its records on other than an accrual basis, the recipient shall not be required to establish an accrual accounting system. These recipients may develop such accrual data for its reports on the basis of an analysis of the documentation on hand.

(2) Records that identify adequately the source and application of funds for federally-sponsored activities. These records shall contain information pertaining to Federal awards, authorizations, obligations, unobligated balances, assets, outlays, income and interest.

(3) Effective control over and accountability for all funds, property and other assets. Recipients shall adequately safeguard all such assets and assure they are used solely for authorized purposes.

(4) Comparison of outlays with budget amounts for each award. Whenever appropriate, financial information should be related to performance and unit cost data.

(5) Written procedures to minimize the time elapsing between the transfer of funds to the recipient from the U.S. Treasury and the issuance or redemption of checks, warrants or payments by other means for program purposes by the recipient. To the extent that the provisions of the Cash Management Improvement Act (CMIA) (Pub. L. 101–453) govern, payment methods of State agencies, instrumentalities, and fiscal agents shall be consistent with CMIA Treasury-State Agreements or the CMIA default procedures codified at 31 CFR part 205, "Withdrawal of Cash from the Treasury for Advances under Federal Grant and Other Programs."

(6) Written procedures for determining the reasonableness, allocability and allowability of costs in accordance with the provisions of the applicable Federal cost principles and the terms and conditions of the award.

(7) Accounting records including cost accounting records that are supported by source documentation.

(c) Where the DoC guarantees or insures the repayment of money borrowed by the recipient, the Grants Officer may require adequate bonding and insurance if the bonding and insurance requirements of the recipient are not deemed adequate to protect the interest of the Federal Government.

(d) The Grants Officer may require adequate fidelity bond coverage where the recipient lacks sufficient coverage to protect the Federal Government's interest.

(e) Where bonds are required in the situations described above, the bonds shall be obtained from companies holding certificates of authority as acceptable sureties, as prescribed in 31 CFR part 223, "Surety Companies Doing Business with the United States."

§ 14.22 Payment.

(a) Payment methods shall minimize the time elapsing between the transfer of funds from the United States Treasury and the issuance or redemption of checks, warrants, or payment by other means by the recipients. Payment methods of State agencies or instrumentalities shall be consistent with Treasury-State CMIA agreements or default procedures codified at 31 CFR part 205. Federal payments to recipients shall be made by electronic funds transfer in accordance with the Debt Collection Improvement Act of 1996, unless waived in accordance with the provisions of this Act.

(b) Recipients are to be paid in advance, provided they maintain or demonstrate the willingness to maintain: written procedures that minimize the time elapsing between the transfer of funds and disbursement by the recipient, and financial management systems that meet the standards for fund control and accountability as established in § 14.21. Advances of funds to a recipient organization shall be limited to the minimum amounts needed and be timed to be in accordance with the actual, immediate cash requirements of the recipient organization in carrying out the purpose of the approved program or project. The timing and amount of advances of funds shall be as close as is administratively feasible to the actual disbursements by the recipient organization for direct program or project costs and the proportionate share of any allowable indirect costs.

(c) Whenever possible, advances may be consolidated to cover anticipated cash needs for all awards made by the DoC operating unit to the recipient.

(1) Advance payment mechanisms include, but are not limited to, electronic funds transfer and Treasury check when the electronic funds transfer requirement is waived.

(2) Advance payment mechanisms are subject to 31 CFR part 205.

(3) Recipients may submit requests for advances and reimbursements on a monthly basis.

(d) Requests for advance payment shall be submitted on SF–270, "Request for Advance or Reimbursement," or other forms as may be authorized by OMB. This form is not to be used when advance payments are made to the recipient automatically through the use of a predetermined payment schedule or if precluded by special DoC instructions for electronic funds transfer.

(e) Reimbursement is the preferred method when the requirements in paragraph (b) of this section cannot be met. The Grants Officer may also use this method on any construction agreement, or if the major portion of the construction project is accomplished through private market financing or Federal loans, and the Federal assistance constitutes a minor portion of the project.

(1) When the reimbursement method is used, the DoC shall make payment within 30 days after receipt of the billing, unless the billing is improper.

(2) Recipients are authorized to submit request for reimbursement at least monthly when electronic funds transfers are not used.

(f) If a recipient cannot meet the criteria for advance payments and the Grants Officer after coordination with the operating unit has determined that reimbursement is not feasible because the recipient lacks sufficient working capital, the Grants Officer may authorize payment on a working capital advance basis. Under this procedure, the Grants Officer shall provide for advancing funds to the recipient to cover its estimated disbursement needs for an initial period generally geared to the awardee's disbursing cycle. Thereafter, payments shall be provided by reimbursing the recipient for its actual cash disbursements. The working capital advance method of payment shall not be used for recipients unwilling or unable to provide timely advances to their subrecipient to meet the subrecipient's actual cash disbursements.

(g) To the extent available, recipients shall disburse funds available from repayments to and interest earned on a revolving fund, program income, rebates, refunds, contract settlements, audit recoveries and interest earned on such funds before requesting additional payments.

(h) Unless otherwise required by statute, Grants Officers shall not withhold payments for proper charges made by recipients at any time during the project period unless paragraph (h) (1) or (2) of this section apply.

(1) A recipient has failed to comply with the project objectives, the terms and conditions of the award, or Federal reporting requirements.

(2) The recipient or subrecipient is delinquent in a debt to the United States as defined in OMB Circular A–129, "Managing Federal Credit Programs." Under such conditions, the Grants Officer may, upon reasonable notice, inform the recipient that payments shall not be made for obligations incurred after a specified date until the conditions are corrected or the indebtedness to the Federal Government is liquidated.

(i) Standards governing the use of banks and other institutions as depositories of funds advanced under awards are as follows.

(1) Except for situations described in paragraph (i)(2) of this section, the DoC shall not require separate depository

accounts for funds provided to a recipient or establish any eligibility requirements for depositories for funds provided to a recipient. However, recipients must be able to account for the receipt, obligation and expenditure of funds.

(2) Advances of Federal funds shall be deposited and maintained in insured accounts whenever possible.

(j) Consistent with the national goal of expanding the opportunities for women-owned and minority-owned business enterprises, recipients shall be encouraged to use women-owned and minority-owned banks (a bank which is owned at least 50 percent by women or minority group members).

(k) Recipients shall maintain advances of Federal funds in interest bearing accounts, unless paragraph (k) (1), (2) or (3) of this section apply.

(1) The recipient receives less than $120,000 in Federal awards per year.

(2) The best reasonably available interest bearing account would not be expected to earn interest in excess of $250 per year on Federal cash balances.

(3) The depository would require an average or minimum balance so high that it would not be feasible within the expected Federal and non-Federal cash resources.

(l) For those entities where CMIA and its implementing regulations do not apply, interest earned on Federal advances deposited in interest bearing accounts shall be remitted annually to Department of Health and Human Services, Payment Management System, Rockville, MD 20852. Interest amounts up to $250 per year may be retained by the recipient for administrative expense. State universities and hospitals shall comply with CMIA, as it pertains to interest. If an entity subject to CMIA uses its own funds to pay pre-award costs for discretionary awards without prior written approval from the Grants Officer, it waives its right to recover the interest under CMIA.

(m) Except as noted elsewhere in this part, only the following forms shall be authorized for the recipients in requesting advances and reimbursements. Grants Officers shall not require more than an original and two copies of these forms.

(1) SF–270, Request for Advance or Reimbursement. DoC has adopted the SF–270 as a standard form for all nonconstruction programs when predetermined advance methods are not used. The Grants Officer, however, may waive the requirement to use the SF–270 for requesting funds under grants and cooperative agreements. Grants Officers have the option of using this form for construction programs in lieu of the SF–271, "Outlay Report and Request for Reimbursement for Construction Programs."

(2) SF–271, Outlay Report and Request for Reimbursement for Construction Programs. DoC has adopted the SF–271 as the standard form to be used for requesting reimbursement for construction programs. However, the Grants Officer may substitute the SF–270 when the Grants Officer determines that the SF–270 provides adequate information to meet Federal needs.

§ 14.23 Cost sharing or matching.

(a) All contributions, including cash and third party in-kind, shall be accepted as part of the recipient's cost sharing or matching when such contributions meet all of the following criteria:

(1) Are verifiable from the recipient's records.

(2) Are not included as contributions for any other federally assisted project or program.

(3) Are necessary and reasonable for proper and efficient accomplishment of project or program objectives.

(4) Are allowable under the applicable cost principles.

(5) Are not paid by the Federal Government under another award, except where authorized by Federal statute to be used for cost sharing or matching.

(6) Are provided for in the approved budget.

(7) Conform to other provisions of this part, as applicable.

(b) Unrecovered indirect costs may be included as part of cost sharing or matching only with the prior approval of the Grants Officer.

(c) Values for recipient contributions of services and property shall be established in accordance with the applicable cost principles. If DoC authorizes recipients to donate buildings or land for construction/facilities acquisition projects or long-term use, the value of the donated property for cost sharing or matching shall be the lesser of paragraph (c) (1) or (2).

(1) The certified value of the remaining life of the property recorded in the recipient's accounting records at the time of donation.

(2) The current fair market value. However, when there is sufficient justification, the Grants Officer may approve the use of the current fair market value of the donated property, even if it exceeds the certified value at the time of donation to the project.

(d) Volunteer services furnished by professional and technical personnel, consultants, and other skilled and unskilled labor may be counted as cost sharing or matching if the service is an integral and necessary part of an approved project or program. Rates for volunteer services shall be consistent with those paid for similar work in the recipient's organization. In those instances in which the required skills are not found in the recipient organization, rates shall be consistent with those paid for similar work in the labor market in which the recipient competes for the kind of services involved. In either case, paid fringe benefits that are reasonable, allowable, and allocable may be included in the valuation.

(e) When an employer other than the recipient furnishes the services of an employee, these services shall be valued at the employee's regular rate of pay (plus an amount of fringe benefits that are reasonable, allowable, and allocable, but exclusive of overhead costs), provided these services are in the same skill for which the employee is normally paid.

(f) Donated supplies may include such items as expendable equipment, office supplies, laboratory supplies or workshop and classroom supplies. Value assessed to donated supplies included in the cost sharing or matching share shall be reasonable and shall not exceed the fair market value of the property at the time of the donation.

(g) The method used for determining cost sharing or matching for donated equipment, buildings and land for which title passes to the recipient may differ according to the purpose of the award, if paragraph (g) (1) or (2) of this section applies.

(1) If the purpose of the award is to assist the recipient in the acquisition of equipment, buildings or land, the total value of the donated property may be claimed as cost sharing or matching.

(2) If the purpose of the award is to support activities that require the use of equipment, buildings or land, normally only depreciation or use charges for equipment and buildings may be made. However, the full value of equipment or other capital assets and fair rental charges for land may be allowed, provided that the Grants Officer has approved the charges.

(h) The value of donated property shall be determined in accordance with the usual accounting policies of the recipient, with the following qualifications:

(1) The value of donated land and buildings shall not exceed its fair market value at the time of donation to the recipient as established by an independent appraiser (e.g., certified real property appraiser or General Services Administration representative) and certified by a responsible official of the recipient.

(2) The value of donated equipment shall not exceed the fair market value of equipment of the same age and condition at the time of donation.

(3) The value of donated space shall not exceed the fair rental value of comparable space as established by an independent appraisal of comparable space and facilities in a privately-owned building in the same locality.

(4) The value of loaned equipment shall not exceed its fair rental value.

(5) The following requirements pertain to the recipient's supporting records for in-kind contributions from third parties:

(i) Volunteer services shall be documented and, to the extent feasible, supported by the same methods used by the recipient for its own employees.

(ii) The basis for determining the valuation for personal service, material, equipment, buildings and land shall be documented.

§ 14.24 Program income.

(a) The standards set forth in this section shall apply in requiring recipient organizations to account for program income related to projects financed in whole or in part with Federal funds.

(b) Except as provided in paragraph (h) of this section, program income earned during the project period shall be retained by the recipient and, in accordance with DoC regulations or the terms and conditions of the award, shall be used in one or more of the ways listed in the following:

(1) Added to funds committed to the project by the DoC and recipient and used to further eligible project objectives.

(2) Used to finance the non-Federal share of the project.

(3) Deducted from the total project allowable cost in determining the net allowable costs on which the Federal share of costs is based.

(c) When an agency authorizes the disposition of program income as described in paragraph (b)(1) or (b)(2) of this section, program income in excess of any limits stipulated shall be used in accordance with paragraph (b)(3) of this section.

(d) In the event that the DoC does not specify in its regulations or the terms and conditions of the award how program income is to be used, paragraph (b)(1) of this section shall apply automatically to all projects or programs.

(e) Unless DoC regulations or the terms and conditions of the award provide otherwise, recipients shall have no obligation to the Federal Government regarding program income earned after the end of the project period.

(f) Costs incident to the generation of program income may be deducted from gross income to determine program income, provided these costs have not been charged to the award.

(g) Proceeds from the sale of property shall be handled in accordance with the requirements of the Property Standards (See §§ 14.30 through 14.37).

(h) Unless DoC regulations or the terms and conditions of the award provide otherwise, recipients shall have no obligation to the Federal Government with respect to program income earned from license fees and royalties for copyrighted material, patents, patent applications, trademarks, and inventions produced under an award. However, Patent and Trademark Amendments (35 U.S.C. 18) apply to inventions made under an experimental, developmental, or research award.

§ 14.25 Revision of budget and program plans.

(a) The budget plan is the financial expression of the project or program as approved during the award process. It may include either the Federal and non-Federal share, or only the Federal share, depending upon DoC requirements. It shall be related to performance for program evaluation purposes whenever appropriate.

(b) Recipients are required to report deviations from budget and program plans, and request prior approvals for budget and program plan revisions, in accordance with this section.

(c) For nonconstruction awards, recipients shall request prior approvals from the Grants Officer for one or more of the following program or budget related reasons. Approvals will be provided in writing by the Grants Officer.

(1) Change in the scope or the objective of the project or program (even if there is no associated budget revision requiring prior written approval).

(2) Change in a key person specified in the application or award document.

(3) The absence for more than three months, or a 25 percent reduction in time devoted to the project, by the approved project director or principal investigator.

(4) The need for additional Federal funding.

(5) The transfer of amounts budgeted for indirect costs to absorb increases in direct costs, or vice versa, if approval is required by the DoC.

(6) The inclusion, unless waived by the DoC, of costs that require prior approval in accordance with OMB Circular A–21, "Cost Principles for Educational Institutions," OMB Circular A–122, "Cost Principles for Non-Profit Organizations," 45 CFR part 74 Appendix E, "Principles for Determining Costs Applicable to Research and Development under Grants and Contracts with Hospitals," or 48 CFR part 31,

"Contract Cost Principles and Procedures," as applicable.

(7) The transfer of funds allotted for training allowances (direct payment to trainees) to other categories of expense.

(8) Unless described in the application and funded in the approved awards, the subaward, transfer or contracting out of any work under an award. This provision does not apply to the purchase of supplies, material, equipment or general support services.

(d) For nonconstruction awards, no other prior approval requirements for specific items may be imposed unless a deviation has been approved by OMB.

(e) Except for requirements listed in paragraphs (c)(1) and (c)(4) of this section, the Grants Officer may waive cost-related and administrative prior written approvals required by this part and OMB Circulars A–21 and A–122. Such waivers may include authorizing recipients to do any one or more of the following:

(1) Incur pre-award costs 90 calendar days prior to award or more than 90 calendar days with the prior approval of the Grants Officer after coordination with the DoC operating unit. All pre-award costs are incurred at the recipient's risk (*i.e.*, the DoC is under no obligation to reimburse such costs if for any reason the recipient does not receive an award or if the award is less than anticipated and inadequate to cover such costs).

(2) Initiate a one-time extension of the expiration date of the award of up to 12 months unless one or more of the following conditions apply. For one-time extensions, the recipient must notify the Grants Officer in writing with the supporting reasons and revised expiration date at least 10 days before the expiration date specified in the award. This one-time extension may not be exercised merely for the purpose of using unobligated balances.

(i) The terms and conditions of award prohibit the extension.

(ii) The extension requires additional Federal funds.

(iii) The extension involves any change in the approved objectives or scope of the project.

(3) Carry forward unobligated balances to subsequent funding periods.

(4) For awards that support research, unless the DoC provides otherwise in the award or in the DoC regulations, the prior approval requirements described in paragraph (e) of this section are automatically waived (*i.e.*, recipients need not obtain such prior approvals) unless one of the conditions included in paragraph (e)(2) of this section applies.

(f) The recipient may not transfer funds among direct cost categories or programs, functions and activities for awards in which the Federal share of the project exceeds $100,000 and the cumulative amount of such transfers exceeds or is expected to exceed 10 percent of the total Federal and non-Federal funds authorized by the Grants Officer. This does not prohibit the recipient from requesting Grants Officer approval for revisions to the budget. No transfers are permitted that would cause any Federal appropriation or part thereof to be used for purposes other than those consistent with the original intent of the appropriation.

(g) All other changes to nonconstruction budgets, except for the changes described in paragraph (j) of this section, do not require prior approval.

(h) For construction awards, recipients shall request prior written approval promptly from the Grants Officer for budget revisions whenever paragraph (h) (1), (2) or (3) apply. Approvals will be provided in writing by the Grants Officer.

(1) The revision results from changes in the scope or the objective of the project or program.

(2) The need arises for additional Federal funds to complete the project.

(3) A revision is desired which involves specific costs for which prior written approval requirements may be imposed consistent with applicable OMB cost principles listed in § 14.27.

(i) For construction awards, no other prior approval requirements for specific items may be imposed unless a deviation has been approved by OMB.

(j) When the DoC makes an award that provides support for both construction and nonconstruction work, the Grants Officer may require the recipient to request prior approval from the Grants Officer before making any fund or budget transfers between the two types of work supported. Approvals will be provided in writing by the Grants Officer.

(k) For both construction and non-construction awards, the DoC shall require recipients to notify the Grants Officer in writing promptly whenever the amount of Federal authorized funds is expected to exceed the needs of the recipient for the project period by more than $5000 or five percent of the Federal award, whichever is greater. This notification shall not be required if an application for additional funding is submitted for a continuation award.

(l) When requesting approval for budget revisions, recipients shall use the budget forms that were used in the application unless the Grants Officer indicates a letter of request suffices.

(m) Within 30 calendar days from the date of receipt of the request for budget revisions, DoC shall review the request and the Grants Officer shall notify the recipient in writing whether the budget revisions have been approved. If the revision is still under consideration at the end of 30 calendar days, the Grants Officer shall inform the recipient in writing of the date when the recipient may expect the decision.

[63 FR 47156, Sept. 4, 1998, as amended at 66 FR 49828, Oct. 1, 2001]

§ 14.26 Non-Federal audits.

(a) Recipients and subrecipients that are institutions of higher education or other non-profit organizations (including hospitals) shall be subject to the audit requirements contained in the Single Audit Act Amendments of 1996 (31 U.S.C. 7501–7507) and revised OMB Circular A–133, "Audits of States, Local Governments, and Non-Profit Organizations."

(b) State and local governments shall be subject to the audit requirements contained in the Single Audit Act Amendments of 1996 (31 U.S.C. 7501–7507) and revised OMB Circular A–133, "Audits of States, Local Governments, and Non-Profit Organizations."

(c) For-profit hospitals not covered by the audit provisions of revised OMB Circular A–133 shall be subject to the audit requirements as stipulated in the award document.

(d) Commercial and other organizations not covered by paragraph (a), (b), or (c) of this section shall be subject to the audit requirements as stipulated in the award document or the prime recipient as stipulated in the sub-award document.

§ 14.27 Allowable costs.

For each kind of recipient, there is a set of Federal principles for determining allowable costs. Allowability of costs shall be determined in accordance with the cost principles applicable to the entity incurring the costs. Thus, allowability of costs incurred by State, local or federally-recognized Indian tribal governments is determined in accordance with the provisions of OMB Circular A–87, "Cost Principles for State, Local and Indian Tribal Governments." The allowability of costs incurred by non-profit organizations is determined in accordance with the provisions of OMB Circular A–122, "Cost Principles for Non-Profit Organizations." The allowability of costs incurred by institutions of higher education is determined in accordance with the provisions of OMB Circular A–21, "Cost Principles for Educational Institutions." The allowability of costs incurred by hospitals is determined in accordance with the provisions of Appendix E of 45 CFR part 74, "Principles for Determining Costs Applicable to Research and Development Under Grants and Contracts with Hospitals." The allowability of costs incurred by commercial organizations and those non-profit organizations listed in Attachment C to Circular A–122 is determined in accordance with the provisions of the Federal Acquisition Regulation (FAR) at 48 CFR part 31.

§ 14.28 Period of availability of funds.

Where a funding period is specified, a recipient may charge to the grant only allowable costs resulting from obligations incurred during the funding period and any pre-award costs authorized by the Grants Officer.

PROPERTY STANDARDS

§ 14.30 Purpose of property standards.

Sections 14.31 through 14.37 set forth uniform standards governing management and disposition of property furnished by the Federal Government whose cost was charged to a project supported by a Federal award. The DoC shall require recipients to observe these standards under awards and shall not impose additional requirements, unless specifically required by Federal statute. The recipient may use its own property management standards and procedures provided it observes the provisions of §§ 14.31 through 14.37.

§ 14.31 Insurance coverage.

Recipients shall, at a minimum, provide the equivalent insurance coverage for real property and equipment acquired with Federal funds as provided to property owned by the recipient. Federally-owned property need not be insured unless required by the terms and conditions of the award.

§ 14.32 Real property.

The DoC award shall prescribe requirements for recipients concerning the use and disposition of real property acquired in whole or in part under awards. Unless otherwise provided by statute, such requirements, at a minimum, shall contain the following:

(a) Title to real property shall vest in the recipient subject to the condition that the recipient shall use the real property for the authorized purpose of the project as long as it is needed, provided that, in lieu of title, with the approval of the Grants Officer, the recipient may hold a leasehold or other interest in the property appropriate to the project purpose. The recipient shall not dispose of or encumber the property or any interest therein without approval of the Grants Officer.

(b) The recipient shall obtain written approval by the Grants Officer for the use of real property in other federally-sponsored projects when the recipient determines that the property is no longer needed for the purpose of the original project. Use in other projects shall be limited to those under federally-sponsored projects (*i.e.*, awards) or programs that have purposes consistent with those authorized for support by the DoC.

(c) When the real property is no longer needed as provided in paragraphs (a) and (b) of this section, the recipient shall request disposition instructions from the DoC or its successor Federal awarding agency. The responsible Federal agency shall observe one or more of the following disposition instructions:

(1) The recipient may be permitted to retain title without further obligation to the Federal Government after it compensates the Federal Government for that percentage of the current fair market value of the property attributable to the Federal participation in the project.

(2) The recipient may be directed to sell the property under guidelines provided by the Grants Officer and pay the Federal Government for that percentage of the current fair market value of the property attributable to the Federal participation in the project (after deducting actual and reasonable selling and fix-up expenses, if any, from the sales proceeds). When the recipient is authorized or required to sell the property, proper sales procedures shall be established that provide for competition to the extent practicable and result in the highest possible return.

(3) The recipient may be directed to transfer title to the property to the Federal Government or to an eligible third party provided that, in such cases, the recipient shall be entitled to compensation for its attributable percentage of the current fair market value of the property.

§ 14.33 Federally-owned and exempt property.

(a) *Federally-owned property.* (1) Title to federally-owned property remains vested in the Federal Government. Recipients shall submit annually an inventory listing of federally-owned property in their custody to the DoC operating unit. Upon completion of the award or when the property is no longer needed, the recipient shall report the property to the DoC operating unit for further Federal agency utilization.

(2) If the DoC operating unit has no further need for the property, it shall

be declared excess and reported to the General Services Administration, unless the DoC has statutory authority to dispose of the property by alternative methods (e.g., the authority provided by the Federal Technology Transfer Act (15 U.S.C. 3710(I)) to donate research equipment to educational and non-profit organizations in accordance with E.O. 12821, "Improving Mathematics and Science Education in Support of the National Education Goals.") Appropriate instructions shall be issued to the recipient by the Grants Officer.

(b) *Exempt property*. When statutory authority exists, the DoC has the option to vest title to property acquired with Federal funds in the recipient without further obligation to the Federal Government and under conditions the DoC considers appropriate. Such property is "exempt property." Should the DoC not establish conditions, title to exempt property upon acquisition shall vest in the recipient without further obligation to the Federal Government.

§ 14.34 Equipment.

(a) Title to equipment acquired by a recipient with Federal funds shall vest in the recipient, subject to conditions of this section.

(b) The recipient shall not use equipment acquired with Federal funds to provide services to non-Federal outside organizations for a fee that is less than private companies charge for equivalent services, unless specifically authorized by Federal statute, for as long as the Federal Government retains an interest in the equipment.

(c) The recipient shall use the equipment in the project or program for which it was acquired as long as needed, whether or not the project or program continues to be supported by Federal funds and shall not encumber the property without approval of the DoC. When no longer needed for the original project or program, the recipient shall use the equipment in connection with its other federally-sponsored activities, in the following order of priority:

(1) Activities sponsored by the DoC operating unit which funded the original project;

(2) Activities sponsored by other DoC operating units; then

(3) Activities sponsored by other Federal awarding agencies.

(d) During the time that equipment is used on the project or program for which it was acquired, the recipient shall make it available for use on other projects or programs if such other use will not interfere with the work on the project or program for which the equipment was originally acquired. First preference for such other use shall be given to other projects or programs sponsored by the DoC operating unit that financed the equipment; second preference shall be given to projects or programs sponsored by other DoC operating units, and third preference shall be given to projects or programs sponsored by other Federal awarding agencies. If the equipment is owned by the Federal Government, use on other activities not sponsored by the Federal Government shall be permissible if authorized by the Grants Officer after coordination with the DoC operating unit. User charges shall be treated as program income.

(e) When acquiring replacement equipment, the recipient may use the equipment to be replaced as trade-in or sell the equipment and use the proceeds to offset the costs of the replacement equipment subject to the approval of the Grants Officer after coordination with the DoC operating unit.

(f) The recipient's property management standards for equipment acquired with Federal funds and federally-owned equipment shall include all of the following:

(1) Equipment records shall be maintained accurately and shall include the following information:

(i) A description of the equipment.

(ii) Manufacturer's serial number, model number, Federal stock number, national stock number, or other identification number.

(iii) Source of the equipment, including the award number.

(iv) Whether title vests in the recipient or the Federal Government.

(v) Acquisition date (or date received, if the equipment was furnished by the Federal Government) and cost.

(vi) Information from which one can calculate the percentage of Federal participation in the cost of the equipment (not applicable to equipment furnished by the Federal Government).

(vii) Location and condition of the equipment and the date the information was reported.

(viii) Unit acquisition cost.

(ix) Ultimate disposition data, including date of disposal and sales price or the method used to determine current fair market value where a recipient compensates the DoC for its share.

(2) Equipment owned by the Federal Government shall be identified to indicate Federal ownership.

(3) A physical inventory of equipment shall be taken and the results reconciled with the equipment records at least once every two years. Any differences between quantities determined by the physical inspection and those shown in the accounting records shall be investigated to determine the causes of the difference. The recipient shall, in connection with the inventory, verify the existence, current utilization, and continued need for the equipment.

(4) A control system shall be in effect to insure adequate safeguards to prevent loss, damage, or theft of the equipment. Any loss, damage, or theft of equipment shall be investigated and fully documented; if the equipment was owned by the Federal Government, the recipient shall promptly notify the Grants Officer.

(5) Adequate maintenance procedures shall be implemented to keep the equipment in good condition.

(6) Where the recipient is authorized or required to sell the equipment, proper sales procedures shall be established which provide for competition to the extent practicable and result in the highest possible return.

(g) When the recipient no longer needs the equipment, the equipment may be used for other activities in accordance with the following standards. Equipment with a current per-unit fair market value of less than $5000 may be retained, sold, or otherwise disposed of with no further obligation to the awarding agency. For equipment with a current per unit fair market value of $5000 or more, the recipient may retain the equipment for other uses provided that compensation is made to the DoC operating unit or its successor. The amount of compensation shall be computed by applying the percentage of Federal participation in the cost of the original project or program to the current fair market value of the equipment. If the recipient has no need for the equipment, the recipient shall request disposition instructions from the Grants Officer. The Grants Officer shall determine whether the equipment can be used to meet the agency's requirements. If no requirement exists within that agency, the availability of the equipment shall be reported to the General Services Administration by the Grants Officer to determine whether a requirement for the equipment exists in other Federal agencies. The Grants Officer shall issue instructions to the recipient no later than 120 calendar days after the recipient's request and the following procedures shall govern:

(1) If so instructed or if disposition instructions are not issued within 120 calendar days after the recipient's request, the recipient shall sell the equipment and reimburse the DoC an amount computed by applying to the sales proceeds the percentage of Federal participation in the cost of the original project or program. However, the recipient shall be permitted to deduct and retain from the Federal share $500 or ten percent of the proceeds, whichever is less, for the recipient's selling and handling expenses.

(2) If the recipient is instructed to ship the equipment elsewhere, the recipient shall be reimbursed by the Federal Government by an amount which is computed by applying the percentage of the recipient's participation in the cost of the original project or program to the current fair market value of the equipment, plus any reasonable shipping or interim storage costs incurred.

(3) If the recipient is instructed to otherwise dispose of the equipment, the recipient shall be reimbursed by the DoC for such costs incurred in its disposition.

(h) The DoC reserves the right to transfer the title to the Federal Government or to a third party named by the Federal Government when such third party is otherwise eligible under existing statutes. Such transfer shall be subject to the following standards:

(1) The equipment shall be appropriately identified in the award or otherwise made known to the recipient in writing.

(2) The Grants Officer shall issue disposition instructions within 120 calendar days after receipt of a final inventory. The final inventory shall list all equipment acquired with grant funds and federally-owned equipment. If the Grants Officer fails to issue written disposition instructions within the 120 calendar day period, the recipient shall apply the standards of this section, as appropriate.

(3) When the DoC exercises its right to take title, the equipment shall be subject to the provisions for federally-owned equipment.

§ 14.35 Supplies and other expendable property.

(a) Title to supplies and other expendable property shall vest in the recipient upon acquisition. If there is a residual inventory of supplies exceeding $5000 in total aggregate value upon termination or completion of the project or program and the supplies are not needed for any other federally-sponsored project or program, the recipient shall retain the supplies for use on non-Federal sponsored activities or sell them, but shall, in either case, compensate the Federal Government for its share. The amount of compensation shall be computed in the same manner as for equipment.

(b) The recipient shall not use supplies acquired with Federal funds to provide services to non-Federal outside organizations for a fee that is less than private companies charge for equivalent services, unless specifically authorized by Federal statute as long as the Federal Government retains an interest in the supplies.

§ 14.36 Intangible property.

(a) The recipient may copyright any work that is subject to copyright and was developed, or for which ownership was purchased, under an award. The DoC reserves a royalty-free, nonexclusive and irrevocable right to reproduce, publish, or otherwise use the work for Federal purposes, and to authorize others to do so.

(b) Recipients are subject to applicable regulations governing patents and inventions, including government-wide regulations issued by the DoC at 37 CFR part 401, "Rights to Inventions Made by Nonprofit Organizations and Small Business Firms Under Government Grants, Contracts and Cooperative Agreements."

(c) The Federal Government has the right to:

(1) Obtain, reproduce, publish or otherwise use the data first produced under an award; and

(2) Authorize others to receive, reproduce, publish, or otherwise use such data for Federal purposes.

(d)(1) In addition, in response to a Freedom of Information Act (FOIA) request for research data relating to published research findings produced under an award that were used by the Federal Government in developing an agency action that has the force and effect of law, the DoC shall request, and the recipient shall provide, within a reasonable time, the research data so that they can be made available to the public through the procedures established under the FOIA. If the DoC obtains the research data solely in response to a FOIA request, the agency may charge the requester a reasonable fee equaling the full incremental cost of obtaining the research data. This fee should reflect costs incurred by the agency, the recipient, and applicable subrecipients. This fee is in addition to any fees the agency may assess under the FOIA (5 U.S.C. 552(a)(4)(A)).

(2) The following definitions apply for purposes of this paragraph (d):

(i) *Research data* is defined as the recorded factual material commonly accepted in the scientific community as necessary to validate research findings, but not any of the following: preliminary analyses, drafts of scientific papers, plans for future research, peer reviews, or communications with colleagues. This "recorded" material excludes physical objects (e.g., laboratory samples). *Research data* also do not include:

(A) Trade secrets, commercial information, materials necessary to be held confidential by a researcher until they are published, or similar information which is protected under law; and

(B) Personnel and medical information and similar information the disclosure of which would constitute a clearly unwarranted invasion of personal privacy, such as information that could be used to identify a particular person in a research study.

(ii) *Published* is defined as either when:

(A) Research findings are published in a peer-reviewed scientific or technical journal; or

(B) A Federal agency publicly and officially cites the research findings in support of an agency action that has the force and effect of law.

(iii) *Used by the Federal Government in developing an agency action that has the force and effect of law* is defined as when an agency publicly and officially cites the research findings in support of an agency action that has the force and effect of law.

(e) Title to intangible property and debt instruments acquired under an award or subaward vests upon acquisition in the recipient. The recipient shall use that property for the originally-authorized purpose, and the recipient shall not encumber the property without written approval from the Grants Officer. When no longer needed for the originally authorized purpose, disposition of the intangible property shall occur in accordance with the provisions of §14.34(g).

[63 FR 47156, Sept. 4, 1998, as amended at 65 FR 14407, 14409, Mar. 16, 2000]

§14.37 Property trust relationship.

Real property, equipment, intangible property and debt instruments that are acquired or improved with Federal funds shall be held in trust by the recipient as trustee for the beneficiaries of the project or program under which the property was acquired or improved. The Grants Officer may require recipients to record liens or other appropriate notices of record to indicate that personal or real property has been acquired or improved with Federal funds and that use and disposition conditions apply to the property.

Procurement Standards

§14.40 Purpose of procurement standards.

Sections 14.41 through 14.48 set forth standards for use by recipients in establishing procedures for the procurement of supplies and other expendable property, equipment, real property and other services with Federal funds. These standards are furnished to ensure that such materials and services are obtained in an effective manner and in compliance with the provisions of applicable Federal statutes and executive orders. No additional procurement standards or requirements shall be imposed by the DoC upon recipients, unless specifically required by Federal statute or executive order or approved by OMB.

§14.41 Recipient responsibilities.

The standards contained in this section do not relieve the recipient of the contractual responsibilities arising under its contract(s). The recipient is the responsible authority, without recourse to the DoC, regarding the settlement and satisfaction of all contractual and administrative issues arising out of procurements entered into in support of an award or other agreement. This includes disputes, claims, protests of award, source evaluation or other matters of a contractual nature. Matters concerning violation of statute are to be referred to such Federal, State or local authority as may have proper jurisdiction.

§14.42 Codes of conduct.

The recipient shall maintain written standards of conduct governing the performance of its employees engaged in the award and administration of contracts. No employee, officer, or agent shall participate in the selection, award, or administration of a contract supported by Federal funds if a real or apparent conflict of interest would be involved. Such a conflict would arise when the employee, officer, or agent, any member of his or her immediate family, his or her partner, or an organization which employs or is about to employ any of the parties indicated herein, has a financial or other interest in the firm selected for an award. The officers, employees, and agents of the recipient shall neither solicit nor accept gratuities, favors, or anything of monetary value from contractors, or parties to subagreements. However, recipients may set standards for situations in which the financial interest is not substantial or the gift is an unsolicited item of nominal value. The standards of conduct shall provide for disciplinary actions to be applied for violations of such standards by officers, employees, or agents of the recipient.

§ 14.43 Competition.

All procurement transactions shall be conducted in a manner to provide, to the maximum extent practical, open and free competition. The recipient shall be alert to organizational conflicts of interest as well as noncompetitive practices among contractors that may restrict or eliminate competition or otherwise restrain trade. In order to ensure objective contractor performance and eliminate unfair competitive advantage, contractors that develop or draft specifications, requirements, statements of work, invitations for bids and/or requests for proposals shall be excluded from competing for such procurements. Awards shall be made to the bidder or offeror whose bid or offer is responsive to the solicitation and is most advantageous to the recipient, price, quality and other factors considered. Solicitations shall clearly set forth all requirements that the bidder or offeror shall fulfill in order for the bid or offer to be evaluated by the recipient. Any and all bids or offers may be rejected when it is in the recipient's interest to do so.

§ 14.44 Procurement procedures.

(a) All recipients shall establish written procurement procedures. These procedures shall provide for, at a minimum, that:

(1) Recipients avoid purchasing unnecessary items;

(2) Where appropriate, an analysis is made of lease and purchase alternatives to determine which would be the most economical and practical procurement for the Federal Government; and

(3) Solicitations for goods and services provide for all of the following:

(i) A clear and accurate description of the technical requirements for the material, product or service to be procured. In competitive procurements, such a description shall not contain features which unduly restrict competition.

(ii) Requirements which the bidder/offeror must fulfill and all other factors to be used in evaluating bids or proposals.

(iii) A description, whenever practicable, of technical requirements in terms of functions to be performed or performance required, including the range of acceptable characteristics or minimum acceptable standards.

(iv) The specific features of "brand name or equal" descriptions that bidders are required to meet when such items are included in the solicitation.

(v) The acceptance, to the extent practicable and economically feasible, of products and services dimensioned in the metric system of measurement.

(vi) Preference, to the extent practicable and economically feasible, for products and services that conserve natural resources and protect the environment and are energy efficient.

(b) Positive efforts shall be made by recipients to utilize small businesses, minority-owned firms, and women's business enterprises, whenever possible. Recipients of Federal awards shall take all of the following steps to further this goal:

(1) Ensure that small businesses, minority-owned firms, and women's business enterprises are used to the fullest extent practicable.

(2) Make information on forthcoming opportunities available and arrange time frames for purchases and contracts to encourage and facilitate participation by small businesses, minority-owned firms, and women's business enterprises.

(3) Consider in the contract process whether firms competing for larger contracts intend to subcontract with small businesses, minority-owned firms, and women's business enterprises.

(4) Encourage contracting with consortiums of small businesses, minority-

owned firms and women's business enterprises when a contract is too large for one of these firms to handle individually.

(5) Use the services and assistance, as appropriate, of such organizations as the Small Business Administration and the DoC's Minority Business Development Agency in the solicitation and utilization of small businesses, minority-owned firms and women's business enterprises.

(c) The type of procuring instruments used (e.g., fixed price contracts, cost reimbursable contracts, purchase orders, and incentive contracts) shall be determined by the recipient but shall be appropriate for the particular procurement and for promoting the best interest of the program or project involved. The "cost-plus-a-percentage-of-cost" or "percentage of construction cost" methods of contracting shall not be used.

(d) Contracts shall be made only with responsible contractors who possess the potential ability to perform successfully under the terms and conditions of the proposed procurement. Consideration shall be given to such matters as contractor integrity, record of past performance, financial and technical resources or accessibility to other necessary resources. In certain circumstances, contracts with certain parties are restricted by agencies' implementation of E.O.s 12549 and 12689, "Debarment and Suspension," as implemented by DoC regulations at 15 CFR part 26.

(e) Recipients shall, on request, make available for the Grants Officer, pre-award review and procurement documents, such as request for proposals or invitations for bids, independent cost estimates, etc., when any of the following conditions apply:

(1) A recipient's procurement procedures or operation fails to comply with the procurement standards in this part.

(2) The procurement is expected to exceed the simplified acquisition threshold fixed at 41 U.S.C. 403 (11) (currently $100,000) and is to be awarded without competition or only one bid or offer is received in response to a solicitation.

(3) The procurement, which is expected to exceed the simplified acquisition threshold, specifies a "brand name" product.

(4) The proposed award over the simplified acquisition threshold is to be awarded to other than the apparent low bidder under a sealed bid procurement.

(5) A proposed contract modification changes the scope of a contract or increases the contract amount by more than the amount of the simplified acquisition threshold.

§ 14.45 Cost and price analysis.

Some form of cost or price analysis shall be made and documented in the procurement files in connection with every procurement action. Price analysis may be accomplished in various ways, including the comparison of price quotations submitted, market prices and similar indicia, together with discounts. Cost analysis is the review and evaluation of each element of cost to determine reasonableness, allocability and allowability.

§ 14.46 Procurement records.

Procurement records and files for purchases in excess of the simplified acquisition threshold shall include the following at a minimum:

(a) Basis for contractor selection;

(b) Justification for lack of competition when competitive bids or offers are not obtained; and

(c) Basis for award cost or price.

§ 14.47 Contract administration.

A system for contract administration shall be maintained to ensure contractor conformance with the terms, conditions and specifications of the contract and to ensure adequate and timely follow up of all purchases. Recipients shall evaluate contractor performance and document, as appropriate, whether contractors have met the terms, conditions and specifications of the contract.

§ 14.48 Contract provisions.

The recipient shall include, in addition to provisions to define a sound and complete agreement, the following provisions in all contracts. The following provisions shall also be applied to subcontracts:

(a) Contracts in excess of the simplified acquisition threshold shall contain contractual provisions or conditions that allow for administrative, contractual, or legal remedies in instances in which a contractor violates or breaches the contract terms, and provide for such remedial actions as may be appropriate.

(b) All contracts in excess of the simplified acquisition threshold shall contain suitable provisions for termination by the recipient, including the manner by which termination shall be effected and the basis for settlement. In addition, such contracts shall describe conditions under which the contract may be terminated for default as well as conditions where the contract may be terminated because of circumstances beyond the control of the contractor.

(c) Except as otherwise required by statute, an award that requires the contracting (or subcontracting) for construction or facility improvements shall provide for the recipient to follow its own requirements relating to bid guarantees, performance bonds, and payment bonds unless the construction contract or subcontract exceeds $100,000. For those contracts or subcontracts exceeding $100,000, the DoC may accept the bonding policy and requirements of the recipient, provided the Grants Officer has made a determination that the Federal Government's interest is adequately protected. If such a determination has not been made, the minimum requirements shall be as follows:

(1) A bid guarantee from each bidder equivalent to five percent of the bid price. The "bid guarantee" shall consist of a firm commitment such as a bid bond, certified check, or other negotiable instrument accompanying a bid as assurance that the bidder shall, upon acceptance of his bid, execute such contractual documents as may be required within the time specified.

(2) A performance bond on the part of the contractor for 100 percent of the contract price. A "performance bond" is one executed in connection with a contract to secure fulfillment of all the contractor's obligations under such contract.

(3) A payment bond on the part of the contractor for 100 percent of the contract price. A "payment bond" is one executed in connection with a contract to assure payment as required by statute of all persons supplying labor and material in the execution of the work provided for in the contract.

(4) Where bonds are required in the situations described in this part, the bonds shall be obtained from companies holding certificates of authority as acceptable sureties pursuant to 31 CFR part 223, "Surety Companies Doing Business with the United States."

(d) All negotiated contracts (except those for less than the simplified acquisition threshold) awarded by recipients shall include a provision to the effect that the recipient, the DoC, the Comptroller General of the United States, or any of their duly authorized representatives, shall have access to any books, documents, papers and records of the contractor which are directly pertinent to a specific program for the purpose of making audits, examinations, excerpts and transcriptions.

(e) All contracts, including small purchases, awarded by recipients and their contractors shall contain the procurement provisions of Appendix A to this part, as applicable.

REPORTS AND RECORDS

§ 14.50 Purpose of reports and records.

Sections 14.51 through 14.53 set forth the procedures for monitoring and reporting on the recipient's financial and program performance and the necessary standard reporting forms. They also set forth record retention requirements.

§ 14.51 Monitoring and reporting program performance.

(a) Recipients are responsible for managing and monitoring each project, program, subaward, function or activity supported by the award. Recipients shall monitor subawards to ensure subrecipients have met the audit requirements as delineated in § 14.26.

(b) The Grants Officer after coordination with the DoC operating unit shall prescribe the frequency with which the performance reports shall be submitted. Except as provided in paragraph (f) of this section, performance reports shall not be required more frequently than quarterly or, less frequently than annually. Annual reports shall be due 90 calendar days after the grant year; quarterly or semi-annual reports shall be due 30 days after the reporting period. The Grants Officer may require annual reports before the anniversary dates of multiple year awards in lieu of these requirements. The final performance reports are due 90 calendar days after the expiration or termination of the award.

(c) If inappropriate, a final technical or performance report shall not be required after completion of the project.

(d) When required, performance reports shall generally contain, for each award, brief information on each of the following:

(1) A comparison of actual accomplishments with the goals and objectives established for the period, the findings of the investigator, or both. Whenever appropriate and the output of programs or projects can be readily quantified, such quantitative data should be related to cost data for computation of unit costs.

(2) Reasons why established goals were not met, if appropriate.

(3) Other pertinent information including, when appropriate, analysis and explanation of cost overruns or high unit costs.

(e) Recipients shall not be required to submit more than the original and two copies of performance reports.

(f) Recipients shall immediately notify the DoC operating unit of developments that have a significant impact on the award-supported activities. Also, notification shall be given in the case of problems, delays, or adverse conditions which materially impair the ability to meet the objectives of the award. This notification shall include a statement of the action taken or contemplated, and any assistance needed to resolve the situation.

(g) The DoC may make site visits, as needed.

(h) Federal awarding agencies shall comply with clearance requirements of 5 CFR part 1320 when requesting performance data from recipients.

§ 14.52 Financial reporting.

(a) The following forms or such other forms as may be approved by OMB are authorized for obtaining financial information from recipients:

(1) SF-269 or SF-269A, Financial Status Report.

(i) Each DoC award shall require recipients to use the SF-269 or SF-269A to report the status of funds for all nonconstruction projects or programs. The DoC, however, has the option of not requiring the SF-269 or SF-269A when the SF-270, Request for Advance or Reimbursement, or SF-272, Report of Federal Cash Transactions, is determined to provide adequate information to meet its needs, except that a final SF-269 or SF-269A shall be required at the completion of the project when the SF-270 is used only for advances.

(ii) The DoC shall prescribe whether the report shall be on a cash or accrual basis. If the DoC requires accrual information and the recipient's accounting records are not normally kept on the accrual basis, the recipient shall not be required to convert its accounting system, but shall develop such accrual information through best estimates based on an analysis of the documentation on hand.

(iii) The DoC shall determine the frequency of the Financial Status Report for each project or program, considering the size and complexity of the particular project or program. However, the report shall not be required more frequently than quarterly or less frequently than annually. A final report shall be required at the completion of the agreement.

(iv) The DoC shall require recipients to submit the SF-269 or SF-269A (an original and no more than two copies) no later than 30 days after the end of each specified reporting period for quarterly and semi-annual reports, and 90 calendar days for annual and final reports. Extensions of reporting due dates may be approved by the Grants Officer upon request of the recipient.

(2) SF-272, Report of Federal Cash Transactions.

(i) When funds are advanced to recipients the DoC shall require each recipient to submit the SF-272 and, when necessary, its continuation sheet, SF-272a. The DoC shall use this report to monitor funds advanced to recipients and to obtain disbursement information for each agreement with the recipients.

(ii) The DoC may require forecasts of Federal funds requirements in the "Remarks" section of the report.

(iii) When practical and deemed necessary, the DoC may require recipients to report in the "Remarks" section the amount of advances received in excess of three days. Recipients shall provide short narrative explanations of actions taken to reduce the excess balances.

(iv) Recipients shall be required to submit not more than the original and two copies of the SF–272 15 calendar days following the end of each quarter. The Grants Officer may require a monthly report from those recipients receiving advances totaling $1 million or more per year.

(v) The Grants Officer may waive the requirement for submission of the SF–272 for any one of the following reasons:

(A) When monthly advances do not exceed $25,000 per recipient, provided that such advances are monitored through other forms contained in this section;

(B) If, in the Grants Officer's opinion, the recipient's accounting controls are adequate to minimize excessive Federal advances; or

(C) When the electronic payment mechanisms provide adequate data.

(b) When the DoC needs additional information or more frequent reports, the following shall be observed:

(1) When additional information is needed to comply with legislative requirements, the Grants Officer shall issue instructions to require recipients to submit such information under the "Remarks" section of the reports.

(2) When the DoC determines that a recipient's accounting system does not meet the standards in § 14.21, additional pertinent information to further monitor awards may be obtained upon written notice to the recipient until such time as the system is brought up to standard. The DoC, in obtaining this information, shall comply with report clearance requirements of 5 CFR part 1320.

(3) Grants Officers are encouraged to shade out any line item on any report if not necessary.

(4) The DoC may accept the identical information from the recipients in machine readable format or computer printouts or electronic outputs in lieu of prescribed formats.

(5) The DoC may provide computer or electronic outputs to recipients when such expedites or contributes to the accuracy of reporting.

§ 14.53 Retention and access requirements for records.

(a) This section sets forth requirements for record retention and access to records for awards to recipients. The DoC shall not impose any other record retention or access requirements upon recipients.

(b) Financial records, supporting documents, statistical records, and all other records pertinent to an award shall be retained for a period of three years from the date of submission of the final expenditure report or, for awards that are renewed quarterly or annually, from the date of the submission of the quarterly or annual financial report, as authorized by the DoC. The only exceptions are the following:

(1) If any litigation, claim, or audit is started before the expiration of the 3-year period, the records shall be retained until all litigation, claims or audit findings involving the records have been resolved and final action taken.

(2) Records for real property and equipment acquired with Federal funds shall be retained for 3 years after final disposition.

(3) When records are transferred to or maintained by the DoC, the 3-year retention requirement is not applicable to the recipient.

(4) Indirect cost rate proposals, cost allocations plans, etc. as specified in paragraph (g) of this section.

(c) Copies of original records may be substituted for the original records if authorized by the DoC.

(d) The Grants Officer after coordination with the DoC operating unit shall request transfer of certain records to its custody from recipients when it determines that the records possess long term retention value. However, in order to avoid duplicate recordkeeping, a DoC operating unit or Grants Officer may make arrangements for recipients to retain any records that are continuously needed for joint use.

(e) The DoC, the Inspector General, Comptroller General of the United States, or any of their duly authorized representatives, have the right of timely and unrestricted access to any books, documents, papers, or other records of recipients that are pertinent to the awards, in order to make audits, examinations, excerpts, transcripts and copies of such documents. This right also includes timely and reasonable access to a recipient's personnel for the purpose of interview and discussion related to such documents. The rights of access in this paragraph are not limited to the required retention period, but shall last as long as records are retained.

(f) Unless required by statute, no DoC operating unit shall place restrictions on recipients that limit public access to the records of recipients that are pertinent to an award, except when the DoC operating unit can demonstrate that such records shall be kept confidential and would have been exempted from disclosure pursuant to the Freedom of Information Act (5 U.S.C. 552) if the records had belonged to the DoC operating unit.

(g) Paragraphs (g)(1) and (g)(2) of this section apply to the following types of documents, and their supporting records: indirect cost rate computations or proposals, cost allocation plans, and any similar accounting computations of the rate at which a particular group of costs is chargeable (such as computer usage chargeback rates or composite fringe benefit rates).

(1) If the recipient submits to the Federal awarding agency responsible for negotiating the recipient's indirect cost rate or the subrecipient submits to the recipient the proposal, plan, or other computation to form the basis for negotiation of the rate, then the 3-year retention period for its supporting records starts on the date of such submission.

(2) If the recipient is not required to submit to the cognizant Federal awarding agency or the subrecipient is not required to submit to the recipient the proposal, plan, or other computation for negotiation purposes, then the 3-year retention period for the proposal, plan, or other computation and its supporting records starts at the end of the fiscal year (or other accounting period) covered by the proposal, plan, or other computation.

TERMINATION AND ENFORCEMENT

§ 14.60 Purpose of termination and enforcement.

Sections 14.61 and 14.62 set forth uniform suspension, termination and enforcement procedures.

§ 14.61 Termination.

(a) Awards may be terminated in whole or in part only if paragraph (a)(1), (2) or (3) apply.

(1) By the Grants Officer, if a recipient materially fails to comply with the terms and conditions of an award.

(2) By the Grants Officer with the consent of the recipient, in which case the two parties shall agree upon the termination conditions, including the effective date and, in the case of partial termination, the portion to be terminated.

(3) By the recipient upon sending to the Grants Officer written notification setting forth the reasons for such termination, the effective date, and, in the case of partial termination, the portion to be terminated. However, if the Grants Officer determines in the case of partial termination that the reduced or modified portion of the grant will not accomplish the purposes for which the grant was made, it may terminate the grant in its entirety under either paragraph (a)(1) or (2).

(b) If costs are allowed under an award, the responsibilities of the recipient referred to in § 14.71(a), including those for property management as applicable, shall be considered in the termination of the award, and provision shall be made for continuing responsibilities of the recipient after termination, as appropriate.

§ 14.62 Enforcement.

(a) *Remedies for noncompliance.* If a recipient materially fails to comply with the terms and conditions of an award, whether stated in a Federal statute, regulation, assurance, application, or notice of award, the Grants Officer may, in addition to imposing any of the special conditions outlined in § 14.14, take one or more of the following actions, as appropriate in the circumstances:

(1) Temporarily withhold payments of funds pending correction of the deficiency by the recipient or more severe enforcement action by the Grants Officer after coordination with the DoC operating unit.

(2) Disallow (that is, deny both use of funds and any applicable matching credit for) all or part of the cost of the activity or action not in compliance.

(3) Wholly or partly suspend or terminate the current award.

(4) Withhold further awards for the project or program.

(5) Take other remedies that may be legally available.

(b) *Hearings and appeals.* In taking an enforcement action, the awarding agency shall provide the recipient an opportunity for hearing, appeal, or other administrative proceeding to which the recipient is entitled under any statute or regulation applicable to the action involved.

(c) *Effects of suspension and termination.* Costs of a recipient resulting from obligations incurred by the recipient during a suspension or after termination of an award are not allowable unless the awarding agency expressly authorizes them in the notice of suspension or termination or subsequently. Other recipient costs during suspension or after termination which are necessary and not reasonably avoidable are allowable if paragraphs (c) (1) and (2) of this section apply.

(1) The costs result from obligations which were properly incurred by the recipient before the effective date of suspension or termination, are not in anticipation of it, and in the case of a termination, are noncancellable.

(2) The costs would be allowable if the award were not suspended or expired normally at the end of the funding period in which the termination takes effect.

(d) *Relationship to debarment and suspension.* The enforcement remedies identified in this section, including suspension and termination, do not preclude a recipient from being subject to debarment and suspension under E.O.s 12549 and 12689 and the DoC implementing regulations (see § 14.13) at 15 CFR part 26.

Subpart D—After-the-Award Requirements

§ 14.70 Purpose.

Sections 14.71 through 14.73 contain closeout procedures and other procedures for subsequent disallowances and adjustments.

§ 14.71 Closeout procedures.

(a) Recipients shall submit, within 90 calendar days after the date of completion of the award, all financial, performance, and other reports as required by the terms and conditions of the award. The Grants Officer may approve extensions when requested by the recipient.

(b) Unless the Grants Officer authorizes an extension, a recipient shall liquidate all obligations incurred under the award not later than 90 calendar days after the funding period or the date of completion as specified in the terms and conditions of the award or in agency implementing instructions.

(c) The Grants Officer shall authorize and the DoC shall make prompt payments to a recipient for allowable reimbursable costs under the award being closed out.

(d) The recipient shall promptly refund any balances of unobligated funds that the DoC has advanced or paid and that is not authorized to be retained by the recipient for use in other projects. OMB Circular A–129 governs unreturned amounts that become delinquent debts.

(e) When authorized by the terms and conditions of the award, the Grants Officer shall make a settlement for any upward or downward adjustments to the Federal share of costs after closeout reports are received.

(f) The recipient shall account for any real and personal property acquired with Federal funds or received from the Federal Government in accordance with §§ 14.31 through 14.37.

(g) In the event a final audit has not been performed prior to the closeout of an award, the DoC shall retain the right to recover an appropriate amount after fully considering the recommendations on disallowed costs resulting from the final audit.

§ 14.72 Subsequent adjustments and continuing responsibilities.

(a) The closeout of an award does not affect any of the following:

(1) The right of the DoC to disallow costs and recover funds on the basis of a later audit or other review.

(2) The obligation of the recipient to return any funds due as a result of later refunds, corrections, or other transactions.

(3) Audit requirements in § 14.26.

(4) Property management requirements in §§ 14.31 through 14.37.

(5) Records retention as required in § 14.53.

(b) After closeout of an award, a relationship created under an award may be modified or ended in whole or in part with the consent of the DoC and the recipient, provided the responsibilities of the recipient referred to in § 14.73(a), including those for property management as applicable, are considered and provisions made for continuing responsibilities of the recipient, as appropriate.

§ 14.73 Collection of amounts due.

(a) Any funds paid to a recipient in excess of the amount to which the recipient is finally determined to be entitled under the terms and conditions of the award constitute a debt to the Federal Government. If not paid within a reasonable period after the demand for payment, the Grants Officer may reduce the debt by:

(1) Making an administrative offset against other requests for reimbursements;

(2) Withholding advance payments otherwise due to the recipient; or

(3) Taking other action permitted by statute.

(b) Except as otherwise provided by law, the DoC shall charge interest on an overdue debt in accordance with 4 CFR Chapter II, "Federal Claims Collection Standards."

Appendix A to Part 14—Contract Provisions

All contracts, awarded by a recipient including small purchases, shall contain the following provisions as applicable:

1. *Equal Employment Opportunity*—All contracts shall contain a provision requiring compliance with E.O. 11246, "Equal Employment Opportunity," as amended by E.O. 11375, "Amending Executive Order 11246 Relating to Equal Employment Opportunity," and as supplemented by regulations at 41 CFR part 60, "Office of Federal Contract Compliance Programs, Equal Employment Opportunity, Department of Labor."

2. *Copeland "Anti-Kickback" Act (18 U.S.C. 874 and 40 U.S.C. 276c)*—All contracts and subgrants in excess of $2000 for construction or repair awarded by recipients and subrecipients shall include a provision for compliance with the Copeland "Anti-Kickback" Act (18 U.S.C. 874), as supplemented by Department of Labor regulations (29 CFR part 3, "Contractors and Subcontractors on Public Building or Public Work Financed in Whole or in Part by Loans or Grants from the United States"). The Act provides that each contractor or subrecipient shall be prohibited from inducing, by any means, any person employed in the construction, completion, or repair of public work, to give up any part of the compensation to which he is otherwise entitled. The recipient shall report all suspected or reported violations to the DoC operating unit.

3. *Davis-Bacon Act, as amended (40 U.S.C. 276a to a–7)*—When required by Federal program legislation, all construction contracts awarded by the recipients and subrecipients of more than $2000 shall include a provision for compliance with the Davis-Bacon Act (40 U.S.C. 276a to a–7) and as supplemented by Department of Labor regulations (29 CFR part 5, "Labor Standards Provisions Applicable to Contracts Governing Federally Financed and Assisted Construction"). Under this Act, contractors shall be required to pay wages to laborers and mechanics at a rate not less than the minimum wages specified in a wage determination made by the Secretary of Labor. In addition, contractors shall be required to pay wages not less than once a week. The recipient shall place a copy of the current prevailing wage determination issued by the Department of Labor in each solicitation and the award of a contract shall be conditioned upon the acceptance of the wage determination. The recipient shall report all suspected or reported violations to the DoC operating unit.

4. *Contract Work Hours and Safety Standards Act (40 U.S.C. 327–333)*—Where applicable, all contracts awarded by recipients exceeding $100,000 for construction contracts and for other contracts that involve the employment

of mechanics or laborers shall include a provision for compliance with Sections 102 and 107 of the Contract Work Hours and Safety Standards Act (40 U.S.C. 327–333), as supplemented by Department of Labor regulations (29 CFR Part 5). Under Section 102 of the Act, each contractor shall be required to compute the wages of every mechanic and laborer on the basis of a standard work week of 40 hours. Work in excess of the standard work week is permissible provided that the worker is compensated at a rate of not less than 1½ times the basic rate of pay for all hours worked in excess of 40 hours in the work week. Section 107 of the Act is applicable to construction work and provides that no laborer or mechanic shall be required to work in surroundings or under working conditions which are unsanitary, hazardous or dangerous. These requirements do not apply to the purchases of supplies or materials or articles ordinarily available on the open market, or contracts for transportation or transmission of intelligence.

5. *Rights to Inventions Made Under a Contract or Agreement*—Contracts or agreements for the performance of experimental, developmental, or research work shall provide for the rights of the Federal Government and the recipient in any resulting invention in accordance with 37 CFR part 401, "Rights to Inventions Made by Nonprofit Organizations and Small Business Firms Under Government Grants, Contracts and Cooperative Agreements," and any implementing regulations issued by the awarding agency.

6. *Clean Air Act (42 U.S.C. 7401 et seq.) and the Federal Water Pollution Control Act (33 U.S.C. 1251 et seq.), as amended*—Contracts and subgrants of amounts in excess of $100,000 shall contain a provision that requires the recipient to agree to comply with all applicable standards, orders or regulations issued pursuant to the Clean Air Act (42 U.S.C. 7401 *et seq.*) and the Federal Water Pollution Control Act as amended (33 U.S.C. 1251 *et seq.*). Violations shall be reported to the DoC operating unit and the Regional Office of the Environmental Protection Agency (EPA).

7. *Byrd Anti-Lobbying Amendment (31 U.S.C. 1352)*—Contractors who apply or bid for an award exceeding $100,000 shall file the required certification. Each tier certifies to the tier above that it will not and has not used Federal appropriated funds to pay any person or organization for influencing or attempting to influence an officer or employee of any agency, a member of Congress, officer or employee of Congress, or an employee of a member of Congress in connection with obtaining any Federal contract, grant or any other award covered by 31 U.S.C. 1352. Each tier shall also disclose any lobbying with non-Federal funds that takes place in connection with obtaining any Federal award. Such disclosures are forwarded from tier to tier up to the recipient.

8. *Debarment and Suspension (E.O.s 12549 and 12689)*—No contract shall be made to parties listed on the General Services Administration's List of Parties Excluded from Federal Procurement or Nonprocurement Programs in accordance with E.O.s 12549 and 12689, "Debarment and Suspension" as implemented by DoC regulations at 15 CFR part 26. This list contains the names of parties debarred, suspended, or otherwise excluded by agencies, and contractors declared ineligible under statutory or regulatory authority other than E.O. 12549. Contractors with awards that exceed the simplified acquisition threshold shall provide the required certification regarding its exclusion status and that of its principal employees.

[63 FR 47156, Sept. 4, 1998, as amended at 66 FR 49828, Oct. 1, 2001]

PART 15—LEGAL PROCEEDINGS

Subpart A—Service of Process

Subpart B—Testimony by Employees and the Production of Documents in Legal Proceedings

Subpart C—Involuntary Child and Spousal Support Allotments of NOAA Corps Officers

Subpart D—Statement of Policy and Procedures Regarding Indemnification of Department of Commerce Employees

15.32 Procedures for the handling of lawsuits against Department employees arising within the scope of their office or employment.

AUTHORITY: 5 U.S.C. 301; 15 U.S.C. 1501, 1512, 1513, 1515 and 1518; Reorganization Plan No. 5 of 1950; 3 CFR, 1949–1953 Comp., p. 1004; 44 U.S.C. 3101; subpart C is issued under 37 U.S.C. 101, 706; 15 U.S.C. 1673; 42 U.S.C. 665.

EDITORIAL NOTE: Nomenclature changes to part 15 appear at 62 FR 19669, Apr. 23, 1997.

Subpart A—Service of Process

SOURCE: 53 FR 41318, Oct. 21, 1988, unless otherwise noted. Redesignated at 62 FR 19669, Apr. 23, 1997.

§ 15.1 Scope and purpose.

(a) This subpart sets forth the procedures to be followed when a summons or complaint is served on the Department, a component, or the Secretary or a Department employee in his or her official capacity.

(b) This subpart is intended to ensure the orderly execution of the affairs of the Department and not to impede any legal proceeding.

(c) This subpart does not apply to subpoenas. The procedures to be followed with respect to subpoenas are set out in subpart B.

(d) This subpart does not apply to service of process made on a Department employee personally on matters not related to official business of the Department or to the official responsibilities of the Department employee.

[53 FR 41318, Oct. 21, 1988. Redesignated and amended at 62 FR 19669, 19670, Apr. 23, 1997]

§ 15.2 Definitions.

For the purpose of this subpart:

(a) *General Counsel* means the General Counsel of the United States Department of Commerce or other Department employee to whom the General Counsel has delegated authority to act under this subpart, or the chief legal officer (or designee) of the Department of Commerce component concerned.

(b) *Component* means Office of the Secretary or an operating unit of the Department as defined in Department Organization Order 1–1.

(c) *Department* means the Department of Commerce.

(d) *Department employee* means any officer or employee of the Department, including commissioned officers of the National Oceanic and Atmospheric Administration.

(e) *Legal proceeding* means a proceeding before a tribunal constituted by law, including a court, an administrative body or commission, or an administrative law judge or hearing officer.

(f) *Official business* means the authorized business of the Department.

(g) *Secretary* means Secretary of Commerce.

§ 15.3 Acceptance of service of process.

(a) Except as otherwise provided in this subpart, any summons or complaint to be served in person or by registered or certified mail or as otherwise authorized by law on the Department, a component or the Secretary or a Department employee in their official capacity, shall be served on the General Counsel of the United States Department of Commerce, Washington, DC 20230.

(b) Any summons or complaint to be served in person or by registered or certified mail or as otherwise authorized by law on the Patent and Trademark Office or the Commissioner of Patents and Trademarks or an employee of the Patent and Trademark Office in his or her official capacity, shall be served on the Solicitor for the Patent and Trademark Office or a Department employee designated by the Solicitor.

(c) Except as otherwise provided in this subpart, any component or Department employee served with a summons or complaint shall immediately notify and deliver the summons or complaint to the office of the General Counsel. Any employee of the Patent and Trademark Office served with a summons or complaint shall immediately notify and deliver the summons or complaint to the office of the Solicitor.

(d) Any Department employee receiving a summons or complaint shall note on the summons or complaint the date, hour, and place of service and whether service was by personal delivery or by mail.

(e) When a legal proceeding is brought to hold a Department employee personally liable in connection with an action taken in the conduct of official business, rather than liable in an official capacity, the Department employee by law is to be served personally with process. Service of process in this case is inadequate when made upon the General Counsel or the Solicitor or their designees. Except as otherwise provided in this subpart, a Department employee sued personally for an action taken in the conduct of official business shall immediately notify and deliver a copy of the summons or complaint to the office of the General Counsel. Any employee of the Patent and Trademark Office sued personally for an action taken in the conduct of official business shall immediately notify and deliver a copy of the summons or complaint to the Office of the Solicitor.

(f) A Department employee sued personally in connection with official business may be represented by the Department of Justice at its discretion. See 28 CFR 50.15 and 50.16 (1987).

(g) The General Counsel or Solicitor or Department employee designated by either, when accepting service of process for a Department employee in an official capacity, shall endorse on the Marshal's or server's return of service form or receipt for registered or certified mail the following statement: "Service accepted in official capacity only." The statement may be placed on the form or receipt with a rubber stamp.

(h) Upon acceptance of service or receiving notification of service, as provided in this section, the General Counsel and Solicitor shall take appropriate steps to protect the rights of the Department, component, the Secretary or Department employee involved.

Subpart B—Testimony by Employees and the Production of Documents in Legal Proceedings

SOURCE: 60 FR 9291, Feb. 17, 1995, unless otherwise noted. Redesignated at 62 FR 19669, Apr. 23, 1997.

§ 15.11 Scope.

(a) This subpart sets forth the policies and procedures of the Department of Commerce regarding the testimony of employees, and former employees, as witnesses in legal proceedings and the production or disclosure of information contained in Department of Commerce documents for use in legal proceedings pursuant to a request, order, or subpoena (collectively referred to in this subpart as a "demand").

(b) This subpart does not apply to any legal proceeding in which an employee is to testify while on leave status, regarding facts or events that are unrelated to the official business of the Department.

(c) This subpart in no way affects the rights and procedures governing public access to records pursuant to the Freedom of Information Act, the Privacy Act or the Trade Secrets Act.

(d) This subpart is not intended to be relied upon to, and does not, create any right or benefit, substantive or procedural, enforceable at law by any party against the United States.

§ 15.12 Definitions.

For the purpose of this subpart:

(a) *Agency counsel* means the chief legal officer (or his/her designee) of an agency within the Department of Commerce.

(b) *Component* means Office of the Secretary or an operating unit of the Department as defined in Department Organization Order 1–1.

(c) *Demand* means a request, order, or subpoena for testimony or documents for use in a legal proceeding.

(d) *Department* means the United States Department of Commerce and its constituent agencies.

(e) *Document* means any record, paper and other property held by the Department, including without limitation, official letters, telegrams, memoranda, reports, studies, calendar and diary entries, maps, graphs, pamphlets, notes, charts, tabulations, analyses, statistical or informational accumulations, any kind of summaries of meetings and conversations, film impressions, magnetic tapes and sound or mechanical reproductions.

(f) *Employee* means all current or former employees or officers of the Department, including commissioned officers of the National Oceanic and Atmospheric Administration and any other individual who has been appointed by, or subject to the supervision, jurisdiction or control of the Secretary of the Department of Commerce.

(g) *General Counsel* means the General Counsel of the Department or other Department employee to whom the General Counsel has delegated authority to act under this subpart.

(h) *Legal proceeding* means all pretrial, trial and post trial stages of all existing or reasonably anticipated judicial or administrative actions, hearings, investigations, or similar proceedings before courts, commissions, boards or other tribunals, foreign or domestic. This phrase includes all phases of discovery as well as responses to formal or informal requests by attorneys or others involved in legal proceedings.

(i) *Official business* means the authorized business of the Department.

(j) *Secretary* means the Secretary of the Department of Commerce.

(k) *Solicitor* means the Solicitor of the Patent and Trademark Office.

(l) *Testimony* means a statement in any form, including personal appearances before a court or other legal tribunal, interviews, depositions, telephonic, televised, or videotaped statements or any responses given during discovery or similar proceedings, which response would involve more than the production of documents.

(m) *United States* means the Federal Government, its departments and agencies, and individuals acting on behalf of the Federal Government.

§15.13 Demand for testimony or production of documents: Department policy.

No employee shall in response to a demand, produce any documents, or provide testimony regarding any information relating to, or based upon Department of Commerce documents, or disclose any information or produce materials acquired as part of the performance of that employee's official duties, or because of that employee's official status without the prior authorization of the General Counsel, or the Solicitor, or the appropriate agency counsel. The reasons for this policy are as follows:

(a) To conserve the time of Department employees for conducting official business;

(b) To minimize the possibility of involving the Department in controversial issues that are not related to the Department's mission;

(c) To prevent the possibility that the public will misconstrue variances between personal opinions of Department employees and Department policy;

(d) To avoid spending the time and money of the United States for private purposes;

(e) To preserve the integrity of the administrative process; and

(f) To protect confidential, sensitive information and the deliberative process of the Department.

§15.14 Demand for testimony or production of documents: Department procedures.

(a) Whenever a demand for testimony or for the production of documents is made upon an employee, the employee shall immediately notify the General Counsel (Room 5890, U. S. Department of Commerce, Washington, DC 20230, (202) 482–1067) or appropriate agency counsel. When a demand for testimony or for the production of documents is made upon an employee of the Patent and Trademark Office, the employee should immediately notify the Solicitor, by phone, (703) 305–9035; by mailed addressed Solicitor, Box 8, Patent and Trademark Office, Washington, DC 20231; or in person to 2121 Crystal Drive, Crystal Park 2, Suite 918, Arlington, Virginia 22215.

(b) A Department employee may not give testimony, produce documents, or answer inquiries from a person not employed by the Department regarding testimony or documents subject to a demand or a potential demand under the provisions of this subpart without the approval of the General Counsel, or the Solicitor, or the appropriate agency counsel. A Department employee shall immediately refer all inquiries and Demands to the General Counsel, or the Solicitor, or appropriate agency counsel. Where appropriate, the General Counsel, or the Solicitor, or appropriate agency counsel, may instruct the Department employee, orally or in writing, not to give testimony or produce documents.

(c)(1) *Demand for testimony or documents.* A demand for the testimony of a Department employee shall be addressed to the General Counsel, Room 5890, Department of Commerce, Washington, DC 20230 or appropriate agency counsel. A demand for testimony of an employee of the Patent and Trademark Office shall be mail addressed to the Solicitor, Box 8, Patent and Trademark Office, Washington, DC 20231; or in person to 2121 Crystal Drive, Crystal Park 2, Suite 918, Arlington, Virginia 22215.

(2) *Subpoenas.* A subpoena for testimony by a Department employee or a document shall be served in accordance with the Federal Rules of Civil or Criminal Procedure or applicable state procedure and a copy of the subpoena shall be sent to the General Counsel, or the Solicitor, or appropriate agency counsel.

(3) *Affidavit.* Except when the United States is a party, every demand shall be accompanied by an affidavit or declaration under 28 U.S.C. 1746 or, if an affidavit is not feasible, a statement setting forth the title of the legal proceeding, the forum, the requesting party's interest in the legal proceeding, the reason for the demand, a showing that the desired testimony or document is not reasonably available from any other source, and if testimony is requested, the intended use of the testimony, a general summary of the desired testimony, and a showing that no document could be provided and used in lieu of testimony. The purpose of this requirement is to assist the General Counsel, or the Solicitor, or appropriate agency counsel in making an informed decision regarding whether testimony or the production of a document(s) should be authorized.

(d) A certified copy of a document for use in a legal proceeding may be provided upon written request and payment of applicable fees. Written requests for certification shall be addressed to the agency counsel for the component having possession, custody, or control of the document. Unless governed by another applicable provision of law or component regulation, the applicable fee includes charges for certification and reproduction as set out in 15 CFR part 4.9. Other reproduction costs and postage fees, as appropriate, must also be borne by the requester.

(e) The Secretary retains the authority to authorize and direct testimony in those cases where a statute or Presidential order mandates a personal decision by the Secretary.

(f) The General Counsel, or the Solicitor, or appropriate agency counsel may consult or negotiate with an attorney for a party or the party if not represented by an attorney, to refine or limit a demand so that compliance is less burdensome or obtain information necessary to make the determination required by paragraph (b) of this section. Failure of the attorney to cooperate in good faith to enable the General Counsel, or the Solicitor, or the Secretary, or the appropriate agency counsel to make an informed determination under this subpart may serve, where appropriate, as a basis for a determination not to comply with the demand.

(g) A determination under this subpart to comply or not to comply with a demand is not an assertion or waiver of privilege, lack of relevance, technical deficiency or any other ground for noncompliance.

(h) The General Counsel, or the Solicitor, or appropriate agency counsel may waive any requirements set forth under this section when circumstances warrant.

§ 15.15 Procedures when a Department employee receives a subpoena.

(a) A Department employee who receives a subpoena shall immediately forward the subpoena to the General Counsel, or the appropriate agency counsel. In the case of an employee of the Patent and Trademark Office, the subpoena shall immediately be forwarded to the Solicitor. The General Counsel, or the Solicitor, or appropriate agency counsel will determine the extent to which a Department employee will comply with the subpoena.

(b) If an employee is served with a subpoena that the General Counsel, or the Solicitor, or appropriate agency counsel determines should not be complied with, the General Counsel, Solicitor or appropriate agency counsel will attempt to have the subpoena withdrawn or modified. If this cannot be done, the General Counsel, Solicitor or appropriate agency counsel will attempt to obtain Department of Justice representation for the employee and move to have the subpoena modified or quashed. If, because of time constraints, this is not possible prior to the compliance date specified in the subpoena, the employee should appear at the time and place set forth in the subpoena. If legal counsel cannot appear on behalf of the employee, the employee should produce a copy of the Department's regulations and inform the legal tribunal that he/she has been advised by counsel not to provide the requested testimony and/or produce documents. If the legal tribunal rules that the demand in the subpoena must be complied with, the employee shall respectfully decline to comply with the demand. *United States ex rel. Touhy* v. *Ragen*, 340 U. S. 462 (1951).

(c) Where the Department employee is an employee of the Office of the Inspector General, the Inspector General in consultation with the General Counsel, will make a determination under paragraphs (a) and (b) of this section.

§15.16 Legal proceedings between private litigants: Expert or opinion testimony.

In addition to the policies and procedures as outlined in §§15.11 through 15.16, the following applies to legal proceedings between private litigants:

(a) If a Department employee is authorized to give testimony in a legal proceeding not involving the United States, the testimony, if otherwise proper, shall be limited to facts within the personal knowledge of the Department employee. Employees, with or without compensation, shall not provide expert testimony in any legal proceedings regarding Department information, subjects or activities except on behalf of the United States or a party represented by the United States Department of Justice. However, upon a showing by the requester that there are exceptional circumstances and that the anticipated testimony will not be adverse to the interest of the Department or the United States, the General Counsel, or the Solicitor, or appropriate agency counsel may, in writing grant special authorization for the employee to appear and give the expert or opinion testimony.

(b)(1) If, while testifying in any legal proceeding, an employee is asked for expert or opinion testimony regarding official DOC information, subjects or activities, which testimony has not been approved in advance in accordance with the regulations in this subpart, the witness shall:

(i) Respectfully decline to answer on the grounds that such expert or opinion testimony is forbidden by the regulations in this subpart;

(ii) Request an opportunity to consult with the General Counsel, or the Solicitor, or appropriate agency counsel before giving such testimony; and

(iii) Explain that upon such consultation, approval for such testimony may be provided.

(2) If the witness is then ordered by the body conducting the proceeding to provide expert or opinion testimony regarding official DOC information, subjects or activities without the opportunity to consult with either the General Counsel, or the Solicitor, or appropriate agency counsel, the witness shall respectfully refuse to provide such testimony. See *United States ex rel. Touhy* v. *Ragen*, 340 U. S. 462 (1951).

(c) If an employee is unaware of the regulations in this subpart and provides expert or opinion testimony regarding official DOC information, subjects or activities in a legal proceeding without the aforementioned consultation, the witness shall, as soon after testifying as possible, inform the General Counsel, or the Solicitor, or appropriate agency counsel that such testimony was given and provide a written summary of the expert or opinion testimony provided.

[60 FR 9291, Feb. 17, 1995. Redesignated and amended at 62 FR 19669, 19670, Apr. 23, 1997]

§ 15.17 Demands or requests in legal proceedings for records protected by confidentiality statutes.

Demands in legal proceedings for the production of records, or for the testimony of Department employees regarding information protected by the Privacy Act, 5 U.S.C. 552a, the Trade Secrets Act, 18 U.S.C. 1905 or other confidentiality statutes, must satisfy the requirements for disclosure set forth in those statutes before the records may be provided or testimony given. The General Counsel, or the Solicitor, or appropriate agency counsel should first determine if there is a legal basis to provide the testimony or records sought under applicable confidentiality statutes before applying §§ 15.11 through 15.18. Where an applicable confidentiality statute mandates disclosure, §§ 15.11 through 15.18 will not apply.

[60 FR 9291, Feb. 17, 1995. Redesignated and amended at 62 FR 19669, 19670, Apr. 23, 1997]

§ 15.18 Testimony of Department employees in proceedings involving the United States.

The following applies in legal proceedings in which the United States is a party:

(a) A Department employee may not testify as an expert or opinion witness for any other party other than the United States.

(b) Whenever, in any legal proceeding involving the United States, a request is made by an attorney representing or acting under the authority of the United States, the General Counsel, or the Solicitor, or appropriate agency counsel will make all necessary arrangements for the Department employee to give testimony on behalf of the United States. Where appropriate, the General Counsel, or the Solicitor, or appropriate agency counsel may require reimbursement to the Department of the expenses associated with a Department employee giving testimony on behalf of the United States.

Subpart C—Involuntary Child and Spousal Support Allotments of NOAA Corps Officers

SOURCE: 53 FR 15548, May 2, 1988, unless otherwise noted. Redesignated at 62 FR 19669, Apr. 23, 1997.

§ 15.21 Purpose.

This subpart provides implementing policies governing involuntary child or child and spousal support allotments for officers of the uniformed service of the National Oceanic and Atmospheric Administration (NOAA), and prescribes applicable procedures.

§ 15.22 Applicability and scope.

This subpart applies to Commissioned Officers of the NOAA Corps on active duty.

§ 15.23 Definitions.

(a) *Active duty.* Full-time duty in the NOAA Corps.

(b) *Authorized person.* Any agent or attorney of any state having in effect a plan approved under part D of title IV of the Social Security Act (42 U.S.C. 651–664), who has the duty or authority to seek recovery of any amounts owed as child or child and spousal support (including, when authorized under the state plan, any official of a political subdivision); and the court that has authority to issue an order against a member for the support and maintenance of a child or any agent of such court.

(c) *Child support.* Periodic payments for the support and maintenance of a child or children, subject to and in accordance with state or local law. This includes but is not limited to, payments to provide for health, education, recreation, and clothing or to meet other specific needs of such a child or children.

(d) *Designated official.* The official who is designated to receive notices of failure to make payments from an authorized person (as defined in paragraph (b) of this section). For the Department of Commerce this official is the Assistant General Counsel for Administration.

(e) *Notice.* A court order, letter, or similar documentation issued by an authorized person providing notification that a member has failed to make periodic support payments under a support order.

(f) *Spousal support.* Periodic payments for the support and maintenance of a spouse or former spouse, in accordance with state and local law. It includes, but is not limited to, separate maintenance, alimony while litigation continues, and maintenance. Spousal support does not include any payment for transfer of property or its value by an individual to his or her spouse or former spouse in compliance with any community property settlement, equitable distribution of property, or other division of property between spouses or former spouses.

(g) *Support order.* Any order for the support of any person issued by a court of competent jurisdiction or by administrative procedures established under state law that affords substantial due process and is subject to judicial review. A court of competent jurisdiction includes: (1) Indian tribal courts within any state, territory, or possession of the United States and the District of Columbia; and (2) a court in any foreign country with which the United States has entered into an agreement that requires the United States to honor the notice.

§ 15.24 Policy.

(a) It is the policy of the Department of Commerce to require Commissioned Officers of the NOAA Corps on active duty to make involuntary allotments from pay and allowances as payment of child, or child and spousal, support payments when the officer has failed to make periodic payments under a support order in a total amount equal to the support payable for two months or longer. Failure to make such payments shall be established by notice from an authorized person to the designated official. Such notice shall specify the name and address of the person to whom the allotment is payable. The amount of the allotment shall be the amount necessary to comply with the support order. If requested, the allotment may include arrearages as well as amounts for current support, except that the amount of the allotment, together with any other amounts withheld for support from the officer as a percentage of pay, shall not exceed the limits prescribed in section 303 (b) and (c) of the Consumer Credit Protection Act (15 U.S.C. 1673). An allotment under this subpart shall be adjusted or discontinued upon notice from an authorized person.

(b) Notwithstanding the above, no action shall be taken to require an allotment from the pay and allowances of any officer until such officer has had a consultation with an attorney from the Office of the Assistant General Counsel for Administration, in person, to discuss the legal and other factors involved with respect to the officer's support obligation and his/her failure to make payments. Where it has not been possible, despite continuing good faith efforts to arrange such a consultation, the allotment shall start the first pay period beginning after 30 days have elapsed since the notice required in paragraph (d)(1) of § 15.25 is given to the affected officer.

[53 FR 15548, May 2, 1988. Redesignated and amended at 62 FR 19669, 19670, Apr. 23, 1997]

§ 15.25 Procedures.

(a) *Service of notice.* (1) An authorized person shall send to the designated official a signed notice that includes:

(i) A statement that delinquent support payments equal or exceed the amount of support payable for 2 months under a support order, and a request that an allotment be initiated pursuant to 42 U.S.C. 665.

(ii) A certified copy of the support order.

(iii) The amount of the monthly support payment. Such amount may include arrearages, if a support order specifies the payment of such arrearages. The notice shall indicate how much of the amount payable shall be applied toward liquidation of the arrearages.

(iv) Sufficient information identifying the officer to enable processing by the designated official. The following information is requested:

(A) Full name;

(B) Social Security Number;

(C) Date of birth; and

(D) Duty station location.

(v) The full name and address of the allottee. The allottee shall be an authorized person, the authorized person's designee, or the recipient named in the support order.

(vi) Any limitations on the duration of the support allotment.

(vii) A certificate that the official sending the notice is an authorized person.

(viii) A statement that delinquent support payments are more than 12 weeks in arrears, if appropriate.

(2) The notice shall be accomplished by certified or registered mail, return receipt requested, or by personal service, upon the appropriate designated official, who shall note the date and time of receipt on the notice.

(3) The notice is effective when it is received in the office of the designated official.

(4) When the information submitted is not sufficient to identify the officer, the notice shall be returned directly to the authorized person with an explanation of the deficiency. However, prior to returning the notice if there is sufficient time, an attempt should be made to inform the authorized person who caused the notice to be served, that it will not be honored unless adequate information is supplied.

(5) Upon receipt of effective notice of delinquent support payments, together with all required supplementary documents and information, the designated official shall identify the officer from whom moneys are due and payable. The allotment shall be established in the amount necessary to comply with the support order and to liquidate arrearages if provided by a support order when the maximum amount to be allotted under this provision, together with any other moneys withheld for support from the officer, does not exceed:

(i) 50 percent of the officer's disposable earnings for any month where the officer asserts by affidavit or other acceptable evidence, that he/she is supporting a spouse and/or dependent child, other than a party in the support order. When the officer submits evidence, copies shall be sent to the authorized person, together with notification that the officer's support claim will be honored. If the support claim is contested by the authorized person, that authorized person may refer this matter to the appropriate court or other authority for resolution.

(ii) 60 percent of the officer's disposable earnings for any month where the officer fails to assert by affidavit or other acceptable evidence that he/she is supporting a spouse and/or dependent child.

(iii) Regardless of the limitations above, an additional 5 percent of the officer's disposable earnings shall be withheld when it is stated in the notice that the officer is in arrears in an amount equivalent to 12 or more weeks' support.

(b) *Disposable earnings.* The following moneys are subject to inclusion in computation of the officer's disposable earnings:

(1) Basic pay.

(2) Special pay (including enlistment and reenlistment bonuses).

(3) Accrued leave payments (basic pay portions only).

(4) Aviation career incentive pay.

(5) Incentive pay for Hazardous Duty.

(6) Readjustment pay.

(7) Diving pay.

(8) Sea pay.

(9) Severance pay (including disability severance pay).

(10) Retired pay (including disability retired pay).

(c) *Exclusions.* In determining the amount of any moneys due from or payable by the United States to any individual, there shall be excluded amounts which are:

(1) Owed by the officer to the United States.

(2) Required by law to be deducted from the remuneration or other payment involved, including, but not limited to:

(i) Amounts withheld from benefits payable under Title II of the Social Security Act where the withholding is required by law.

(ii) Federal employment taxes.

(3) Properly withheld for federal and state income tax purposes if the withholding of the amounts is authorized by law and if amounts withheld are not greater than would be the case if the individual claimed all dependents to

which he/she were entitled. The withholding of additional amounts pursuant to section 3402(i) of Title 26 of the United States Code may be permitted only when the officer presents evidence of a tax obligation which supports the additional withholding.

(4) Deducted for servicemen's Group Life Insurance coverage.

(5) Advances of pay that may be due and payable by the officer at some future date.

(d) *Officer notification.* (1) As soon as possible, but not later than 15 calendar days after the date of receipt of notice, the designated official shall send to the officer, at his/her duty station or last known address, written notice:

(i) That notice has been received from an authorized person, including a copy of the documents submitted;

(ii) Of the maximum limitations set forth, with a request that the officer submit supporting affidavits or other documentation necessary for determining the applicable percentage limitation;

(iii) That the officer may submit supporting affidavits or other documentation as evidence that the information contained in the notice is in error;

(iv) That by submitting supporting affidavits or other necessary documentation, the officer consents to the disclosure of such information to the party requesting the support allotment;

(v) Of the amount or percentage that will be deducted if the officer fails to submit the documentation necessary to enable the designated official to respond to the notice within the prescribed time limits;

(vi) That legal counsel will be provided by the Office of the Assistant General Counsel for Administration; and

(vii) Of the date that the allotment is scheduled to begin.

(2) The officer shall be provided with the following:

(i) A consultation in person with an attorney from the Office of the Assistant General Counsel for Administration, to discuss the legal and other factors involved with the officer's support obligation and his/her failures to make payment.

(ii) Copies of any other documents submitted with the notice.

(3) The Office of the Assistant General Counsel for Administration will make every effort to see that the officer receives a consultation concerning the support obligation and the consequences of failure to make payments within 30 days of the notice required in paragraph (d)(1). In the event such consultation is not possible, despite continuing good faith efforts to arrange a consultation, no action shall be taken to require an allotment from the pay and allowances of any NOAA Corps Officer until 30 days have elapsed after the notice described in paragraph (d)(1) is given to the affected officer.

(4) If, within 30 days of the date of the notice, the officer has furnished the designated official affidavits or other documentation showing the information in the notice to be in error, the designated official shall consider the officer's response. The designated official may return to the authorized person, without action, the notice for a statutorily required support allotment together with the member's affidavit and other documentation, if the member submits substantial proof of error, such as:

(i) The support payments are not delinquent.

(ii) The underlying support order in the notice has been amended, superseded, or set aside.

(e) *Absence of funds.* (1) When notice is served and the identified officer is found not to be entitled to moneys due from or payable by NOAA, the designated official shall return the notice to the authorized person, and advise that no moneys are due from or payable by NOAA to the named individual.

(2) Where it appears that moneys are only temporarily exhausted or otherwise unavailable, the authorized person shall be fully advised as to why, and for how long, the money will be unavailable.

(3) In instances where the officer separates from active duty service, the authorized person shall be informed by the Office of Commissioned Personnel, NOAA Corps that the allotment is discontinued.

(4) Payment of statutorily required allotments shall be enforced over other

voluntary deductions and allotments when the gross amount of pay and allowances is not sufficient to permit all authorized deductions and collections.

(f) *Allotment of funds.* (1) The authorized person or allottee shall notify the designated official promptly if the operative court order upon which the allotment is based is vacated, modified, or set aside. The designated official shall also be notified of any events affecting the allottee's eligibility to receive the allotment, such as the former spouse's remarriage, if a part of the payment is for spousal support, and notice of a change in eligibility for child support payments under circumstances of death, emancipation, adoption, or attainment of majority of a child whose support is provided through the allotment.

(2) An allotment established under this Directive shall be adjusted or discontinued upon notice from the authorized person.

(3) Neither the Department of Commerce nor any officer or employee thereof, shall be liable for any payment made from moneys due from, or payable by, the Department of Commerce to any individuals pursuant to notice regular on its face, if such payment is made in accordance with this subpart. If a designated official receives notice based on support which, on its face, appears to conform to the law of the jurisdiction from which it was issued, the designated official shall not be required to ascertain whether the authority that issued the orde had obtained personal jurisdiction over the member.

(4) *Effective date of allotment.* The allotment shall start with the first pay period beginning after the officer has had a consultation with an attorney from the Office of the Assistant General Counsel for Administration but not later than the first pay period beginning after 30 days have elapsed since the notice required in paragraph (d)(1) of this section is given to the affected officer. The Department of Commerce shall not be required to vary its normal NOAA Corps allotment payment cycle to comply with the notice.

(g) *Designated official.* Notice should be sent to: The Assistant General Counsel for Administration, Office of the General Counsel, U.S. Department of Commerce, Washington, DC 20230, (202) 377–5387.

Subpart D—Statement of Policy and Procedures Regarding Indemnification of Department of Commerce Employees

SOURCE: 62 FR 19670, Apr. 23, 1997, unless otherwise noted.

§ 15.31 Policy.

(a) The Department of Commerce may indemnify a present or former Department employee who is personally named as a defendant in any civil suit in state or federal court, or other legal proceeding seeking damages against a present or former Department employee personally, for any verdict, judgment or other monetary award which is rendered against such employee, provided that the conduct giving rise to the verdict, judgment or award was taken within the scope of his/her employment and that such indemnification is in the interest of the Department as determined by the Secretary or his/her designee.

(b) The Department may settle or compromise a personal damage claim against a present or former employee by the payment of available funds at any time provided the alleged conduct giving rise to the personal property claim was taken within the employee's scope of employment and such settlement is in the interest of the Department as determined by the Secretary or his/her designee.

(c) Absent exceptional circumstances, as determined by the Secretary or his/her designee, the Department will not consider a request either to indemnify or to settle a personal damage claim before entry of an adverse verdict, judgment or award.

(d) Any payment under this section either to indemnify a present or former Department employee or to settle a personal damage claim shall be contingent upon the availability of appropriated funds of the Department of Commerce.

§ 15.32 Procedures for the handling of lawsuits against Department employees arising within the scope of their office or employment.

The following procedures shall be followed in the event that a civil action or proceeding is brought, in any court, against a present or former employee of the Department (or against his/her estate) for personal injury, loss of property or death, resulting from the Department employee's activities while acting within the scope of his/her office or employment:

(a) After being served with process or pleadings in such an action or proceeding, the employee (or the executor(rix) or administrator(rix)) of the estate shall within five (5) calendar days of receipt, deliver all such process and pleadings or an attested true copy thereof, together with a fully detailed report of the circumstances of the incident giving rise to the court action or proceeding to the General Counsel. Where appropriate, the General Counsel, or his/her designee, may request that the Department of Justice provide legal representation for the present or former Department employee.

(b)(1) Only if a present or former employee of the Department has satisfied the requirements of paragraph (a) of this section in a timely fashion, may the employee subsequently request indemnification to satisfy a verdict, judgment, or award entered against that employee.

(2) No request for indemnification will be considered unless the employee has submitted a written request, with appropriate documentation, including copies of the verdict, judgment, appeal bond, award, or settlement proposal through the employee's supervisory chain to the head of the employee's component. The written request will include an explanation by the employee of how the employee was working within the scope of employment and whether the employee has insurance or any other source of indemnification.

(3) The head of the component or his/her designee will forward the employee's request with a recommendation to the General Counsel for review. The request for indemnification shall include a detailed analysis of the basis for the recommendation. The head of the component will also certify to the General Counsel that the component has funds available to pay the indemnification.

(c) The General Counsel or his/her designee will review the circumstances of the incident giving rise to the action or proceeding, and all data bearing upon the question of whether the employee was acting within the scope of his/her employment. Where appropriate, the agency shall seek the views of the Department of Justice and/or the U.S. Attorney for the district embracing the place where the action or proceeding is brought.

(d) The General Counsel shall forward the request, the accompanying documentation, and the General Counsel's recommendation to the Secretary or his/her designee for decision.

PART 16—PROCEDURES FOR A VOLUNTARY CONSUMER PRODUCT INFORMATION LABELING PROGRAM

AUTHORITY: Sec. 2, 31 Stat. 1449, as amended; sec. 1, 64 Stat. 371, (15 U.S.C. 272); Reorganization Plan No. 3 of 1946, Part VI.

SOURCE: 42 FR 26648, May 25, 1977, unless otherwise noted.

§ 16.1 Purpose.

The purpose of this part is to establish procedures under which a voluntary consumer product information labeling program administered by the Department of Commerce will function.

§ 16.2 Description and goal of program.

(a) The Department's Voluntary Consumer Product Information Labeling Program makes available to consumers, at the point of sale, information on consumer product performance in an understandable and useful form so as to facilitate accurate consumer purchasing decisions and enhance consumer satisfaction. It also educates consumers, distributors and retailers in the use of the product performance information displayed and provides manufacturers and other persons who participate in the program with an opportunity to convey to the public the particular advantages of their products. These objectives are accomplished by:

(1) Selecting or developing standardized test methods by which selected product performance characteristics can be measured;

(2) Developing labeling methods by which information concerning product performance can be transmitted in useful form to consumers at the point of sale;

(3) Encouraging manufacturers and other participants in the program voluntarily to test and label their products according to the selected or developed methods; and

(4) Encouraging consumers through various informational and educational programs to utilize the product performance information provided.

(b) The program involves voluntary labeling by enrolled participants of selected categories of consumer products with information concerning selected performance characteristics of those products. The performance characteristics selected are those that are of demonstrable importance to consumers, that consumers cannot evaluate through mere inspection of the product, and that can be measured objectively and reported understandably to consumers. The consumer products covered include those for which incorrect purchase decision can result in financial loss, dissatisfaction, or inconvenience. The program seeks to avoid the duplication of other Federal programs under which performance characteristics are labeled by exempting those performance characteristics from this program. However, where the Federal agency concerned agrees, the Department of Commerce may include information about those performance characteristics in CPILP labels if, by doing so, product comparison at the point of sale is simplified for consumers, and the complexity of product labeling is reduced for the manufacturers by enabling them to comply with the labeling requirements of other Federal agencies through participation in CPILP.

(c) For selected categories of consumer products, the program includes advertising guidelines covering situations where quantitative performance values are stated in advertising or where qualitative comparisons are made of the performance of different products.

[42 FR 26648, May 25, 1977, as amended at 43 FR 8255, Mar. 1, 1978]

§ 16.3 Definitions.

(a) The term *Secretary* means the Secretary of Commerce or her designee.

(b) The term *consumer* means the first person who purchases a consumer product for purposes other than resale.

(c) The term *participant* means a manufacturer, assembler or private brand labeler of consumer products or an importer of such products for resale and who participates in the program.

(d) The term *consumer product* means any article produced or distributed for sale to a consumer for the use, consumption, or enjoyment of such consumer. The term does not include products customarily intended primarily for business, commercial, or industrial use.

(e) The term *person* means an individual; a manufacturer; distributor; retailer; importer; private brand labeler; government agency at the Federal (including any agency of the Department of Commerce), State and local level; consumer organization; trade association; standards writing body; professional society; testing laboratory; or educational institution.

(f) The term *performance characteristic* means a performance characteristic of a consumer product that can be measured in an objective manner with respect to a given consumer product.

(g) The term *Specification* means a Performance Information Labeling Specification developed under § 16.5.

(h) The term *label* means printed matter affixed to or otherwise provided with a consumer product and containing all of the performance characteristics as prescribed by the Specification applicable to that product.

(i) The term *designated agent* means a person as defined in paragraph (e) of this section, who has been designated by the Secretary to carry out appropriate operational procedures on behalf of more than one participant in this program in accordance with rules set out under § 16.9.

§ 16.4 Finding of need to establish a specification for labeling a consumer product.

(a) Any person may request the Secretary to find that there is a need to label a particular consumer product with information concerning one or more specific performance characteristics of that product.

(b) Such a request shall be in writing and will, to the extent practicable, include the following information:

(1) Identification of the consumer product;

(2) Extent that the product identified in paragraph (b)(1) of this section is used by the public and, if known, what the production or sales volume is of such product;

(3) Nature and extent of difficulty experienced by consumers in making informed purchase decisions because of a lack of knowledge regarding the performance characteristics of the identified consumer product;

(4) Potential or actual loss to consumers as a result of an incorrect decision based on an inadequate understanding of the performance characteristics of the identified consumer product;

(5) Extent of incidence of consumer complaints arising from or reasonably traceable to lack of knowledge regarding the performance characteristics of the identified consumer product;

(6) If known, whether there currently exist test methods which could be used to test the performance characteristics of the identified consumer product and an identification of those test methods;

(7) Reasons why it is felt, in cases where existing test methods are identified in responding to paragraph (b)(6) of this section, that such test methods are suitable for making objective measurements of the performance characteristics of the identified consumer product; and

(8) Estimated cost to participants to test and label the product.

(c) The Secretary may ask for more information to support a request made under paragraph (a) of this section if she feels it is necessary to do so, or, if she deems it to be in the public interest, may develop such information herself as by consultation on a one-time basis with consumers, consumer organizations, and others. The Secretary shall act expeditiously on all requests and shall notify the requester of her decision in writing. If the Secretary determines that there is no need to establish a Specification for labeling the requested consumer product performance characteristics, or because of a lack of resources, she will decline to act further on the request. In those instances where the Secretary declines a request, she shall state the reasons for so declining.

(d) If the Secretary finds that a need exists to establish a Specification for labeling a consumer product under this program, she shall publish a notice in the FEDERAL REGISTER setting out such finding and its basis and stating that she is developing a proposed Specification in accordance with § 16.5.

§ 16.5 Development of performance information labeling specifications.

(a) If the Secretary makes a finding of need pursuant to § 16.4, she will publish a proposed Performance Information Labeling Specification in the FEDERAL REGISTER with a notice giving the complete text of the proposed Specification and any other pertinent information. The notice will invite any interested person to submit written comments on the proposed Specification within 45 days after its publication in the FEDERAL REGISTER, unless another time limit is provided by the Secretary. Interested persons wanting to express their views in an informal hearing may do so, if within 15 days after the proposed Specification is published in the FEDERAL REGISTER, they request the Secretary to hold a hearing. Such informal hearings shall be held so as to give all interested persons an opportunity for the oral presentation of data, views, or arguments in addition to the opportunity to make written submissions. Notice of such hearings shall be published in the FEDERAL REGISTER. A transcript shall be kept of any oral presentations.

(b) Each Specification shall as a minimum include:

(1) A description of the performance characteristics of the consumer product covered;

(2) An identification by reference of the test methods to be used in measuring the performance characteristics. The test methods, where they exist and are deemed appropriate for inclusion in the particular Specification involved, shall be those which are described in nationally-recognized voluntary standards. Where appropriate test methods do not exist, they will be developed by the Department of Commerce in cooperation with interested parties and set out in full in the Specification;

(3) A prototype label and directions for displaying the label on or with the consumer product concerned. Such directions will not prohibit the display of additional information by the participant on space adjacent to the marked boundaries of the label; and

(4) Conditions of participation.

(c) The Secretary, after consideration of all written and oral comments and other materials received in accordance with paragraph (a) of this section, shall publish in the FEDERAL REGISTER within 30 days after the final date for receipt of comments, or as soon as practicable thereafter, a notice either:

(1) Giving the complete text of a final Specification, including conditions of use, and stating that any prospective participant in the program desiring voluntarily to use the Department of Commerce Mark developed under § 16.10 must advise the Department of Commerce: or

(2) Stating that the proposed Specification will be further developed before final publication; or

(3) Withdrawing the proposed Specification from further consideration.

§ 16.6 Establishment of fees and charges.

(a) The Secretary in conjunction with the use of the Working Capital Fund of the National Institute of Standards & Technology, as authorized under section 12 of the Act of March 3, 1901, as amended (15 U.S.C. 278b), for this program, shall establish fees and charges for use of the Department of Commerce Label and Mark on each product. Such fees and charges shall be related to the number of units of products labeled, where appropriate. The fees and charges established by the Secretary, which may be revised by her when she deems it appropriate to do so, shall be in amounts calculated to make the operation of this program as self-sufficient as reasonable. A separate notice will be published in the FEDERAL REGISTER simultaneously with the notice of each proposed Specification referred to in § 16.5(a). Such notice will set out a schedule of estimated fees and charges the Secretary proposes to establish. The notice would be furnished for informational and guidance purposes only in order that the public may evaluate the proposed Specification in light of the expected fees to be charged.

(b) At such time as the Secretary publishes the notice announcing the final Specification referred to in § 16.5(c)(1), she shall simultaneously publish a separate notice in the FEDERAL REGISTER setting forth the final schedule of fees that will be charged participants in the program. The effective date of such final schedule of fees shall be the same as the date on which the final Specification takes effect.

(c) Revisions, if any, to the fees and charges established by the Secretary under paragraph (b) of this section shall be published in subsequent FEDERAL REGISTER notices and shall take effect not less than thirty (30) days after the date of publication of such notice.

(d) The establishment of fees and charges under this section may, at any time, be suspended by the Secretary for any length of time.

[42 FR 26648, May 25, 1977, as amended at 42 FR 57686, Nov. 4, 1977; 55 FR 38315, Sept. 18, 1990]

§ 16.7 Participation in program.

(a) Any manufacturer, assembler, or private brand labeler of consumer products or importer of such products for resale, desiring to participate in this program will so notify the Secretary. The notification will identify the particular Specification to be used and the prospective participant's identification and model numbers for the products to be labeled. The notification must include a statement that if accepted as a participant in the program by the Secretary, the prospective participant will:

(1) Abide by all conditions imposed by these procedures:

(2) Abide by the conditions contained in the Specification, as prescribed in paragraph (d) of this section;

(3) Pay the fees and charges established by the Secretary; and

(4) Desist from using the Department of Commerce label and Mark if his participation is terminated under § 16.8.

(b) The Secretary shall act expeditiously on all requests to participate in the program and shall notify each prospective participant of her decision in writing. In those instances where the Secretary declines a request, she shall state the reasons for so declining.

(c) If a prospective participant seeking to participate in the program is notified by the Secretary that she proposes to deny that prospective participant the right to participate, that prospective participant shall have thirty (30) days from the receipt of such notification to request a hearing under the provisions of 5 U.S.C. 556. The Secretary's proposed denial shall become final through the issuance of a written decision to such prospective participant in the event that he does not appeal such notification by the end of the thirty (30) day period. If however, such prospective participant requests a hearing within that thirty (30) day period, the Secretary's proposed denial shall be stayed pending the outcome of the hearing held pursuant to 5 U.S.C. 556.

(d) The conditions set out in each Specification will include, but not be limited to, the following:

(1) Prior to the use of a Label, the participant will make or have made the measurements to obtain the information required for inclusion on the Label and, if requested, will forward within 30 days such measurement data to the Secretary. Such measurement data will be kept on file by the participant or his agent for two years after that product is no longer manufactured unless otherwise provided in the Specification.

(2) The participant will describe the test results on the Label as prescribed in the Specification.

(3) The participant will display or arrange to display, in accordance with the appropriate Specification, the Label on or with each individual product of the type covered except for units exported from the U.S. Participants who utilized more than one brand name may participate by labeling some or all of the brand names. All models with the same brand name must be included in the program unless they are for export only.

(4) The participant agrees at his expense to comply with any reasonable request of the Secretary to have consumer products manufactured, assembled, imported, or privately brand labeled by him tested to determine that testing has been done according to the relevant Specification.

(5) Participants may reproduce the Department of Commerce Label and Mark in advertising: *Provided*, That the entire Label, complete with all information required to be displayed at the point of retail sale, is shown legibly and is not combined or associated directly with any other mark or logo.

§ 16.8 Termination of participation.

(a) The Secretary upon finding that a participant is not complying with the conditions set out in these procedures or in a Specification may terminate upon 30 days notice the participant's right to continue his participation in the program: *Provided*, That the participant shall first by given an opportunity to show cause why the participation should not be terminated.

(b) Upon receipt of a notice from the Secretary of the proposed termination, which notice shall set forth the reasons for such proposed termination, the participant shall have thirty (30) days from the date of receipt of such notification to request a hearing under the provisions of 5 U.S.C. 556. The Secretary's proposed termination shall become final through the issuance of a written decision to the participant in the event such participant does not appeal the proposed termination within the thirty (30) day period. If, however, the participant requests a hearing within the thirty (30) day period, the Secretary's proposed termination shall be stayed pending the outcome of the hearing held pursuant to 5 U.S.C. 556.

(c) A participant may at any time terminate his participation and responsibilities under this program with regard to a specific type of product by giving written notice to the Secretary that he has discontinued use of the Department of Commerce Label and Mark for all consumer products of the type involved.

§ 16.9 Rules governing designated agents.

(a) The following rules, requirements and tasks shall be applicable with respect to the seeking of designated agent status and the performance of that role after such status has been obtained. Each person desiring to be designated as a designated agent under this program shall:

(1) Make written application to the Secretary;

(2) Provide appropriate information showing his qualifications to represent members within a given product area and that more than one prospective participant in that product area is agreeable to such representation; and

(3) Agree to service any participant in this program in the agent's cognizant product area whether or not such participant is a member of the organization or body which that agent represents.

(b) The Secretary may require a person seeking designated agent status to supply further information before granting such status to that person. The Secretary will notify each person seeking designated agent status, in writing, as expeditiously as possible after evaluating such person's application.

(c) Each person granted designated agent status shall:

(1) Provide the Secretary with a list of the participants that the designated agent services under the program. The Secretary shall also be provided an updated list as soon thereafter as may be practicable whenever there are any changes in the list;

(2) Collect fees and charges from the participants serviced under this program, consolidate such sums, and transmit those fees and charges required under § 16.6 to the Secreatry;

(3) Distribute Department of Commerce Marks developed under § 16.10 or instructions for the printing of such Marks to the participants that the designated agent services under this program;

(4) Gather and consolidate such statistical information as may be required by the Secretary from individual participants serviced;

(5) Provide the Secretary with reports, including the consolidate statistical information referred to in paragraph (c)(4) of this section, as may be called for by her, relative to the activities of the participants the designated agent is servicing; and

(6) Perform any additional tasks mutually agreed upon by the designated agent and the Secretary.

(d) If a person seeking designated agent status is notified by the Secretary that she proposes to deny that person such status, that person shall have thirty (30) days from the date of receipt of such notification to request a hearing under the provisions of 5 U.S.C. 556. The Secretary's proposed denial shall become final through the issuance of a written decision to such person in the event that he does not appeal such notification by the end of that thirty (30) day period. If, however, such person requests a hearing within that thirty (30) day period, the Secretary proposed denial shall be stayed pending the outcome of the hearing held pursuant to 5 U.S.C. 556.

(e) If the Secretary finds that a designated agent has violated the terms of paragraph (c) of this section, she may, after consultations with such designated agent, notify such person that she proposes to revoke his status as a designated agent.

(f) Upon receipt of a notice from the Secretary of the proposed revocation, which notice shall set forth the reasons for such proposed revocation, the designated agent shall have thirty (30) days from the date of receipt of such notification to request a hearing under the provisions of U.S.C. 556. The Secretary's proposed revocation shall become final through the issuance of a written decision to the designated agent in the event such designated agent does not appeal the proposed revocation within that thirty (30) day period. If, however, the designated agent requires a hearing within that thirty (30) day period, the Secretary's proposed revocation shall be stayed pending the outcome of the hearing held pursuant to 5 U.S.C. 556.

§ 16.10 The Department of Commerce Mark.

The Department of Commerce shall develop a Mark which shall be registered in the U.S. Patent and Trademark Office under 15 U.S.C. 1054 for use on each Label described in a Specification.

§ 16.11 Amendment or revision of a performance information labeling specification.

The Secretary may by order amend or revise any Specification published under § 16.5. The procedure applicable to the establishment of a Specification under § 16.5 shall be followed in amending or revising such Specification. Such amendment or revision shall not apply to consumer products manufactured prior to the effective date of the amendment or revision.

§ 16.12 Consumer education.

The Secretary, in close cooperation and coordination with interested Government agencies, appropriate trade associations and industry members, consumer organizations, and other interested persons shall carry out a program to educate consumers relative to the significance of the labeling program. Some elements of this program shall also be directed toward informing retailers and other interested groups about the program.

§ 16.13 Coordination with State and local programs.

The Secretary will establish and maintain an active program of communication with appropriate State and local government offices and agencies and will furnish and make available information and assistance that will promote uniformity in State and local programs for the labeling of performance characteristics of consumer products.

§ 16.14 Annual report.

The Secretary will prepare an annual report of activities under the program, including an evaluation of the program and a list of participants, designated agents, and types of consumer products covered.

PART 17—LICENSING OF GOVERNMENT-OWNED INVENTIONS IN THE CUSTODY OF THE DEPARTMENT OF COMMERCE

AUTHORITY: Sec. 205(c), 63 Stat. 390 (40 U.S.C. 486(c)).

EDITORIAL NOTE: 41 CFR Part 101–4 referred to in this part was removed at 50 FR 28402, July 12, 1985.

Subpart A—Licensing of Rights in Domestic Patents and Patent Applications

§ 17.1 Licensing rules.

(a) The Government-wide rules for the licensing of rights in domestic patents and patent applications vested in the United States of America, found at 41 CFR 101–4.1, are applicable to all such licensing activities of the Department of Commerce, subject to the following minor clarifications:

(1) The term "Government agency" as defined at 41 CFR 101–4.102(c) means the United States Department of Commerce or a designated operating unit within the Department.

(2) The term "The head of the Government agency", as defined at 41 CFR 101–4.102(d), means the Secretary of Commerce or a designee.

(b) [Reserved]

[42 FR 54415, Oct. 6, 1977]

Subpart B—Licensing of Rights in Foreign Patents and Patent Applications [Reserved]

Subpart C—Appeal Procedures for Licensing Department of Commerce Patents

SOURCE: 49 FR 7986, Mar. 5, 1984, unless otherwise noted.

§ 17.21 Purpose.

This subpart describes the terms, conditions and procedures under which a party may appeal from a decision of the Director of the National Technical Information Service concerning the grant, denial, interpretation, modification or termination of a license of any patent in the custody of the Department of Commerce.

§ 17.22 Definitions.

(a) 41 CFR Part 101–4 shall mean the General Services Administration Final Rule concerning "Patents: Licensing of Federally Owned Inventions" which was originally published in the FEDERAL REGISTER, volume 47, number 152, Friday, August 6, 1982 at pages 34148 through 34151.

(b) Director shall mean the Director of the National Technical Information Service, and operating agency within the U.S. Department of Commerce.

(c) Under Secretary means the Under Secretary for Technology who is an officer appointed by the President and confirmed by the Senate and is an official to whom the Director reports within the Department of Commerce.

[49 FR 7986, Mar. 5, 1984, as amended at 55 FR 38983, Sept. 24, 1990]

§ 17.23 Authority to grant licenses.

The Director has been duly delegated authority to make any decision or determination concerning the granting, denial, interpretation, modification or termination of any license of any patent in the custody and control of the U.S. Department of Commerce. The decision and determination of the Director is final and conclusive on behalf of this Department unless the procedures for appeal set forth below are initiated.

§ 17.24 Persons who may appeal.

The following person(s) may appeal to the Under Secretary any decision or determination concerning the grant, denial, interpretation, modification or termination of a license:

(a) A person whose application for a license has been denied;

(b) A licensee whose license has been modified or terminated in whole or in part; or

(c) A person who has timely filed a written objection in response to the notice published in the FEDERAL REGISTER as required by 41 CFR 101–4.104–3(a)(1)(c)(i) or 101–4.104–3(b)(1)(i) and who can demonstrate to the satisfaction of the Under Secretary that such person may be damaged by the Director's determination.

[49 FR 7986, Mar. 5, 1984, as amended at 55 FR 38983, Sept. 24, 1990]

§ 17.25 Procedures.

(a) Any appellant party(ies) who was denied a license by the Director under § 17.24(a) shall not be entitled to an adversary hearing. Such party(ies) shall file appropriate documents no later than 30 days from the receipt of the Director's decision unless the Under Secretary grants for good cause an extension of time. The notice, in concise and brief terms, should state the grounds for appeal and include copies of all pertinent documents. Accompanying the notice should be concise arguments as to why the Director's decision should be rejected or modified.

(b) The Under Secretary shall render a written opinion within 30 days of receiving all required documentation in a non-adversary appeal.

(c) Judicial review is available as the law permits.

[49 FR 7986, Mar. 5, 1984, as amended at 55 FR 38983, Sept. 24, 1990]

§17.26 Adjudicatory.

(a) Any appellant party who seeks review of the Director's decision based upon a modification or termination of a license by the Director under §17.24(b), or who has filed a timely objection and can demonstrate damages as provided in §17.24(c), shall be entitled to an adversary hearing in accord with the provisions of the Administrative Procedures Act (5 U.S.C. 554–557). A party may waive an adversary hearing by filing a written waiver with the Under Secretary.

(b) When an adversary hearing is required under §17.24 (b) or (c) the Under Secretary shall appoint as promptly as possible an Administrative Law Judge who shall hold hearings no later than 45 days from the date of the appointment. The hearings will be conducted in conformity with the objectives of the Administrative Procedure Act. The Administrative Law Judge shall submit a written recommendation to the Under Secretary no later than 30 days subsequent to the hearing and/or the filing of any required written arguments or documentation.

(c) The Under Secretary shall render a final written decision on behalf of the Department based upon the appeal file which shall include the hearing record, exhibits, written submissions of the party(ies), and the recommendation of the Administrative Law Judge. The Under Secretary's decision shall include the reasons which form the basis of the determination. The final decision may uphold, overrule, or modify the Director's decision or take any action deemed appropriate.

(d) Judicial review is available as the law permits.

[49 FR 7986, Mar. 5, 1984, as amended at 55 FR 38983, Sept. 24, 1990]

PART 18—ATTORNEY'S FEES AND OTHER EXPENSES

GENERAL PROVISIONS

Sec.

AUTHORITY: 5 U.S.C. 504(c)(1).

SOURCE: 47 FR 13510, Mar. 31, 1982, unless otherwise noted.

GENERAL PROVISIONS

§18.1 Purpose of these rules.

The Equal Access to Justice Act, 5 U.S.C. 504 (called "the Act" in this part), provides for the award of attorney fees and other expenses to eligible individuals and entities who are parties to certain administrative proceedings (called "adversary adjudications") before the Department of Commerce (the word Department includes its component agencies). An eligible party may receive an award when it prevails over the Department, unless the Department's position in the proceeding was substantially justified or special circumstances make an award unjust. The rules in this part describe the parties that are eligible for awards and the Department's proceedings that are covered by the Act. They also explain how to apply for awards, and the procedures and standards that the Department will use to make them.

§18.2 Definitions.

As used in this part:

(a) *Adversary adjudication* means an adjudication under 5 U.S.C. 554 in which the position of the United States is represented by counsel or otherwise, but excludes an adjudication for the purpose of establishing or fixing a rate or for the purpose of granting or renewing a license.

(b) *Adjudicative officer* means the official, without regard to whether the official is designated as an administrative law judge, a hearing officer or examiner, or otherwise, who presided at the adversary adjudication.

§ 18.3 When the Act applies.

The Act applies to any adversary adjudication pending or commenced before the Department on or after August 5, 1985. It also applies to any adversary adjudication commenced on or after October 1, 1984, and finally disposed of before August 5, 1985, provided that an application for fees and expenses, as described in §§ 18.11 through 18.14 of this part, has been filed with the Department within 30 days after August 5, 1985, and to any adversary adjudication pending on or commenced on or after October 1, 1981, in which an application for fees and other expenses was timely filed and was dismissed for lack of jurisdiction.

[53 FR 6798, Mar. 3, 1988]

§ 18.4 Proceedings covered.

(a) The Act applies to adversary adjudications conducted by the Department and to appeals of decisions of contracting officers of the Department made pursuant to section 6 of the Contract Disputes Act of 1978 (41 U.S.C. 605) before agency boards of contract appeals as provided in section 8 of that Act (41 U.S.C. 607). Adversary adjudications conducted by the Department are adjudications under 5 U.S.C. 554 in which the position of this or any other agency of the United States, or any component of an agency, is presented by an attorney or other representative who enters an appearance and participates in the proceeding. Pursuant to section 8(c) of the Contract Disputes Act (41 U.S.C. 607(c)), the Department has arranged for appeals from decisions by contracting officers of the Department to be decided by the General Services Administration Board of Contract Appeals. This Board, in accordance with its own procedures, shall be responsible for making determinations on applications pursuant to the Act relating to appeals to the Board from decisions of contracting officers of the Department. Such determinations are final, subject to appeal under § 18.23. Any proceeding in which the Department may prescribe a lawful present or future rate is not covered by the Act. Proceedings to grant or renew licenses are also excluded, but proceedings to modify, suspend, or revoke licenses are covered if they are otherwise "adversary adjudications." The Department proceedings covered are:

(1) *Department-wide.* (i) Title VI Civil Rights hearings conducted by the Department under 42 U.S.C. 2000d–1 and 15 CFR 8.12(d).

(ii) Handicap discrimination hearings conducted by the Department under 29 U.S.C. 794(a) and 15 CFR 8.12(d).

(2) National Oceanic and Atmospheric Administration ("NOAA")

(i) Proceedings concerning suspension, revocation, or modification of a permit or license issued by NOAA.

(ii) Proceedings to assess civil penalties under any of the statutes administered by NOAA.

(3) *International Trade Administration.* Enforcement proceedings under the AntiBoycott provisions of the Export Administration Act of 1979, 50 U.S.C. app. 2407.

(4) *Patent and Trademark Office.* Disbarment proceedings of attorneys and agents under 35 U.S.C. 32.

(b) The Department may also designate a proceeding not listed in paragraph (a) of this section as an adversary adjudication for purposes of the Act by so stating in an order initiating the proceeding or designating the matter for hearing. The Department's failure to designate a proceeding as an adversary adjudication shall not preclude the filing of an application by a party who believes the proceeding is covered by the Act; whether the proceeding is covered will then be an issue for resolution in proceedings on the application.

(c) If a proceeding includes both matters covered by the Act and matters specifically excluded from coverage, any award made will include only fees and expenses related to covered issues.

[47 FR 13510, Mar. 31, 1982, as amended at 53 FR 6798, Mar. 3, 1988]

§ 18.5 Eligibility of applicants.

(a) To be eligible for an award of attorney fees and other expenses under the Act, the applicant must be a party to the adversary adjudication for which it seeks an award. The term "party" is defined in 5 U.S.C. 551(3). The applicant must show that it meets all conditions of eligibility set out in this part.

(b) The types of eligible applicants are as follows:

(1) An individual with a net worth of not more than $2 million;

(2) The sole owner of an unincorporated business who has a net worth of not more than $7 million, including both personal and business interests, and not more than 500 employees;

(3) A charitable or other tax-exempt organization described in section 501(c)(3) of the Internal Revenue Code (26 U.S.C. 501(c)(3)) with not more than 500 employees;

(4) A cooperative association as defined in section 15(a) of the Agricultural Marketing Act (12 U.S.C. 1141j(a)) with not more than 500 employees; and

(5) Any other partnership, corporation, association, unit of local government, or organization with a net worth of not more than $7 million and not more than 500 employees.

(c) For the purpose of eligibility, the net worth and number of employees of an applicant shall be determined as of the date the proceeding was initiated.

(d) An applicant who owns an unincorporated business will be considered as an "individual" rather than a "sole owner of an unincorporated business" if the issues on which the applicant prevails are related primarily to personal interests rather than to business interests.

(e) The employees of an applicant include all persons who regularly perform services for remuneration for the applicant, under the applicant's direction and control. Part-time employees shall be included on a proportional basis.

(f) The net worth and number of employees of the applicant and all of its affiliates shall be aggregated to determine eligibility. Any individual, corporation or other entity that directly or indirectly controls or owns a majority of the voting shares or other interest of the applicant, or any corporation or other entity of which the applicant directly or indirectly owns or controls a majority of the voting shares or other interest, will be considered an affiliate for purposes of this part, unless the adjudicative officer determines that such treatment would be unjust and contrary to the purposes of the Act in light of the actual relationship between the affiliated entities. In addition, the adjudicative officer may determine that financial relationships of the applicant other than those described in this paragraph constitute special circumstances that would make an award unjust.

(g) An applicant that participates in a proceeding primarily on behalf of one or more other persons or entities that would be ineligible is not itself eligible for an award.

[47 FR 13510, Mar. 31, 1982, as amended at 53 FR 6798, Mar. 3, 1988]

§ 18.6 Standards for awards.

(a) A prevailing applicant may receive an award for fees and expenses incurred in connection with a proceeding, or in a significant and discrete substantive portion of the proceedings, unless the position of the Department over which the applicant has prevailed was substantially justified. The position of the Department includes, in addition to the position taken by the Department in the adversary adjudication, the action or failure to act by the Department upon which the adversary adjudication is based. The burden of proof that an award should not be made to an eligible prevailing applicant because the Department's position was substantially justified is on the agency counsel.

(b) An award will be reduced or denied if the applicant has unduly or unreasonably protracted the proceeding or if special circumstances make the award sought unjust.

[47 FR 13510, Mar. 31, 1982, as amended at 53 FR 6799, Mar. 3, 1988]

§ 18.7 Allowable fees and expenses.

(a) Awards will be based on rates customarily charged by persons engaged in the business of acting as attorneys, agents and expert witnesses, even if the services were made available without charge or at a reduced rate to the applicant.

(b) No award for the fee of an attorney or agent under this rule may exceed $75.00 per hour. No award to compensate an expert witness may exceed the highest rate at which the Department pays expert witnesses. However, an award may also include the reasonable expenses of the attorney, agent, or witness as a separate item, if the attorney, agent, or witness ordinarily charges clients separately for such expenses.

(c) In determining the reasonableness of the fee sought for an attorney, agent, or expert witness, the adjudicative officer shall consider the following:

(1) If the attorney, agent, or witness is in private practice, his or her customary fee for similar services, or, if an employee of the applicant, the fully allocated cost of the services;

(2) The prevailing rate for similar services in the community in which the attorney, agent or witness ordinarily performs services;

(3) The time actually spent in the representation of the applicant;

(4) The time reasonably spent in light of the difficulty or complexity of the issues in the proceedings; and

(5) Such other factors as may bear on the value of the services provided.

(d) The reasonable cost of any study, analysis, engineering report, test, project, or similar matter prepared on behalf of a party may be awarded, to the extent that the charge for the service does not exceed the prevailing rate for similar services, and the study or other matter was necessary for preparation of the applicant's case.

[47 FR 13510, Mar. 31, 1982, as amended at 53 FR 6799, Mar. 3, 1988]

§ 18.8 Rulemaking on maximum rates for attorney fees.

(a) If warranted by an increase in the cost of living or by special circumstances (such as limited availability of attorneys qualified to handle certain types of proceedings), the Department may adopt regulations providing that attorney fees may be awarded at a rate higher than the ceiling set forth in § 18.7(b) in some or all of the types of proceedings covered by this part. The Department will conduct any rulemaking proceedings for this purpose under the informal rulemaking procedures of the Administrative Procedure Act.

(b) Any person may file with the Department a petition for rulemaking to increase the maximum rate for attorney fees. The petition should be sent to the General Counsel, Department of Commerce, 14th Street and Constitution Avenue, Room 5870, Washington, D.C. 20230. The petition should identify the rate the petitioner believes the Department should establish and the types of proceedings in which the rate should be used. It should also explain fully the reasons why higher rate is warranted. The Department will respond to the petition within 60 days after it is filed, by initiating a rulemaking proceeding, denying the petition, or taking other appropriate action.

§ 18.9 Awards against other agencies.

If an applicant is entitled to an award because it prevailed over another agency of the United States that participated in a proceeding before the Department and took a position that was not substantially justified, the award or an appropriate portion of the award shall be made against that agency.

§ 18.10 Delegations of authority.

The Secretary delegates to the General Counsel the authority to take final action on matters pertaining to the Act.

INFORMATION REQUIRED FROM APPLICANTS

§ 18.11 Contents of application.

(a) An application for an award of fees and expenses under the Act shall identify the applicant and the proceeding for which an award is sought. The application shall show that the applicant has prevailed and identify the position of the Department or other agency in the proceeding that the applicant alleges was not substantially justified. Unless the applicant is an individual, the application shall also state the number of employees of the applicant and describe briefly the type and purpose of its organization or business.

(b) The application shall also include a statement that the applicant's net worth does not exceed $2 million (if an individual) or $7 million (for all other applicants, including their affiliates). However, an applicant may omit this statement if:

(1) It attaches a copy of a ruling by the Internal Revenue Service that it qualifies as an organization described in section 501(c)(3) of the Internal Revenue Code (26 U.S.C. 501(c)(3)), or, in the case of a tax-exempt organization not required to obtain a ruling from the Internal Revenue Service on its exempt status, a statement that describes the basis for the applicant's belief that it qualifies under such section; or

(2) It states that it is a cooperative association as defined in section 15(a) of the Agricultural Marketing Act (12 U.S.C. 1141j(a)) and includes a copy of its charter or articles of incorporation.

(c) The application shall state the amount of fees and expenses for which an award is sought.

(d) The application may also include any other matters that the applicant wishes the adjudicative officer to consider in determining whether and in what amount an award should be made.

(e) The application shall be signed by the applicant or an authorized officer or attorney of the applicant. It shall also contain or be accompanied by a written verification under oath or under penalty of perjury that the information provided in the application is true and correct.

[47 FR 13510, Mar. 31, 1982, as amended at 53 FR 6799, Mar. 3, 1988]

§ 18.12 Net worth exhibit.

(a) Each applicant except a qualified tax-exempt organization or cooperative association must provide with its application a detailed exhibit showing the net worth of the applicant and any affiliates (as defined in § 18.5(f) of this part) when the proceeding was initiated. Unless regulations issued by a component of the Department establish particular requirements, the exhibit may be in any form convenient to the applicant that provides full disclosure of the applicant's and its affiliates' assets and liabilities and is sufficient to determine whether the applicant qualifies under the standards in this part. The adjudicative officer may require an applicant to file additional information to determine its eligibility for an award.

(b) Ordinarily, the net worth exhibit will be included in the public record of the proceeding. However, an applicant that objects to public disclosure of information in any portion of the exhibit and believes there are legal grounds for withholding it from disclosure may submit that portion of the exhibit directly to the adjudicative officer in a sealed envelope labeled "Confidential Financial Information," accompanied by a motion to withhold the information from public disclosure. The motion shall describe the information sought to be withheld and explain, in detail, why it falls within one or more of the specific exemptions from mandatory disclosure under the Freedom of Information Act, 5 U.S.C. 552(b)(1)–(9), why public disclosure of the information would adeversely affect the applicant, and why disclosure is not required in the public interest. The material in question shall be served on counsel representing the agency against which the applicant seeks an award, but need not be served on any other party to the proceeding. If the adjudicative officer finds that the information should not be withheld from disclosure, it shall be placed in the public record of the proceeding. Otherwise, any request to inspect or copy the exhibit shall be disposed of in accordance with the Department's established procedures under the Freedom of Information Act (15 CFR Part 4).

[47 FR 13510, Mar. 31, 1982, as amended at 53 FR 6799, Mar. 3, 1988]

§ 18.13 Documentation of fees and expenses.

The application shall be accompanied by full documentation of the fees and expenses, including the cost of any study, analysis, engineering report, test, project, or similar matter for which an award is sought. A separate itemized statement shall be submitted for each professional firm or individual whose services are covered by the application, showing the hours spent in connection with the proceeding by each individual, a description of the specific services performed, the rate at which each fee has been computed, any expenses for which reimbursement is sought, the total amount claimed, and the total amount paid or payable by the applicant or by any other person or entity for the services provided. The adjudicative officer may require the applicant to provide vouchers, receipts, or other substantiation for any expenses claimed.

§ 18.14 When an application may be filed.

(a) An application may be filed whenever the applicant has prevailed in the proceeding or in a significant and discrete substantive portion of the proceeding, but in no case later than 30 days after the Department's final disposition of the proceeding.

(b) For purposes of this rule, final disposition means the date on which a decision or order disposing of the merits of the proceeding or any other complete resolution of the proceeding, such as a settlement or voluntary dismissal, becomes final and unappealable, both within the agency and to the courts.

(c) If review or reconsideration is sought or taken of a decision as to which an applicant believes it has prevailed, proceedings for the award of fees shall be stayed pending final disposition of the underlying controversy. When the United States appeals the underlying merits of an adversary adjudication to a court, no decision on an application for fees and other expenses in connection with that adversary adjudication shall be made until a final and unreviewable decision is rendered by the court on the appeal or until the underlying merits of the case have been finally determined pursuant to the appeal.

[47 FR 13510, Mar. 31, 1982, as amended at 53 FR 6799, Mar. 3, 1988]

PROCEDURES FOR CONSIDERING APPLICATIONS

§ 18.15 Filing and service of documents.

Any application for an award or other pleading or document related to an application shall be filed and served on all parties to the proceeding in the same manner as other pleadings in the proceeding, except as provided in § 18.12(b) for confidential financial information.

§ 18.16 Answer to application.

(a) Within 30 calendar days after service of an application, counsel representing the agency against which an award is sought may file an answer to the application. Unless agency counsel requests an extension of time for filing (an extension for an additional 30 days is available as a matter of right) or files a statement of intent to negotiate under paragraph (b) of this section, failure to file an answer within the 30 calendar day period may be treated as a consent to the award requested.

(b) If agency counsel and the applicant believe that the issues in the fee application can be settled, they may jointly file a statement of their intent to negotiate a settlement. The filing of this statement shall extend the time for filing an answer for an additional 30 days, and further extensions may be granted by the adjudicative officer upon request by agency counsel and the applicant.

(c) The answer shall explain in detail any objections to the award requested and identify the facts relied on in support of the agency counsel's position. If the answer is based on any alleged facts not already in the record of the proceeding, agency counsel shall include with the answer either supporting affidavits or a request for further proceedings under § 18.20.

[47 FR 13510, Mar. 31, 1982, as amended at 53 FR 6799, Mar. 3, 1988]

§ 18.17 Reply.

Within 15 calendar days after service of an answer, the applicant may file a reply. If the reply is based on any alleged facts not already in the record of the proceeding, the applicant shall include with the reply either supporting affidavits or a request for further proceedings under § 18.20.

§ 18.18 Comments by other parties.

Any party to a proceeding other than the applicant and the agency counsel may file comments on an application within 30 calendar days after it is served or on an answer within 15 calendar days after it is served. A commenting party may not participate further in proceedings on the application unless the adjudicative officer determines that the public interest requires such participation in order to permit full exploration of matters raised in the comments.

[47 FR 13510, Mar. 31, 1982, as amended at 53 FR 6799, Mar. 3, 1988]

§ 18.19 Settlement.

The applicant and agency counsel may agree on a proposed settlement of the award before final action on the application, either in connection with a settlement of the underlying proceeding, or after the underlying proceeding has been concluded, in accordance with the component agency's standard settlement procedure. If a prevailing party and agency counsel agree on a proposed settlement of an award before an application has been filed, the application shall be filed with the proposed settlement.

[47 FR 13510, Mar. 31, 1982, as amended at 53 FR 6799, Mar. 3, 1988]

§ 18.20 Further proceedings.

(a) Ordinarily, the determination of an award will be made on the basis of the written record. However, on request of either the applicant or agency counsel, or on his or her own initiative, the adjudicative officer may order further proceedings, such as an informal conference, oral argument, additional written submissions or, as to issues other than substantial justification (such as the applicant's eligibility or substantiation of fees and expenses), pertinent discovery or an evidentiary hearing. Such further proceedings shall be held only when necessary for full and fair resolution of the issues arising from the application, and shall be conducted as promptly as possible. Whether or not the position of the agency was substantially justified shall be determined on the basis of the administrative record, as a whole, which is made in the adversary adjudication for which fees and other expenses are sought.

(b) A request that the adjudicative officer order further proceedings under this section shall specifically identify the information sought or the disputed issues and shall explain why the additional proceedings are necessary to resolve the issues.

[47 FR 13510, Mar. 31, 1982, as amended at 53 FR 6799, Mar. 3, 1988]

§ 18.21 Decision.

The adjudicative officer shall issue an initial decision on the application within 30 calendar days after completion of proceedings on the application. The initial decision of the adjudicative officer shall include written findings and conclusions on the applicant's eligibility and status as a prevailing party, and an explanation of the reasons for any difference between the amount requested and the amount awarded. The decision shall also include, if at issue, findings on whether the Department's position was substantially justified, whether the applicant unduly protracted the proceedings, or whether special circumstances make an award unjust. If the applicant has sought an award against more than one agency, the decision shall allocate responsibility for payment of any award made among the agencies, and shall explain the reasons for the allocation made.

[47 FR 13510, Mar. 31, 1982, as amended at 53 FR 6799, Mar. 3, 1988]

§ 18.22 Agency review.

Either the applicant or agency counsel may file a petition for review of the initial decision on the fee application, or the Department may decide to review the decision on its own initiative. The petition must be filed with the General Counsel, Office of the Assistant General Counsel for Administration, Rm. 5882, U.S. Department of Commerce, 14th Street and Pennsylvania Avenue NW., Washington, DC 20230, not later than 30 calendar days after the initial decision is issued. For purposes of this section, a document will be considered filed with the General Counsel as of the date of the postmark (or for government penalty mail, as shown by a certificate of mailing), if mailed, or if not mailed, as of the date actually delivered to the Office of General Counsel. A petition for review must be accompanied by a full written statement in support thereof, including a precise statement of why the petitioner believes the initial decision should be reversed or modified, and proof of service upon all parties. A response to the petition may be filed by another party to the proceeding and must be filed with the General Counsel at the above address not more than 30 calendar days after the date of service of the petition for review. The General Counsel may request any further submissions deemed helpful in resolving the petition for review. If neither the applicant nor agency counsel seeks review and the Department does not take review on its own initiative, the initial decision on the application shall become a final decision of the Department 30 calendar days after it is issued. Whether to review a decision is a matter within the discretion of the General Counsel. If review is taken, the General Counsel will issue the Department's final decision on the application or remand the application to the adjudicative officer for further proceedings. The standard of review exercised by the General Counsel shall be that which was required for the highest level of Departmental review which could have been exercised on the underlying covered proceeding.

[53 FR 6799, Mar. 3, 1988]

§ 18.23 Judicial review.

Judicial review of final agency decisions on awards may be sought as provided in 5 U.S.C. 504(c)(2).

§ 18.24 Payment of award.

An applicant seeking payment of an award by the Department shall submit a copy of the final decision granting the award, accompanied by a certification that the applicant will not seek review of the decision in the United States courts to the General Counsel, U.S. Department of Commerce, 14th Street and Constitution Avenue, NW., Room 5870, Washington, D.C. 20230. The Department will pay the amount awarded to the applicant within 60 calendar days, unless judicial review of the award or of the underlying decision of the adversary adjudication has been sought by the applicant or any other party to the proceeding.

[47 FR 13510, Mar. 31, 1982, as amended at 53 FR 6800, Mar. 3, 1988]

PART 19—COMMERCE DEBT COLLECTION

Subpart A—General Provisions

Sec.

Subpart B—Procedures To Collect Commerce Debts

AUTHORITY: 31 U.S.C. 3701, *et seq.*

SOURCE: 72 FR 18871, Apr. 16, 2007, unless otherwise noted.

Subpart A—General Provisions

§ 19.1 What definitions apply to the regulations in this Part?

As used in this Part:

Administrative offset or *offset* means withholding funds payable by the United States (including funds payable by the United States on behalf of a state government) to, or held by the United States for, a person to satisfy a debt owed by the person. The term "administrative offset" can include, but is not limited to, the offset of Federal salary, vendor, retirement, and Social Security benefit payments. The terms "centralized administrative offset" and "centralized offset" refer to the process by which the Treasury Department's Financial Management Service offsets Federal payments through the Treasury Offset Program.

Administrative wage garnishment means the process by which a Federal agency orders a non-Federal employer to withhold amounts from a debtor's wages to satisfy a debt, as authorized by 31 U.S.C. 3720D, 31 CFR 285.11, and this Part.

Agency or *Federal agency* means a department, agency, court, court administrative office, or instrumentality in the executive, judicial, or legislative branch of the Federal Government, including government corporations.

Commerce debt means a debt owed to a Commerce entity by a person.

Commerce Department means the United States Department of Commerce.

Commerce entity means a component of the Commerce Department, including offices or bureaus. Commerce offices currently include the Office of the Secretary of Commerce, and the Office of Inspector General. Commerce bureaus currently include the Bureau of Industry and Security, the Economics and Statistics Administration (including the Bureau of Economic Analysis, and the Bureau of the Census), the Economic Development Administration, the International Trade Administration, the Minority Business Development Agency, the National Oceanic and Atmospheric Administration, the National Telecommunications and Information Administration, the U.S. Patent and Trademark Office, and the Technology Administration (including the National Institute of Standards and Technology, and the National Technical Information Service).

Creditor agency means any Federal agency that is owed a debt.

Day means calendar day except when express reference is made to business day, which reference shall mean Monday through Friday. For purposes of time computation, the last day of the period provided will be included in the calculation unless that day is a Saturday, a Sunday, or a Federal legal holiday; in which case, the next business day will be included.

Debt means any amount of money, funds or property that has been determined by an appropriate official of the Federal Government to be owed to the United States by a person. As used in this Part, the term "debt" can include a Commerce debt but does not include debts arising under the Internal Revenue Code of 1986 (26 U.S.C. 1 *et seq.*).

Debtor means a person who owes a debt to the United States.

Delinquent debt means a debt that has not been paid by the date specified in the agency's initial written demand for payment or applicable agreement or instrument (including a post-delinquency payment agreement) unless other satisfactory payment arrangements have been made.

Delinquent Commerce debt means a delinquent debt owed to a Commerce entity.

Disposable pay has the same meaning as that term is defined in 5 CFR 550.1103.

Employee or *Federal employee* means a current employee of the Commerce Department or other Federal agency, including a current member of the uniformed services, including the Army, Navy, Air Force, Marine Corps, Coast Guard, Commissioned Corps of the National Oceanic and Atmospheric Administration, and Commissioned Corps of the Public Health Service, including the National Guard and the reserve forces of the uniformed services.

FCCS means the Federal Claims Collection Standards, which were jointly published by the Departments of the Treasury and Justice and codified at 31 CFR Parts 900–904.

Financial Management Service means the Financial Management Service, a bureau of the Treasury Department, which is responsible for the centralized collection of delinquent debts through the offset of Federal payments and other means.

Payment agency or *Federal payment agency* means any Federal agency that transmits payment requests in the form of certified payment vouchers, or other similar forms, to a disbursing official for disbursement. The payment agency may be the agency that employs the debtor. In some cases, the Commerce Department may be both the creditor agency and payment agency.

Person means an individual, corporation, partnership, association, organization, State or local government or any other type of entity other than a Federal agency.

Salary offset means a type of administrative offset to collect a debt under 5 CFR 5514 by deductions(s) at one or more officially established pay intervals from the current pay account of an employee without his or her consent.

Secretary means the Secretary of Commerce.

Tax refund offset is defined in 31 CFR 285.2(a).

§ 19.2 Why has the Commerce Department issuing these regulations and what do they cover?

(a) *Scope.* This Part provides procedures for the collection of Commerce debts. This Part also provides procedures for collection of other debts owed to the United States when a request for offset of a payment for which Commerce is the payment agency is received by the Commerce Department from another agency (for example, when a Commerce Department employee owes a debt to the United States Department of Education).

(b) *Applicability.* (1) This Part applies to the Commerce Department when collecting a Commerce debt, to persons who owe Commerce debts, to persons controlled by or controlling persons who owe Federal agency debts, and to Federal agencies requesting offset of a payment issued by the Commerce Department as a payment agency (including salary payments to Commerce Department employees).

(2) This Part does not apply to tax debts nor to any debt for which there is an indication of fraud or misrepresentation, as described in § 900.3 of the FCCS, unless the debt is returned by the Department of Justice to the Commerce Department for handling.

(3) Nothing in this Part precludes collection or disposition of any debt under statutes and regulations other than those described in this Part. See, for example, 5 U.S.C. 5705, Advancements and Deductions, which authorizes Commerce entities to recover travel advances by offset of up to 100% of a Federal employee's accrued pay. See, also, 5 U.S.C. 4108, governing the collection of training expenses. To the extent that the provisions of laws, other regulations, and Commerce Department enforcement policies differ from the provisions of this Part, those provisions of law, other regulations, and Commerce Department enforcement policies apply to the remission or mitigation of fines, penalties, and forfeitures, and to debts arising under the tariff laws of the United States, rather than the provisions of this Part.

(c) *Additional policies and procedures.* Commerce entities may, but are not required to, promulgate additional policies and procedures consistent with this Part, the FCCS, and other applicable Federal law, policies, and procedures, subject to the approval of Deputy Chief Financial Officer.

(d) *Duplication not required.* Nothing in this Part requires a Commerce entity to duplicate notices or administrative proceedings required by contract, this Part, or other laws or regulations, including but not limited to those required by financial assistance awards such as grants, cooperative agreements, loans or loan guarantees.

(e) *Use of multiple collection remedies allowed.* Commerce entities and other Federal agencies may simultaneously use multiple collection remedies to collect a debt, except as prohibited by law. This Part is intended to promote aggressive debt collection, using for each debt all available and appropriate collection remedies. These remedies are not listed in any prescribed order to provide Commerce entities with flexibility in determining which remedies will be most efficient in collecting the particular debt.

(f) All citations in this Part, such as to statutes, regulations and the Department of Commerce Credit and Debt Management Operating Procedures Handbook, are intended to be references to cited sources as each currently stands and as each may be amended from time to time.

§ 19.3 Do these regulations adopt the Federal Claims Collection Standards (FCCS)?

This Part adopts and incorporates all provisions of the FCCS. This Part also supplements the FCCS by prescribing procedures consistent with the FCCS, as necessary and appropriate for Commerce Department operations.

Subpart B—Procedures To Collect Commerce Debts

§ 19.4 What notice will Commerce entities send to a debtor when collecting a Commerce debt?

(a) *Notice requirements.* Commerce entities shall aggressively collect Commerce debts. Commerce entities shall promptly send at least one written notice to a debtor informing the debtor of the consequences of failing to pay or otherwise resolve a Commerce debt. The notice(s) shall be sent to the debtor at the most current address of the debtor in the records of the Commerce entity collecting the Commerce debt. Generally, before starting the collection actions described in §§ 19.5 and 19.9 through 19.17 of this Part, Commerce entities will send no more than two written notices to the debtor. The notice(s) explain why the Commerce debt is owed, the amount of the Commerce debt, how a debtor may pay the Commerce debt or make alternate repayment arrangements, how a debtor may review non-privileged documents related to the Commerce debt, how a debtor may dispute the Commerce debt, the collection remedies available to Commerce entities if the debtor refuses or otherwise fails to pay the Commerce debt, and other consequences to the debtor if the Commerce debt is not paid. Except as otherwise provided in paragraph (b) of this section, the written notice(s) shall explain to the debtor:

(1) The nature and amount of the Commerce debt, and the facts giving rise to the Commerce debt;

(2) How interest, penalties, and administrative costs are added to the Commerce debt, the date by which payment should be made to avoid such charges, and that such assessments must be made unless excused in accordance with 31 CFR 901.9 (see § 19.5 of this Part);

(3) The date by which payment should be made to avoid the enforced collection actions described in paragraph (a)(6) of this section;

(4) The Commerce entity's willingness to discuss alternative payment arrangements and how the debtor may enter into a written agreement to repay the Commerce debt under terms acceptable to the Commerce entity (see § 19.6 of this Part);

(5) The name, address, and telephone number of a contact person or office within the Commerce entity;

(6) The Commerce entity's intention to enforce collection by taking one or more of the following actions if the

debtor fails to pay or otherwise resolve the Commerce debt:

(i) *Offset.* Offset the debtor's Federal payments, including income tax refunds, salary, certain benefit payments (such as Social Security), retirement, vendor, travel reimbursements and advances, and other Federal payments (see §§ 19.10 through 19.12 of this Part);

(ii) *Private collection agency.* Refer the Commerce debt to a private collection agency (see § 19.15 of this Part);

(iii) *Credit bureau reporting.* Report the Commerce debt to a credit bureau (see § 19.14 of this Part);

(iv) *Administrative wage garnishment.* Garnish the individual debtor's wages through administrative wage garnishment (see § 19.13 of this Part);

(v) *Litigation.* Refer the Commerce debt to the Department of Justice to initiate litigation to collect the Commerce debt (see § 19.16 of this Part);

(vi) *Treasury Department's Financial Management Service.* Refer the Commerce debt to the Financial Management Service for collection (see § 19.9 of this Part);

(7) That Commerce debts over 180 days delinquent must be referred to the Financial Management Service for the collection actions described in paragraph (a)(6) of this section (see § 19.9 of this Part);

(8) How the debtor may inspect and copy non-privileged records related to the Commerce debt;

(9) How the debtor may request a review of the Commerce entity's determination that the debtor owes a Commerce debt and present evidence that the Commerce debt is not delinquent or legally enforceable (see §§ 19.10(c) and 19.11(c) of this Part);

(10) How a debtor who is an individual may request a hearing if the Commerce entity intends to garnish the debtor's private sector (*i.e.*, non-Federal) wages (see § 19.13(a) of this Part), including:

(i) The method and time period for requesting a hearing;

(ii) That a request for a hearing, timely filed on or before the 15th business day following the date of the mailing of the notice, will stay the commencement of administrative wage garnishment, but not other collection procedures; and

(iii) The name and address of the office to which the request for a hearing should be sent.

(11) How a debtor who is an individual and a Federal employee subject to Federal salary offset may request a hearing (see § 19.12(e) of this Part), including:

(i) The method and time period for requesting a hearing;

(ii) That a request for a hearing, timely filed on or before the 15th day following receipt of the notice, will stay the commencement of salary offset, but not other collection procedures;

(iii) The name and address of the office to which the request for a hearing should be sent;

(iv) That the Commerce entity will refer the Commerce debt to the debtor's employing agency or to the Financial Management Service to implement salary offset, unless the employee files a timely request for a hearing;

(v) That a final decision on the hearing, if requested, will be issued at the earliest practical date, but not later than 60 days after the filing of the request for a hearing, unless the employee requests and the hearing official grants a delay in the proceedings;

(vi) That any knowingly false or frivolous statements, representations, or evidence may subject the Federal employee to penalties under the False Claims Act (31 U.S.C. 3729–3731) or other applicable statutory authority, and criminal penalties under 18 U.S.C. 286, 287, 1001, and 1002, or other applicable statutory authority;

(vii) That unless prohibited by contract or statute, amounts paid on or deducted for the Commerce debt which are later waived or found not owed to the United States will be promptly refunded to the employee; and

(viii) That proceedings with respect to such Commerce debt are governed by 5 U.S.C. 5514 and 31 U.S.C. 3716.

(12) How the debtor may request a waiver of the Commerce debt, if applicable. See, for example, § 19.5 and § 19.12(f) of this Part.

(13) How the debtor's spouse may claim his or her share of a joint income tax refund by filing Form 8379 with the Internal Revenue Service (see *http://www.irs.gov*);

(14) How the debtor may exercise other rights and remedies, if any, available to the debtor under programmatic statutory or regulatory authority under which the Commerce debt arose.

(15) That certain debtors and, if applicable, persons controlled by or controlling such debtors, may be ineligible for Federal Government loans, guaranties and insurance, grants, cooperative agreements or other sources of Federal funds (see 28 U.S.C. 3201(e); 31 U.S.C. 3720B, 31 CFR 285.13, and § 19.17(a) of this Part);

(16) If applicable, the Commerce entity's intention to deny, suspend or revoke licenses, permits or privileges (see § 19.17(b) of this Part); and

(17) That the debtor should advise the Commerce entity of a bankruptcy proceeding of the debtor or another person liable for the Commerce debt being collected.

(b) *Exceptions to notice requirements.* A Commerce entity may omit from a notice to a debtor one or more of the provisions contained in paragraphs (a)(6) through (a)(17) of this section if the Commerce entity, in consultation with its legal counsel, determines that any provision is not legally required given the collection remedies to be applied to a particular Commerce debt.

(c) *Respond to debtors; comply with FCCS.* Commerce entities should respond promptly to communications from debtors and comply with other FCCS provisions applicable to the administrative collection of debts. See 31 CFR part 901.

§ 19.5 How will Commerce entities add interest, penalty charges, and administrative costs to a Commerce debt?

(a) *Assessment and notice.* Commerce entities shall assess interest, penalties and administrative costs on Commerce debts in accordance with the provisions of 31 U.S.C. 3717 and 31 CFR 901.9. Interest shall be charged in accordance with the requirements of 31 U.S.C. 3717(a). Penalties shall accrue at a rate of not more than 6% per year or such other higher rate as authorized by law. Administrative costs, that is, the costs of processing and handling a delinquent debt, shall be determined by the Commerce entity collecting the debt, as directed by the Office of the Deputy Chief Financial Officer. Commerce entities may have additional policies regarding how interest, penalties, and administrative costs are assessed on particular types of debts, subject to the approval of the Deputy Chief Financial Officer. Commerce entities are required to explain in the notice to the debtor described in § 19.4 of this Part how interest, penalties, costs, and other charges are assessed, unless the requirements are included in a contract or other legally binding agreement.

(b) *Waiver of interest, penalties, and administrative costs.* Unless otherwise required by law or contract, Commerce entities may not charge interest if the amount due on the Commerce debt is paid within 30 days after the date from which the interest accrues. See 31 U.S.C. 3717(d). Commerce entities may waive interest, penalties, and administrative costs, or any portion thereof, when it would be against equity and good conscience or not in the United States' best interest to collect such charges, in accordance with Commerce guidelines for such waivers. Legal counsel approval to waive such charges is required. See Department of Commerce Credit and Debt Management Operating Standards and Procedures Handbook (currently at *http://www.osec.doc.gov/ofm/credit/cover.htm).*

(c) *Accrual during suspension of debt collection.* In most cases, interest, penalties and administrative costs will continue to accrue during any period when collection has been suspended for any reason (for example, when the debtor has requested a hearing). Commerce entities may suspend accrual of any or all of these charges when accrual would be against equity and good conscience or not in the United States' best interest, in accordance with Commerce guidelines for such waivers. See Department of Commerce Credit and Debt Management Operating Standards and Procedures Handbook (currently at *http://www.osec.doc.gov/ofm/credit/cover.htm*).

§ 19.6 When will Commerce entities allow a debtor to pay a Commerce debt in installments instead of one lump sum?

If a debtor is financially unable to pay the Commerce debt in one lump sum, a Commerce entity may accept payment of a Commerce debt in regular installments, in accordance with the provisions of 31 CFR 901.8 and the Commerce entity's policies and procedures.

§ 19.7 When will Commerce entities compromise a Commerce debt?

If a Commerce entity cannot collect the full amount of a Commerce debt, the Commerce entity may compromise the Commerce debt in accordance with the provisions of 31 CFR part 902 and the Commerce entity's policies and procedures. Legal counsel approval to compromise a Commerce debt is required as described in Department of Commerce Credit and Debt Management Operating Standards and Procedures Handbook (currently at *http://www.osec.doc.gov/ofm/credit/cover.htm*).

§ 19.8 When will Commerce entities suspend or terminate debt collection on a Commerce debt?

If, after pursuing all appropriate means of collection, a Commerce entity determines that a Commerce debt is uncollectible, the Commerce entity may suspend or terminate debt collection activity in accordance with the provisions of 31 CFR part 903 and the Commerce entity's policies and procedures. Legal counsel approval to suspend or terminate collection on a Commerce debt is required as described in Department of Commerce Credit and Debt Management Operating Standards and Procedures Handbook (currently at *http://www.osec.doc.gov/ofm/credit/cover.htm*). Termination of debt collection activity by a Commerce entity does not discharge the indebtedness.

§ 19.9 When will Commerce entities transfer a Commerce debt to the Treasury Department's Financial Management Service for collection?

(a) Commerce entities will transfer any Commerce debt that is more than 180 days delinquent to the Financial Management Service for debt collection services, a process known as "cross-servicing." See 31 U.S.C. 3711(g) and 31 CFR 285.12. Commerce entities may transfer Commerce debts delinquent 180 days or less to the Financial Management Service in accordance with the procedures described in 31 CFR 285.12. The Financial Management Service takes appropriate action to collect or compromise the transferred Commerce debt, or to suspend or terminate collection action thereon, in accordance with the statutory and regulatory requirements and authorities applicable to the Commerce debt and the collection action to be taken. See 31 CFR 285.12(b) and 285.12(c)(2). Appropriate action can include, but is not limited to, contact with the debtor, referral of the Commerce debt to the Treasury Offset Program, private collection agencies or the Department of Justice, reporting of the Commerce debt to credit bureaus, and administrative wage garnishment.

(b) At least sixty (60) days prior to transferring a Commerce debt to the Financial Management Service, Commerce entities will send notice to the debtor as required by § 19.4 of this Part. Commerce entities will certify to the Financial Management Service, in writing, that the Commerce debt is valid, delinquent, legally enforceable, and that there are no legal bars to collection. In addition, Commerce entities will certify their compliance with all applicable due process and other requirements as described in this Part and other Federal laws. See 31 CFR 285.12(i) regarding the certification requirement.

(c) As part of its debt collection process, the Financial Management Service uses the Treasury Offset Program to collect Commerce debts by administrative and tax refund offset. See 31 CFR 285.12(g). The Treasury Offset Program is a centralized offset program administered by the Financial Management Service to collect delinquent debts owed to Federal agencies and states (including past-due child support). Under the Treasury Offset Program, before a Federal payment is disbursed, the Financial Management Service compares the name and taxpayer identification number (TIN) of the payee with the names and TINs of debtors that have been submitted by Federal agencies and states to the Treasury Offset Program database. If there is a match, the Financial Management Service (or, in some cases, another Federal disbursing agency) offsets all or a portion of the Federal payment, disburses any remaining payment to the payee, and pays the offset amount to the creditor agency. Federal payments eligible for offset include, but are not limited to, income tax refunds, salary, travel advances and reimbursements, retirement and vendor payments, and Social Security and other benefit payments.

§ 19.10 How will Commerce entities use administrative offset (offset of non-tax Federal payments) to collect a Commerce debt?

(a) *Centralized administrative offset through the Treasury Offset Program.* (1) In most cases, the Financial Management Service uses the Treasury Offset Program to collect Commerce debts by the offset of Federal payments. See § 19.9(c) of this Part. If not already transferred to the Financial Management Service under § 19.9 of this Part, Commerce entities will refer Commerce debt over 180 days delinquent to the Treasury Offset Program for collection by centralized administrative offset. See 31 U.S.C. 3716(c)(6); 31 CFR part 285, subpart A; and 31 CFR 901.3(b). Commerce entities may refer to the Treasury Offset Program for offset any Commerce debt that has been delinquent for 180 days or less.

(2) At least sixty (60) days prior to referring a Commerce debt to the Treasury Offset Program, in accordance with paragraph (a)(1) of this section, Commerce entities will send notice to the debtor in accordance with the requirements of § 19.4 of this Part. Commerce entities will certify to the Financial Management Service, in writing, that the Commerce debt is valid, delinquent, legally enforceable, and that there are no legal bars to collection by offset. In addition, Commerce entities will certify their compliance with the requirements described in this Part.

(b) *Non-centralized administrative offset for Commerce debts.* (1) When centralized administrative offset through the Treasury Offset Program is not available or appropriate, Commerce entities may collect past-due, legally enforceable Commerce debts through non-centralized administrative offset. See 31 CFR 901.3(c). In these cases, Commerce entities may offset a payment internally or make an offset request directly to a Federal payment agency. If the Federal payment agency is another Commerce entity, the Commerce entity making the request shall do so through the Deputy Chief Financial Officer as described in § 19.20(c) of this Part.

(2) At least thirty (30) days prior to offsetting a payment internally or requesting a Federal payment agency to offset a payment, Commerce entities will send notice to the debtor in accordance with the requirements of § 19.4 of this Part. When referring a Commerce debt for offset under this paragraph (b), Commerce entities making the request will certify, in writing, that the Commerce debt is valid, delinquent, legally enforceable, and that there are no legal bars to collection by offset. In addition, Commerce entities will certify their compliance with these regulations concerning administrative offset. See 31 CFR 901.3(c)(2)(ii).

(c) *Administrative review.* The notice described in § 19.4 of this Part shall explain to the debtor how to request an administrative review of a Commerce entity's determination that the debtor owes a Commerce debt and how to present evidence that the Commerce debt is not delinquent or legally enforceable. In addition to challenging the existence and amount of the Commerce debt, the debtor may seek a review of the terms of repayment. In most cases, Commerce entities will provide the debtor with a "paper hearing" based upon a review of the written record, including documentation provided by the debtor. Commerce entities shall provide the debtor with a reasonable opportunity for an oral hearing when the debtor requests reconsideration of the Commerce debt and the Commerce entity determines that the question of the indebtedness cannot be resolved by review of the documentary evidence, for example, when the validity of the Commerce debt turns on an issue of credibility or veracity. Unless otherwise required by law, an oral hearing under this section is not required to be a formal evidentiary hearing, although Commerce entities should carefully document all significant matters discussed at the hearing. Commerce entities may suspend collection through administrative offset and/or other collection actions pending the resolution of a debtor's dispute.

(d) *Procedures for expedited offset.* Under the circumstances described in 31 CFR 901.3(b)(4)(iii), Commerce entities may effect an offset against a payment to be made to the debtor prior to sending a notice to the debtor, as described in § 19.4 of this Part, or completing the procedures described in paragraph (b)(2) and (c) of this section. Commerce entities shall give the debtor notice and an opportunity for review as soon as practicable and promptly refund any money ultimately found not to have been owed to the Government. Legal counsel approval to effect such pre-notice offset is required as described in Department of Commerce Credit and Debt Management Operating Standards and Procedures Handbook (currently at *http://www.osec.doc.gov/ofm/credit/cover.htm*).

§ 19.11 How will Commerce entities use tax refund offset to collect a Commerce debt?

(a) *Tax refund offset.* In most cases, the Financial Management Service uses the Treasury Offset Program to collect Commerce debts by the offset of tax refunds and other Federal payments. See § 19.9(c) of this Part. If not already transferred to the Financial Management Service under § 19.9 of this Part, Commerce entities will refer to the Treasury Offset Program any past-due, legally enforceable Commerce debt for collection by tax refund offset. See 26 U.S.C. 6402(d), 31 U.S.C. 3720A and 31 CFR 285.2.

(b) *Notice.* At least sixty (60) days prior to referring a Commerce debt to the Treasury Offset Program, Commerce entities will send notice to the debtor in accordance with the requirements of § 19.4 of this Part. Commerce entities will certify to the Financial Management Service's Treasury Offset Program, in writing, that the Commerce debt is past due and legally enforceable in the amount submitted and that the Commerce entities have made reasonable efforts to obtain payment of the Commerce debt as described in 31 CFR 285.2(d). In addition, Commerce entities will certify their compliance with all applicable due process and other requirements described in this Part and other Federal laws. See 31 U.S.C. 3720A(b) and 31 CFR 285.2.

(c) *Administrative review.* The notice described in § 19.4 of this Part shall provide the debtor with at least 60 days prior to the initiation of tax refund offset to request an administrative review as described in § 19.10(c) of this Part. Commerce entities may suspend collection through tax refund offset and/or other collection actions pending the resolution of the debtor's dispute.

§ 19.12 How will Commerce entities offset a Federal employee's salary to collect a Commerce debt?

(a) *Federal salary offset.* (1) Salary offset is used to collect debts owed to the United States by Commerce Department and other Federal employees. If a Federal employee owes a Commerce debt, Commerce entities may offset the employee's Federal salary to collect the Commerce debt in the manner described in this section. For information on how a Federal agency other than a Commerce entity may collect debt from the salary of a Commerce Department employee, see §§ 19.20 and 19.21, subpart C, of this Part.

(2) Nothing in this Part requires a Commerce entity to collect a Commerce debt in accordance with the provisions of this section if Federal law allows otherwise. See, for example, 5 U.S.C. 5705 (travel advances not used for allowable travel expenses are recoverable from the employee or his estate by setoff against accrued pay and other means) and 5 U.S.C. 4108 (recovery of training expenses).

(3) Commerce entities may use the administrative wage garnishment procedure described in § 19.13 of this Part to collect a Commerce debt from an individual's non-Federal wages.

(b) *Centralized salary offset through the Treasury Offset Program.* As described in § 19.9(a) of this Part, Commerce entities will refer Commerce debts to the Financial Management Service for collection by administrative offset, including salary offset, through the Treasury Offset Program. When possible, Commerce entities should attempt salary offset through the Treasury Offset Program before applying the procedures in paragraph (c) of this section. See 5 CFR 550.1108 and 550.1109.

(c) *Non-centralized salary offset for Commerce debts.* When centralized salary offset through the Treasury Offset Program is not available or appropriate, Commerce entities may collect delinquent Commerce debts through non-centralized salary offset. See 5 CFR 550.1109. In these cases, Commerce entities may offset a payment internally or make a request directly to a Federal payment agency to offset a salary payment to collect a delinquent Commerce debt owed by a Federal employee. If the Federal payment agency is another Commerce entity, the Commerce entity making the request shall do so through the Deputy Chief Financial Officer as described in § 19.20(c) of this Part. At least thirty (30) days prior to offsetting internally or requesting a Federal agency to offset a salary payment, Commerce entities will send notice to the debtor in accordance with the requirements of § 19.4 of this Part. When referring a Commerce debt for offset, Commerce entities will certify to the payment agency, in writing, that the Commerce debt is valid, delinquent and legally enforceable in the amount stated, and there are no legal bars to collection by salary offset. In addition, Commerce entities will certify that all due process and other prerequisites to salary offset have been met. See 5 U.S.C. 5514, 31 U.S.C. 3716(a), and this section for a description of the due process and other prerequisites for salary offset.

(d) *When prior notice not required.* Commerce entities are not required to provide prior notice to an employee when the following adjustments are made by a Commerce entity to a Commerce employee's pay:

(1) Any adjustment to pay arising out of any employee's election of coverage or a change in coverage under a Federal benefits program requiring periodic deductions from pay, if the amount to be recovered was accumulated over four pay periods or less;

(2) A routine intra-agency adjustment of pay that is made to correct an overpayment of pay attributable to clerical or administrative errors or delays in processing pay documents, if the overpayment occurred within the four pay periods preceding the adjustment, and, at the time of such adjustment, or as soon thereafter as practical, the individual is provided written notice of the nature and the amount of the adjustment and point of contact for contesting such adjustment; or

(3) Any adjustment to collect a Commerce debt amounting to $50 or less, if, at the time of such adjustment, or as soon thereafter as practical, the individual is provided written notice of the nature and the amount of the adjustment and a point of contact for contesting such adjustment.

(e) *Hearing procedures*—(1) *Request for a hearing.* A Federal employee who has received a notice that his or her Commerce debt will be collected by means of salary offset may request a hearing concerning the existence or amount of the Commerce debt. The Federal employee also may request a hearing concerning the amount proposed to be deducted from the employee's pay each pay period. The employee must send any request for hearing, in writing, to the office designated in the notice described in § 19.4. See § 19.4(a)(11). The request must be received by the designated office on or before the 15th day following the employee's receipt of the notice. The employee must sign the request and specify whether an oral or paper hearing is requested. If an oral hearing is requested, the employee must explain why the matter cannot be resolved by review of the documentary evidence alone. All travel expenses incurred by the Federal employee in connection with an in-person hearing will be borne by the employee. See 31 CFR 901.3(a)(7).

(2) *Failure to submit timely request for hearing.* If the employee fails to submit a request for hearing within the time period described in paragraph (e)(1) of this section, the employee will have waived the right to a hearing, and salary offset may be initiated. However, Commerce entities should accept a late request for hearing if the employee can

show that the late request was the result of circumstances beyond the employee's control or because of a failure to receive actual notice of the filing deadline.

(3) *Hearing official.* Commerce entities must obtain the services of a hearing official who is not under the supervision or control of the Secretary. Commerce entities may contact the Deputy Chief Financial Officer as described in § 19.20(c) of this Part or an agent of any Commerce agency designated in Appendix A to 5 CFR part 581 (List of Agents Designated to Accept Legal Process) to request a hearing official.

(4) *Notice of hearing.* After the employee requests a hearing, the designated hearing official shall inform the employee of the form of the hearing to be provided. For oral hearings, the notice shall set forth the date, time and location of the hearing. For paper hearings, the notice shall notify the employee of the date by which he or she should submit written arguments to the designated hearing official. The hearing official shall give the employee reasonable time to submit documentation in support of the employee's position. The hearing official shall schedule a new hearing date if requested by both parties. The hearing official shall give both parties reasonable notice of the time and place of a rescheduled hearing.

(5) *Oral hearing.* The hearing official will conduct an oral hearing if he or she determines that the matter cannot be resolved by review of documentary evidence alone (for example, when an issue of credibility or veracity is involved). The hearing need not take the form of an evidentiary hearing, but may be conducted in a manner determined by the hearing official, including but not limited to:

(i) Informal conferences with the hearing official, in which the employee and agency representative will be given full opportunity to present evidence, witnesses and argument;

(ii) Informal meetings with an interview of the employee by the hearing official; or

(iii) Formal written submissions, with an opportunity for oral presentation.

(6) *Paper hearing.* If the hearing official determines that an oral hearing is not necessary, he or she will make the determination based upon a review of the available written record, including any documentation submitted by the employee in support of his or her position. See 31 CFR 901.3(a)(7).

(7) *Failure to appear or submit documentary evidence.* In the absence of good cause shown (for example, excused illness), if the employee fails to appear at an oral hearing or fails to submit documentary evidence as required for a paper hearing, the employee will have waived the right to a hearing, and salary offset may be initiated. Further, the employee will have been deemed to admit the existence and amount of the Commerce debt as described in the notice of intent to offset. If the Commerce entity representative fails to appear at an oral hearing, the hearing official shall proceed with the hearing as scheduled, and make his or her determination based upon the oral testimony presented and the documentary evidence submitted by both parties.

(8) *Burden of proof.* Commerce entities will have the initial burden to prove the existence and amount of the Commerce debt. Thereafter, if the employee disputes the existence or amount of the Commerce debt, the employee must prove by a preponderance of the evidence that no such Commerce debt exists or that the amount of the Commerce debt is incorrect. In addition, the employee may present evidence that the proposed terms of the repayment schedule are unlawful, would cause a financial hardship to the employee, or that collection of the Commerce debt may not be pursued due to operation of law.

(9) *Record.* The hearing official shall maintain a summary record of any hearing provided by this Part. Witnesses will testify under oath or affirmation in oral hearings. See 31 CFR 901.3(a)(7).

(10) *Date of decision.* The hearing official shall issue a written opinion stating his or her decision, based upon documentary evidence and information developed at the hearing, as soon as practicable after the hearing, but not later than 60 days after the date on which the request for hearing was received by

the Commerce entity. If the employee requests a delay in the proceedings, the deadline for the decision may be postponed by the number of days by which the hearing was postponed. When a decision is not timely rendered, the Commerce entity shall waive interest and penalties applied to the Commerce debt for the period beginning with the date the decision is due and ending on the date the decision is issued.

(11) *Content of decision.* The written decision shall include:

(i) A statement of the facts presented to support the origin, nature, and amount of the Commerce debt;

(ii) The hearing official's findings, analysis, and conclusions; and

(iii) The terms of any repayment schedules, if applicable.

(12) *Final agency action.* The hearing official's decision shall be final.

(f) *Waiver not precluded.* Nothing in this Part precludes an employee from requesting waiver of an overpayment under 5 U.S.C. 5584 or 8346(b), 10 U.S.C. 2774, 32 U.S.C. 716, or other statutory authority. Commerce entities may grant such waivers when it would be against equity and good conscience or not in the United States' best interest to collect such Commerce debts, in accordance with those authorities, 5 CFR 550.1102(b)(2), and Commerce policies and procedures. See Department of Commerce Credit and Debt Management Operating Standards and Procedures Handbook (currently at *http://www.osec.doc.gov/ofm/credit/cover.htm*).

(g) *Salary offset process*—(1) *Determination of disposable pay.* The Deputy Chief Financial Officer will consult with the appropriate Commerce entity payroll office to determine the amount of a Commerce Department employee's disposable pay (as defined in § 19.1 of this Part) and will implement salary offset when requested to do so by a Commerce entity, as described in paragraph (c) of this section, or another agency, as described in § 19.20 of this Part. If the debtor is not employed by the Commerce Department, the agency employing the debtor will determine the amount of the employee's disposable pay and will implement salary offset upon request.

(2) *When salary offset begins.* Deductions shall begin within three official pay periods following receipt of the creditor agency's request for offset.

(3) *Amount of salary offset.* The amount to be offset from each salary payment will be up to 15 percent of a debtor's disposable pay, as follows:

(i) If the amount of the Commerce debt is equal to or less than 15 percent of the disposable pay, such Commerce debt generally will be collected in one lump sum payment;

(ii) Installment deductions will be made over a period of no greater than the anticipated period of employment. An installment deduction will not exceed 15 percent of the disposable pay from which the deduction is made unless the employee has agreed in writing to the deduction of a greater amount or the creditor agency has determined that smaller deductions are appropriate based on the employee's ability to pay.

(4) *Final salary payment.* After the employee has separated either voluntarily or involuntarily from the payment agency, the payment agency may make a lump sum deduction exceeding 15 percent of disposable pay from any final salary or other payments pursuant to 31 U.S.C. 3716 in order to satisfy a Commerce debt.

(h) *Payment agency's responsibilities.* (1) As required by 5 CFR 550.1109, if the employee separates from the payment agency from which a Commerce entity has requested salary offset, the payment agency must certify the total amount of its collection and notify the Commerce entity and the employee of the amounts collected. If the payment agency is aware that the employee is entitled to payments from the Civil Service Retirement Fund and Disability Fund, the Federal Employee Retirement System, or other similar payments, it must provide written notification to the payment agency responsible for making such payments that the debtor owes a Commerce debt, the amount of the Commerce debt, and that the Commerce entity has complied with the provisions of this section. Commerce entities must submit a properly certified claim to the new payment agency before the collection can be made.

(2) If the employee is already separated from employment and all payments due from his or her former payment agency have been made, Commerce entities may request that money due and payable to the employee from the Civil Service Retirement Fund and Disability Fund, the Federal Employee Retirement System, or other similar funds, be administratively offset to collect the Commerce debt. Generally, Commerce entities will collect such monies through the Treasury Offset Program as described in § 19.9(c) of this Part.

(3) When an employee transfers to another agency, Commerce entities should resume collection with the employee's new payment agency in order to continue salary offset.

§ 19.13 How will Commerce entities use administrative wage garnishment to collect a Commerce debt from a debtor's wages?

(a) Commerce entities are authorized to collect Commerce debts from an individual debtor's wages by means of administrative wage garnishment in accordance with the requirements of 31 U.S.C. 3720D and 31 CFR 285.11. This Part adopts and incorporates all of the provisions of 31 CFR 285.11 concerning administrative wage garnishment, including the hearing procedures described in 31 CFR 285.11(f). Commerce entities may use administrative wage garnishment to collect a delinquent Commerce debt unless the debtor is making timely payments under an agreement to pay the Commerce debt in installments (see § 19.6 of this Part). At least thirty (30) days prior to initiating an administrative wage garnishment, Commerce entities will send notice to the debtor in accordance with the requirements of § 19.4 of this Part, including the requirements of § 19.4(a)(10) of this Part. For Commerce debts referred to the Financial Management Service under § 19.9 of this Part, Commerce entities may authorize the Financial Management Service to send a notice informing the debtor that administrative wage garnishment will be initiated and how the debtor may request a hearing as described in § 19.4(a)(10) of this Part. If a debtor makes a timely request for a hearing, administrative wage garnishment will not begin until a hearing is held and a decision is sent to the debtor. See 31 CFR 285.11(f)(4). Even if a debtor's hearing request is not timely, Commerce entities may suspend collection by administrative wage garnishment in accordance with the provisions of 31 CFR 285.11(f)(5). All travel expenses incurred by the debtor in connection with an in-person hearing will be borne by the debtor.

(b) This section does not apply to Federal salary offset, the process by which Commerce entities collect Commerce debts from the salaries of Federal employees (see § 19.12 of this Part).

§ 19.14 How will Commerce entities report Commerce debts to credit bureaus?

Commerce entities shall report delinquent Commerce debts to credit bureaus in accordance with the provisions of 31 U.S.C. 3711(e), 31 CFR 901.4, and the Office of Management and Budget Circular A–129, "Policies for Federal Credit Programs and Non-tax Receivables." For additional information, see Financial Management Service's "Guide to the Federal Credit Bureau Program," which currently may be found at *http://www.fms.treas.gov/debt*. At least sixty (60) days prior to reporting a delinquent Commerce debt to a consumer reporting agency, Commerce entities will send notice to the debtor in accordance with the requirements of § 19.4 of this Part. Commerce entities may authorize the Financial Management Service to report to credit bureaus those delinquent Commerce debts that have been transferred to the Financial Management Service under § 19.9 of this Part.

§ 19.15 How will Commerce entities refer Commerce debts to private collection agencies?

Commerce entities will transfer delinquent Commerce debts to the Financial Management Service to obtain debt collection services provided by private collection agencies. See § 19.9 of this Part.

§ 19.16 When will Commerce entities refer Commerce debts to the Department of Justice?

(a) *Compromise or suspension or termination of collection activity.* Commerce entities shall refer Commerce debts having a principal balance over $100,000, or such higher amount as authorized by the Attorney General, to the Department of Justice for approval of any compromise of a Commerce debt or suspension or termination of collection activity. See §§ 19.7 and 19.8 of this Part; 31 CFR 902.1; 31 CFR 903.1.

(b) *Litigation.* Commerce entities shall promptly refer to the Department of Justice for litigation delinquent Commerce debts on which aggressive collection activity has been taken in accordance with this Part and that should not be compromised, and on which collection activity should not be suspended or terminated. See 31 CFR part 904. Commerce entities may authorize the Financial Management Service to refer to the Department of Justice for litigation those delinquent Commerce debts that have been transferred to the Financial Management Service under § 19.9 of this Part.

§ 19.17 Will a debtor who owes a Commerce or other Federal agency debt, and persons controlled by or controlling such debtors, be ineligible for Federal loan assistance, grants, cooperative agreements, or other sources of Federal funds or for Federal licenses, permits or privileges?

(a) Delinquent debtors are ineligible for and barred from obtaining Federal loans or loan insurance or guaranties. As required by 31 U.S.C. 3720B and 31 CFR 901.6, Commerce entities will not extend financial assistance in the form of a loan, loan guarantee, or loan insurance to any person delinquent on a debt owed to a Federal agency. The Commerce Department may issue standards under which the Commerce Department may determine that persons controlled by or controlling such delinquent debtors are similarly ineligible in accordance with 31 CFR 285.13(c)(2). This prohibition does not apply to disaster loans. Commerce entities may extend credit after the delinquency has been resolved. See 31 CFR 285.13. Waivers of ineligibility may be granted by the Secretary or designee on a person by person basis in accordance with 31 CFR 285.13(g). However, such authority may not be delegated below the Deputy Chief Financial Officer.

(b) A debtor who has a judgment lien against the debtor's property for a debt to the United States is not eligible to receive grants, loans or funds directly or indirectly from the United States until the judgment is paid in full or otherwise satisfied. This prohibition does not apply to funds to which the debtor is entitled as beneficiary. The Commerce Department may promulgate regulations to allow for waivers of this ineligibility. See 28 U.S.C. 3201(e).

(c) Suspension or revocation of eligibility for licenses, permits, or privileges. Unless prohibited by law, Commerce entities with the authority to do so under the circumstances should deny, suspend or revoke licenses, permits, or other privileges for any inexcusable or willful failure of a debtor to pay a debt. The Commerce entity responsible for distributing the licenses, permits, or other privileges will establish policies and procedures governing suspension and revocation for delinquent debtors. If applicable, Commerce entities will advise the debtor in the notice required by § 19.4 of this Part of the Commerce entities' ability to deny, suspend or revoke licenses, permits or privileges. See § 19.4(a)(16) of this Part.

(d) To the extent that a person delinquent on a Commerce debt is not otherwise barred under § 19.17(a)(c) of this Part from becoming or remaining a recipient of a Commerce grant or cooperative agreement, it is Commerce policy that no award of Federal funds shall be made to a Commerce grant or cooperative agreement applicant who has an outstanding delinquent Commerce debt until:

(1) The delinquent Commerce debt is paid in full,

(2) A negotiated repayment schedule acceptable to Commerce is established and at least one payment is received, or

(3) Other arrangements satisfactory to Commerce are made.

§ 19.18 How does a debtor request a special review based on a change in circumstances such as catastrophic illness, divorce, death, or disability?

(a) *Material change in circumstances.* A debtor who owes a Commerce debt may, at any time, request a special review by the applicable Commerce entity of the amount of any offset, administrative wage garnishment, or voluntary payment, based on materially changed circumstances beyond the control of the debtor such as, but not limited to, catastrophic illness, divorce, death, or disability.

(b) *Inability to pay.* For purposes of this section, in determining whether an involuntary or voluntary payment would prevent the debtor from meeting essential subsistence expenses (e.g., costs incurred for food, housing, clothing, transportation, and medical care), the debtor shall submit a detailed statement and supporting documents for the debtor, his or her spouse, and dependents, indicating:

(1) Income from all sources;

(2) Assets;

(3) Liabilities;

(4) Number of dependents;

(5) Expenses for food, housing, clothing, and transportation;

(6) Medical expenses;

(7) Exceptional expenses, if any; and

(8) Any additional materials and information that the Commerce entity may request relating to ability or inability to pay the amount(s) currently required.

(c) *Alternative payment arrangement.* If the debtor requests a special review under this section, the debtor shall submit an alternative proposed payment schedule and a statement to the Commerce entity collecting the Commerce debt, with supporting documents, showing why the current offset, garnishment or repayment schedule imposes an extreme financial hardship on the debtor. The Commerce entity will evaluate the statement and documentation and determine whether the current offset, garnishment, or repayment schedule imposes extreme financial hardship on the debtor. The Commerce entity shall notify the debtor in writing of such determination, including, if appropriate, a revised offset, garnishment, or payment schedule. If the special review results in a revised offset, garnishment, or repayment schedule, the Commerce entity will notify the appropriate Federal agency or other persons about the new terms.

§ 19.19 Will Commerce entities issue a refund if money is erroneously collected on a Commerce debt?

Commerce entities shall promptly refund to a debtor any amount collected on a Commerce debt when the Commerce debt is waived or otherwise found not to be owed to the United States, or as otherwise required by law. Refunds under this Part shall not bear interest unless required by law.

Subpart C—Procedures for Offset of Commerce Department Payments To Collect Debts Owed to Other Federal Agencies

§ 19.20 How do other Federal agencies use the offset process to collect debts from payments issued by a Commerce entity?

(a) *Offset of Commerce entity payments to collect debts owed to other Federal agencies.* (1) In most cases, Federal agencies submit debts to the Treasury Offset Program to collect delinquent debts from payments issued by Commerce entities and other Federal agencies, a process known as "centralized offset." When centralized offset is not available or appropriate, any Federal agency may ask a Commerce entity (when acting as a "payment agency") to collect a debt owed to such agency by offsetting funds payable to a debtor by the Commerce entity, including salary payments issued to Commerce entity employees. This section and § 19.21 of this subpart C apply when a Federal agency asks a Commerce entity to offset a payment issued by the Commerce entity to a person who owes a debt to the United States.

(2) This subpart C does not apply to Commerce debts. See §§ 19.10 through 19.12 of this Part for offset procedures applicable to Commerce debts.

(3) This subpart C does not apply to the collection of non-Commerce debts through tax refund offset. See 31 CFR 285.2 for tax refund offset procedures.

(b) *Administrative offset (including salary offset); certification.* A Commerce entity will initiate a requested offset only upon receipt of written certification from the creditor agency that the debtor owes the past-due, legally enforceable debt in the amount stated, and that the creditor agency has fully complied with all applicable due process and other requirements contained in 31 U.S.C. 3716, 5 U.S.C. 5514, and the creditor agency's regulations, as applicable. Offsets will continue until the debt is paid in full or otherwise resolved to the satisfaction of the creditor agency.

(c) *Where a creditor agency makes requests for offset.* Requests for offset under this section shall be sent to the Department of Commerce, ATTN: Deputy Chief Financial Officer, 1401 Constitution Avenue, NW., Room 6827, Washington, DC 20230. The Deputy Chief Financial Officer will forward the request to the appropriate Commerce entity for processing in accordance with this subpart C.

(d) *Incomplete certification.* A Commerce entity will return an incomplete debt certification to the creditor agency with notice that the creditor agency must comply with paragraph (b) of this section before action will be taken to collect a debt from a payment issued by a Commerce entity.

(e) *Review.* A Commerce entity is not authorized to review the merits of the creditor agency's determination with respect to the amount or validity of the debt certified by the creditor agency.

(f) *When Commerce entities will not comply with offset request.* A Commerce entity will comply with the offset request of another agency unless the Commerce entity determines that the offset would not be in the best interests of the United States, or would otherwise be contrary to law.

(g) *Multiple debts.* When two or more creditor agencies are seeking offsets from payments made to the same person, or when two or more debts are owed to a single creditor agency, the Commerce entity that has been asked to offset the payments may determine the order in which the debts will be collected or whether one or more debts should be collected by offset simultaneously.

(h) *Priority of debts owed to Commerce entity.* For purposes of this section, debts owed to a Commerce entity generally take precedence over debts owed to other agencies. The Commerce entity that has been asked to offset the payments may determine whether to pay debts owed to other agencies before paying a debt owed to a Commerce entity. The Commerce entity that has been asked to offset the payments will determine the order in which the debts will be collected based on the best interests of the United States.

§ 19.21 What does a Commerce entity do upon receipt of a request to offset the salary of a Commerce entity employee to collect a debt owed by the employee to another Federal agency?

(a) *Notice to the Commerce employee.* When a Commerce entity receives proper certification of a debt owed by one of its employees, the Commerce entity will begin deductions from the employee's pay at the next officially established pay interval. The Commerce entity will send a written notice to the employee indicating that a certified debt claim has been received from the creditor agency, the amount of the debt claimed to be owed by the creditor agency, the date deductions from salary will begin, and the amount of such deductions.

(b) *Amount of deductions from Commerce employee's salary.* The amount deducted under § 19.20(b) of this Part will be the lesser of the amount of the debt certified by the creditor agency or an amount up to 15% of the debtor's disposable pay. Deductions shall continue until the Commerce entity knows that the debt is paid in full or until otherwise instructed by the creditor agency. Alternatively, the amount offset may be an amount agreed upon, in writing, by the debtor and the creditor agency. See § 19.12(g) (salary offset process).

(c) *When the debtor is no longer employed by the Commerce entity*—(1) *Offset of final and subsequent payments.* If a Commerce entity employee retires or resigns or if his or her employment ends before collection of the debt is complete, the Commerce entity will continue to offset, under 31 U.S.C. 3716, up to 100% of an employee's subsequent payments until the debt is paid or otherwise resolved. Such payments include a debtor's final salary payment, lump-sum leave payment, and other payments payable to the debtor by the Commerce entity. See 31 U.S.C. 3716 and 5 CFR 550.1104(l) and 550.1104(m).

(2) *Notice to the creditor agency.* If the employee is separated from the Commerce entity before the debt is paid in full, the Commerce entity will certify to the creditor agency the total amount of its collection. If the Commerce entity is aware that the employee is entitled to payments from the Civil Service Retirement and Disability Fund, Federal Employee Retirement System, or other similar payments, the Commerce entity will provide written notice to the agency making such payments that the debtor owes a debt (including the amount) and that the provisions of 5 CFR 550.1109 have been fully complied with. The creditor agency is responsible for submitting a certified claim to the agency responsible for making such payments before collection may begin. Generally, creditor agencies will collect such monies through the Treasury Offset Program as described in §19.9(c) of this Part.

(3) *Notice to the debtor.* The Commerce entity will provide to the debtor a copy of any notices sent to the creditor agency under paragraph (c)(2) of this section.

(d) *When the debtor transfers to another Federal agency*—(1) *Notice to the creditor agency.* If the debtor transfers to another Federal agency before the debt is paid in full, the Commerce entity will notify the creditor agency and will certify the total amount of its collection on the debt. The Commerce entity will provide a copy of the certification to the creditor agency. The creditor agency is responsible for submitting a certified claim to the debtor's new employing agency before collection may begin.

(2) *Notice to the debtor.* The Commerce entity will provide to the debtor a copy of any notices and certifications sent to the creditor agency under paragraph (d)(1) of this section.

(e) *Request for hearing official.* A Commerce entity will provide a hearing official upon the creditor agency's request with respect to a Commerce entity employee. See 5 CFR 550.1107(a).

PART 20—NONDISCRIMINATION ON THE BASIS OF AGE IN PROGRAMS OR ACTIVITIES RECEIVING FEDERAL FINANCIAL ASSISTANCE

Subpart A—General

Subpart B—Standards for Determining Age Discrimination

Subpart C—Responsibilities of DOC Recipients

Subpart D—Investigation, Conciliation, and Enforcement Procedures

AUTHORITY: Age Discrimination Act of 1975, as amended, 42 U.S.C. sec. 6101 *et seq.* and the government-wide regulations implementing the Act, 45 CFR Part 90.

SOURCE: 51 FR 28926, Aug. 13, 1986, unless otherwise noted.

EDITORIAL NOTE: Nomenclature changes to part 20 appear at 68 FR 51355, Aug. 26, 2003.

Subpart A—General

§20.1 The purpose of DOC's age discrimination regulations.

The purpose of these regulations is to set out DOC's policies and procedures under the Age Discrimination Act of 1975 and the general age discrimination regulations at 45 CFR Part 90. The Act and the general regulations prohibit discrimination on the basis of age in programs or activities receiving Federal financial assistance. The Act and the general regulations permit federally assisted programs or activities, and recipients of Federal funds, to continue to use age distinctions and factors other than age which meet the requirements of the Act and its implementing regulations.

§20.2 Programs or activities to which these regulations apply.

(a) The Act and these regulations apply to each DOC recipient and to each program or activity operated by the recipient which receives Federal financial assistance provided by any entity of DOC.

(b) The Act and these regulations do not apply to:

(1) An age distinction contained in that part of a Federal, State, or local statute or ordinance adopted by an elected, general purpose legislative body which:

(i) Provides benefits or assistance to persons based on age; or

(ii) Establishes criteria for participation in age-related terms; or

(iii) Describes intended beneficiaries or target groups in age-related terms.

(2) Any employment practice or any employer, employment agency, labor organization, or any labor-management joint apprenticeship training program, except for any program or activity receiving Federal financial assistance for public service employment.

§20.3 Definitions.

As used in these regulations, the following terms are defined as follows:

(a) *Act* means the Age Discrimination Act of 1975, as amended (Title III of Pub. L. 94–135).

(b) *Action* means any act, activity, policy, rule, standard, or method of administration; or the use of any policy, rule, standard, or method of administration.

(c) *Age* means how old a person is, or the number of years from the date of a person's birth.

(d) *Age distinction* means any action using age or an age-related term.

(e) *Age-related term* means a word or words which necessarily imply a particular age or range of ages (for example: "children," "adult," "older persons," but not "student").

(f) *Agency* means a Federal department or agency that is empowered to extend financial assistance.

(g) *DOC* means the U.S. Department of Commerce.

(h) *Federal financial assistance* means any grant, entitlement, loan, cooperative agreement, contract (other than a procurement contract or a contract of insurance or guaranty), or any other arrangement by which the agency provides or otherwise makes available assistance in the form of:

(1) Funds; or

(2) Services of Federal personnel; or

(3) Real and personal property or any interest in or use of property, including:

(i) Transfers or leases of property for less than fair market value or for reduced considerations; and

(ii) Proceeds from a subsequent transfer or lease of property if the Federal share of its fair market value is not returned to the Federal Government.

(i) *Normal operation* means the operation of a program or activity without significant changes that would impair its ability to meet its objectives.

(j) *Program or activity* means all of the operations of any entity described in paragraphs (j)(1) through (4) of this section, any part of which is extended Federal financial assistance:

(1)(i) A department, agency, special purpose district, or other instrumentality of a State or of a local government; or

(ii) The entity of such State or local government that distributes such assistance and each such department or agency (and each other State or local government entity) to which the assistance is extended, in the case of assistance to a State or local government;

(2)(i) A college, university, or other postsecondary institution, or a public system of higher education; or

(ii) A local educational agency (as defined in 20 U.S.C. 7801), system of vocational education, or other school system;

(3)(i) An entire corporation, partnership, or other private organization, or an entire sole proprietorship—

(A) If assistance is extended to such corporation, partnership, private organization, or sole proprietorship as a whole; or

(B) Which is principally engaged in the business of providing education, health care, housing, social services, or parks and recreation; or

(ii) The entire plant or other comparable, geographically separate facility to which Federal financial assistance is extended, in the case of any other corporation, partnership, private organization, or sole proprietorship; or

(4) Any other entity which is established by two or more of the entities described in paragraph (j)(1),(2), or (3) of this section.

(k) *Recipient* means any State or its political subdivision, any instrumentality of a State or its political sub-division, any public or private agency, institution, organization, or other entity, or any person to which Federal financial assistance is extended, directly or through another recipient. Recipient includes any successor, assignee, or transferee, but excludes the ultimate beneficiary of the assistance.

(l) *Secretary* means the Secretary of Commerce or his or her designee.

(m) *Statutory objective* means any purpose of a program or activity expressly stated in any Federal statute, State statute, or local statute or ordinance adopted by an elected, general purpose legislative body.

(n) *Subrecipient* means any of the entities in the definition of "recipient" to which a recipient extends or passes on Federal financial assistance. A subrecipient is generally regarded as a recipient of Federal financial assistance and has all the duties of a recipient in these regulations.

(o) *United States* means the fifty States, the District of Columbia, Puerto Rico, the Virgin Islands, American Samoa, Guam, Wake Island, the Canal Zone, the Northern Marianas, and the territories and possessions of the United States.

[51 FR 28926, Aug. 13, 1986, as amended at 68 FR 51354, Aug. 26, 2003]

Subpart B—Standards for Determining Age Discrimination

§ 20.4 Rules against age discrimination.

The rules stated in this section are limited by the exceptions contained in § 20.5.

(a) General rule: No person in the United States shall, on the basis of age, be excluded from participation in, be denied the benefits of, or be subjected to discrimination under any program or activity receiving Federal financial assistance.

(b) Specific rules: A recipient may not, in any program or activity receiving Federal financial assistance, directly or through contractual licensing, or other arrangements, use age distinctions or take any other actions which have the effect, on the basis of age, of:

(1) Excluding individuals from, denying them the benefits of, or subjecting them to discrimination under, a program or activity receiving Federal financial assistance, or

(2) Denying or limiting individuals in their opportunity to participate in any program or activity receiving Federal financial assistance.

(c) The specific forms of age discrimination listed in paragaph (b) of this section do not necessarily constitute a complete list.

(d) If a recipient operating a program or activity provides special benefits to the elderly or to children, such use of age distinctions shall be presumed to be necessary to the normal operation of the program or activity, notwithstanding the provisions of § 20.5.

§ 20.5 Exceptions to the rules.

(a) *Normal operations or statutory objective of any program or activity.* A recipient is permitted to take an action otherwise prohibited by § 20.4 if the action reasonably considers age as a factor necessary to the normal operation or the achievement of any statutory objective of a program or activity. An action meets this standard if:

(1) Age is used as a measure or approximation of one or more other characteristics; and

(2) The other characteristic(s) must be measured or approximated in order for the normal operation of the program or activity to continue, or to achieve any statutory objective or the program or activity; and

(3) The other characteristic(s) can be reasonably measured or approximated by the use of age; and

(4) The other characteristic(s) are impractical to measure directly on an individual bases.

(b) *Reasonable factors other than age.* A recipient is permitted to take an action otherwise prohibited by §20.4 which is based on a factor other than age, even though that action may have a disproportionate effect on persons of different ages. An action may be based on a factor other than age only if the factor bears a direct and substantial relationship to the normal operation of the program or activity or to the achievement of a statutory objective.

§20.6 Burden of proof.

The burden of proving that an age distinction or other action falls within the exceptions outlined in §20.5 is on the recipient of Federal financial assistance.

Subpart C—Responsibilities of DOC Recipients

§20.7 General responsibilities.

Each DOC recipient has primary responsibility to ensure that its programs or activities are in compliance with the Act, the general regulations, and these regulations, and shall take steps to eliminate violation of the Act.

(a) Each DOC recipient will provide an assurance that the program or activity for which it is receiving Federal financial assistance will be conducted in compliance with all requirements for the Act and these and other DOC regulations. A recipient also has responsibility to maintain records, provide information, and to afford DOC reasonable access to its records and facilities to the extent necessary to determine whether it is in compliance with the Act and these regulations.

(b) *Recipient assessment of age distinctions.* (1) To assess the recipient's compliance with the Act, DOC may, as part of a compliance review under §20.10 or a complaint investigation under §20.11, require a recipient employing the equivalent or 15 or more employees, to complete, in a manner specified by the responsible Department official, a written self-evaluation of any age distinction imposed in its program or activity receiving Federal financial assistance from DOC.

(2) Whenever an assessment indicates a violation of the Act and the DOC regulations, the recipient shall take corrective action.

§20.8 Notice to subrecipients.

Where a recipient passes on Federal financial assistant from DOC to subrecipients, the recipient shall give subrecipients written notice of their obligations under the Act and these regulations.

§20.9 Information requirements.

Upon DOC's request, each recipient shall provide access and make information available for DOC to determine whether the recipient is complying with the Act and these regulations.

Subpart D—Investigation, Conciliation, and Enforcement Procedures

§20.10 Compliance reviews.

(a) DOC may conduct compliance reviews and pre-award reviews or use other similar procedures that will permit it to investigate and correct violations of the Act and these regulations. DOC may conduct such review even in the absence of a complaint against a recipient. The review may be as comprehensive as necessary to determine whether a violation of the Act and these regulations has occurred.

(b) If a compliance review of pre-award review indicates a violation of the Act or these regulations, DOC will attempt to achieve voluntary compliance with the Act. If voluntary compliance cannot be achieved, DOC will arrange for enforcement as described in § 20.15.

§ 20.11 Complaints.

(a) Any person, individually, or as a member of a class, or on behalf of others, may file a complaint with DOC alleging discrimination prohibited by the Act or these regulations based on an action occurring on or after July 1, 1979. A complainant shall file a complaint within 180 days from the date the complainant first had knowledge of the alleged act of discrimination. However, for good cause shown, DOC may extend this time limit.

(b) DOC will attempt to facilitate the filing of complaints wherever possible, including taking the following measures:

(1) Accepting as a sufficient complaint, any written statement which: identifies the parties involved and the date the complainant first had knowledge of the alleged violation; describes generally the action or practice complained of; and is signed by the complainant;

(2) Freely permitting a complainant to add information to the complaint to meet the requirements of a sufficient complaint;

(3) Considering as the filing date, the date on which a complaint is sufficient to be processed;

(4) Notifiying the complainant and the recipient of their rights and obligations under the compliant procedure, including the right to have a representative at all stages of the process;

(5) Notifying the complainant and the recipient (or their representatives) of their right to contact DOC for information and assistance regarding the complaint resolution process.

(c) DOC will return to the complainant any complaint outside the jurisdiction of these regulations, and will state the reason(s) why it is outside the jurisdiction of these regulations.

§ 20.12 Mediation.

(a) DOC will refer to a mediation service designated by the Secretary all sufficient complaints that:

(1) Fall within the jurisdiction of the Act and these regulations, unless the age distinction complained of is clearly within an exception; and

(2) Contain all information necessary for further processing.

(b) Both the complainant and the recipient shall participate in the mediation process to the extent necessary to reach an agreement or to make an informed judgment that an agreement is not possible.

(c) If the complainant and the recipient reach an agreement, the mediator shall prepare a written statement of the agreement and have the complainant and the recipient sign it. The mediator shall send a copy of the agreement to DOC. DOC will take no further action on the complaint unless the complainant or the recipient fails to comply with the agreement.

(d) The mediator is required to protect the confidentiality of all information obtained in the course of the mediation process. No mediator shall testify in any adjudicative proceeding, produce any document, or otherwise disclose any information obtained, in the course of the mediation process without prior approval of the head or the mediation service.

(e) The mediation will proceed for a maximum of 60 days after a complaint is filed with DOC. Mediation ends if:

(1) 60 days elapse from the time DOC receives the complaint; *or*

(2) Prior to the end of that 60-day period, an agreement is reached; *or*

(3) Prior to the end of that 60-day period, the mediator determines that an agreement cannot be reached.

(f) The mediator shall return unresolved complaints to DOC.

§ 20.13 Investigation.

(a) Informal investigation:

(1) DOC will investigate complaints that are unresolved after mediation or are reopended because of a violation of a mediation agreement.

(2) As part of the initial investigation, DOC will use informal factfinding methods, including joint or separate discussions with the complainant and recipient, to establish the facts and, if possible, settle the complaint on terms

that are mutually agreeable to the parties. DOC may seek the assistance of any involved State agency.

(3) DOC will put any agreement in writing and have it signed by the parties and an authorized offical at DOC.

(4) The settlement shall not affect the operation of any other enforcement effort of DOC, including compliance reviews and investigation or other complaints which may involve the recipient.

(5) The settlement is not a finding of discrimination against a recipient.

(b) Formal investigation: If DOC cannot resolve the complaint through informal investigation, it will begin to develop formal findings through further investigation of the complaint. If the investigation indicates a violation of these regulations, DOC will attempt to obtain voluntary compliance. If DOC cannot obtain voluntary compliance, it will begin enforcement as described in §8a.15.

§20.14 Prohibition against intimidation or retaliation.

A recipient may not engage in acts of intimidation or retaliation against any person who:

(a) Attempts to assert a right protected by the Act or these regulations; or

(b) Cooperates in any mediation, investigation, hearing, or other part of DOC's investigation, conciliation, and enforcement process.

§20.15 Compliance procedure.

(a) DOC may enforce the Act and these regulations by:

(1) Terminating the Federal financial assistance to the recipient under the program or activity found to have violated the Act or these regulations. The determination of the recipient's violation may be made only after a recipient has had an opportunity for a hearing on the record before an administrative law judge. If a case is settled during mediation, or prior to hearing, Federal financial assistance to the program or activity will not be terminated.

(2) Any other means authorized by law including but not limited to:

(i) Referral to the Department of Justice for proceedings to enforce any rights of the United States or obligations of the recipient created by the Act or these regulations.

(ii) Use of any requirement of or referral to any Federal, State, or local government agency that will have the effect of correcting a violation of the Act or these regulations.

(b) DOC will limit any termination under this section to the particular recipient and particular program or activity or part of such program or activity DOC finds in violation of these regulations. DOC will not base any part of a termination on a finding with respect to any program or activity of the recipient which does not receive Federal financial assistance from DOC.

(c) DOC will take no action under paragraph (a) until:

(1) The head of the organization providing the financial assistance has advised the recipient of its failure to comply with the Act and these regulations and has determined that voluntary compliance cannot be obtained.

(2) Thirty days have elapsed after the Secretary has sent a written report of the circumstances and grounds of the action to the committees of the Congress having legislative jurisdiction over the program or activity involved. The Secretary will file a report whenever any action is taken under paragraph (a).

(d) DOC also may defer granting new Federal financial assistance to a recipient when a hearing under §20.16 is initiated.

(1) New Federal financial assistance from DOC includes all assistance for which DOC requires an application or approval, including renewal or continuation of existing activities, or authorization of new activities, during the deferral period. New Federal financial assistance from DOC does not include increases in funding as a result of changed computation of formula awards or assistance approved prior to the beginning of a hearing under §20.16.

(2) DOC will not begin a deferral until the recipient has received a notice of an opportunity for a hearing under §20.16. DOC will not continue a deferral for more than 60 days unless a hearing has begun within that time, or the time for beginning the hearing has been extended by mutual consent of

the recipient and the head of the organization providing Federal financial assistance. DOC will not continue a deferral for more than 30 days after the close of the hearing, unless the hearing results in a finding against the recipient.

(3) DOC will limit any deferral to the particular recipient and particular program or activity or part of such program or activity DOC finds in violation of these regulations. DOC will not base any part of a deferral on a finding with respect to any program or activity of the recipient which does not, and would not in connection with the new funds, receive Federal financial assistance for DOC.

§ 20.16 Hearings, decisions, post-termination proceedings.

Certain DOC procedural provisions applicable to Title VI of the Civil Rights Act of 1964 apply to DOC enforcement of these regulations. They are found in 15 CFR Part 8, § 8.12 and § 8.13.

§ 20.17 Remedial action by recipients.

(a) Where DOC finds that a recipient has discriminated on the basis of age, the recipient shall take any remedial action that DOC may require to overcome the effects of the discrimination. If another recipient exercises control over the recipient that has discriminated, DOC may require both recipients to take remedial action.

(b) Even in the absence of a finding of discrimination, a recipient may take affirmative action to overcome the effects of conditions that resulted in limited participation in the recipient's program or activity on the basis of age.

§ 20.18 Alternative funds disbursal procedure.

(a) When, under the provisions of these regulations, DOC terminates the funding of a recipient, the Secretary may, using undisbursed funds from the terminated award, make a new award to an alternate recipient, *i.e.* any public or non-profit private organization or agency, or State or political subdivision of the State.

(b) The Secretary will require any alternate recipient to demonstrate:

(1) The ability to comply with these regulations; and

(2) The ability to achieve the goals of the Federal statute authorizing the Federal financial assistance.

§ 20.19 Private lawsuits after exhaustion of administrative remedies.

(a) A complainant may file a civil action following the exhaustion of administrative remedies under the Act. Administrative remedies are exhausted if:

(1) 180 days have elapsed since the complainant filed the complaint and DOC has made no finding with regard to the complaint; or

(2) DOC issues any finding in favor of the recipient.

(b) If DOC fails to make a finding within 180 days or issues a finding in favor of recipient, DOC shall:

(1) Promptly advise the complainant of this fact; and

(2) Advise the complainant of his or her right to bring civil action for injunctive relief; and

(3) Inform the complainant that:

(i) The complainant may bring a civil action only in a United States district court for the district in which the recipient is located or transacts business;

(ii) A complainant prevailing in a civil action has the right to be awarded the costs of the action, including reasonable attorney's fees, but that the complainant must demand these costs in the complaint;

(iii) Before commencing the action, the complainant shall give 30 days notice by registered mail to the Secretary, the Attorney General of the United States, and the recipient;

(iv) The notice shall contain the alleged violation of the Act, the relief requested, the court in which the complainant is bringing the action, and whether or not attorney's fees are demanded in the event the complainant prevails; and

(v) The complainant may not bring an action if the same alleged violation of the Act by the same recipient is the subject of a pending action in any court of the United States.

PARTS 21–22 [RESERVED]

PART 23—USE OF PENALTY MAIL IN THE LOCATION AND RECOVERY OF MISSING CHILDREN

AUTHORITY: 39 U.S.C. 3220(a)(2); 5 U.S.C. 301.

SOURCE: 51 FR 46614, Dec. 24, 1986, unless otherwise noted.

§23.1 Purpose.

These regulations are intended to comply with 39 U.S.C. 3220(a)(2), and the Office of Juvenile Justice and Delinquency Prevention (OJJDP) guidelines (50 FR 46622), to assist in the location and recovery of missing children through the use of penalty mail.

§23.2 Contact person.

Tim Coss, Office of Administrative Services Operations, U.S. Department of Commerce (H2063), 14th and Constitution Ave., NW., Washington, DC 20230, Telephone (202) 377–2108.

§23.3 Plan.

(a) The Department of Commerce will supplement and expand the national effort to assist in the location and recovery of missing children through the economical use of missing children information in domestic penalty mail directed to the public and Federal employees.

(b) The Department of Commerce may include, on or inside authorized types of penalty mail, pictures and biographical data related to missing children, provided such use is determined to be cost effective. The authorized types of penalty mail include:

(1) All envelopes; and

(2) Self-mailer publications (newsletters, bulletins, etc.) with a shelf-life of no more than 90 days.

(c) The manner in which pictures and biographical data may be used includes:

(1) Printing on envelopes at the time they are initially printed with the United States Postal Service (USPS) required postal code identification;

(2) Printed inserts that are placed in envelopes along with other mailing material;

(3) Stickers that are printed and placed on envelopes prior to mailing; and

(4) Printing as part of the content of self-mailers such as bureau newsletters, bulletins, etc.

(d) Missing children information will not be placed on letter-size envelopes in the areas described as the "Penalty Indicia Area," "OCR Read Area," "Bar Code Read Area," and "Return Address Area" per Appendix A of the OJJDP guidelines.

(e) The National Center for Missing and Exploited Children (National Center) will be the sole source from which the Department of Commerce will obtain the camera-ready and other photographic and biographical materials for use by organizational units. Photographs which were reasonably current as of the time of the child's disappearance shall be the only acceptable form of visual media or pictorial likeness used on or in penalty mail.

(f) The Department of Commerce will remove all printed penalty mail envelopes and other materials from circulation or other use (*i.e.*, use or destroy) within 90 days of notification by the National Center of the need to withdraw penalty mail envelopes and other materials related to a particular child from circulation. The Department of Commerce will not include missing children information on blank pages or covers of items such as those to be included in the Superintendent of Documents' Sales Program, or to be distributed to Depository Libraries, as such material generally could not be withdrawn from use within 90 days of notification. The National Center will be responsible for immediately notifying the Department Contact Person, in writing, of the need to withdraw from circulation penalty mail envelopes and other materials related to a particular child.

(g) The Department of Commerce will give priority:

(1) To penalty mail that is addressed to the public for receipt in the United States, its territories and possessions; and

(2) To inter- and intra-agency publications and other media that will be widely disseminated to and viewed by Federal employees.

(h) All suggestions and/or recommendations for innovative, cost-effective techniques should be forwarded to the Department Contact Person. The Department Contact Person shall conduct biannual meetings of departmental representatives to discuss the current plan and recommendations for future plans.

(i) This shall be the sole regulation implementing this program for the Department of Commerce.

§ 23.4 Cost and percentage estimates.

It is estimated that this program will cost the Department of Commerce $39,530 in the first year. It is the Department of Commerce's estimate that 9% of its penalty mail will transmit missing children photographs and information when the program is fully implemented.

§ 23.5 Report to the Office of Juvenile Justice and Delinquency Prevention.

The Department of Commerce will compile and submit a consolidated report to OJJDP, by June 30, 1987, on its experience in implementation of 39 U.S.C. 3220(a) (2), the OJJDP guidelines, and the Department of Commerce's regulation. This report will cover the period from December 24, 1986 through March 31, 1987, and provide detail on:

(a) The Department of Commerce's experience in implementation (including problems encountered), successful and/or innovative methods adopted to use missing children photographs and information on or in penalty mail, the estimated number of pieces of penalty mail containing such information, and the percentage of total penalty mail directed to the public which included missing children information.

(b) The estimated total cost to implement the program, with supporting detail, and

(c) Recommendations for changes in the program to make it more effective.

§ 23.6 Definitions.

(a) *Operating units.* Bureaus and other organizational entities outside the Office of the Secretary charged with carrying out specified substantive functions (*i.e.*, programs).

(b) *Organizational units.* The organizational units within the Department of Commerce are:

Office of the Secretary
Bureau of Economic Analysis
Economic Development Administration
Bureau of the Census
International Trade Administration
Minority Business Development Agency
National Bureau of Standards
National Oceanic and Atmospheric Administration
National Telecommunications and Information Administration
National Technical Information Service
Patent and Trademark Office
United States Travel and Tourism Administration

§ 23.7 Notice to Department of Commerce organizational units of implementation and procedures.

Following are roles and responsibilities for the program within the Department of Commerce.

(a) The Department Contact Person shall:

(1) Serve as the Department of Commerce's sole representative for ordering materials, including camera-ready negatives, from the National Center,

(2) Serve as the Department of Commerce's sole supplier of materials to Operating Units,

(3) Maintain a current list of personnel within each Operating Unit who are authorized to order materials,

(4) Notify Operating Units whenever permission to use information on a missing child has been withdrawn,

(5) Ensure that only current missing children materials are distributed to Operating Units, and that only those requests from authorized departmental representatives are filled,

(6) Prepare all required departmental reports on the program,

(7) Promulgate any departmentwide operating instructions deemed appropriate for the program, and

(8) Chair biannual meetings of departmental representatives to discuss

the program and identify additional opportunities to use the missing children data with penalty mail.

(b) The Head of each Operating Unit (and for the Office of the Secretary, the Director of the Office of Administrative Services Operations), or his/her representative, shall:

(1) Designate a single person to act as the Operating Unit's representative to the Department for requesting and controlling missing children materials and receiving notification to withdraw materials from use (an alternative may be designated to act in the representative's absence),

(2) Provide the Department Contact Person with the name, title, telephone number, and room number of the Operating Unit's representative for the program (and also for the alternate, if one is designated), and notify the Department of changes when they occur,

(3) Ensure that the shelf-life of printed penalty mail materials containing missing children information is limited to a maximum of three months,

(4) Ensure that information on a child is not used once permission has been withdrawn and the shelf-life for the material would keep the information available for greater than 90 days after the date that permission to use it was withdrawn,

(5) Direct that the Operating Unit representative (or alternate) order missing children information, as appropriate, only from the Department Contact Person,

(6) Comply with policies, procedures, and operating instructions issued by the Department,

(7) Maintain necessary information to prepare required reports and submit them in accordance with requirements,

(8) Provide only current camera-ready and other photographic and biographical materials to printers, including those at the Administrative Support Centers, and

(9) Otherwise determine and control the use of missing children materials and information by the Operating Unit.

(c) The Director of each Administrative Support Center, or his/her representatives, shall:

(1) Cooperate with serviced Operating Units to promote the use of missing children information on penalty mail,

(2) As directed by an Operating Unit, utilize camera-ready and other photographic and biographical material provided by the Operating Unit in preparation of material for use with penalty mail, and

(3) Assure that any printing performed or procured under its direction is in accordance with the type of material and the manner of presentation as prescribed in this regulation.

PART 24—UNIFORM ADMINISTRATIVE REQUIREMENTS FOR GRANTS AND COOPERATIVE AGREEMENTS TO STATE AND LOCAL GOVERNMENTS

Subpart A—General

Subpart B—Pre-Award Requirements

Subpart C—Post-Award Requirements

FINANCIAL ADMINISTRATION

CHANGES, PROPERTY, AND SUBAWARDS

REPORTS, RECORDS, RETENTION, AND ENFORCEMENT

Subpart D—After-the-Grant Requirements

Subpart E—Entitlements [Reserved]

AUTHORITY: 5 U.S.C. 301.

SOURCE: 53 FR 8048, 8087, Mar. 11, 1988, unless otherwise noted.

Subpart A—General

§ 24.1 Purpose and scope of this part.

This part establishes uniform administrative rules for Federal grants and cooperative agreements and subawards to State, local and Indian tribal governments.

§ 24.2 Scope of subpart.

This subpart contains general rules pertaining to this part and procedures for control of exceptions from this part.

§ 24.3 Definitions.

As used in this part:

Accrued expenditures mean the charges incurred by the grantee during a given period requiring the provision of funds for: (1) Goods and other tangible property received; (2) services performed by employees, contractors, subgrantees, subcontractors, and other payees; and (3) other amounts becoming owed under programs for which no current services or performance is required, such as annuities, insurance claims, and other benefit payments.

Accrued income means the sum of: (1) Earnings during a given period from services performed by the grantee and goods and other tangible property delivered to purchasers, and (2) amounts becoming owed to the grantee for which no current services or performance is required by the grantee.

Acquisition cost of an item of purchased equipment means the net invoice unit price of the property including the cost of modifications, attachments, accessories, or auxiliary apparatus necessary to make the property usable for the purpose for which it was acquired. Other charges such as the cost of installation, transportation, taxes, duty or protective in-transit insurance, shall be included or excluded from the unit acquisition cost in accordance with the grantee's regular accounting practices.

Administrative requirements mean those matters common to grants in general, such as financial management, kinds and frequency of reports, and retention of records. These are distinguished from *programmatic* requirements, which concern matters that can be treated only on a program-by-program or grant-by-grant basis, such as kinds of activities that can be supported by grants under a particular program.

Awarding agency means (1) with respect to a grant, the Federal agency, and (2) with respect to a subgrant, the party that awarded the subgrant.

Cash contributions means the grantee's cash outlay, including the outlay of money contributed to the grantee or subgrantee by other public agencies and institutions, and private organizations and individuals. When authorized by Federal legislation, Federal funds received from other assistance agreements may be considered as grantee or subgrantee cash contributions.

Contract means (except as used in the definitions for *grant* and *subgrant* in this section and except where qualified by *Federal*) a procurement contract under a grant or subgrant, and means a procurement subcontract under a contract.

Cost sharing or matching means the value of the third party in-kind contributions and the portion of the costs of a federally assisted project or program not borne by the Federal Government.

Cost-type contract means a contract or subcontract under a grant in which the contractor or subcontractor is paid on the basis of the costs it incurs, with or without a fee.

Equipment means tangible, nonexpendable, personal property having a useful life of more than one year and an acquisition cost of $5,000 or more per unit. A grantee may use its own definition of equipment provided that such definition would at least include all equipment defined above.

Expenditure report means: (1) For nonconstruction grants, the SF–269 "Financial Status Report" (or other equivalent report); (2) for construction grants, the SF–271 "Outlay Report and Request for Reimbursement" (or other equivalent report).

Federally recognized Indian tribal government means the governing body or a governmental agency of any Indian tribe, band, nation, or other organized group or community (including any Native village as defined in section 3 of the Alaska Native Claims Settlement Act, 85 Stat 688) certified by the Secretary of the Interior as eligible for the special programs and services provided by him through the Bureau of Indian Affairs.

Government means a State or local government or a federally recognized Indian tribal government.

Grant means an award of financial assistance, including cooperative agreements, in the form of money, or property in lieu of money, by the Federal Government to an eligible grantee. The term does not include technical assistance which provides services instead of money, or other assistance in the form of revenue sharing, loans, loan guarantees, interest subsidies, insurance, or direct appropriations. Also, the term does not include assistance, such as a fellowship or other lump sum award, which the grantee is not required to account for.

Grantee means the government to which a grant is awarded and which is accountable for the use of the funds provided. The grantee is the entire legal entity even if only a particular component of the entity is designated in the grant award document.

Local government means a county, municipality, city, town, township, local public authority (including any public and Indian housing agency under the United States Housing Act of 1937) school district, special district, intrastate district, council of governments (whether or not incorporated as a nonprofit corporation under State law), any other regional or interstate government entity, or any agency or instrumentality of a local government.

Obligations means the amounts of orders placed, contracts and subgrants awarded, goods and services received, and similar transactions during a given period that will require payment by the grantee during the same or a future period.

OMB means the United States Office of Management and Budget.

Outlays (expenditures) mean charges made to the project or program. They may be reported on a cash or accrual basis. For reports prepared on a cash basis, outlays are the sum of actual cash disbursement for direct charges for goods and services, the amount of indirect expense incurred, the value of in-kind contributions applied, and the amount of cash advances and payments made to contractors and subgrantees. For reports prepared on an accrued expenditure basis, outlays are the sum of actual cash disbursements, the amount of indirect expense incurred, the value of inkind contributions applied, and the new increase (or decrease) in the amounts owed by the grantee for goods and other property received, for services performed by employees, contractors, subgrantees, subcontractors, and other payees, and other amounts becoming owed under programs for which no current services or performance are required, such as annuities, insurance claims, and other benefit payments.

Percentage of completion method refers to a system under which payments are made for construction work according to the percentage of completion of the work, rather than to the grantee's cost incurred.

Prior approval means documentation evidencing consent prior to incurring specific cost.

Real property means land, including land improvements, structures and appurtenances thereto, excluding movable machinery and equipment.

Share, when referring to the awarding agency's portion of real property, equipment or supplies, means the same percentage as the awarding agency's portion of the acquiring party's total costs under the grant to which the acquisition costs under the grant to which the acquisition cost of the property was charged. Only costs are to be counted—not the value of third-party in-kind contributions.

State means any of the several States of the United States, the District of Columbia, the Commonwealth of Puerto Rico, any territory or possession of the United States, or any agency or instrumentality of a State exclusive of local governments. The term does not include any public and Indian housing agency under United States Housing Act of 1937.

Subgrant means an award of financial assistance in the form of money, or property in lieu of money, made under a grant by a grantee to an eligible subgrantee. The term includes financial assistance when provided by contractual legal agreement, but does not include procurement purchases, nor does it include any form of assistance which is excluded from the definition of *grant* in this part.

Subgrantee means the government or other legal entity to which a subgrant is awarded and which is accountable to the grantee for the use of the funds provided.

Supplies means all tangible personal property other than *equipment* as defined in this part.

Suspension means depending on the context, either (1) temporary withdrawal of the authority to obligate grant funds pending corrective action by the grantee or subgrantee or a decision to terminate the grant, or (2) an action taken by a suspending official in accordance with agency regulations implementing E.O. 12549 to immediately exclude a person from participating in grant transactions for a period, pending completion of an investigation and such legal or debarment proceedings as may ensue.

Termination means permanent withdrawal of the authority to obligate previously-awarded grant funds before that authority would otherwise expire. It also means the voluntary relinquishment of that authority by the grantee or subgrantee. *Termination* does not include: (1) Withdrawal of funds awarded on the basis of the grantee's underestimate of the unobligated balance in a prior period; (2) Withdrawal of the unobligated balance as of the expiration of a grant; (3) Refusal to extend a grant or award additional funds, to make a competing or noncompeting continuation, renewal, extension, or supplemental award; or (4) voiding of a grant upon determination that the award was obtained fraudulently, or was otherwise illegal or invalid from inception.

Terms of a grant or subgrant mean all requirements of the grant or subgrant, whether in statute, regulations, or the award document.

Third party in-kind contributions mean property or services which benefit a federally assisted project or program and which are contributed by non-Federal third parties without charge to the grantee, or a cost-type contractor under the grant agreement.

Unliquidated obligations for reports prepared on a cash basis mean the amount of obligations incurred by the grantee that has not been paid. For reports prepared on an accrued expenditure basis, they represent the amount of obligations incurred by the grantee for which an outlay has not been recorded.

Unobligated balance means the portion of the funds authorized by the Federal agency that has not been obligated by the grantee and is determined by deducting the cumulative obligations from the cumulative funds authorized.

§24.4 Applicability.

(a) *General.* Subparts A through D of this part apply to all grants and subgrants to governments, except where inconsistent with Federal statutes or with regulations authorized in accordance with the exception provision of §24.6, or:

(1) Grants and subgrants to State and local institutions of higher education or State and local hospitals.

(2) The block grants authorized by the Omnibus Budget Reconciliation Act of 1981 (Community Services; Preventive Health and Health Services; Alcohol, Drug Abuse, and Mental Health Services; Maternal and Child Health Services; Social Services; Low-Income Home Energy Assistance; States' Program of Community Development Block Grants for Small Cities; and Elementary and Secondary Education other than programs administered by the Secretary of Education under Title V, Subtitle D, Chapter 2, Section 583—the Secretary's discretionary grant program) and Titles I-III of the Job

Training Partnership Act of 1982 and under the Public Health Services Act (Section 1921), Alcohol and Drug Abuse Treatment and Rehabilitation Block Grant and Part C of Title V, Mental Health Service for the Homeless Block Grant).

(3) Entitlement grants to carry out the following programs of the Social Security Act:

(i) Aid to Needy Families with Dependent Children (Title IV-A of the Act, not including the Work Incentive Program (WIN) authorized by section 402(a)19(G); HHS grants for WIN are subject to this part);

(ii) Child Support Enforcement and Establishment of Paternity (Title IV-D of the Act);

(iii) Foster Care and Adoption Assistance (Title IV-E of the Act);

(iv) Aid to the Aged, Blind, and Disabled (Titles I, X, XIV, and XVI-AABD of the Act); and

(v) Medical Assistance (Medicaid) (Title XIX of the Act) not including the State Medicaid Fraud Control program authorized by section 1903(a)(6)(B).

(4) Entitlement grants under the following programs of The National School Lunch Act:

(i) School Lunch (section 4 of the Act),

(ii) Commodity Assistance (section 6 of the Act),

(iii) Special Meal Assistance (section 11 of the Act),

(iv) Summer Food Service for Children (section 13 of the Act), and

(v) Child Care Food Program (section 17 of the Act).

(5) Entitlement grants under the following programs of The Child Nutrition Act of 1966:

(i) Special Milk (section 3 of the Act), and

(ii) School Breakfast (section 4 of the Act).

(6) Entitlement grants for State Administrative expenses under The Food Stamp Act of 1977 (section 16 of the Act).

(7) A grant for an experimental, pilot, or demonstration project that is also supported by a grant listed in paragraph (a)(3) of this section;

(8) Grant funds awarded under subsection 412(e) of the Immigration and Nationality Act (8 U.S.C. 1522(e)) and subsection 501(a) of the Refugee Education Assistance Act of 1980 (Pub. L. 96–422, 94 Stat. 1809), for cash assistance, medical assistance, and supplemental security income benefits to refugees and entrants and the administrative costs of providing the assistance and benefits;

(9) Grants to local education agencies under 20 U.S.C. 236 through 241–1(a), and 242 through 244 (portions of the Impact Aid program), except for 20 U.S.C. 238(d)(2)(c) and 240(f) (Entitlement Increase for Handicapped Children); and

(10) Payments under the Veterans Administration's State Home Per Diem Program (38 U.S.C. 641(a)).

(b) *Entitlement programs.* Entitlement programs enumerated above in §24.4(a) (3) through (8) are subject to subpart E.

§24.5 Effect on other issuances.

All other grants administration provisions of codified program regulations, program manuals, handbooks and other nonregulatory materials which are inconsistent with this part are superseded, except to the extent they are required by statute, or authorized in accordance with the exception provision in §24.6.

§24.6 Additions and exceptions.

(a) For classes of grants and grantees subject to this part, Federal agencies may not impose additional administrative requirements except in codified regulations published in the FEDERAL REGISTER.

(b) Exceptions for classes of grants or grantees may be authorized only by OMB.

(c) Exceptions on a case-by-case basis and for subgrantees may be authorized by the affected Federal agencies.

Subpart B—Pre-Award Requirements

§24.10 Forms for applying for grants.

(a) *Scope.* (1) This section prescribes forms and instructions to be used by governmental organizations (except hospitals and institutions of higher education operated by a government) in applying for grants. This section is not applicable, however, to formula grant programs which do not require applicants to apply for funds on a project basis.

(2) This section applies only to applications to Federal agencies for grants, and is not required to be applied by grantees in dealing with applicants for subgrants. However, grantees are encouraged to avoid more detailed or burdensome application requirements for subgrants.

(b) *Authorized forms and instructions for governmental organizations.* (1) In applying for grants, applicants shall only use standard application forms or those prescribed by the granting agency with the approval of OMB under the Paperwork Reduction Act of 1980.

(2) Applicants are not required to submit more than the original and two copies of preapplications or applications.

(3) Applicants must follow all applicable instructions that bear OMB clearance numbers. Federal agencies may specify and describe the programs, functions, or activities that will be used to plan, budget, and evaluate the work under a grant. Other supplementary instructions may be issued only with the approval of OMB to the extent required under the Paperwork Reduction Act of 1980. For any standard form, except the SF–424 facesheet, Federal agencies may shade out or instruct the applicant to disregard any line item that is not needed.

(4) When a grantee applies for additional funding (such as a continuation or supplemental award) or amends a previously submitted application, only the affected pages need be submitted. Previously submitted pages with information that is still current need not be resubmitted.

§ 24.11 State plans.

(a) *Scope.* The statutes for some programs require States to submit plans before receiving grants. Under regulations implementing Executive Order 12372, "Intergovernmental Review of Federal Programs," States are allowed to simplify, consolidate and substitute plans. This section contains additional provisions for plans that are subject to regulations implementing the Executive order.

(b) *Requirements.* A State need meet only Federal administrative or programmatic requirements for a plan that are in statutes or codified regulations.

(c) *Assurances.* In each plan the State will include an assurance that the State shall comply with all applicable Federal statutes and regulations in effect with respect to the periods for which it receives grant funding. For this assurance and other assurances required in the plan, the State may:

(1) Cite by number the statutory or regulatory provisions requiring the assurances and affirm that it gives the assurances required by those provisions,

(2) Repeat the assurance language in the statutes or regulations, or

(3) Develop its own language to the extent permitted by law.

(d) *Amendments.* A State will amend a plan whenever necessary to reflect: (1) New or revised Federal statutes or regulations or (2) a material change in any State law, organization, policy, or State agency operation. The State will obtain approval for the amendment and its effective date but need submit for approval only the amended portions of the plan.

§ 24.12 Special grant or subgrant conditions for "high-risk" grantees.

(a) A grantee or subgrantee may be considered "high risk" if an awarding agency determines that a grantee or subgrantee:

(1) Has a history of unsatisfactory performance, or

(2) Is not financially stable, or

(3) Has a management system which does not meet the management standards set forth in this part, or

(4) Has not conformed to terms and conditions of previous awards, or

(5) Is otherwise not responsible; and if the awarding agency determines that an award will be made, special conditions and/or restrictions shall correspond to the high risk condition and shall be included in the award.

(b) Special conditions or restrictions may include:

(1) Payment on a reimbursement basis;

(2) Withholding authority to proceed to the next phase until receipt of evidence of acceptable performance within a given funding period;

(3) Requiring additional, more detailed financial reports;

(4) Additional project monitoring;

(5) Requiring the grantee or subgrantee to obtain technical or management assistance; or

(6) Establishing additional prior approvals.

(c) If an awarding agency decides to impose such conditions, the awarding official will notify the grantee or subgrantee as early as possible, in writing, of:

(1) The nature of the special conditions/restrictions;

(2) The reason(s) for imposing them;

(3) The corrective actions which must be taken before they will be removed and the time allowed for completing the corrective actions, and

(4) The method of requesting reconsideration of the conditions/restrictions imposed.

Subpart C—Post-Award Requirements

FINANCIAL ADMINISTRATION

§24.20 Standards for financial management systems.

(a) A State must expand and account for grant funds in accordance with State laws and procedures for expending and accounting for its own funds. Fiscal control and accounting procedures of the State, as well as its subgrantees and cost-type contractors, must be sufficient to—

(1) Permit preparation of reports required by this part and the statutes authorizing the grant, and

(2) Permit the tracing of funds to a level of expenditures adequate to establish that such funds have not been used in violation of the restrictions and prohibitions of applicable statutes.

(b) The financial management systems of other grantees and subgrantees must meet the following standards:

(1) *Financial reporting.* Accurate, current, and complete disclosure of the financial results of financially assisted activities must be made in accordance with the financial reporting requirements of the grant or subgrant.

(2) *Accounting records.* Grantees and subgrantees must maintain records which adequately identify the source and application of funds provided for financially-assisted activities. These records must contain information pertaining to grant or subgrant awards and authorizations, obligations, unobligated balances, assets, liabilities, outlays or expenditures, and income.

(3) *Internal control.* Effective control and accountability must be maintained for all grant and subgrant cash, real and personal property, and other assets. Grantees and subgrantees must adequately safeguard all such property and must assure that it is used solely for authorized purposes.

(4) *Budget control.* Actual expenditures or outlays must be compared with budgeted amounts for each grant or subgrant. Financial information must be related to performance or productivity data, including the development of unit cost information whenever appropriate or specifically required in the grant or subgrant agreement. If unit cost data are required, estimates based on available documentation will be accepted whenever possible.

(5) *Allowable cost.* Applicable OMB cost principles, agency program regulations, and the terms of grant and subgrant agreements will be followed in determining the reasonableness, allowability, and allocability of costs.

(6) *Source documentation.* Accounting records must be supported by such source documentation as cancelled checks, paid bills, payrolls, time and attendance records, contract and subgrant award documents, etc.

(7) *Cash management.* Procedures for minimizing the time elapsing between the transfer of funds from the U.S. Treasury and disbursement by grantees and subgrantees must be followed whenever advance payment procedures are used. Grantees must establish reasonable procedures to ensure the receipt of reports on subgrantees' cash balances and cash disbursements in sufficient time to enable them to prepare complete and accurate cash transactions reports to the awarding agency. When advances are made by letter-of-credit or electronic transfer of funds methods, the grantee must make drawdowns as close as possible to the time of making disbursements. Grantees must monitor cash drawdowns by

their subgrantees to assure that they conform substantially to the same standards of timing and amount as apply to advances to the grantees.

(c) An awarding agency may review the adequacy of the financial management system of any applicant for financial assistance as part of a preaward review or at any time subsequent to award.

§ 24.21 Payment.

(a) *Scope.* This section prescribes the basic standard and the methods under which a Federal agency will make payments to grantees, and grantees will make payments to subgrantees and contractors.

(b) *Basic standard.* Methods and procedures for payment shall minimize the time elapsing between the transfer of funds and disbursement by the grantee or subgrantee, in accordance with Treasury regulations at 31 CFR Part 205.

(c) *Advances.* Grantees and subgrantees shall be paid in advance, provided they maintain or demonstrate the willingness and ability to maintain procedures to minimize the time elapsing between the transfer of the funds and their disbursement by the grantee or subgrantee.

(d) *Reimbursement.* Reimbursement shall be the preferred method when the requirements in paragraph (c) of this section are not met. Grantees and subgrantees may also be paid by reimbursement for any construction grant. Except as otherwise specified in regulation, Federal agencies shall not use the percentage of completion method to pay construction grants. The grantee or subgrantee may use that method to pay its construction contractor, and if it does, the awarding agency's payments to the grantee or subgrantee will be based on the grantee's or subgrantee's actual rate of disbursement.

(e) *Working capital advances.* If a grantee cannot meet the criteria for advance payments described in paragraph (c) of this section, and the Federal agency has determined that reimbursement is not feasible because the grantee lacks sufficient working capital, the awarding agency may provide cash or a working capital advance basis. Under this procedure the awarding agency shall advance cash to the grantee to cover its estimated disbursement needs for an initial period generally geared to the grantee's disbursing cycle. Thereafter, the awarding agency shall reimburse the grantee for its actual cash disbursements. The working capital advance method of payment shall not be used by grantees or subgrantees if the reason for using such method is the unwillingness or inability of the grantee to provide timely advances to the subgrantee to meet the subgrantee's actual cash disbursements.

(f) *Effect of program income, refunds, and audit recoveries on payment.* (1) Grantees and subgrantees shall disburse repayments to and interest earned on a revolving fund before requesting additional cash payments for the same activity.

(2) Except as provided in paragraph (f)(1) of this section, grantees and subgrantees shall disburse program income, rebates, refunds, contract settlements, audit recoveries and interest earned on such funds before requesting additional cash payments.

(g) *Withholding payments.* (1) Unless otherwise required by Federal statute, awarding agencies shall not withhold payments for proper charges incurred by grantees or subgrantees unless—

(i) The grantee or subgrantee has failed to comply with grant award conditions or

(ii) The grantee or subgrantee is indebted to the United States.

(2) Cash withheld for failure to comply with grant award condition, but without suspension of the grant, shall be released to the grantee upon subsequent compliance. When a grant is suspended, payment adjustments will be made in accordance with § 24.43(c).

(3) A Federal agency shall not make payment to grantees for amounts that are withheld by grantees or subgrantees from payment to contractors to assure satisfactory completion of work. Payments shall be made by the Federal agency when the grantees or subgrantees actually disburse the withheld funds to the contractors or to escrow accounts established to assure satisfactory completion of work.

(h) *Cash depositories.* (1) Consistent with the national goal of expanding the opportunities for minority business enterprises, grantees and subgrantees are encouraged to use minority banks (a bank which is owned at least 50 percent by minority group members). A list of minority owned banks can be obtained from the Minority Business Development Agency, Department of Commerce, Washington, DC 20230.

(2) A grantee or subgrantee shall maintain a separate bank account only when required by Federal-State agreement.

(i) *Interest earned on advances.* Except for interest earned on advances of funds exempt under the Intergovernmental Cooperation Act (31 U.S.C. 6501 *et seq.*) and the Indian Self-Determination Act (23 U.S.C. 450), grantees and subgrantees shall promptly, but at least quarterly, remit interest earned on advances to the Federal agency. The grantee or subgrantee may keep interest amounts up to $100 per year for administrative expenses.

§ 24.22 Allowable costs.

(a) *Limitation on use of funds.* Grant funds may be used only for:

(1) The allowable costs of the grantees, subgrantees and cost-type contractors, including allowable costs in the form of payments to fixed-price contractors; and

(2) Reasonable fees or profit to cost-type contractors but not any fee or profit (or other increment above allowable costs) to the grantee or subgrantee.

(b) *Applicable cost principles.* For each kind of organization, there is a set of Federal principles for determining allowable costs. Allowable costs will be determined in accordance with the cost principles applicable to the organization incurring the costs. The following chart lists the kinds of organizations and the applicable cost principles.

For the costs of a—	Use the principles in—
State, local or Indian tribal government.	OMB Circular A–87.
Private nonprofit organization other than an (1) institution of higher education, (2) hospital, or (3) organization named in OMB Circular A–122 as not subject to that circular.	OMB Circular A–122.
Educational institutions.	OMB Circular A–21.
For-profit organization other than a hospital and an organization named in OBM Circular A–122 as not subject to that circular.	48 CFR Part 31. Contract Cost Principles and Procedures, or uniform cost accounting standards that comply with cost principles acceptable to the Federal agency.

§ 24.23 Period of availability of funds.

(a) *General.* Where a funding period is specified, a grantee may charge to the award only costs resulting from obligations of the funding period unless carryover of unobligated balances is permitted, in which case the carryover balances may be charged for costs resulting from obligations of the subsequent funding period.

(b) *Liquidation of obligations.* A grantee must liquidate all obligations incurred under the award not later than 90 days after the end of the funding period (or as specified in a program regulation) to coincide with the submission of the annual Financial Status Report (SF–269). The Federal agency may extend this deadline at the request of the grantee.

§ 24.24 Matching or cost sharing.

(a) *Basic rule: Costs and contributions acceptable.* With the qualifications and exceptions listed in paragraph (b) of this section, a matching or cost sharing requirement may be satisfied by either or both of the following:

(1) Allowable costs incurred by the grantee, subgrantee or a cost-type contractor under the assistance agreement. This includes allowable costs borne by non-Federal grants or by others cash donations from non-Federal third parties.

(2) The value of third party in-kind contributions applicable to the period to which the cost sharing or matching requirements applies.

(b) *Qualifications and exceptions*—(1) *Costs borne by other Federal grant agreements.* Except as provided by Federal statute, a cost sharing or matching requirement may not be met by costs borne by another Federal grant. This prohibition does not apply to income earned by a grantee or subgrantee from a contract awarded under another Federal grant.

(2) *General revenue sharing.* For the purpose of this section, general revenue sharing funds distributed under 31 U.S.C. 6702 are not considered Federal grant funds.

(3) *Cost or contributions counted towards other Federal costs-sharing requirements.* Neither costs nor the values of third party in-kind contributions may count towards satisfying a cost sharing or matching requirement of a grant agreement if they have been or will be counted towards satisfying a cost sharing or matching requirement of another Federal grant agreement, a Federal procurement contract, or any other award of Federal funds.

(4) *Costs financed by program income.* Costs financed by program income, as defined in § 24.25, shall not count towards satisfying a cost sharing or matching requirement unless they are expressly permitted in the terms of the assistance agreement. (This use of general program income is described in § 24.25(g).)

(5) *Services or property financed by income earned by contractors.* Contractors under a grant may earn income from the activities carried out under the contract in addition to the amounts earned from the party awarding the contract. No costs of services or property supported by this income may count toward satisfying a cost sharing or matching requirement unless other provisions of the grant agreement expressly permit this kind of income to be used to meet the requirement.

(6) *Records.* Costs and third party in-kind contributions counting towards satisfying a cost sharing or matching requirement must be verifiable from the records of grantees and subgrantee or cost-type contractors. These records must show how the value placed on third party in-kind contributions was derived. To the extent feasible, volunteer services will be supported by the same methods that the organization uses to support the allocability of regular personnel costs.

(7) *Special standards for third party in-kind contributions.* (i) Third party in-kind contributions count towards satisfying a cost sharing or matching requirement only where, if the party receiving the contributions were to pay for them, the payments would be allowable costs.

(ii) Some third party in-kind contributions are goods and services that, if the grantee, subgrantee, or contractor receiving the contribution had to pay for them, the payments would have been an indirect costs. Costs sharing or matching credit for such contributions shall be given only if the grantee, subgrantee, or contractor has established, along with its regular indirect cost rate, a special rate for allocating to individual projects or programs the value of the contributions.

(iii) A third party in-kind contribution to a fixed-price contract may count towards satisfying a cost sharing or matching requirement only if it results in:

(A) An increase in the services or property provided under the contract (without additional cost to the grantee or subgrantee) or

(B) A cost savings to the grantee or subgrantee.

(iv) The values placed on third party in-kind contributions for cost sharing or matching purposes will conform to the rules in the succeeding sections of this part. If a third party in-kind contribution is a type not treated in those sections, the value placed upon it shall be fair and reasonable.

(c) *Valuation of donated services*—(1) *Volunteer services.* Unpaid services provided to a grantee or subgrantee by individuals will be valued at rates consistent with those ordinarily paid for similar work in the grantee's or subgrantee's organization. If the grantee or subgrantee does not have employees performing similar work, the rates will be consistent with those ordinarily paid by other employers for similar work in the same labor market. In either case, a reasonable amount for fringe benefits may be included in the valuation.

(2) *Employees of other organizations.* When an employer other than a grantee, subgrantee, or cost-type contractor furnishes free of charge the services of an employee in the employee's normal line of work, the services will be valued at the employee's regular rate of pay exclusive of the employee's fringe benefits and overhead costs. If the services

are in a different line of work, paragraph (c)(1) of this section applies.

(d) *Valuation of third party donated supplies and loaned equipment or space.* (1) If a third party donates supplies, the contribution will be valued at the market value of the supplies at the time of donation.

(2) If a third party donates the use of equipment or space in a building but retains title, the contribution will be valued at the fair rental rate of the equipment or space.

(e) *Valuation of third party donated equipment, buildings, and land.* If a third party donates equipment, buildings, or land, and title passes to a grantee or subgrantee, the treatment of the donated property will depend upon the purpose of the grant or subgrant, as follows:

(1) *Awards for capital expenditures.* If the purpose of the grant or subgrant is to assist the grantee or subgrantee in the acquisition of property, the market value of that property at the time of donation may be counted as cost sharing or matching,

(2) *Other awards.* If assisting in the acquisition of property is not the purpose of the grant or subgrant, paragraphs (e)(2) (i) and (ii) of this section apply:

(i) If approval is obtained from the awarding agency, the market value at the time of donation of the donated equipment or buildings and the fair rental rate of the donated land may be counted as cost sharing or matching. In the case of a subgrant, the terms of the grant agreement may require that the approval be obtained from the Federal agency as well as the grantee. In all cases, the approval may be given only if a purchase of the equipment or rental of the land would be approved as an allowable direct cost. If any part of the donated property was acquired with Federal funds, only the non-federal share of the property may be counted as cost-sharing or matching.

(ii) If approval is not obtained under paragraph (e)(2)(i) of this section, no amount may be counted for donated land, and only depreciation or use allowances may be counted for donated equipment and buildings. The depreciation or use allowances for this property are not treated as third party in-kind contributions. Instead, they are treated as costs incurred by the grantee or subgrantee. They are computed and allocated (usually as indirect costs) in accordance with the cost principles specified in §24.22, in the same way as depreciation or use allowances for purchased equipment and buildings. The amount of depreciation or use allowances for donated equipment and buildings is based on the property's market value at the time it was donated.

(f) *Valuation of grantee or subgrantee donated real property for construction/acquisition.* If a grantee or subgrantee donates real property for a construction or facilities acquisition project, the current market value of that property may be counted as cost sharing or matching. If any part of the donated property was acquired with Federal funds, only the non-federal share of the property may be counted as cost sharing or matching.

(g) *Appraisal of real property.* In some cases under paragraphs (d), (e) and (f) of this section, it will be necessary to establish the market value of land or a building or the fair rental rate of land or of space in a building. In these cases, the Federal agency may require the market value or fair rental value be set by an independent appraiser, and that the value or rate be certified by the grantee. This requirement will also be imposed by the grantee on subgrantees.

§24.25 Program income.

(a) *General.* Grantees are encouraged to earn income to defray program costs. Program income includes income from fees for services performed, from the use or rental of real or personal property acquired with grant funds, from the sale of commodities or items fabricated under a grant agreement, and from payments of principal and interest on loans made with grant funds. Except as otherwise provided in regulations of the Federal agency, program income does not include interest on grant funds, rebates, credits, discounts, refunds, etc. and interest earned on any of them.

(b) *Definition of program income.* Program income means gross income received by the grantee or subgrantee directly generated by a grant supported activity, or earned only as a result of the grant agreement during the grant period. "During the grant period" is the time between the effective date of the award and the ending date of the award reflected in the final financial report.

(c) *Cost of generating program income.* If authorized by Federal regulations or the grant agreement, costs incident to the generation of program income may be deducted from gross income to determine program income.

(d) *Governmental revenues.* Taxes, special assessments, levies, fines, and other such revenues raised by a grantee or subgrantee are not program income unless the revenues are specifically identified in the grant agreement or Federal agency regulations as program income.

(e) *Royalties.* Income from royalties and license fees for copyrighted material, patents, and inventions developed by a grantee or subgrantee is program income only if the revenues are specifically identified in the grant agreement or Federal agency regulations as program income. (See § 24.34.)

(f) *Property.* Proceeds from the sale of real property or equipment will be handled in accordance with the requirements of §§ 24.31 and 24.32.

(g) *Use of program income.* Program income shall be deducted from outlays which may be both Federal and non-Federal as described below, unless the Federal agency regulations or the grant agreement specify another alternative (or a combination of the alternatives). In specifying alternatives, the Federal agency may distinguish between income earned by the grantee and income earned by subgrantees and between the sources, kinds, or amounts of income. When Federal agencies authorize the alternatives in paragraphs (g) (2) and (3) of this section, program income in excess of any limits stipulated shall also be deducted from outlays.

(1) *Deduction.* Ordinarily program income shall be deducted from total allowable costs to determine the net allowable costs. Program income shall be used for current costs unless the Federal agency authorizes otherwise. Program income which the grantee did not anticipate at the time of the award shall be used to reduce the Federal agency and grantee contributions rather than to increase the funds committed to the project.

(2) *Addition.* When authorized, program income may be added to the funds committed to the grant agreement by the Federal agency and the grantee. The program income shall be used for the purposes and under the conditions of the grant agreement.

(3) *Cost sharing or matching.* When authorized, program income may be used to meet the cost sharing or matching requirement of the grant agreement. The amount of the Federal grant award remains the same.

(h) *Income after the award period.* There are no Federal requirements governing the disposition of program income earned after the end of the award period (*i.e.*, until the ending date of the final financial report, see paragraph (a) of this section), unless the terms of the agreement or the Federal agency regulations provide otherwise.

§ 24.26 Non-Federal audit.

(a) *Basic rule.* Grantees and subgrantees are responsible for obtaining audits in accordance with the Single Audit Act Amendments of 1996 (31 U.S.C. 7501–7507) and revised OMB Circular A–133, "Audits of States, Local Governments, and Non-Profit Organizations." The audits shall be made by an independent auditor in accordance with generally accepted government auditing standards covering financial audits.

(b) *Subgrantees.* State or local governments, as those terms are defined for purposes of the Single Audit Act Amendments of 1996, that provide Federal awards to a subgrantee, which expends $300,000 or more (or other amount as specified by OMB) in Federal awards in a fiscal year, shall:

(1) Determine whether State or local subgrantees have met the audit requirements of the Act and whether subgrantees covered by OMB Circular A–110, "Uniform Administrative Requirements for Grants and Agreements with Institutions of Higher Education, Hospitals, and Other Non-Profit Organizations," have met the audit requirements of the Act. Commercial contractors (private for-profit and private and governmental organizations) providing

goods and services to State and local governments are not required to have a single audit performed. State and local governments should use their own procedures to ensure that the contractor has complied with laws and regulations affecting the expenditure of Federal funds;

(2) Determine whether the subgrantee spent Federal assistance funds provided in accordance with applicable laws and regulations. This may be accomplished by reviewing an audit of the subgrantee made in accordance with the Act, Circular A–110, or through other means (e.g., program reviews) if the subgrantee has not had such an audit;

(3) Ensure that appropriate corrective action is taken within six months after receipt of the audit report in instance of noncompliance with Federal laws and regulations;

(4) Consider whether subgrantee audits necessitate adjustment of the grantee's own records; and

(5) Require each subgrantee to permit independent auditors to have access to the records and financial statements.

(c) *Auditor selection.* In arranging for audit services, §24.36 shall be followed.

[53 FR 8048, 8087, Mar. 11, 1988, as amended at 62 FR 45939, 45940, Aug. 29, 1997]

CHANGES, PROPERTY, AND SUBAWARDS

§24.30 Changes.

(a) *General.* Grantees and subgrantees are permitted to rebudget within the approved direct cost budget to meet unanticipated requirements and may make limited program changes to the approved project. However, unless waived by the awarding agency, certain types of post-award changes in budgets and projects shall require the prior written approval of the awarding agency.

(b) *Relation to cost principles.* The applicable cost principles (see §24.22) contain requirements for prior approval of certain types of costs. Except where waived, those requirements apply to all grants and subgrants even if paragraphs (c) through (f) of this section do not.

(c) *Budget changes*—(1) *Nonconstruction projects.* Except as stated in other regulations or an award document, grantees or subgrantees shall obtain the prior approval of the awarding agency whenever any of the following changes is anticipated under a nonconstruction award:

(i) Any revision which would result in the need for additional funding.

(ii) Unless waived by the awarding agency, cumulative transfers among direct cost categories, or, if applicable, among separately budgeted programs, projects, functions, or activities which exceed or are expected to exceed ten percent of the current total approved budget, whenever the awarding agency's share exceeds $100,000.

(iii) Transfer of funds allotted for training allowances (*i.e.*, from direct payments to trainees to other expense categories).

(2) *Construction projects.* Grantees and subgrantees shall obtain prior written approval for any budget revision which would result in the need for additional funds.

(3) *Combined construction and nonconstruction projects.* When a grant or subgrant provides funding for both construction and nonconstruction activities, the grantee or subgrantee must obtain prior written approval from the awarding agency before making any fund or budget transfer from nonconstruction to construction or vice versa.

(d) *Programmatic changes.* Grantees or subgrantees must obtain the prior approval of the awarding agency whenever any of the following actions is anticipated:

(1) Any revision of the scope or objectives of the project (regardless of whether there is an associated budget revision requiring prior approval).

(2) Need to extend the period of availability of funds.

(3) Changes in key persons in cases where specified in an application or a grant award. In research projects, a change in the project director or principal investigator shall always require approval unless waived by the awarding agency.

(4) Under nonconstruction projects, contracting out, subgranting (if authorized by law) or otherwise obtaining the services of a third party to perform

activities which are central to the purposes of the award. This approval requirement is in addition to the approval requirements of § 24.36 but does not apply to the procurement of equipment, supplies, and general support services.

(e) *Additional prior approval requirements.* The awarding agency may not require prior approval for any budget revision which is not described in paragraph (c) of this section.

(f) *Requesting prior approval.* (1) A request for prior approval of any budget revision will be in the same budget formal the grantee used in its application and shall be accompanied by a narrative justification for the proposed revision.

(2) A request for a prior approval under the applicable Federal cost principles (see § 24.22) may be made by letter.

(3) A request by a subgrantee for prior approval will be addressed in writing to the grantee. The grantee will promptly review such request and shall approve or disapprove the request in writing. A grantee will not approve any budget or project revision which is inconsistent with the purpose or terms and conditions of the Federal grant to the grantee. If the revision, requested by the subgrantee would result in a change to the grantee's approved project which requires Federal prior approval, the grantee will obtain the Federal agency's approval before approving the subgrantee's request.

§ 24.31 Real property.

(a) *Title.* Subject to the obligations and conditions set forth in this section, title to real property acquired under a grant or subgrant will vest upon acquisition in the grantee or subgrantee respectively.

(b) *Use.* Except as otherwise provided by Federal statutes, real property will be used for the originally authorized purposes as long as needed for that purposes, and the grantee or subgrantee shall not dispose of or encumber its title or other interests.

(1) The Federal awarding agency may require the placing of appropriate notices of record to advise that property has been acquired or improved with Federal financial assistance, and that use and disposition conditions apply to the property.

(2) [Reserved]

(c) *Disposition.* When real property is no longer needed for the originally authorized purpose, the grantee or subgrantee will request disposition instructions from the awarding agency. The instructions will provide for one of the following alternatives:

(1) *Retention of title.* Retain title after compensating the awarding agency. The amount paid to the awarding agency will be computed by applying the awarding agency's percentage of participation in the cost of the original purchase to the fair market value of the property. However, in those situations where a grantee or subgrantee is disposing of real property acquired with grant funds and acquiring replacement real property under the same program, the net proceeds from the disposition may be used as an offset to the cost of the replacement property.

(2) *Sale of property.* Sell the property and compensate the awarding agency. The amount due to the awarding agency will be calculated by applying the awarding agency's percentage of participation in the cost of the original purchase to the proceeds of the sale after deduction of any actual and reasonable selling and fixing-up expenses. If the grant is still active, the net proceeds from sale may be offset against the original cost of the property. When a grantee or subgrantee is directed to sell property, sales procedures shall be followed that provide for competition to the extent practicable and result in the highest possible return.

(3) *Transfer of title.* Transfer title to the awarding agency or to a third-party designated/approved by the awarding agency. The grantee or subgrantee shall be paid an amount calculated by applying the grantee or subgrantee's percentage of participation in the purchase of the real property to the current fair market value of the property.

[53 FR 8048, Mar. 11, 1988, as amended at 53 FR 8049, Mar. 11, 1988]

§ 24.32 Equipment.

(a) *Title.* Subject to the obligations and conditions set forth in this section, title to equipment acquired under a grant or subgrant will vest upon acquisition in the grantee or subgrantee respectively.

(b) *States*. A State will use, manage, and dispose of equipment acquired under a grant by the State in accordance with State laws and procedures. Other grantees and subgrantees will follow paragraphs (c) through (e) of this section.

(c) *Use*. (1) Equipment shall be used by the grantee or subgrantee in the program or project for which it was acquired as long as needed, whether or not the project or program continues to be supported by Federal funds. When no longer needed for the original program or project, the equipment may be used in other activities currently or previously supported by a Federal agency.

(2) The grantee or subgrantee shall also make equipment available for use on other projects or programs currently or previously supported by the Federal Government, providing such use will not interfere with the work on the projects or program for which it was originally acquired. First preference for other use shall be given to other programs or projects supported by the awarding agency. User fees should be considered if appropriate.

(3) Notwithstanding the encouragement in §24.25(a) to earn program income, the grantee or subgrantee must not use equipment acquired with grant funds to provide services for a fee to compete unfairly with private companies that provide equivalent services, unless specifically permitted or contemplated by Federal statute.

(4) When acquiring replacement equipment, the grantee or subgrantee may use the equipment to be replaced as a trade-in or sell the property and use the proceeds to offset the cost of the replacement property, subject to the approval of the awarding agency.

(d) *Management requirements*. Procedures for managing equipment (including replacement equipment), whether acquired in whole or in part with grant funds, until disposition takes place will, as a minimum, meet the following requirements:

(1) Property records must be maintained that include a description of the property, a serial number or other identification number, the source of property, who holds title, the acquisition date, and cost of the property, percentage of Federal participation in the cost of the property, the location, use and condition of the property, and any ultimate disposition data including the date of disposal and sale price of the property.

(2) A physical inventory of the property must be taken and the results reconciled with the property records at least once every two years.

(3) A control system must be developed to ensure adequate safeguards to prevent loss, damage, or theft of the property. Any loss, damage, or theft shall be investigated.

(4) Adequate maintenance procedures must be developed to keep the property in good condition.

(5) If the grantee or subgrantee is authorized or required to sell the property, proper sales procedures must be established to ensure the highest possible return.

(e) *Disposition*. When original or replacement equipment acquired under a grant or subgrant is no longer needed for the original project or program or for other activities currently or previously supported by a Federal agency, disposition of the equipment will be made as follows:

(1) Items of equipment with a current per-unit fair market value of less than $5,000 may be retained, sold or otherwise disposed of with no further obligation to the awarding agency.

(2) Items of equipment with a current per unit fair market value in excess of $5,000 may be retained or sold and the awarding agency shall have a right to an amount calculated by multiplying the current market value or proceeds from sale by the awarding agency's share of the equipment.

(3) In cases where a grantee or subgrantee fails to take appropriate disposition actions, the awarding agency may direct the grantee or subgrantee to take excess and disposition actions.

(f) *Federal equipment*. In the event a grantee or subgrantee is provided federally-owned equipment:

(1) Title will remain vested in the Federal Government.

(2) Grantees or subgrantees will manage the equipment in accordance with

Federal agency rules and procedures, and submit an annual inventory listing.

(3) When the equipment is no longer needed, the grantee or subgrantee will request disposition instructions from the Federal agency.

(g) *Right to transfer title.* The Federal awarding agency may reserve the right to transfer title to the Federal Government or a third part named by the awarding agency when such a third party is otherwise eligible under existing statutes. Such transfers shall be subject to the following standards:

(1) The property shall be identified in the grant or otherwise made known to the grantee in writing.

(2) The Federal awarding agency shall issue disposition instruction within 120 calendar days after the end of the Federal support of the project for which it was acquired. If the Federal awarding agency fails to issue disposition instructions within the 120 calendar-day period the grantee shall follow § 24.32(e).

(3) When title to equipment is transferred, the grantee shall be paid an amount calculated by applying the percentage of participation in the purchase to the current fair market value of the property.

§ 24.33 Supplies.

(a) *Title.* Title to supplies acquired under a grant or subgrant will vest, upon acquisition, in the grantee or subgrantee respectively.

(b) *Disposition.* If there is a residual inventory of unused supplies exceeding $5,000 in total aggregate fair market value upon termination or completion of the award, and if the supplies are not needed for any other federally sponsored programs or projects, the grantee or subgrantee shall compensate the awarding agency for its share.

§ 24.34 Other property.

(a) *Copyrights.* The Federal awarding agency reserves a royalty-free, nonexclusive, and irrevocable license to reproduce, publish or otherwise use, and to authorize others to use, for Federal Government purposes:

(1) The copyright in any work developed under a grant, subgrant, or contract under a grant or subgrant; and

(2) Any rights of copyright to which a grantee, subgrantee, or a contractor purchases ownership with grant support.

(b) *Intangible property.* Title to such property as loans, notes, and other debt instruments (whether considered tangible or intangible) acquired under a grant or subgrant will vest upon acquisition in the grantee or subgrantee respectively. Such property will be used for the originally authorized purpose as long as needed for that purpose, and the grantee or subgrantee shall not dispose of or encumber its title or other interests. When no longer needed for the originally authorized purpose, disposition of such property will be made as provided in § 24.32(e).

[53 FR 8049, Mar. 11, 1988]

§ 24.35 Subawards to debarred and suspended parties.

Grantees and subgrantees must not make any award or permit any award (subgrant or contract) at any tier to any party which is debarred or suspended or is otherwise excluded from or ineligible for participation in Federal assistance programs under Executive Order 12549, ''Debarment and Suspension.''

§ 24.36 Procurement.

(a) *States.* When procuring property and services under a grant, a State will follow the same policies and procedures it uses for procurements from its non-Federal funds. The State will ensure that every purchase order or other contract includes any clauses required by Federal statutes and executive orders and their implementing regulations. Other grantees and subgrantees will follow paragraphs (b) through (i) in this section.

(b) *Procurement standards.* (1) Grantees and subgrantees will use their own procurement procedures which reflect applicable State and local laws and regulations, provided that the procurements conform to applicable Federal law and the standards identified in this section.

(2) Grantees and subgrantees will maintain a contract administration

system which ensures that contractors perform in accordance with the terms, conditions, and specifications of their contracts or purchase orders.

(3) Grantees and subgrantees will maintain a written code of standards of conduct governing the performance of their employees engaged in the award and administration of contracts. No employee, officer or agent of the grantee or subgrantee shall participate in selection, or in the award or administration of a contract supported by Federal funds if a conflict of interest, real or apparent, would be involved. Such a conflict would arise when:

(i) The employee, officer or agent,

(ii) Any member of his immediate family,

(iii) His or her partner, or

(iv) An organization which employs, or is about to employ, any of the above, has a financial or other interest in the firm selected for award. The grantee's or subgrantee's officers, employees or agents will neither solicit nor accept gratuities, favors or anything of monetary value from contractors, potential contractors, or parties to subagreements. Grantee and subgrantees may set minimum rules where the financial interest is not substantial or the gift is an unsolicited item of nominal intrinsic value. To the extent permitted by State or local law or regulations, such standards or conduct will provide for penalties, sanctions, or other disciplinary actions for violations of such standards by the grantee's and subgrantee's officers, employees, or agents, or by contractors or their agents. The awarding agency may in regulation provide additional prohibitions relative to real, apparent, or potential conflicts of interest.

(4) Grantee and subgrantee procedures will provide for a review of proposed procurements to avoid purchase of unnecessary or duplicative items. Consideration should be given to consolidating or breaking out procurements to obtain a more economical purchase. Where appropriate, an analysis will be made of lease versus purchase alternatives, and any other appropriate analysis to determine the most economical approach.

(5) To foster greater economy and efficiency, grantees and subgrantees are encouraged to enter into State and local intergovernmental agreements for procurement or use of common goods and services.

(6) Grantees and subgrantees are encouraged to use Federal excess and surplus property in lieu of purchasing new equipment and property whenever such use is feasible and reduces project costs.

(7) Grantees and subgrantees are encouraged to use value engineering clauses in contracts for construction projects of sufficient size to offer reasonable opportunities for cost reductions. Value engineering is a systematic and creative anaylsis of each contract item or task to ensure that its essential function is provided at the overall lower cost.

(8) Grantees and subgrantees will make awards only to responsible contractors possessing the ability to perform successfully under the terms and conditions of a proposed procurement. Consideration will be given to such matters as contractor integrity, compliance with public policy, record of past performance, and financial and technical resources.

(9) Grantees and subgrantees will maintain records sufficient to detail the significant history of a procurement. These records will include, but are not necessarily limited to the following: rationale for the method of procurement, selection of contract type, contractor selection or rejection, and the basis for the contract price.

(10) Grantees and subgrantees will use time and material type contracts only—

(i) After a determination that no other contract is suitable, and

(ii) If the contract includes a ceiling price that the contractor exceeds at its own risk.

(11) Grantees and subgrantees alone will be responsible, in accordance with good administrative practice and sound business judgment, for the settlement of all contractual and administrative issues arising out of procurements. These issues include, but are not limited to source evaluation, protests, disputes, and claims. These standards do not relieve the grantee or subgrantee of any contractual responsibilities under its contracts. Federal agencies

will not substitute their judgment for that of the grantee or subgrantee unless the matter is primarily a Federal concern. Violations of law will be referred to the local, State, or Federal authority having proper jurisdiction.

(12) Grantees and subgrantees will have protest procedures to handle and resolve disputes relating to their procurements and shall in all instances disclose information regarding the protest to the awarding agency. A protestor must exhaust all administrative remedies with the grantee and subgrantee before pursuing a protest with the Federal agency. Reviews of protests by the Federal agency will be limited to:

(i) Violations of Federal law or regulations and the standards of this section (violations of State or local law will be under the jurisdiction of State or local authorities) and

(ii) Violations of the grantee's or subgrantee's protest procedures for failure to review a complaint or protest. Protests received by the Federal agency other than those specified above will be referred to the grantee or subgrantee.

(c) *Competition.* (1) All procurement transactions will be conducted in a manner providing full and open competition consistent with the standards of § 24.36. Some of the situations considered to be restrictive of competition include but are not limited to:

(i) Placing unreasonable requirements on firms in order for them to qualify to do business,

(ii) Requiring unnecessary experience and excessive bonding,

(iii) Noncompetitive pricing practices between firms or between affiliated companies,

(iv) Noncompetitive awards to consultants that are on retainer contracts,

(v) Organizational conflicts of interest,

(vi) Specifying only a "brand name" product instead of allowing "an equal" product to be offered and describing the performance of other relevant requirements of the procurement, and

(vii) Any arbitrary action in the procurement process.

(2) Grantees and subgrantees will conduct procurements in a manner that prohibits the use of statutorily or administratively imposed in-State or local geographical preferences in the evaluation of bids or proposals, except in those cases where applicable Federal statutes expressly mandate or encourage geographic preference. Nothing in this section preempts State licensing laws. When contracting for architectural and engineering (A/E) services, geographic location may be a selection criteria provided its application leaves an appropriate number of qualified firms, given the nature and size of the project, to compete for the contract.

(3) Grantees will have written selection procedures for procurement transactions. These procedures will ensure that all solicitations:

(i) Incorporate a clear and accurate description of the technical requirements for the material, product, or service to be procured. Such description shall not, in competitive procurements, contain features which unduly restrict competition. The description may include a statement of the qualitative nature of the material, product or service to be procured, and when necessary, shall set forth those minimum essential characteristics and standards to which it must conform if it is to satisfy its intended use. Detailed product specifications should be avoided if at all possible. When it is impractical or uneconomical to make a clear and accurate description of the technical requirements, a "brand name or equal" description may be used as a means to define the performance or other salient requirements of a procurement. The specific features of the named brand which must be met by offerors shall be clearly stated; and

(ii) Identify all requirements which the offerors must fulfill and all other factors to be used in evaluating bids or proposals.

(4) Grantees and subgrantees will ensure that all prequalified lists of persons, firms, or products which are used in acquiring goods and services are current and include enough qualified sources to ensure maximum open and free competition. Also, grantees and subgrantees will not preclude potential bidders from qualifying during the solicitation period.

(d) *Methods of procurement to be followed.* (1) Procurement by *small purchase procedures.* Small purchase procedures are those relatively simple and informal procurement methods for securing services, supplies, or other property that do not cost more than the simplified acquisition threshold fixed at 41 U.S.C. 403(11) (currently set at $100,000). If small purchase procedures are used, price or rate quotations shall be obtained from an adequate number of qualified sources.

(2) Procurement by *sealed bids* (formal advertising). Bids are publicly solicited and a firm-fixed-price contract (lump sum or unit price) is awarded to the responsible bidder whose bid, conforming with all the material terms and conditions of the invitation for bids, is the lowest in price. The sealed bid method is the preferred method for procuring construction, if the conditions in § 24.36(d)(2)(i) apply.

(i) In order for sealed bidding to be feasible, the following conditions should be present:

(A) A complete, adequate, and realistic specification or purchase description is available;

(B) Two or more responsible bidders are willing and able to compete effectively and for the business; and

(C) The procurement lends itself to a firm fixed price contract and the selection of the successful bidder can be made principally on the basis of price.

(ii) If sealed bids are used, the following requirements apply:

(A) The invitation for bids will be publicly advertised and bids shall be solicited from an adequate number of known suppliers, providing them sufficient time prior to the date set for opening the bids;

(B) The invitation for bids, which will include any specifications and pertinent attachments, shall define the items or services in order for the bidder to properly respond;

(C) All bids will be publicly opened at the time and place prescribed in the invitation for bids;

(D) A firm fixed-price contract award will be made in writing to the lowest responsive and responsible bidder. Where specified in bidding documents, factors such as discounts, transportation cost, and life cycle costs shall be considered in determining which bid is lowest. Payment discounts will only be used to determine the low bid when prior experience indicates that such discounts are usually taken advantage of; and

(E) Any or all bids may be rejected if there is a sound documented reason.

(3) Procurement by *competitive proposals.* The technique of competitive proposals is normally conducted with more than one source submitting an offer, and either a fixed-price or cost-reimbursement type contract is awarded. It is generally used when conditions are not appropriate for the use of sealed bids. If this method is used, the following requirements apply:

(i) Requests for proposals will be publicized and identify all evaluation factors and their relative importance. Any response to publicized requests for proposals shall be honored to the maximum extent practical;

(ii) Proposals will be solicited from an adequate number of qualified sources;

(iii) Grantees and subgrantees will have a method for conducting technical evaluations of the proposals received and for selecting awardees;

(iv) Awards will be made to the responsible firm whose proposal is most advantageous to the program, with price and other factors considered; and

(v) Grantees and subgrantees may use competitive proposal procedures for qualifications-based procurement of architectural/engineering (A/E) professional services whereby competitors' qualifications are evaluated and the most qualified competitor is selected, subject to negotiation of fair and reasonable compensation. The method, where price is not used as a selection factor, can only be used in procurement of A/E professional services. It cannot be used to purchase other types of services though A/E firms are a potential source to perform the proposed effort.

(4) Procurement by *noncompetitive proposals* is procurement through solicitation of a proposal from only one source, or after solicitation of a number of sources, competition is determined inadequate.

(i) Procurement by noncompetitive proposals may be used only when the award of a contract is infeasible under small purchase procedures, sealed bids or competitive proposals and one of the following circumstances applies:

(A) The item is available only from a single source;

(B) The public exigency or emergency for the requirement will not permit a delay resulting from competitive solicitation;

(C) The awarding agency authorizes noncompetitive proposals; or

(D) After solicitation of a number of sources, competition is determined inadequate.

(ii) Cost analysis, *i.e.*, verifying the proposed cost data, the projections of the data, and the evaluation of the specific elements of costs and profits, is required.

(iii) Grantees and subgrantees may be required to submit the proposed procurement to the awarding agency for pre-award review in accordance with paragraph (g) of this section.

(e) *Contracting with small and minority firms, women's business enterprise and labor surplus area firms.* (1) The grantee and subgrantee will take all necessary affirmative steps to assure that minority firms, women's business enterprises, and labor surplus area firms are used when possible.

(2) Affirmative steps shall include:

(i) Placing qualified small and minority businesses and women's business enterprises on solicitation lists;

(ii) Assuring that small and minority businesses, and women's business enterprises are solicited whenever they are potential sources;

(iii) Dividing total requirements, when economically feasible, into smaller tasks or quantities to permit maximum participation by small and minority business, and women's business enterprises;

(iv) Establishing delivery schedules, where the requirement permits, which encourage participation by small and minority business, and women's business enterprises;

(v) Using the services and assistance of the Small Business Administration, and the Minority Business Development Agency of the Department of Commerce; and

(vi) Requiring the prime contractor, if subcontracts are to be let, to take the affirmative steps listed in paragraphs (e)(2) (i) through (v) of this section.

(f) *Contract cost and price.* (1) Grantees and subgrantees must perform a cost or price analysis in connection with every procurement action including contract modifications. The method and degree of analysis is dependent on the facts surrounding the particular procurement situation, but as a starting point, grantees must make independent estimates before receiving bids or proposals. A cost analysis must be performed when the offeror is required to submit the elements of his estimated cost, e.g., under professional, consulting, and architectural engineering services contracts. A cost analysis will be necessary when adequate price competition is lacking, and for sole source procurements, including contract modifications or change orders, unless price resonableness can be established on the basis of a catalog or market price of a commercial product sold in substantial quantities to the general public or based on prices set by law or regulation. A price analysis will be used in all other instances to determine the reasonableness of the proposed contract price.

(2) Grantees and subgrantees will negotiate profit as a separate element of the price for each contract in which there is no price competition and in all cases where cost analysis is performed. To establish a fair and reasonable profit, consideration will be given to the complexity of the work to be performed, the risk borne by the contractor, the contractor's investment, the amount of subcontracting, the quality of its record of past performance, and industry profit rates in the surrounding geographical area for similar work.

(3) Costs or prices based on estimated costs for contracts under grants will be allowable only to the extent that costs incurred or cost estimates included in negotiated prices are consistent with Federal cost principles (see § 24.22). Grantees may reference their own cost principles that comply with the applicable Federal cost principles.

(4) The cost plus a percentage of cost and percentage of construction cost

methods of contracting shall not be used.

(g) *Awarding agency review.* (1) Grantees and subgrantees must make available, upon request of the awarding agency, technical specifications on proposed procurements where the awarding agency believes such review is needed to ensure that the item and/or service specified is the one being proposed for purchase. This review generally will take place prior to the time the specification is incorporated into a solicitation document. However, if the grantee or subgrantee desires to have the review accomplished after a solicitation has been developed, the awarding agency may still review the specifications, with such review usually limited to the technical aspects of the proposed purchase.

(2) Grantees and subgrantees must on request make available for awarding agency pre-award review procurement documents, such as requests for proposals or invitations for bids, independent cost estimates, etc. when:

(i) A grantee's or subgrantee's procurement procedures or operation fails to comply with the procurement standards in this section; or

(ii) The procurement is expected to exceed the simplified acquisition threshold and is to be awarded without competition or only one bid or offer is received in response to a solicitation; or

(iii) The procurement, which is expected to exceed the simplified acquisition threshold, specifies a "brand name" product; or

(iv) The proposed award is more than the simplified acquisition threshold and is to be awarded to other than the apparent low bidder under a sealed bid procurement; or

(v) A proposed contract modification changes the scope of a contract or increases the contract amount by more than the simplified acquisition threshold.

(3) A grantee or subgrantee will be exempt from the pre-award review in paragraph (g)(2) of this section if the awarding agency determines that its procurement systems comply with the standards of this section.

(i) A grantee or subgrantee may request that its procurement system be reviewed by the awarding agency to determine whether its system meets these standards in order for its system to be certified. Generally, these reviews shall occur where there is a continuous high-dollar funding, and third-party contracts are awarded on a regular basis.

(ii) A grantee or subgrantee may self-certify its procurement system. Such self-certification shall not limit the awarding agency's right to survey the system. Under a self-certification procedure, awarding agencies may wish to rely on written assurances from the grantee or subgrantee that it is complying with these standards. A grantee or subgrantee will cite specific procedures, regulations, standards, etc., as being in compliance with these requirements and have its system available for review.

(h) *Bonding requirements.* For construction or facility improvement contracts or subcontracts exceeding the simplified acquisition threshold, the awarding agency may accept the bonding policy and requirements of the grantee or subgrantee provided the awarding agency has made a determination that the awarding agency's interest is adequately protected. If such a determination has not been made, the minimum requirements shall be as follows:

(1) *A bid guarantee from each bidder equivalent to five percent of the bid price.* The "bid guarantee" shall consist of a firm commitment such as a bid bond, certified check, or other negotiable instrument accompanying a bid as assurance that the bidder will, upon acceptance of his bid, execute such contractual documents as may be required within the time specified.

(2) *A performance bond on the part of the contractor for 100 percent of the contract price.* A "performance bond" is one executed in connection with a contract to secure fulfillment of all the contractor's obligations under such contract.

(3) *A payment bond on the part of the contractor for 100 percent of the contract price.* A "payment bond" is one executed in connection with a contract to assure payment as required by law of

all persons supplying labor and material in the execution of the work provided for in the contract.

(i) *Contract provisions.* A grantee's and subgrantee's contracts must contain provisions in paragraph (i) of this section. Federal agencies are permitted to require changes, remedies, changed conditions, access and records retention, suspension of work, and other clauses approved by the Office of Federal Procurement Policy.

(1) Administrative, contractual, or legal remedies in instances where contractors violate or breach contract terms, and provide for such sanctions and penalties as may be appropriate. (Contracts more than the simplified acquisition threshold)

(2) Termination for cause and for convenience by the grantee or subgrantee including the manner by which it will be effected and the basis for settlement. (All contracts in excess of $10,000)

(3) Compliance with Executive Order 11246 of September 24, 1965, entitled "Equal Employment Opportunity," as amended by Executive Order 11375 of October 13, 1967, and as supplemented in Department of Labor regulations (41 CFR chapter 60). (All construction contracts awarded in excess of $10,000 by grantees and their contractors or subgrantees)

(4) Compliance with the Copeland "Anti-Kickback" Act (18 U.S.C. 874) as supplemented in Department of Labor regulations (29 CFR Part 3). (All contracts and subgrants for construction or repair)

(5) Compliance with the Davis-Bacon Act (40 U.S.C. 276a to 276a–7) as supplemented by Department of Labor regulations (29 CFR Part 5). (Construction contracts in excess of $2000 awarded by grantees and subgrantees when required by Federal grant program legislation)

(6) Compliance with Sections 103 and 107 of the Contract Work Hours and Safety Standards Act (40 U.S.C. 327–330) as supplemented by Department of Labor regulations (29 CFR Part 5). (Construction contracts awarded by grantees and subgrantees in excess of $2000, and in excess of $2500 for other contracts which involve the employment of mechanics or laborers)

(7) Notice of awarding agency requirements and regulations pertaining to reporting.

(8) Notice of awarding agency requirements and regulations pertaining to patent rights with respect to any discovery or invention which arises or is developed in the course of or under such contract.

(9) Awarding agency requirements and regulations pertaining to copyrights and rights in data.

(10) Access by the grantee, the subgrantee, the Federal grantor agency, the Comptroller General of the United States, or any of their duly authorized representatives to any books, documents, papers, and records of the contractor which are directly pertinent to that specific contract for the purpose of making audit, examination, excerpts, and transcriptions.

(11) Retention of all required records for three years after grantees or subgrantees make final payments and all other pending matters are closed.

(12) Compliance with all applicable standards, orders, or requirements issued under section 306 of the Clean Air Act (42 U.S.C. 1857(h)), section 508 of the Clean Water Act (33 U.S.C. 1368), Executive Order 11738, and Environmental Protection Agency regulations (40 CFR part 15). (Contracts, subcontracts, and subgrants of amounts in excess of $100,000).

(13) Mandatory standards and policies relating to energy efficiency which are contained in the state energy conservation plan issued in compliance with the Energy Policy and Conservation Act (Pub. L. 94–163, 89 Stat. 871).

[53 FR 8048, 8087, Mar. 11, 1988, as amended at 60 FR 19639, 19642, Apr. 19, 1995]

§ 24.37 Subgrants.

(a) *States.* States shall follow state law and procedures when awarding and administering subgrants (whether on a cost reimbursement or fixed amount basis) of financial assistance to local and Indian tribal governments. States shall:

(1) Ensure that every subgrant includes any clauses required by Federal statute and executive orders and their implementing regulations;

(2) Ensure that subgrantees are aware of requirements imposed upon

them by Federal statute and regulation;

(3) Ensure that a provision for compliance with § 24.42 is placed in every cost reimbursement subgrant; and

(4) Conform any advances of grant funds to subgrantees substantially to the same standards of timing and amount that apply to cash advances by Federal agencies.

(b) *All other grantees.* All other grantees shall follow the provisions of this part which are applicable to awarding agencies when awarding and administering subgrants (whether on a cost reimbursement or fixed amount basis) of financial assistance to local and Indian tribal governments. Grantees shall:

(1) Ensure that every subgrant includes a provision for compliance with this part;

(2) Ensure that every subgrant includes any clauses required by Federal statute and executive orders and their implementing regulations; and

(3) Ensure that subgrantees are aware of requirements imposed upon them by Federal statutes and regulations.

(c) *Exceptions.* By their own terms, certain provisions of this part do not apply to the award and administration of subgrants:

(1) Section 24.10;

(2) Section 24.11;

(3) The letter-of-credit procedures specified in Treasury Regulations at 31 CFR Part 205, cited in § 24.21; and

(4) Section 24.50.

REPORTS, RECORDS, RETENTION, AND ENFORCEMENT

§ 24.40 Monitoring and reporting program performance.

(a) *Monitoring by grantees.* Grantees are responsible for managing the day-to-day operations of grant and subgrant supported activities. Grantees must monitor grant and subgrant supported activities to assure compliance with applicable Federal requirements and that performance goals are being achieved. Grantee monitoring must cover each program, function or activity.

(b) *Nonconstruction performance reports.* The Federal agency may, if it decides that performance information available from subsequent applications contains sufficient information to meet its programmatic needs, require the grantee to submit a performance report only upon expiration or termination of grant support. Unless waived by the Federal agency this report will be due on the same date as the final Financial Status Report.

(1) Grantees shall submit annual performance reports unless the awarding agency requires quarterly or semi-annual reports. However, performance reports will not be required more frequently than quarterly. Annual reports shall be due 90 days after the grant year, quarterly or semi-annual reports shall be due 30 days after the reporting period. The final performance report will be due 90 days after the expiration or termination of grant support. If a justified request is submitted by a grantee, the Federal agency may extend the due date for any performance report. Additionally, requirements for unnecessary performance reports may be waived by the Federal agency.

(2) Performance reports will contain, for each grant, brief information on the following:

(i) A comparison of actual accomplishments to the objectives established for the period. Where the output of the project can be quantified, a computation of the cost per unit of output may be required if that information will be useful.

(ii) The reasons for slippage if established objectives were not met.

(iii) Additional pertinent information including, when appropriate, analysis and explanation of cost overruns or high unit costs.

(3) Grantees will not be required to submit more than the original and two copies of performance reports.

(4) Grantees will adhere to the standards in this section in prescribing performance reporting requirements for subgrantees.

(c) *Construction performance reports.* For the most part, on-site technical inspections and certified percentage-of-completion data are relied on heavily by Federal agencies to monitor progress under construction grants and subgrants. The Federal agency will require additional formal performance reports only when considered necessary, and never more frequently than quarterly.

(d) *Significant developments.* Events may occur between the scheduled performance reporting dates which have significant impact upon the grant or subgrant supported activity. In such cases, the grantee must inform the Federal agency as soon as the following types of conditions become known:

(1) Problems, delays, or adverse conditions which will materially impair the ability to meet the objective of the award. This disclosure must include a statement of the action taken, or contemplated, and any assistance needed to resolve the situation.

(2) Favorable developments which enable meeting time schedules and objectives sooner or at less cost than anticipated or producing more beneficial results than originally planned.

(e) Federal agencies may make site visits as warranted by program needs.

(f) *Waivers, extensions.* (1) Federal agencies may waive any performance report required by this part if not needed.

(2) The grantee may waive any performance report from a subgrantee when not needed. The grantee may extend the due date for any performance report from a subgrantee if the grantee will still be able to meet its performance reporting obligations to the Federal agency.

§ 24.41 Financial reporting.

(a) *General.* (1) Except as provided in paragraphs (a) (2) and (5) of this section, grantees will use only the forms specified in paragraphs (a) through (e) of this section, and such supplementary or other forms as may from time to time be authorized by OMB, for:

(i) Submitting financial reports to Federal agencies, or

(ii) Requesting advances or reimbursements when letters of credit are not used.

(2) Grantees need not apply the forms prescribed in this section in dealing with their subgrantees. However, grantees shall not impose more burdensome requirements on subgrantees.

(3) Grantees shall follow all applicable standard and supplemental Federal agency instructions approved by OMB to the extend required under the Paperwork Reduction Act of 1980 for use in connection with forms specified in paragraphs (b) through (e) of this section. Federal agencies may issue substantive supplementary instructions only with the approval of OMB. Federal agencies may shade out or instruct the grantee to disregard any line item that the Federal agency finds unnecessary for its decisionmaking purposes.

(4) Grantees will not be required to submit more than the original and two copies of forms required under this part.

(5) Federal agencies may provide computer outputs to grantees to expedite or contribute to the accuracy of reporting. Federal agencies may accept the required information from grantees in machine usable format or computer printouts instead of prescribed forms.

(6) Federal agencies may waive any report required by this section if not needed.

(7) Federal agencies may extend the due date of any financial report upon receiving a justified request from a grantee.

(b) *Financial Status Report*—(1) *Form.* Grantees will use Standard Form 269 or 269A, Financial Status Report, to report the status of funds for all nonconstruction grants and for construction grants when required in accordance with § 24.41(e)(2)(iii) of this section.

(2) *Accounting basis.* Each grantee will report program outlays and program income on a cash or accrual basis as prescribed by the awarding agency. If the Federal agency requires accrual information and the grantee's accounting records are not normally kept on the accural basis, the grantee shall not be required to convert its accounting system but shall develop such accrual information through and analysis of the documentation on hand.

(3) *Frequency.* The Federal agency may prescribe the frequency of the report for each project or program. However, the report will not be required more frequently than quarterly. If the Federal agency does not specify the frequency of the report, it will be submitted annually. A final report will be

required upon expiration or termination of grant support.

(4) *Due date.* When reports are required on a quarterly or semiannual basis, they will be due 30 days after the reporting period. When required on an annual basis, they will be due 90 days after the grant year. Final reports will be due 90 days after the expiration or termination of grant support.

(c) *Federal Cash Transactions Report*—(1) *Form.* (i) For grants paid by letter or credit, Treasury check advances or electronic transfer of funds, the grantee will submit the Standard Form 272, Federal Cash Transactions Report, and when necessary, its continuation sheet, Standard Form 272a, unless the terms of the award exempt the grantee from this requirement.

(ii) These reports will be used by the Federal agency to monitor cash advanced to grantees and to obtain disbursement or outlay information for each grant from grantees. The format of the report may be adapted as appropriate when reporting is to be accomplished with the assistance of automatic data processing equipment provided that the information to be submitted is not changed in substance.

(2) *Forecasts of Federal cash requirements.* Forecasts of Federal cash requirements may be required in the "Remarks" section of the report.

(3) *Cash in hands of subgrantees.* When considered necessary and feasible by the Federal agency, grantees may be required to report the amount of cash advances in excess of three days' needs in the hands of their subgrantees or contractors and to provide short narrative explanations of actions taken by the grantee to reduce the excess balances.

(4) *Frequency and due date.* Grantees must submit the report no later than 15 working days following the end of each quarter. However, where an advance either by letter of credit or electronic transfer of funds is authorized at an annualized rate of one million dollars or more, the Federal agency may require the report to be submitted within 15 working days following the end of each month.

(d) *Request for advance or reimbursement*—(1) *Advance payments.* Requests for Treasury check advance payments will be submitted on Standard Form 270, Request for Advance or Reimbursement. (This form will not be used for drawdowns under a letter of credit, electronic funds transfer or when Treasury check advance payments are made to the grantee automatically on a predetermined basis.)

(2) *Reimbursements.* Requests for reimbursement under nonconstruction grants will also be submitted on Standard Form 270. (For reimbursement requests under construction grants, see paragraph (e)(1) of this section.)

(3) The frequency for submitting payment requests is treated in §24.41(b)(3).

(e) *Outlay report and request for reimbursement for construction programs.* (1) Grants that support construction activities paid by reimbursement method.

(i) Requests for reimbursement under construction grants will be submitted on Standard Form 271, Outlay Report and Request for Reimbursement for Construction Programs. Federal agencies may, however, prescribe the Request for Advance or Reimbursement form, specified in §24.41(d), instead of this form.

(ii) The frequency for submitting reimbursement requests is treated in §24.41(b)(3).

(2) Grants that support construction activities paid by letter of credit, electronic funds transfer or Treasury check advance.

(i) When a construction grant is paid by letter of credit, electronic funds transfer or Treasury check advances, the grantee will report its outlays to the Federal agency using Standard Form 271, Outlay Report and Request for Reimbursement for Construction Programs. The Federal agency will provide any necessary special instruction. However, frequency and due date shall be governed by §24.41(b) (3) and (4).

(ii) When a construction grant is paid by Treasury check advances based on periodic requests from the grantee, the advances will be requested on the form specified in §24.41(d).

(iii) The Federal agency may substitute the Financial Status Report specified in §24.41(b) for the Outlay Report and Request for Reimbursement for Construction Programs.

(3) *Accounting basis.* The accounting basis for the Outlay Report and Request for Reimbursement for Construction Programs shall be governed by §24.41(b)(2).

§ 24.42 Retention and access requirements for records.

(a) *Applicability.* (1) This section applies to all financial and programmatic records, supporting documents, statistical records, and other records of grantees or subgrantees which are:

(i) Required to be maintained by the terms of this part, program regulations or the grant agreement, or

(ii) Otherwise reasonably considered as pertinent to program regulations or the grant agreement.

(2) This section does not apply to records maintained by contractors or subcontractors. For a requirement to place a provision concerning records in certain kinds of contracts, see §24.36(i)(10).

(b) *Length of retention period.* (1) Except as otherwise provided, records must be retained for three years from the starting date specified in paragraph (c) of this section.

(2) If any litigation, claim, negotiation, audit or other action involving the records has been started before the expiration of the 3-year period, the records must be retained until completion of the action and resolution of all issues which arise from it, or until the end of the regular 3-year period, whichever is later.

(3) To avoid duplicate recordkeeping, awarding agencies may make special arrangements with grantees and subgrantees to retain any records which are continuously needed for joint use. The awarding agency will request transfer of records to its custody when it determines that the records possess long-term retention value. When the records are transferred to or maintained by the Federal agency, the 3-year retention requirement is not applicable to the grantee or subgrantee.

(c) *Starting date of retention period*—(1) *General.* When grant support is continued or renewed at annual or other intervals, the retention period for the records of each funding period starts on the day the grantee or subgrantee submits to the awarding agency its single or last expenditure report for that period. However, if grant support is continued or renewed quarterly, the retention period for each year's records starts on the day the grantee submits its expenditure report for the last quarter of the Federal fiscal year. In all other cases, the retention period starts on the day the grantee submits its final expenditure report. If an expenditure report has been waived, the retention period starts on the day the report would have been due.

(2) *Real property and equipment records.* The retention period for real property and equipment records starts from the date of the disposition or replacement or transfer at the direction of the awarding agency.

(3) *Records for income transactions after grant or subgrant support.* In some cases grantees must report income after the period of grant support. Where there is such a requirement, the retention period for the records pertaining to the earning of the income starts from the end of the grantee's fiscal year in which the income is earned.

(4) *Indirect cost rate proposals, cost allocations plans, etc.* This paragraph applies to the following types of documents, and their supporting records: indirect cost rate computations or proposals, cost allocation plans, and any similar accounting computations of the rate at which a particular group of costs is chargeable (such as computer usage chargeback rates or composite fringe benefit rates).

(i) *If submitted for negotiation.* If the proposal, plan, or other computation is required to be submitted to the Federal Government (or to the grantee) to form the basis for negotiation of the rate, then the 3-year retention period for its supporting records starts from the date of such submission.

(ii) *If not submitted for negotiation.* If the proposal, plan, or other computation is not required to be submitted to the Federal Government (or to the grantee) for negotiation purposes, then the 3-year retention period for the proposal plan, or computation and its supporting records starts from end of the fiscal year (or other accounting period) covered by the proposal, plan, or other computation.

(d) *Substitution of microfilm.* Copies made by microfilming, photocopying, or similar methods may be substituted for the original records.

(e) *Access to records*—(1) *Records of grantees and subgrantees.* The awarding agency and the Comptroller General of the United States, or any of their authorized representatives, shall have the right of access to any pertinent books, documents, papers, or other records of grantees and subgrantees which are pertinent to the grant, in order to make audits, examinations, excerpts, and transcripts.

(2) *Expiration of right of access.* The rights of access in this section must not be limited to the required retention period but shall last as long as the records are retained.

(f) *Restrictions on public access.* The Federal Freedom of Information Act (5 U.S.C. 552) does not apply to records unless required by Federal, State, or local law, grantees and subgrantees are not required to permit public access to their records.

§24.43 Enforcement.

(a) *Remedies for noncompliance.* If a grantee or subgrantee materially fails to comply with any term of an award, whether stated in a Federal statute or regulation, an assurance, in a State plan or application, a notice of award, or elsewhere, the awarding agency may take one or more of the following actions, as appropriate in the circumstances:

(1) Temporarily withhold cash payments pending correction of the deficiency by the grantee or subgrantee or more severe enforcement action by the awarding agency,

(2) Disallow (that is, deny both use of funds and matching credit for) all or part of the cost of the activity or action not in compliance,

(3) Wholly or partly suspend or terminate the current award for the grantee's or subgrantee's program,

(4) Withhold further awards for the program, or

(5) Take other remedies that may be legally available.

(b) *Hearings, appeals.* In taking an enforcement action, the awarding agency will provide the grantee or subgrantee an opportunity for such hearing, appeal, or other administrative proceeding to which the grantee or subgrantee is entitled under any statute or regulation applicable to the action involved.

(c) *Effects of suspension and termination.* Costs of grantee or subgrantee resulting from obligations incurred by the grantee or subgrantee during a suspension or after termination of an award are not allowable unless the awarding agency expressly authorizes them in the notice of suspension or termination or subsequently. Other grantee or subgrantee costs during suspension or after termination which are necessary and not reasonably avoidable are allowable if:

(1) The costs result from obligations which were properly incurred by the grantee or subgrantee before the effective date of suspension or termination, are not in anticipation of it, and, in the case of a termination, are noncancellable, and,

(2) The costs would be allowable if the award were not suspended or expired normally at the end of the funding period in which the termination takes effect.

(d) *Relationship to debarment and suspension.* The enforcement remedies identified in this section, including suspension and termination, do not preclude grantee or subgrantee from being subject to "Debarment and Suspension" under E.O. 12549 (see §24.35).

§24.44 Termination for convenience.

Except as provided in §24.43 awards may be terminated in whole or in part only as follows:

(a) By the awarding agency with the consent of the grantee or subgrantee in which case the two parties shall agree upon the termination conditions, including the effective date and in the case of partial termination, the portion to be terminated, or

(b) By the grantee or subgrantee upon written notification to the awarding agency, setting forth the reasons for such termination, the effective date, and in the case of partial termination, the portion to be terminated. However, if, in the case of a partial termination, the awarding agency determines that the remaining portion of the award will not accomplish the purposes for which the award was made, the awarding agency may terminate the award in its entirety under either § 24.43 or paragraph (a) of this section.

Subpart D—After-the-Grant Requirements

§ 24.50 Closeout.

(a) *General.* The Federal agency will close out the award when it determines that all applicable administrative actions and all required work of the grant has been completed.

(b) *Reports.* Within 90 days after the expiration or termination of the grant, the grantee must submit all financial, performance, and other reports required as a condition of the grant. Upon request by the grantee, Federal agencies may extend this timeframe. These may include but are not limited to:

(1) *Final performance or progress report.*

(2) *Financial Status Report (SF 269) or Outlay Report and Request for Reimbursement for Construction Programs (SF–271) (as applicable).*

(3) *Final request for payment (SF–270) (if applicable).*

(4) *Invention disclosure (if applicable).*

(5) *Federally-owned property report:*

In accordance with § 24.32(f), a grantee must submit an inventory of all federally owned property (as distinct from property acquired with grant funds) for which it is accountable and request disposition instructions from the Federal agency of property no longer needed.

(c) *Cost adjustment.* The Federal agency will, within 90 days after receipt of reports in paragraph (b) of this section, make upward or downward adjustments to the allowable costs.

(d) *Cash adjustments.* (1) The Federal agency will make prompt payment to the grantee for allowable reimbursable costs.

(2) The grantee must immediately refund to the Federal agency any balance of unobligated (unencumbered) cash advanced that is not authorized to be retained for use on other grants.

§ 24.51 Later disallowances and adjustments.

The closeout of a grant does not affect:

(a) The Federal agency's right to disallow costs and recover funds on the basis of a later audit or other review;

(b) The grantee's obligation to return any funds due as a result of later refunds, corrections, or other transactions;

(c) Records retention as required in § 24.42;

(d) Property management requirements in §§ 24.31 and 24.32; and

(e) Audit requirements in § 24.26.

§ 24.52 Collection of amounts due.

(a) Any funds paid to a grantee in excess of the amount to which the grantee is finally determined to be entitled under the terms of the award constitute a debt to the Federal Government. If not paid within a reasonable period after demand, the Federal agency may reduce the debt by:

(1) Making an adminstrative offset against other requests for reimbursements,

(2) Withholding advance payments otherwise due to the grantee, or

(3) Other action permitted by law.

(b) Except where otherwise provided by statutes or regulations, the Federal agency will charge interest on an overdue debt in accordance with the Federal Claims Collection Standards (4 CFR Chapter II). The date from which interest is computed is not extended by litigation or the filing of any form of appeal.

Subpart E—Entitlements [Reserved]

PART 25—PROGRAM FRAUD CIVIL REMEDIES

Sec.

AUTHORITY: Secs. 6101–6104, Pub. L. 99–509, 100 Stat. 1874 (31 U.S.C. 3801–3812); Sec. 4, as amended, and sec. 5, Pub. L. 101–410, 104 Stat. 890 (28 U.S.C. 2461 note); Pub. L. 104–134, 110 Stat. 1321, 28 U.S.C. 2461 note.

SOURCE: 55 FR 47854, Nov. 16, 1990, unless otherwise noted.

FRAUD CIVIL REMEDIES

§25.1 Basis and purpose.

(a) *Basis.* This part implements the Program Fraud Civil Remedies Act of 1986, Public Law 99–509, section 6101–6104, 100 Stat. 1874 (October 21, 1986), to be codified at 31 U.S.C. 3801–3812. 31 U.S.C. 3809 of the statute requires each authority head to promulgate regulations necessary to implement the provisions of the statute.

(b) *Purpose.* This part (1) establishes administrative procedures for imposing civil penalties and assessments against persons who make, submit, or present, or cause to be made, submitted, or presented, false, fictitious, or fraudulent claims or written statements to authorities or to their agents, and (2) specifies the hearing and appeal rights of persons subject to allegations of liability for such penalties and assessments.

§25.2 Definitions.

ALJ means an Administrative Law Judge in the authority appointed pursuant to 5 U.S.C. 3105 or detailed to the authority pursuant to 5 U.S.C. 3344.

Authority means the Department of Commerce.

Authority head means the Secretary of the Department of Commerce, or designee.

Benefit means, except as the context otherwise requires, anything of value, including but not limited to any advantage, preference, privilege, license, permit, favorable decision, ruling, status, or loan guarantee.

Claim means any request, demand, or submission—

(a) Made to the authority for property, services, or money (including money representing grants, loans, insurance, or benefits);

(b) Made to a recipient of property, services, or money from the authority or to a party to a contract with the authority—

(1) For property or services if the United States—

(i) Provided such property or services;

(ii) Provided any portion of the funds for the purchase of such property or services; or

(iii) Will reimburse such recipient or party for the purchase of such property or services; or

(2) For the payment of money (including money representing grants, loans, insurance, or benefits) if the United States—

(i) Provided any portion of the money requested or demanded; or

(ii) Will reimburse such recipient or party for any portion of the money paid on such request or demand; or

(c) Made to the authority which has the effect of decreasing an obligation to pay or account for property, services, or money.

Complaint means the administrative complaint served by the reviewing official on the respondent under §25.7.

Department means the Department of Commerce.

Government means the United States Government.

Individual means a natural person.

Initial decision means the written decision of the ALJ required by §§25.10 or 25.37, and includes a revised initial decision issued following a remand or a motion for reconsideration.

Investigating official means the Inspector General of the Department of Commerce or an officer or employee of the Office of the Inspector General designated by the Inspector General and serving in a position for which the rate of basic pay is not less than the minimum rate of basic pay for grade GS–16 under the General Schedule.

Knows or has reason to know, means that a person, with respect to a claim or statement—

(a) Has actual knowledge that the claim or statement is false, fictitious, or fraudulent;

(b) Acts in deliberative ignorance of the truth or falsity of the claim or statement; or

(c) Acts in reckless disregard of the truth or falsity of the claim or statement.

Makes, wherever it appears, shall include the terms presents, submits, and causes to be made, presented, or submitted. As the context requires, *making* or *made*, shall likewise include the corresponding forms of such terms.

Person means any individual, partnership, corporation, association, or private organization and includes the plural of that term.

Representative means any attorney who is a member in good standing of the bar of any State, Territory, or possession of the United States or of the District of Columbia or the Commonwealth of Puerto Rico.

Respondent means any person alleged in a complaint under §25.7 to be liable for a civil penalty or assessment under §25.3.

Reviewing official means the General Counsel of the Department or his or her designee who is serving in a position for which the rate of basic pay is not less than the minimum rate of basic pay for grade GS–16 under the General Schedule.

Statement means any representation, certification, affirmation, document, record, or accounting or bookkeeping entry made—

(a) With respect to a claim or to obtain the approval or payment of a claim (including relating to eligibility to make a claim); or

(b) With respect to (including relating to eligibility for)—

(1) A contract with, or a bid or proposal for a contract with; or

(2) A grant, loan, or benefit from,

the authority, or any State, political subdivision of a State, or other party, if the United States Government provides any portion of the money or property under such contract or for such grant, loan, or benefit, or if the Government will reimburse such State, political subdivision, or party for any portion of the money or property under such contract or for such grant, loan, or benefit.

§25.3 Basis for civil penalties and assessments.

(a) *Claims*. (1) Any person who makes a claim that the person knows or has reason to know—

(i) Is false, fictitious, or fraudulent;

(ii) Includes, or is supported by, any written statement which asserts a material fact which is false, fictitious, or fraudulent;

(iii) Includes, or is supported by, any written statement that—

(A) Omits a material fact;

(B) Is false, fictitious, or fraudulent as a result of such omission; and

(C) Is a statement in which the person making such statement has a duty to include such material fact; or

(iv) Is for payment for the provision of property or services which the person has not provided as claimed, shall be subject, in addition to any other remedy that may be prescribed by law, to a civil penalty of not more than $5,000 for each such claim made on or before October 23, 1996, and of not more than $5,500 for each such claim made after October 23, 1996.

(2) Each voucher, invoice, claim form, or other individual request or demand for property, services, or money constitutes a separate claim.

(3) A claim shall be considered made to the authority, recipient, or party when such claim is actually made to an agent, fiscal intermediary, or other entity, including any State or political subdivision thereof, acting for or on behalf of the authority, recipient, or party.

(4) Each claim for property, services, or money is subject to a civil penalty regardless of whether such property, services, or money is actually delivered or paid.

(5) If the Government has made payment (including transferred property or provided services) or a claim, a person subject to a civil penalty under paragraph (a)(1) of this section shall also be subject to an assessment of not more than twice the amount of such claim or that portion thereof that is determined to be in violation of paragraph (a)(1) of the section. Such assessment shall be in lieu of damages sustained by the Government because of such claim.

(b) *Statements.* (1) Any person who makes a written statement that—

(i) The person knows or has reason to know—

(A) Asserts a material fact which is false, fictitious, or fraudulent; or

(B) Is false, fictitious, or fraudulent because it omits a material fact that the person making the statement has a duty to include in such statement; and

(ii) Contains, or is accompanied by, an express certification or affirmation of the truthfulness and accuracy of the contents of the statement, shall be subject, in addition to any other remedy that may be prescribed by law, to a civil penalty of not more than $5,000 for each such statement made on or before October 23, 1996, and of not more than $5,500 for each such statement made after October 23, 1996.

(2) Each written representation, certification, or affirmation constitutes a separate statement.

(3) A statement shall be considered made to the authority when such statement is actually made to an agent, fiscal intermediary, or other entity, including any State or political subdivision thereof, acting for or on behalf of the authority.

(c) No proof of specific intent to defraud is required to establish liability under this section.

(d) In any case in which it is determined that more than one person is liable for making a claim or statement under this section, each such person may be held liable for a civil penalty.

(e) In any case in which it is determined that more than one person is liable for making a claim under this section on which the Government has made payment (including transferred property or provide services), an assessment may be imposed against any such person or jointly and severally against any combination of such persons.

[55 FR 47854, Nov. 16, 1990, as amended at 61 FR 55094, Oct. 24, 1996]

§ 25.4 Investigation.

(a) If an investigating official concludes that a subpoena pursuant to the authority conferred by 31 U.S.C. 3804(a) is warranted—

(1) The subpoena so issued shall notify the person to whom it is addressed of the authority under which the subpoena is issued and shall identify the records or documents sought;

(2) The investigating official may designate a person to act on his or her behalf to receive the documents sought; and

(3) The person receiving such subpoena shall be required to tender to the investigating official, or the person designated to receive the documents, a certification that—

(i) The documents sought have been produced;

(ii) Such documents are not available and the reasons therefore; or

(iii) Such documents, suitably identified, have been withheld based upon the assertion of an identified privilege.

(b) If the investigating official concludes that an action under the Program Fraud Civil Remedies Act may be warranted, the investigating official shall submit a report containing the findings and conclusions of such investigation to the reviewing official.

(c) Nothing in this section shall preclude or limit an investigating official's discretion to refer allegations directly to the Department of Justice for suit under the False Claims Act or other civil relief, or to defer or postpone a report or referral to avoid interference with a criminal investigation or prosecution.

(d) Nothing in this section modifies any responsibility of an investigating official to report violations of criminal law to the Attorney General.

§ 25.5 Review by the reviewing official.

(a) If, based on the report of the investigating official under § 25.4(b), the reviewing official determines that there is adequate evidence to believe that a person is liable under § 25.3, the reviewing official shall transmit to the Attorney General a written notice of the reviewing official's intention to issue a complaint under § 25.7.

(b) Such notice shall include—

(1) A statement of the reviewing official's reasons for issuing a complaint;

(2) A statement specifying the evidence that supports the allegations of liability;

(3) A description of the claims or statements upon which the allegations of liability are based;

(4) An estimate of the amount of money, or the value of property, services, or other benefits, requested or demanded in violation of § 25.3 of this part;

(5) A statement of any exculpatory or mitigating circumstances that may relate to the claims or statements known by the reviewing official or the investigating official; and

(6) A statement that there is a reasonable prospect of collecting an appropriate amount of penalties and assessments. Such a statement may be based upon information then known or an absence of any information indicating that the person may be unable to pay such an amount.

§ 25.6 Prerequisites for issuing a complaint.

(a) The reviewing official may issue a complaint under § 25.7 only if—

(1) The Department of Justice approved the issuance of a complaint in a written statement described in 31 U.S.C. 3803(b)(1), and

(2) In the case of allegations of liability under § 25.3(a) with respect to a claim, the reviewing official determines that, with respect to such claim or a group of related claims submitted at the same time such claim is submitted (as defined in paragraph (b) of this section), the amount of money, or the value of property or services, demanded or requested in violation of § 25.3(a) does not exceed $150,000.

(b) For the purposes of this section, a related group of claims submitted at the same time shall include only those claims arising from the same transaction (e.g., grant, loan, application, or contract) that are submitted simultaneously as part of a single request, demand, or submission.

(c) Nothing in this section shall be construed to limit the reviewing official's authority to join in a single complaint against a person claims that are unrelated or were not submitted simultaneously, regardless of the amount of money, or the value of property or services, demanded or requested.

§ 25.7 Complaint.

(a) On or after the date the Department of Justice approves the issuance of a complaint in accordance with 31 U.S.C. 3803(b)(1), the reviewing official may serve a complaint on the respondent, as provided in § 25.8.

(b) The complaint shall state—

(1) The allegations of liability against the respondent, including the statutory basis for liability, an identification of the claims or statements that are the basis for the alleged liability, and the reasons why liability allegedly arises from such claims or statements;

(2) The maximum amount of penalties and assessments for which the respondent may be held liable;

(3) Instructions for filing an answer to request a hearing, including a specific statement of the respondent's right to request a hearing by filing an answer and to be represented by a representative; and

(4) That failure to file an answer within 30 days of service of the complaint will result in the imposition of

the maximum amount of penalties and assessments without right to appeal.

(c) At the same time the reviewing official serves the complaint, he or she shall serve the respondent with a copy of these regulations.

§25.8 Service of complaint.

(a) Service of a complaint must be made by certified or registered mail or by delivery in any manner authorized by Rule 4(d) of the Federal Rules of Civil Procedure.

(b) Proof of service, stating the name and address of the person on whom the complaint was served, and the manner and date of service, may be made by—

(1) Affidavit of the individual making service;

(2) An acknowledged United States Postal Service return receipt card; or

(3) Written acknowledgment of the respondent or his or her representative.

§25.9 Answer.

(a) The respondent may request a hearing by filing an answer with the reviewing official within 30 days of service of the complaint. An answer shall be deemed to be a request for hearing.

(b) In the answer, the respondent—

(1) Shall admit or deny each of the allegations of liability made in the complaint;

(2) Shall state any defense on which the respondent intends to rely;

(3) May state any reasons why the respondent contends that the penalties and assessments should be less than the statutory maximum; and

(4) Shall state the name, address, and telephone number of the person authorized by the respondent to act as respondent's representative, if any.

§25.10 Default upon failure to file an answer.

(a) If the respondent does not file an answer within the time prescribed in §25.9(a), the reviewing official may refer the complaint to the ALJ along with the proof of service, as provided in §25.8(b).

(b) Upon the referral of the complaint, the ALJ shall promptly serve on the respondent in the manner prescribed in §25.8, a notice that an initial decision will be issued under this section.

(c) The ALJ shall assume the facts alleged in the complaint to be true and, if such facts establish liability under §25.3, the ALJ shall issue an initial decision imposing the maximum amount of penalties and assessments allowed under the statute.

(d) Except as otherwise provided in this section, by failing to file a timely answer, the respondent waives any right to further review of the penalties and assessments imposed under paragraph (c) of this section, and the initial decision shall become final binding upon the parties 30 days after it is issued.

(e) If, before such an initial decision becomes final, the respondent files motion with the ALJ seeking to reopen on the grounds that extraordinary circumstances prevented the respondent from filing an answer, the initial decision shall be stayed pending the ALJ's decision on the motion.

(f) If, on such motion, the respondent can demonstrate extraordinary circumstances excusing the failure to file a timely answer, the ALJ shall withdraw the initial decision in paragraph (c) of this section, if such a decision has been issued, and shall grant the respondent an opportunity to answer the complaint.

(g) A decision of the ALJ denying a respondent's motion under paragraph (e) of this section is not subject to reconsideration under §25.38.

(h) The respondent may appeal to the authority head the decision denying a motion to reopen by filing a notice of appeal with the authority head within 15 days after the ALJ denies the motion. The timely filing of a notice of appeal shall stay the initial decision until the authority head decides the issue.

(i) If the respondent files a timely notice of appeal with the authority head, the ALJ shall forward the record of the proceeding to the authority head.

(j) The authority head shall decide expeditiously whether extraordinary circumstances excuse the respondent's failure to file a timely answer based solely on the record before the ALJ.

(k) If the authority head decides that extraordinary circumstances excused the respondent's failure to file a timely answer, the authority head shall remand the case of the ALJ with instructions to grant the respondent an opportunity to answer.

(l) If the authority head decides that the respondent's failure to file a timely answer is not excused, the authority head shall reinstate the initial decision of the ALJ, which shall become final and binding upon the parties 30 days after the authority head issues such decision.

§ 25.11 Referral of complaint and answer to the ALJ.

Upon receipt of an answer, the reviewing official shall file the complaint and answer with the ALJ.

§ 25.12 Notice of hearing.

(a) When the ALJ receives the complaint and answer, the ALJ shall promptly serve a notice of hearing upon the respondent in the manner prescribed by § 25.8. At the same time, the ALJ shall send a copy of such notice to the representative for the Government.

(b) Such notice shall include—

(1) The tentative time and place, and the nature of the hearing;

(2) The legal authority and jurisdiction under which the hearing is to be held;

(3) The matters of fact and law to be asserted;

(4) A description of the procedures for the conduct of the hearing;

(5) The name, address, and telephone number of the representative of the Government and of the respondent, if any; and

(6) Such other matters as the ALJ deems appropriate.

§ 25.13 Parties to the hearing.

(a) The parties to the hearing shall be the respondent and the authority.

(b) Pursuant to 31 U.S.C. 3730(c)(5), a private plaintiff under the False Claims Act may participate in these proceedings to the extent authorized by the provisions of that Act.

§ 25.14 Separation of functions.

(a) The investigating official, the reviewing official, and any employee or agent of the authority who takes part in investigating, preparing, or presenting a particular case may not, in such case or a factually related case—

(1) Participate in the hearing as the ALJ;

(2) Participate or advise in the initial decision or the review of the initial decision by the authority head, except as a witness or a representative in public proceedings; or

(3) Make the collection of penalties and assessments under 31 U.S.C. 3806.

(b) The ALJ shall not be responsible to, or subject to the supervision or direction of, the investigating official or the reviewing official.

(c) The reviewing official shall, after consulting with the Inspector General, designate the representative for the Government, who shall be an attorney with either the Office of General Counsel or the Office of the Inspector General. The reviewing official's decision is final.

§ 25.15 Ex parte contacts.

No party or person (except employees of the ALJ's office) shall communicate in any way with the ALJ on any matter at issue in a case, unless on notice and opportunity for all parties to participate. This provision does not prohibit a person or party from inquiring about the status of a case or asking routine questions concerning administrative functions or procedures.

§ 25.16 Disqualification of reviewing official or ALJ.

(a) A reviewing official or ALJ in a particular case may disqualify himself or herself at any time.

(b) A party may file with the ALJ a motion for disqualification of a reviewing official or an ALJ. Such motion shall be accompanied by an affidavit alleging personal bias or other reason for disqualification.

(c) Such motion and affidavit shall be filed promptly upon the party's discovery of reasons requiring disqualification, or such objections shall be deemed waived.

(d) Such affidavit shall state specific facts that support the party's belief that personal bias or other reason for disqualification exists and the time and circumstances of the party's discovery of such facts. It shall be accompanied by a certificate of the representative of record that it is made in good faith.

(e) Upon the filing of such a motion and affidavit, the ALJ shall proceed no further in the case until he or she resolves the matter of disqualification in accordance with paragraph (f) of this section.

(f)(1) If the ALJ determines that a reviewing official is disqualified, the ALJ shall dismiss the complaint without prejudice.

(2) If the ALJ disqualifies himself or herself, the case shall be reassigned promptly to another ALJ.

(3) If the ALJ denies a motion to disqualify, the authority head may determine the matter only as part of his or her review of the initial decision upon appeal, if any.

§25.17 Rights of parties.

Except as otherwise limited by this part, all parties may—

(a) Be accompanied, represented, and advised by a representative;

(b) Participate in any conference held by the ALJ;

(c) Conduct discovery;

(d) Agree to stipulations of fact or law, which shall be made part of the record;

(e) Present evidence relevant to the issues at the hearing;

(f) Present and cross-examine witnesses;

(g) Present oral arguments at the hearing as permitted by the ALJ; and

(h) Submit written briefs and proposed findings of fact and conclusions of law after the hearing.

§25.18 Authority of the ALJ.

(a) The ALJ shall conduct a fair and impartial hearing, avoid delay, maintain order, and assure that a record of the proceeding is made.

(b) The ALJ has the authority to—

(1) Set and change the date, time, and place of the hearing upon reasonable notice to the parties;

(2) Continue or recess the hearing in whole or in part for a reasonable period of time;

(3) Hold conferences to identify or simplify the issues, or to consider other matters that may aid in the expeditious disposition of the proceeding;

(4) Administer oaths and affirmations;

(5) Issue subpoenas requiring the attendance of witnesses and the production of documents at depositions or at hearings;

(6) Rule on motions and other procedural matters;

(7) Regulate the scope and timing of discovery;

(8) Regulate the course of the hearing and the conduct of representatives and parties;

(9) Examine witnesses;

(10) Receive, rule on, exclude, or limit evidence;

(11) Upon motion of a party, take official notice of facts;

(12) Upon motion of a party, decide cases, in whole or in part, by summary judgment where there is no disputed issue of material fact;

(13) Conduct any conference, argument, or hearing on motions in person or by telephone; and

(14) Exercise such other authority as is necessary to carry out the responsibilities of the ALJ under this part.

(c) The ALJ does not have the authority to find Federal statutes or regulations invalid.

§25.19 Prehearing conferences.

(a) The ALJ may schedule prehearing conferences as appropriate.

(b) Upon the motion of any party, the ALJ shall schedule at least one prehearing conference at a reasonable time in advance of the hearing.

(c) The ALJ may use prehearing conferences to discuss the following:

(1) Simplification of the issues;

(2) The necessity or desirability of amendments to the pleadings, including the need for a more definite statement;

(3) Stipulations and admissions of fact or as to the contents and authenticity of documents;

(4) Whether the parties can agree to submission of the case on a stipulated record;

(5) Whether a party chooses to waive appearance at an oral hearing and to submit only documentary evidence (subject to the objection of other parties) and written argument;

(6) Limitation of the number of witnesses;

(7) Scheduling dates for the exchange of witness lists and of proposed exhibits;

(8) Discovery;

(9) The time and place for the hearing; and

(10) Such other matters as may tend to expedite the fair and just disposition of the proceedings.

(d) The ALJ may issue an order containing all matters agreed upon by the parties or ordered by the ALJ at a prehearing conference.

§ 25.20 Disclosure of documents.

(a) Upon written request to the reviewing official, the respondent may review any relevant and material documents, transcripts, records, and other materials that related to the allegations set out in the complaint and upon which the findings and conclusions of the investigating official under § 25.4(b) are based, unless such documents are subject to a privilege under Federal law. Upon payment of fees for duplication, the respondent may obtain copies of such documents.

(b) Upon written request to the reviewing official, the respondent also may obtain a copy of all exculpatory information in the possession of the reviewing official or investigating official relating to the allegations in the complaint, even if it is contained in a document that would otherwise be privileged. If the document would otherwise be privileged, only that portion containing exculpatory information must be disclosed.

(c) The notice sent to the Attorney General from the reviewing official as described in § 25.5 is not discoverable under any circumstances.

(d) The respondents may file a motion to compel dosclosure of the documents subject to the provisions of this section. Such a motion may only be filed with the ALJ following the filing of an answer pursuant to § 25.9.

§ 25.21 Discovery.

(a) The following types of discovery are authorized:

(1) Requests for production of documents for inspection and copying;

(2) Requests for admissions of the authenticity of any relevant document or of the truth of any relevant fact;

(3) Written interrogatories; and

(4) Depositions.

(b) For the purpose of this section and §§ 25.22 and 25.23, the term "documents" includes information, documents, reports, answers, records, accounts, papers, and other data and documentary evidence. Nothing contained herein shall be interpreted to require the creation of a document.

(c) Unless mutually agreed to by the parties, discovery is available only as ordered by the ALJ. The ALJ shall regulate the timing of discovery.

(d) *Motions for discovery.* (1) A party seeking discovery may file a motion with the ALJ. Such a motion shall be accompanied by a copy of the requested discovery, or in the case of depositions, a summary of the scope of the proposed deposition.

(2) Within two days of service, a party may file an opposition to the motion and/or a motion for protective order as provided in § 25.34.

(3) The ALJ may grant a motion for discovery only if he or she finds that the discovery sought—

(i) Is necessary for the expeditious, fair, and reasonable consideration of the issues;

(ii) Is not unduly costly or burdensome;

(iii) Will not unduly delay the proceeding; and

(iv) Does not seek privileged information.

(4) The burden of showing that discovery should be allowed is on the party seeking discovery.

(5) The ALJ may grant discovery subject to a protective order under § 25.24.

(e) *Depositions.* (1) If a motion for deposition is granted, the ALJ shall issue a subpoena for the deponent, which may require the deponent to produce documents. The subpoena shall specify the time and place at which the deposition will be held.

(2) The party seeking to depose shall serve the subpoena in the manner prescribed in § 25.8.

(3) The deponent may file with the ALJ a motion to quash the subpoena or a motion for a protective order within ten days of service.

(4) The party seeking to depose shall provide for the taking of a verbatim transcript of the deposition, which it shall make available to all other parties for inspection and copying.

(f) Each party shall bear its own costs of discovery.

§25.22 Exchange of witness lists, statements, and exhibits.

(a) At least 15 days before the hearing or at such other time as may be ordered by the ALJ, the parties shall exchange witness lists, copies of prior statements of proposed witnesses, and copies of proposed hearing exhibits, including copies of any written statements that the party intends to offer in lieu of live testimony in accordance with §25.33(b). At the time the above documents are exchanged, any party that intends to rely on the transcript of deposition testimony in lieu of live testimony at the hearing, if permitted by the ALJ, shall provide each party with a copy of the specific pages of the transcript it intends to introduce into evidence.

(b) If a party objects, the ALJ shall not admit into evidence the testimony of any witness whose name does not appear on the witness list or any exhibit not provided to the opposing party as provided above unless the ALJ finds good cause for the failure or that there is no prejudice to the objecting party.

(c) Unless another party objects within the time set by the ALJ, documents exchanged in accordance with paragraph (a) of this section shall be deemed to be authentic for the purpose of admissibility at the hearing.

§25.23 Subpoena for attendance at hearing.

(a) A party wishing to procure the appearance and testimony of any individual at the hearing may request that the ALJ issue a subpoena.

(b) A subpoena requiring the attendance and testimony of an individual may also require the individual to produce documents at the hearing.

(c) A party seeking a subpoena shall file a written request therefore not less than 15 days before the date fixed for the hearing unless otherwise allowed by the ALJ for good cause shown: Such request shall specify any documents to be produced and shall designate the witnesses and describe the address and location thereof with sufficient particularity to permit such witnesses to be found.

(d) The subpoena shall specify the time and place at which the witness is to appear and any documents the witness is to produce.

(e) The party seeking the subpoena shall serve it in the manner prescribed in §25.8. A subpoena on a party or upon an individual under the control of a party may be served by first class mail.

(f) A party or the individual to whom the subpoena is directed may file with the ALJ a motion to quash the subpoena within ten days after service or on or before the time specified in the subpoena for compliance if it is less than ten days after service.

§25.24 Protective order.

(a) A party of a prospective witness or deponent may file a motion for a protective order with respect to discovery sought by an opposing party or with respect to the hearing, seeking to limit the availability or disclosure of evidence.

(b) In issuing a protective order, the ALJ may make any order which justice requires to protect a party or person from annoyance, embarrassment, oppression, or undue burden or expense, including one or more of the following:

(1) That the discovery not be had;

(2) That the discovery may be had only on specified terms and conditions, including a designation of the time or place;

(3) That the discovery may be had only through a method of discovery other than that requested;

(4) That certain matters not be inquired into, or that the scope of discovery be limited to certain matters;

(5) That discovery be conducted with no one present except persons designated by the ALJ;

(6) That the contents of discovery or evidence be sealed;

(7) That a deposition after being sealed be opened only by order of the ALJ;

(8) That a trade secret or other confidential research, development, commercial information, or facts pertaining to any criminal investigation,

proceeding, or other administrative investigation not be disclosed or be disclosed only in a designated way; or

(9) That the parties simultaneously file specified documents or information enclosed in sealed envelopes to be opened as direct by the ALJ.

§ 25.25 Fees.

The party requesting a subpoena shall pay the cost of the fees and mileage of any witness subpoenaed in the amounts that would be payable to a witness in a proceeding in United States District Court. A check for witness fees and mileage shall accompany the subpoena when served, except that when a subpoena is issued on behalf of the Department of Commerce, a check for witness fees and mileage need not accompany the subpoena.

§ 25.26 Form, filing and service of papers.

(a) *Form.* (1) Documents filed with the ALJ shall include an original and one copy.

(2) Every pleading and paper filed in the proceeding shall contain a caption setting forth the title of the action, the case number assigned by the ALJ, and a designation of the paper (e.g., motion to quash subpoena).

(3) Every pleading and paper shall be signed by, and shall contain the address and telephone number of, the party of the person on whose behalf the paper was filed, or his or her representative.

(4) Papers are considered filed when they are mailed. Date of mailing may be established by a certificate from the party or its representative or by proof that the document was sent by certified or registered mail.

(b) *Service.* A party filing a document with the ALJ shall, at the time of filing, serve a copy of such document on every other party. Service upon any party of any document other than the complaint or notice of hearing shall be made by deliverying or mailing a copy to the party's last known address. When a party is represented by a representative, service shall be made upon such representative in lieu of the actual party.

(c) *Proof of service.* A certificate of the individual serving the document by personal delivery or by mail, setting forth the manner of service, shall be proof of service.

§ 25.27 Computation of time.

(a) In computing any period of time under this part or in an order issued thereunder, the time begins with the day following the act, event, or default, and includes the last day of the period, unless it is a Saturday, Sunday, or legal holiday observed by the Federal government, in which event it includes the next business day.

(b) When the period of time allowed is less than seven days, intermediate Saturdays, Sundays, and legal holidays observed by the Federal government shall be excluded from the computation.

(c) Where a document has been served or issued by mail, an additional five days will be added to the time permitted for any response.

§ 25.28 Motions.

(a) Any application to the ALJ for an order or ruling shall be by motion. Motions shall state the relief sought, the authority relied upon, and the facts alleged, and shall be filed with the ALJ and served on all other parties.

(b) Except for motions made during a prehearing conference or at the hearing, all motions shall be in writing. The ALJ may require that oral motions be reduced to writing.

(c) Within 15 days after a written motion is served, or such other time as may be fixed by the ALJ, any party may file a response to such motion.

(d) The ALJ may not grant a written motion before the time for filing responses thereto has expired, except upon consent of the parties or following a hearing on the motion, but may overrule or deny such motion without awaiting a response.

(e) The ALJ shall make a reasonable effort to dispose of all outstanding motions prior to the beginning of the hearing.

§ 25.29 Sanctions.

(a) The ALJ may sanction a person, including any party or representative, for—

(1) Failing to comply with an order, rule, or procedure governing the proceeding;

(2) Failing to prosecute or defend an action; or

(3) Engaging in other misconduct that interferes with the speedy, orderly, or fair conduct of the hearing.

(b) Any such sanction, including but not limited to those listed in paragraphs (c), (d), and (e) of this section, shall reasonably relate to the severity and nature of the failure or misconduct.

(c) When a party fails to comply with an order, including an order for taking a deposition, the production of evidence within the party's control, or a request for admission, the ALJ may—

(1) Draw an inference in favor of the requesting party with regard to the information sought;

(2) In the case of requests for admission, deem each matter of which an admission is requested to be admitted;

(3) Prohibit the party failing to comply with such order from introducing evidence concerning, or otherwise relying upon, testimony relating to the information sought; and

(4) Strike any part of the pleadings or other submissions of the party failing to comply with such request.

(d) If a party fails to prosecute or defend an action under this part commenced by service of a notice of hearing, the ALJ may dismiss the action or may issue an initial decision imposing penalties and assessments.

(e) The ALJ may refuse to consider any motion, request, response, brief or other document which is not filed in a timely fashion.

§25.30 The hearing and burden of proof.

(a) The ALJ shall conduct a hearing on the record in order to determine whether the respondent is liable for a civil penalty or assessment under §25.3 and, if so, the appropriate amount of any such civil penalty or assessment considering any aggravating or mitigating factors.

(b) The authority shall prove respondent's liability and any aggravating factors by a preponderance of the evidence.

(c) The respondent shall prove any affirmative defenses and any mitigating factors by a preponderance of the evidence.

(d) The hearing shall be open to the public unless otherwise ordered by the ALJ for good cause shown.

§25.31 Determining the amount of penalties and assessments.

(a) In determining an appropriate amount of civil penalties and assessments, the ALJ and the authority head, upon appeal, should evaluate any circumstances that mitigate or aggravate the violation and should articulate in their opinions the reasons that support the penalties and assessments they impose. Because of the intangible costs of fraud, the expense of investigating such conduct, and the need to deter others who might be similarly tempted ordinarily double assessment, in lieu of damages, and a significant civil penalty should be imposed.

(b) Although not exhaustive, the following factors are among those that may influence the ALJ and the authority head in determining the amount of penalties and assessments to impose with respect to the misconduct (*i.e.*, the false, fictitious, or fraudulent claims or statements) charged in the complaint:

(1) The number of false, fictitious, or fraudulent claims or statements;

(2) The time period over which such claims or statements were made;

(3) The degree of the respondent's culpability with respect to the misconduct;

(4) The amount of money or the value of the property, services, or benefit falsely claimed;

(5) The value of the Government's actual loss as a result of the misconduct, including foreseeable consequential damages and the costs of investigation;

(6) The relationship of the amount imposed as civil penalties to the amount of the Government's loss;

(7) The potential or actual impact of the misconduct upon national defense, public health or safety, or public confidence in the management of Government programs and operations, including particularly the impact on the intended beneficiaries of such program;

(8) Whether the respondent has engaged in a pattern of the same or similar misconduct;

(9) Whether the respondent attempted to conceal the misconduct;

(10) The degree to which the respondent has involved others in the misconduct or in concealing it;

(11) Where the misconduct of employees or agents is imputed to the respondent, the extent to which the respondent's practices fostered or attempted to preclude such misconduct;

(12) Whether the respondent cooperated in or obstructed an investigation of the misconduct;

(13) Whether the respondent assisted in identifying and prosecuting other wrongdoers;

(14) The complexity of the program or transaction, and the degree of the respondent's sophistication with respect to it, including the extent of the respondent's prior participation in the program or in similar transactions;

(15) Whether the respondent has been found, in any criminal, civil, or administrative proceeding to have engaged in similar misconduct or to have dealt dishonestly with the Government of the United States or of a State directly or indirectly; and

(16) The need to deter the respondent and others from engaging in the same or similar misconduct.

(c) Nothing in this section shall be construed to limit the ALJ or the authority head from considering any other factors that in any given case may mitigate or aggravate the offense for which penalties and assessments are imposed.

§ 25.32 Location of hearing.

(a) The hearing may be held—

(1) In any judicial district of the United States in which the respondent resides or transacts business;

(2) In any judicial district of the United States in which the claim or statement in issue was made; or

(3) In such other place as may be agreed upon by the respondent and the ALJ.

(b) Each party shall have the opportunity to present arguments with respect to the location of the hearing.

(c) The hearing shall be held at the place and at the time ordered by the ALJ.

§ 25.33 Witnesses.

(a) Except as provided in paragraph (b) of this section, testimony at the hearing shall be given orally by witnesses under oath or affirmation.

(b) At the discretion of the ALJ, testimony may be admitted in the form of a written statement or deposition. Any such written statements must be provided to all other parties along with the last known address of such witness, in a manner which allows sufficient time for other parties to subpoena such witness for cross-examination at the hearing. Prior written statements of witnesses proposed to testify at the hearing and deposition transcripts shall be exchanged as provided in § 25.22(a).

(c) The ALJ shall exercise reasonable control over the mode and order of interrogating witnesses and presenting evidence so as to—

(1) Make the interrogation and presentation effective for the ascertainment of the truth;

(2) Avoid needless consumption of time; and

(3) Protect witnesses from harassment or undue embarrassment.

(d) The ALJ shall permit the parties to conduct such cross-examination as may be required for a full and true disclosure of the facts.

(e) At the discretion of the ALJ, a witness may be cross-examined on matters relevant to the proceeding without regard to the scope of his or her direct examination. To the extent permitted by the ALJ, cross-examination on matters outside the scope of direct examination shall be conducted in the manner of direct examination and may proceed by leading questions only if the witness is a hostile witness, an adverse party or a witness identified with an adverse party.

(f) Upon motion of any party, the ALJ shall order witnesses excluded so that they cannot hear the testimony of other witnesses. This rule does not authorize exclusion of—

(1) A party who is an individual;

(2) In the case of a party that is not an individual, an officer or employee of

the party designated by the party's representative; or

(3) An individual whose presence is shown by a party to be essential to the presentation of its case, including an individual employed by the Government engaged in assisting the representative for the Government.

§ 25.34 Evidence.

(a) The ALJ shall determine the admissibility of evidence.

(b) Except as provided in this part, the ALJ shall not be bound by the Federal Rules of Evidence. However, the ALJ may apply the Federal Rules of Evidence where appropriate, e.g., to exclude unreliable evidence.

(c) The ALJ shall exclude irrelevant and inmaterial evidence.

(d) Although relevant, evidence may be excluded if its probative value is substantially outweighed by the danger of unfair prejudice, confusion of the issues, or by considerations of undue delay or needless presentation of cumulative evidence.

(e) Although relevant, evidence may be excluded if it is privileged under Federal law.

(f) Evidence concerning offers of compromise or settlement shall be inadmissible to the extent provided in Rule 408 of the Federal Rules of Evidence.

(g) The ALJ shall permit the parties to introduce rebuttal witnesses and evidence.

(h) All documents and other evidence offered or taken for the record shall be open to examination by all parties, unless otherwise ordered by the ALJ pursuant to § 25.24.

§ 25.35 The record.

(a) The hearing will be recorded and transcribed. Transcripts may be obtained following the hearing from the ALJ at a cost not to exceed the actual cost of duplication.

(b) The transcript of testimony, exhibits and other evidence admitted at the hearing, and all papers and requests filed in the proceeding constitute the record for the decision by the ALJ and the authority head.

(c) The record may be inspected and copied (upon payment of a reasonable fee) by anyone, unless otherwise ordered by the ALJ pursuant to § 25.24.

§ 25.36 Post-hearing briefs.

The ALJ may require the parties to file post-hearing briefs. In any event, any party may file a post-hearing brief. The ALJ shall fix the time for filing such briefs, not to exceed 60 days from the date the parties receive the transcript of the hearing or, if applicable, the stipulated record. Such briefs may be accompanied by proposed findings of fact and conclusions of law. The ALJ may permit the parties to file reply briefs.

§ 25.37 Initial decision.

(a) The ALJ shall issue an initial decision based only on the record, which shall contain findings of fact, conclusions of law, and the amount of any penalties and assessments imposed.

(b) The findings of fact shall include a finding on each of the following issues:

(1) Whether the claims or statements identified in the complaint, or any portions thereof, violate § 25.3.

(2) If the person is liable for penalties or assessments, the appropriate amount of any such penalties or assessments considering any mitigating or aggravating factors that he or she finds in the case, such as those described in § 25.31.

(c) The ALJ shall promptly serve the initial decision on all parties within 90 days after the time for submission of post-hearing briefs and reply briefs (if permitted) has expired. The ALJ shall as the same time serve all respondents with a statement describing the right of any respondent determined to be liable for a civil penalty or assessment to file a motion for reconsideration with the ALJ or a notice of appeal with the authority head. If the ALJ fails to meet the deadline contained in this paragraph, he or she shall notify the parties of the reason for the delay and shall set a new deadline.

(d) Unless the initial decision of the ALJ is timely appealed to the authority head, or a motion for reconsideration of the initial decision is timely filed, the initial decision shall constitute the final decision of the authority head and shall be final and binding on the parties 30 days after it is issued by the ALJ.

§25.38 Reconsideration of initial decision.

(a) Except as provided in paragraph (d) of this section, any party may file a motion for reconsideration of the initial decision within 20 days of receipt of the initial decision. If service was made by mail, receipt will be presumed to be five days from the date of mailing in the absence of contrary proof.

(b) Every such motion must set forth the matters claimed to have been erroneously decided and the nature of the alleged errors. Such motion shall be accompanied by a supporting brief.

(c) Responses to such motions shall be allowed only upon request of the ALJ.

(d) No party may file a motion for reconsideration of an initial decision that has been revised in response to a previous motion for reconsideration.

(e) The ALJ may dispose of a motion for reconsideration by denying it or by issuing a revised initial decision.

(f) If the ALJ denies a motion for reconsideration, the initial decision shall constitute the final decision of the authority head and shall be final and binding on the parties 30 days after the ALJ denies the motion, unless the initial decision is timely appealed to the authority head in accordance with §25.39.

(g) If the ALJ issues a revised initial decision, that decision shall constitute the final decision of the authority head and shall be final and binding on the parties 30 days after it is issued, unless it is timely appealed to the authority head in accordance with §25.39.

§25.39 Appeal to authority head.

(a) Any respondent who has filed a timely answer and who is determined in an initial decision to be liable for a civil penalty or assessment may appeal such decision to the authority head by filing a notice of appeal with the authority head in accordance with this section.

(b)(1) No notice of appeal may be filed until the time period for filing a motion for reconsideration under §25.38 has expired.

(2) If a motion for reconsideration is timely filed, a notice of appeal must be filed within 30 days after the ALJ denies the motion or issues a revised initial decision, whichever applies.

(3) If no motion for reconsideration is timely filed, a notice of appeal must be filed within 30 days after the ALJ issues the initial decision.

(4) The authority head may extend the initial 30 day period for an additional 30 days if the respondent files with the authority head a request for an extension within the initial 30 day period and shows good cause.

(c) If the respondent files a timely notice of appeal with the authority head, the ALJ shall forward the record of the proceeding to the authority head.

(d) A notice of appeal shall be accompanied by a written brief specifying exceptions to the initial decision and reasons supporting the exceptions.

(e) The representative for the Government may file a brief in opposition to exceptions within 30 days of receiving the notice of appeal and accompanying brief.

(f) There is no right to appear personally before the authority head.

(g) There is no right to appeal any interlocutory ruling by the ALJ.

(h) In reviewing the initial decision, the authority head shall not consider any objection that was not raised before the ALJ unless a demonstration is made of extraordinary circumstances causing the failure to raise the objection.

(i) If any party demonstrates to the satisfaction of the authority head that additional evidence not presented at such hearing is material and that there was reasonable grounds for the failure to present such evidence at such hearing, the authority head shall remand the matter to the ALJ for consideration of such additional evidence.

(j) The authority head may affirm, reduce, reverse, compromise, remand, or settle any penalty or assessment determined by the ALJ in any initial decision.

(k) The authority head shall promptly serve each party to the appeal with a copy of the decision of the authority head and a statement describing the right of any person determined to be liable for a penalty or assessment to seek judicial review.

(l) Unless a petition for review is filed as provided in 31 U.S.C. 3805 after a respondent has exhausted all administrative remedies under this part and within 60 days after the date on which the authority head serves the respondent with a copy of the authority head's decision, a determination that a respondent is liable under §25.3 is final and is not subject to judicial review.

§25.40 Stays ordered by the Department of Justice.

If at any time the Attorney General or an Assistant Attorney General designated by the Attorney General transmits to the authority head a written finding that continuation of the administrative process described in this part with respect to a claim or statement may adversely affect any pending or potential criminal or civil action related to such claim or statement, the authority head shall stay the process and it shall be resumed only upon receipt of the written authorization of the Attorney General.

§25.41 Stay pending appeal.

(a) An initial decision is stayed automatically pending disposition of a motion for reconsideration or of an appeal to the authority head.

(b) No administrative stay is available following a final decision of the authority head.

§25.42 Judicial review.

Section 3805 of title 31, United States Code, authorized judicial review by an appropriate United States District Court of a final decision of the authority head imposing penalties or assessments under this part and specifies the procedures for such review.

§25.43 Collection of civil penalties and assessments.

Sections 3806 and 3808(b) of title 31, United States Code, authorize actions for collection of civil penalties and assessments imposed under this part and specify the procedures for such actions.

§25.44 Right to administrative offset.

The amount of any penalty or assessment which has become final, or for which a judgment has been entered under §§25.42 and 25.43, or any amount agreed upon in a compromise or settlement under §25.46, may be collected by administrative offset under 31 U.S.C. 3716, except that an administrative offset may not be made under this subsection against a refund of an overpayment of Federal taxes, then or later owing by the United States to the respondent.

§25.45 Deposit in Treasury of United States.

All amounts collected pursuant to this part shall be deposited as miscellaneous receipts in the Treasury of the United States, except as provided in 31 U.S.C. 3806(g).

§25.46 Compromise or settlement.

(a) Parties may make offers of compromise or settlement at any time.

(b) The reviewing official has the exclusive authority to compromise or settle a case under this part at any time after the date on which the reviewing official is permitted to issue a complaint and before the date on which the ALJ issues an initial decision. If the designated representative of the Government is not with the Office of General Counsel, the representative shall forward all settlement offers to the reviewing official and cannot negotiate a compromise or settlement with the respondent except as directed by the reviewing official.

(c) The authority head has exclusive authority to compromise or settle a case under this part at any time after the date on which the ALJ issues an initial decision, except during the pendency of any review under §25.42 or during the pendency of any action to collect penalties and assessments under §25.43.

(d) The Attorney General has exclusive authority to compromise or settle a case under this part during the pendency of any review under §25.42 or of any action to recover penalties and assessments under 31 U.S.C. 3806.

(e) The investigating official may recommend settlement terms to the reviewing official, the authority head, or the Attorney General, as appropriate. The reviewing official may recommend settlement terms to the authority head, or the Attorney General, as appropriate.

(f) Any compromise or settlement must be in writing.

§ 25.47 Limitations.

(a) The notice of hearing with respect to a claim or statement must be served in the manner specified in § 25.8 within 6 years after the date on which such claim or statement is made.

(b) If the respondent fails to file a timely answer, service of a notice under § 25.10(b) shall be deemed a notice of hearing for purposes of this section.

(c) The statute of limitations may be extended by agreement of the parties.

PART 26 [RESERVED]

PART 27—PROTECTION OF HUMAN SUBJECTS

AUTHORITY: 5 U.S.C. 301; 42 U.S.C. 300v–1(b).

SOURCE: 56 FR 28012, 28019, June 18, 1991, unless otherwise noted.

§ 27.101 To what does this policy apply?

(a) Except as provided in paragraph (b) of this section, this policy applies to all research involving human subjects conducted, supported or otherwise subject to regulation by any federal department or agency which takes appropriate administrative action to make the policy applicable to such research. This includes research conducted by federal civilian employees or military personnel, except that each department or agency head may adopt such procedural modifications as may be appropriate from an administrative standpoint. It also includes research conducted, supported, or otherwise subject to regulation by the federal government outside the United States.

(1) Research that is conducted or supported by a federal department or agency, whether or not it is regulated as defined in § 27.102(e), must comply with all sections of this policy.

(2) Research that is neither conducted nor supported by a federal department or agency but is subject to regulation as defined in § 27.102(e) must be reviewed and approved, in compliance with § 27.101, § 27.102, and § 27.107 through § 27.117 of this policy, by an institutional review board (IRB) that operates in accordance with the pertinent requirements of this policy.

(b) Unless otherwise required by department or agency heads, research activities in which the only involvement of human subjects will be in one or more of the following categories are exempt from this policy:

(1) Research conducted in established or commonly accepted educational settings, involving normal educational practices, such as (i) research on regular and special education instructional strategies, or (ii) research on the effectiveness of or the comparison among instructional techniques, curricula, or classroom management methods.

(2) Research involving the use of educational tests (cognitive, diagnostic, aptitude, achievement), survey procedures, interview procedures or observation of public behavior, unless:

(i) Information obtained is recorded in such a manner that human subjects can be identified, directly or through identifiers linked to the subjects; and

(ii) Any disclosure of the human subjects' responses outside the research could reasonably place the subjects at risk of criminal or civil liability or be damaging to the subjects' financial standing, employability, or reputation.

(3) Research involving the use of educational tests (cognitive, diagnostic, aptitude, achievement), survey procedures, interview procedures, or observation of public behavior that is not exempt under paragraph (b)(2) of this section, if:

(i) The human subjects are elected or appointed public officials or candidates for public office; or

(ii) Federal statute(s) require(s) without exception that the confidentiality of the personally identifiable information will be maintained throughout the research and thereafter.

(4) Research, involving the collection or study of existing data, documents, records, pathological specimens, or diagnostic specimens, if these sources are publicly available or if the information is recorded by the investigator in such a manner that subjects cannot be identified, directly or through identifiers linked to the subjects.

(5) Research and demonstration projects which are conducted by or subject to the approval of department or agency heads, and which are designed to study, evaluate, or otherwise examine:

(i) Public benefit or service programs;

(ii) Procedures for obtaining benefits or services under those programs;

(iii) Possible changes in or alternatives to those programs or procedures; or

(iv) Possible changes in methods or levels of payment for benefits or services under those programs.

(6) Taste and food quality evaluation and consumer acceptance studies,

(i) If wholesome foods without additives are consumed or

(ii) If a food is consumed that contains a food ingredient at or below the level and for a use found to be safe, or agricultural chemical or environmental contaminant at or below the level found to be safe, by the Food and Drug Administration or approved by the Environmental Protection Agency or the Food Safety and Inspection Service of the U.S. Department of Agriculture.

(c) Department or agency heads retain final judgment as to whether a particular activity is covered by this policy.

(d) Department or agency heads may require that specific research activities or classes of research activities conducted, supported, or otherwise subject to regulation by the department or agency but not otherwise covered by this policy, comply with some or all of the requirements of this policy.

(e) Compliance with this policy requires compliance with pertinent federal laws or regulations which provide additional protections for human subjects.

(f) This policy does not affect any state or local laws or regulations which may otherwise be applicable and which provide additional protections for human subjects.

(g) This policy does not affect any foreign laws or regulations which may otherwise be applicable and which provide additional protections to human subjects of research.

(h) When research covered by this policy takes place in foreign countries, procedures normally followed in the foreign countries to protect human subjects may differ from those set forth in this policy. [An example is a foreign institution which complies with guidelines consistent with the World Medical Assembly Declaration (Declaration of Helsinki amended 1989) issued either by sovereign states or by an organization whose function for the protection of human research subjects is internationally recognized.] In these circumstances, if a department or agency head determines that the procedures prescribed by the institution afford protections that are at least equivalent to those provided in this policy, the department or agency head may approve the substitution of the foreign procedures in lieu of the procedural requirements provided in this policy. Except when otherwise required by statute, Executive Order, or the department or agency head, notices of these actions as they occur will be published in the FEDERAL REGISTER or will be otherwise published as provided in department or agency procedures.

(i) Unless otherwise required by law, department or agency heads may waive the applicability of some or all of the provisions of this policy to specific research activities or classes of research activities otherwise covered by this policy. Except when otherwise required by statute or Executive Order, the department or agency head shall forward advance notices of these actions to the Office for Human Research Protections, Department of Health and Human Services (HHS), or any successor office, and shall also publish them in the FEDERAL REGISTER or in such other manner as provided in department or agency procedures.[1]

[56 FR 28012, 28019, June 18, 1991; 56 FR 29756, June 28, 1991, as amended at 70 FR 36328, June 23, 2005]

§27.102 Definitions.

(a) *Department or agency head* means the head of any federal department or agency and any other officer or employee of any department or agency to whom authority has been delegated.

(b) *Institution* means any public or private entity or agency (including federal, state, and other agencies).

(c) *Legally authorized representative* means an individual or judicial or other body authorized under applicable law to consent on behalf of a prospective subject to the subject's participation in the procedure(s) involved in the research.

(d) *Research* means a systematic investigation, including research development, testing and evaluation, designed to develop or contribute to generalizable knowledge. Activities which meet this definition constitute research for purposes of this policy, whether or not they are conducted or supported under a program which is considered research for other purposes. For example, some demonstration and service programs may include research activities.

(e) *Research subject to regulation,* and similar terms are intended to encompass those research activities for which a federal department or agency has specific responsibility for regulating as a research activity, (for example, Investigational New Drug requirements administered by the Food and Drug Administration). It does not include research activities which are incidentally regulated by a federal department or agency solely as part of the department's or agency's broader responsibility to regulate certain types of activities whether research or non-research in nature (for example, Wage and Hour requirements administered by the Department of Labor).

(f) *Human subject* means a living individual about whom an investigator (whether professional or student) conducting research obtains

(1) Data through intervention or interaction with the individual, or

(2) Identifiable private information.

Intervention includes both physical procedures by which data are gathered (for example, venipuncture) and manipulations of the subject or the subject's environment that are performed for research purposes. Interaction includes communication or interpersonal contact between investigator and subject. "Private information" includes information about behavior that occurs in a context in which an individual can reasonably expect that no observation or recording is taking place, and information which has been provided for specific purposes by an individual and which the individual can reasonably expect will not be made public (for example, a medical record). Private information must be individually identifiable (*i.e.*, the identity of the subject is or may readily be ascertained by the investigator or associated with the information) in order for obtaining the information to constitute research involving human subjects.

[1] Institutions with HHS-approved assurances on file will abide by provisions of title 45 CFR part 46 subparts A–D. Some of the other Departments and Agencies have incorporated all provisions of title 45 CFR part 46 into their policies and procedures as well. However, the exemptions at 45 CFR part 46.101(b) do not apply to research involving prisoners, subpart C. The exemption at 45 CFR part 46.101(b)(2), for research involving survey or interview procedures or observation of public behavior, does not apply to research with children, subpart D, except for research involving observations of public behavior when the investigator(s) do not participate in the activities being observed.

(g) *IRB* means an institutional review board established in accord with and for the purposes expressed in this policy.

(h) *IRB approval* means the determination of the IRB that the research has been reviewed and may be conducted at an institution within the constraints set forth by the IRB and by other institutional and federal requirements.

(i) *Minimal risk* means that the probability and magnitude of harm or discomfort anticipated in the research are not greater in and of themselves than those ordinarily encountered in daily life or during the performance of routine physical or psychological examinations or tests.

(j) *Certification* means the official notification by the institution to the supporting department or agency, in accordance with the requirements of this policy, that a research project or activity involving human subjects has been reviewed and approved by an IRB in accordance with an approved assurance.

§ 27.103 Assuring compliance with this policy—research conducted or supported by any Federal Department or Agency.

(a) Each institution engaged in research which is covered by this policy and which is conducted or supported by a federal department or agency shall provide written assurance satisfactory to the department or agency head that it will comply with the requirements set forth in this policy. In lieu of requiring submission of an assurance, individual department or agency heads shall accept the existence of a current assurance, appropriate for the research in question, on file with the Office for Human Research Protections, HHS, or any successor office, and approved for federalwide use by that office. When the existence of an HHS-approved assurance is accepted in lieu of requiring submission of an assurance, reports (except certification) required by this policy to be made to department and agency heads shall also be made to the Office for Human Research Protections, HHS, or any successor office.

(b) Departments and agencies will conduct or support research covered by this policy only if the institution has an assurance approved as provided in this section, and only if the institution has certified to the department or agency head that the research has been reviewed and approved by an IRB provided for in the assurance, and will be subject to continuing review by the IRB. Assurances applicable to federally supported or conducted research shall at a minimum include:

(1) A statement of principles governing the institution in the discharge of its responsibilities for protecting the rights and welfare of human subjects of research conducted at or sponsored by the institution, regardless of whether the research is subject to federal regulation. This may include an appropriate existing code, declaration, or statement of ethical principles, or a statement formulated by the institution itself. This requirement does not preempt provisions of this policy applicable to department- or agency-supported or regulated research and need not be applicable to any research exempted or waived under § 27.101 (b) or (i).

(2) Designation of one or more IRBs established in accordance with the requirements of this policy, and for which provisions are made for meeting space and sufficient staff to support the IRB's review and recordkeeping duties.

(3) A list of IRB members identified by name; earned degrees; representative capacity; indications of experience such as board certifications, licenses, etc., sufficient to describe each member's chief anticipated contributions to IRB deliberations; and any employment or other relationship between each member and the institution; for example: full-time employee, part-time employee, member of governing panel or board, stockholder, paid or unpaid consultant. Changes in IRB membership shall be reported to the department or agency head, unless in accord with § 27.103(a) of this policy, the existence of an HHS-approved assurance is accepted. In this case, change in IRB membership shall be reported to the Office for Human Research Protections, HHS, or any successor office.

(4) Written procedures which the IRB will follow (i) for conducting its initial and continuing review of research and

for reporting its findings and actions to the investigator and the institution; (ii) for determining which projects require review more often than annually and which projects need verification from sources other than the investigators that no material changes have occurred since previous IRB review; and (iii) for ensuring prompt reporting to the IRB of proposed changes in a research activity, and for ensuring that such changes in approved research, during the period for which IRB approval has already been given, may not be initiated without IRB review and approval except when necessary to eliminate apparent immediate hazards to the subject.

(5) Written procedures for ensuring prompt reporting to the IRB, appropriate institutional officials, and the department or agency head of (i) any unanticipated problems involving risks to subjects or others or any serious or continuing noncompliance with this policy or the requirements or determinations of the IRB and (ii) any suspension or termination of IRB approval.

(c) The assurance shall be executed by an individual authorized to act for the institution and to assume on behalf of the institution the obligations imposed by this policy and shall be filed in such form and manner as the department or agency head prescribes.

(d) The department or agency head will evaluate all assurances submitted in accordance with this policy through such officers and employees of the department or agency and such experts or consultants engaged for this purpose as the department or agency head determines to be appropriate. The department or agency head's evaluation will take into consideration the adequacy of the proposed IRB in light of the anticipated scope of the institution's research activities and the types of subject populations likely to be involved, the appropriateness of the proposed initial and continuing review procedures in light of the probable risks, and the size and complexity of the institution.

(e) On the basis of this evaluation, the department or agency head may approve or disapprove the assurance, or enter into negotiations to develop an approvable one. The department or agency head may limit the period during which any particular approved assurance or class of approved assurances shall remain effective or otherwise condition or restrict approval.

(f) Certification is required when the research is supported by a federal department or agency and not otherwise exempted or waived under § 27.101 (b) or (i). An institution with an approved assurance shall certify that each application or proposal for research covered by the assurance and by § 27.103 of this Policy has been reviewed and approved by the IRB. Such certification must be submitted with the application or proposal or by such later date as may be prescribed by the department or agency to which the application or proposal is submitted. Under no condition shall research covered by § 27.103 of the Policy be supported prior to receipt of the certification that the research has been reviewed and approved by the IRB. Institutions without an approved assurance covering the research shall certify within 30 days after receipt of a request for such a certification from the department or agency, that the application or proposal has been approved by the IRB. If the certification is not submitted within these time limits, the application or proposal may be returned to the institution.

(Approved by the Office of Management and Budget under control number 0990–0260)

[56 FR 28012, 28019, June 18, 1991; 56 FR 29756, June 28, 1991, as amended at 70 FR 36328, June 23, 2005]

§§ 27.104–27.106 [Reserved]

§ 27.107 IRB membership.

(a) Each IRB shall have at least five members, with varying backgrounds to promote complete and adequate review of research activities commonly conducted by the institution. The IRB shall be sufficiently qualified through the experience and expertise of its members, and the diversity of the members, including consideration of race, gender, and cultural backgrounds and sensitivity to such issues as community attitudes, to promote respect for its advice and counsel in safeguarding the rights and welfare of human subjects. In addition to possessing the professional competence necessary to review specific research activities, the IRB shall be able to ascertain the acceptability of proposed research in terms of institutional commitments and regulations, applicable law, and standards of professional conduct and practice. The IRB shall therefore include persons knowledgeable in these areas. If an IRB regularly reviews research that involves a vulnerable category of subjects, such as children, prisoners, pregnant women, or handicapped or mentally disabled persons, consideration shall be given to the inclusion of one or more individuals who are knowledgeable about and experienced in working with these subjects.

(b) Every nondiscriminatory effort will be made to ensure that no IRB consists entirely of men or entirely of women, including the institution's consideration of qualified persons of both sexes, so long as no selection is made to the IRB on the basis of gender. No IRB may consist entirely of members of one profession.

(c) Each IRB shall include at least one member whose primary concerns are in scientific areas and at least one member whose primary concerns are in nonscientific areas.

(d) Each IRB shall include at least one member who is not otherwise affiliated with the institution and who is not part of the immediate family of a person who is affiliated with the institution.

(e) No IRB may have a member participate in the IRB's initial or continuing review of any project in which the member has a conflicting interest, except to provide information requested by the IRB.

(f) An IRB may, in its discretion, invite individuals with competence in special areas to assist in the review of issues which require expertise beyond or in addition to that available on the IRB. These individuals may not vote with the IRB.

§27.108 IRB functions and operations.

In order to fulfill the requirements of this policy each IRB shall:

(a) Follow written procedures in the same detail as described in §27.103(b)(4) and, to the extent required by, §27.103(b)(5).

(b) Except when an expedited review procedure is used (see §27.110), review proposed research at convened meetings at which a majority of the members of the IRB are present, including at least one member whose primary concerns are in nonscientific areas. In order for the research to be approved, it shall receive the approval of a majority of those members present at the meeting.

§27.109 IRB review of research.

(a) An IRB shall review and have authority to approve, require modifications in (to secure approval), or disapprove all research activities covered by this policy.

(b) An IRB shall require that information given to subjects as part of informed consent is in accordance with §27.116. The IRB may require that information, in addition to that specifically mentioned in §27.116, be given to the subjects when in the IRB's judgment the information would meaningfully add to the protection of the rights and welfare of subjects.

(c) An IRB shall require documentation of informed consent or may waive documentation in accordance with §27.117.

(d) An IRB shall notify investigators and the institution in writing of its decision to approve or disapprove the proposed research activity, or of modifications required to secure IRB approval of the research activity. If the IRB decides to disapprove a research activity, it shall include in its written notification a statement of the reasons for its decision and give the investigator an opportunity to respond in person or in writing.

(e) An IRB shall conduct continuing review of research covered by this policy at intervals appropriate to the degree of risk, but not less than once per year, and shall have authority to observe or have a third party observe the consent process and the research.

(Approved by the Office of Management and Budget under control number 0990–0260)

[56 FR 28012, 28019, June 18, 1991, as amended at 70 FR 36328, June 23, 2005]

§27.110 Expedited review procedures for certain kinds of research involving no more than minimal risk, and for minor changes in approved research.

(a) The Secretary, HHS, has established, and published as a Notice in the FEDERAL REGISTER, a list of categories of research that may be reviewed by the IRB through an expedited review procedure. The list will be amended, as appropriate after consultation with other departments and agencies, through periodic republication by the Secretary, HHS, in the FEDERAL REGISTER. A copy of the list is available from the Office for Human Research Protections, HHS, or any successor office.

(b) An IRB may use the expedited review procedure to review either or both of the following:

(1) Some or all of the research appearing on the list and found by the reviewer(s) to involve no more than minimal risk,

(2) Minor changes in previously approved research during the period (of one year or less) for which approval is authorized.

Under an expedited review procedure, the review may be carried out by the IRB chairperson or by one or more experienced reviewers designated by the chairperson from among members of the IRB. In reviewing the research, the reviewers may exercise all of the authorities of the IRB except that the reviewers may not disapprove the research. A research activity may be disapproved only after review in accordance with the non-expedited procedure set forth in §27.108(b).

(c) Each IRB which uses an expedited review procedure shall adopt a method for keeping all members advised of research proposals which have been approved under the procedure.

(d) The department or agency head may restrict, suspend, terminate, or choose not to authorize an institution's or IRB's use of the expedited review procedure.

[56 FR 28012, 28019, June 18, 1991, as amended at 70 FR 36328, June 23, 2005]

§27.111 Criteria for IRB approval of research.

(a) In order to approve research covered by this policy the IRB shall determine that all of the following requirements are satisfied:

(1) Risks to subjects are minimized: (i) By using procedures which are consistent with sound research design and which do not unnecessarily expose subjects to risk, and (ii) whenever appropriate, by using procedures already being performed on the subjects for diagnostic or treatment purposes.

(2) Risks to subjects are reasonable in relation to anticipated benefits, if any, to subjects, and the importance of the knowledge that may reasonably be expected to result. In evaluating risks and benefits, the IRB should consider only those risks and benefits that may result from the research (as distinguished from risks and benefits of therapies subjects would receive even if not participating in the research). The IRB should not consider possible long-range effects of applying knowledge gained in the research (for example, the possible effects of the research on public policy) as among those research risks that fall within the purview of its responsibility.

(3) Selection of subjects is equitable. In making this assessment the IRB should take into account the purposes of the research and the setting in which the research will be conducted and should be particularly cognizant of the special problems of research involving vulnerable populations, such as children, prisoners, pregnant women, mentally disabled persons, or economically or educationally disadvantaged persons.

(4) Informed consent will be sought from each prospective subject or the subject's legally authorized representative, in accordance with, and to the extent required by §27.116.

(5) Informed consent will be appropriately documented, in accordance with, and to the extent required by §27.117.

(6) When appropriate, the research plan makes adequate provision for monitoring the data collected to ensure the safety of subjects.

(7) When appropriate, there are adequate provisions to protect the privacy

of subjects and to maintain the confidentiality of data.

(b) When some or all of the subjects are likely to be vulnerable to coercion or undue influence, such as children, prisoners, pregnant women, mentally disabled persons, or economically or educationally disadvantaged persons, additional safeguards have been included in the study to protect the rights and welfare of these subjects.

§27.112 Review by institution.

Research covered by this policy that has been approved by an IRB may be subject to further appropriate review and approval or disapproval by officials of the institution. However, those officials may not approve the research if it has not been approved by an IRB.

§27.113 Suspension or termination of IRB approval of research.

An IRB shall have authority to suspend or terminate approval of research that is not being conducted in accordance with the IRB's requirements or that has been associated with unexpected serious harm to subjects. Any suspension or termination of approval shall include a statement of the reasons for the IRB's action and shall be reported promptly to the investigator, appropriate institutional officials, and the department or agency head.

(Approved by the Office of Management and Budget under control number 0990–0260)

[56 FR 28012, 28019, June 18, 1991, as amended at 70 FR 36328, June 23, 2005]

§27.114 Cooperative research.

Cooperative research projects are those projects covered by this policy which involve more than one institution. In the conduct of cooperative research projects, each institution is responsible for safeguarding the rights and welfare of human subjects and for complying with this policy. With the approval of the department or agency head, an institution participating in a cooperative project may enter into a joint review arrangement, rely upon the review of another qualified IRB, or make similar arrangements for avoiding duplication of effort.

§27.115 IRB records.

(a) An institution, or when appropriate an IRB, shall prepare and maintain adequate documentation of IRB activities, including the following:

(1) Copies of all research proposals reviewed, scientific evaluations, if any, that accompany the proposals, approved sample consent documents, progress reports submitted by investigators, and reports of injuries to subjects.

(2) Minutes of IRB meetings which shall be in sufficient detail to show attendance at the meetings; actions taken by the IRB; the vote on these actions including the number of members voting for, against, and abstaining; the basis for requiring changes in or disapproving research; and a written summary of the discussion of controverted issues and their resolution.

(3) Records of continuing review activities.

(4) Copies of all correspondence between the IRB and the investigators.

(5) A list of IRB members in the same detail as described is §27.103(b)(3).

(6) Written procedures for the IRB in the same detail as described in §27.103(b)(4) and §27.103(b)(5).

(7) Statements of significant new findings provided to subjects, as required by §27.116(b)(5).

(b) The records required by this policy shall be retained for at least 3 years, and records relating to research which is conducted shall be retained for at least 3 years after completion of the research. All records shall be accessible for inspection and copying by authorized representatives of the department or agency at reasonable times and in a reasonable manner.

(Approved by the Office of Management and Budget under control number 0990–0260)

[56 FR 28012, 28019, June 18, 1991, as amended at 70 FR 36328, June 23, 2005]

§27.116 General requirements for informed consent.

Except as provided elsewhere in this policy, no investigator may involve a human being as a subject in research covered by this policy unless the investigator has obtained the legally effective informed consent of the subject or the subject's legally authorized representative. An investigator shall seek such consent only under circumstances that provide the prospective subject or the representative sufficient opportunity to consider whether or not to participate and that minimize the possibility of coercion or undue influence. The information that is given to the subject or the representative shall be in language understandable to the subject or the representative. No informed consent, whether oral or written, may include any exculpatory language through which the subject or the representative is made to waive or appear to waive any of the subject's legal rights, or releases or appears to release the investigator, the sponsor, the institution or its agents from liability for negligence.

(a) Basic elements of informed consent. Except as provided in paragraph (c) or (d) of this section, in seeking informed consent the following information shall be provided to each subject:

(1) A statement that the study involves research, an explanation of the purposes of the research and the expected duration of the subject's participation, a description of the procedures to be followed, and identification of any procedures which are experimental;

(2) A description of any reasonably foreseeable risks or discomforts to the subject;

(3) A description of any benefits to the subject or to others which may reasonably be expected from the research;

(4) A disclosure of appropriate alternative procedures or courses of treatment, if any, that might be advantageous to the subject;

(5) A statement describing the extent, if any, to which confidentiality of records identifying the subject will be maintained;

(6) For research involving more than minimal risk, an explanation as to whether any compensation and an explanation as to whether any medical treatments are available if injury occurs and, if so, what they consist of, or where further information may be obtained;

(7) An explanation of whom to contact for answers to pertinent questions about the research and research subjects' rights, and whom to contact in the event of a research-related injury to the subject; and

(8) A statement that participation is voluntary, refusal to participate will involve no penalty or loss of benefits to which the subject is otherwise entitled, and the subject may discontinue participation at any time without penalty or loss of benefits to which the subject is otherwise entitled.

(b) Additional elements of informed consent. When appropriate, one or more of the following elements of information shall also be provided to each subject:

(1) A statement that the particular treatment or procedure may involve risks to the subject (or to the embryo or fetus, if the subject is or may become pregnant) which are currently unforeseeable;

(2) Anticipated circumstances under which the subject's participation may be terminated by the investigator without regard to the subject's consent;

(3) Any additional costs to the subject that may result from participation in the research;

(4) The consequences of a subject's decision to withdraw from the research and procedures for orderly termination of participation by the subject;

(5) A statement that significant new findings developed during the course of the research which may relate to the subject's willingness to continue participation will be provided to the subject; and

(6) The approximate number of subjects involved in the study.

(c) An IRB may approve a consent procedure which does not include, or which alters, some or all of the elements of informed consent set forth above, or waive the requirement to obtain informed consent provided the IRB finds and documents that:

(1) The research or demonstration project is to be conducted by or subject to the approval of state or local government officials and is designed to study, evaluate, or otherwise examine: (i) Public benefit of service programs; (ii) procedures for obtaining benefits or services under those programs; (iii) possible changes in or alternatives to those programs or procedures; or (iv)

possible changes in methods or levels of payment for benefits or services under those programs; and

(2) The research could not practicably be carried out without the waiver or alteration.

(d) An IRB may approve a consent procedure which does not include, or which alters, some or all of the elements of informed consent set forth in this section, or waive the requirements to obtain informed consent provided the IRB finds and documents that:

(1) The research involves no more than minimal risk to the subjects;

(2) The waiver or alteration will not adversely affect the rights and welfare of the subjects;

(3) The research could not practicably be carried out without the waiver or alteration; and

(4) Whenever appropriate, the subjects will be provided with additional pertinent information after participation.

(e) The informed consent requirements in this policy are not intended to preempt any applicable federal, state, or local laws which require additional information to be disclosed in order for informed consent to be legally effective.

(f) Nothing in this policy is intended to limit the authority of a physician to provide emergency medical care, to the extent the physician is permitted to do so under applicable federal, state, or local law.

(Approved by the Office of Management and Budget under control number 0990–0260)

[56 FR 28012, 28019, June 18, 1991, as amended at 70 FR 36328, June 23, 2005]

§27.117 Documentation of informed consent.

(a) Except as provided in paragraph (c) of this section, informed consent shall be documented by the use of a written consent form approved by the IRB and signed by the subject or the subject's legally authorized representative. A copy shall be given to the person signing the form.

(b) Except as provided in paragraph (c) of this section, the consent form may be either of the following:

(1) A written consent document that embodies the elements of informed consent required by §27.116. This form may be read to the subject or the subject's legally authorized representative, but in any event, the investigator shall give either the subject or the representative adequate opportunity to read it before it is signed; or

(2) A short form written consent document stating that the elements of informed consent required by §27.116 have been presented orally to the subject or the subject's legally authorized representative. When this method is used, there shall be a witness to the oral presentation. Also, the IRB shall approve a written summary of what is to be said to the subject or the representative. Only the short form itself is to be signed by the subject or the representative. However, the witness shall sign both the short form and a copy of the summary, and the person actually obtaining consent shall sign a copy of the summary. A copy of the summary shall be given to the subject or the representative, in addition to a copy of the short form.

(c) An IRB may waive the requirement for the investigator to obtain a signed consent form for some or all subjects if it finds either:

(1) That the only record linking the subject and the research would be the consent document and the principal risk would be potential harm resulting from a breach of confidentiality. Each subject will be asked whether the subject wants documentation linking the subject with the research, and the subject's wishes will govern; or

(2) That the research presents no more than minimal risk of harm to subjects and involves no procedures for which written consent is normally required outside of the research context.

In cases in which the documentation requirement is waived, the IRB may require the investigator to provide subjects with a written statement regarding the research.

(Approved by the Office of Management and Budget under control number 0990–0260)

[56 FR 28012, 28019, June 18, 1991, as amended at 70 FR 36328, June 23, 2005]

§ 27.118 Applications and proposals lacking definite plans for involvement of human subjects.

Certain types of applications for grants, cooperative agreements, or contracts are submitted to departments or agencies with the knowledge that subjects may be involved within the period of support, but definite plans would not normally be set forth in the application or proposal. These include activities such as institutional type grants when selection of specific projects is the institution's responsibility; research training grants in which the activities involving subjects remain to be selected; and projects in which human subject's involvement will depend upon completion of instruments, prior animal studies, or purification of compounds. These applications need not be reviewed by an IRB before an award may be made. However, except for research exempted or waived under § 27.101 (b) or (i), no human subjects may be involved in any project supported by these awards until the project has been reviewed and approved by the IRB, as provided in this policy, and certification submitted, by the institution, to the department or agency.

§ 27.119 Research undertaken without the intention of involving human subjects.

In the event research is undertaken without the intention of involving human subjects, but it is later proposed to involve human subjects in the research, the research shall first be reviewed and approved by an IRB, as provided in this policy, a certification submitted, by the institution, to the department or agency, and final approval given to the proposed change by the department or agency.

§ 27.120 Evaluation and disposition of applications and proposals for research to be conducted or supported by a Federal Department or Agency.

(a) The department or agency head will evaluate all applications and proposals involving human subjects submitted to the department or agency through such officers and employees of the department or agency and such experts and consultants as the department or agency head determines to be appropriate. This evaluation will take into consideration the risks to the subjects, the adequacy of protection against these risks, the potential benefits of the research to the subjects and others, and the importance of the knowledge gained or to be gained.

(b) On the basis of this evaluation, the department or agency head may approve or disapprove the application or proposal, or enter into negotiations to develop an approvable one.

§ 27.121 [Reserved]

§ 27.122 Use of Federal funds.

Federal funds administered by a department or agency may not be expended for research involving human subjects unless the requirements of this policy have been satisfied.

§ 27.123 Early termination of research support: Evaluation of applications and proposals.

(a) The department or agency head may require that department or agency support for any project be terminated or suspended in the manner prescribed in applicable program requirements, when the department or agency head finds an institution has materially failed to comply with the terms of this policy.

(b) In making decisions about supporting or approving applications or proposals covered by this policy the department or agency head may take into account, in addition to all other eligibility requirements and program criteria, factors such as whether the applicant has been subject to a termination or suspension under paragraph (a) of this section and whether the applicant or the person or persons who would direct or has have directed the scientific and technical aspects of an activity has have, in the judgment of the department or agency head, materially failed to discharge responsibility for the protection of the rights and welfare of human subjects (whether or not the research was subject to federal regulation).

§ 27.124 Conditions.

With respect to any research project or any class of research projects the department or agency head may impose additional conditions prior to or at the time of approval when in the judgment of the department or agency head additional conditions are necessary for the protection of human subjects.

PART 28—NEW RESTRICTIONS ON LOBBYING

AUTHORITY: Sec. 319, Pub. L. 101–121 (31 U.S.C. 1352; 5 U.S.C. 301; Sec. 4, as amended, and sec. 5, Pub. L. 101–410, 104 Stat. 890 (28 U.S.C. 2461 note); Pub. L. 104–134, 110 Stat. 1321, 28 U.S.C. 2461 note.

SOURCE: 55 FR 6737, 6748, Feb. 26, 1990, unless otherwise noted.

CROSS REFERENCE: See also Office of Management and Budget notice published at 54 FR 52306, December 20, 1989.

Subpart A—General

§ 28.100 Conditions on use of funds.

(a) No appropriated funds may be expended by the recipient of a Federal contract, grant, loan, or cooperative agreement to pay any person for influencing or attempting to influence an officer or employee of any agency, a Member of Congress, an officer or employee of Congress, or an employee of a Member of Congress in connection with any of the following covered Federal actions: the awarding of any Federal contract, the making of any Federal grant, the making of any Federal loan, the entering into of any cooperative agreement, and the extension, continuation, renewal, amendment, or modification of any Federal contract, grant, loan, or cooperative agreement.

(b) Each person who requests or receives from an agency a Federal contract, grant, loan, or cooperative agreement shall file with that agency a certification, set forth in Appendix A, that the person has not made, and will not make, any payment prohibited by paragraph (a) of this section.

(c) Each person who requests or receives from an agency a Federal contract, grant, loan, or a cooperative agreement shall file with that agency a disclosure form, set forth in Appendix B, if such person has made or has agreed to make any payment using nonappropriated funds (to include profits from any covered Federal action), which would be prohibited under paragraph (a) of this section if paid for with appropriated funds.

(d) Each person who requests or receives from an agency a commitment providing for the United States to insure or guarantee a loan shall file with that agency a statement, set forth in Appendix A, whether that person has made or has agreed to make any payment to influence or attempt to influence an officer or employee of any agency, a Member of Congress, an officer or employee of Congress, or an employee of a Member of Congress in connection with that loan insurance or guarantee.

(e) Each person who requests or receives from an agency a commitment providing for the United States to insure or guarantee a loan shall file with that agency a disclosure form, set forth in Appendix B, if that person has made or has agreed to make any payment to influence or attempt to influence an officer or employee of any agency, a Member of Congress, an officer or employee of Congress, or an employee of a Member of Congress in connection with that loan insurance or guarantee.

§ 28.105 Definitions.

For purposes of this part:

(a) *Agency*, as defined in 5 U.S.C. 552(f), includes Federal executive departments and agencies as well as independent regulatory commissions and Government corporations, as defined in 31 U.S.C. 9101(1).

(b) *Covered Federal action* means any of the following Federal actions:

(1) The awarding of any Federal contract;

(2) The making of any Federal grant;

(3) The making of any Federal loan;

(4) The entering into of any cooperative agreement; and,

(5) The extension, continuation, renewal, amendment, or modification of any Federal contract, grant, loan, or cooperative agreement.

Covered Federal action does not include receiving from an agency a commitment providing for the United States to insure or guarantee a loan. Loan guarantees and loan insurance are addressed independently within this part.

(c) *Federal contract* means an acquisition contract awarded by an agency, including those subject to the Federal Acquisition Regulation (FAR), and any other acquisition contract for real or personal property or services not subject to the FAR.

(d) *Federal cooperative agreement* means a cooperative agreement entered into by an agency.

(e) *Federal grant* means an award of financial assistance in the form of money, or property in lieu of money, by the Federal Government or a direct appropriation made by law to any person. The term does not include technical assistance which provides services instead of money, or other assistance in the form of revenue sharing, loans, loan guarantees, loan insurance, interest subsidies, insurance, or direct United States cash assistance to an individual.

(f) *Federal loan* means a loan made by an agency. The term does not include loan guarantee or loan insurance.

(g) *Indian tribe* and *tribal organization* have the meaning provided in section 4 of the Indian Self-Determination and Education Assistance Act (25 U.S.C. 450B). Alaskan Natives are included under the definitions of Indian tribes in that Act.

(h) *Influencing or attempting to influence* means making, with the intent to influence, any communication to or appearance before an officer or employee or any agency, a Member of Congress, an officer or employee of Congress, or an employee of a Member of Congress in connection with any covered Federal action.

(i) *Loan guarantee* and *loan insurance* means an agency's guarantee or insurance of a loan made by a person.

(j) *Local government* means a unit of government in a State and, if chartered, established, or otherwise recognized by a State for the performance of a governmental duty, including a local public authority, a special district, an intrastate district, a council of governments, a sponsor group representative organization, and any other instrumentality of a local government.

(k) *Officer or employee of an agency* includes the following individuals who are employed by an agency:

(1) An individual who is appointed to a position in the Government under title 5, U.S. Code, including a position under a temporary appointment;

(2) A member of the uniformed services as defined in section 101(3), title 37, U.S. Code;

(3) A special Government employee as defined in section 202, title 18, U.S. Code; and,

(4) An individual who is a member of a Federal advisory committee, as defined by the Federal Advisory Committee Act, title 5, U.S. Code appendix 2.

(l) *Person* means an individual, corporation, company, association, authority, firm, partnership, society, State, and local government, regardless of whether such entity is operated for profit or not for profit. This term excludes an Indian tribe, tribal organization, or any other Indian organization with respect to expenditures specifically permitted by other Federal law.

(m) *Reasonable compensation* means, with respect to a regularly employed officer or employee of any person, compensation that is consistent with the normal compensation for such officer or employee for work that is not furnished to, not funded by, or not furnished in cooperation with the Federal Government.

(n) *Reasonable payment* means, with respect to perfessional and other technical services, a payment in an amount that is consistent with the amount normally paid for such services in the private sector.

(o) *Recipient* includes all contractors, subcontractors at any tier, and subgrantees at any tier of the recipient of funds received in connection with a Federal contract, grant, loan, or cooperative agreement. The term excludes an Indian tribe, tribal organization, or any other Indian organization with respect to expenditures specifically permitted by other Federal law.

(p) *Regularly employed* means, with respect to an officer or employee of a person requesting or receiving a Federal contract, grant, loan, or cooperative agreement or a commitment providing for the United States to insure or guarantee a loan, an officer or employee who is employed by such person for at least 130 working days within one year immediately preceding the date of the submission that initiates agency consideration of such person for receipt of such contract, grant, loan, cooperative agreement, loan insurance commitment, or loan guarantee commitment. An officer or employee who is employed by such person for less than 130 working days within one year immediately preceding the date of the submission that initiates agency consideration of such person shall be considered to be regularly employed as soon as he or she is employed by such person for 130 working days.

(q) *State* means a State of the United States, the District of Columbia, the Commonwealth of Puerto Rico, a territory or possession of the United States, an agency or instrumentality of a State, and a multi-State, regional, or interstate entity having governmental duties and powers.

§28.110 Certification and disclosure.

(a) Each person shall file a certification, and a disclosure form, if required, with each submission that initiates agency consideration of such person for:

(1) Award of a Federal contract, grant, or cooperative agreement exceeding $100,000; or

(2) An award of a Federal loan or a commitment providing for the United States to insure or guarantee a loan exceeding $150,000.

(b) Each person shall file a certification, and a disclosure form, if required, upon receipt by such person of:

(1) A Federal contract, grant, or cooperative agreement exceeding $100,000; or

(2) A Federal loan or a commitment providing for the United States to insure or guarantee a loan exceeding $150,000,

unless such person previously filed a certification, and a disclosure form, if required, under paragraph (a) of this section.

(c) Each person shall file a disclosure form at the end of each calendar quarter in which there occurs any event that requires disclosure or that materially affects the accuracy of the information contained in any disclosure form previously filed by such person under paragraphs (a) or (b) of this section. An event that materially affects the accuracy of the information reported includes:

(1) A cumulative increase of $25,000 or more in the amount paid or expected to be paid for influencing or attempting to influence a covered Federal action; or

(2) A change in the person(s) or individual(s) influencing or attempting to influence a covered Federal action; or,

(3) A change in the officer(s), employee(s), or Member(s) contacted to influence or attempt to influence a covered Federal action.

(d) Any person who requests or receives from a person referred to in paragraphs (a) or (b) of this section:

(1) A subcontract exceeding $100,000 at any tier under a Federal contract;

(2) A subgrant, contract, or subcontract exceeding $100,000 at any tier under a Federal grant;

(3) A contract or subcontract exceeding $100,000 at any tier under a Federal loan exceeding $150,000; or,

(4) A contract or subcontract exceeding $100,000 at any tier under a Federal cooperative agreement,

shall file a certification, and a disclosure form, if required, to the next tier above.

(e) All disclosure forms, but not certifications, shall be forwarded from tier to tier until received by the person referred to in paragraphs (a) or (b) of this section. That person shall forward all disclosure forms to the agency.

(f) Any certification or disclosure form filed under paragraph (e) of this section shall be treated as a material representation of fact upon which all receiving tiers shall rely. All liability arising from an erroneous representation shall be borne solely by the tier filing that representation and shall not be shared by any tier to which the erroneous representation is forwarded. Submitting an erroneous certification or disclosure constitutes a failure to file the required certification or disclosure, respectively. If a person fails to file a required certification or disclosure, the United States may pursue all available remedies, including those authorized by section 1352, title 31, U.S. Code.

(g) For awards and commitments in process prior to December 23, 1989, but not made before that date, certifications shall be required at award or commitment, covering activities occurring between December 23, 1989, and the date of award or commitment. However, for awards and commitments in process prior to the December 23, 1989 effective date of these provisions, but not made before December 23, 1989, disclosure forms shall not be required at time of award or commitment but shall be filed within 30 days.

(h) No reporting is required for an activity paid for with appropriated funds if that activity is allowable under either subpart B or C.

Subpart B—Activities by Own Employees

§ 28.200 Agency and legislative liaison.

(a) The prohibition on the use of appropriated funds, in § 28.100 (a), does not apply in the case of a payment of reasonable compensation made to an officer or employee of a person requesting or receiving a Federal contract, grant, loan, or cooperative agreement if the payment is for agency and legislative liaison activities not directly related to a covered Federal action.

(b) For purposes of paragraph (a) of this section, providing any information specifically requested by an agency or Congress is allowable at any time.

(c) For purposes of paragraph (a) of this section, the following agency and legislative liaison activities are allowable at any time only where they are not related to a specific solicitation for any covered Federal action:

(1) Discussing with an agency (including individual demonstrations) the qualities and characteristics of the person's products or services, conditions or terms of sale, and service capabilities; and,

(2) Technical discussions and other activities regarding the application or adaptation of the person's products or services for an agency's use.

(d) For purposes of paragraph (a) of this section, the following agencies and legislative liaison activities are allowable only where they are prior to formal solicitation of any covered Federal action:

(1) Providing any information not specifically requested but necessary for an agency to make an informed decision about initiation of a covered Federal action;

(2) Technical discussions regarding the preparation of an unsolicited proposal prior to its official submission; and,

(3) Capability presentations by persons seeking awards from an agency pursuant to the provisions of the Small Business Act, as amended by Public Law 95–507 and other subsequent amendments.

(e) Only those activities expressly authorized by this section are allowable under this section.

§ 28.205 Professional and technical services.

(a) The prohibition on the use of appropriated funds, in § 28.100(a), does not apply in the case of a payment of reasonable compensation made to an officer or employee of a person requesting or receiving a Federal contract, grant, loan, or cooperative agreement or an extension, continuation, renewal, amendment, or modification of a Federal contract, grant, loan, or cooperative agreement if payment is for professional or technical services rendered directly in the preparation, submission, or negotiation of any bid, proposal, or application for that Federal contract, grant, loan, or cooperative agreement or for meeting requirements imposed by or pursuant to law as a condition for receiving that Federal contract, grant, loan, or cooperative agreement.

(b) For purposes of paragraph (a) of this section, "professional and technical services" shall be limited to advice and analysis directly applying any professional or technical discipline. For example, drafting of a legal document accompanying a bid or proposal by a lawyer is allowable. Similarly, technical advice provided by an engineer on the performance or operational capability of a piece of equipment rendered directly in the negotiation of a contract is allowable. However, communications with the intent to influence made by a professional (such as a licensed lawyer) or a technical person (such as a licensed accountant) are not allowable under this section unless they provide advice and analysis directly applying their professional or technical expertise and unless the advice or analysis is rendered directly and solely in the preparation, submission or negotiation of a covered Federal action. Thus, for example, communications with the intent to influence made by a lawyer that do not provide legal advice or analysis directly and solely related to the legal aspects of his or her client's proposal, but generally advocate one proposal over another are not allowable under this section because the lawyer is not providing professional legal services. Similarly, communications with the intent to influence made by an engineer providing an engineering analysis prior to the preparation or submission of a bid or proposal are not allowable under this section since the engineer is providing technical services but not directly in the preparation, submission or negotiation of a covered Federal action.

(c) Requirements imposed by or pursuant to law as a condition for receiving a covered Federal award include those required by law or regulation, or reasonably expected to be required by law or regulation, and any other requirements in the actual award documents.

(d) Only those services expressly authorized by this section are allowable under this section.

§ 28.210 Reporting.

No reporting is required with respect to payments of reasonable compensation made to regularly employed officers or employees of a person.

Subpart C—Activities by Other Than Own Employees

§ 28.300 Professional and technical services.

(a) The prohibition on the use of appropriated funds, in § 28.100 (a), does not apply in the case of any reasonable payment to a person, other than an officer or employee of a person requesting or receiving a covered Federal action, if the payment is for professional or technical services rendered directly in the preparation, submission, or negotiation of any bid, proposal, or application for that Federal contract, grant, loan, or cooperative agreement or for meeting requirements imposed by or pursuant to law as a condition for receiving that Federal contract, grant, loan, or cooperative agreement.

(b) The reporting requirements in § 28.110 (a) and (b) regarding filing a disclosure form by each person, if required, shall not apply with respect to professional or technical services rendered directly in the preparation, submission, or negotiation of any commitment providing for the United States to insure or guarantee a loan.

(c) For purposes of paragraph (a) of this section, "professional and technical services" shall be limited to advice and analysis directly applying any professional or technical discipline. For example, drafting or a legal document accompanying a bid or proposal by a lawyer is allowable. Similarly, technical advice provided by an engineer on the performance or operational capability of a piece of equipment rendered directly in the negotiation of a contract is allowable. However, communications with the intent to influence made by a professional (such as a licensed lawyer) or a technical person (such as a licensed accountant) are not allowable under this section unless they provide advice and analysis directly applying their professional or technical expertise and unless the advice or analysis is rendered directly and solely in the preparation, submission or negotiation of a covered Federal action. Thus, for example, communications with the intent to influence made by a lawyer that do not provide legal advice or analysis directly and solely related to the legal aspects of his or her client's proposal, but generally advocate one proposal over another are not allowable under this section because the lawyer is not providing professional legal services. Similarly, communications with the intent to influence made by an engineer providing an engineering analysis prior to the preparation or submission of a bid or proposal are not allowable under this section since the engineer is providing technical services but not directly in the preparation, submission or negotiation of a covered Federal action.

(d) Requirements imposed by or pursuant to law as a condition for receiving a covered Federal award include those required by law or regulation, or reasonably expected to be required by law or regulation, and any other requirements in the actual award documents.

(e) Persons other than officers or employees of a person requesting or receiving a covered Federal action include consultants and trade associations.

(f) Only those services expressly authorized by this section are allowable under this section.

Subpart D—Penalties and Enforcement

§ 28.400 Penalties.

(a) Any person who makes an expenditure prohibited herein shall be subject to a civil penalty of not less than $10,000 and not more than $100,000 for each such expenditure made on or before October 23, 1996, and of not less than $11,000 and not more than $110,000 for each such expenditure made after October 23, 1996.

(b) Any person who fails to file or amend the disclosure form (see Appendix B of this part) to be filed or amended if required herein, shall be subject to a civil penalty of not less than $10,000 and not more than $100,000 for each such failure occurring on or before October 23, 1996, and of not less than $11,000 and not more than $110,000 for each such failure occurring after October 23, 1996.

(c) A filing or amended filing on or after the date on which an administrative action for the imposition of a civil penalty is commenced does not prevent the imposition of such civil penalty for a failure occurring before that date. An administrative action is commenced with respect to a failure when an investigating official determines in writing to commence an investigation of an allegation of such failure.

(d) In determining whether to impose a civil penalty, and the amount of any such penalty, by reason of a violation by any person, the agency shall consider the nature, circumstances, extent, and gravity of the violation, the effect on the ability of such person to continue in business, any prior violations by such person, the degree of culpability of such person, the ability of the person to pay the penalty, and such other matters as may be appropriate.

(e) First offenders under paragraphs (a) or (b) of this section shall be subject to a civil penalty of $10,000, absent aggravating circumstances for each such offense committed on or before October 23, 1996, and $11,000 for each such offense committed after October 23, 1996.

Second and subsequent offenses by persons shall be subject to an appropriate civil penalty between $10,000 and $100,000 for each such offense committed on or before October 23, 1996, and between $11,000 and $110,000 for each such offense committed after October 23, 1996, as determined by the agency head or his or her designee.

(f) An imposition of a civil penalty under this section does not prevent the United States from seeking any other remedy that may apply to the same conduct that is the basis for the imposition of such civil penalty.

[55 FR 6737, 6748, Feb. 26, 1990, as amended at 61 FR 55095, Oct. 24, 1996]

§ 28.405 Penalty procedures.

Agencies shall impose and collect civil penalties pursuant to the provisions of the Program Fraud and Civil Remedies Act, 31 U.S.C. sections 3803 (except subsection (c)), 3804, 3805, 3806, 3807, 3808, and 3812, insofar as these provisions are not inconsistent with the requirements herein.

§ 28.410 Enforcement.

The head of each agency shall take such actions as are necessary to ensure that the provisions herein are vigorously implemented and enforced in that agency.

Subpart E—Exemptions

§ 28.500 Secretary of Defense.

(a) The Secretary of Defense may exempt, on a case-by-case basis, a covered Federal action from the prohibition whenever the Secretary determines, in writing, that such an exemption is in the national interest. The Secretary shall transmit a copy of each such written exemption to Congress immediately after making such a determination.

(b) The Department of Defense may issue supplemental regulations to implement paragraph (a) of this section.

Subpart F—Agency Reports

§ 28.600 Semi-annual compilation.

(a) The head of each agency shall collect and compile the disclosure reports (see Appendix B) and, on May 31 and November 30 of each year, submit to the Secretary of the Senate and the Clerk of the House of Representatives a report containing a compilation of the information contained in the disclosure reports received during the six-month period ending on March 31 or September 30, respectively, of that year.

(b) The report, including the compilation, shall be available for public inspection 30 days after receipt of the report by the Secretary and the Clerk.

(c) Information that involves intelligence matters shall be reported only to the Select Committee on Intelligence of the Senate, the Permanent Select Committee on Intelligence of the House of Representatives, and the Committees on Appropriations of the Senate and the House of Representatives in accordance with procedures agreed to by such committees. Such information shall not be available for public inspection.

(d) Information that is classified under Executive Order 12356 or any successor order shall be reported only to the Committee on Foreign Relations of the Senate and the Committee on Foreign Affairs of the House of Representatives or the Committees on Armed Services of the Senate and the House of Representatives (whichever such committees have jurisdiction of matters involving such information) and to the Committees on Appropriations of the Senate and the House of Representatives in accordance with procedures agreed to by such committees. Such information shall not be available for public inspection.

(e) The first semi-annual compilation shall be submitted on May 31, 1990, and shall contain a compilation of the disclosure reports received from December 23, 1989 to March 31, 1990.

(f) Major agencies, designated by the Office of Management and Budget (OMB), are required to provide machine-readable compilations to the Secretary of the Senate and the Clerk of the House of Representatives no later than with the compilations due on May 31, 1991. OMB shall provide detailed specifications in a memorandum to these agencies.

(g) Non-major agencies are requested to provide machine-readable compilations to the Secretary of the Senate and the Clerk of the House of Representatives.

(h) Agencies shall keep the originals of all disclosure reports in the official files of the agency.

§ 28.605 Inspector General report.

(a) The Inspector General, or other official as specified in paragraph (b) of this section, of each agency shall prepare and submit to Congress each year, commencing with submission of the President's Budget in 1991, an evaluation of the compliance of that agency with, and the effectiveness of, the requirements herein. The evaluation may include any recommended changes that may be necessary to strengthen or improve the requirements.

(b) In the case of an agency that does not have an Inspector General, the agency official comparable to an Inspector General shall prepare and submit the annual report, or, if there is no such comparable official, the head of the agency shall prepare and submit the annual report.

(c) The annual report shall be submitted at the same time the agency submits its annual budget justifications to Congress.

(d) The annual report shall include the following: All alleged violations relating to the agency's covered Federal actions during the year covered by the report, the actions taken by the head of the agency in the year covered by the report with respect to those alleged violations and alleged violations in previous years, and the amounts of civil penalties imposed by the agency in the year covered by the report.

Appendix A to Part 28—Certification Regarding Lobbying

Certification for Contracts, Grants, Loans, and Cooperative Agreements

The undersigned certifies, to the best of his or her knowledge and belief, that:

(1) No Federal appropriated funds have been paid or will be paid, by or on behalf of the undersigned, to any person for influencing or attempting to influence an officer or employee of an agency, a Member of Congress, an officer or employee of Congress, or an employee of a Member of Congress in connection with the awarding of any Federal contract, the making of any Federal grant, the making of any Federal loan, the entering into of any cooperative agreement, and the extension, continuation, renewal, amendment, or modification of any Federal contract, grant, loan, or cooperative agreement.

(2) If any funds other than Federal appropriated funds have been paid or will be paid to any person for influencing or attempting to influence an officer or employee of any agency, a Member of Congress, an officer or employee of Congress, or an employee of a Member of Congress in connection with this Federal contract, grant, loan, or cooperative agreement, the undersigned shall complete and submit Standard Form-LLL, "Disclosure Form to Report Lobbying," in accordance with its instructions.

(3) The undersigned shall require that the language of this certification be included in the award documents for all subawards at all tiers (including subcontracts, subgrants, and contracts under grants, loans, and cooperative agreements) and that all subrecipients shall certify and disclose accordingly.

This certification is a material representation of fact upon which reliance was placed when this transaction was made or entered into. Submission of this certification is a prerequisite for making or entering into this transaction imposed by section 1352, title 31, U.S. Code. Any person who fails to file the required certification shall be subject to a civil penalty of not less than $10,000 and not more than $100,000 for each such failure occurring on or before October 23, 1996, and of not less than $11,000 and not more than $110,000 for each such failure occurring after October 23, 1996.

Statement for Loan Guarantees and Loan Insurance

The undersigned states, to the best of his or her knowledge and belief, that:

If any funds have been paid or will be paid to any person for influencing or attempting to influence an officer or employee of any agency, a Member of Congress, an officer or employee of Congress, or an employee of a Member of Congress in connection with this commitment providing for the United States to insure or guarantee a loan, the undersigned shall complete and submit Standard Form-LLL, "Disclosure Form to Report Lobbying," in accordance with its instructions.

Submission of this statement is a prerequisite for making or entering into this transaction imposed by section 1352, title 31, U.S. Code. Any person who fails to file the required statement shall be subject to a civil penalty of not less than $10,000 and not more than $100,000 for each such failure occurring on or before October 23, 1996, and of not less than $11,000 and not more than $110,000 for each such failure occurring after October 23, 1996.

[55 FR 6737, 6748, Feb. 26, 1990, as amended at 61 FR 55095, Oct. 24, 1996]

APPENDIX B TO PART 28—DISCLOSURE FORM TO REPORT LOBBYING

DISCLOSURE OF LOBBYING ACTIVITIES

Approved by OMB 0348-0046

Complete this form to disclose lobbying activities pursuant to 31 U.S.C. 1352
(See reverse for public burden disclosure.)

1. Type of Federal Action:
☐ a. contract
b. grant
c. cooperative agreement
d. loan
e. loan guarantee
f. loan insurance

2. Status of Federal Action:
☐ a. bid/offer/application
b. initial award
c. post-award

3. Report Type:
☐ a. initial filing
b. material change
For Material Change Only:
year ______ quarter ____
date of last report ________

4. Name and Address of Reporting Entity:
☐ Prime ☐ Subawardee
Tier ____, *if known*:

Congressional District, *if known*:

5. If Reporting Entity in No. 4 is Subawardee, Enter Name and Address of Prime:

Congressional District, *if known*:

6. Federal Department/Agency:

7. Federal Program Name/Description:

CFDA Number, *if applicable*: ____________

8. Federal Action Number, *if known*:

9. Award Amount, *if known*:
$

10. a. Name and Address of Lobbying Entity *(if individual, last name, first name, MI)*:

b. Individuals Performing Services *(including address if different from No. 10a) (last name, first name, MI)*:

(attach Continuation Sheet(s) SF-LLL-A, if necessary)

11. Amount of Payment *(check all that apply)*:
$ ______________ ☐ actual ☐ planned

12. Form of Payment *(check all that apply)*:
☐ a. cash
☐ b. in-kind; specify: nature ______________
value ______________

13. Type of Payment *(check all that apply)*:
☐ a. retainer
☐ b. one-time fee
☐ c. commission
☐ d. contingent fee
☐ e. deferred
☐ f. other; specify: ______________

14. Brief Description of Services Performed or to be Performed and Date(s) of Service, including officer(s), employee(s), or Member(s) contacted, for Payment Indicated in Item 11:

(attach Continuation Sheet(s) SF-LLL-A, if necessary)

15. Continuation Sheet(s) SF-LLL-A attached: ☐ Yes ☐ No

16. Information requested through this form is authorized by title 31 U.S.C. section 1352. This disclosure of lobbying activities is a material representation of fact upon which reliance was placed by the tier above when this transaction was made or entered into. This disclosure is required pursuant to 31 U.S.C. 1352. This information will be reported to the Congress semi-annually and will be available for public inspection. Any person who fails to file the required disclosure shall be subject to a civil penalty of not less than $10,000 and not more than $100,000 for each such failure.

Signature: ______________
Print Name: ______________
Title: ______________
Telephone No.: ____________ **Date:** ____________

Federal Use Only:

Authorized for Local Reproduction
Standard Form - LLL

INSTRUCTIONS FOR COMPLETION OF SF-LLL, DISCLOSURE OF LOBBYING ACTIVITIES

This disclosure form shall be completed by the reporting entity, whether subawardee or prime Federal recipient, at the initiation or receipt of a covered Federal action, or a material change to a previous filing, pursuant to title 31 U.S.C. section 1352. The filing of a form is required for each payment or agreement to make payment to any lobbying entity for influencing or attempting to influence an officer or employee of any agency, a Member of Congress, an officer or employee of Congress, or an employee of a Member of Congress in connection with a covered Federal action. Use the SF-LLL-A Continuation Sheet for additional information if the space on the form is inadequate. Complete all items that apply for both the initial filing and material change report. Refer to the implementing guidance published by the Office of Management and Budget for additional information.

1. Identify the type of covered Federal action for which lobbying activity is and/or has been secured to influence the outcome of a covered Federal action.

2. Identify the status of the covered Federal action.

3. Identify the appropriate classification of this report. If this is a followup report caused by a material change to the information previously reported, enter the year and quarter in which the change occurred. Enter the date of the last previously submitted report by this reporting entity for this covered Federal action.

4. Enter the full name, address, city, state and zip code of the reporting entity. Include Congressional District, if known. Check the appropriate classification of the reporting entity that designates if it is, or expects to be, a prime or subaward recipient. Identify the tier of the subawardee, e.g., the first subawardee of the prime is the 1st tier. Subawards include but are not limited to subcontracts, subgrants and contract awards under grants.

5. If the organization filing the report in item 4 checks "Subawardee", then enter the full name, address, city, state and zip code of the prime Federal recipient. Include Congressional District, if known.

6. Enter the name of the Federal agency making the award or loan commitment. Include at least one organizational level below agency name, if known. For example, Department of Transportation, United States Coast Guard.

7. Enter the Federal program name or description for the covered Federal action (item 1). If known, enter the full Catalog of Federal Domestic Assistance (CFDA) number for grants, cooperative agreements, loans, and loan commitments.

8. Enter the most appropriate Federal identifying number available for the Federal action identified in item 1 (e.g., Request for Proposal (RFP) number; Invitation for Bid (IFB) number; grant announcement number; the contract, grant, or loan award number; the application/proposal control number assigned by the Federal agency). Include prefixes, e.g., "RFP-DE-90-001."

9. For a covered Federal action where there has been an award or loan commitment by the Federal agency, enter the Federal amount of the award/loan commitment for the prime entity identified in item 4 or 5.

10. (a) Enter the full name, address, city, state and zip code of the lobbying entity engaged by the reporting entity identified in item 4 to influence the covered Federal action.

    (b) Enter the full names of the individual(s) performing services, and include full address if different from 10 (a). Enter Last Name, First Name, and Middle Initial (MI).

11. Enter the amount of compensation paid or reasonably expected to be paid by the reporting entity (item 4) to the lobbying entity (item 10). Indicate whether the payment has been made (actual) or will be made (planned). Check all boxes that apply. If this is a material change report, enter the cumulative amount of payment made or planned to be made.

12. Check the appropriate box(es). Check all boxes that apply. If payment is made through an in-kind contribution, specify the nature and value of the in-kind payment.

13. Check the appropriate box(es). Check all boxes that apply. If other, specify nature.

14. Provide a specific and detailed description of the services that the lobbyist has performed, or will be expected to perform, and the date(s) of any services rendered. Include all preparatory and related activity, not just time spent in actual contact with Federal officials. Identify the Federal official(s) or employee(s) contacted or the officer(s), employee(s), or Member(s) of Congress that were contacted.

15. Check whether or not a SF-LLL-A Continuation Sheet(s) is attached.

16. The certifying official shall sign and date the form, print his/her name, title, and telephone number.

Public reporting burden for this collection of information is estimated to average 30 mintues per response, including time for reviewing instructions, searching existing data sources, gathering and maintaining the data needed, and completing and reviewing the collection of information. Send comments regarding the burden estimate or any other aspect of this collection of information, including suggestions for reducing this burden, to the Office of Management and Budget, Paperwork Reduction Project (0348-0046), Washington, D.C. 20503.

DISCLOSURE OF LOBBYING ACTIVITIES
CONTINUATION SHEET

Approved by OMB
0348-0046

Reporting Entity: ______________________ **Page** ____ **of** ____

Authorized for Local Reproduction
Standard Form - LLL-A

PART 29—GOVERNMENTWIDE REQUIREMENTS FOR DRUG-FREE WORKPLACE (FINANCIAL ASSISTANCE)

Subpart A—Purpose and Coverage

Subpart B—Requirements for Recipients Other Than Individuals

AUTHORITY: 5 U.S.C. 301; 41 U.S.C. 701 *et seq.*

SOURCE: 68 FR 66557, 66577, Nov. 26, 2003, unless otherwise noted.

EDITORIAL NOTE: Nomenclature changes to part 29 appear at 68 FR 66577, Nov. 26, 2003.

Subpart A—Purpose and Coverage

§ 29.100 What does this part do?

This part carries out the portion of the Drug-Free Workplace Act of 1988 (41 U.S.C. 701 *et seq.*, as amended) that applies to grants. It also applies the provisions of the Act to cooperative agreements and other financial assistance awards, as a matter of Federal Government policy.

§ 29.105 Does this part apply to me?

(a) Portions of this part apply to you if you are either—

(1) A recipient of an assistance award from the Department of Commerce; or

(2) A(n) DoC awarding official. (See definitions of award and recipient in §§ 29.605 and 29.660, respectively.)

(b) The following table shows the subparts that apply to you:

If you are	see subparts
(1) A recipient who is not an individual	A, B and E.
(2) A recipient who is an individual	A, C and E.
(3) A(n) DoC awarding official	A, D and E.

§ 29.110 Are any of my Federal assistance awards exempt from this part?

This part does not apply to any award that the Secretary of Commerce or designee determines that the application of this part would be inconsistent with the international obligations of the United States or the laws or regulations of a foreign government.

§ 29.115 Does this part affect the Federal contracts that I receive?

It will affect future contract awards indirectly if you are debarred or suspended for a violation of the requirements of this part, as described in § 29.510(c). However, this part does not apply directly to procurement contracts. The portion of the Drug-Free Workplace Act of 1988 that applies to

Federal procurement contracts is carried out through the Federal Acquisition Regulation in chapter 1 of Title 48 of the Code of Federal Regulations (the drug-free workplace coverage currently is in 48 CFR part 23, subpart 23.5).

Subpart B—Requirements for Recipients Other Than Individuals

§ 29.200 What must I do to comply with this part?

There are two general requirements if you are a recipient other than an individual.

(a) First, you must make a good faith effort, on a continuing basis, to maintain a drug-free workplace. You must agree to do so as a condition for receiving any award covered by this part. The specific measures that you must take in this regard are described in more detail in subsequent sections of this subpart. Briefly, those measures are to—

(1) Publish a drug-free workplace statement and establish a drug-free awareness program for your employees (see §§ 29.205 through 29.220); and

(2) Take actions concerning employees who are convicted of violating drug statutes in the workplace (see § 29.225).

(b) Second, you must identify all known workplaces under your Federal awards (see § 29.230).

§ 29.205 What must I include in my drug-free workplace statement?

You must publish a statement that—

(a) Tells your employees that the unlawful manufacture, distribution, dispensing, possession, or use of a controlled substance is prohibited in your workplace;

(b) Specifies the actions that you will take against employees for violating that prohibition; and

(c) Lets each employee know that, as a condition of employment under any award, he or she:

(1) Will abide by the terms of the statement; and

(2) Must notify you in writing if he or she is convicted for a violation of a criminal drug statute occurring in the workplace and must do so no more than five calendar days after the conviction.

§ 29.210 To whom must I distribute my drug-free workplace statement?

You must require that a copy of the statement described in § 29.205 be given to each employee who will be engaged in the performance of any Federal award.

§ 29.215 What must I include in my drug-free awareness program?

You must establish an ongoing drug-free awareness program to inform employees about—

(a) The dangers of drug abuse in the workplace;

(b) Your policy of maintaining a drug-free workplace;

(c) Any available drug counseling, rehabilitation, and employee assistance programs; and

(d) The penalties that you may impose upon them for drug abuse violations occurring in the workplace.

§ 29.220 By when must I publish my drug-free workplace statement and establish my drug-free awareness program?

If you are a new recipient that does not already have a policy statement as described in § 29.205 and an ongoing awareness program as described in § 29.215, you must publish the statement and establish the program by the time given in the following table:

If	then you
(a) The performance period of the award is less than 30 days	must have the policy statement and program in place as soon as possible, but before the date on which performance is expected to be completed.
(b) The performance period of the award is 30 days or more ...	must have the policy statement and program in place within 30 days after award.
(c) You believe there are extraordinary circumstances that will require more than 30 days for you to publish the policy statement and establish the awareness program.	may ask the DoC awarding official to give you more time to do so. The amount of additional time, if any, to be given is at the discretion of the awarding official.

§ 29.225 What actions must I take concerning employees who are convicted of drug violations in the workplace?

There are two actions you must take if an employee is convicted of a drug violation in the workplace:

(a) First, you must notify Federal agencies if an employee who is engaged in the performance of an award informs you about a conviction, as required by § 29.205(c)(2), or you otherwise learn of the conviction. Your notification to the Federal agencies must__

(1) Be in writing;

(2) Include the employee's position title;

(3) Include the identification number(s) of each affected award;

(4) Be sent within ten calendar days after you learn of the conviction; and

(5) Be sent to every Federal agency on whose award the convicted employee was working. It must be sent to every awarding official or his or her official designee, unless the Federal agency has specified a central point for the receipt of the notices.

(b) Second, within 30 calendar days of learning about an employee's conviction, you must either__

(1) Take appropriate personnel action against the employee, up to and including termination, consistent with the requirements of the Rehabilitation Act of 1973 (29 U.S.C. 794), as amended; or

(2) Require the employee to participate satisfactorily in a drug abuse assistance or rehabilitation program approved for these purposes by a Federal, State or local health, law enforcement, or other appropriate agency.

§ 29.230 How and when must I identify workplaces?

(a) You must identify all known workplaces under each DoC award. A failure to do so is a violation of your drug-free workplace requirements. You may identify the workplaces__

(1) To the DoC official that is making the award, either at the time of application or upon award; or

(2) In documents that you keep on file in your offices during the performance of the award, in which case you must make the information available for inspection upon request by DoC officials or their designated representatives.

(b) Your workplace identification for an award must include the actual address of buildings (or parts of buildings) or other sites where work under the award takes place. Categorical descriptions may be used (e.g., all vehicles of a mass transit authority or State highway department while in operation, State employees in each local unemployment office, performers in concert halls or radio studios).

(c) If you identified workplaces to the DoC awarding official at the time of application or award, as described in paragraph (a)(1) of this section, and any workplace that you identified changes during the performance of the award, you must inform the DoC awarding official.

Subpart C—Requirements for Recipients Who Are Individuals

§ 29.300 What must I do to comply with this part if I am an individual recipient?

As a condition of receiving a(n) DoC award, if you are an individual recipient, you must agree that—

(a) You will not engage in the unlawful manufacture, distribution, dispensing, possession, or use of a controlled substance in conducting any activity related to the award; and

(b) If you are convicted of a criminal drug offense resulting from a violation occurring during the conduct of any award activity, you will report the conviction:

(1) In writing.

(2) Within 10 calendar days of the conviction.

(3) To the DoC awarding official or other designee for each award that you currently have, unless § 29.301 or the award document designates a central point for the receipt of the notices. When notice is made to a central point, it must include the identification number(s) of each affected award.

§ 29.301 [Reserved]

Subpart D—Responsibilities of DoC Awarding Officials

§ 29.400 What are my responsibilities as a DoC awarding official?

As a DoC awarding official, you must obtain each recipient's agreement, as a condition of the award, to comply with the requirements in—

(a) Subpart B of this part, if the recipient is not an individual; or

(b) Subpart C of this part, if the recipient is an individual.

Subpart E—Violations of This Part and Consequences

§ 29.500 How are violations of this part determined for recipients other than individuals?

A recipient other than an individual is in violation of the requirements of this part if the Secretary of Commerce or designee determines, in writing, that—

(a) The recipient has violated the requirements of subpart B of this part; or

(b) The number of convictions of the recipient's employees for violating criminal drug statutes in the workplace is large enough to indicate that the recipient has failed to make a good faith effort to provide a drug-free workplace.

§ 29.505 How are violations of this part determined for recipients who are individuals?

An individual recipient is in violation of the requirements of this part if the Secretary of Commerce or designee determines, in writing, that—

(a) The recipient has violated the requirements of subpart C of this part; or

(b) The recipient is convicted of a criminal drug offense resulting from a violation occurring during the conduct of any award activity.

§ 29.510 What actions will the Federal Government take against a recipient determined to have violated this part?

If a recipient is determined to have violated this part, as described in § 29.500 or § 29.505, the Department of Commerce may take one or more of the following actions—

(a) Suspension of payments under the award;

(b) Suspension or termination of the award; and

(c) Suspension or debarment of the recipient under 15 CFR Part 26, for a period not to exceed five years.

§ 29.515 Are there any exceptions to those actions?

The Secretary of Commerce may waive with respect to a particular award, in writing, a suspension of payments under an award, suspension or termination of an award, or suspension or debarment of a recipient if the Secretary of Commerce determines that such a waiver would be in the public interest. This exception authority cannot be delegated to any other official.

Subpart F—Definitions

§ 29.605 Award.

Award means an award of financial assistance by the Department of Commerce or other Federal agency directly to a recipient.

(a) The term award includes:

(1) A Federal grant or cooperative agreement, in the form of money or property in lieu of money.

(2) A block grant or a grant in an entitlement program, whether or not the grant is exempted from coverage under the Governmentwide rule 15 CFR Part 24 that implements OMB Circular A–102 (for availability, see 5 CFR 1310.3) and specifies uniform administrative requirements.

(b) The term award does not include:

(1) Technical assistance that provides services instead of money.

(2) Loans.

(3) Loan guarantees.

(4) Interest subsidies.

(5) Insurance.

(6) Direct appropriations.

(7) Veterans' benefits to individuals (*i.e.*, any benefit to veterans, their families, or survivors by virtue of the service of a veteran in the Armed Forces of the United States).

§ 29.610 Controlled substance.

Controlled substance means a controlled substance in schedules I through V of the Controlled Substances Act (21 U.S.C. 812), and as further defined by regulation at 21 CFR 1308.11 through 1308.15.

§29.615 Conviction.

Conviction means a finding of guilt (including a plea of nolo contendere) or imposition of sentence, or both, by any judicial body charged with the responsibility to determine violations of the Federal or State criminal drug statutes.

§29.620 Cooperative agreement.

Cooperative agreement means an award of financial assistance that, consistent with 31 U.S.C. 6305, is used to enter into the same kind of relationship as a grant (see definition of grant in §29.650), except that substantial involvement is expected between the Federal agency and the recipient when carrying out the activity contemplated by the award. The term does not include cooperative research and development agreements as defined in 15 U.S.C. 3710a.

§29.625 Criminal drug statute.

Criminal drug statute means a Federal or non-Federal criminal statute involving the manufacture, distribution, dispensing, use, or possession of any controlled substance.

§29.630 Debarment.

Debarment means an action taken by a Federal agency to prohibit a recipient from participating in Federal Government procurement contracts and covered nonprocurement transactions. A recipient so prohibited is debarred, in accordance with the Federal Acquisition Regulation for procurement contracts (48 CFR part 9, subpart 9.4) and the common rule, Government-wide Debarment and Suspension (Nonprocurement), that implements Executive Order 12549 and Executive Order 12689.

§29.635 Drug-free workplace.

Drug-free workplace means a site for the performance of work done in connection with a specific award at which employees of the recipient are prohibited from engaging in the unlawful manufacture, distribution, dispensing, possession, or use of a controlled substance.

§29.640 Employee.

(a) *Employee* means the employee of a recipient directly engaged in the performance of work under the award, including—

(1) All direct charge employees;

(2) All indirect charge employees, unless their impact or involvement in the performance of work under the award is insignificant to the performance of the award; and

(3) Temporary personnel and consultants who are directly engaged in the performance of work under the award and who are on the recipient's payroll.

(b) This definition does not include workers not on the payroll of the recipient (e.g., volunteers, even if used to meet a matching requirement; consultants or independent contractors not on the payroll; or employees of subrecipients or subcontractors in covered workplaces).

§29.645 Federal agency or agency.

Federal agency or agency means any United States executive department, military department, government corporation, government controlled corporation, any other establishment in the executive branch (including the Executive Office of the President), or any independent regulatory agency.

§29.650 Grant.

Grant means an award of financial assistance that, consistent with 31 U.S.C. 6304, is used to enter into a relationship—

(a) The principal purpose of which is to transfer a thing of value to the recipient to carry out a public purpose of support or stimulation authorized by a law of the United States, rather than to acquire property or services for the Federal Government's direct benefit or use; and

(b) In which substantial involvement is not expected between the Federal agency and the recipient when carrying out the activity contemplated by the award.

§29.655 Individual.

Individual means a natural person.

§ 29.660 Recipient.

Recipient means any individual, corporation, partnership, association, unit of government (except a Federal agency) or legal entity, however organized, that receives an award directly from a Federal agency.

§ 29.665 State.

State means any of the States of the United States, the District of Columbia, the Commonwealth of Puerto Rico, or any territory or possession of the United States.

§ 29.670 Suspension.

Suspension means an action taken by a Federal agency that immediately prohibits a recipient from participating in Federal Government procurement contracts and covered nonprocurement transactions for a temporary period, pending completion of an investigation and any judicial or administrative proceedings that may ensue. A recipient so prohibited is suspended, in accordance with the Federal Acquisition Regulation for procurement contracts (48 CFR part 9, subpart 9.4) and the common rule, Governmentwide Debarment and Suspension (Nonprocurement), that implements Executive Order 12549 and Executive Order 12689. Suspension of a recipient is a distinct and separate action from suspension of an award or suspension of payments under an award.

Subtitle B—Regulations Relating to Commerce and Foreign Trade

CHAPTER I—BUREAU OF THE CENSUS, DEPARTMENT OF COMMERCE

PART 30—FOREIGN TRADE REGULATIONS

Subpart A—General Requirements

Subpart B—Export Control and Licensing Requirements

Subpart C—Special Provisions and Specific-Type Transactions

Subpart D—Exemptions From the Requirements for the Filing of Electronic Export Information

Subpart E—General Carrier and Manifest Requirements

Subpart F—Import Requirements

Subpart G—General Administrative Provisions

Subpart H—Penalties

AUTHORITY: 5 U.S.C. 301; 13 U.S.C. 301–307; Reorganization plan No. 5 of 1990 (3 CFR 1949–1953 Comp., p.1004); Department of Commerce Organization Order No. 35–2A, July 22, 1987, as amended and No. 35–2B, December 20, 1996, as amended; Public Law 107–228, 116 Stat. 1350.

SOURCE: 73 FR 31555, June 2, 2008, unless otherwise noted.

Subpart A—General Requirements

§30.1 Purpose and definitions.

(a) This part sets forth the Foreign Trade Regulations (FTR) as required under the provisions of Title 13, United States Code (U.S.C.), Chapter 9, section 301. These regulations are revised pursuant to provisions of the Foreign Relations Authorization Act, Public Law 107–228 (the Act). This Act authorizes the Secretary of Commerce, with the concurrence of the Secretary of State and the Secretary of Homeland Security, to publish regulations mandating that all persons who are required to file export information under Chapter 9 of 13 U.S.C., file such information through the Automated Export System (AES) for all shipments where a Shipper's Export Declaration (SED) was previously required. The law further authorizes the Secretary of Commerce to issue regulations regarding imposition of civil and criminal penalties for violations of the provisions of the Act and these regulations.

(b) Electronic filing through the AES strengthens the U.S. government's ability to prevent the export of certain items to unauthorized destinations and/or end users because the AES aids in targeting, identifying, and when necessary confiscating suspicious or illegal shipments prior to exportation.

(c) Definitions used in the FTR. As used in this part, the following definitions apply:

AES applicant. The USPPI or authorized agent who applies to the Census Bureau for authorization to report export information electronically to the AES, or through AES*Direct* or its related applications.

AES*Direct.* A free Internet application supported by the Census Bureau that allows USPPIs, their authorized agent, or the authorized agent of the FPPI to transmit EEI through the AES via the Internet at *http://www.aesdirect.gov.*

AES downtime filing citation. A statement used in place of a proof of filing citation when the AES or AES*Direct* computer systems experiences a major failure. The downtime filing citation must appear on the bill of lading, air waybill, export shipping instructions, or other commercial loading documents.

AES participant application (APA). An electronic submission of an individual or a company's desire to participate in the AES. It sets forth a commitment to develop, maintain, and adhere to CBP and Census Bureau performance requirements and operational standards.

Air waybill. The shipping document used for the transportation of air freight includes conditions, limitations of liability, shipping instructions, description of commodity, and applicable transportation charges. It is generally similar to a straight non-negotiable bill of lading and is used for similar purposes.

Annotation. An explanatory note (e.g., proof of filing citation, postdeparture filing citation, AES downtime filing citation, exemption, or exclusion legend) placed on the bill of lading, air waybill, export shipping instructions, or other loading document.

Authorized agent. An individual or legal entity physically located in or otherwise under the jurisdiction of the United States that has obtained power of attorney or written authorization from a USPPI or FPPI to act on its behalf, and for purposes of this part, to complete and file the EEI.

Automated Broker Interface (ABI). A CBP system through which an importer or licensed customs broker can electronically file entry and entry summary data on goods imported into the United States.

Automated Export System (AES). The system, including AESDirect, for collecting EEI information (or any successor document) from persons exporting goods from the United States, Puerto Rico, or the U.S. Virgin Islands; between Puerto Rico and the United States; and to the U.S. Virgin Islands from the United States or Puerto Rico.

Automated Export System Trade Interface Requirements (AESTIR). The document that describes the operational requirements of the AES. The AESTIR presents record formats and other reference information used in the AES.

Automated Foreign Trade Zone Reporting Program (AFTZRP). The electronic reporting program used to transmit statistical data on goods admitted into a FTZ directly to the Census Bureau.

Bill of lading (BL). A document that establishes the terms of a contract between a shipper and a transportation company under which freight is to be moved between specified points for a specified charge. Usually prepared by the authorized agent on forms issued by the carrier, it serves as a document of title, a contract of carriage, and a receipt for goods.

Bond. An instrument used by CBP as security to ensure the payment of duties, taxes and fees and/or compliance with certain requirements such as the submission of manifest information.

Bonded warehouse. An approved private warehouse used for the storage of goods until duties or taxes are paid and the goods are properly released by CBP. Bonds must be posted by the warehouse proprietor and by the importer to indemnify the government if the goods are released improperly.

Booking. A reservation made with a carrier for a shipment of goods on a specific voyage, flight, truck or train.

Bureau of Industry and Security (BIS). This bureau within the U.S. Department of Commerce is concerned with the advancement of U.S. national security, foreign policy, and economic interests. The BIS is responsible for regulating the export of sensitive goods and technologies; enforcing export control, antiboycott, and public safety laws; cooperating with and assisting other countries on export control and strategic trade issues; and assisting U.S. industry to comply with international arms control agreements.

Buyer. The principal in the export transaction that purchases the commodities for delivery to the ultimate consignee. The buyer and ultimate consignee may be the same.

Cargo. Goods being transported.

Carnet. An international customs document that allows the carnet holder to import into the United States or export to foreign countries certain goods on a temporary basis without the payment of duties.

Carrier. An individual or legal entity in the business of transporting passengers or goods. Airlines, trucking companies, railroad companies, shipping lines, pipeline companies, and slot charterers are all examples of carriers.

Civil penalty. A monetary penalty imposed on a USPPI, authorized agent, FPPI, carrier, or other party to the transaction for violating the FTR, including failing to file export information, filing false or misleading information, filing information late, and/or using the AES to further any illegal activity, and/or violating any other regulations of this part.

Commerce Control List (CCL). A list of items found in Supplement No. 1 to Part 774 of the EAR. Supplement No. 2 to Part 774 of the EAR contains the General Technology and Software Notes relevant to entries contained in the CCL.

Compliance alert. An electronic response sent to the filer by the AES when the shipment was not reported in accordance with this part (e.g., late filing). The filer is required to review their filing practices and take steps to conform with export reporting requirements.

Consignee. The person or entity named in a freight contract, a contract of carriage that designates to whom goods have been consigned, and that has the legal right to claim the goods at the destination.

Consignment. Delivery of goods from a USPPI (the consignor) to an agent (consignee) under agreement that the agent sells the goods for the account of the USPPI.

Container. A uniform, reusable metal "box" in which goods are shipped by vessel, truck, or rail as defined in the

International Convention for Safe Containers, as amended (TIAS 9037; 29 U.S.T. 3709).

Controlling agency. The agency responsible for the license determination on specified goods exported from the United States.

Cost of goods sold. Cost of goods is the sum of expenses incurred in the USPPI acquisition or production of the goods.

Country of origin. The country where the goods were mined, grown, or manufactured or where each foreign material used or incorporated in a good underwent a change in tariff classification indicating a substantial transformation under the applicable rule of origin for the good. The country of origin for U.S. imports are reported in terms of the International Standards Organization (ISO) codes designated in the Schedule C, Classification of Country and Territory Designations.

Country of ultimate destination. The country where the goods are to be consumed, further processed, stored, or manufactured, as known to the USPPI at the time of export.

Criminal penalty. For the purpose of this part, a penalty imposed for knowingly or willfully violating the FTR, including failing to file export information, filing false or misleading information, filing information late, and/or using the AES to further illegal activity. The criminal penalty includes fines, imprisonment, and/or forfeiture.

Customs broker. An individual or entity licensed to enter and clear imported goods through CBP for another individual or entity.

Destination. The foreign location to which a shipment is consigned.

Distributor. An agent who sells directly for a supplier and maintains an inventory of the supplier's products.

Domestic exports. Goods that are grown, produced, or manufactured in the United States, and commodities of foreign origin that have been changed in the United States, including changes made in a U.S. FTZ, from the form in which they were imported, or that have been enhanced in value or improved in condition by further processing or manufacturing in the United States.

Drayage. The charge made for hauling freight, carts, drays, or trucks.

Dun & Bradstreet Number (DUNS). The DUNS Number is a unique 9-digit identification sequence that provides identifiers to single business entities while linking corporate family structures together.

Dunnage. Materials placed around cargo to prevent shifting or damage while in transit.

Duty. A charge imposed on the import of goods. Duties are generally based on the value of the goods (ad valorem duties), some other factor, such as weight or quantity (specific duties), or a combination of value and other factors (compound duties).

Electronic export information (EEI). The electronic export data as filed in the AES. This is the electronic equivalent of the export data formerly collected as Shipper's Export Declaration (SED) information and now mandated to be filed through the AES or AESDirect.

Employer identification number (EIN). The USPPI's Internal Revenue Service (IRS) EIN is the 9-digit numerical code as reported on the Employer's Quarterly Federal Tax Return, Treasury Form 941.

End user. The person abroad that receives and ultimately uses the exported or reexported items. The end user is not an authorized agent or intermediary, but may be the FPPI or ultimate consignee.

Enhancement. A change or modification to goods that increases their value or improves their condition.

Entry number. Consists of a three-position entry filer code and a seven-position transaction code, plus a check digit assigned by the entry filer as a tracking number for goods entered into the United States.

Equipment number. The identification number for shipping equipment, such as container or igloo (Unit Load Device (ULD)) number, truck license number, or rail car number.

Exclusions. Transactions outside of the scope of the FTR that are excluded from the requirement of filing EEI.

Exemption. A specific reason as cited within this part that eliminates the requirement for filing EEI.

Exemption legend. A notation placed on the bill of lading, air waybill, export shipping instructions, or other commercial loading document that describes the basis for not filing EEI for an export transaction. The exemption legend shall reference the number of the section or provision in the FTR where the particular exemption is provided (See Appendix D to this part).

Export. To send or transport goods out of a country.

Export Administration Regulations (EAR). Regulations administered by the BIS that, among other things, provide specific instructions on the use and types of export licenses required for certain commodities, software, and technology. These regulations are located in 15 CFR parts 730 through 774.

Export control. Governmental control of exports for statistical or strategic and short supply or national security purposes, and/or for foreign policy purposes.

Export Control Classification Number (ECCN). The number used to identify items on the CCL, Supplement No. 1 to Part 774 of the EAR. The ECCN consists of a set of digits and a letter. Items that are not classified under an ECCN are designated "EAR99." Section 738.2 of the EAR describes the ECCN format.

Export license. A controlling agency's document authorizing export of particular goods in specific quantities or values to a particular destination. Issuing agencies include, but are not limited to, the U.S. State Department; the BIS; the Bureau of Alcohol, Tobacco, and Firearms; and the Drug Enforcement Administration permit to export.

Export statistics. The measure of quantity and value of goods (except for shipments to U.S. military forces overseas) moving out of the United States to foreign countries, whether such goods are exported from within the Customs territory of the United States, a CBP bonded warehouse, or a U.S. Foreign Trade Zone (FTZ).

Export value. The value of the goods at the U.S. port of export. The value shall be the selling price (or the cost if the goods are not sold), including inland or domestic freight, insurance, and other charges to the U.S. seaport, airport, or land border port of export. Cost of goods is the sum of expenses incurred in the USPPI's acquisition or production of the goods. (See §30.6(a)(17)).

Fatal error message. An electronic response sent to the filer by the AES when invalid or missing data has been encountered, the EEI has been rejected, and the information is not on file in the AES. The filer is required to immediately correct the problem, correct the data, and retransmit the EEI.

Filers. Those USPPIs or authorized agents (of either the USPPI or the FPPI) who have been approved to file EEI directly in the AES system or AES*Direct* Internet application.

Filing electronic export information. The act of entering the EEI in the AES.

Foreign entity. A person that temporarily enters into the United States and purchases or obtains goods for export. This person does not physically maintain an office or residence in the United States. This is a special class of USPPI.

Foreign exports. Commodities of foreign origin that have entered the United States for consumption, for entry into a CBP bonded warehouse or U.S. FTZ, and which, at the time of exportation, are in substantially the same condition as when imported.

Foreign principal party in interest (FPPI). The party shown on the transportation document to whom final delivery or end-use of the goods will be made. This party may be the ultimate consignee.

Foreign Trade Zone (FTZ). Specially licensed commercial and industrial areas in or near ports of entry where foreign and domestic goods, including raw materials, components, and finished goods, may be brought in without being subject to payment of customs duties. Goods brought into these zones may be stored, sold, exhibited, repacked, assembled, sorted, graded, cleaned, or otherwise manipulated prior to reexport or entry into the country's customs territory.

Forwarding agent. The person in the United States who is authorized by the principal party in interest to facilitate the movement of the cargo from the United States to the foreign destination and/or prepare and file the required documentation.

Goods. Merchandise, supplies, raw materials, and products or any other item identified by a Harmonized Tariff System (HTS) code.

Harmonized system. A method of classifying goods for international trade developed by the Customs Cooperation Council (now the World Customs Organization).

Harmonized Tariff Schedule of the United States (HTSUS). An organized listing of goods and their duty rates, developed by the U.S. International Trade Commission, which is used by CBP as the basis for classifying imported products, including establishing the duty to be charged and providing statistical information about imports and exports.

Imports. All goods physically brought into the United States, including:

(1) Goods of foreign origin, and

(2) Goods of domestic origin returned to the United States without substantial transformation affecting a change in tariff classification under an applicable rule of origin.

Inbond. A procedure administered by CBP under which goods are transported or warehoused under CBP supervision until the goods are either formally entered into the customs territory of the United States and duties are paid, or until they are exported from the United States. The procedure is so named because the cargo moves under a bond (financial liability assured by the principal on the bond) from the gateway seaport, airport, or land border port and remains "inbond" until CBP releases the cargo at the inland Customs point or at the port of export.

Inland freight. The cost to ship goods between points inland and the seaport, airport, or land border port of exportation, other than baggage, express mail, or regular mail.

Intermediate consignee. The person or entity in the foreign country who acts as an agent for the principal party in interest with the purpose of effecting delivery of items to the ultimate consignee. The intermediate consignee may be a bank, forwarding agent, or other person who acts as an agent for a principal party in interest.

Internal Transaction Number (ITN). The AES generated number assigned to a shipment confirming that an EEI transaction was accepted and is on file in the AES.

International Standards Organization (ISO) Country Codes. The 2-position alphabetic ISO code for countries used to identify countries for which shipments are reportable.

International Traffic in Arms Regulations (ITAR). Regulations administered by the Directorate of Defense Trade Controls within the U.S. State Department that provide for the control of the export and temporary import of defense articles and defense services. These regulations are located in 22 CFR 120–130.

Interplant correspondence. Records or documents from a U.S. firm to its subsidiary or affiliate, whether in the United States or overseas.

In-transit. Goods shipped through the United States, Puerto Rico, or the U.S. Virgin Islands from one foreign country or area to another foreign country or area without entering the consumption channels of the United States.

License applicant. The person who applies for an export or reexport license. (For example, obtaining a license for commodities, software, or technology that are listed on the CCL.)

License exception. An authorization that allows a USPPI or other appropriate party to export or reexport under stated conditions, items subject to the EAR that would otherwise require a license under the EAR. The BIS License Exceptions are currently contained in Part 740 of the EAR (15 CFR part 740).

Loading document. A document that establishes the terms of a contract between a shipper and a transportation company under which freight is to be moved between points for a specific charge. It is usually prepared by the shipper and actuated by the carrier and serves as a document of title, a contract of carriage, and a receipt for goods. Examples of loading documents include the air waybill, inland bill of lading, ocean bill of lading, and through bill of lading.

Manifest. A collection of documents, including forms, such as the cargo declaration and annotated bills of lading, that lists and describes the cargo contents of a carrier, container, or warehouse. Carriers required to file manifests with CBP Port Director must include an AES filing citation, or exemption or exclusion legend for all cargo being transported.

Merchandise. Goods, wares, and chattels of every description, and includes merchandise the exportation of which is prohibited, and monetary instruments as defined in 31 U.S.C. 5312.

Method of transportation. The method by which goods arrive in or are exported from the United States by way of seaports, airports, or land border crossing points. Methods of transportation include vessel, air, truck, rail, or other.

North American Free Trade Agreement (NAFTA). The formal agreement, or treaty, among Canada, Mexico, and the United States to promote trade amongst the three countries. It includes measures for the elimination of tariffs and nontariff barriers to trade, as well as numerous specific provisions concerning the conduct of trade and investment.

Office of Foreign Assets Control (OFAC). An agency within the U.S. Department of the Treasury that administers and enforces economic and trade sanctions based on U.S. foreign policy and national security goals against targeted foreign countries, terrorists, international narcotics traffickers, and those engaged in activities related to the proliferation of weapons of mass destruction. The OFAC acts under Presidential wartime and national emergency powers, as well as authority granted by specific legislation, to impose controls on transactions and freeze foreign assets under U.S. jurisdiction.

Order party. The person in the United States that conducts the direct negotiations or correspondence with the foreign purchaser or ultimate consignee and who, as a result of these negotiations, receives the order from the FPPI. If a U.S. order party directly arranges for the sale and export of goods to the FPPI, the U.S. order party shall be listed as the USPPI in the EEI.

Packing list. A list showing the number and kinds of items being shipped, as well as other information needed for transportation purposes.

Partnership agencies. U.S. government agencies that have statistical and analytical reporting and/or monitoring and enforcement responsibilities related to AES postdeparture filing privileges.

Party ID type. Identifies whether the Party ID is an EIN, DUNS, or Foreign Entity reported to the AES, for example, E=EIN, D=DUNS, T=Foreign Entity.

Person. Any natural person, corporation partnership or other legal entity of any kind, domestic or foreign.

Port of export. The seaport or airport where the goods are loaded on the exporting carrier that is taking the goods out of the United States, or the port where exports by overland transportation cross the U.S. border into a foreign country. In the case of an export by mail, use port code 8000.

Postdeparture filing. The privilege granted to approved USPPIs for their EEI to be filed up to 10 calendar days after the date of export, *i.e.*, the date the goods are scheduled to cross the U.S. border.

Postdeparture filing citation. A notation placed on the bill of lading, air waybill, export shipping instructions, or other commercial loading documents that states that the EEI will be filed after departure of the carrier. (See Appendix D of this part.)

Power of attorney. A legal authorization, in writing, from a USPPI or FPPI stating that the agent has authority to act as the principal party's true and lawful agent for purposes of preparing and filing the EEI in accordance with the laws and regulations of the United States.

Primary benefit. Receiving the majority payment or exchange of item of value or other legal consideration resulting from an export trade transaction; usually monetary.

Principal parties in interest. Those persons in a transaction that receive the primary benefit, monetary or otherwise, from the transaction. Generally, the principals in a transaction are the seller and the buyer. In most cases, the forwarding or other agent is not a principal party in interest.

Proof of filing citation. A notation placed on the bill of lading, air waybill, export shipping instructions, or other commercial loading document, usually for carrier use, that provides evidence that the EEI has been filed and accepted in the AES.

Reexport. For statistical purposes: These are exports of foreign-origin goods that have previously entered the United States, Puerto Rico, or the U.S. Virgin Islands for consumption, entry into a CBP bonded warehouse, or a U.S. FTZ, and at the time of exportation, have undergone no change in form or condition or enhancement in value by further manufacturing in the United States, Puerto Rico, the U.S. Virgin Islands, or U.S. FTZs. For the purpose of goods subject to export controls (e.g., U.S. Munitions List (USML) articles) these are shipments of U.S.-origin products from one foreign destination to another.

Related party transaction. A transaction involving trade between a USPPI and an ultimate consignee where either party owns directly or indirectly 10 percent or more of the other party.

Remission. The cancellation or release from a penalty, including fines, and/or forfeiture, under this part.

Retention. The necessary act of keeping all documentation pertaining to an export transaction for a period of at least five years for an EEI filing, or a time frame designated by the controlling agency for licensed shipments, whichever is longer.

Routed export transaction. A transaction in which the FPPI authorizes a U.S. agent to facilitate export of items from the United States on its behalf and prepare and file the EEI.

Schedule B. The Statistical Classification of Domestic and Foreign Commodities Exported from the United States. These 10-digit commodity classification numbers are administered by the Census Bureau and cover everything from live animals and food products to computers and airplanes. It should also be noted that all import and export codes used by the United States are based on the Harmonized Tariff System.

Schedule C. The Classification of Country and Territory Designations. The Schedule C provides a list of country of origin codes. The country of origin is reported in terms of the International Standards Organization codes.

Schedule D. The Classification of CBP districts and ports. The Schedule D provides a list of CBP districts and ports and the corresponding numeric codes used in compiling U.S. foreign trade statistics.

Schedule K. The Classification of Foreign Ports by Geographic Trade Area and Country. The Schedule K lists the major seaports of the world that directly handle waterborne shipments in the foreign trade of the United States, and includes numeric codes to identify these ports. This schedule is maintained by the U.S. Army Corps of Engineers.

Seller. A principal in the transaction, usually the manufacturer, producer, wholesaler, or distributor of the goods, that receives the monetary benefit or other consideration for the exported goods.

Service center. A company, entity, or organization which has been certified and approved to only transmit complete EEI to the AES.

Shipment. Unless as otherwise provided, all goods being sent from one USPPI to one consignee to a single country of destination on a single conveyance and on the same day.

Shipment reference number. A unique identification number assigned to the shipment by the filer for reference purposes. This number must remain unique for a period of five years.

Shipper's Export Declaration. The DOC paper form used under the FTSR to collect information from a person exporting from the United States. This form was used for compiling the official U.S. export statistics for the United States and for export control purposes.

Shipping weight. The total weight of a shipment in kilograms including goods and packaging.

Split shipment. A shipment booked for export on one aircraft, but split by the carrier and sent on two or more aircrafts of the same carrier.

Subzone. A special purpose foreign trade zone established as part of a foreign trade zone project with a limited purpose that cannot be accommodated within an existing zone. Subzones are often established to serve the needs of a specific company and may be located within an existing facility of the company.

Tariff schedule. A comprehensive list or schedule of goods with applicable duty rates to be paid or charged for each listed article as it enters or leaves a country.

Transmitting electronic export information. The act of sending the completed EEI to the AES.

Transportation reference number. A reservation number assigned by the carrier to hold space on the carrier for cargo being shipped. It is the booking number for vessel shipments and the master air waybill number for air shipments, the bill of lading number for rail shipments, and the freight or pro bill for truck shipments.

Ultimate consignee. The person, party, or designee that is located abroad and actually receives the export shipment. This party may be the end user or the FPPI.

United States Munitions List (USML). Articles and services designated for defense purposes under the ITAR and specified in 22 CFR 121.

Unlading. The physical removal of cargo from an aircraft, truck, rail, or vessel.

U.S. Customs and Border Protection (CBP). CBP is the unified border agency within the DHS charged with the management, control, and protection of our Nation's borders at and between the official ports of entry to the United States. CBP is charged with keeping terrorist and terrorist weapons from entering the country and enforcing customs, immigration, agricultural and countless other laws of the United States.

U.S. Immigration and Customs Enforcement (ICE). An agency within the DHS that is responsible for enforcing customs, immigration and related laws and investigating violations of laws to secure the Nation's borders.

U.S. principal party in interest (USPPI). The person or legal entity in the United States that receives the primary benefit, monetary or otherwise, from the export transaction. Generally, that person or entity is the U.S. seller, manufacturer, or order party, or the foreign entity while in the United States when purchasing or obtaining the goods for export.

Vehicle Identification Number (VIN). A number issued by the manufacturer and used for the identification of a self-propelled vehicle.

Verify message. An electronic response sent to the filer by the AES when an unlikely condition is found.

Violation of the FTR. Failure of the USPPI, FPPI, authorized agent of the USPPI, FPPI, carrier, or other party to the transaction to comply with the requirements set forth in 15 CFR 30, for each export shipment.

Warning message. An electronic response sent to the filer by the AES when certain incomplete and conflicting data reporting conditions are encountered.

Wholesaler/distributor. An agent who sells directly for a supplier and maintains an inventory of the supplier's products.

Written authorization. A legal authorization, in writing, by the USPPI or FPPI stating that the agent has authority to act as the USPPI's or FPPI's true and lawful agent for purposes of preparing and filing the EEI in accordance with the laws and regulations of the United States.

Zone admission number. A unique and sequential number assigned by a FTZ operator or user for shipments admitted to a zone.

[73 FR 31555, June 2, 2008, as amended at 74 FR 38916, Aug. 5, 2009]

EFFECTIVE DATE NOTE: At 78 FR 16373, Mar. 14, 2013, §30.1 was amended in paragraph (c) by revising the terms and definitions for "AES downtime filing citation," "Annotation," "Automated Export System Trade Interface Requirements (AESTIR)," "Country of ultimate destination," "Filers," "Foreign Export," "Foreign principal party in interest (FPPI)," "Foreign Trade Zone," "Harmonized Tariff Schedule of the United States Annotated (HTSUSA)," "Method of transportation," "Port of export," "Postdeparture filing," "Power of attorney," "Shipment," "Shipment reference number," "Shipper's Export Declaration (SED)," "Split shipment," "U.S. Customs and Border Protection (CBP)," and "Written Authorization;" and removing the definition for "Automated Foreign Trade Zone Reporting Program (AFTZRP)," "Loading Document,"

"Export Value"; and by adding alphabetically the definitions for "Commercial loading document," "Diplomatic pouch," "Electronic CBP Form 214 Admissions (e214)," "Filer ID," "Foreign port of unlading," "Household goods," "International waters," "Issued banknote," "Mass-market software," "Non Vessel Operating Common Carrier (NVOCC)," "Shipping documents," "Transshipment," "Value," and "Voluntary Self-Disclosure (VSD)", effective Jan. 8, 2014. At 78 FR 67928, Nov. 13, 2013, the effective date was delayed until Apr. 5, 2014. For the convenience of the user, the added and revised text is set forth as follows:

§ 30.1 Purpose and definitions.

* * * * *

(c) * * *

AES downtime filing citation. A statement used in place of a proof of filing citation when the AES or AES *Direct* computer systems experience a major failure. The citation must appear on the bill of lading, air waybill, export shipping instructions, or other commercial loading documents. The downtime filing citation is not to be used when the filer's system is down or experiencing delays.

* * * * *

Annotation. An explanatory note (e.g., proof of filing citation, postdeparture filing citation, AES downtime filing citation, exemption or exclusion legend) placed on the bill of lading, air waybill, export shipping instructions, or other commercial loading documents.

* * * * *

Automated Export System Trade Interface Requirements (AESTIR). The document that describes the technical and operational requirements of the AES. The AESTIR presents record formats and other reference information used in the AES.

* * * * *

Commercial loading document. A document that establishes the terms of a contract between a shipper and a transportation company under which freight is to be moved between points for a specific charge. It is usually prepared by the shipper or the shipper's agent or the carrier and serves as a contract of carriage. Examples of commercial loading documents include the air waybill, ocean bill of lading, truck bill and rail bill of lading.

* * * * *

Country of ultimate destination. The country where the goods are to be consumed, further processed, stored, or manufactured, as known to the USPPI at the time of export. (See § 30.6(a)(5).

* * * * *

Diplomatic pouch. Any properly identified and sealed pouch, package, envelope, bag, or other container that is used to transport official correspondence, documents, and articles intended for official use, between embassies, legations, or consulates, and the foreign office of any government.

* * * * *

Electronic CBP Form 214 Admissions (e214). An automated CBP mechanism that allows importers, brokers, and zone operators to report FTZ admission information electronically via the CBP's Automated Broker Interface. The e214 is the electronic mechanism that replaced the Census Bureau's Automated Foreign Trade Zone Reporting Program (AFTZRP).

* * * * *

Filers. Those USPPIs or authorized agents (of either the USPPI or the FPPI) who have been approved to file EEI directly in the AES or AES*Direct* Internet application.

Filer ID. The Employer Identification Number or Dun & Bradstreet Number of the company or individual filing the export information in the Automated Export System.

* * * * *

Foreign exports. Commodities of foreign origin that have previously been admitted to a U.S. FTZ or entered the United States for consumption, including entry into a CBP bonded warehouse, and which, at the time of exportation, are in substantially the same condition as when imported.

Foreign port of unlading. The port in a foreign country where the goods are removed from the exporting carrier. The foreign port does not have to be located in the country of destination. The foreign port of unlading shall be reported in terms of the Schedule K, "Classification of CBP Foreign Ports by Geographic Trade Area and Country."

Foreign Principal Party in Interest (FPPI). The party abroad who purchases the goods for export or to whom final delivery or end-use of the goods will be made. This party may be the Ultimate Consignee.

Foreign Trade Zone (FTZ). Specially licensed commercial and industrial areas in or near ports of entry where foreign and domestic goods, including raw materials, components, and finished goods, may be brought in without being subject to payment of customs duties. Goods brought into these zones may be stored, sold, exhibited, repacked, assembled, sorted, graded, cleaned, manufactured, or otherwise manipulated prior to reexport or entry into the country's customs territory.

* * * * *

Harmonized Tariff Schedule of the United States Annotated (HTSUSA). An organized listing of goods and their duty rates, developed by the U.S. International Trade Commission, as the basis for classifying imported products.

Household goods. Usual and reasonable kinds and quantities of personal property necessary and appropriate for use by the USPPI in the USPPI's dwelling in a foreign country that are shipped under a bill of lading or an air waybill and are not intended for sale.

* * * * *

International waters. Waters located outside the U.S. territorial sea, which extends 12 nautical miles measured from the baselines of the United States, and outside the territory of any foreign country, including the territorial waters thereof. Note that vessels, platforms, buoys, undersea systems, and other similar structures that are located in international waters, but are attached permanently or temporarily to a country's continental shelf, are considered to be within the territory of that country.

* * * * *

Issued banknote. A promissory note intended to circulate as money, usually printed on paper or plastic, issued by a bank with a specific denomination, payable to an individual, entity or the bearer.

* * * * *

Kimberley Process Certificate (KPC). The document used to certify the origin of rough diamonds from sources which are free of conflict.

* * * * *

Mass-market software. Software that is produced in large numbers and made available to the public. It does not include software that is customized for a specific user.

* * * * *

Method of transportation. The method by which goods are exported from the United States by way of seaports, airports, or land border crossing points. Methods of transportation include vessel, air, truck, rail, mail or other. Method of transportation is synonymous with mode of transportation.

* * * * *

Non-Vessel Operating Common Carrier (NVOCC). A freight forwarder that acts as common carrier but does not operate the vessels by which ocean transportation is provided, and is a shipper in relation to the involved ocean common carrier.

* * * * *

Port of export. The port of export is the U.S. Customs and Border Protection (CBP) seaport or airport where the goods are loaded on the aircraft or vessel that is taking the goods out of the United States, or the CBP port where exports by overland transportation cross the U.S. border into Canada or Mexico. For EEI reporting purposes only, for goods loaded aboard an aircraft or vessel that stops at several ports before clearing to the foreign country, the port of export is the first CBP port where the goods were loaded. For goods off-loaded from the original conveyance to another conveyance (even if the aircraft or vessel belongs to the same carrier) at any of the ports, the port where the goods were loaded on the last conveyance before going foreign is the port of export. The port of export is reported in terms of Schedule D, "Classification of CBP Districts and Ports." Use port code 8000 for shipments by mail.

* * * * *

Postdeparture filing. The privilege granted to approved USPPIs for their EEI to be filed up to five (5) calendar days after the date of export.

* * * * *

Power of attorney. A legal authorization, in writing, from a USPPI or FPPI stating that an agent has authority to act as the principal party's true and lawful agent for purposes of preparing and filing the EEI in accordance with the laws and regulations of the United States. (See Appendix A of this part.)

* * * * *

Shipment. All goods being sent from one USPPI to one consignee located in a single country of destination on a single conveyance and on the same day. Except as noted in §30.2(a)(1)(iv), the EEI shall be filed when the value of the goods is over $2,500 per Schedule B or HTSUSA commodity classification code.

Shipment reference number. A unique identification number assigned to the shipment by the filer for reference purposes. The reuse of the shipment reference number is prohibited.

Shipper's Export Declaration (SED). The Department of Commerce paper form used under the Foreign Trade Statistics Regulations to collect information from an entity exporting from the United States. This form was used for compiling the official U.S. export statistics for the United States and for export control purposes. The SED became obsolete on October 1, 2008, with the implementation of the Foreign Trade Regulations (FTR) and has been superseded by the EEI filed in the AES or through the AES*Direct.*

Shipping documents. Documents that include but are not limited to commercial invoices, export shipping instructions, packing lists, bill of ladings and air waybills.

* * * * *

Split shipment. A shipment booked for export that is divided by the carrier in two or more shipments by the same mode of transportation from the same port within 24 hours.

* * * * *

Transshipment. The transfer of merchandise from the country or countries of origin through an intermediary country or countries to the country of ultimate destination.

* * * * *

U.S. Customs and Border Protection (CBP). The border agency within the Department of Homeland Security (DHS) charged with the management, control, and protection of our Nation's borders at and between the official ports of entry of the United States.

* * * * *

Value. The selling price (or the cost if the goods are not sold) in U.S. dollars, plus inland or domestic freight, insurance, and other charges to the U.S. seaport, airport, or land border port of export. Cost of goods is the sum of expenses incurred in the USPPI's acquisition or production of the goods. (See § 30.6(a)(17)).

* * * * *

Voluntary Self-Disclosure (VSD). A narrative account with supporting documentation that sufficiently describes suspected violations of the FTR. A VSD reflects due diligence in detecting, and correcting potential violation(s) when required information was not reported or when incorrect information was provided that violates the FTR.

* * * * *

Written authorization. An authorization, in writing, by the USPPI or FPPI stating that the agent has authority to act as the USPPI's or FPPI's true and lawful agent for purposes of preparing and filing the EEI in accordance with the laws and regulations of the United States. (See Appendix A of this part.)

§ 30.2 General requirements for filing Electronic Export Information (EEI).

(a) *Filing requirements*—(1) The EEI shall be filed through the AES by the United States Principal Party In Interest (USPPI), the USPPI's authorized agent, or the authorized U.S. agent of the Foreign Principal Party In Interest (FPPI) for all exports of physical goods, including shipments moving pursuant to orders received over the Internet. The Automated Export System (AES) is the electronic system for collecting Shipper's Export Declaration (SED) (or any successor document) information from persons exporting goods from the United States, Puerto Rico, Foreign Trade Zones (FTZs) located in the United States or Puerto Rico, the U.S. Virgin Islands, between Puerto Rico and the United States, and to the U.S. Virgin Islands from the United States or Puerto Rico. Exceptions, exclusions, and exemptions to this requirement are provided for in paragraph (d) of this section and Subpart D of this part. References to the AES also shall apply to AES*Direct* unless otherwise specified. For purposes of the regulations in this part, the SED information shall be referred to as EEI. Filing through the AES shall be done in accordance with the definitions, specifications, and requirements of the regulations in this part for all export shipments, except as specifically excluded in § 30.2(d) or exempted in Subpart D of this part, when shipped as follows:

(i) To foreign countries or areas, including free (foreign trade) zones located therein (see § 30.36 for exemptions for shipments from the United States to Canada) from any of the following:

(A) The United States, including the 50 states and the District of Columbia.

(B) Puerto Rico.

(C) FTZs located in the United States or Puerto Rico.

(D) The U.S. Virgin Islands.

(ii) Between any of the following nonforeign areas including goods previously admitted to customs warehouses or FTZs and moving under a U.S. Customs and Border Protection (CBP) bond:

(A) To Puerto Rico from the United States.

(B) To the United States from Puerto Rico.

(C) To the U.S. Virgin Islands from the United States or Puerto Rico.

(iii) The EEI shall be filed for goods moving as described in paragraphs (a)(1)(i) and (ii) of this section by any mode of transportation. (Instructions for filing EEI for vessels, aircraft, railway cars, and other carriers when sold while outside the areas described in paragraphs (a)(1)(i) and (ii) are covered in § 30.26.)

(iv) Notwithstanding exemptions in Subpart D, EEI shall be filed for the following types of export shipments, regardless of value:

(A) Requiring a Department of Commerce, Bureau of Industry and Security (BIS) license (15 CFR 730–774).

(B) Requiring a Department of State, Directorate of Defense Trade Controls (DDTC) license under the International Traffic in Arms Regulations (ITAR) (22 CFR Parts 120 through 130).

(C) Subject to the ITAR, but exempt from license requirements.

(D) Requiring a Department of Justice, Drug Enforcement Administration (DEA) export permit (21 CFR 1312).

(E) Destined for a country listed in Country Group E:1 as set forth in Supplement 1 to 15 CFR 740.

(F) Requiring an export license issued by any other federal government agency.

(G) Classified as rough diamonds under 6-digit HS subheadings 7102.10, 7102.21, and 7102.31.

(2) *Filing methods.* The USPPI has four means for filing EEI: use AES*Direct*; develop AES software using the AESTIR (see *http://www.cbp.gov/xp/cgov/export/aes/*); purchase software developed by certified vendors using the AESTIR; or use an authorized agent. An FPPI can only use an authorized agent in a routed export transaction.

(b) *General requirements*—(1) The EEI shall be filed prior to exportation (see § 30.4) unless the USPPI has been approved to submit export data on a postdeparture basis (see § 30.5(c)). Shipments requiring a license or license exemption may be filed postdeparture only when the appropriate licensing agency has granted the USPPI authorization. See Subpart B of this part.

(2) Specific data elements required for EEI filing are contained in § 30.6.

(3) The AES downtime procedures provide uniform instructions for processing export transactions when the AES or AES*Direct* or the computer system of an AES participant is unavailable for transmission. (See § 30.4(b)(1) and § 30.4(b)(3).)

(4) Instructions for particular types of transactions and exemptions from these requirements are found in Subparts C and D of this part.

(5) The EEI is required to be filed in the AES prior to export for shipments by vessel going directly to the countries identified in U.S. Customs and Border Protection regulations 19 CFR 4.75(c) and by aircraft going directly or indirectly to those countries. (See U.S. Customs and Border Protection regulations 19 CFR 122.74(b)(2).)

(c) *Certification and filing requirements.* Filers of EEI shall be required to meet application, certification, and filing requirements before being approved to submit EEI. Steps leading toward approval for the AES or the AES*Direct* filing include the following processes: (See § 30.5 for specific application, certification, and filing standards applicable to AES and AES*Direct* submissions.)

(1) Submission of an electronic AES Participant Application (APA) for AES filing or submission of an online registration for filing through *http://www.census.gov/aes*.

(2) Successful completion of certification testing for AES or for AES*Direct* filing.

(d) *Exclusions from filing EEI.* The following types of transactions are outside the scope of this part and shall be excluded from EEI filing:

(1) Goods shipped under CBP bond through the United States, Puerto Rico, or the U.S. Virgin Islands from one foreign country or area to another where such goods do not enter the consumption channels of the United States.

(2) Goods shipped from the U.S. territories and goods shipped between the United States and these territories do not require EEI filing. However, goods transiting U.S. territories to foreign destinations require EEI filing.

(3) Electronic transmissions and intangible transfers. (See Subpart B of this part for export control requirements for these types of transactions.)

(4) Goods shipped to Guantanamo Bay Naval Base in Cuba from the United States, Puerto Rico, or the U.S. Virgin Islands and from Guantanamo Bay Naval Base to the United States, Puerto Rico, or the U.S. Virgin Islands. (See § 30.39 for filing requirements for shipments exported by the U.S. Armed Services.)

(e) *Penalties*. Failure of the USPPI, the authorized agent of either the USPPI or the FPPI, the exporting carrier, or any other person subject thereto to comply with any of the requirements of the regulations in this part renders such persons subject to the penalties provided for in Subpart H of this part.

EFFECTIVE DATE NOTE: At 78 FR 16375, Mar. 14, 2013, § 30.2 was amended by revising paragraph (a)(1)(iv)(E); adding paragraph (a)(1)(iv)(H); adding a note to (a)(1)(iv); revising paragraphs (a)(2) and (b)(3); revising paragraph (d) introductory text, (d)(2), and (d)(4); and adding paragraph (d)(5), effective Jan. 8, 2014. At 78 FR 67928, Nov. 13, 2013, the effective date was delayed until Apr. 5, 2014. For the convenience of the user, the added and revised text is set forth as follows:

§ 30.2 General requirements for filing Electronic Export Information (EEI).

(a) * * *

(1) * * *

(iv) * * *

(E) Requiring a general or specific export license issued by the U.S. Nuclear Regulatory Commission under 10 CFR part 110.

* * * * *

(H) Used self-propelled vehicles as defined in 19 CFR 192.1 of U.S. Customs and Border Protection regulations, except as noted in CBP regulations.

Note to Paragraph (a)(1)(iv): For the filing requirement for exports destined for a country in Country Group E:1 as set forth in the Supplement No. 1 to 15 CFR part 740, see FTR § 30.16.

(2) *Filing methods*. The USPPI has four means for filing EEI: use AES*Direct;* develop AES software using the AESTIR (see *<www.cbp.gov/xp/cgov/trade/automated/aes/tech_docs/aestir/>*); purchase software developed by certified vendors using the AESTIR; or use an authorized agent. An FPPI can only use an authorized agent in a routed transaction.

(b) * * *

(3) The AES downtime procedures provide uniform instructions for processing export transactions when the government's AES or AES*Direct* is unavailable for transmission. (See § 30.4(b)(1) and § 30.4(b)(3).)

* * * * *

(d) *Exclusions from filing EEI*. The following types of transactions are outside the scope of this part and shall be excluded from EEI filing.

* * * * *

(2) Except Puerto Rico and the U.S. Virgin Islands, goods shipped from the U.S. territories and goods shipped between the United States and these territories do not require EEI filing. However, goods transiting U.S. territories to foreign destinations require EEI filing.

* * * * *

(4) Goods shipped to Guantanamo Bay Naval Base in Cuba from the United States, Puerto Rico, or the U.S. Virgin Islands and from Guantanamo Bay Naval Base to the United States, Puerto Rico, or the U.S. Virgin Islands. (See § 30.39 for filing requirements for shipments exported to the U.S. Armed Services.)

(5) Goods licensed by a U.S. federal government agency where the country of ultimate destination is the United States or goods destined to international waters where the person(s) or entity assuming control of the item(s) is a citizen or permanent resident alien of the United States or a juridical entity organized under the laws of the United States or a jurisdiction within the United States.

* * * * *

§ 30.3 Electronic Export Information filer requirements, parties to export transactions, and responsibilities of parties to export transactions.

(a) *General requirements*. The filer of EEI for export transactions is either the USPPI, or the U.S. authorized agent. All EEI submitted to the AES shall be complete, correct, and based on personal knowledge of the facts stated or on information furnished by the parties to the export transaction.

The filer shall be physically located in the United States at the time of filing, have an EIN or DUNS and be certified to report in the AES. In the event that the filer does not have an EIN or DUNS, the filer must obtain an EIN from the Internal Revenue Service. The filer is responsible for the truth, accuracy, and completeness of the EEI, except insofar as that party can demonstrate that it reasonably relied on information furnished by other responsible persons participating in the transaction. All parties involved in export transactions, including U.S. authorized agents, should be aware that invoices and other commercial documents may not necessarily contain all the information needed to prepare the EEI. The parties shall ensure that all information needed for reporting to the AES, including correct export licensing information, is provided to the U.S. authorized agent for the purpose of correctly preparing the EEI.

(b) *Parties to the export transaction*—(1) *Principal parties in interest.* Those persons in a transaction that receive the primary benefit, monetary or otherwise, are considered principal parties to the transaction. Generally, the principal parties in interest in a transaction are the seller and buyer. In most cases, the forwarding or other agent is not a principal party in interest.

(2) *USPPI.* For purposes of filing EEI, the USPPI is the person or legal entity in the United States that receives the primary benefit, monetary or otherwise, from the transaction. Generally, that person or entity is the U.S. seller, manufacturer, order party, or foreign entity purchasing or obtaining goods for export. The foreign entity shall be listed as the USPPI if it is in the United States when the items are purchased or obtained for export. The foreign entity shall then follow the provisions for filing the EEI specified in § 30.3 and § 30.6 pertaining to the USPPI.

(i) If a U.S. manufacturer sells goods directly to an entity in a foreign area, the U.S. manufacturer shall be listed as the USPPI in the EEI.

(ii) If a U.S. manufacturer sells goods, as a domestic sale, to a U.S. buyer (wholesaler/distributor) and that U.S. buyer sells the goods for export to a FPPI, the U.S. buyer (wholesaler/distributor) shall be listed as the USPPI in the EEI.

(iii) If a U.S. order party directly arranges for the sale and export of goods to a foreign entity, the U.S. order party shall be listed as the USPPI in the EEI.

(iv) If a customs broker is listed as the importer of record when entering goods into the United States for immediate consumption or warehousing entry, the customs broker may be listed as the USPPI in the EEI if the goods are subsequently exported without change or enhancement.

(v) If a foreign person is listed as the importer of record when entering goods into the United States for immediate consumption or warehousing entry, the customs broker who entered the goods, may be listed as the USPPI in the EEI if the goods are subsequently exported without change or enhancement.

(3) *Authorized agent.* The agent shall be authorized by the USPPI or, in the case of a routed export transaction, the agent shall be authorized by the FPPI to prepare and file the EEI. In a routed export transaction, the authorized agent can be the "exporter" for export control purposes as defined in 15 CFR 772.1 of the U.S. Department of Commerce EAR. However, the authorized agent shall not be shown as the USPPI in the EEI unless the agent acts as a USPPI in the export transaction as defined in paragraphs (b)(2)(iii), (iv), and (v) of this section.

(c) *General responsibilities of parties in export transactions*—(1) *USPPI responsibilities.* (i) The USPPI can prepare and file the EEI itself, or it can authorize an agent to prepare and file the EEI on its behalf. If the USPPI prepares the EEI itself, the USPPI is responsible for the accuracy and timely transmission of all the export information reported to the AES.

(ii) When the USPPI authorizes an agent to file the EEI on its behalf, the USPPI is responsible for:

(A) Providing the authorized agent with accurate and timely export information necessary to file the EEI.

(B) Providing the authorized agent with a power of attorney or written authorization to file the EEI (see paragraph (f) of this section for written authorization requirements for agents).

(C) Retaining documentation to support the information provided to the authorized agent for filing the EEI, as specified in § 30.10.

(2) *Authorized agent responsibilities.* The agent, when authorized by a USPPI to prepare and file the EEI for an export transaction, is responsible for performing the following activities:

(i) Accurate preparation and timely filing of the EEI based on information received from the USPPI and other parties involved in the transaction.

(ii) Obtaining a power of attorney or written authorization to file the EEI.

(iii) Retaining documentation to support the information reported to the AES, as specified in § 30.10.

(iv) Upon request, providing the USPPI with a copy of the export information filed in a mutually agreed upon format.

(d) *Filer responsibilities.* Responsibilities of USPPIs and authorized agents filing EEI are as follows:

(1) Filing complete and accurate information (see § 30.4 for a delineation of filing responsibilities of USPPIs and authorized agents).

(2) Filing information in a timely manner in accordance with the provisions and requirements contained in this part.

(3) Responding to fatal errors, warning, verify and reminder messages, and compliance alerts generated by the AES in accordance with provisions and requirements contained in this part.

(4) Providing the exporting carrier with the required proof of filing citations or exemption legends in accordance with provisions contained in this part.

(5) Promptly filing corrections or cancellations to EEI in accordance with provisions contained in § 30.9.

(6) Retaining all necessary and proper documentation related to EEI transactions in accordance with provisions contained in this part (see § 30.10 for specific requirements for retaining and producing documentation for export shipments).

(e) *Responsibilities of parties in a routed export transaction.* The Census Bureau recognizes "routed export transactions" as a subset of export transactions. A routed export transaction is a transaction in which the FPPI authorizes a U.S. agent to facilitate the export of items from the United States and to prepare and file EEI.

(1) *USPPI responsibilities.* In a routed export transaction, the FPPI may authorize or agree to allow the USPPI to prepare and file the EEI. If the FPPI agrees to allow the USPPI to file the EEI, the FPPI must provide a written authorization to the USPPI assuming the responsibility for filing. The USPPI may authorize an agent to file the EEI on its behalf. If the USPPI or its agent prepares and files the EEI, it shall retain documentation to support the EEI filed. If the FPPI agrees to allow the USPPI to file EEI, the filing of the export transaction shall be treated as a routed export transaction. If the FPPI authorizes an agent to prepare and file the EEI, the USPPI shall retain documentation to support the information provided to the agent for preparing the EEI as specified in § 30.10 and provide the agent with the following information to assist in preparing the EEI:

(i) Name and address of the USPPI.

(ii) USPPI's EIN or DUNS

(iii) State of origin (State).

(iv) FTZ if applicable.

(v) Commercial description of commodities.

(vi) Origin of goods indicator: Domestic (D) or Foreign (F).

(vii) Schedule B or HTSUSA, Classification Commodity Code.

(viii) Quantities/units of measure.

(ix) Value.

(x) Export Control Classification Number (ECCN) or sufficient technical information to determine the ECCN.

(xi) All licensing information necessary to file the EEI for commodities where the Department of State, the Department of Commerce, or other U.S. government agency issues a license for the commodities being exported, or the merchandise is being exported under a license exemption or license exception.

(xii) Any information that it knows will affect the determination of license authorization (see Subpart B of this part for additional information on licensing requirements).

NOTE TO PARAGRAPH (e)(1) OF THIS SECTION: For items in paragraph (e) (1) (ix), (x),(xi) and (xii) of this section, where the FPPI has assumed responsibility for determining and obtaining license authority see requirements set forth in 15 CFR 758.3 of the EAR.

(2) *Authorized agent responsibilities.* In a routed export transaction, if an authorized agent is preparing and filing the EEI on behalf of the FPPI, the authorized agent must obtain a power of attorney or written authorization from the FPPI and prepare and file the EEI based on information obtained from the USPPI or other parties involved in the transaction. The authorized agent shall be responsible for filing the EEI accurately and timely in accordance with the FTR. Upon request, the authorized agent will provide the USPPI with a copy of the power of attorney or written authorization from the FPPI. The authorized agent shall also retain documentation to support the EEI reported through the AES. The agents shall upon request, provide the USPPI with the data elements in paragraphs (e)(1)(i) through (xii) of this section as submitted through the AES. The authorized agent shall provide the following export information through the AES:

(i) Date of export.

(ii) Transportation Reference Number.

(iii) Ultimate consignee.

(iv) Intermediate consignee, if applicable.

(v) Authorized agent name and address.

(vi) EIN or DUNS of the authorized agent.

(vii) Country of ultimate destination.

(viii) Method of transportation.

(ix) Carrier identification and conveyance name.

(x) Port of export.

(xi) Foreign port of unloading.

(xii) Shipping weight.

(xiii) ECCN.

(xiv) License or license exemption information.

NOTE TO PARAGRAPH (e)(2) OF THIS SECTION: For items in paragraphs (e)(2)(xiii) and (xiv) of this section, where the FPPI has assumed responsibility for determining and obtaining license authority, see requirements set forth in 15 CFR 758.3 of the EAR.

(f) *Authorizing an agent.* In a power of attorney or other written authorization, authority is conferred upon an agent to perform certain specified acts or kinds of acts on behalf of a principal (see 15 CFR 758.1(h) of the EAR). In cases where an authorized agent is filing EEI to the AES, the agent shall obtain a power of attorney or written authorization from a principal party in interest to file the information on its behalf. A power of attorney or written authorization should specify the responsibilities of the parties with particularity and should state that the agent has authority to act on behalf of a principal party in interest as its true and lawful agent for purposes of creating and filing EEI in accordance with the laws and regulations of the United States. In routed export transactions the USPPI is not required to provide an agent of the FPPI with a power of attorney or written authorization.

NOTE TO §30.3: The EAR defines the "exporter" as the person in the United States who has the authority of a principal party in interest to determine and control the sending of items out of the United States (see 15 CFR 772 of the EAR). For statistical purposes "exporter" is not defined in the FTR. Instead, however, the USPPI is defined in the FTR.

For purposes of licensing responsibility under the EAR, the U.S. agent of the FPPI may be the "exporter" or applicant on the license in certain routed export transactions (see 15 CFR 758.3 of the EAR). Therefore, due to the differences in export reporting requirements among Federal agencies, conformity of documentation is not required in the FTR.

[73 FR 31555, June 2, 2008, as amended at 74 FR 38916, Aug. 5, 2009]

EFFECTIVE DATE NOTE: At 78 FR 16375, Mar. 14, 2013, §30.3 was amended by revising paragraphs (b)(2) introductory text, (b)(2)(iii), and (c)(2)(ii), and adding paragraphs (b)(4) and (c)(3), effective Jan. 8, 2014. At 78 FR 67928, Nov. 13, 2013, the effective date was delayed until Apr. 5, 2014. For the convenience of the user, the added and revised text is set forth as follows:

§ 30.3 Electronic Export Information filer requirements, parties to export transactions, and responsibilities of parties to export transactions.

* * * * *

(b) * * *

(2) *USPPI.* For purposes of filing EEI, the USPPI is the person or legal entity in the United States that receives the primary benefit, monetary or otherwise, from the transaction. Generally, that person or entity is the U.S. seller, manufacturer, order party, or foreign entity if in the United States at the time goods are purchased or obtained for export. The foreign entity shall be listed as the USPPI if it is in the United States when the items are purchased or obtained for export. The foreign entity shall then follow the provisions for filing the EEI specified in §§ 30.3 and 30.6 pertaining to the USPPI.

* * * * *

(iii) If a U.S. order party directly arranges for the sale and export of goods to the FPPI, the U.S. order party shall be listed as the USPPI in the EEI.

* * * * *

(4) *Carrier.* A carrier is an individual or legal entity in the business of transporting passengers or goods. Airlines, trucking companies, railroad companies, shipping lines, and pipeline companies are all examples of carriers.

(c) * * *

(2) * * *

(ii) Obtaining a power of attorney or written authorization from the USPPI to file the EEI.

* * * * *

(3) *Carrier responsibilities.* (i) The carrier must not load or move cargo unless the required documentation, from the USPPI or authorized agent, contains the required AES proof of filing, postdeparture, downtime, exclusion or exemption citations. This information must be cited on the first page of the bill of lading, air waybill, or other commercial loading documents.

(ii) The carrier must annotate the AES proof of filing, postdeparture, downtime, exclusion or exemption citations on the carrier's outbound manifest when required.

(iii) The carrier is responsible for presenting the required AES proof of filing, postdeparture, downtime, exclusion or exemption citations to the CBP Port Director at the port of export as stated in Subpart E of this part. Such presentation shall be without material change or amendment of the proof of filing, postdeparture, downtime, exclusion or exemption citation.

(iv) The carrier shall notify the USPPI or the authorized agent of changes to the transportation data, and the USPPI or the authorized agent shall electronically transmit the corrections, cancellations, or amendments as soon as the corrections are known in accordance with § 30.9. Manifest amendments must be made in accordance with CBP regulations.

(v) Retain documents pertaining to the export shipment as specified in § 30.10.

* * * * *

§ 30.4 Electronic Export Information filing procedures, deadlines, and certification statements.

Two electronic filing options (predeparture and postdeparture) for transmitting EEI are available to the USPPI or authorized agent. The electronic postdeparture filing takes into account that complete information concerning export shipments may not always be available prior to exportation and accommodates these circumstances by providing, when authorized, for filing of EEI after departure. For example, for exports of seasonal and agricultural commodities, only estimated quantities, values, and consignees may be known prior to exportation. The procedures for obtaining certification as an AES filer and for applying for authorization to file on a postdeparture basis are described in § 30.5.

(a) *EEI transmitted predeparture.* The EEI shall always be transmitted prior to departure for the following types of shipments:

(1) Used self-propelled vehicles as defined in 19 CFR 192.1 of U.S. Customs and Border Protection regulations.

(2) Essential and precursor chemicals requiring a permit from the DEA;

(3) Shipments defined as "sensitive" by Executive Order;

(4) Shipments where a U.S. government agency requires predeparture filing;

(5) Shipments defined as "routed export transactions" (see § 30.3(e));

(6) Shipments to countries where complete outbound manifests are required prior to clearing vessels or aircraft for export (see U.S. Customs and Border Protection regulations 19 CFR 4.75(c) and 122.74(b)(2) for a listing of these countries);

(7) Items identified on the USML of the ITAR (22 CFR 121);

(8) Exports that require a license from the BIS, unless the BIS has approved postdeparture filing privileges for the USPPI;

(9) Shipments of rough diamonds classified under HS subheadings 7102.10, 7102.21, and 7102.31 and exported (reexported) in accordance with the Kimberley Process; and

(10) Shipments for which the USPPI has not been approved for postdeparture filing.

(b) *Filing deadlines for EEI transmitted predeparture.* The USPPI or the authorized agent shall file the required EEI and have received the AES ITN no later than the time period specified as follows:

(1) For USML shipments, refer to the ITAR (22 CFR 120 through 130) for specific requirements concerning predeparture filing time frames. In addition, if a filer is unable to acquire an ITN because the AES is not operating, the filer shall not export until the AES is operating and an ITN is acquired.

(2) For non-USML shipments, file the EEI and provide the ITN as follows:

(i) For vessel cargo, the USPPI or the authorized agent shall file the EEI required by § 30.6 and provide the filing citation or exemption legend to the exporting carrier twenty-four hours prior to loading cargo on the vessel at the U.S. port where the cargo is laden.

(ii) For air cargo, including cargo being transported by Air Express Couriers, the USPPI or the authorized agent shall file the EEI required by § 30.6 and provide the filing citation or exemption legend to the exporting carrier no later than two (2) hours prior to the scheduled departure time of the aircraft.

(iii) For truck cargo, including cargo departing by Express Consignment Couriers, the USPPI or the authorized agent shall file the EEI required by § 30.6 and provide the filing citation or exemption legend to the exporting carrier no later than one (1) hour prior to the arrival of the truck at the United States border to go foreign.

(iv) For rail cargo, the USPPI or the authorized agent shall file the EEI required by § 30.6 and provide the filing citation or exemption legend to the exporting carrier no later than two (2) hours prior to the time the train arrives at the U.S. border to go foreign.

(v) For mail and cargo shipped by other methods, except pipeline, the USPPI or the authorized agent shall file the EEI required by § 30.6 and provide the filing citation or exemption legend to the exporting carrier no later than two (2) hours prior to exportation. (See § 30.46 for filing deadlines for shipments sent by pipeline.)

(vi) For all other modes, the USPPI or the authorized agent shall file the required EEI no later than two (2) hours prior to exportation.

(3) For non-USML shipments when the AES is unavailable, use the following instructions:

(i) If the participant's AES is unavailable, the filer must delay the export of the goods or find an alternative filing method;

(ii) If AES or AES*Direct* is unavailable, the goods may be exported and the filer must:

(A) Provide the appropriate downtime filing citation as described in § 30.7(b) and Appendix D; and

(B) Report the EEI at the first opportunity AES is available.

(c) *EEI transmitted postdeparture.* Postdeparture filing is only available for approved USPPIs and provides for the electronic filing of the data elements required by § 30.6 no later than ten calendar days from the date of exportation. For USPPIs approved for postdeparture filing, all shipments (other than those for which predeparture filing is specifically required), by all methods of transportation, may be exported with the filing of EEI made postdeparture. Certified AES authorized agents or service centers may transmit information postdeparture on behalf of USPPIs approved for postdeparture filing, or the approved USPPI may transmit the data postdeparture itself. However, authorized agents or service centers will not be approved for postdeparture filing.

(d) *Proof of filing citation and exemption and exclusion legends.* The USPPI or the authorized agent shall provide the exporting carrier with the proof of filing citation and exemption and exclusion legends as described in § 30.7.

EFFECTIVE DATE NOTE: At 78 FR 16376, Mar. 14, 2013, § 30.4 was amended by revising paragraphs (a)(6) and (8); redesignating paragraphs (a)(9) and (10) as paragraphs (a)(10) and (11); adding new paragraph (a)(9); revising paragraph (b)(1) and paragraph (b)(2) introductory text; redesignating paragraph (b)(3) as (b)(4); adding a new paragraph (b)(3); revising newly redesignated paragraph (b)(4); adding paragraph (b)(5); and revising paragraph (c), effective Jan. 8, 2014. At 78 FR 67928, Nov. 13, 2013, the effective date was delayed until Apr. 5, 2014. For the convenience of the user, the added and revised text is set forth as follows:

§ 30.4 Electronic Export Information filing procedures, deadlines, and certification statements.

* * * * *

(a) * * *

(6) Shipments where complete outbound manifests are required prior to clearing vessels going directly to the countries identified in U.S. Customs and Border Protection regulations 19 CFR 4.75(c) and aircraft going directly or indirectly to those countries. (See U.S. Customs and Border Protection regulation 19 CFR 122.74(b)(2));

* * * * *

(8) Shipments that require a license from the BIS and exports listed under BIS's grounds for denial of postdeparture filing status (see 15 CFR 758.2);

(9) Shipments that require a license from the Nuclear Regulatory Commission.

* * * * *

(b) * * *

(1) For USML shipments, refer to the ITAR (22 CFR 123.22(b)(1)) for specific requirements concerning predeparture filing time frames. In addition, if a filer is unable to acquire an ITN because the AES or AES*Direct* is not operating, the filer shall not export until the AES is operating and an ITN is acquired. The downtime filing citation is not to be used when the filer's system is down or experiencing delays.

(2) For non-USML shipments, except shipments between the United States and Puerto Rico, file the EEI and provide the ITN as follows (See § 30.4(b)(3), for filing timeframes for shipments between the United States and Puerto Rico):

* * * * *

(3) For shipments between the United States and Puerto Rico, the AES proof of filing citation, postdeparture filing citation, or exemption citation must be presented to the carrier by the time the shipment arrives at the port of unloading.

(4) For non-USML shipments when the AES or AES*Direct* is unavailable, use the following instructions:

(i) If the participant's AES is unavailable, the filer must delay the export of the goods or find an alternative filing method;

(ii) If AES or AES*Direct* is unavailable, the goods may be exported and the filer must:

(A) Provide the appropriate downtime filing citation as described in § 30.7(b) and Appendix D; and

(B) Report the EEI at the first opportunity AES or AES*Direct* is available.

(5) For used self-propelled vehicles as defined in 19 CFR 192.1 of U.S. Customs and Border Protection regulations, the USPPI or the authorized agent shall file the EEI as required by § 30.6 and provide the filing citation to the CBP at least 72 hours prior to export. The filer must also provide the carrier with the filing citation as required by paragraph (b) of this section.

(c) *EEI transmitted postdeparture.* Postdeparture filing is only available for approved USPPIs and provides for the electronic filing of the data elements required by § 30.6 no later than five (5) calendar days after the date of exportation. For USPPIs approved for postdeparture filing, all shipments (other than those for which predeparture filing is specifically required), by all methods of transportation, may be exported with the filing of EEI made postdeparture. Authorized agents or service centers may transmit information postdeparture on behalf of USPPIs approved for postdeparture filing, or the approved USPPI may transmit the data postdeparture itself.

* * * * *

§ 30.5 Electronic Export Information filing application and certification processes and standards.

Prior to filing EEI, the USPPI or the authorized agent must be certified to file through the AES. A service center shall be certified to transmit electronically to the AES. The USPPI, authorized agent, or service center may use a software package designed by a certified vendor to file EEI through the AES. Once an authorized agent has successfully completed the certification process, any USPPI using that agent does not have to be certified. The certified authorized agent shall have a properly executed power of attorney or written authorization from the USPPI or FPPI, and be physically located in the United States to file EEI through the AES. The USPPI or authorized agent that utilizes a certified software vendor or service center shall complete certification testing. Service centers may only transmit export information; they may not prepare and file export information unless they have authorization from the USPPI in the form of a power of attorney or written authorization, thus making them authorized agents. The USPPI seeking approval for postdeparture filing privileges shall be approved before they or their authorized agent may file on a postdeparture basis.

(a) *AES application process*—(1) *AES Participation Application.* The USPPI or authorized agent who chooses to file through the AES and seek approval for postdeparture filing privileges, must submit a complete on-line LOI at *http://www.census.gov/aes.*

(2) *AESDirect registration.* The USPPI or authorized agent who chooses to file through AES*Direct* shall also complete the online AES*Direct* registration form at *http://www.aesdirect.gov.* After submitting the registration, an AES*Direct* filing account is created for the filing company. The person designated as the account administrator is responsible for activating the account and completing the certification process as discussed in paragraph (b)(2) of this section.

(b) *Certification process*—(1) *AES certification process.* The USPPI or authorized agent shall perform an initial two-part communication test to ascertain whether its system is capable of both transmitting data to, and receiving data from, the AES. The USPPI or authorized agent shall demonstrate specific system application capabilities. The capability to correctly handle these system applications is the prerequisite to certification for participation in the AES. The USPPI or authorized agent shall successfully transmit the AES certification test. CBP's and/or Census Bureau's client representatives provide assistance during certification testing. These representatives make the sole determination as to whether or not the USPPI or authorized agent qualifies for certification. Upon successful completion of certification testing, the USPPI's or authorized agent's status is moved from testing mode to operational status. The AES filers may be required to repeat the certification testing process at any time. The Census Bureau will provide the AES filer with a certification notice after the USPPI or authorized agent has been approved for operational status. The certification notice will include:

(i) The date that filers may begin transmitting data;

(ii) Reporting instructions; and

(iii) Examples of the required AES proof of filing citations, postdeparture filing citations, AES downtime filing citation, and exemption legends.

(2) AES*Direct certification process.* To become certified for AES*Direct*, filers shall demonstrate knowledge of this part and the ability to successfully transmit EEI. Upon successful completion of the certification testing, notification by e-mail will be sent to the account administrator when an account is fully activated for filing via AES*Direct*. Certified filers should print and retain the page congratulating the filer on passing the test.

(c) *Postdeparture filing approval process.* The USPPI may apply for postdeparture filing privileges by submitting a postdeparture filing application at *http://www.census.gov/aes.* An authorized agent may not apply on behalf of a USPPI. The Census Bureau will distribute the LOI to CBP and the other federal government partnership agencies participating in the AES postdeparture filing review process. Failure to meet the standards of the Census Bureau, CBP or any of the partnership agencies is reason for denial of the AES applicant for postdeparture filing privileges. Each partnership agency will develop its own internal postdeparture filing acceptance standards, and each agency will notify the Census Bureau of the USPPI's success or failure to meet that agency's acceptance standards. Any partnership agency may require additional information from USPPIs that are applying for postdeparture filing. The Census Bureau will notify the USPPI of the decision to either deny or approve their application for postdeparture filing privileges within thirty (30) calendar days of receipt of the postdeparture filing application by the Census Bureau, or if a decision cannot be reached at that time, the USPPI will be notified of an extension for a final decision as soon as possible after the thirty (30) calendar days.

(1) *Grounds for denial of postdeparture filing status.* The Census Bureau may deny a USPPI's application for postdeparture filing privileges for any of the following reasons:

(i) There is no history of filing for the USPPI through the AES.

(ii) The USPPI's volume of EEI reported through the AES does not warrant participation in postdeparture filing.

(iii) The USPPI or its authorized agent has failed to submit EEI through the AES in a timely and accurate manner.

(iv) The USPPI has a history of noncompliance with the Census Bureau export regulations contained in this part.

(v) The USPPI has been indicted, convicted, or is currently under investigation for a felony involving a violation of federal export laws or regulations and the Census Bureau has evidence of probable cause supporting such violation, or the USPPI is in violation of Census Bureau export regulations contained in this part.

(vi) The USPPI has made or caused to be made in the LOI a false or misleading statement or omission with respect to any material fact.

(vii) The USPPI would pose a significant threat to national security interests such that its participation in postdeparture filing should be denied.

(viii) The USPPI has multiple violations of either the EAR (15 CFR 730 through 774) or the ITAR (22 CFR 120 through 130) within the last three (3) years.

(2) *Notice of denial.* A USPPI denied postdeparture filing privileges by other agencies shall contact those agencies regarding the specific reason(s) for nonselection and for their appeal procedures. A USPPI denied postdeparture filing status by the Census Bureau will be provided with a specific reason for nonselection and a Census Bureau point of contact in an electronic notification letter. A USPPI may appeal the Census Bureau's nonselection decision by following the appeal procedure and reapplication procedure provided in paragraph (c)(5) of this section.

(3) *Revocation of postdeparture filing privileges*—(i) *Revocation by the Census Bureau.* The Census Bureau may revoke postdeparture filing privileges of an approved USPPI for the following reasons:

(A) The USPPI's volume of EEI reported in the AES does not warrant continued participation in postdeparture filing;

(B) The USPPI or its authorized agent has failed to submit EEI through the AES in a timely and accurate manner;

(C) The USPPI has made or caused to be made in the LOI a false or misleading statement or omission with respect to material fact;

(D) The USPPI submitting the LOI has been indicted, convicted, or is currently under investigation for a felony involving a violation of federal export laws or regulations and the Census Bureau has evidence of probable cause supporting such violation, or the AES applicant is in violation of export rules and regulations contained in this part;

(E) The USPPI has failed to comply with existing export regulations or has failed to pay any outstanding penalties assessed in connection with such noncompliance; or

(F) The USPPI would pose a significant threat to national security interests such that its continued participation in postdeparture filing should be terminated.

(ii) *Revocation by other agencies.* Any of the other agencies may revoke a USPPI's postdeparture filing privileges with respect to transactions subject to the jurisdiction of that agency. When doing so, the agency shall notify both the Census Bureau and the USPPI whose authorization is being revoked.

(4) *Notice of revocation.* Approved postdeparture filing USPPIs whose postdeparture filing privileges have been revoked by other agencies shall contact those agencies for their specific revocation and appeal procedures. When the Census Bureau makes a determination to revoke an approved USPPI's postdeparture filing privileges, the USPPI will be notified electronically of the reason(s) for the decision. In most cases, the revocation

shall become effective when the USPPI has either exhausted all appeal procedures, or thirty (30) calendar days after receipt of the notice of revocation, if no appeal is filed. However, in cases judged to affect national security, revocations shall become effective immediately upon notification.

(5) *Appeal procedure.* Any USPPI whose request for postdeparture filing privileges has been denied by the Census Bureau or whose postdeparture filing privileges have been revoked by the Census Bureau may appeal the decision by filing an appeal within thirty (30) calendar days of receipt of the notice of decision. Appeals should be addressed to the Chief, Foreign Trade Division, U.S. Census Bureau, Washington, DC 20233–6700. The Census Bureau will issue a written decision to the USPPI within thirty (30) calendar days from the date of receipt of the appeal by the Census Bureau. If a written decision is not issued within thirty (30) calendar days, the Census Bureau will forward to the USPPI a notice of extension within that time period. The USPPI will be provided with the reasons for the extension of this time period and an expected date of decision. The USPPIs who have had their postdeparture filing status denied or revoked may not reapply for this privilege for one year following written notification of the denial or revocation.

(d) *Electronic Export Information filing standards.* The data elements required for filing EEI are contained in §30.6. When filing EEI, the USPPI or authorized agent shall comply with the data transmission procedures determined by CBP and the Census Bureau and shall agree to stay in complete compliance with all export rules and regulations in this part. Failure of the USPPI or the authorized agent of either the USPPI or FPPI to comply with these requirements constitutes a violation of the regulations in this part, and renders such principal party or the authorized agent subject to the penalties provided for in Subpart H of this part. In the case of AES*Direct*, when submitting a registration form to AES*Direct*, the registering company is certifying that it will be in compliance with all applicable export rules and regulations. This includes complying with the following security requirements:

(1) AES*Direct* user names, administrator codes, and passwords are to be kept secure by the account administrator and not disclosed to any unauthorized user or any persons outside the registered company.

(2) Registered companies are responsible for those persons having access to the user name, administrator code, and password. If an employee with direct access to the user name, administrator code, and password leaves the company or otherwise is no longer an authorized user, the company shall immediately change the password and administrator code in the system to ensure the integrity and confidentiality of Title 13 data.

(3) Antivirus software shall be installed and set to run automatically on all computers that access AES*Direct*. All AES*Direct* registered companies will maintain subscriptions with their antivirus software vendor to keep antivirus lists current. Registered companies are responsible for performing full scans of these systems on a regular basis, but not less than every thirty (30) days, to ensure the elimination of any virus contamination. If the registered company's computer system is infected with a virus, the company shall contact the Census Bureau's Foreign Trade Division Computer Security Officer and refrain from using AES*Direct* until it is virus free. Failure to comply with these requirements will result in immediate loss of privilege to use AES*Direct* until the registered company can establish to the satisfaction of the Census Bureau's Foreign Trade Division Computer Security Officer that the company's computer systems accessing AES*Direct* are virus free.

(e) *Monitoring the filing of EEI.* The USPPI's or the authorized agent's AES filings will be monitored and reviewed for quality, timeliness, and coverage. The Census Bureau will provide performance reports to USPPIs and authorized agents who file EEI. The Census Bureau will take appropriate action to correct specific situations where the USPPI or authorized agent fails to maintain acceptable levels of data quality, timeliness, or coverage.

(f) *Support.* The Census Bureau provides online services that allow the USPPI and the authorized agent to seek assistance pertaining to AES and this part. For AES assistance, filers may send an e-mail to *ASKAES@census.gov* and for FTR assistance, filers may send an e-mail to *FTDREGS@census.gov.* AES*Direct* is supported by a help desk available twelve (12) hours a day from 7 a.m. to 7 p.m. EST, seven (7) days a week. Filers can obtain contact information from the Web site *http://www.aesdirect.gov.*

EFFECTIVE DATE NOTE: At 78 FR 16376, Mar. 14, 2013, § 30.5 was amended by revising paragraph (c) introductory text, adding paragraphs (c)(1)(ix) and (c)(3)(i)(G), and revising paragraphs (d)(1) and (2), effective Jan. 8, 2013. At 78 FR 67928, Nov. 13, 2013, the effective date was delayed until Apr. 5, 2014. For the convenience of the user, the added and revised text is set forth as follows:

§ 30.5 Electronic Export Information filing application and certification processes and standards.

* * * * *

(c) *Postdeparture filing approval process.* Postdeparture filing is a privilege granted to approved USPPIs for their EEI to be filed up to five (5) calendar days after the date of export. The USPPI or its authorized agent may not transmit EEI postdeparture for certain types of shipments that are identified in § 30.4(a). The USPPI may apply for postdeparture filing privileges by submitting a postdeparture filing application at *www.census.gov/aes.* An authorized agent may not apply on behalf of a USPPI. The Census Bureau will distribute the applications submitted by USPPI's who are applying for postdeparture to the CBP and the other federal government partnership agencies for their review and approval. Failure to meet the standards of the Census Bureau, CBP or any of the partnership agencies is reason for denial of the AES applicant for postdeparture filing privileges. Each partnership agency will develop its own internal postdeparture filing acceptance standards, and each agency will notify the Census Bureau of the USPPI's success or failure to meet that agency's acceptance standards. Any partnership agency may require additional information from USPPIs that are applying for postdeparture filing. The Census Bureau will notify the USPPI of the decision to either deny or approve its application for postdeparture filing privileges within ninety (90) calendar days of receipt of the postdeparture filing application by the Census Bureau.

(1) * * *

(ix) The USPPI fails to demonstrate the ability to meet the AES predeparture filing requirements.

* * * * *

(3) * * *

(i) * * *

(G) The USPPI or its authorized agent files postdeparture for commodities that are identified in § 30.4(a).

* * * * *

(d) * * *

(1) AES*Direct* user names and passwords are to be kept secure by the account administrator and not disclosed to any unauthorized user or any persons outside the registered company.

(2) Registered companies are responsible for those persons having a user name and password. If an employee with a user name and password leaves the company or otherwise is no longer an authorized user, the company shall immediately deactivate that username in the system to ensure the integrity and confidentiality of Title 13 data.

* * * * *

§ 30.6 Electronic Export Information data elements.

The information specified in this section is required for shipments transmitted to the AES. The data elements identified as "mandatory" shall be reported for each transaction. The data elements identified as "conditional" shall be reported if they are required for or apply to the specific shipment. The data elements identified as "optional" may be reported at the discretion of the USPPI or the authorized agent.

(a) Mandatory data elements are as follows:

(1) *USPPI and USPPI identification.* The name, address, identification, and contact information of the USPPI shall be reported to the AES as follows:

(i) *Name of the USPPI.* In all export transactions, the name listed in the USPPI field in the EEI shall be the USPPI in the transaction. (See § 30.1 for the definition of the USPPI and § 30.3 for details on the USPPI's reporting responsibilities.)

(ii) *Address of the USPPI.* In all EEI filings, the USPPI shall report the address or location (no post office box number) from which the goods actually begin the journey to the port of export. For example, the EEI covering goods laden aboard a truck at a warehouse in Georgia for transport to Florida for loading onto a vessel for export to a foreign country shall show the address of the warehouse in Georgia. For shipments with multiple origins, report the address from which the commodity with the greatest value begins its export journey. If such information is not known, report the address in state in which the commodities are consolidated for export.

(iii) *USPPI identification number.* The USPPI shall report its own IRS EIN in the USPPI field of the EEI. If the USPPI has only one EIN, report that EIN. If the USPPI has more than one EIN, report the EIN that the USPPI uses to report employee wages and withholdings, and not the EIN that is used to report only company earnings or receipts. If the USPPI does not have an EIN, the USPPI must obtain an EIN for reporting to the AES. Use of another company's or individual's EIN or other identification number is prohibited. The appropriate Party type code shall be reported through the AES. When a foreign entity is in the United States when the items are purchased or obtained for export, the foreign entity is the USPPI for filing purposes. In such situations, the foreign entity shall report a DUNS, border crossing number, passport number, or any number assigned by CBP.

(iv) *Contact information.* Show contact name and telephone number.

(2) *Date of export.* The date of export is the date when goods are scheduled to leave the port of export on the exporting carrier that is taking the goods out of the United States.

(3) *Ultimate consignee.* The ultimate consignee is the person, party, or designee that is located abroad and actually receives the export shipment. The name and address of the ultimate consignee, whether by sale in the United States or abroad or by consignment, shall be reported in the EEI. The ultimate consignee as known at the time of export shall be reported. For shipments requiring an export license, the ultimate consignee shall be the person so designated on the export license or authorized to be the ultimate consignee under the applicable license exemption in conformance with the EAR or ITAR, as applicable. For goods sold en route, report the appropriate "To be Sold En Route" indicator in the EEI, and report corrected information as soon as it is known (see § 30.9 for procedures on correcting AES information).

(4) *U.S. state of origin.* The U.S. state of origin is the 2-character postal code for the state in which the goods begin their journey to the port of export. For example, a shipment covering goods laden aboard a truck at a warehouse in Georgia for transport to Florida for loading onto a vessel for export to a foreign country shall show Georgia as the state of origin. The U.S. state of origin may be different from the U.S. state where the goods were produced, mined, or grown. For shipments of multi-state origin, reported as a single shipment, report the U.S. state of the commodity with the greatest value. If such information is not known, report the state in which the commodities are consolidated for export.

(5) *Country of ultimate destination.* The country of ultimate destination is the country in which the goods are to be consumed or further processed or manufactured. The country of ultimate destination is the code issued by the ISO.

(i) *Shipments under an export license or license exemption.* For shipments under an export license or license exemption issued by the Department of State, DDTC, or the Department of Commerce, BIS, the country of ultimate destination shall conform to the country of ultimate destination as shown on the license. In the case of a Department of State license, the country of ultimate destination is the country specified with respect to the end user. For goods licensed by other government agencies refer to their specific requirements concerning providing country of destination information.

(ii) *Shipments not moving under an export license.* The country of ultimate destination is the country known to the USPPI at the time of exportation. The country to which the goods are being shipped is not the country of ultimate destination if the USPPI has knowledge at the time the goods leave the United States that they are intended for reexport or transshipment in their present form to another known country. For goods shipped to Canada, Mexico, Panama, Hong Kong, Belgium, United Arab Emirates, The Netherlands, or Singapore, for example, special care should be exercised before reporting these countries as the ultimate destination, since these are countries through which goods from the United States are frequently transshipped. If the USPPI does not know the ultimate destination of the goods, the country of destination to be shown is the last country, as known to the USPPI at the time of shipment from the United States, to which the goods are to be shipped in their present form. (For instructions as to the reporting of country of destination for vessels sold or transferred from the United States to foreign ownership, see §30.26.)

(iii) For goods to be sold en route, report the country of the first port of call and then report corrected information as soon as it is known.

(6) *Method of transportation.* The method of transportation is the means by which the goods are exported from the United States.

(i) *Conveyances exported under their own power.* The mode of transportation for aircraft, vessels, or locomotives (railroad stock) transferring ownership or title and moving out of the United States under its own power is the mode of transportation by which the conveyance moves out of the United States.

(ii) *Exports through Canada, Mexico, or other foreign countries for transshipment to another destination.* For transshipments through Canada, Mexico, or another foreign country, the mode of transportation is the mode of the carrier transporting the goods out of the United States.

(7) *Conveyance name/carrier name.* The conveyance name/carrier name is the name of the conveyance/carrier transporting the goods out of the United States as known at the time of exportation. For exports by sea, the conveyance name is the vessel name. For exports by air, rail, or truck, the carrier name is that which corresponds to the carrier identification as specified in paragraph (a)(8) of this section. Terms, such as airplane, train, rail, truck, vessel, barge, or international footbridge are not acceptable. For shipments by other methods of transportation, including mail, fixed methods (pipeline), the conveyance/carrier name is not required.

(8) *Carrier identification.* The carrier identification specifies the carrier that transports the goods out of the United States. The carrier transporting the goods to the port of export and the carrier transporting the goods out of the United States may be different. For transshipments through Canada, Mexico, or another foreign country, the carrier identification is that of the carrier that transports the goods out of the United States. The carrier identification is the Standard Carrier Alpha Code (SCAC) for vessel, rail, and truck shipments or the International Air Transport Association (IATA) code for air shipments. For other valid method of transportation, including mail, fixed modes (pipeline), and passenger, hand carried the carrier identification is not required. The National Motor Freight Traffic Association (NMFTA) issues and maintains the SCAC. (See *http://www.nmfta.org.*) The IATA issues and maintains the IATA codes. (See *http://www.census.gov/trade* for a list of IATA codes.)

(9) *Port of export.* The port of export is the seaport or airport where the goods are loaded on the exporting carrier that is taking the goods out of the United States, or the port where exports by overland transportation cross the U.S. border into a foreign country. The port of export shall be reported in terms of Schedule D, "Classification of CBP Districts and Ports." Use port code 8000 for shipments by mail.

(i) *Vessel and air exports involving several ports of exportation.* For goods loaded aboard a carrier in a port of lading, where the carrier stops at several ports before clearing to the foreign country, the port of export is the first port where the goods were loaded on the exporting carrier. For goods off-loaded from the original conveyance to another conveyance (even if the aircraft or vessel belongs to the same carrier) at any of the ports, the port where the goods were loaded on the last conveyance before going foreign is the port of export.

(ii) *Exports through Canada, Mexico, or other foreign countries for transshipment to another destination.* For transshipments through Canada, Mexico, or another foreign country to a third country, the port of export is the location where the goods are loaded on the carrier that is taking the goods out of the United States.

(10) *Related party indicator.* Used to indicate when a transaction involving trade between a USPPI and an ultimate consignee where either party owns directly or indirectly 10 percent or more of the other party.

(11) *Domestic or foreign indicator.* Indicates if the goods exported are of domestic or foreign origin. Report foreign goods separately from goods of domestic production even if the commodity classification number is the same.

(i) *Domestic.* Exports of domestic goods include: Those commodities that are grown, produced, or manufactured (including commodities incorporating foreign components) in the United States, including goods exported from U.S. FTZs, Puerto Rico, or the U.S. Virgin Islands; and those articles of foreign origin that have been enhanced in value or changed from the form in which they were originally imported by further manufacture or processing in the United States, including goods exported from U.S. FTZs, Puerto Rico, or the U.S. Virgin Islands.

(ii) *Foreign.* Exports of foreign goods include those commodities that are grown, produced, or manufactured in foreign countries that entered the United States including goods admitted to U.S. FTZs as imports and that, at the time of exportation, have undergone no change in form or condition or enhancement in value by further manufacture in the United States, in U.S. FTZs, in Puerto Rico, or in the U.S. Virgin Islands.

(12) *Commodity classification number.* Report the 10-digit commodity classification number as provided in Schedule B, *Statistical Classification of Domestic and Foreign Commodities Exported from the United States* in the EEI. The 10-digit commodity classification number provided in the Harmonized Tariff Schedule of the United States (HTSUSA) may be reported in lieu of the Schedule B commodity classification number except as noted in the headnotes of the HTSUSA. The HTSUSA is a global classification system used to describe most world trade in goods. Furnishing the correct Schedule B or HTSUSA number does not relieve the USPPI or the authorized agent of furnishing a complete and accurate commodity description. When reporting the Schedule B number or HTSUSA number, the decimals shall be omitted. (See *http://www.census.gov/trade* for a list of Schedule B classification numbers.)

(13) *Commodity description.* Report the description of the goods shipped in English in sufficient detail to permit verification of the Schedule B or HTSUSA number. Clearly and fully state the name of the commodity in terms that can be identified or associated with the language used in Schedule B or HTSUSA (usually the commercial name of the commodity), and any and all characteristics of the commodity that distinguish it from commodities of the same name covered by other Schedule B or HTSUSA classifications. If the shipment requires a license, the description reported in the EEI shall conform with that shown on the license. If the shipment qualifies for a license exemption, the description shall be sufficient to ensure compliance with that license exemption. However, where the description on the license does not state all of the characteristics of the commodity that are needed to completely verify the commodity classification number, as described in this paragraph, report the missing characteristics, as well as the description shown on the license, in the commodity description field of the EEI.

(14) *Primary unit of measure.* The unit of measure shall correspond to the primary quantity as prescribed in the Schedule B or HTSUSA. If neither Schedule B nor HTSUSA specifies a unit of measure for the item, an "X" is required in the unit of measure field.

(15) *Primary quantity.* The quantity is the total number of units that correspond to the first unit of measure specified in the Schedule B or

HTSUSA. Where the unit of measure is in terms of weight (grams, kilograms, metric tons, etc.), the quantity reflects the net weight, not including the weight of barrels, boxes, or other bulky coverings, and not including salt or pickle in the case of salted or pickled fish or meats. For a few commodities where "content grams" or "content kilograms" or some similar weight unit is specified in Schedule B or HTSUSA, the quantity may be less than the net weight. The quantity is reported as a whole unit only, without commas or decimals. If the quantity contains a fraction of a whole unit, round fractions of one-half unit or more up and fractions of less than one-half unit down to the nearest whole unit. (For example, where the unit for a given commodity is in terms of "tons," a net quantity of 8.4 tons would be reported as 8 for the quantity. If the quantity is less than one unit, the quantity is 1.)

(16) *Shipping weight.* The shipping weight is the weight in kilograms, which includes the weight of the commodity, as well as the weight of normal packaging, such as boxes, crates, barrels, etc. The shipping weight is required for exports by air, vessel, rail, and truck, and required for exports of household goods transported by all methods. For exports (except household goods) by mail, fixed transport (pipeline), or other valid methods, the shipping weight is not required and shall be reported as zero. For containerized cargo in lift vans, cargo vans, or similar substantial outer containers, the weight of such containers is not included in the shipping weight. If the shipping weight is not available for each Schedule B or HTSUSA item included in one or more containers, the approximate shipping weight for each item is estimated and reported. The total of these estimated weights equals the actual shipping weight of the entire container or containers.

(17) *Value.* In general, the value to be reported in the EEI shall be the value of the goods at the U.S. port of export. The value shall be the selling price as defined in this paragraph (or the cost if the goods are not sold), including inland or domestic freight, insurance, and other charges to the U.S. seaport, airport, or land border port of export. Cost of goods is the sum of expenses incurred in the USPPI acquisition or production of the goods. Report the value to the nearest dollar; omit cents. Fractions of a dollar less than 50 cents should be ignored, and fractions of 50 cents or more should be rounded up to the next dollar.

(i) *Selling price.* The selling price for goods exported pursuant to sale, and the value to be reported in the EEI, is the USPPI's price to the FPPI (the foreign buyer). Deduct from the selling price any unconditional discounts, but do not deduct discounts that are conditional upon a particular act or performance on the part of the foreign buyer. For goods shipped on consignment without a sale actually having been made at the time of export, the selling price to be reported in the EEI is the market value at the time of export at the U.S. port.

(ii) *Adjustments.* When necessary, make the following adjustments to obtain the value.

(A) Where goods are sold at a point other than the port of export, freight, insurance, and other charges required in moving the goods from their U.S. point of origin to the exporting carrier at the port of export or border crossing point shall be added to the selling price (as defined in paragraph (a)(17)(i) of this section) for purposes of reporting the value in the EEI.

(B) Where the actual amount of freight, insurance, and other domestic costs is not available, an estimate of the domestic costs shall be made and added to the cost of the goods or selling price to derive the value to be reported in the EEI. Add the estimated domestic costs to the cost or selling price of the goods to obtain the value to be reported in the EEI.

(C) Where goods are sold at a "delivered" price to the foreign destination, the cost of loading the goods on the exporting carrier, if any, and freight, insurance, and other costs beyond the port of export shall be subtracted from the selling price for purposes of reporting value in the EEI. If the actual amount of such costs is not available, an estimate of the costs should be subtracted from the selling price.

(D) Costs added to or subtracted from the selling price in accordance with the instructions in this paragraph (a)(17)(ii) should not be shown separately in the EEI, but the value reported should be the value after making such adjustments, where required, to arrive at the value of the goods at the U.S. port of export.

(iii) *Exclusions.* Exclude the following from the selling price of goods exported.

(A) Commissions to be paid by the USPPI to its agent abroad or commissions to be deducted from the selling price by the USPPI's agent abroad.

(B) The cost of loading goods on the exporting carrier at the port of export.

(C) Freight, insurance, and any other charges or transportation costs beyond the port of export.

(D) Any duties, taxes, or other assessments imposed by foreign countries.

(iv) For definitions of the value to be reported in the EEI for special types of transactions where goods are not being exported pursuant to commercial sales, or where subsidies, government financing or participation, or other unusual conditions are involved, see Subpart C of this part.

(18) *Export information code.* A code that identifies the type of export shipment or condition of the exported items (e.g., goods donated for relief or charity, impelled shipments, shipments under the Foreign Military Sales program, household goods, and all other shipments). (For the list of the codes see Appendix B.)

(19) *Shipment reference number.* A unique identification number assigned by the filer that allows for the identification of the shipment in the filer's system. The number must be unique for five years.

(20) *Line number.* A number that identifies the specific commodity line item within a shipment.

(21) *Hazardous material indicator.* An indicator that identifies whether the shipment is hazardous as defined by the Department of Transportation.

(22) *Inbond code.* The code indicating whether the shipment is being transported under bond.

(23) *License code/license exemption code.* The code that identifies the commodity as having a federal government agency requirement for a license, permit, license exception or exemption or that no license is required.

(24) *Routed export transaction indicator.* An indicator that identifies that the shipment is a routed export transaction as defined in § 30.3.

(25) *Shipment filing action request indicator.* An indicator that allows the filer to add, change, replace, or cancel an export shipment transaction.

(26) *Line item filing action request indicator.* An indicator that allows the filer to add, change, or delete a commodity line within an export shipment transaction.

(27) *Filing option indicator.* An indicator of whether the filer is reporting export information predeparture or postdeparture. See § 30.4 for more information on EEI filing options.

(b) Conditional data elements are as follows:

(1) *Authorized agent and authorized agent identification.* If an authorized agent is used to prepare and file the EEI, the following information shall be provided to the AES.

(i) *U.S. Authorized agent's identification number.* Report the U.S. authorized agent's own EIN or DUNS for the first shipment and for each subsequent shipment. Use of another company's or individual's EIN or other identification number is prohibited. The party ID type of agent identification (E=EIN, D=DUNS) shall be indicated.

(ii) *Name of the authorized agent.* Report the name of the authorized agent. The authorized agent is that person or entity in the United States that is authorized by the USPPI or the FPPI to prepare and file the EEI or the person or entity, if any, named on the export license. (See § 30.3 for details on the specific reporting responsibilities of authorized agents and Subpart B of this part for export control licensing requirements for authorized agents.)

(iii) *Address of the authorized agent.* Report the address or location (no post office box number) of the authorized agent. The authorized agent's address shall be reported with the initial shipment. Subsequent shipments may be identified by the agent's identification number.

(iv) *Contact information.* Report the contact name and telephone number.

(2) *Intermediate consignee.* The name and address of the intermediate consignee (if any) shall be reported. The intermediate consignee acts in a foreign country as an agent for the principal party in interest or the ultimate consignee for the purpose of effecting delivery of the export shipment to the ultimate consignee. The intermediate consignee is the person named as such on the export license or authorized to act as such under the applicable general license and in conformity with the EAR.

(3) *FTZ identifier.* If goods are removed from the FTZ and not entered for consumption, report the FTZ identifier. This is the unique identifier assigned by the Foreign Trade Zone Board that identifies the FTZ, subzone or site from which goods are withdrawn for export.

(4) *Foreign port of unlading.* The foreign port of unlading is the foreign port in the country where the goods are removed from the exporting carrier. The foreign port does not have to be located in the country of destination. For exports by sea to foreign countries, not including Puerto Rico, the foreign port of unlading is the code in terms of Schedule K, *Classification of Foreign Ports by Geographic Trade Area and Country.* For exports by sea or air between the United States and Puerto Rico, the foreign port of unlading is the code in terms of Schedule D, *Classification of CBP Districts and Ports.* The foreign port of unlading is not required for exports by other modes of transportation, including rail, truck, mail, fixed (pipeline), or air (unless between the U.S. and Puerto Rico).

(5) *Export license number/CFR citation/KPC number.* License number, permit number, citation, or authorization number assigned by the Department of Commerce, BIS; Department of State, DDTC; Department of the Treasury, OFAC; Department of Justice, DEA; Nuclear Regulatory Commission; or any other federal government agency.

(6) *Export Control Classification Number (ECCN).* The number used to identify items on the CCL, Supplement No. 1 to Part 774 of the EAR. The ECCN consists of a set of digits and a letter. Items that are not classified under an ECCN are designated "EAR99".

(7) *Secondary unit of measure.* The unit of measure that corresponds to the secondary quantity as prescribed in the Schedule B or HTSUSA. If neither Schedule B nor HTSUSA specifies a secondary unit of measure for the item, the unit of measure is not required.

(8) *Secondary quantity.* The total number of units that correspond to the secondary unit of measure, if any, specified in the Schedule B or HTSUSA. See the definition of primary quantity for specific instructions on reporting the quantity as a weight and whole unit, rounding fractions.

(9) *Vehicle Identification Number (VIN)/Product ID.* The identification number found on the reported used vehicle. For used self-propelled vehicles that do not have a VIN, the Product ID is reported. "Used" vehicle refers to any self-propelled vehicle where the equitable or legal title to which has been transferred by a manufacturer, distributor, or dealer to an ultimate purchaser. See U.S. Customs and Border Protection regulations 19 CFR 192.1 for more information on exports of used vehicles.

(10) *Vehicle ID qualifier.* The qualifier that identifies the type of used vehicle number reported. The valid codes are V for VIN and P for Product ID.

(11) *Vehicle title number.* The number issued by the Motor Vehicle Administration.

(12) *Vehicle title state code.* The 2-character postal code for the state or territory that issued the vehicle title.

(13) *Entry number.* The entry number must be reported for goods that are entered in lieu of being transported under bond for which the importer of record is a foreign entity or, for reexports of goods withdrawn from a FTZ for which a NAFTA deferred duty claim (entry type 08) could have been made, but that the importer elected to enter for consumption under CBP entry type 06. For goods imported into the United States for export to a third country of ultimate destination, where the importer of record on the entry is a foreign entity, the USPPI will be the authorized agent designated by the foreign importer for service of process. The USPPI, in this circumstance, is required to report the import entry number.

(14) *Transportation reference number (TRN).* The TRN is as follows:

(i) *Vessel shipments.* Report the booking number for vessel shipments. The booking number is the reservation number assigned by the carrier to hold space on the vessel for cargo being exported. The TRN is required for all vessel shipments.

(ii) *Air shipments.* Report the master air waybill number for air shipments. The air waybill number is the reservation number assigned by the carrier to hold space on the aircraft for cargo being exported. The TRN is optional for air shipments.

(iii) *Rail shipments.* Report the bill of lading (BL) number for rail shipments. The BL number is the reservation number assigned by the carrier to hold space on the rail car for cargo being exported. The TRN is optional for rail shipments.

(iv) *Truck shipments.* Report the freight or pro bill number for truck shipments. The freight or pro bill number is the number assigned by the carrier to hold space on the truck for cargo being exported. The freight or pro bill number correlates to a bill of lading number, air waybill number or trip number for multimodal shipments. The TRN is optional for truck shipments.

(15) *Department of State requirements*—(i) *DDTC registration number.* The number assigned by the DDTC to persons who are required to register per Part 122 of the ITAR (22 CFR 120 through 130), and have an authorization (license or exemption) from DDTC to export the article.

(ii) *DDTC Significant Military Equipment (SME) indicator.* A term used to designate articles on the USML (22 CFR 121) for which special export controls are warranted because of their capacity for substantial military utility or capability. See §120.7 of the ITAR 22 CFR 120 through 130 for a definition of SME and §121.1 for items designated as SME articles.

(iii) *DDTC eligible party certification indicator.* Certification by the U.S. exporter that the exporter is an eligible party to participate in defense trade. See 22 CFR 120.1(c). This certification is required only when an exemption is claimed.

(iv) *DDTC USML category code.* The USML category of the article being exported (22 CFR 121).

(v) *DDTC Unit of Measure (UOM).* This unit of measure is the UOM covering the article being shipped as described on the export authorization or declared under an ITAR exemption.

(vi) *DDTC quantity.* This quantity is for the article being shipped. The quantity is the total number of units that corresponds to the DDTC UOM code.

(vii) *DDTC exemption number.* The exemption number is the specific citation from the ITAR (22 CFR 120 through 130) that exempts the shipment from the requirements for a license or other written authorization from DDTC.

(viii) *DDTC export license line number.* The line number of the State Department export license that corresponds to the article being exported.

(16) *Kimberley Process Certificate (KPC) number.* The unique identifying number on the KPC issued by the United States KPC authority that must accompany any export shipment of rough diamonds. Rough diamonds are classified under 6-digit HS subheadings 7102.10, 7102.21, and 7102.31. Enter the KPC number in the license number field excluding the 2-digit U.S. ISO country code.

(c) *Optional data elements:*

(1) *Seal number.* The security seal number placed on the equipment or container.

(2) *Equipment number.* Report the identification number for the shipping equipment, such as container or igloo number (Unit Load Device (ULD)), truck license number, or rail car number.

[73 FR 31555, June 2, 2008, as amended at 74 FR 38916, Aug. 5, 2009]

EFFECTIVE DATE NOTE: At 78 FR 16376, Mar. 14, 2013, §30.6 was amended by revising paragraphs (a)(1)(ii), (a)(3), (a)(5) introductory text, (a)(5)(i), (a)(8), (a)(9), (a)(17) introductory text, (a)(19), and (a)(23); adding paragraph (a)(28); revising paragraph (b)(1) introductory text, (b)(1)(ii), and (b)(3); redesignating paragraphs (b)(15) and (16) as (b)(16) and (17), respectively, and revising them; adding a new paragraph (b)(15); and revising paragraph (c)(2), effective Jan. 8, 2014. At 78 FR 67928, Nov. 13, 2013, the effective date was delayed until Apr. 5, 2014. For the convenience of the user, the added and revised text is set forth as follows:

§ 30.6 Electronic Export Information data elements.

* * * * *

(a) * * *

(1) * * *

(ii) *Address of the USPPI.* In all EEI filings, the USPPI shall report the address or location (no post office box number) from which the goods actually begin the journey to the port of export even if the USPPI does not own/lease the facility. For example, the EEI covering goods laden aboard a truck at a warehouse in Georgia for transport to Florida for loading onto a vessel for export to a foreign country shall show the address of the warehouse in Georgia. For shipments with multiple origins, report the address from which the commodity with the greatest value begins its export journey. If such information is not known, report the address in the state where the commodities are consolidated for export.

* * * * *

(3) *Ultimate consignee.* The ultimate consignee is the person, party, or designee that is located abroad and actually receives the export shipment. The name and address of the ultimate consignee, whether by sale in the United States or abroad or by consignment, shall be reported in the EEI. The ultimate consignee as known at the time of export shall be reported. For shipments requiring an export license including shipments to international waters, the ultimate consignee reported in the AES shall be the person so designated on the export license or authorized to be the ultimate consignee under the applicable license exemption or exception in conformance with the EAR or ITAR, as applicable. For goods sold en route, report the appropriate "To be Sold En Route" indicator in the EEI, and report corrected information as soon as it is known (see § 30.9 for procedures on correcting AES information).

* * * * *

(5) *Country of ultimate destination.* The country of ultimate destination is the country in which goods are to be consumed, further processed, stored, or manufactured, as known to the USPPI at the time of export. The country of ultimate destination is the code issued by the ISO. (i) *Shipments under an export license, license exception or license exemption.* For shipments under an export license or license exemption issued by the Department of State, DDTC or export license or license exception issued by the Department of Commerce, BIS, the country of ultimate destination shall conform to the country of ultimate destination as shown on the license. In the case of a Department of State license, the country of ultimate destination is the country specified with respect to the end user. For goods licensed by other government agencies, refer to their specific requirements concerning providing country of destination information. For shipments to international waters for items that are being exported pursuant to a BIS license exception or No License Required (NLR), the country of destination to be reported is the nationality of the person(s) or entity assuming control of the item(s) subject to the Export Administration Regulations that are being exported.

* * * * *

(8) *Carrier identification.* The carrier identification is the Standard Carrier Alpha Code (SCAC) for vessel, rail, and truck shipments or the International Air Transport Association (IATA) code for air shipments. The carrier identification specifies the carrier that transports the goods out of the United States. The carrier transporting the goods to the port of export and the carrier transporting the goods out of the United States may be different. For vessel shipments, report the carrier identification code of the party whose booking number was reported in the AES. For transshipments through Canada, Mexico, or another foreign country, the carrier identification is that of the carrier that transports the goods out of the United States. For modes other than vessel, air, rail and truck valid methods of transportation, including but not limited to mail, fixed transport (pipeline), and passenger hand carried, the carrier identification is not required. The National Motor Freight Traffic Association (NMFTA) issues and maintains the SCAC. (See *www.nmfta.org.*) The IATA issues and maintains the IATA codes. (See *www.census.gov/trade* for a list of IATA codes.)

(9) *Port of export.* The port of export is the U.S. Customs and Border Protection (CBP) seaport or airport where the goods are loaded on the carrier that is taking the goods out of the United States, or the CBP port where exports by overland transportation cross the U.S. border into Canada or Mexico. For EEI reporting purposes only, for goods loaded aboard a conveyance (aircraft or vessel) that stops at several ports before clearing to the foreign country, the port of export is the first port where the goods were loaded on this conveyance. For goods off-loaded from the original conveyance to another conveyance (even if the aircraft or vessel belongs to the same carrier) at any of the ports, the port where the goods were loaded on the last conveyance before going foreign is the port

of export. The port of export shall be reported in terms of Schedule D, "Classification of CBP Districts and Ports." Use port code 8000 for shipments by mail.

* * * * *

(17) *Value.* In general, the value to be reported in the EEI shall be the value of the goods at the U.S. port of export in U.S. dollars. The value shall be the selling price (or the cost, if the goods are not sold), plus inland or domestic freight, insurance, and other charges to the U.S. seaport, airport, or land border port of export. Cost of goods is the sum of expenses incurred in the USPPI's acquisition or production of the goods. Report the value to the nearest dollar, omit cents. Fractions of a dollar less than 50 cents should be ignored, and fractions of 50 cents or more should be rounded up to the next dollar.

* * * * *

(19) *Shipment reference number.* A unique identification number assigned by the filer that allows for the identification of the shipment in the filer's system. The reuse of the shipment reference number is prohibited.

* * * * *

(23) *License code/license exemption code.* The code that identifies the commodity as having a federal government agency requirement for a license, permit, authorization, license exception or exemption or that no license is required.

* * * * *

(28) *Ultimate consignee type.* Provide the business function of the ultimate consignee that most often applies. If more than one type applies to the ultimate consignee, report the type that applies most often. For purposes of this paragraph, the ultimate consignee will be designated as a Direct Consumer, Government Entity, Reseller, or Other/Unknown, defined as follows:

(i) Direct Consumer—a non-government institution, enterprise, or company that will consume or use the exported good as a consumable, for its own internal processes, as an input to the production of another good or as machinery or equipment that is part of a manufacturing process or a provision of services and will not resell or distribute the good.

(ii) Government Entity—a government-owned or government-controlled agency, institution, enterprise, or company.

(iii) Reseller—a non-government reseller, retailer, wholesaler, distributor, distribution center or trading company.

(iv) Other/Unknown—an entity that is not a Direct Consumer, Government Entity or Reseller, as defined above, or whose ultimate consignee type is not known at the time of export.

(b) * * *

(1) *Authorized agent and authorized agent identification.* The authorized agent is the person or entity in the United States who is authorized by the USPPI or the FPPI to prepare and file the EEI or the person or entity, if any, named on the export license. If an authorized agent is used, the following information shall be provided to the AES:

* * * * *

(ii) *Name of the authorized agent.* Report the name of the authorized agent. (See §30.3 for details on the specific reporting responsibilities of authorized agents and Subpart B of this part for export control licensing requirements for authorized agents.)

* * * * *

(3) *FTZ identifier.* If goods are removed from a FTZ and not entered for consumption, report the FTZ identifier. This is the unique 7-digit alphanumeric identifier assigned by the Foreign Trade Zone Board that identifies the FTZ, subzone or site from which goods are withdrawn for export.

* * * * *

(15) *License value.* For shipments requiring an export license, report the value designated on the export license that corresponds to the commodity being exported.

(16) *Department of State requirements.* (i) *Directorate of Defense Trade Controls (DDTC) registration number.* The number assigned by the DDTC to persons who are required to register per part 122 of the ITAR (22 CFR parts 120 through 130), and have an authorization (license or exemption) from DDTC to export the article.

(ii) *DDTC Significant Military Equipment (SME) indicator.* A term used to designate articles on the USML (22 CFR part 121) for which special export controls are warranted because of their capacity for substantial military utility or capability. See §120.7 of the ITAR 22 CFR parts 120 through 130 for a definition of SME and §121.1 for items designated as SME articles.

(iii) *DDTC eligible party certification indicator.* Certification by the U.S. exporter that the exporter is an eligible party to participate in defense trade. See 22 CFR 120.1(c). This certification is required only when an exemption is claimed.

(iv) *DDTC United States Munitions List (USML) category code.* The USML category of the article being exported (22 CFR part 121).

(v) *DDTC Unit of Measure (UOM)*. This unit of measure is the UOM covering the article being shipped as described on the export authorization or declared under an ITAR exemption.

(vi) *DDTC quantity*. This quantity is the number of articles being shipped. The quantity is the total number of units that corresponds to the DDTC UOM code.

(vii) *DDTC exemption number*. The exemption number is the specific citation from the ITAR (22 CFR parts 120 through 130) that exempts the shipment from the requirements for a license or other written authorization from DDTC.

(viii) *DDTC export license line number*. The line number of the State Department export license that corresponds to the article being exported.

(17) *Kimberley Process Certificate (KPC) number*. The unique identifying number on the KPC issued by the United States Kimberley Process Authority that must accompany all export shipments of rough diamonds. Rough diamonds are classified under 6-digit HS subheadings 7102.10, 7102.21, and 7102.31. Enter the KPC number in the license number field excluding the 2-digit ISO country code for the United States.

(c) * * *

(2) *Equipment number*. Report the identification number for the shipping equipment, such as container or igloo number (Unit Load Device (ULD)), truck license number, rail car number, or container number for containerized vessel cargo.

§ 30.7 Annotating the bill of lading, air waybill, or other commercial loading documents with proof of filing citations, and exemption legends.

(a) Items identified on the USML shall meet the predeparture reporting requirements identified in the ITAR (22 CFR 120 through 130) for the U.S. State Department requirements concerning the time and place of filing. For USML shipments, the proof of filing citations shall include the statement in "AES," followed by the returned confirmation number provided by the AES when the transmission is accepted, referred to as the ITN.

(b) For shipments other than USML, the USPPI or the authorized agent is responsible for annotating the proper proof of filing citation or exemption legend on the first page of the bill of lading, air waybill, export shipping instructions or other commercial loading documents. The USPPI or the authorized agent must provide the proof of filing citation or exemption legend to the exporting carrier. The carrier must annotate the proof of filing citation, exemption or exclusion legends on the carrier's outbound manifest when required. The carrier is responsible for presenting the appropriate proof of filing citation or exemption legend to CBP Port Director at the port of export as stated in Subpart E of this part. Such presentation shall be without material change or amendment of the proof of filing citation, postdeparture filing citation, AES downtime filing citation, or exemption legend as provided to the carrier by the USPPI or the authorized agent. The proof of filing citation will identify that the export information has been accepted as transmitted. The postdeparture filing citation, AES downtime filing citation, or exemption legend will identify that no filing is required prior to export. The proof of filing citations, postdeparture filing citations, or exemption legends shall appear on the bill of lading, air waybill or other commercial loading documentation and shall be clearly visible. The AES filing citation, exemption or exclusion legends are provided for in Appendix D. The exporting carrier shall annotate the manifest or other carrier documentation with the AES filing citations, exemption or exclusions legends.

(c) Exports of rough diamonds classified under HS subheadings 7102.10, 7102.21, and 7102.31, in accordance with the Clean Diamond Trade Act, will require the proof of filing citation, as stated in paragraph (b) of this section, and report the proof of filing citation on the KPC.

EFFECTIVE DATE NOTE: At 78 FR 16378, Mar. 14, 2013, § 30.7 was amended by revising paragraph (c), effective Jan. 8, 2014. At 78 FR 67928, Nov. 13, 2013, the effective date was delayed until Apr. 5, 2014. For the convenience of the user, the revised text is set forth as follows:

§ 30.7 Annotating the bill of lading, air waybill, or other commercial loading documents with proof of filing citations, and exemption legends.

* * * * *

(c) Exports of rough diamonds classified under HS subheading 7102.10, 7102.21, 7102.31, in accordance with the Clean Diamond Trade Act, will require the proof of filing citation, as stated in paragraph (b) of this section, and report the proof of filing citation on the

KPC. In addition, the KPC must be faxed prior to exportation to the Census Bureau on (800) 457–7328 or provided by other methods as permitted by the Census Bureau.

§30.8 Time and place for presenting proof of filing citations, and exemption and exclusions legends.

The following conditions govern the time and place to present proof of filing citations, postdeparture filing citations, AES downtime filing citation, exemption or exclusion legends. The USPPI or the authorized agent is required to deliver the proof of filing citations, postdeparture filing citations, AES downtime filing citation, exemption or exclusion legends required in §30.4(e) to the exporting carrier. See Appendix D of this part for the properly formatted proof of filing citations, exemption or exclusion legends. Failure of the USPPI or the authorized agent of either the USPPI or FPPI to comply with these requirements constitutes a violation of the regulations in this part and renders such principal party or the authorized agent subject to the penalties provided for in Subpart H of this part.

(a) *Postal exports.* The proof of filing citations, postdeparture filing citations, AES downtime filing citation, and/or exemption and exclusions legends for items being sent by mail, as required in §30.2, shall be presented to the postmaster with the packages at the time of mailing. The postmaster is required to deliver the proof of filing citations and/or exemption legends prior to export.

(b) *Pipeline exports.* The proof of filing citations or exemption and exclusion legends for items being sent by pipeline shall be presented to the operator of a pipeline no later than four calendar days after the close of the month.

(c) *Exports by other methods of transportation.* For exports sent other than by mail or pipeline, the USPPI or the authorized agent is required to deliver the proof of filing citations, and/or exemption and exclusion legends to the exporting carrier in accord with the time periods set forth in §30.4(b).

EFFECTIVE DATE NOTE: At 78 FR 16378, Mar. 14, 2013, §30.8 was revised, effective Jan. 8, 2014. At 78 FR 67928, Nov. 13, 2013, the effective date was delayed until Apr. 5, 2014. For the convenience of the user, the revised text is set forth as follows:

§30.8 Time and place for presenting proof of filing citations and exemption legends.

The following conditions govern the time and place to present proof of filing citations, postdeparture filing citations, AES downtime filing citation, exemption, or exclusion legends. The USPPI or the authorized agent is required to deliver the proof of filing citations, postdeparture filing citations, AES downtime filing citations, exemption, or exclusion legends required in §30.7 to the exporting carrier. See Appendix D of this part for the properly formatted proof of filing citations, exemption, or exclusion legends. Failure of the USPPI or the authorized agent of either the USPPI or FPPI to comply with these requirements constitutes a violation of the regulations in this part and renders such principal party or the authorized agent subject to the penalties provided for in Subpart H of this part.

(a) *Postal exports.* The proof of filing citations, postdeparture filing citations, AES downtime filing citation, and/or exemption and exclusions legends for items being sent by mail, as required in §30.4(b), shall be presented to the appropriate Postal Service personnel with the packages at the time of mailing. The postmaster is required to deliver the proof of filing citations or exemption legends prior to export.

(b) *Pipeline exports.* The proof of filing citations or exemption and exclusion legends for items being sent by pipeline shall be presented to the operator of a pipeline no later than four calendar days after the close of the month. See §30.46 for requirements for the filing of export information by pipeline carriers.

(c) *Exports by other methods of transportation.* For exports sent other than by mail or pipeline, the USPPI or the authorized agent is required to deliver the proof of filing citations and/or exemption and exclusion legends to the exporting carrier in accord with the time periods set forth in §30.4(b).

§30.9 Transmitting and correcting Electronic Export Information.

(a) The USPPI or the authorized filing agent is responsible for electronically transmitting accurate EEI as known at the time of filing in the AES and transmitting any changes to that information as soon as they are known. Corrections, cancellations, or amendments to that information shall be electronically identified and transmitted to the AES for all required fields as soon as possible. The provisions of this paragraph relating to the reporting of corrections, cancellations, or amendments to EEI, shall not be construed as a relaxation of the requirements of the rules and regulations pertaining to the preparation and filing of EEI. Failure to correct the EEI is a violation of the provisions of this part.

(b) For shipments where the USPPI or the authorized agent has received an error message from AES, the corrections shall take place as required. Fatal error messages are sent to filers when EEI is not accepted in the AES. These errors must be corrected and EEI resubmitted prior to export for shipments filed predeparture and as soon as possible for shipments filed postdeparture but not later than ten calendar days after departure. Failure to respond to fatal error messages or otherwise transmit corrections to the AES constitutes a violation of the regulations in this part and renders such principal party or authorized agent subject to the penalties provided for in Subpart H of this part. For EEI that generates a warning message, the correction shall be made within four (4) calendar days of receipt of the original transmission. For EEI that generates a verify message, the correction, when warranted, shall be made within four calendar days of receipt of the message. A compliance alert indicates that the shipment was not reported in accordance with regulation. The USPPI or the authorized agent is required to review filing practices and take whatever corrective actions are required to conform with export reporting requirements.

EFFECTIVE DATE NOTE: At 78 FR 16378, Mar. 14, 2013, § 30.9 was amended by revising paragraph (b), effective Jan. 8, 2014. At 78 FR 67928, Nov. 13, 2013, the effective date was delayed until Apr. 5, 2014. For the convenience of the user, the revised text is set forth as follows:

§ 30.9 Transmitting and correcting Electronic Export Information.

* * * * *

(b) For shipments where the USPPI or the authorized agent has received an error message from AES, the corrections shall take place as required. Fatal error messages are sent to filers when EEI is not accepted in the AES and update rejected messages are sent when a correction is not accepted in the AES. Fatal errors must be corrected and EEI resubmitted prior to export for shipments filed predeparture and for post-departure shipments but not later than five (5) calendar days after the date of export. Failure to respond to fatal error messages for shipments filed predeparture prior to export of the cargo subjects the principal party or authorized agent to penalties provided for in Subpart H of this part. Failing to transmit corrections to the AES constitutes a violation of the regulations in this part and renders such principal party or authorized agent subject to the penalties provided for in Subpart H of this part. Update rejected messages must be corrected as soon as possible. For EEI that generates a warning message, the correction shall be made within four (4) calendar days of receipt of the original transmission. For EEI that generates a verify message, the correction, when warranted, shall be made within four (4) calendar days of receipt of the message. A compliance alert indicates that the shipment was not reported in accordance with the FTR. The USPPI or the authorized agent is required to review its filing practices and take required corrective actions to conform with export reporting requirements.

§ 30.10 Retention of export information and the authority to require production of documents.

(a) *Retention of export information.* All parties to the export transaction (owners and operators of export carriers, USPPIs, FPPIs and/or authorized agents) shall retain documents pertaining to the export shipment for five years from the date of export. If the Department of State or other regulatory agency has recordkeeping requirements for exports that exceed the retention period specified in this part, then those requirements prevail. The USPPI or the authorized agent of the USPPI or FPPI may request a copy of the electronic record or submission from the Census Bureau as provided for in Subpart G of this part. The Census Bureau's retention and maintenance of AES records does not relieve filers from requirements in § 30.10.

(1) AES filers shall retain a copy of the electronic certification notice from the Census Bureau showing the filer's approved operational status. The electronic certification notice shall be retained for as long as the filer submits EEI through the AES.

(2) AES*Direct* filers shall retain a copy of the electronic certification notice obtained during the AES*Direct* certification. The electronic certification

notice shall be retained for as long as the filer submits EEI through AES*Direct*.

(b) *Authority to require production of documents.* For purposes of verifying the completeness and accuracy of information reported as required under § 30.6, and for other purposes under the regulations in this part, all parties to the export transaction (owners and operators of the exporting carriers, USPPIs, FPPIs, and/or authorized agents) shall provide upon request to the Census Bureau, CBP, ICE, BIS and other participating agencies EEI, shipping documents, invoices, orders, packing lists, and correspondence as well as any other relevant information bearing upon a specific export transaction at anytime within the five year time period.

NOTE TO § 30.10: Section 1252(b)(2) of Public Law 106–113, Proliferation Prevention Enhancement Act of 1999, required the Department of Commerce to print and maintain on file a paper copy or other acceptable back-up record of the individual's submission at a location selected by the Secretary of Commerce. The Census Bureau will maintain a data base of EEI filed in AES to ensure that requirements of Public Law 106–113 are met and that all filers can obtain a validated record of their submissions.

§§ 30.11–30.14 [Reserved]

Subpart B—Export Control and Licensing Requirements

§ 30.15 Introduction.

(a) For export shipments to foreign countries, the EEI is used both for statistical and for export control purposes. All parties to an export transaction must comply with all relevant export control regulations, as well as the requirements of the statistical regulations of this part. For convenience, references to provisions of the EAR, ITAR, CBP, and OFAC regulations that affect the statistical reporting requirements of this part have been incorporated into this part. For regulations and information concerning other agencies that exercise export control and licensing authority for particular types of commodity shipments, a USPPI, its authorized agent, or other party to the transaction shall consult the appropriate agency regulations.

(b) In addition to the reporting requirements set forth in § 30.6, further information may be required for export control purposes by the regulations of CBP, BIS, State Department, or the U.S. Postal Service under particular circumstances.

(c) This part requires the retention of documents or records pertaining to a shipment for five years from the date of export. All records concerning license exceptions or license exemptions shall be retained in the format (including electronic or hard copy) required by the controlling agency's regulations. For information on recordkeeping retention requirements exceeding the requirements of this part, refer to the regulations of the agency exercising export control authority for the specific shipment.

(d) In accordance with the provisions of Subpart G of this part, information from the EEI is used solely for official purposes, as authorized by the Secretary of Commerce, and any unauthorized use is not permitted.

§ 30.16 Export Administration Regulations.

The EAR issued by the U.S. Department of Commerce, BIS, also contain some additional reporting requirements pertaining to EEI (see 15 CFR 730–774).

(a) The EAR requires that export information be filed for shipments from U.S. Possessions to foreign countries or areas. (see 15 CFR 758.1(b) and 772.1, definition of the United States.)

(b) Requirements to place certain export control information in the EEI are found in the EAR.

EFFECTIVE DATE NOTE: At 78 FR 16379, Mar. 14, 2013, § 30.16 was amended by revising the introductory text and paragraph (b) and adding paragraphs (c), (d), and (e), effective Jan. 8, 2014. At 78 FR 67928, Nov. 13, 2013, the effective date was delayed until Apr. 5, 2014. For the convenience of the user, the added and revised text is set forth as follows:

§ 30.16 Export Administration Regulations.

The Export Administration Regulations (EAR) issued by the U.S. Department of Commerce, BIS, contain additional reporting requirements pertaining to EEI (see 15 CFR parts 730–774).

* * * * *

(b) Requirements to place certain export control information in the EEI are found in the EAR. (See 15 CFR 758.1(g) and 15 CFR 758.2).

(c) Requirements to place certain export control information on export control documents for shipments exempt from AES filing requirements. (See 15 CFR 758.1(d)).

(d) A shipment destined for a country listed in Country Group E:1 as set forth in Supplement No. 1 to 15 CFR part 740 shall require EEI filings regardless of value unless such shipment is eligible for an exemption in § 30.37(y) of this part and does not require a license by BIS or any other Federal Government Agency.

(e) Goods licensed by BIS where the country of ultimate destination is the United States or goods destined to international waters where the person(s) or entity assuming control of the item(s) is a citizen or permanent resident alien of the United States or a juridical entity organized under the laws of the United States or a jurisdiction within the United States shall be excluded from EEI filing.

§ 30.17 Customs and Border Protection regulations.

Refer to the DHS's CBP regulations, 19 CFR 192, for information referencing the advanced electronic submission of cargo information on exports for screening and targeting purposes pursuant to the Trade Act of 2002. The regulations also prohibit postdeparture filing of export information for certain shipments, and contain other regulatory provisions affecting the reporting of EEI. CBP's regulations can be obtained from the U.S. Government Printing Office's Web site at *www.gpoaccess.gov*.

§ 30.18 Department of State regulations.

(a) The USPPI or the authorized agent shall file export information, when required, for items on the USML of the ITAR (22 CFR 121). Information for items identified on the USML, including those exported under an export license exemption, shall be filed prior to export.

(b) Refer to the ITAR 22 CFR 120–130 for requirements regarding information required for electronically reporting export information for USML shipments and filing time requirements.

(c) Department of State regulations can be found at *http://www.state.gov*.

EFFECTIVE DATE NOTE: At 78 FR 16370, Mar. 14, 2013, § 30.18 was amended by revising paragraph (a), effective Jan. 8, 2014. At 78 FR 67928, Nov. 13, 2013, the effective date was delayed until Apr. 5, 2014. For the convenience of the user, the revised text is set forth as follows:

§ 30.18 Department of State regulations.

(a) The USPPI or the authorized agent shall file export information, as required, for items on the USML of the International Traffic in Arms Regulations (ITAR) (22 CFR part 121). Information for items identified on the USML, including those exported under an export license or license exemption, shall be filed prior to export. Items identified on the USML, including those exported under an export license or license exemption, ultimately destined to a location in the United States are not required to be reported in the AES.

* * * * *

§ 30.19 Other Federal agency regulations.

Other Federal agencies have requirements regarding the reporting of certain types of export transactions. The USPPIs and/or authorized agents are responsible for adhering to these requirements.

§§ 30.20–30.24 [Reserved]

Subpart C—Special Provisions and Specific-Type Transactions

§ 30.25 Values for certain types of transactions.

Special procedures govern the values to be reported for shipments of the following unusual types:

(a) *Subsidized exports of agricultural products*. Where provision is made for the payment to the USPPI for the exportation of agricultural commodities under a program of the Department of Agriculture, the value required to be reported for EEI is the selling price paid by the foreign buyer minus the subsidy.

(b) *General Services Administration (GSA) exports of excess personal property*. For exports of GSA excess personal property, the value to be shown in the EEI will be "fair market value," plus charges when applicable, at which the property was transferred to GSA by the holding agency. These charges include packing, rehabilitation, inland freight, or drayage. The estimated "fair market value" may be zero, or it may be a percentage of the original or estimated acquisition costs. (Bill of lading, air waybill, and other commercial loading documents for such shipments will bear the notation "Excess Personal Property, GSA Regulations 1–III, 303.03.")

EFFECTIVE DATE NOTE: At 78 FR 16379, Mar. 14, 2013, §30.25 was amended by adding paragraph (c), effective Jan. 8, 2014. At 78 FR 67928, Nov. 13, 2013, the effective date was delayed until Apr. 5, 2014. For the convenience of the user, the added text is set forth as follows:

§30.25 Values for certain types of transactions.

* * * * *

(c) *Goods rejected after entry.* For imported goods that are cleared by CBP but subsequently rejected, an EEI must be filed to export the goods. The value to be reported in the AES is the declared import value of the goods.

§30.26 Reporting of vessels, aircraft, cargo vans, and other carriers and containers.

(a) Vessels, locomotives, aircraft, rail cars, trucks, other vehicles, trailers, pallets, cargo vans, lift vans, or similar shipping containers are not considered "shipped" in terms of the regulations in this part, when they are moving, either loaded or empty, without transfer of ownership or title, in their capacity as carriers of goods or as instruments of such carriers, and EEI is not required.

(b) However, EEI shall be filed for such items, when moving as goods pursuant to sale or other transfer from ownership in the United States to ownership abroad. If a vessel, car, aircraft, locomotive, rail car, vehicle, or container, whether in service or newly built or manufactured, is sold or transferred to foreign ownership while in the Customs territory of the United States or at a port in such area, EEI shall be reported in accordance with the general requirements of the regulations in this part, identifying the port through or from which the vessel, aircraft, locomotive, rail car, car, vehicle, or container first leaves the United States after sale or transfer. If the vessel, aircraft, locomotive, rail car, car, vehicle, or shipping container is outside the Customs territory of the United States at the time of sale or transfer to foreign ownership, EEI shall be reported identifying the last port of clearance or departure from the United States prior to sale or transfer. The country of destination to be shown in the EEI for vessels sold foreign is the country of new ownership. The country for which the vessel clears, or the country of registry of the vessel, should not be reported as the country of destination in the EEI unless such country is the country of new ownership.

EFFECTIVE DATE NOTE: At 78 FR 16379, Mar. 14, 2013, §30.26 was revised, effective Jan. 8, 2014. At 78 FR 67928, Nov. 13, 2013, the effective date was delayed until Apr. 5, 2014. For the convenience of the user, the revised text is set forth as follows:

§30.26 Reporting of vessels, aircraft, cargo vans, and other carriers and containers.

(a) Export information shall be filed in the AES for all vessels, locomotives, aircraft, rail cars, trucks, other vehicles, trailers, pallets, cargo vans, lift vans, or similar shipping containers when these items are moving as goods pursuant to sale or other transfer from ownership in the United States to ownership abroad. If the vessel, car, aircraft, locomotive, rail car, vehicle, or shipping container is outside Customs territory of the United States at the time of sale or transfer to foreign ownership, EEI shall be reported identifying the last port of clearance or departure from the United States prior to sale or transfer. The date of export shall be the date of sale.

(b) The country of destination to be shown in the EEI for vessels sold foreign is the country of new ownership. The country for which the vessel clears, or the country of registry of the vessel, should not be reported as the country of destination in the EEI unless such country is the country of new ownership.

§30.27 Return of exported cargo to the United States prior to reaching its final destination.

When goods reported as exported from the United States are not exported or are returned without having been entered into a foreign destination, the filer shall cancel the EEI.

§30.28 "Split shipments" by air.

When a shipment by air covered by a single EEI submission is divided by the exporting carrier at the port of export where the manifest is filed, and part of the shipment is exported on one aircraft and part on another aircraft of the same carrier, the following procedures shall apply:

(a) The carrier shall deliver the manifest to CBP Port Director with the manifest covering the flight on which the first part of the split shipment is exported and shall make no changes to the EEI. However, the manifest shall show in the "number of packages" column the actual portion of the declared total quantity being carried and shall carry a notation to indicate "Split Shipment." All manifests with the notation "Split Shipment" will have identical ITNs.

(b) On each subsequent manifest covering a flight on which any part of a split shipment is exported, a prominent notation "SPLIT SHIPMENT" shall be made on the manifest for identification. On the last shipment, the notation shall read "SPLIT SHIPMENT, FINAL." Each subsequent manifest covering a part of a split shipment shall also show in the "number of packages" column only the goods carried on that particular flight and a reference to the total amount originally declared for export (for example, 5 of 11, or 5/11). Immediately following the line showing the portion of the split shipment carried on that flight, a notation will be made showing the air waybill number shown in the original EEI and the portions of the originally declared total carried on each previous flight, together with the number and date of each such previous flight (for example, air waybill 123; 1 of 2, flight 36A, June 6 SPLIT SHIPMENT; 2 of 2, flight 40X, June 6 SPLIT SHIPMENT, FINAL).

(c) Since the complete EEI was filed for the entire shipment initially, additional electronic reporting will not be required for these subsequent shipments.

EFFECTIVE DATE NOTE: At 78 FR 16379, Mar. 14, 2013, § 30.28 was amended by revising the section heading, introductory text, and paragraphs (a) and (b), effective Jan. 8, 2014. At 78 FR 67928, Nov. 13, 2013, the effective date was delayed until Apr. 5, 2014. For the convenience of the user, the revised text is set forth as follows:

§ 30.28 Split shipments.

A shipment covered by a single EEI transmission booked for export on one conveyance, but divided prior to export where the exporting carrier at the port of export will file the manifest indicating that the cargo was sent on two or more of the same conveyances leaving from the same port of export of the same carrier within 24 hours. For the succeeding parts of the shipment that are not exported within 24 hours, a new EEI must be filed and amendments must be made to the original AES record. The following procedures apply for split shipments:

(a) The carrier shall deliver the manifest to the CBP Port Director with the manifest covering the conveyance on which the first part of the split shipment is exported and shall make no changes to the EEI. However, the manifest shall show in the "number of packages" column the actual portion of the declared total quantity being carried and shall carry a notation to indicate "Split Shipment."e.g., "3 of 10—Split Shipment" All associated manifests with the notation "Split Shipment" will have identical ITNs if exported within 24 hours.

(b) On each subsequent manifest covering a conveyance on which any part of a split shipment is exported, a prominent notation "SPLIT SHIPMENT", e.g. "4 of 10—Split shipment" shall be made on the manifest for identification. On the last shipment, the notation shall read "SPLIT SHIPMENT, FINAL, e.g., "10 of 10 Split Shipment, Final"." Each subsequent manifest covering a part of a split shipment shall also show in the "number of packages" column only the goods carried on that particular conveyance and a reference to the total number originally declared for export (for example, 5 of 11, or 5/11). Immediately following the line showing the portion of the split shipment carried on that conveyance, a notation will be made showing the bill of lading number, air waybill number, or other commercial loading documents shown in the original EEI and the portions of the originally declared total carried on each previous conveyance, together with the number and date of each such previous conveyance.

* * * * *

§ 30.29 Reporting of repairs and replacements.

These guidelines will govern the reporting of the following:

(a) The return of goods previously imported for repair and alteration only and other returns to the foreign shipper of temporary imported goods (declared as such on importation) shall have Schedule B or HTSUSA classification commodity number 9801.10.0000. The value reported in the EEI shall include parts and labor. The value of the original product shall not be included.

(b) *Goods that are covered under warranty.* (1) Goods that are reexported after repair under warranty shall follow the procedures in paragraph (a) of this section. It is recommended that the bill of lading, air waybill, or other loading documents include the statement, "This product was repaired under warranty."

(2) Goods that are replaced under warranty at no charge to the customer shall include the statement, "Product replaced under warranty, value for EEI purposes" on the bill of lading, air waybill, or other commercial-loading documents. Place the notation below the proof of filing citation or exemption legend on the commercial document. Report the value of the replacement parts only.

EFFECTIVE DATE NOTE: At 78 FR 16380, Mar. 14, 2013, § 30.29 was amended by revising paragraphs (a), (b)(1), and (b)(2), effective Jan. 8, 2014. At 78 FR 67928, Nov. 13, 2013, the effective date was delayed until Apr. 5, 2014. For the convenience of the user, the revised text is set forth as follows:

§ 30.29 Reporting of repairs and replacements.

* * * * *

(a) The return of goods previously imported only for repair and alteration.

(1) The return of non-USML goods temporarily imported for repair and alteration and declared as such on importation shall have Schedule B number 9801.10.0000. The value reported shall only include parts and labor. The value of the original product shall not be included. If the value of the parts and labor is over $2,500 per Schedule B number, then EEI must be filed.

(2) The return of USML goods temporarily imported for repair and alteration and declared as such on importation shall have Schedule B number 9801.10.0000. In the value field, report the value of the parts and labor, in the license value field, report the value designated on the export license that corresponds to the commodity being exported. An EEI must be filed regardless of value.

(b) * * *

(1) Goods that are reexported after repair under warranty shall follow the procedures in paragraph (a)(1) or (2) of this section as appropriate. It is recommended that the bill of lading, air waybill, or other loading documents include the statement, "This product was repaired under warranty."

(2) Goods that are replaced under warranty at no charge to the customer shall include the statement, "Product replaced under warranty, value for EEI purposes" on the bill of lading, air waybill, or other commercial loading documents. Place the notation below the proof of filing citation or exemption legend on the commercial document. Report the Schedule B number or HTSUSA classification commodity number of the replacement parts. For non-USML goods, report the value of the replacement parts in accordance with § 30.6(a)(17). For USML shipments report the value in accordance to § 30.6(a)(17) and (b)(15).

§§ 30.30–30.34 [Reserved]

Subpart D—Exemptions From the Requirements for the Filing of Electronic Export Information

§ 30.35 Procedure for shipments exempt from filing requirements.

Where an exemption from the filing requirement is provided in this subpart of this part, a legend describing the basis for the exemption shall be made on the first page of the bill of lading, air waybill, or other commercial loading document for carrier use, or on the carrier's outbound manifest. The exemption legend shall reference the number of the section or provision in this part where the particular exemption is provided (see Appendix D of this part).

EFFECTIVE DATE NOTE: At 78 FR 16380, Mar. 14, 2013, § 30.35 was revised, effective Jan. 8, 2013. At 78 FR 67928, Nov. 13, 2013, the effective date was delayed until Apr. 5, 2014. For the convenience of the user, the revised text is set forth as follows:

§ 30.35 Procedure for shipments exempt from filing requirements.

Except as noted in § 30.2(a)(1)(iv), where an exemption from the filing requirement is provided in this subpart of this part, a legend describing the basis for the exemption shall be made on the first page of the bill of lading, air waybill, or other commercial loading document, and on the carrier's outbound manifest. The exemption legend shall reference the number of the section or provision in this part where the particular exemption is provided (see Appendix D of this part).

§ 30.36 Exemption for shipments destined to Canada.

(a) Except as noted in § 30.2(a)(1)(iv), and in paragraph (b) of this section, shipments originating in the United States where the country of ultimate destination is Canada are exempt from the EEI reporting requirements of this part.

(b) This exemption does not apply to the following types of export shipments:

(1) Sent for storage in Canada, but ultimately destined for third countries.

(2) Exports moving from the United States through Canada to a third destination shall be reported in the same manner as for all other exports. The USPPI or authorized agent shall follow the instructions as contained in this part for preparing and filing the EEI.

(3) Requiring a Department of State, DDTC, export license under the ITAR (22 CFR 120–130).

(4) Requiring a Department of Commerce, BIS, export license under the EAR (15 CFR 730–774).

(5) Subject to the ITAR, but exempt from license requirements.

(6) Classified as rough diamonds under the 6-digit HS subheadings (7102.10, 7102.21, or 7102.31).

EFFECTIVE DATE NOTE: At 78 FR 16380, Mar, 14, 2013, § 30.36 was amended by revising paragraph (b) introductory text and paragraph (b)(2); and adding paragraph (b)(7), effective Jan. 8, 2013. At 78 FR 67928, Nov. 13, 2013, the effective date was delayed until Apr. 5, 2014. For the convenience of the user, the added and revised text is set forth as follows:

§ 30.36 Exemption for shipments destined to Canada.

* * * * *

(b) This exemption does not apply to the following types of export shipments (These shipments shall be reported in the same manner as for all other exports, except household goods, which require limited reporting):

* * * * *

(2) Exports moving from the United States through Canada to a third destination.

* * * * *

(7) Used self-propelled vehicles as defined in 19 CFR 192.1 of U.S. Customs and Border Protection regulations, regardless of value or country of destination.

§ 30.37 Miscellaneous exemptions.

Filing EEI is not required for the following kinds of shipments. However, the Census Bureau has the authority to periodically require the reporting of shipments that are normally exempt from filing.

(a) Except as noted in § 30.2(a)(1)(iv), exports of commodities where the value of the commodities shipped from one USPPI to one consignee on a single exporting carrier, classified under an individual Schedule B or HTSUSA commodity classification code, is $2,500 or less. This exemption applies to individual Schedule B or HTSUSA commodity classification codes regardless of the total shipment value. In instances where a shipment contains a mixture of individual Schedule B or HTSUSA commodity codes valued $2,500 or less and individual Schedule B or HTSUSA commodity classification codes valued over $2,500, only those commodity classification codes valued over $2,500 need to be reported. If the filer reports multiple items of the same Schedule B or HTSUSA code, this exemption only applies if the total value of exports for the Schedule B or HTSUSA code is $2,500 or less.

(b) Tools of trade and their containers that are usual and reasonable kinds and quantities of commodities and software intended for use by individual USPPIs or by employees or representatives of the exporting company in furthering the enterprises and undertakings of the USPPI abroad. Commodities and software eligible for this exemption are those that do not require an export license or that are exported as tools of the trade under a license exception of the EAR (15 CFR 740.9), and are subject to the following provisions:

(1) Are owned by the individual USPPI or exporting company.

(2) Accompany the individual USPPI, employee, or representative of the exporting company.

(3) Are necessary and appropriate and intended for the personal and/or business use of the individual USPPI, employee, or representative of the company or business.

(4) Are not for sale.

(5) Are returned to the United States no later than one (1) year from the date of export.

(6) Are not shipped under a bill of lading or an air waybill.

(c) Shipments from one point in the United States to another point in the United States by routes passing through Canada or Mexico.

(d) Shipments from one point in Canada or Mexico to another point in the same country by routes through the United States.

(e) Shipments transported inbond through the United States and exported from another U.S. port or transshipped and exported directly from the port of arrival. (When goods are shipped through the United States for export to a third country of ultimate destination, but are first entered for consumption or for warehousing in the United States, the EEI shall be filed when the goods are exported from the United States.) Shipments transported inbond through the United States by vessel are subject to the filing requirements of the U.S. Army Corps of Engineers. Shipments transported inbond through the United States which require an export license are subject to the filing requirements of the licensing Federal agency.

(f) Exports of technology and software as defined in 15 CFR 772 of the EAR that do not require an export license are exempt from filing requirements. However, EEI is required for mass-market software. For purposes of this part, mass-market software is defined as software that is generally available to the public by being sold at retail selling points, or directly from the software developer or supplier, by means of over-the-counter transactions, mail-order transactions, telephone transactions, or electronic mail-order transactions, and designed for installation by the user without further substantial technical support by the developer or supplier.

(g) Shipments to foreign libraries, government establishments, or similar institutions, as provided in § 30.40(d).

(h) Shipments as authorized under License Exception GFT for gift parcels and humanitarian donations (see 15 CFR 740.12 of the EAR).

(i) Diplomatic pouches and their contents.

(j) Human remains and accompanying appropriate receptacles and flowers.

(k) Shipments of interplant correspondence, executed invoices and other documents, and other shipments of company business records from a U.S. firm to its subsidiary or affiliate. This excludes highly technical plans, correspondence, etc. that could be licensed.

(l) Shipments of pets as baggage, accompanied or unaccompanied, of persons leaving the United States, including members of crews on vessels and aircraft.

(m) Carriers' stores, not shipped under a bill of lading or an air waybill (including goods carried in ships aboard carriers for sale to passengers), supplies, and equipment for departing vessels, planes, or other carriers, including usual and reasonable kinds and quantities of bunker fuel, deck engine and steward department stores, provisions and supplies, medicinal and surgical supplies, food stores, slop chest articles, and saloon stores or supplies for use or consumption on board and not intended for unlading in a foreign country, and including usual and reasonable kinds and quantities of equipment and spare parts for permanent use on the carrier when necessary for proper operation of such carrier and not intended for unlading in a foreign country. Hay, straw, feed, and other appurtenances necessary to the care and feeding of livestock while en route to a foreign destination are considered part of carriers' stores of carrying vessels, trains, planes, etc.

(n) Dunnage, not shipped under a bill of lading or an air waybill, of usual and reasonable kinds and quantities necessary and appropriate to stow or secure cargo on the outgoing or any immediate return voyage of an exporting carrier, when exported solely for use as dunnage and not intended for unlading in a foreign country.

(o) Shipments of aircraft parts and equipment; food, saloon, slop chest, and related stores; and provisions and supplies for use on aircraft by a U.S. airline to its own installations, aircraft, and agents abroad, under EAR

License Exception AVS for aircraft and vessels (see 15 CFR 740.15(c)).

(p) Filing EEI is not required for the following types of commodities when they are not shipped as cargo under a bill of lading or an air waybill and do not require an export license, but the USPPI shall be prepared to make an oral declaration to CBP Port Director, when required: baggage and personal effects, accompanied or unaccompanied, of persons leaving the United States, including members of crews on vessels and aircraft.

(q) Temporary exports, except those that require licensing, whether shipped or hand carried, (e.g., carnet) that are exported from and returned to the United States in less than one year (12 months) from the date of export.

(r) Goods previously imported under a Temporary Import Bond for return in the same condition as when imported including: goods for testing, experimentation, or demonstration; goods imported for exhibition; samples and models imported for review or for taking orders; goods imported for participation in races or contests, and animals imported for breeding or exhibition and goods imported for use by representatives of foreign governments or international organizations or by members of the armed forces of a foreign country. Goods that were imported under bond for processing and reexportation are not covered by this exemption.

(s) Issued banknotes and securities, and coins in circulation exported as evidence of financial claims. The EEI must be filed for unissued bank notes and securities and coins not in circulation (such as banknotes printed in the United States and exported in fulfillment of the printing contract, or as parts of collections), which should be reported at their commercial or current value.

(t) Documents used in international transactions, documents moving out of the United States to facilitate international transactions including airline tickets, internal revenue stamps, liquor stamps, and advertising literature. Exports of such documents in fulfillment of a contract for their production, however, are not exempt and must be reported at the transaction value for their production.

EFFECTIVE DATE NOTE: At 78 FR 16380, Mar. 14, 2013, § 30.37 was amended by revising the introductory text and paragraph (a); removing and reserving paragraph (e); revising paragraphs (g) and (h); removing and reserving paragraphs (q) and (r); and adding paragraphs (u), (v), (w), (x) and (y), effective Jan. 8, 2013. At 78 FR 67928, Nov. 13, 2013, the effective date was delayed until Apr. 5, 2014. For the convenience of the user, the added and revised text is set forth as follows:

§ 30.37 Miscellaneous exemptions.

Except as noted in § 30.2(a)(1)(iv), filing EEI is not required for the following kinds of shipments. However, the Census Bureau has the authority to periodically require the reporting of shipments that are normally exempt from filing.

(a) Exports of commodities where the value of the commodities shipped from one USPPI to one consignee on a single exporting conveyance, classified under an individual Schedule B number or HTSUSA commodity classification code is $2,500 or less. This exemption applies to individual Schedule B numbers or HTSUSA commodity classification codes regardless of the total shipment value. In instances where a shipment contains a mixture of individual Schedule B numbers or HTSUSA commodity classification codes valued at $2,500 or less and individual Schedule B numbers or HTSUSA commodity classification codes valued over $2,500, only those Schedule B numbers or HTSUSA commodity classification codes valued over $2,500 are required to be reported. If the filer reports multiple items of the same Schedule B number or HTSUSA commodity classification code, this exemption only applies if the total value of exports for the Schedule B number or HTSUSA commodity classification code is $2,500 or less. Items of domestic and foreign origin under the same commodity classification number must be reported separately and EEI filing is required when either is over $2,500. For the reporting of household goods see § 30.38. NOTE: this exemption does not apply to the export of vehicles. The export information for vehicles must be filed in AES regardless of value or country of destination.

* * * * *

(g) Shipments of books, maps, charts, pamphlets, and similar articles to foreign libraries, government establishments, or similar institutions.

(h) Shipments as authorized under License Exception GFT for gift parcels and humanitarian donations (15 CFR 740.12(a) and (b)).

* * * * *

(u) Exports of technical data and defense service exemptions as cited in 22 CFR 123.22(b)(3)(iii) of the ITAR.

(v) Vessels, locomotives, aircraft, rail cars, trucks, other vehicles, trailers, pallets, cargo vans, lift vans, or similar shipping containers not considered "shipped" in terms of the regulations in this part, when they are moving, either loaded or empty, without transfer of ownership or title, in their capacity as carriers of goods or as instruments of such carriers.

(w) Shipments to Army Post Office, Diplomatic Post Office, Fleet Post Office.

(x) Shipments exported under license exception Baggage (BAG) (15 CFR 740.14).

(y) The following types of shipments destined for a country listed in Country Group E:1 as set forth in Supplement No. 1 to 15 CFR part 740 are not required to be filed in the AES:

(1) Shipments of published books, software, maps, charts, pamphlets, or any other similar media available for general distribution, as described in 15 CFR 731.7 to foreign libraries, or similar institutions.

(2) Shipments to U.S. government agencies and employees that are lawfully exported under License Exception GOV (15 CFR 740.11(b)(2)(i) or (ii)) valued at $2500 or less per Schedule B Number.

(3) Personal effects as described in 15 CFR 740.14(b)(1) being lawfully exported under License Exception BAG (15 CFR 740.14).

(4) Individual gift parcels and humanitarian donations being lawfully exported under License Exception GFT (15 CFR 740.12(a) and (b)).

(5) Vessels and aircraft lawfully leaving the United States for temporary sojourn to or in a Country Group E:1 country under License Exception AVS (15 CFR 740.15).

(6) Tools of trade that will be used by a person traveling to a Country Group E:1 destination, that will be returned to the United States within one year and that are lawfully being exported to a Country Group E:1 destination under License Exception BAG (15 CFR 740.14) or License Exception TMP (15 CFR 740.9(a)).

§30.38 Exemption from the requirements for reporting complete commodity information.

The following type of shipments will require limited reporting of EEI when goods are shipped under a bill of lading or an air waybill. In such cases, Schedule B or HTSUSA commodity classification codes and domestic/foreign indicator shall not be required.

(a) Usual and reasonable kinds and quantities of wearing apparel, articles of personal adornment, toilet articles, medicinal supplies, food, souvenirs, games, and similar personal effects and their containers.

(b) Usual and reasonable kinds and quantities of furniture, household effects, household furnishings, and their containers.

(c) Usual and reasonable kinds and quantities of vehicles, such as passenger cars, station wagons, trucks, trailers, motorcycles, bicycles, tricycles, baby carriages, strollers, and their containers provided that the above-indicated baggage, personal effects, and vehicular property: (See U.S. Customs and Border Protection regulations 19 CFR 192 for separate CBP requirements for the exportation of used self-propelled vehicles.)

(1) Shall include only such articles as are owned by such person or members of his/her immediate family;

(2) Shall be in his/her possession at the time of or prior to his/her departure from the United States for the foreign country;

(3) Are necessary and appropriate for the use of such person or his/her immediate family;

(4) Are intended for his/her use or the use of his/her immediate family; and

(5) Are not intended for sale.

EFFECTIVE DATE NOTE: At 78 FR 16380, Mar. 14, 2013, §30.38 was revised, effective Jan. 8, 2013. At 78 FR 67928, Nov. 13, 2013, the effective date was delayed until Apr. 5, 2014. For the convenience of the user, the revised text is set forth as follows:

§30.38 Exemption from the requirements for reporting complete commodity information.

Except as noted in §30.2(a)(1)(iv), report EEI for household goods. Household goods are usual and reasonable kinds and quantities of personal property necessary and appropriate for use by the USPPI in the USPPI's dwelling in a foreign country. Household goods include, but are not limited to items such as furniture, large and small appliances, kitchenware, electronics, toys, bicycles, clothing, personal adornments, and associated containers. These goods should be for use by the USPPI, not intended for sale; and shipped under a bill of lading or an air waybill. In such cases, Schedule B or HTSUSA commodity classification codes and domestic/foreign indicator shall not be required.

§ 30.39 Special exemptions for shipments to the U.S. Armed Services.

Filing of EEI is not required for any and all commodities, whether shipped commercially or through government channels, consigned to the U.S. Armed Services for their exclusive use, including shipments to armed services exchange systems. This exemption does not apply to articles that are on the USML and thus controlled by the ITAR and shipments that are not consigned to the U.S. Armed Services, regardless of whether they may be for their ultimate and exclusive use.

EFFECTIVE DATE NOTE: At 78 FR 16381, Mar. 14, 2013, § 30.39 was revised, effective Jan. 8, 2013. At 78 FR 67928, Nov. 13, 2013, the effective date was delayed until Apr. 5, 2014. For the convenience of the user, the revised text is set forth as follows:

§ 30.39 Special exemptions for shipments to the U.S. Armed Services.

Except as noted in § 30.2 (a)(1)(iv), filing of EEI is not required for any and all commodities, whether shipped commercially or through government channels, consigned to the U.S. Armed Services for their exclusive use, including shipments to armed services exchange systems. This exemption does not apply to articles that are on the USML and thus controlled by the ITAR and/or shipments that are not consigned to the U.S. Armed Services, regardless of whether they may be for their ultimate and exclusive use.

§ 30.40 Special exemptions for certain shipments to U.S. government agencies and employees.

Filing EEI is not required for the following types of shipments to U.S. government agencies and employees:

(a) Office furniture, office equipment, and office supplies shipped to and for the exclusive use of U.S. government offices.

(b) Household goods and personal property shipped to and for the exclusive and personal use of U.S. government employees.

(c) Food, medicines, and related items and other commissary supplies shipped to U.S. government offices or employees for the exclusive use of such employees, or to U.S. government employee cooperatives or other associations for subsequent sale or other distribution to such employees.

(d) Books, maps, charts, pamphlets, and similar articles shipped by U.S. government offices to U.S. or foreign libraries, government establishments, or similar institutions.

EFFECTIVE DATE NOTE: At 78 FR 16381, Mar. 14, 2013, § 30.40 was amended by revising the introductory text and removing paragraph (d), effective Jan. 8, 2013. At 78 FR 67928, Nov. 13, 2013, the effective date was delayed until Apr. 5, 2014. For the convenience of the user, the revised text is set forth as follows:

§ 30.40 Special exemptions for certain shipments to U.S. government agencies and employees.

Except as noted in § 30.2(a)(1)(iv), filing EEI is not required for the following types of shipments to U.S. government agencies and employees:

* * * * *

§§ 30.41–30.44 [Reserved]

Subpart E—General Carrier and Manifest Requirements

§ 30.45 General statement of requirements for the filing of carrier manifests with proof of filing citations for the electronic submission of export information or exemption legends when Electronic Export Information filing is not required.

(a) *Requirement for filing carrier manifest.* Carriers transporting goods from the United States, Puerto Rico, or the U.S. Virgin Islands to foreign countries; from the United States or Puerto Rico to the U.S. Virgin Islands; or between the United States and Puerto Rico; shall not be granted clearance and shall not depart until complete manifests or other required documentation (for ocean, air, and rail carriers) have been delivered to CBP Port Director in accordance with all applicable requirements under CBP regulations. CBP may require any of the following: bill of lading, air waybill, export shipping instructions, manifest, train consist, or other commercial loading document. The required document shall contain the appropriate AES proof of filing citations, covering all cargo for which the EEI is required, or exemption legends, covering cargo for which EEI need not be filed by the regulations of this part. Such annotation shall be without material change or amendment of proof of filing citations or exemption and exclusion legends as provided to the carrier by the USPPI or its authorized agent.

(1) *Vessels.* Vessels transporting goods as specified (except vessels exempted by paragraph (a)(4) of this section) shall file a complete manifest. Manifests may be filed via paper or electronically through the AES Vessel Transportation Module as provided in CBP Regulations, 19 CFR 4.63 and 4.76.

(i) *Bunker fuel.* The manifest (including vessels taking bunker fuel to be laden aboard vessels on the high seas) clearing for foreign countries shall show the quantities and values of bunker fuel taken aboard at that port for fueling use of the vessel, apart from such quantities as may have been laden on vessels as cargo.

(ii) *Coal and fuel oil.* The quantity of coal shall be reported in metric tons (1000 kgs or 2240 pounds), and the quantity of fuel oil shall be reported in barrels of 158.98 liters (42 gallons). Fuel oil shall be described in such manner as to identify diesel oil as distinguished from other types of fuel oil.

(2) *Aircraft.* Aircraft transporting goods shall file a complete manifest as required in CBP Regulations 19 CFR 122.72–122.76. The manifest shall be filed with CBP Port Director at the port where the goods are laden. For shipments from the United States to Puerto Rico, the manifests shall be filed with CBP Port Director at the port where the goods are unladed in Puerto Rico.

(3) *Rail carriers.* Rail carriers transporting goods shall file a car manifest or train consist with CBP Port Director at the border port of export in accordance with 19 CFR 123.

(4) *Carriers not required to file manifests.* Carriers exempted from filing manifests under applicable CBP regulations are required, upon request, to present to CBP Port Director, the proof of filing citation or exemption and exclusion legends for each shipment.

(5) *Penalties.* Failure of the carrier to file a manifest as required constitutes a violation of the regulations in this part and renders such carrier subject to the penalties provided for in Subpart H of this part.

(b) *Partially exported shipments.* Except as provided in paragraph (c) of this section, when a carrier identifies, prior to filing the manifest, that a portion of the goods covered by a single EEI transaction has not been exported on the intended carrier, it shall be noted on the manifest submitted to CBP. The carrier shall notify the USPPI or the authorized agent of changes to the commodity data, and the USPPI or the authorized agent shall electronically transmit the corrections, cancellations, or amendments as soon as they are known in accordance with §30.9. Failure by the carrier to correct the manifest constitutes a violation of the provisions of the regulations in this part and renders the carrier subject to the penalties provided for in Subpart H of this part.

(c) *"Split shipments" by air.* When a shipment by air covered by a single EEI transmission is exported in more than one aircraft of the carrier, the "split shipment" procedure provided in §30.28 shall be followed by the carrier in delivering manifests with the proof of filing citation or exemption legend to CBP Port Director.

(d) *Attachment of commercial documents.* The manifest shall carry a notation that values stated are as presented on the bills of lading, cargo lists, export shipping documents or other commercial documents. The bills of lading, cargo lists, export shipping documents or other commercial documents shall be securely attached to the manifest in such a manner as to constitute one document. The manifest shall reference the statement "Cargo as per bills of lading attached" or "Cargo as per commercial forms attached." Also required on the face of each bill of lading shall be the information required by the manifest for cargo covered by that document.

(e) *Exempt items.* For any item for which EEI is not required by the regulations in this part, a notation on the manifest shall be made by the carrier as to the basis for the exemption. In cases where a manifest is not required and EEI is not required, an oral declaration to CBP Port Director shall be made as to the basis for the exemption.

(f) *Proof of filing citations and exemption legends.* (1) Ocean and air exporting carriers shall not accept paper SEDs under any circumstances nor load cargo that does not have all proof of filing citations, exemption or exclusion legends as provided for in Appendix D.

(2) Ocean and air exporting carriers are subject to the penalties provided for in Subpart H of this part if the exporting carrier;

(i) Accepts paper SEDs for cargo or,

(ii) Loads cargo without all proof of filing citations, exemption or exclusion legends as provided for in Appendix D.

(3) Truck exporting carriers shall not accept paper SEDs under any circumstances nor cross the border into a foreign country without a proof of filing citations, exemption or exclusion legends for cargo being exported as provided for in Appendix D. Truck exporting carriers accepting paper SEDs for cargo being exported into foreign countries, or carrying cargo into foreign countries without a proof of filing citation, exemption or exclusion legends in their possession are subject to the penalties provided for in Subpart H of this part.

(4) Rail exporting carriers shall not accept paper SEDs under any circumstance nor cross the border into a foreign country without a proof of filing citations, exemption or exclusion legends for cargo being exported as provided in Appendix D. Rail exporting carriers accepting paper SEDs for cargo being exported into foreign countries, or carrying cargo into foreign countries without required proof of filing citations, exemption or exclusion legends in their possession are subject to the penalties provided for in Subpart H of this part.

EFFECTIVE DATE NOTE: At 78 FR 16381, Mar. 14, 2013, § 30.45 was amended by revising paragraph (a) introductory text and paragraphs (a)(2), (a)(4), (c), (d), and (f)(1) and (2); and removing paragraphs (f)(3) and (4), effective Jan. 8, 2013. At 78 FR 67928, Nov. 13, 2013, the effective date was delayed until Apr. 5, 2014. For the convenience of the user, the revised text is set forth as follows:

§ 30.45 General statement of requirements for the filing of carrier manifests with proof of filing citations for the electronic submission of export information or exemption legends when Electronic Export Information filing is not required.

(a) *Requirement for filing carrier manifest.* Carriers transporting goods from the United States, Puerto Rico, or the U.S. Virgin Islands to foreign countries; from the United States or Puerto Rico to the U.S. Virgin Islands; or between the United States and Puerto Rico may not be granted clearance and may not depart until complete manifests or other required documentation (for ocean, air, and rail carriers) have been delivered to CBP Port Director in accordance with all applicable requirements under CBP regulations. The CBP may require any document it determines necessary to ensure compliance with U.S. export control laws, such as: bill of lading, air waybill, export shipping instructions, manifest, train consist, or other commercial loading documents. The required documents shall contain the appropriate AES proof of filing citations, covering all cargo for which the EEI is required; or exemption legends, covering cargo for which EEI need not be filed by the regulations of this part. Such annotation shall be without material change or amendment of proof of filing citations or exemption and exclusion legends as provided to the carrier by the USPPI or its authorized agent.

* * * * *

(2) *Aircraft.* Aircraft transporting goods shall file a complete manifest in accordance with all applicable requirements under CBP regulations. The manifest shall be filed with the CBP Port Director at the CBP port of exit. For shipments from the United States to Puerto Rico, the manifests shall be filed with the CBP Port Director at the port where the goods are unladen in Puerto Rico.

* * * * *

(4) *Carriers not required to file manifests.* Carriers allowed to file incomplete manifests under applicable CBP regulations are required, upon request, to present to the CBP Port Director the proof of filing citation, exemption or exclusion legends for each shipment, prior to departure of the vessel, aircraft, train, truck or other means of conveyance.

* * * * *

(c) *Split shipments.* When a shipment is divided by the carrier and is covered by a single EEI transmission, the split shipment procedure provided in § 30.28 shall be followed by the carrier in delivering manifests with the proof of filing citation or exemption legend to the CBP Port Director.

(d) *Attachment of commercial documents.* The manifest shall carry a notation that values stated are as presented on the bills of lading, cargo lists, export shipping documents or other commercial documents. The bills of lading, cargo lists, export shipping documents or other commercial documents shall be securely attached to the manifest in such a manner as to constitute one document and otherwise comply with CBP regulations.

* * * * *

(f) * * *

(1) Except as noted in § 30.4(b)(2), ocean, rail, truck and air exporting carriers shall not load cargo that does not have all proof of filing citations, exemption, exclusion legends, or postdeparture citations as provided for in Appendix D.

(2) Except as noted in § 30.4(b)(2), ocean, rail, truck and air exporting carriers are subject to the penalties provided for in Subpart H of this part if the exporting carrier;

* * * * *

§ 30.46 Requirements for the filing of export information by pipeline carriers.

The operator of a pipeline may transport goods to a foreign country without the prior filing of the proof of filing citations, exemption or exclusion legends, on the condition that within four calendar days following the end of each calendar month the operator will deliver to CBP Port Director the proof of filing citations, exemption or exclusion legends covering all exports through the pipeline to each consignee during the month.

EFFECTIVE DATE NOTE: At 78 FR 16381, Mar. 14, 2013, § 30.46 was revised, effective Jan. 0, 2014. At 78 FR 67928, Nov. 13, 2013, the effective date was delayed until Apr. 5, 2014. For the convenience of the user, the revised text is set forth as follows:

§ 30.46 Requirements for the filing of export information by pipeline carriers.

The operator of a pipeline may transport goods to a foreign country without the prior filing of the proof of filing citations, exemption, or exclusion legends, on the condition that within four calendar days following the end of each calendar month the operator will deliver to CBP Port Director the proof of filing citations, exemption, or exclusion legends covering all exports through the pipeline to each consignee during the month.

§ 30.47 Clearance or departure of carriers under bond on incomplete manifest.

(a) For purposes of the regulations in this part, except when carriers are transporting merchandise from the United States to Puerto Rico, clearance (where clearance is required) or permission to depart (where clearance is not required) may be granted to any carrier by CBP Port Director prior to filing of a complete manifest as required under the regulations of this part or prior to filing by the carrier of all filing U.S. Customs and Border Protection regulations citations, exclusion, and/or exemption legends, provided there is a bond as specified in 19 CFR 4.75, 4.76, and 122.74. The conditions of the bond shall be that a complete manifest, where a manifest is required by the regulations in this part and all required filing citations, exclusion, and/or exemption legends shall be filed by the carrier no later than the fourth business day after clearance (where clearance is required) or departure (where clearance is not required) of the carrier except as otherwise specifically provided in paragraph (a)(1), (2), and (3) of this section.

(1) For manifests submitted electronically through AES, the condition of the bond shall be that the manifest and all required filing citations, exclusion, and/or exemption legends shall be completed not later than the tenth business day after departure from each port.

(2) For rail carriers to Canada, the conditions of the bond shall be that manifest and all filing citations, exclusion, and/or exemption legends shall be filed not later than the fifteenth business day after departure.

(3) For carriers under bond on incomplete manifest, the carrier must file prior to departure a list of filing citations, exclusion, and/or exemption legends for export shipments aboard the conveyance. The list of filing citations, exclusion and/or exemption legends shall be presented to a CBP Export Control Officer at the port of exit prior to departure.

(b) In the event that any required manifest and all required filing citations, exclusion and/or exemption legends are not filed by the carrier within the period provided by the bond, then a penalty of $1,100 shall be exacted for each day's delinquency beyond the prescribed period, but not more than $10,000 per violation.

(c) Remission or mitigation of the penalties for manifest violations provided herein may be granted by CBP as the Administering Authority. Prior disclosure of a manifest violation of this section shall be made in writing to CBP Port Director in the port of export as the Administering Authority.

EFFECTIVE DATE NOTE: At 78 FR 16381, Mar. 14, 2013, § 30.47 was amended by revising paragraph (a), effective Jan. 8, 2013. At 78 FR 67928, Nov. 13, 2013, the effective date was delayed until Apr. 5, 2014. For the convenience of the user, the revised text is set forth as follows:

§ 30.47 Clearance or departure of carriers under bond on incomplete manifest.

(a) For purposes of the regulations in this part, except when carriers are transporting merchandise from the United States to Puerto Rico, clearance or permission to depart may be granted to any carrier by a CBP Port Director prior to filing of a complete manifest as required under the CBP regulations or prior to filing by the carrier of all required filing citations, exclusion and/or exemption legends, provided there is a bond as specified in 19 CFR 4.75, 4.76, and 122.74. The conditions of the bond shall be that a complete manifest, where a manifest is required by the regulations in this part and all required filing citations, exclusion and/or exemption legends shall be filed by the carrier in accordance with all applicable requirements under CBP regulations.

(1) For manifests submitted electronically through the AES, the condition of the bond shall be that the manifest and all required filing citations, exclusion, and/or exemption legends shall be completed in accordance with all applicable requirements under CBP regulations.

(2) For rail carriers to Canada, the conditions of the bond shall be that the manifest and all filing citations, exclusion, and/or exemption legends shall be filed with CBP in accordance with all applicable requirements under CBP regulations.

(3) For carriers under bond on incomplete manifest, upon request, a list of filing citations, exclusion, and/or exemption legends must be presented to a CBP Export Control Officer at the port of export prior to departure by the carrier.

* * * * *

§§ 30.48–30.49 [Reserved]

Subpart F—Import Requirements

§ 30.50 General requirements for filing import entries.

Electronic entry summary filing through the ABI, paper import entry summaries (CBP–7501), or paper record of vessel foreign repair or equipment purchase (CBP–226) shall be completed by the importer or its licensed import broker and filed directly with CBP in accordance with 19 CFR. Information on all mail and informal entries required for statistical and CBP purposes shall be reported, including value not subject to duty. Upon request, the importer or import broker shall provide the Census Bureau with information or documentation necessary to verify the accuracy of the reported information, or to resolve problems regarding the reported import transaction received by the Census Bureau.

(a) Import information for statistical purposes shall be filed for goods shipped as follows:

(1) Entering the United States from foreign countries.

(2) Admitted to U.S. FTZs.

(3) From the U.S. Virgin Islands.

(4) From other nonforeign areas (except Puerto Rico).

(b) Sources for collecting import statistics include the following:

(1) CBP's ABI Program (see 19 CFR Subpart A, Part 143).

(2) CBP–7501 paper entry summaries required for individual transactions (see 19 CFR Subpart B, Part 142).

(3) CBP–226, Record of Vessel Foreign Repair or Equipment Purchase (see 19 CFR 4.7 and 4.14).

(4) CBP–214, Application for Foreign Trade Zone Admission and/or Status Designation (Statistical copy).

(5) Automated Foreign Trade Zone Reporting Program (AFTZRP).

EFFECTIVE DATE NOTE: At 78 FR 16382, Mar. 14, 2013, § 30.50 was amended by revising paragraph (b)(5) and adding paragraph (c), effective Jan 8, 2014. At 78 FR 67928, Nov. 13, 2013, the effective date was delayed until Apr. 5, 2014. For the convenience of the user, the added and revised text is set forth as follows:

§ 30.50 General requirements for filing import entries.

* * * * *

(b) * * *

(5) Electronic CBP Form 214 Admissions (e214).

(c) The Kimberley Process Certificates must be faxed prior to exportation to the Census Bureau on (800) 457–7328 or provided by other methods as permitted by the Census Bureau.

§30.51 Statistical information required for import entries.

The information required for statistical purposes is, in most cases, also required by CBP regulations for other purposes. Refer to CBP Web site at *http://www.cbp.gov* to download "Instructions for Preparation of CBP–7501," for completing the paper entry summary documentation (CBP–7501). Refer to the Customs and Trade Automated Interface Requirements for instructions on submitting an ABI electronic record, or instructions for completing CBP–226 for declaring any equipment, repair parts, materials purchased, or expense for repairs incurred outside of the United States.

§30.52 Foreign Trade Zones.

Foreign goods admitted into FTZs shall be reported as a general import. When goods are withdrawn from a FTZ for export to a foreign country, the export shall be reported in accordance with §30.2. When goods are withdrawn for domestic consumption or entry into a bonded warehouse, the withdrawal shall be reported on CBP–7501 or through the ABI in accordance with CBP regulations. (This section emphasizes the reporting requirements contained in CBP regulations 19 CFR 146, "Foreign Trade Zones.") When foreign goods are admitted into a FTZ, the zone operator is required to file CBP–214, "Application for Foreign Trade Zone Admission and/or Status Designation." Refer to CBP Web site for instructions on completing CBP–214. Per 19 CFR 146.32(a), the applicant for admission shall present CBP–214 to the Port Director and shall include the statistical (pink) copy, CBP–214(A), for transmittal to the Census Bureau, unless the applicant makes arrangements for the electronic transmission of statistical information to the Census Bureau through the AFTZRP. Companies operating in FTZs interested in reporting CBP–214 statistical information electronically on a monthly basis shall apply directly to the Census Bureau. Monthly electronic reports shall be filed with the Census Bureau no later than the tenth (10) calendar day of the month following the report month. Participation in the Census Bureau program does not relieve companies of the responsibility to file CBP–214 with CBP. The following data items are required to be filed, in the AFTZRP, for statistical purposes. (Use the instructions and definitions provided in 19 CFR 146 for completing these fields.):

(a) HTSUSA Classification Code.

(b) Country of Origin.

(c) Country Sub-code.

(d) U.S. Port of Entry.

(e) U.S. Port of Unlading.

(f) Transaction Type.

(g) Statistical Month.

(h) Method of Transportation.

(i) Company Authorization Symbol.

(j) Carrier Code.

(k) Foreign Port of Lading.

(l) Date of Exportation.

(m) Date of Importation.

(n) Special Program Indicator Field.

(o) Unit of Quantity.

(p) CBP (dutiable) Value.

(q) Gross (shipping) Weight.

(r) Charges.

(s) U.S. Value.

(t) FTZ/Subzone Number.

(u) Zone Admission Number.

(v) Vessel Name.

(w) Serial Number.

(x) Trade Identification.

(y) Admission Date.

EFFECTIVE DATE NOTE: At 78 FR 16382, Mar. 14, 2013, §30.52 was revised, effective Jan. 8, 2013. At 78 FR 67928, Nov. 13, 2013, the effective date was delayed until Apr. 5, 2014. For the convenience of the user, the revised text is set forth as follows:

§30.52 Foreign Trade Zones (FTZ).

When goods are withdrawn from a FTZ for export to a foreign country, the export shall be reported in accordance with §30.2. Foreign goods admitted into FTZs shall be reported as a general import. Statistical requirements for zone admissions are provided to the Census Bureau via CBP's Automated Broker Interface (ABI) electronic 214 (e214) program or the CBP Form 214A Application for Foreign Trade Zone Admission and/or Status Designation. Refer to CBP Web site at *www.cbp.gov* to download the "Foreign Trade Zone Manual" where instructions for completing the paper CBP Form 214A documents are provided in Appendix C. When goods are withdrawn for domestic consumption or entry into a bonded warehouse, the withdrawal shall be reported on CBP 7501 or through the ABI in accordance with CBP regulations. The instructions and definitions for completing the e214 are provided in 19 CFR 146. The following data items are required to be filed on the 214A, for statistical purposes:

(a) Zone Number and Location (Address)
(b) Port Code
(c) Importing Vessel and Flag/Other Carrier
(d) Export Date
(e) Import Date
(f) Zone Admission Number
(g) U.S. Port of Unlading
(h) In-bond Carrier
(i) Foreign Port of Lading
(j) Bill of Lading/AWB Number
(k) Number of Packages & Country of Origin
(l) Description of Merchandise
(m) HTSUSA Number
(n) Quantity (HTSUSA)
(o) Gross Weight
(p) Separate Value and Aggregate Charges
(q) Status Designation

§ 30.53 Import of goods returned for repair.

Import entries covering U.S. goods imported temporarily for repair or alteration and reexport are required to show the following statement: "Imported for Repair and Reexport" on CBP–7501 or in the ABI entry. Whenever goods are returned to the United States after undergoing either repair, alteration, or assembly under HTS heading 9802, the country of origin shall be shown as the country in which the repair, alteration, or assembly is performed. When the goods are for reexport and meet all of the requirements for filing the EEI, file according to the instructions provided in § 30.2, except for the following data items:

(a) *Value.* Report the value of the repairs, including parts and labor. Do not report the value of the original product. If goods are repaired under warranty, at no charge to the customer, report the cost to repair as if the customer were being charged.

(b) *Schedule B Classification Code.* Report Schedule B commodity classification code 9801.10.0000 for goods reexported after repair.

§ 30.54 Special provisions for imports from Canada.

(a) When certain softwood lumber products described under HTSUSA subheadings 4407.1001, 4409.1010, 4409.1090, and 4409.1020 are imported from Canada, import entry records are required to show a valid Canadian region of manufacture code. The Canadian region of manufacture is determined on a first mill basis (the point at which the item was first manufactured into a covered lumber product). Canadian region of manufacture is the first region where the subject goods underwent a change in tariff classification to the tariff classes cited in this paragraph. The Canadian region code should be transmitted in the electronic ABI summaries. The Canadian region of manufacture code should replace the region of origin code on CBP–7501, entry summary form. These requirements apply only for imports of certain softwood lumber products for which the region of origin is Canada.

(b) All other imports from Canada, including certain softwood lumber products not covered in paragraph (a) of this section, will require the twoletter designation of the Canadian region of origin to be reported on U.S. entry summary records. This information is required only for U.S. imports that under applicable CBP rules of origin are determined to originate in Canada. For nonmanufactured goods determined to be of Canadian origin, the region of origin is defined as the region where the exported goods were originally grown, mined, or otherwise produced. For goods of Canadian origin that are manufactured or assembled in Canada, with the exception of the certain softwood lumber products described in paragraph (a) of this section, the region of origin is that in which the final manufacture or assembly is performed prior to exporting that good to the United States. In cases where the region in which the goods were manufactured, assembled, grown, mined, or otherwise produced is unknown, the region in which the Canadian vendor is located can be reported. For those reporting on paper forms the region of origin code replaces the region of origin code on the CBP–7501, entry summary form.

(c) All electronic ABI entry summaries for imports originating in Canada also require the Canadian region of origin code to be transmitted for each entry summary line item.

(d) The region of origin code replaces the region of origin code only for imports that have been determined, under applicable CBP rules, to originate in Canada. Valid Canadian region/territory codes are:

XA—Alberta

XB—New Brunswick
XD—British Columbia Coastal
XE—British Columbia Interior
XM—Manitoba
XN—Nova Scotia
XO—Ontario
XP—Prince Edward Island
XQ—Quebec
XS—Saskatchewan
XT—Northwest Territories
XV—Nunavut
XW—Newfoundland
XY—Yukon

EFFECTIVE DATE NOTE: At 78 FR 16382, Mar. 14, 2013, §30.54 was amended by revising paragraph (b), effective Jan. 8, 2014. At 78 FR 67928, Nov. 13, 2013, the effective date was delayed until Apr. 5, 2014. For the convenience of the user, the revised text is set forth as follows:

§30.54 Special provisions for imports from Canada.

* * * * *

(b) All other imports from Canada, including certain softwood lumber products not covered in paragraph (a) of this section, will require the two letter designation of the Canadian province of origin to be reported on U.S. entry summary records. This information is required only for U.S. imports that under applicable CBP rules of origin are determined to originate in Canada. For nonmanufactured goods determined to be of Canadian origin, the province of origin is defined as the region where the exported goods were originally grown, mined, or otherwise produced. For goods of Canadian origin that are manufactured or assembled in Canada, with the exception of the certain softwood lumber products described in paragraph (a) of this section, the region of origin is that in which the final manufacture or assembly is performed prior to exporting that good to the United States. In cases where the region in which the goods were manufactured, assembled, grown, mined, or otherwise produced is unknown, the province in which the Canadian vendor is located can be reported. For those reporting on paper forms the region of origin code replaces the country of origin code on CBP Form 7501, entry summary form.

* * * * *

§30.55 Confidential information, import entries, and withdrawals.

The contents of the statistical copies of import entries and withdrawals on file with the Census Bureau are treated as confidential and will not be released without authorization by CBP, in accordance with 19 CFR 103.5 relating to the copies on file in CBP offices. The importer or import broker must provide the Census Bureau with information or documentation necessary to verify the accuracy or resolve problems regarding the reported import transaction.

(a) The basic responsibility for obtaining and providing the information required by the general statistical headnotes of the HTSUSA rests with the person filing the import entry. This is provided for in section 484(a) of the Tariff Act, 19 CFR 141.61(e) of CBP regulations, and §30.50 of this subpart. CBP Regulations 19 CFR 141.61(a) specify that the entry summary data clearly set forth all information required.

(b) 19 CFR 141.61(e) of CBP regulations provides that penalty procedures relating to erroneous statistical information shall not be invoked against any person who attempts to comply with the statistical requirements of the General Statistical Notes of the HTSUSA. However, in those instances where there is evidence that statistical suffixes are misstated to avoid quota action, or a misstatement of facts is made to avoid import controls or restrictions related to specific commodities, the importer or its licensed broker should be aware that the appropriate actions will be taken under 19 U.S.C. 1592, as amended.

§§30.56–30.59 [Reserved]

Subpart G—General Administrative Provisions

§30.60 Confidentiality of Electronic Export Information.

(a) *Confidential status*. The EEI collected pursuant to this Part is confidential, to be used solely for official purposes as authorized by the Secretary of Commerce. The collection of EEI by the Department of Commerce has been approved by the Office of Management and Budget (OMB). The information collected is used by the Census Bureau for statistical purposes only and by the BIS for export control purposes. In addition, EEI is used by other federal government agencies, such as the Department of State, CBP, and ICE for export control and other federal government agencies such as the Bureau of Economic Analysis, Bureau of Labor Statistics, and Bureau of Transportation Statistics for statistical purposes. Except as provided for in paragraph (e) of this section, information collected pursuant to this Part shall not be disclosed to anyone by any officer, employee, contractor, agent of the federal government or other parties with access to the EEI other than to the USPPI, or the authorized agent of the USPPI or the transporting carrier. Such disclosure shall be limited to that information provided by each party pursuant to this Part.

(b) *Supplying EEI for official purposes.* (1) The EEI may be supplied to federal agencies for official purposes, defined to include, but not limited to:

(i) Verification and investigation of export shipments, including penalty assessments, for export control and compliance purposes,

(ii) Providing proof of export; and

(iii) Statistical purposes;

(iv) Circumstances to be determined in the national interest pursuant to 13 U.S.C., § 301(g) and paragraph (e) of this section.

(2) The EEI may be supplied to the USPPI, or authorized agents of USPPI and carriers for compliance and audit purposes. Such disclosure shall be limited to that information provided to the AES by each party.

(c) *Supplying EEI for nonofficial purposes.* The official report of the EEI submitted to the United States Government shall not be disclosed by the USPPI, or the authorized agent, or representative of the USPPI for "nonofficial purposes," either in whole or in part, or in any form including but not limited to electronic transmission, paper printout, or certified reproduction. "Nonofficial purposes" are defined to include but not limited to use of the official EEI:

(1) In support of claims by the USPPI or its authorized agent for exemption from Federal or state taxation;

(2) By the U.S. Internal Revenue Service for purposes not related to export control or compliance;

(3) By state and local government agencies, and nongovernmental entities or individuals for any purpose; and

(4) By foreign governments for any purposes.

(d) *Copying of information to manifests.* Because the ocean manifest can be made public under provision of CBP regulations, no information from the EEI, except the ITN, filing citation, exemptions or exclusion legends, shall be copied to the outward manifest of ocean carriers.

(e) *Determination by the Secretary of Commerce.* Under 13 U.S.C. 301(g), the EEI is exempt from public disclosure unless the Secretary or delegate determines that such exemption would be contrary to the national interest. The Secretary or his or her delegate may make such information available, if he or she determines it is in the national interest, taking such safeguards and precautions to limit dissemination as deemed appropriate under the circumstances. In recommendations or decisions regarding such actions, it shall be presumed to be contrary to the national interest to provide EEI for purposes set forth in paragraph (c) of this section. In determining whether, under a particular set of circumstances, it is contrary to the national interest to apply the exemption, the maintenance of confidentiality and national security shall be considered as important elements of national interest. The unauthorized disclosure of confidential EEI granted under National Interest Determination renders such persons subject to the civil penalties provided for in Subpart H of this part.

(f) *Penalties.* Disclosure of confidential EEI by any officer, employee, contractor, or agent of the federal government, except as provided for in paragraphs (a) and (e) of this section renders such persons subject to the civil penalties provided for in Subpart H of this part.

§ 30.61 Statistical classification schedules.

The following statistical classification schedules are referenced in this part. These schedules, may be accessed through the Census Bureau's Web site at *http://www.census.gov/trade.*

(a) *Schedule B—Statistical Classification for Domestic and Foreign Commodities Exported from the United States,* shows the detailed commodity classification requirements and 10-digit statistical reporting numbers to be used in preparing EEI, as required by these regulations.

(b) *Harmonized Tariff Schedules of the United States Annotated for Statistical Reporting*, shows the 10-digit statistical reporting number to be used in preparing import entries and withdrawal forms.

(c) *Schedule C*—Classification of Country and Territory Designations for U.S. Foreign Trade Statistics.

(d) *Schedule D*—Classification of CBP Districts and Ports.

(e) *Schedule K*—Classification of Foreign Ports by Geographic Trade Area and Country.

(f) *International Air Transport Association (IATA)*—Code of the carrier for air shipments. These are the air carrier codes to be used in reporting EEI, as required by the regulations in this part.

(g) *Standard Carrier Alpha Code (SCAC)*—Classification of the carrier for vessel, rail and truck shipments, showing the carrier codes necessary to prepare EEI, as required by the regulations in this part.

§30.62 Emergency exceptions.

The Census Bureau and CBP may jointly authorize the postponement of or exception to the requirements of the regulations in this Part as warranted by the circumstances in individual cases of emergency where strict enforcement of the regulations would create a hardship. In cases where export control requirements also are involved, the concurrence of the regulatory agency and CBP also will be obtained.

§30.63 Office of Management and Budget control numbers assigned pursuant to the Paperwork Reduction Act.

(a) *Purpose.* This subpart will comply with the requirements of the Paperwork Reduction Act (PRA), 44 U.S.C. 3507(f), which requires that agencies display a current control number assigned by the Director of OMB for each agency information collection requirement.

(b) *Display.*

15 CFR section where identified and described	Current OMB control No.
§§30.1 through 30.99	0607–0152

§§30.64–30.69 [Reserved]

Subpart H—Penalties

§30.70 Violation of the Clean Diamond Trade Act.

Public Law 108–19, the Clean Diamond Trade Act (the Act), section 8(c), authorizes CBP and ICE, as appropriate, to enforce the laws and regulations governing exports of rough diamonds, including those with respect to the validation of the Kimberley Process Certificate by the exporting authority. The Treasury Department's OFAC also has enforcement authority pursuant to section 5(a) of the Act, Executive Order 13312, and Rough Diamonds Control Regulations (31 CFR 592). CBP, ICE, and the OFAC, pursuant to section 5(a) of the Act, are further authorized to enforce provisions of section 8(a) of the Act, that provide for the following civil and criminal penalties:

(a) *Civil penalties.* A civil penalty not to exceed $10,000 may be imposed on any person who violates, or attempts to violate, any order or regulation issued under the Act.

(b) *Criminal penalties.* For the willful violation or attempted violation of any license, order, or regulation issued under the Act, a fine not to exceed $50,000, shall be imposed upon conviction or:

(1) If a natural person, imprisoned for not more than ten years, or both;

(2) If an officer, director, or agent of any corporation, who willfully participates in such violation, imprisoned for not more than ten years, or both.

§30.71 False or fraudulent reporting on or misuse of the Automated Export System.

(a) *Criminal penalties*—(1) *Failure to file; submission of false or misleading information.* Any person, including USPPIs, authorized agents or carriers, who knowingly fails to file or knowingly submits, directly or indirectly, to the U.S. Government, false or misleading export information through the AES, shall be subject to a fine not to exceed $10,000 or imprisonment for not more than five years, or both, for each violation.

(2) *Furtherance of illegal activities.* Any person, including USPPIs, authorized agents or carriers, who knowingly reports, directly or indirectly, to the U.S. Government any information through or otherwise uses the AES to further any illegal activity shall be subject to a fine not to exceed $10,000 or imprisonment for not more than five years, or both, for each violation.

(3) *Forfeiture penalties.* Any person who is convicted under this subpart shall, in addition to any other penalty, be subject to forfeiting to the United States:

(i) Any of that person's interest in, security of, claim against, or property or contractual rights of any kind in the goods or tangible items that were the subject of the violation.

(ii) Any of that person's interest in, security of, claim against, or property or contractual rights of any kind in tangible property that was used in the export or attempt to export that was the subject of the violation.

(iii) Any of that person's property constituting, or derived from, any proceeds obtained directly or indirectly as a result of this violation.

(4) *Exemption.* The criminal fines provided for in this subpart are exempt from the provisions of 18 U.S.C. 3571.

(b) *Civil penalties*—(1) *Failure to file or delayed filing violations.* A civil penalty not to exceed $1,100 for each day of delinquency beyond the applicable period prescribed in § 30.4, but not more than $10,000 per violation, may be imposed for failure to file information or reports in connection with the exportation or transportation of cargo.

(2) *Filing false/misleading information, furtherance of illegal activities and penalties for other violations.* A civil penalty not to exceed $10,000 per violation may be imposed for each violation of provisions of this part other than any violation encompassed by paragraph (b)(1) of this section. Such penalty may be in addition to any other penalty imposed by law.

(3) *Forfeiture penalties.* In addition to any other civil penalties specified in this section, any property involved in a violation may be subject to forfeiture under applicable law.

NOTE TO PARAGRAPH (b): The Civil Monetary Penalties; Adjustment for Inflation Final Rule effective December 14, 2004, adjusted the penalty in Title 13, Chapter 9, Section 304, United States Code from $1,000 to $10,000 to $1,100 to $10,000.

EFFECTIVE DATE NOTE: At 78 FR 16382, Mar. 14, 2013, § 30.71 was amended by revising paragraph (b)(1), redesignating paragraphs (b)(2) and (3) as paragraphs (b)(3) and (4), revising the newly redesignated (b)(3) and adding new paragraph (b)(2), effective Jan. 8, 2013. At 78 FR 67928, Nov. 13, 2013, the effective date was delayed until Apr. 5, 2014. For the convenience of the user, the added and revised text is set forth as follows:

§ 30.71 False or fraudulent reporting on or misuse of the Automated Export System.

* * * * *

(b) * * *

(1) *Failure to file violations.* A failure to file violation occurs if the government discovers that there is no AES record for an export transaction by the applicable period prescribed in § 30.4 of this part. Any AES record filed later than ten (10) calendar days after the due date will also be considered a failure to file regardless of whether the violation was or was not discovered by the government. A civil penalty not to exceed $10,000 may be imposed for a failure to file violation.

(2) *Late filing violations.* A late filing violation occurs when an AES record is filed after the applicable period prescribed in § 30.4 of this part. A civil penalty not to exceed $1,100 for each day of delinquency, but not more than $10,000 per violation, may be imposed for failure to file timely export information or reports in connection with the exportation or transportation of cargo. (See 19 CFR part 192)

(3) *Filing false/misleading information, furtherance of illegal activities and penalties for other violations.* A civil penalty not to exceed $10,000 per violation may be imposed for each violation of provisions of this part other than any violation encompassed by paragraph (b)(1) or (b)(2) of this section. Such penalty may be in addition to any other penalty imposed by law.

* * * * *

§ 30.72 Civil penalty procedures.

(a) *General.* Whenever a civil penalty is sought for a violation of this part, the charged party is entitled to receive a formal complaint specifying the charges and, at his or her request, to contest the charges in a hearing before an administrative law judge. Any such hearing shall be conducted in accordance with 5 U.S.C. 556 and 557.

(b) *Applicable law for delegated function.* If, pursuant to 13 U.S.C. 306, the Secretary delegates functions addressed in this part to another agency, the provisions of law of that agency relating to penalty assessment, remission or mitigation of such penalties, collection of such penalties, and limitations of action and compromise of claims shall apply.

(c) *Commencement of civil actions.* If any person fails to pay a civil penalty imposed under this subpart, the Secretary may request the Attorney General to commence a civil action in an appropriate district court of the United States to recover the amount imposed (plus interest at currently prevailing rates from the date of the final order). No such action may be commenced more than five years after the date the order imposing the civil penalty becomes final. In such action, the validity, amount, and appropriateness of such penalty shall not be subject to review.

(d) *Remission and mitigation.* Any penalties imposed under §30.71(b)(1) and (b)(2) may be remitted or mitigated, if:

(1) The penalties were incurred without willful negligence or fraud; or

(2) Other circumstances exist that justify a remission or mitigation.

(e) *Deposit of payments in General Fund of the Treasury.* Any amount paid in satisfaction of a civil penalty imposed under this subpart shall be deposited into the general fund of the Treasury and credited as miscellaneous receipts, other than a payment to remit a forfeiture which shall be deposited into the Treasury Forfeiture fund.

§30.73 Enforcement.

(a) *Department of Commerce.* The BIS's OEE may conduct investigations pursuant to this part. In conducting investigations, BIS may, to the extent necessary or appropriate to the enforcement of this part, exercise such authorities as are conferred upon BIS by other laws of the United States, subject, as appropriate, to policies and procedures approved by the Attorney General.

(b) *Department of Homeland Security (DHS).* ICE and CBP may enforce the provisions of this part and ICE, as assisted by CBP may conduct investigations under this part.

§30.74 Voluntary self-disclosure.

(a) *General policy.* The Census Bureau strongly encourages disclosure of any violation or suspected violation of the FTR. Voluntary self-disclosure is a mitigating factor in determining what administrative sanctions, if any, will be sought. The Secretary of Commerce has delegated all enforcement authority under 13 U.S.C. Chapter 9, to the BIS and the DHS.

(b) *Limitations.* (1) The provisions of this section apply only when information is provided to the Census Bureau for its review in determining whether to seek administrative action for violations of the FTR.

(2) The provisions of this section apply only when information is received by the Census Bureau for review prior to the time that the Census Bureau, or any other agency of the United States Government, has learned the same or substantially similar information from another source and has commenced an investigation or inquiry in connection with that information.

(3) While voluntary self-disclosure is a mitigating factor in determining what corrective actions will be required by the Census Bureau and/or whether the violation will be referred to the BIS to determine what administrative sanctions, if any, will be sought, it is a factor that is considered together with all other factors in a case. The weight given to voluntary self-disclosure is within the discretion of the Census Bureau and the BIS, and the mitigating effect of voluntary self-disclosure may be outweighed by aggravating factors. Voluntary self-disclosure does not prevent transactions from being referred to the Department of Justice (DOJ) for criminal prosecution. In such a case, the BIS or the DHS would notify the DOJ of the voluntary self-disclosure, but the consideration of that factor is within the discretion of the DOJ.

(4) Any person, including USPPIs, authorized agents, or carriers, will not be deemed to have made a voluntary self-disclosure under this section unless the individual making the disclosure did so

with the full knowledge and authorization of senior management.

(5) The provisions of this section do not, nor should they be relied on to, create, confer, or grant any rights, benefits, privileges, or protection enforceable at law or in equity by any person, business, or entity in any civil, criminal, administrative, or other matter.

(c) *Information to be provided*—(1) *General.* Any person disclosing information that constitutes a voluntary self-disclosure should, in the manner outlined below, if a violation is suspected or a violation is discovered, conduct a thorough review of all export transactions for the past five years where violations of the FTR are suspected and notify the Census Bureau as soon as possible.

(2) *Initial notification.* (i) The initial notification must be in writing and be sent to the address in paragraph (c)(5) of this section. The notification must include the name of the person making the disclosure and a brief description of the suspected violations. The notification should describe the general nature, circumstances, and extent of the violations. If the person making the disclosure subsequently completes the narrative account required by paragraph (c)(3) of this section, the disclosure will be deemed to have been made on the date of the initial notification for purposes of paragraph (b)(2) of this section.

(ii) Disclosure of suspected violations that involve export of items controlled, licensed, or otherwise subject to the jurisdiction by a department or agency of the federal government should be made to the appropriate federal department or agency.

(3) *Narrative account.* After the initial notification, a thorough review should be conducted of all export transactions where possible violations of the FTR are suspected. The Census Bureau recommends that the review cover a period of five years prior to the date of the initial notification. If the review goes back less than five years, there is a risk that violations may not be discovered that later could become the subject of an investigation. Any violations not voluntarily disclosed do not receive consideration under this section. However, the failure to make such disclosures will not be treated as a separate violation unless some other section of the FTR or other provision of law requires disclosure. Upon completion of the review, the Census Bureau should be furnished with a narrative account that sufficiently describes the suspected violations so that their nature and gravity can be assessed. The narrative account should also describe the nature of the review conducted and measures that may have been taken to minimize the likelihood that violations will occur in the future. The narrative account should include:

(i) The kind of violation involved, for example, failure to file EEI, failure to correct fatal errors, failure to file timely corrections;

(ii) Describe all data required to be reported under the FTR that was either not reported or reported incorrectly;

(iii) An explanation of when and how the violations occurred;

(iv) The complete identities and addresses of all individuals and organizations, whether foreign or domestic, involved in the activities giving rise to the violations; and

(v) A description of any mitigating circumstances.

(4) *Electronic export information.* Report all data required under the FTR that was not reported. Report corrections for all data reported incorrectly. All reporting of unreported data or corrections to previously reported data shall be made through the AES.

(5) *Where to make voluntary self-disclosures.* With the exception of voluntary disclosures of manifest violations under § 30.47 (c), the information constituting a voluntary self-disclosure or any other correspondence pertaining to a voluntary self-disclosure may be submitted to: Chief, Foreign Trade Division, U.S. Census Bureau, Room 6K032, Washington, DC 20233–6700, by phone 1–800–549–0595, by fax (301) 763–8835, or by e-mail *FTDRegs@census.gov.*

(d) *Action by the Census Bureau.* After the Census Bureau has been provided with the required narrative, it will promptly notify CBP, ICE, and the OEE of the voluntary disclosure, acknowledge the disclosure by letter, provide the person making the disclosure with a point of contact, and take whatever additional action, including further investigation, it deems appropriate. As quickly as the facts and circumstances of a given case permit, the Census Bureau may take any of the following actions:

(1) Inform the person or company making the voluntary self-disclosure of the action to be taken.

(2) Issue a warning letter or letter setting forth corrective measures required.

(3) Refer the matter, if necessary, to the OEE for the appropriate action.

EFFECTIVE DATE NOTE: At 78 FR 16382, Mar. 14, 2013, §30.74 was amended by revising paragraphs (c)(3)(iv), (c)(3)(v), and (c)(5) and adding paragraphs (c)(3)(vi) and (c)(3)(vii), effective Jan. 8, 2014. At 78 FR 67928, Nov. 13, 2013, the effective date was delayed until Apr. 5, 2014. For the convenience of the user, the added and revised text is set forth as follows:

§30.74 Voluntary self-disclosure.

* * * * *

(c) * * *

(3) * * *

(iv) The complete identities and addresses of all individuals and organizations, whether foreign or domestic, involved in the activities giving rise to the violations;

(v) A description of any mitigating circumstances;

(vi) Corrective measures taken; and

(vii) ITNs of the missed and/or corrected shipments.

* * * * *

(5) *Where to make voluntary self-disclosures.* With the exception of voluntary disclosures of manifest violations under §30.47(c), the information constituting a Voluntary Self-Disclosures or any other correspondence pertaining to a Voluntary Self-Disclosures may be submitted to: Chief, Foreign Trade Division, U.S. Census Bureau, Room 6K032, Washington, DC 20233–6700, or by fax on (301) 763–8835. Additional instructions are found at *www.census.gov/trade.*

* * * * *

§§30.75–30.99 [Reserved]

APPENDIX A TO PART 30—SAMPLE FOR POWER OF ATTORNEY AND WRITTEN AUTHORIZATION

Appendix A to Part 30–Sample for Power of Attorney and Written Authorization
SAMPLE FORMAT: Power of Attorney

POWER OF ATTORNEY
U.S. PRINCIPAL PARTY IN INTEREST/AUTHORIZED AGENT

Know all men by these presents, that______________________________, the
(Name of U.S. Principal Party in Interest (USPPI))
USPPI organized and doing business under the laws of the State or Country of
________________________ and having an office and place of business
at____________________________hereby
(Address of USPPI)
authorizes__________________________, (Authorized Agent)
(Name of Authorized Agent)
of____
(Address of Authorized Agent)
to act for and on its behalf as a true and lawful agent and attorney of the U.S. Principal Party in Interest (USPPI) for, and in the name, place, and stead of the USPPI, from this date, in the United States either in writing, electronically, or by other authorized means to: act as authorized agent for export control, U.S. Census Bureau (Census Bureau) reporting, and U.S. Customs and Border Protection (CBP) purposes. Also, to prepare and transmit any Electronic Export Information (EEI) or other documents or records required to be filed by the Census Bureau, CBP, the Bureau of Industry and Security, or any other U.S. Government agency, and perform any other act that may be required by law or regulation in connection with the exportation or transportation of any goods shipped or consigned by or to the USPPI, and to receive or ship any goods on behalf of the USPPI.

The USPPI hereby certifies that all statements and information contained in the documentation provided to the authorized agent and relating to exportation will be true and correct. Furthermore, the USPPI understands that civil and criminal penalties may be imposed for making false or fraudulent statements or for the violation of any United States laws or regulations on exportation.

This power of attorney is to remain in full force and effect until revocation in writing is duly given by the U.S. Principal Party in Interest and received by the Authorized Agent.

IN WITNESS WHEREOF, ______________________________ caused these
(Full Name of USPPI/USPPI Company)
presents to be sealed and signed:

Witness: ________________________ Signature:____________________
Capacity: ____________________
Date:______________________

Sample Written Authorization
SAMPLE FORMAT: Written Authorization

WRITTEN AUTHORIZATION TO PREPARE OR TRANSMIT ELECTRONIC EXPORT INFORMATION

I, ____, authorize
(Name of U.S. Principal Party in Interest)
____ to act as authorized agent for
(Name of Authorized Agent)
export control, U.S. Customs, and Census Bureau purposes to transmit such export information electronically that may be required by law or regulation in connection with the exportation or transportation of any goods on behalf of said U.S. Principal Party in Interest. The U.S. Principal Party in Interest certifies that necessary and proper documentation to accurately transmit the information electronically is and will be provided to the said Authorized Agent. The U.S. Principal Party in Interest further understands that civil and criminal penalties may be imposed for making false or fraudulent statements or for the violation of any U.S. laws or regulations on exportation and agrees to be bound by all statements of said authorized agent based upon information or documentation provided by the U.S. Principal Party in Interest to said authorized agent.

Signature: ____
(U.S. Principal Party in Interest)
Capacity: ____
Date: ____________________________

APPENDIX B TO PART 30—AES FILING CODES

PART I—METHOD OF TRANSPORTATION CODES

10 Vessel
11 Vessel Containerized
12 Vessel (Barge)
20 Rail
21 Rail Containerized
30 Truck
31 Truck Containerized
32 Auto
33 Pedestrian
34 Road, Other
40 Air
41 Air Containerized
50 Mail
60 Passenger, Hand Carried
70 Fixed Transport (Pipeline and Powerhouse)

PART II—EXPORT INFORMATION CODES

TP Temporary exports of domestic merchandise
IP Shipments of merchandise imported under a Temporary Import Bond for further manufacturing or processing
IR Shipments of merchandise imported under a Temporary Import Bond for repair
CH Shipments of goods donated for charity
FS Foreign Military Sales
OS All other exports
HV Shipments of personally owned vehicles
HH Household and personal effects
TE Temporary exports to be returned to the United States
TL Merchandise leased for less than a year
IS Shipments of merchandise imported under a Temporary Import Bond for return in the same condition
CR Shipments moving under a carnet
GP U.S. Government shipments
MS Shipments consigned to the U.S. Armed Forces
GS Shipments to U.S. Government agencies for their use
UG Gift parcels under Bureau of Industry and Security License Exception GFT
DD Other exemptions:
Currency
Airline tickets
Bank notes
Internal revenue stamps
State liquor stamps
Advertising literature

Shipments of temporary imports by foreign entities for their use
RJ Inadmissible merchandise
(For Manifest Use Only by AES Carriers)
AE Shipment information filed through AES
(See §§30.50 through 30.58 for information on filing exemptions.)

PART III—LICENSE CODES

DEPARTMENT OF COMMERCE, BUREAU OF INDUSTRY AND SECURITY (BIS), LICENSES

C30 Licenses issued by BIS authorizing an export, reexport, or other regulated activity.
C31 SCL—Special Comprehensive License
C32 NLR—No License Required (controlled for other than or in addition to Anti-Terrorism)
C33 NLR—No License Required (All others, including Anti-Terrorism controls ONLY)
C35 LVS—Limited Value Shipments
C36 GBS—Shipments to B Countries
C37 CIV—Civil End Users
C38 TSR—Restricted Technology and Software
C40 TMP—Temporary Imports, Exports, and Re-exports
C41 RPL—Servicing and Replacement of Parts and Equipment
C42 GOV—Government and International Organizations
C43 GFT—Gift Parcels and Humanitarian Donations
C44 TSU—Technology and Software—Unrestricted
C45 BAG—Baggage
C46 AVS—Aircraft and Vessels (AES not required)
C47 APR—Additional Permissive Re-exports
C48 KMI—Key Management Intrastructure
C49 TAPS—Trans-Alaska Pipeline Authorization Act
C50 ENC—Encryption Commodities and Software
C51 AGR—License Exception Agricultural Commodities
C53 APP—Adjusted Peak Performance (Computers)
C54 SS-WRC—Western Red Cedar
C55 SS-Sample—Crude Oil Samples
C56 SS-SPR—Strategic Petroleum Reserves
C57 VEU—Validated End User Authorization

NUCLEAR REGULATORY COMMISSION (NRC) CODES

N01 NRC Form 250/250A—NRC Form 250/250A
N02 NRC General License—NRC 'General' Export License

DEPARTMENT OF STATE, DIRECTORATE OF DEFENSE TRADE CONTROLS (DDTC) CODES

SAG—Agreements
SCA—Canadian ITAR Exemption
S00—License Exemption Citation
S05—DSP-5—Permanent export of unclassified defense articles and services
S61—DSP-61—Temporary import of unclassified articles
S73—DSP-73—Temporary export of unclassified articles
S85—DSP-85—Temporary or permanent import or export of classified articles
S94—DSP-94—Foreign Military Sales

DEPARTMENT OF TREASURY, OFFICE OF FOREIGN ASSETS CONTROL (OFAC) CODES

T10—OFAC Specific License
T11—OFAC General License
T12—Kimberley Process Certificate Number

OTHER LICENSE TYPES

OPA—Other Partnership Agency License

For export license exemptions under International Traffic in Arms Regulations, refer to 22 CFR 120–130 of the ITAR for the list of export license exemptions.

PART IV—IN-BOND CODES

70 Not In Bond
36 Warehouse Withdrawal for Immediate Exportation
37 Warehouse Withdrawal for Transportation and Exportation
67 Immediate Exportation from a Foreign Trade Zone
68 Transportation and Exportation from a Foreign Trade Zone

EFFECTIVE DATE NOTE: At 78 FR 16383, Mar. 14, 2013, Appendix B to Part 30 was amended by revising parts II and III, effective Jan. 8, 2014. At 78 FR 67928, Nov. 13, 2013, the effective date was delayed until Apr. 5, 2014. For the convenience of the user, the revised text is set forth as follows:

APPENDIX B TO PART 30—AES FILING CODES

* * * * *

PART II—EXPORT INFORMATION CODES

TP—Temporary exports of domestic merchandise
IP—Shipments of merchandise imported under a Temporary Import Bond for further manufacturing or processing
IR—Shipments of merchandise imported under a Temporary Import Bond for repair
CH—Shipments of goods donated for charity
FS—Foreign Military Sales
ZD—North American Free Trade Agreements (NAFTA) duty deferral shipments
OS—All other exports
HV—Shipments of personally owned vehicles
HH—Household and personal effects
TE—Temporary exports to be returned to the United States

TL—Merchandise leased for less than a year
IS—Shipments of merchandise imported under a Temporary Import Bond for return in the same condition
CR—Shipments moving under a carnet
GP—U.S. Government shipments
MS—Shipments consigned to the U.S. Armed Forces
GS—Shipments to U.S. Government agencies for their use
UG—Gift parcels under Bureau of Industry and Security License Exception GFT
DD—Other exemptions:
Currency
Airline tickets
Bank notes
Internal revenue stamps
State liquor stamps
Advertising literature
Shipments of temporary imports by foreign entities for their use
IW—International water shipments
CI—Impelled shipments of goods donated for relief or charity
FI—Impelled Foreign Military Sales Program
OI—All other exports (impelled)
(For Manifest Use Only by AES Carriers)
AE Shipment information filed through AES
(See §§30.50 through 30.58 for information on filing exemptions.)

PART III—LICENSE CODES

Department of Commerce, Bureau of Industry and Security (BIS), Licenses

C30 Licenses issued by BIS authorizing an export, reexport, or other regulated activity.
C31 SCL—Special Comprehensive License
C32 NLR—No License Required (controlled for other than or in addition to Anti-Terrorism)
C33 NLR No License Required (All others, including Anti-Terrorism controls ONLY)
C35 LVS—Limited Value Shipments
C36 GBS—Shipments to B Countries
C37 CIV—Civil End Users
C38 TSR—Restricted Technology and Software
C39 CTP—Computers
C40 TMP—Temporary Imports, Exports, and Re-exports
C41 RPL—Servicing and Replacement of Parts and Equipment
C42 GOV—Government and International Organizations
C43 GFT—Gift Parcels and Humanitarian Donations
C44 TSU—Technology and Software—Unrestricted
C45 BAG—Baggage
C46 AVS—Aircraft and Vessels (AES not required)
C49 TAPS —Trans-Alaska Pipeline Authorization Act
C50 ENC—Encryption Commodities and Software
C51 AGR—License Exception Agricultural Commodities
C53 APP—Adjusted Peak Performance (Computers)
C54 SS-WRC—Western Red Cedar
C55 SS-Sample—Crude Oil Samples
C56 SS-SPR—Strategic Petroleum Reserves
C57 VEU—Validated End User Authorization
C58 CCD—Consumer Communication Devices
C59 STA—Strategic Trade Authorization

Department of Energy/National Nuclear Security Administration (DOE/NNSA) Codes

E01—DOE/NNSA

Nuclear Regulatory Commission (NRC) Codes

N01 NRC Form 250/250A—NRC Form 250/250A
N02 NRC General License—NRC 'General' Export License

Department of State, Directorate of Defense Trade Controls (DDTC) Codes

SAG—Agreements
SCA—Canadian ITAR Exemption
S00—License Exemption Citation
S05 DSP-5—Permanent export of unclassified defense articles and services
S61 DSP-61—Temporary import of unclassified articles
S73 DSP-73—Temporary export of unclassified articles
S85 DSP-85—Temporary or permanent import or export of classified articles
S94 DSP 94 Foreign Military Sales

Department of Treasury, Office of Foreign Assets Control (OFAC) Codes

T10—OFAC Specific License
T11—OFAC General License
T12—Kimberley Process Certificate Number

Other License Types

OPA—Other Partnership Agency License

For export license exemptions under International Traffic in Arms Regulations, refer to 22 CFR 120–130 of the ITAR for the list of export license exemptions.

APPENDIX C TO PART 30—SUMMARY OF EXEMPTIONS AND EXCLUSIONS FROM EEI FILING

A. EEI is not required for the following types of shipments: [1]

[1] Exemption from the requirements for reporting complete commodity information is covered in §30.38; Special exemptions for shipments to the U.S. Armed Services and
Continued

1. Exemption for shipments destined to Canada (§ 30.36).

2. Valued $2,500 or less per Schedule B/HTSUSA classification for commodities shipped from one USPPI to one consignee on a single carrier (§ 30.37(a)).

3. Tools of the trade and their containers that are usual and reasonable kinds and quantities of commodities and software intended for use by individual USPPIs or by employees or representatives of the exporting company in furthering the enterprises and undertakings of the USPPI abroad (§ 30.37(b)).

4. Shipments from one point in the United States to another point in the United States by routes passing through Canada or Mexico (§ 30.37(c)).

5. Shipments from one point in Canada or Mexico to another point in the same country by routes through the United States (§ 30.37(d)).

6. Shipments transported inbond through the United States for export to a third country and exported from another U.S. port or transshipped and exported directly from the port of arrival never having made entry into the United States. If entry for consumption or warehousing in the United States is made, then an EEI is required if the goods are then exported to a third country from the United States (§ 30.37(e)).

7. Exports of technology and software as defined in 15 CFR 772 of the EAR that do not require an export license. However, EEI is required for mass-market software (§ 30.37(f)).

8. Shipments to foreign libraries, government establishments, or similar institutions, as provided in FTR Subpart D § 30.40 (d). (§ 30.37(h)).

9. Shipments as authorized under License Exception GFT for gift parcels and humanitarian donations (EAR 15 CFR 740.12); § 30.37(i)).

10. Diplomatic pouches and their contents (§ 30.37(j)).

11. Human remains and accompanying appropriate receptacles and flowers (§ 30.37(k)).

12. Shipments of interplant correspondence, executed invoices and other documents, and other shipments of company business records from a U.S. firm to its subsidiary or affiliate. This excludes highly technical plans, correspondence, etc. that could be licensed (§ 30.37(l)).

13. Shipments of pets as baggage (§ 30.37(m)).

14. Carrier's stores, not shipped under a bill of lading or an air waybill, supplies and equipment, including usual and reasonable kinds and quantities of bunker fuel, deck engine and steward department stores, provisions and supplies, medicinal and surgical supplies, food stores, slop chest articles, and saloon stores or supplies for use or consumption on board and not intended for unlading in a foreign country. (See Table 5 if shipped under a bill of lading or an air waybill (§ 30.37(n)).

15. Dunnage not shipped under a bill of lading or an air waybill, of usual and reasonable kinds and quantities not intended for unlading in a foreign country (§ 30.37(o)).

16. Shipments of aircraft parts and equipment; food, saloon, slop chest, and related stores; and provisions and supplies for use on aircraft by a U.S. airline. (EAR license exception (AVS) for aircraft and vessels 15 CFR 740.15(c); § 30.37(p)).

17. Baggage and personal effects, accompanied or unaccompanied, of persons leaving the United States including members of crews on vessels and aircraft, when they are not shipped as cargo under a bill of lading or an air waybill and do not require an export license (§ 30.37(q)).

18. Temporary exports, whether shipped or hand carried, (e.g., carnet) that are exported from or returned to the United States in less than one year (12 months) from date of export (§ 30.37(r)).

19. Goods previously imported under Temporary Import Bond for return in the same condition as when imported including: goods for testing, experimentation, or demonstration; goods imported for exhibition; samples and models imported for review or for taking orders; goods for imported for participation in races or contests; and animals imported for breeding or exhibition and imported for use by representatives of foreign government or international organizations or by members of the armed forces of a foreign country. Goods that were imported under bond for processing and re-exportation are not covered by this exemption (§ 30.37(s)).

20. Issued banknotes and securities and coins in circulation exported as evidence of financial claims. The EEI must be filed for unissued bank notes and securities and coins not in circulation (such as bank notes printed in the United States and exported in fulfillment of the printing contract or as part of collections), which should be reported at their commercial or current value (§ 30.37(t)).

21. Documents used in international transactions, documents moving out of the United States to facilitate international transactions including airline tickets, internal revenue stamps, liquor stamps, and advertising literature. Export of such documents in fulfillment of a contract for their production, however, are not exempt and must be reported at the transaction value for their production (§ 30.37(u)).

B. The following types of transactions are outside the scope of the FTR and shall be excluded from EEI filing:

covered in § 30.39; and Special exemptions for certain shipments to U.S. Government agencies and employees are covered in § 30.40.

1. Goods shipped under CBP bond through the United States, Puerto Rico, or the U.S. Virgin Islands from one foreign country or area to another where such goods do not enter the consumption channels of the United States.

2. Goods shipped from the U.S. territories of Guam Island, American Samoa, Wake Island, Midway Island, and Northern Mariana Islands to foreign countries or areas, and goods shipped between the U.S. and these territories (§30.2(d)(2)).

3. Electronic transmissions and intangible transfers. See FTR, Subpart B, for export control requirements for these types of transactions (§30.2(d)(3)).

4. Goods shipped to Guantanamo Bay Naval Base in Cuba from the United States, Puerto Rico, or the U.S. Virgin Islands and from Guantanamo Bay Naval Base to the United States, Puerto Rico, or the U.S. Virgin Islands. (See FTR Subpart D §30.39 for filing requirements for shipments exported by the U.S. Armed Services.) (§30.2(d)(4)).

EFFECTIVE DATE NOTE: At 78 FR 16383, Mar. 14, 2013, Appendix C to part 30 was revised, effective Jan. 8, 2014. At 78 FR 67928, Nov. 13, 2013, the effective date was delayed until Apr. 5, 2014. For the convenience of the user, the revised text is set forth as follows:

APPENDIX C TO PART 30—SUMMARY OF EXEMPTIONS AND EXCLUSIONS FROM EEI FILING

A. Except as noted in §30.2 (a)(1)(iv), filing EEI is not required for the following types of shipments:[1]

1. Exemption for shipments destined to Canada (§30.36).

2. Valued $2,500 or less per Schedule B/ HTSUSA classification for commodities shipped from one USPPI to one consignee on a single carrier (§30.37(a)).

3. Tools of the trade and their containers that are usual and reasonable kinds and quantities of commodities and software intended for use by individual USPPIs or by employees or representatives of the exporting company in furthering the enterprises and undertakings of the USPPI abroad (§30.37(b)).

4. Shipments from one point in the United States to another point in the United States by routes passing through Canada or Mexico (§30.37(c)).

5. Shipments from one point in Canada or Mexico to another point in the same country by routes through the United States (§30.37(d)).

6. Exports of technology and software as defined in 15 CFR part 772 of the EAR that do not require an export license. However, EEI is required for mass-market software (§30.37(f)).

7. Shipments of books, maps, charts, pamphlets, and similar articles to foreign libraries, government establishments, or similar institutions (§30.37(g)).

8. Shipments as authorized under License Exception GFT for gift parcels and humanitarian donations (15 CFR 740.12(a) and (b)); §30.37(h).

9. Diplomatic pouches and their contents (§30.37(i)).

10. Human remains and accompanying appropriate receptacles and flowers (§30.37(j)).

11. Shipments of interplant correspondence, executed invoices and other documents, and other shipments of company business records from a U.S. firm to its subsidiary or affiliate. This excludes highly technical plans, correspondence, etc. that could be licensed (§30.37(k)).

12. Shipments of pets as baggage (§30.37(l)).

13. Carrier's stores, not shipped under a bill of lading or an air waybill, supplies and equipment, including usual and reasonable kinds and quantities of bunker fuel, deck engine and steward department stores, provisions and supplies, medicinal and surgical supplies, food stores, slop chest articles, and saloon stores or supplies for use or consumption on board and not intended for unlading in a foreign country (§30.37(m)).

14. Dunnage not shipped under a bill of lading or an air waybill, of usual and reasonable kinds and quantities not intended for unlading in a foreign country (§30.37(n)).

15. Shipments of aircraft parts and equipment; food, saloon, slop chest, and related stores; and provisions and supplies for use on aircraft by a U.S. airline. (EAR license exception (AVS) for aircraft and vessels 15 CFR 740.15(c); §30.37(o)).

16. Baggage and personal effects, accompanied or unaccompanied, of persons leaving the United States including members of crews on vessels and aircraft, when they are not shipped as cargo under a bill of lading or an air waybill or other commercial loading documents and do not require an export license (§30.37(p)).

17. Issued banknotes and securities and coins in circulation exported as evidence of financial claims. The EEI must be filed for unissued bank notes and securities and coins not in circulation (such as bank notes printed in the United States and exported in fulfillment of the printing contract or as part of collections), which should be reported at their commercial or current value (§30.37(s)).

18. Documents used in international transactions, documents moving out of the United

[1] Exemption from the requirements for reporting complete commodity information is covered in §30.38; Special exemptions for shipments to the U.S. Armed Services are covered in §30.39; and special exemptions for certain shipments to U.S. Government agencies and employees are covered in §30.40.

States to facilitate international transactions including airline tickets, internal revenue stamps, liquor stamps, and advertising literature. Export of such documents in fulfillment of a contract for their production, however, are not exempt and must be reported at the transaction value for their production (§30.37(t)).

19. Exports of technical data and defense service exemptions as defined in 22 CFR 123.22(b)(3)(iii) of the ITAR (§30.37(u)).

20. Vessels, locomotives, aircraft, rail cars, trucks, other vehicles, trailers, pallets, cargo vans, lift vans, or similar shipping containers not considered "shipped" in terms of the regulations in this part, when they are moving, either loaded or empty, without transfer of ownership or title, in their capacity as carriers of goods or as instruments of such carriers, and EEI filing is not required. (§30.37(v)).

21. Shipments to APO/DPO/FPO (§30.37(w))

22. Shipments exported under license exception BAG (§30.37(x))

23. Certain shipments destined to Country Group E:1 (§30.37(y))

B. The following types of transactions are outside the scope of the FTR and shall be excluded from EEI filing:

1. Goods shipped under CBP bond through the United States, Puerto Rico, or the U.S. Virgin Islands from one foreign country or area to another where such goods do not enter the consumption channels of the United States.

2. Except Puerto Rico and U.S. Virgin Islands, goods shipped from the U.S. territories, and goods shipped between the United States and these territories do not require EEI filing. However, goods transiting U.S. territories to foreign destinations require EEI filing.

3. Electronic transmissions and intangible transfers. (See Subpart B of this part for export control requirements for these types of transactions.)

4. Goods shipped to Guantanamo Bay Naval Base in Cuba from the United States, Puerto Rico, or the U.S. Virgin Islands and from Guantanamo Bay Naval Base to the United States, Puerto Rico, or the U.S. Virgin Islands. (See §30.39 for filing requirements for shipments exported to the U.S. Armed Services.)

5. Goods licensed by a U.S. Federal Government agency where the country of ultimate destination is the United States or goods destined to international waters where the person(s) or entity assuming control of the item(s) is a citizen or permanent resident alien of the United States or a juridical entity organized under the laws of the United States or a jurisdiction within the United States.

APPENDIX D TO PART 30—AES FILING CITATION, EXEMPTION AND EXCLUSION LEGENDS

I. USML Proof of Filing Citation	AES ITN Example: AES X20060101987654.
II. AES Proof of Filing Citation subpart A §30.7	AES ITN Example: AES X20060101987654.
III. AES Postdeparture Citation-USPPIUSPPI is filing the EEI.	AESPOST USPPI EIN mm/dd/yyyy Example: AESPOST 12345678912 01/01/2006.
IV. Postdeparture Citation-Agent	AESPOST USPPI EIN—Filer ID mm/dd/yyyy Example: AESPOST 12345678912—987654321 01/01/2006.
V. AES Downtime Citation-Use only when AES or AES*Direct* is unavailable.	AESDOWN Filer ID mm/dd/yyyy Example: AESDOWN 123456789 01/01/2006.
VI. Standard Exclusions are found in 15 CFR 30, Subpart A, §30.2(d)(1) through §30.2(d)(4).	
The following types of transactions shall be excluded from EEI filing:	
(1) Goods Shipped from U.S. territories.	NOEEI §30.2(d)(site corresponding number).
(2) Goods Shipped to or from Guantanamo Bay Naval Base in Cuba and the United States.	
(3) Inbond Shipments through the United States, Puerto Rico, and the U.S. Virgin Islands.	
VII. Exemption for Shipments to Canada	NOEEI §30.36.
VIII. Exemption for Low-Value Shipments	NOEEI §30.37(a).

IX. Miscellaneous Exemption Statements are found in 15 CFR 30 Subpart D §30.37(b) through §30.37(u).	NOEEI §30.37 (site corresponding alphabet).
X. Special Exemption for Shipments to the U.S. Armed Forces.	NOEEI §30.39
XI. Special Exemptions for Certain Shipments to U.S. Government Agencies and Employees (Exemption Statements are found in 15 CFR 30 Subpart D §30.40(a) through §30.40(d).	NOEEI §30.40 (site corresponding alphabet).
XII. Split Shipments by Air "Split Shipments" should be referenced as such on the manifest in accordance with provisions contained in §30.28, "Split Shipments by Air." The notation should be easily identifiable on the manifest.	AES ITN SS Example: AES X20060101987654 SS.
It is preferable to include a reference to a split shipment in the exemption statements cited in the example, the notation SS should be included at the end of the appropriate exemption statement.	
Proof of filing citations by pipeline	NOEEI §30.8(b).

EFFECTIVE DATE NOTE: At 78 FR 16384, Mar. 14, 2013, Appendix D to part 30 was revised, effective Jan. 8, 2014. At 78 FR 67928, Nov. 13, 2013, the effective date was delayed until Apr. 5, 2014. For the convenience of the user, the revised text is set forth as follows:

APPENDIX D TO PART 30—AES FILING CITATION AND EXEMPTION LEGENDS

I. USML Proof of Filing Citation	AES ITN; Example: AES X20100101987654.
II. AES Proof of Filing Citation subpart A §30.7	AES ITN; Example: AES X20100101987654.
III. AES Postdeparture Citation—USPPI; USPPI is filing the EEI.	AESPOST USPPI EIN mm/dd/yyyy; Example: AESPOST 12345678912 01/01/2010.
IV. Postdeparture Citation—Agent; Agent is filing the EEI.	AESPOST USPPI EIN—Filer ID mm/dd/yyyy; Example: AESPOST 12345678912—987654321 01/01/2010.
V. AES Downtime Citation—Use only when AES or AES*Direct* is unavailable.	AESDOWN Filer ID mm/dd/yyyy; Example: AESDOWN 123456789 01/01/2010.
VI. Exemption for Shipments to Canada	NOEEI §30.36.
VII. Exemption for Low-Value Shipments	NOEEI §30.37(a).
VIII. Miscellaneous Exemption Statements are found in 15 CFR 30 Subpart D §30.37(b) through §30.37(y).	NOEEI §30.37 (site corresponding alphabet).
IX. Special Exemption for Shipments to the U.S. Armed Forces.	NOEEI §30.39.
X. Special Exemptions for Certain Shipments to U.S. Government Agencies and Employees (Exemption Statements are found in 15 CFR 30 Subpart D §30.40(a) through §30.40(d).	NOEEI §30.40 (site corresponding alphabet).
XI. Split Shipments. Split Shipments should be referenced as such on the manifest in accordance with provisions contained in §30.28, Split Shipments. The notation should be easily identifiable on the manifest. It is preferable to include a reference to a split shipment in the exemption statements cited in the example, the notation SS should be included at the end of the appropriate exemption statement.	AES ITN SS; Example: AES X20100101987654 SS.
XII. Proof of filing citations by pipeline	NOEEI §30.8(b).

APPENDIX E TO PART 30—FTSR TO FTR CONCORDANCE

FTSR	FTSR regulatory topic	FTR	FTR regulatory topic
	Subpart A—General Requirements—USPPI		
30.1	General statement of requirement for Shipper's Export Declarations (SEDs).	30.2	General requirements for filing Electronic Export Information (EEI).
30.1(a)	General requirements for filing SEDs	General requirements for filing EEI..	
30.1(b)	General requirements for reporting regarding method of transportation.	NA..	
30.1(c)	AES as an alternative to SED reporting	NA..	
30.1(d)	Electronic transmissions and intangible transfers.	30.2(d)(3)	Exclusions from filing EEI.
30.2	Related export control requirements	30.15	Export control and licensing requirements introduction.
		30.16	EAR requirements for export information on shipments from U.S. Possessions to foreign destinations or areas.
		30.17	Customs and Border Protection Regulations.
30.3	Shipper's Export Declaration forms	NA..	
30.4	Preparation and signature of Shipper's Export Declarations (SED).	30.3	Electronic Export Information filer requirements, parties to export transactions, responsibilities of parties to export transactions.
30.4(a)	General requirements (SED)	30.3(a)	General Requirements.
		30.3(b)	Parties to the export transaction.
30.4(b)	Responsibilities of parties in export transactions.	30.3(c)	General responsibilities of parties in export transactions.
		30.3(d)	Filer responsibilities.
30.4(c)	Responsibilities of parties in a routed export transactions.	30.3(e)	Responsibilities of parties in a routed export transaction.
30.4(d)	Information on the Shipper's Export Declaration (SED) or Automated Export System (AES) record.	30.3(a)	General requirements.
30.4(e)	Authorizing a forwarding or other agent	30.3(f)	Authorizing an agent.
30.4(f)	Format requirements for SEDs	NA..	
30.5	Number and copies of Shipper's Export Declaration required.	NA..	
30.6	Requirements as to separate Shipper's Export Declarations.	NA..	
30.7	Information required on Shipper's Export Declarations.	NA..	
30.8	Additional information required on shipper's Export Declaration for In-Transit Goods (ENG Form 7513).	NA..	
30.9	Requirements for separation and alignment of items on shipper's Export Declarations.	NA..	
30.10	Continuation sheets for Shipper's Export Declaration.	NA..	
30.11	Authority to require production of document.	30.10(b)	Authority to require production of documents and retaining electronic data.
30.12	Time and place for presenting the SED, exemption legends or proof of filing citations.	30.4	Electronic export information filing procedures, deadlines, and certification statements.
		30.8	Time and place for presenting proof of filing citations, postdeparture filing citations, AES downtime citations, and exemption legends.
30.15	Procedure for presentation of declarations covering shipments from an interior point.	NA..	
30.16	Corrections to Shipper's Export Declarations.	30.9	Transmitting and correcting Electronic Export Information.
	Subpart B—General Requirements—Exporting Carriers		
30.20	General statement of requirement for the filing of manifests * * *.	30.45	General statement of requirements for the filing of carrier manifests with proof of filing.

FTSR	FTSR regulatory topic	FTR	FTR regulatory topic
30.20(a)	Carriers transporting merchandise from the United States, Puerto Rico, or U.S. territories to foreign countries.	30.45(a)	Requirements for filing carrier manifest.
30.20(b)	For carriers transporting merchandise from the United States to Puerto Rico.	30.45(a)	Requirements for filing carrier manifest.
30.20(c)	Except as otherwise specifically provided, declarations should not be filed at the place where the shipment originates.	30.45(a)	Requirements for filing carrier manifest.
30.20(d)	For purposes of these regulations, the port of exportation is defined as * * *.	30.1(c)	Definition used with EEI.
30.21	Requirements for the filing of Manifests	30.45	General statement of requirements for the filing of carrier manifests with proof of filing citations for the electronic submission of export information or exemption legends when EEI is not required.
30.21(a)	Vessel	30.45(a)(1)	Vessel.
30.21(b)	Aircraft	30.45(a)(2)	Aircraft.
30.21(c)	Rail Carrier	30.45(a)(3)	Rail Carrier.
30.21(d)	Carriers not required to file manifests	30.45(a)(4)	Carriers not required to file manifests.
30.22(a)	Requirements for the filing of SEDs or AES exemption legends and AES proof of filing citations by departing carriers.	30.8	Time and place for presenting proof of filing citation, exemption, and exclusion legends.
30.22(b)	The exporting carrier shall be responsible for the accuracy of the following items of information.	NA..	
30.22(c)	Except as provided in paragraph (d) of this section, when a transportation company finds, prior to the filing of declarations and manifest as provided in paragraph (a) of this section, that due to circumstances beyond the control of the transportation company or to inadvertence, a portion of the merchandise covered by an individual Shipper's Export Declaration has not been exported on the intended carrier.	NA..	
30.22(d)	When a shipment by air covered by a single Shipper's Export Declaration is divided by the transportation company and exported in more than one aircraft of the transportation.	30.45(c)	Split shipments by air.
30.22(e)	Exporting carriers are authorized to amend incorrect shipping weights reported on Shipper's Export Declarations.	NA..	
30.23	Requirements for the filing of Shipper's Export Declarations by pipeline carriers.	30.46	Requirements for the filing of export information by pipeline carriers.
30.24	Clearance or departure of carriers under bond on incomplete manifest on Shipper's Export Declarations.	30.47	Clearance or departure of carriers under bond on incomplete manifests.
	Subpart C—Special Provisions Applicable Under Particular Circumstances		
30.30	Values for certain types of transactions	30.25	Values for certain types of transactions.
30.31	Identification of certain nonstatistical and other unusual transactions.	30.29	Reporting of repairs and replacements.
30.31(a)	Merchandise exported for repair only, and other temporary exports.	30.29(a)	The return of goods previously imported for repair * * *.
30.31(b)	The return of merchandise previously imported for repair only.	30.29(b)	Goods that are covered under warranty and other temporary exports.
30.31(c)	Shipments of material in connection with construction, maintenance, and related work being done on projects for the U.S. Armed Forces.	NA..	
30.33	Vessels, planes, cargo vans, and other carriers and containers sold foreign.	30.26	Reporting of vessels, aircraft, cargo vans, and other carriers and containers.
30.34	Return of exported cargo to the United States prior to reaching its final destination.	30.27	Return of exported cargo to the United States prior to reaching its final destination.
30.37	Exceptions from the requirement for reporting complete commodity detail on the Shipper's Export Declaration.	30.38	Exemption from the requirements for reporting complete commodity information.

FTSR	FTSR regulatory topic	FTR	FTR regulatory topic
30.37(a)	Where it can be determined that particular types of U.S. Government shipments, or shipments for government projects, are of such nature that they should not be included in the export statistics.	30.39	Special exemptions for shipments to the U.S. Armed Services. (Note, this section does not specifically address construction materials nor related work being done on projects).
30.37(b)	Special exemptions to specific portions of the requirements of § 30.7 with respect to the reporting of detailed information.	NA..	
30.39	Authorization for reporting statistical information other than by means of individual Shipper's Export Declarations filed for each shipment.	NA..	
30.40	Single declaration for multiple consignees	NA..	
30.41	"Split shipments" by air	30.28	"Split shipments" by air.
Subpart D—Exemptions From the Requirements for the Filing of Shipper's Export Declarations			
30.50	Procedure for shipments exempt from the requirements for Shipper's Export Declarations.	30.35	Procedure for shipments exempt from filing requirements.
30.51	Government shipments not generally exempt.	30.39	Special exemption for shipments to the U.S. Armed Services.
30.52	Special exemptions for shipments to the U.S. Armed Services.	30.39	Special exemptions for shipments to the U.S. Armed Services.
30.53	Special exemptions for certain shipments to U.S. Government agencies and employees.	30.40	Special exemptions for certain shipments to U.S. Government agencies and employees.
30.53(e)	All commodities shipped to and for the exclusive use of the Panama Canal Zone or the Panama Canal Company.	NA..	
30.55	Miscellaneous exemptions	30.37	Miscellaneous exemptions.
30.55(a)	Diplomatic pouches and their contents	30.37(i)	Diplomatic pouches and their contents.
30.55(b)	Human remains and accompanying appropriate receptacles and flowers.	30.37(j)	Human remains and accompanying appropriate receptacles and flowers.
30.55(c)	Shipments from one point in the United States to another thereof by routes passing through Mexico.	30.37(c)	Shipments from one point in the United States to another point in the United States by routes passing through Canada or Mexico.
30.55(d)	Shipments from one point in Mexico to another point thereof by routes through the United States.	30.37(d)	Shipments from one point in Canada or Mexico to another point in the same country by routes through the United States.
30.55(e)	Shipments, other than by vessel, or merchandise for which no validated export licenses are required, transported in-bond through the United States, and exported from another U.S. port, or transshipped and exported directly from the port of arrival.	30.37(e)	Shipments, transported in-bond through the United States, and exported from another U.S. port, or transshipped and exported directly from the port of arrival.
30.55(f)	Shipments to foreign libraries, government establishments, or similar institutions, as provided in § 30.53(d).	30.37(g)	Shipments to foreign libraries, government establishments, or similar institutions, as provided in § 30.40(d).
30.55(g)	Shipments of single gift parcels as authorized by the Bureau of Industry and Security under License Exception GFT, see 15 CFR 740.12 of the EAR.	30.37(h)	Shipments authorized by License Exception GFT for gift parcels, humanitarian donations.
30.55(h)	Except as noted in paragraph (h)(2) of this section, exports of commodities where the value of the commodities shipped from one exporter to one consignee on a single exporting carrier, classified under an individual Schedule B number, is $2,500 or less.	30.37(a)	Except as noted in § 30.2(a)(e)(iv), exports of commodities where the value of the commodities shipped USPPI to one consignee on a single exporting carrier, classified under an individual Schedule B or HTSUSA commodity classification code, is $2,500 or less.
30.55(i)	Shipments of interplant correspondence, executed invoices, and other documents and other shipments of company business records from a U.S. firm to its subsidiary or affiliate.	30.37(k)	Shipments of interplant correspondence, executed invoices, and other documents and other shipments of company business records from a U.S. firm to its subsidiary or affiliate.
30.55(j)	Shipments of pets as baggage, accompanied or unaccompanied, of persons leaving the United States, including members of crews on vessels and aircraft.	30.37(l)	Shipments of pets as baggage, accompanied or unaccompanied, of persons leaving the United States, including members of crews on vessels and aircraft.

FTSR	FTSR regulatory topic	FTR	FTR regulatory topic
30.55(k)	Shipments for use in connection with NASA tracking systems under Office of Export Administration Project License DL–5355–S.	NA..	
30.55(l)	Shipments of aircraft parts and equipment, and food, saloon, slop chest, and related stores, provisions, and supplies for use on aircraft by a U.S. airline to its own installations, aircraft, and agent aboard, under Department of Commerce, Office of Export Administration General License, RCS.	NA..	
30.55(m)	Shipments for use in connection with NOAA operations under the Office of Export Administration General License G–NOAA.	NA..	
30.55(n)	Exports of technology and software as defined in 15 CFR 772 of the EAR that do not require an export license.	30.37(f)	Exports of technology and software as defined in 15 CFR 772 of the EAR that do not require an export license.
30.55(o)	Intangible exports of software and technology, such as downloaded software and technical data, including technology and software that requires an export license and mass market software exported electronically.	30.2(d)(3)	Intangible exports of software and technology, such as downloaded software and technical data, including technology and software that requires an export license and mass market software exported electronically.
30.56	Conditional Exemptions	30.37	Miscellaneous exemptions.
30.56(a)	Baggage and personal effects * * *	30.38	Exemption from the requirements for reporting complete commodity information.
30.56(b)	Tools of trade * * *	30.37(b)	Tools of trade * * *.
30.56(c)	Carriers' stores * * *	30.37(m)	Carriers' stores * * *.
30.56(d)	Dunnage * * *	30.37(n)	Dunnage * * *.
30.57	Information on export declarations for shipments of types of goods covered by § 30.56 not conditionally exempt.	NA..	
30.58	Exemption for shipments from the United States to Canada.	30.36	Exemption for shipments destined to Canada.
	Subpart E—Electronic Filing Requirements—Shipper's Export Information		
30.60	General requirements for filing export and manifest data electronically using the Automated Export System (AES).	30.2	General requirements for filing Electronic Export Information.
30.60(a)	Participation	NA..	
30.60(b)	Letter of Intent	30.5(a)(1)	Postdeparture filing application.
30.60(c)	General filing and transmission requirements.	30.4	NA.
30.60(d)	General responsibilities of exporters, filing agents, and sea carriers—.	30.3	Electronic Export Information filer requirements, parties to export transactions, and responsibilities of parties to export transactions.
30.61	Electronic filing options	30.4	Electronic Export Information filing procedure, deadlines, and certification statement.
30.62	AES Certification, qualifications, and standards.	30.5	EEI filing application and certification processes and standards.
30.63	Information required to be reported electronically through AES (data elements).	30.6	Electronic Export Information data elements.
30.64	Transmitting and correcting AES information.	30.9	Transmitting and correcting Electronic Export Information.
30.65	Annotating the proper exemption legends or proof of filing citations for shipments transmitted electronically.	30.7	Annotating the bill of lading, air waybill, and other commercial loading documents with the proper proof of filing citations, approved postdeparture filing citations, downtime filing citation, or exemption legends.
30.66	Recordkeeping and requirements	30.5(f)	Support.
30.66	Support, documentation, and recordkeeping requirements.	30.10	Retention of export information and the authority to require production of documents.

FTSR	FTSR regulatory topic	FTR	FTR regulatory topic
	Subpart F—General Requirements—Importers		
30.70	Statistical information required on import entries.	30.50	General requirements for filing import entries.
		30.51	Statistical information required for import entries.
30.80	Imports from Canada	30.54	Special provisions for imports from Canada.
30.81	Imports of merchandise into Guam	NA..	
30.82	Identification of U.S. merchandise returned for repair and reexport.	30.53	Import of goods returned for repair.
30.83	Statistical copy of mail and informal entries.	NA..	
	Subpart H—General Administrative Provisions		
30.90	Confidential information, import entries, and withdrawals.	30.55	Confidentiality information, import entries, and withdrawals.
30.91	Confidential information, Shipper's Export Declarations.	30.60	Confidentiality of Electronic Export Information.
30.92	Statistical classification schedules	30.61	Statistical classification schedules.
30.93	Emergency exceptions	30.62	Emergency exceptions.
30.94	Instructions to CBP	NA..	
30.95	Penalties for violations	Subpart H..	
30.95(a)	Exports (reexports) of rough diamonds	30.70	Violation of the Clean Diamond Trade Act.
30.95(b)	Exports of other than rough diamonds	30.71	False or fraudulent reporting.
30.99	OMB control numbers assigned pursuant to the Paperwork Reduction Act.	30.63	Office of Management and Budget control numbers assigned pursuant to the Paperwork Reduction Act.

EFFECTIVE DATE NOTE: At 78 FR 16384, Mar. 14, 2013, Appendix E to Part 30 was revised, effective Jan. 8, 2013. At 78 FR 67928, Nov. 13, 2013, the effective date was delayed until Apr. 5, 2014. For the convenience of the user, the revised text is set forth as follows:

APPENDIX E TO PART 30—FTSR TO FTR CONCORDANCE

FTSR	FTSR Regulatory topic	FTR	FTR Regulatory topic
	Subpart A—General Requirements—USPPI		
30.1	General statement of requirement for Shipper's Export Declarations (SEDs).	30.2	General requirements for filing Electronic Export Information (EEI).
30.1(a)	General requirements for filing SEDs		General requirements for filing EEI.
30.1(b)	General requirements for reporting regarding method of transportation.		NA.
30.1(c)	AES as an alternative to SED reporting		NA.
30.1(d)	Electronic transmissions and intangible transfers	30.2 (d)(3)	Exclusions from filing EEI.
30.2	Related export control requirements	30.15	Export control and licensing requirements introduction.
		30.16	EAR requirements for export information on shipments from U.S. Possessions to foreign destinations or areas.
		30.17	Customs and Border Protection Regulations.
30.3	Shipper's Export Declaration forms		NA.
30.4	Preparation and signature of Shipper's Export Declarations (SED).	30.3	Electronic Export Information filer requirements, parties to export transactions, responsibilities of parties to export transactions.
30.4(a)	General requirements (SED)	30.3(a)	General Requirements.
		30.3(b)	Parties to the export transaction.
30.4(b)	Responsibilities of parties in export transactions	30.3(c)	General responsibilities of parties in export transactions.
		30.3(d)	Filer responsibilities.
30.4(c)	Responsibilities of parties in a routed export transactions.	30.3(e)	Responsibilities of parties in a routed export transaction.
30.4(d)	Information on the Shipper's Export Declaration (SED) or Automated Export System (AES) record.	30.3(a)	General requirements.
30.4(e)	Authorizing a forwarding or other agent	30.3(f)	Authorizing an agent.
30.4(f)	Format requirements for SEDs		NA.
30.5	Number and copies of Shipper's Export Declaration required.		NA.

FTSR	FTSR Regulatory topic	FTR	FTR Regulatory topic
30.6	Requirements as to separate Shipper's Export Declarations.		NA.
30.7	Information required on Shipper's Export Declarations.		NA.
30.8	Additional information required on Shipper's Export Declaration for In-Transit Goods (ENG Form 7513).		NA.
30.9	Requirements for separation and alignment of items on Shipper's Export Declarations.		NA.
30.10	Continuation sheets for Shipper's Export Declaration.		NA.
30.11	Authority to require production of document	30.10(b)	Authority to require production of documents and retaining electronic data.
30.12	Time and place for presenting the SED, exemption legends or proof of filing citations.	30.4	Electronic export information filing procedures, deadlines, and certification statements.
		30.8	Time and place for presenting proof of filing citations, postdeparture filing citations, AES downtime citations, and exemption legends.
30.15	Procedure for presentation of declarations covering shipments from an interior point.		NA.
30.16	Corrections to Shipper's Export Declarations	30.9	Transmitting and correcting Electronic Export Information.
	Subpart B—General Requirements—Exporting Carriers		
30.20	General statement of requirement for the filing of manifests.	30.45	General statement of requirements for the filing of carrier manifests with proof of filing citations.
30.20(a)	Carriers transporting merchandise from the United States, Puerto Rico, or U.S. territories to foreign countries.	30.45(a)	Requirements for filing carrier manifest.
30.20(b)	For carriers transporting merchandise from the United States to Puerto Rico.	30.45(a)	Requirements for filing carrier manifest.
30.20(c)	Except as otherwise specifically provided, declarations should not be filed at the place where the shipment originates.	30.45(a)	Requirements for filing carrier manifest.
30.20(d)	For purposes of these regulations, the port of exportation is defined as.	30.1(c)	Definition used with EEI.
30.21	Requirements for the filing of Manifests	30.45	General statement of requirements for the filing of carrier manifests with proof of filing citations for the electronic submission of export information or exemption legends when EEI is not required.
30.21(a)	Vessel	30.45(a)(1)	Vessel.
30.21(b)	Aircraft	30.45(a)(2)	Aircraft.
30.21(c)	Rail Carrier	30.45(a)(3)	Rail Carrier.
30.21(d)	Carriers not required to file manifests	30.45(a)(4)	Carriers not required to file manifests.
30.22(a)	Requirements for the filing of SEDs or AES exemption legends and AES proof of filing citations by departing carriers.	30.8	Time and place for presenting proof of filing citation, and exemption legends.
30.22(b)	The exporting carrier shall be responsible for the accuracy of the following items of information.		NA.
30.22(c)	Except as provided in paragraph (d) of this section, when a transportation company finds, prior to the filing of declarations and manifest as provided in paragraph (a) of this section, that due to circumstances beyond the control of the transportation company or to inadvertence, a portion of the merchandise covered by an individual Shipper's Export Declaration has not been exported on the intended carrier.		NA.
30.22(d)	When a shipment by air covered by a single Shipper's Export Declaration is divided by the transportation company and exported in more than one aircraft of the transportation.	30.45(c)	Split shipments.
30.22(e)	Exporting carriers are authorized to amend incorrect shipping weights reported on Shipper's Export Declarations.		NA.
30.23	Requirements for the filing of Shipper's Export Declarations by pipeline carriers..	30.46	Requirements for the filing of export information by pipeline carriers.
30.24	Clearance or departure of carriers under bond on incomplete manifest on Shipper's Export Declarations.	30.47	Clearance or departure of carriers under bond on incomplete manifests.

FTSR	FTSR Regulatory topic	FTR	FTR Regulatory topic
Subpart C—Special Provisions Applicable Under Particular Circumstances			
30.30	Values for certain types of transactions	30.25	Values for certain types of transactions.
30.31	Identification of certain nonstatistical and other unusual transactions.	30.29	Reporting of repairs and replacements.
30.31(a) ..	Merchandise exported for repair only, and other temporary exports.	30.29(a)	The return of goods previously imported for repair.
30.31(b) ..	The return of merchandise previously imported for repair only.	30.29(b)	Goods that are covered under warranty and other temporary exports.
30.31(c) ..	Shipments of material in connection with construction, maintenance, and related work being done on projects for the U.S. Armed Forces.	....	NA.
30.33	Vessels, planes, cargo vans, and other carriers and containers sold foreign.	30.26	Reporting of vessels, aircraft, cargo vans, and other carriers and containers.
30.34	Return of exported cargo to the United States prior to reaching its final destination.	30.27	Return of exported cargo to the United States prior to reaching its final destination.
30.37	Exceptions from the requirement for reporting complete commodity detail on the Shipper's Export Declaration.	30.38	Exemption from the requirements for reporting complete commodity information.
30.37(a) ..	Where it can be determined that particular types of U.S. Government shipments, or shipments for government projects, are of such nature that they should not be included in the export statistics.	30.39	Special exemptions for shipments to the U.S. Armed Services. (Note, this section does not specifically address construction materials nor related work being done on projects).
30.37(b) ..	Special exemptions to specific portions of the requirements of § 30.7 with respect to the reporting of detailed information.	....	NA.
30.39	Authorization for reporting statistical information other than by means of individual Shipper's Export Declarations filed for each shipment.	....	NA.
30.40	Single declaration for multiple consignees	....	NA.
30.41	"Split shipments" by air	30.28	Split shipments.
Subpart D—Exemptions from the requirements for the Filing of Shipper's Export Declarations			
30.50	Procedure for shipments exempt from the requirements for Shipper's Export Declarations.	30.35	Procedure for shipments exempt from filing requirements.
30.51	Government shipments not generally exempt	30.39	Special exemption for shipments to the U.S. Armed Services.
30.52	Special exemptions for shipments to the U.S. Armed Services.	30.39	Special exemptions for shipments to the U.S. Armed Services.
30.53	Special exemptions for certain shipments to U.S. Government agencies and employees.	30.40	Special exemptions for certain shipments to U.S. Government agencies and employees.
30.53(e) ..	All commodities shipped to and for the exclusive use of the Panama Canal Zone Government or the Panama Canal Company.	....	NA.
30.55	Miscellaneous exemptions	30.37	Miscellaneous exemptions.
30.55(a) ..	Diplomatic pouches and their contents	30.37(i)	Diplomatic pouches and their contents.
30.55(b) ..	Human remains and accompanying appropriate receptacles and flowers.	30.37(j)	Human remains and accompanying appropriate receptacles and flowers.
30.55(c) ..	Shipments from one point in the United States to another thereof by routes passing through Mexico.	30.37(c)	Shipments from one point in the United States to another point in the United States by routes passing through Canada or Mexico.
30.55(d) ..	Shipments from one point in Mexico to another point thereof by routes through the United States.	30.37(d)	Shipments from one point in Canada or Mexico to another point in the same country by routes through the United States.
30.55(e) ..	Shipments, other than by vessel, or merchandise for which no validated export licenses are required, transported inbond through the United States, and exported from another U.S. port, or transshipped and exported directly from the port of arrival.	30.2(d)(1)	Shipments, transported in-bond through the United States, and exported from another U.S. port, or transshipped and exported directly from the port of arrival.
30.55(f) ...	Shipments to foreign libraries, government establishments, or similar institutions, as provided in § 30.53(d).	30.37(g)	Shipments to foreign libraries, government establishments, or similar institutions, as provided in § 30.40(d).
30.55(g) ..	Shipments of single gift parcels as authorized by the Bureau of Industry and Security under License Exception GFT, see 15 CFR 740.12 of the EAR.	30.37(h)	Shipments authorized by License Exception GFT for gift parcels, humanitarian donations.

FTSR	FTSR Regulatory topic	FTR	FTR Regulatory topic
30.55(h) ..	Except as noted in paragraph (h)(2) of this section, exports of commodities where the value of the commodities shipped from one exporter to one consignee on a single exporting carrier, classified under an individual Schedule B number, is $2,500 or less.	30.37(a)	Except as noted in § 30.2(a)(1)(iv), exports of commodities where the value of the commodities shipped USPPI to one consignee on a single exporting carrier, classified under an individual Schedule B or HTSUSA commodity classification code, is $2,500 or less.
30.55(i) ...	Shipments of interplant correspondence, executed invoices, and other documents and other shipments of company business records from a U.S. firm to its subsidiary or affiliate.	30.37(k)	Shipments of interplant correspondence, executed invoices, and other documents and other shipments of company business records from a U.S. firm to its subsidiary or affiliate.
30.55(j) ...	Shipments of pets as baggage, accompanied or unaccompanied, of persons leaving the United States, including members of crews on vessels and aircraft.	30.37(l)	Shipments of pets as baggage, accompanied or unaccompanied, of persons leaving the United States, including members of crews on vessels and aircraft.
30.55(k) ..	Shipments for use in connection with NASA tracking systems under Office of Export Administration Project License DL–5355–S.	....	NA.
30.55(l) ...	Shipments of aircraft parts and equipment, and food, saloon, slop chest, and related stores, provisions, and supplies for use on aircraft by a U.S. airline to its own installations, aircraft, and agent aboard, under Department of Commerce, Office of Export Administration General License, RCS.	....	NA.
30.55(m)	Shipments for use in connection with NOAA operations under the Office of Export Administration General License G–NOAA.	....	NA.
30.55(n) ..	Exports of technology and software as defined in 15 CFR 772 of the EAR that do not require an export license.	30.37(f)	Exports of technology and software as defined in 15 CFR 772 of the EAR that do not require an export license.
30.55(o) ..	Intangible exports of software and technology, such as downloaded software and technical data, including technology and software that requires an export license and mass market software exported electronically.	30.2(d)(3)	Intangible exports of software and technology, such as downloaded software and technical data, including technology and software that requires an export license and mass market software exported electronically.
30.56	Conditional Exemptions	30.37	Miscellaneous exemptions.
30.56(a) ..	Baggage and personal effects	30.38	Exemption from the requirements for reporting complete commodity information.
30.56(b) ..	Tools of trade	30.37(b)	Tools of trade
30.56(c) ..	Carriers' stores.	30.37(m)	Carriers' stores
30.56(d) ..	Dunnage.	30.37(n)	Dunnage
30.57	Information on export declarations for shipments of types of goods covered by § 30.56 not conditionally exempt.	....	NA.
30.58	Exemption for shipments from the United States to Canada.	30.36	Exemption for shipments destined to Canada.
	Subpart E—Electronic Filing Requirements—Shipper's Export Information		
30.60	General requirements for filing export and manifest data electronically using the Automated Export System (AES).	30.2	General requirements for filing Electronic Export Information.
30.60(a) ..	Participation	....	NA.
30.60(b) ..	Letter of Intent	30.5(a)(1)	Postdeparture filing application.
30.60(c) ..	General filing and transmission requirements	30.4	NA.
30.60(d) ..	General responsibilities of exporters, filing agents, and sea carriers	30.3	Electronic Export Information filer requirements, parties to export transactions, and responsibilities of parties to export transactions.
30.61	Electronic filing options	30.4	Electronic Export Information filing procedure, deadlines, and certification statement.
30.62	AES Certification, qualifications, and standards ...	30.5	EEI filing application and certification processes and standards.
30.63	Information required to be reported electronically through AES (data elements).	30.6	Electronic Export Information data elements.
30.64	Transmitting and correcting AES information	30.9	Transmitting and correcting Electronic Export Information.
30.65	Annotating the proper exemption legends or proof of filing citations for shipments transmitted electronically.	30.7	Annotating the bill of lading, air waybill, and other commercial loading documents with the proper proof of filing citations, approved postdeparture filing citations, downtime filing citation, or exemption legends.
30.66	Recordkeeping and requirements	30.5(f)	Support.

FTSR	FTSR Regulatory topic	FTR	FTR Regulatory topic
30.66	Support, documentation, and recordkeeping requirements.	30.10	Retention of export information and the authority to require production of documents.
	Subpart F—General Requirements—Importers		
30.70	Statistical information required on import entries	30.50	General requirements for filing import entries.
		30.51	Statistical information required for import entries.
30.80	Imports from Canada	30.54	Special provisions for imports from Canada.
30.81	Imports of merchandise into Guam	....	NA.
30.82	Identification of U.S. merchandise returned for repair and reexport.	30.53	Import of goods returned for repair.
30.83	Statistical copy of mail and informal entries	....	NA.
	Subpart H—General Administrative Provisions		
30.90	Confidential information, import entries, and withdrawals.	30.55	Confidentiality information, import entries, and withdrawals.
30.91	Confidential information, Shipper's Export Declarations.	30.60	Confidentiality of Electronic Export Information.
30.92	Statistical classification schedules	30.61	Statistical classification schedules.
30.93	Emergency exceptions	30.62	Emergency exceptions.
30.94	Instructions to CBP	....	NA.
30.95	Penalties for violations	....	Subpart H.
30.95(a) ..	Exports (reexports) of rough diamonds	30.70	Violation of the Clean Diamond Trade Act.
30.95(b) ..	Exports of other than rough diamonds	30.71	False or fraudulent reporting.
30.99	OMB control numbers assigned pursuant to the Paperwork Reduction Act.	30.63	Office of Management and Budget control numbers assigned pursuant to the Paperwork Reduction Act.

Appendix F to Part 30—FTR to FTSR Concordance

FTR	FTR regulatory topic	FTSR	FTSR regulatory topic
	Subpart A—General Requirements		
30.1	Purpose and definitions	NA	NA.
30.2	General requirements for filing Electronic Export Information.	30.1	General statement of requirement for Shipper's Export Declarations.
30.2(a)	Filing Requirements	....	Filing Requirements.
30.2(b)	General requirements.	....	NA.
30.2(c)	Certification and filing requirements	....	NA.
30.2(d)	(d) Exclusions from filing EEI	....	NA.
30.2(e)	(e) Penalties	....	NA.
30.3	Electronic Export Information filer requirements, parties to export transactionns, and responsibilities of parties to export transactions.	30.4	Preparation and signature of Shipper's Export Declaration.
30.4	Electronic Export Information filing procedures, deadlines, and certification statements.	30.61	Electronic filing options.
30.4(a)	EEI transmitted predeparture	30.61(a)	EEI transmitted predeparture.
30.4(b)	Filing deadlines for EEI transmitted predeparture.	....	NA.
30.4(c)	EEI transmitted postdeparture	30.61(b)	EEI transmitted post departure.
30.4(d)	Proof of filing citation or exemption legend	30.12(d)	Exports file via AES.
30.5	Electronic Export Information filing application and certification processes and standards.	30.62	AES Certification, qualifications, and standards.
30.5(a)	AES application process	30.60(b)	AES Participant Application.
30.5(b)	Certification process	30.66	Recordkeeping and requirements.
30.5(c)	Postdeparture filing approval process.		
30.5(d)	Electronic Export Information filing standards.		
30.5(e)	Monitoring the filing of Electronic Export Information		
30.5(f)	Support.		
30.6	Electronic Export Information data elements.	30.63	Information required to be reported electronically through AES (data elements).
30.7	Annotating the bill of lading * * *	30.65	Annotating the proper exemption legends or proof of filing citations * * *.
30.8	Time and place for preenting proof of filing citations, postdeparture filing citations, downtime filing citation, or exemption legends.	30.12	Time and place for presenting the SED, exemption legends, or proof of filing citations.

FTR	FTR regulatory topic	FTSR	FTSR regulatory topic
30.9	Transmitting and correcting Electronic Export Information.	30.64	Transmitting and correcting AES information.
		30.16	Corrections to Shipper's Export Declarations.
30.10(a)	Retention of Export information	30.66	Support, documentation and recordkeeping, and documentation requirements.
30.10(b)	Authority to require production of documents.	30.11	Authority to require production of documents.
Subpart B—Export Control and Licensing Requirements			
30.15	Introduction	30.2	Related export control requirements.
30.16	Export Administration Regulations	30.2	Related export control requirements.
30.17	Customs and Border Protection Regulations.	30.2	Related export control requirements.
30.18	Department of State Regulations	30.2	Related export control requirements.
30.19	Other Federal agency regulations	30.2	Related export control requirements.
Subpart C—Special Provisions and Specific-Type Transactions			
30.25	Values for certain types of transactions	30.30	Values for certain types of transactions.
30.26	Reporting of vessels, aircraft, cargo vans, and other carriers and containers.	30.33	Vessels, planes, cargo vans, and other carriers and containers sold foreign.
30.27	Return of exported cargo to the United States prior to reaching its final destination.	30.34	Return of exported cargo to the United States prior to reaching its final destination.
30.28	"Split shipments" by air	30.41	"Split shipments" by air.
30.29	Reporting of repairs and replacements	30.31	Identification of certain nonstatistical and other unusual transactions.
Subpart D—Exemptions From the Requirements for the Filing of Electronic Export Information			
30.35	Procedure for shipments exempt from filing requirements.	30.50	Procedure for shipments exempt from the requirements for SEDs.
30.36	Exemption for shipments destined to Canada.	30.58	Exemption for shipments from the United states to Canada.
30.37	Miscellaneous exemptions	30.55	Miscellaneous exemptions.
		30.55	Conditional exemptions.
30.37(a)	Except as noted in § 30.2(a)(1)(iv), exports of commodities where the value * * * is $2,500 or less.		Except as noted in paragraph h(2) of this section, exports of commodities where the value * * * is $2,500 or less.
30.37(b)	Tools of trade * * *	30.56(b)	Tools of trade * * *.
30.37(c)	Shipments from one point in the United States to another point in the United States by routes passing through Canada or Mexico	30.55(c)	Shipments from one point in the United States to another thereof by routes passing through Mexico.
		30.58(a)	* * * this exemption also applies to shipments from one point in the United States or Canada to another point thereof * * *.
30.37(d)	Shipments from one point in Canada or Mexico to another point thereof by routes through the United States	30.55(d)	Shipments from one point in Canada or Mexico to another point in the same country by routes through the United States.
		30.58(a)	* * * this exemption also applies to shipments from one point in the United States or Canada to another point thereof * * *.
30.37(e)	Shipments transported inbound through the United States * * *.	30.55(e)	Shipments, other than by vessel, or merchandise for which no validated licenses required, transported inbound through the United States * * *.
30.37(f)	Exports of technology and software as defined in 15 CFR of the EAR that do not require an export license * * *.	30.55(n)	Exports of technology and software as defined in 15 CFR 772 of the EAR that do not require an export license * * *.
30.37(g)	Shipments to foreign libraries, government establishments, or similar institutions, as provided in § 30.40(d).		Shipments to foreign libraries, government establishments, or similar institutions, as provided in § 30.53(d).
30.37(h)	Shipments as authorized under License Exception GFT for gift parcels and humanitarian donations.	30.55(g)	Shipments of single gift parcels as authorized by the Bureau of Industry and Security under license exception GFT.
30.37(i)	Diplomatic pouches and their contents	30.55(a)	Diplomatic pouches and their contents.

FTR	FTR regulatory topic	FTSR	FTSR regulatory topic
30.37(j)	Human remains and accompanying appropriate receptacles and flowers.	30.55(b)	Human remains and accompanying appropriate receptacles and flowers.
30.37(k)	Shipments of interplant correspondence, executed invoices and other documents, and other shipments of company business records from a U.S. firm to its subsidiary or affiliate.	30.55(i)	Shipments of interplant correspondence, executed invoices and other documents, and other shipments of company business records from a U.S. firm to its subsidiary or affiliate.
30.37(l)	Shipments of pets as baggage, accompanied or unaccompanied, of persons leaving the United States, including members of crews on vessels and aircraft.	30.55(j)	Shipments of pets as baggage, accompanied or unaccompanied, of persons leaving the United States, including members of crews on vessels and aircraft.
30.37(m)	Carriers' stores * * *	30.56(c)	Carriers' stores * * *.
30.37(n)	Dunnage * * *	30.56(d)	Dunnage * * *.
30.37(o)	Shipments of aircraft parts and equipment; food, saloon, slop chest, and related stores, * * *.	30.55(l)	Shipments of aircraft parts and equipment; food, saloon, slop chest, and related stores, * * *.
30.37(p)	Baggage and personal effects not shipped as cargo under a bill of lading or an air waybill and not requiring an export license * * *.	30.56(a)	Baggage and personal effects not shipped as cargo under a bill of lading or an air waybill and not requiring an export license * * *.
30.37(q)	Temporary exports, whether shipped or hand carried (e.g., carnet), which are exported from or returned to the United States in less than one year (21 months) from the date of export	30.31(a)	* * * and other temporary exports.
		30.37(a)(2)	Temporary exports by or to U.S. Government agencies.
30.37(r)	Goods previously imported under a Temporary Import Bond for return in the same condition as when imported * * *.	30.31(b)	* * * and other returns to the foreign shipper of other temporarily imported merchandise.
30.37(s)	Issued bank notes and securities and coins in circulation exported as evidence of financial claims.		NA.
30.37(t)	Documents used in international transactions * * *.		NA.
30.38	Exemption from the requirements for reporting complete commodity information.	30.56	Conditional exemptions.
30.38(a)	Usual and reasonable kinds and quantities of wearing apparel, articles of personal adornment, toilet articles, medicinal supplies, food, souvenirs, games, and similar personal effects and their containers.	30.56(a)(1)	Usual and reasonable kinds and quantities of wearing apparel, articles of personal adornment, toilet articles, medicinal supplies, food, souvenirs, games, and similar personal effects and their containers.
30.38(b)	Usual and reasonable kinds and quantities of furniture, household effects, household furnishings, and their containers.	30.56(a)(2)	Usual and reasonable kinds and quantities of furniture, household effects, household furnishings, and their containers.
30.38(c)	Usual and reasonable kinds and quantities of vehicles, such as passenger cars, station wagons, trucks, * * *.	30.56(a)(3)	Usual and reasonable kinds and quantities of vehicles, such as passenger cars, station wagons, trucks, * * *.
30.39	Special exemptions for certain shipments to U.S. Government agencies and employees.	30.53	Special exemptions for certain shipments to U.S. Government agencies and employees
30.40	Special exemptions for certain shipments to U.S. Government agencies and employees.	30.53	Special exemptions for certain shipments to U.S. Government agencies and employees
Subpart E—General Carrier and Manifest Requirements			
30.45	General statement of requirements for the filing of carrier manifests with proof of filing citations	30.20	General statement of requirements for the filing of manifests * * *.
		30.21	Requirements for the filing of manifests.
		30.22	Requirements for filing of Shipper's Export Declarations by departing carriers.
30.46	Requirements for the filing of export information by pipeline carriers.	30.23	Requirement for the filing of Shipper's Export declarations by pipeline carriers.
30.47	Clearance or departure of carriers under bond on incomplete manifests.	30.24	Clearance or departure of carriers under bond on incomplete manifest * * *.

FTR	FTR regulatory topic	FTSR	FTSR regulatory topic
	Subpart F—Import Requirements		
30.50	General requirements for filing import entries.	30.70	Statistical information required on import entries.
30.53	Import of goods returned for repair	30.82	Identification of U.S. merchandise returned for repair and reexport.
30.54	Special provisions for imports from Canada.	30.80	Imports from Canada.
30.55	Confidential information, import entries, and withdrawals.	30.90	Confidential information import entries, and withdrawals.
	Subpart G—General Administrative Provisions		
30.60	Confidentiality of Electronic Export Information.	30.91	Confidential information, Shipper's Export Declaration.
30.61	Statistical classification schedules	30.92	Statistical classification schedules.
30.62	Emergency exceptions	30.93	Emergency exceptions.
30.63	Office of Management and Budget control numbers assigned pursuant to the Paperwork Reduction Act.	30.99	OMB control numbers assigned pursuant to the Paperwork Reduction Act.
	Subpart H—Penalties		
30.70	Violation of the Clean Diamond Trade Act	30.95(a)	Penalties for violations for export (reexport) of rough diamonds.
30.71	False or fraudulent reporting on or misuse of the Automated Export System.	30.95(b)	Penalties for violations of exports other than diamonds.
30.71(a)	Criminal penalties.		
30.71(b)	Civil penalties.		
30.72	Civil penalty procedures		NA.
30.73	Enforcement		NA.
30.73(a)	Department of Commerce.		
30.73(b)	Department of Homeland Security.		
30.74	Voluntary self-disclosure		NA.
30.75–30.99	[Reserved]		

EFFECTIVE DATE NOTE: At 78 FR 16388, Mar. 14, 2013, Appendix F to Part 30 was revised, effective Jan. 8, 2014. At 78 FR 67928, Nov. 13, 2013, the effective date was delayed until Apr. 5, 2014. For the convenience of the user, the revised text is set forth as follows:

APPENDIX F TO PART 30—FTR TO FTSR CONCORDANCE

FTR	FTR Regulatory topic	FTSR	FTSR Regulatory topic
	Subpart A—General Requirements		
30.1	Purpose and definitions	NA	NA.
30.2	General requirements for filing Electronic Export Information.	30.1	General statement of requirement for Shipper's Export Declarations.
30.2(a)	Filing Requirements		Filing Requirements.
30.2(b)	General requirements		NA.
30.2(c)	Certification and filing requirements		NA.
30.2(d)	Exclusions from filing EEI		NA.
30.2(e)	Penalties		NA.
30.3	Electronic Export Information filer requirements, parties to export transactions, and responsibilities of parties to export transactions.	30.4	Preparation and signature of Shipper's Export Declaration.
30.4	Electronic Export Information filing procedures, deadlines, and certification statements.	30.61	Electronic filing options.
30.4(a)	EEI transmitted predeparture	30.61(a)	EEI transmitted predeparture.
30.4(b)	Filing deadlines for EEI transmitted predeparture.		NA.
30.4(c)	EEI transmitted postdeparture	30.61(b)	EEI transmitted postdeparture.
30.4(d)	Proof of filing citation or exemption legend.	30.12(d)	Exports file via AES.
30.5	Electronic Export Information filing application and certification processes and standards.	30.62	AES Certification, qualifications, and standards.
30.5(a)	AES application process	30.60(b)	AES Participant Application.

FTR	FTR Regulatory topic	FTSR	FTSR Regulatory topic
30.5(b)	Certification process	30.66	Record keeping and requirements.
30.5(c)	Postdeparture filing approval process	.	
30.5(d)	Electronic Export Information filing standards.	.	
30.5(e)	Monitoring the filing of Electronic Export Information.	.	
30.5(f)	Support	.	
30.6	Electronic Export Information data elements.	30.63	Information required to be reported electronically through AES (data elements).
30.7	Annotating the bill of lading	30.65	Annotating the proper exemption legends or proof of filing citations.
30.8	Time and place for presenting proof of filing citations, postdeparture filing citations, downtime filing citation, or exemption legends.	30.12	Time and place for presenting the SED, exemption legends, or proof of filing citations.
30.9	Transmitting and correcting Electronic Export Information.	30.64	Transmitting and correcting AES information.
		30.16	Corrections to Shipper's Export Declarations.
30.10(a)	Retention of Export information	30.66	Support, documentation and recordkeeping, and documentation requirements.
30.10(b)	Authority to require production of documents.	30.11	Authority to require production of documents.
Subpart B—Export Control and Licensing Requirements			
30.15	Introduction	30.2	Related export control requirements.
30.16	Bureau of Industry and Security regulations.	30.2	Related export control requirements.
30.17	U.S. Customs and Border Protection regulations.	30.2	Related export control requirements.
30.18	Department of State regulations	30.2	Related export control requirements.
30.19	Other Federal agency regulations	30.2	Related export control requirements.
Subpart C—Special Provisions and Specific-Type Transactions			
30.25	Values for certain types of transactions	30.30	Values for certain types of transactions.
30.26	Reporting of vessels, aircraft, cargo vans, and other carriers and containers.	30.33	Vessels, planes, cargo vans, and other carriers and containers sold foreign.
30.27	Return of exported cargo to the United States prior to reaching its final destination.	30.34	Return of exported cargo to the United States prior to reaching its final destination.
30.28	Split shipments	30.41	"Split shipments" by air.
30.29	Reporting of repairs and replacements	30.31	Identification of certain nonstatistical and other unusual transactions.
Subpart D—Exemptions from the Requirements for the Filing of Electronic Export Information			
30.35	Procedure for shipments exempt from filing requirements.	30.50	Procedure for shipments exempt from the requirements for SEDs.
30.36	Exemption for shipments destined to Canada.	30.58	Exemption for shipments from the United States to Canada.
30.37	Miscellaneous exemptions	30.55	Miscellaneous exemptions.
		30.55	Conditional exemptions.
30.37(a)	Except as noted in §30.2(a)(1)(iv), exports of commodities where the value * * * is $2,500 or less.	30.55(h)	Except as noted in paragraph h(2) of this section, exports of commodities where the value * * * is $2,500 or less.
30.37(b)	Tools of trade	30.56(b)	Tools of trade
30.37(c)	Shipments from one point in the United States to another point in the United States by routes passing through Canada or Mexico.	30.55(c)	Shipments from one point in the United States to another thereof by routes passing through Mexico.
		30.58(a)	* * * this exemption also applies to shipments from one point in the United States or Canada to another point thereof * * *
30.37(d)	Shipments from one point in Canada or Mexico to another point thereof by routes through the United States.	30.55(d)	Shipments from one point in Canada or Mexico to another point in the same country by routes through the United States.

FTR	FTR Regulatory topic	FTSR	FTSR Regulatory topic
		30.58(a)	* * * this exemption also applies to shipments from one point in the United States or Canada to another point thereof * * *
30.37(e)	Reserved		NA.
30.37(f)	Exports of technology and software as defined in 15 CFR of the EAR that do not require an export license.	30.55(n)	Exports of technology and software as defined in 15 CFR 772 of the EAR that do not require an export license
30.37(g)	Shipments to foreign libraries, government establishments, or similar institutions.	30.55(f)	Shipments to foreign libraries, government establishments, or similar institutions, as provided in § 30.53(d).
30.37(h)	Shipments as authorized under License Exception GFT for gift parcels and humanitarian donations.	30.55(g)	Shipments of single gift parcels as authorized by the Bureau of Industry and Security under license exception GFT.
30.37(i)	Diplomatic pouches and their contents	30.55(a)	Diplomatic pouches and their contents.
30.37(j)	Human remains and accompanying appropriate receptacles and flowers.	30.55(b)	Human remains and accompanying appropriate receptacles and flowers.
30.37(k)	Shipments of interplant correspondence, executed invoices and other documents, and other shipments of company business records from a U.S. firm to its subsidiary or affiliate.	30.55(i)	Shipments of interplant correspondence, executed invoices and other documents, and other shipments of company business records from a U.S. firm to its subsidiary or affiliate.
30.37(l)	Shipments of pets as baggage, accompanied or unaccompanied, of persons leaving the United States, including members of crews on vessels and aircraft.	30.55(j)	Shipments of pets as baggage, accompanied or unaccompanied, of persons leaving the United States, including members of crews on vessels and aircraft.
30.37(m)	Carriers' stores * * *	30.56(c)	Carriers' stores * * *
30.37(n)	Dunnage * * *	30.56(d)	Dunnage * * *
30.37(o)	Shipments of aircraft parts and equipment; food, saloon, slop chest, and related stores, * * *	30.55(l)	Shipments of aircraft parts and equipment and food, saloon, slop chest, and related stores, * * *
30.37(p)	Baggage and personal effects not shipped as cargo under a bill of lading or an air waybill and not requiring an export license * * *	30.56(a)	Baggage and personal effects not shipped as cargo under a bill of lading or an air waybill and not requiring an export license * * *
30.37(q)	Reserved		NA.
30.37(r)	Reserved		NA.
30.37(s)	Issued bank notes and securities and coins in circulation exported as evidence of financial claims.		NA
30.37(t)	Documents used in international transaction * * *		NA.
30.37(u)	Exports of technical data and defense service exemptions.		NA.
30.37(v)	Vessels, aircraft, cargo vans and other carriers and containers		NA.
30.37(w)	Shipments to Army Post Office, Diplomatic Post Office, Fleet Post Office.		NA.
30.37(x)	Shipments exported under license exception Baggage (BAG).		NA.
30.37(y)(1)	Shipments of books, maps, charts, pamphlets, and similar articles to foreign libraries, government establishments, or similar institutions..		NA.
30.37(y)(2)	Shipments to U.S. government agencies and employees that are lawfully exported under License Exception GOV of the Export Administration Regulations (15 CFR § 740.11(b)(2)(i) or (ii)) valued at $2500 or less per Schedule B Number.		NA.
30.37(y)(3)	Personal effects as described in 15 CFR § 740.14(b)(1) being lawfully exported under License Exception BAG of the Export Administration Regulations (15 CFR § 740.14).		NA.
30.37(y)(4)	Individual gift parcels and humanitarian donations being lawfully exported under License Exception GFT of the Export Administration Regulations (15 CFR § 740.12(a) and (b)).		NA.

FTR	FTR Regulatory topic	FTSR	FTSR Regulatory topic
30.37(y)(5)	Vessels and aircraft lawfully leaving the United States for temporary sojourn to or in a Country Group E:1 country.		NA.
30.37(y)(6)	Tools of trade that will be used by a person traveling to a Country Group E destination, that will be returned to the United States within one year and that are lawfully being exported to a Country Group E:1 destination under License Exception BAGGAGE (15 CFR 740.14 or License Exception TMP (15 CFR 740.9(a))..		NA.
30.38	Exemption from the requirements for reporting complete commodity information.	30.56	Conditional exemptions.
30.38(a)	Usual and reasonable kinds and quantities of wearing apparel, articles of personal adornment, toilet articles, medicinal supplies, food, souvenirs, games, and similar personal effects and their containers.	30.56(a)(1)	Usual and reasonable kinds and quantities of wearing apparel, articles of personal adornment, toilet articles, medicinal supplies, food, souvenirs, games, and similar personal effects and their containers.
30.38(b)	Usual and reasonable kinds and quantities of furniture, household effects, household furnishings, and their containers.	30.56(a)(2)	Usual and reasonable kinds and quantities of furniture, household effects, household furnishings, and their containers.
30.38(c)	Usual and reasonable kinds and quantities of vehicles, such as passenger cars, station wagons, trucks, * * *	30.56(a)(3)	Usual and reasonable kinds and quantities of vehicles, such as passenger cars, station wagons, trucks, * * *
30.39	Special exemptions for shipments to the U.S. Armed Services.	30.52	Special exemptions for shipments to the U.S. Armed Services.
30.40	Special exemptions for certain shipments to U.S. Government agencies and employees.	30.53	Special exemptions for certain shipments to U.S. Government agencies and employees.
Subpart E—General Carrier and Manifest Requirements			
30.45	General statement of requirements for the filing of carrier manifests with proof of filing citations.	30.20	General statement of requirements for the filing of manifests * * *
		30.21	Requirements for the filing of manifests.
		30.22	Requirements for filing of Shipper's Export Declarations by departing carriers.
30.46	Requirements for the filing of export information by pipeline carriers.	30.23	Requirement for the filing of Shipper's Export Declarations by pipeline carriers.
30.47	Clearance or departure of carriers under bond on incomplete manifest.	30.24	Clearance or departure of carriers under bond on incomplete manifest * * *
Subpart F—Import Requirements			
30.50	General requirements for filing import entries.	30.70	Statistical information required on import entries.
30.51	Statistical information required for import entries.	30.70	Statistical information required for import entries.
30.52	Foreign Trade Zones		NA.
30.53	Import of goods returned for repair	30.82	Identification of U.S. merchandise returned for repair and reexport.
30.54	Special provisions for imports from Canada.	30.80	Imports from Canada.
30.55	Confidential information, import entries, and withdrawals.	30.90	Confidential information import entries, and withdrawals.
Subpart G—General Administrative Provisions			
30.60	Confidentiality of Electronic Export Information.	30.91	Confidential information, Shipper's Export Declaration.
30.61	Statistical classification schedules	30.92	Statistical classification schedules.
30.62	Emergency exceptions	30.93	Emergency exceptions.
30.63	Office of Management and Budget control numbers assigned pursuant to the Paperwork Reduction Act.	30.99	OMB control numbers assigned pursuant to the Paperwork Reduction Act.

FTR	FTR Regulatory topic	FTSR	FTSR Regulatory topic
Subpart H—Penalties			
30.70	Violation of the Clean Diamond Trade Act	30.95(a)	Penalties for violations for export (reexport) of rough diamonds.
30.71	False or fraudulent reporting on or misuse of the Automated Export System.	30.95(b)	Penalties for violations of exports other than diamonds.
30.71(a)	Criminal penalties		
30.71(b)	Civil penalties		
30.72	Civil penalty procedures		NA.
30.73	Enforcement		NA.
30.73(a)	Department of Commerce.		
30.73(b)	Department of Homeland Security.		
30.74	Voluntary self-disclosure		NA.
30.75–30.99	[Reserved].		

PART 40—TRAINING OF FOREIGN PARTICIPANTS IN CENSUS PROCEDURES AND GENERAL STATISTICS

AUTHORITY: 5 U.S.C. 301; 22 U.S.C. 1456; 31 U.S.C. 686. Memorandum of Agreement between the Department of Commerce and the Foreign Operations Administration Concerning Foreign Technical Assistance Work, signed June 10, 1954.

SOURCE: 28 FR 119, Jan. 4, 1963, unless otherwise noted.

§ 40.1 Type of grant.

Training grants will be awarded by the Agency for International Development (AID), in its capacity as the bilateral technical assistance agency for the United States Government, to foreign participants for training, observation, and research in the fields of censuses and statistics at the Bureau of the Census. In compliance with the needs of the participants and consistent with resources of the Bureau, training programs will be developed along the lines of a combined interne-training and/or training-in research types, and may include any or all of the following:

(a) Conference courses designed to provide the trainee with adequate background information on (1) organization and administration of the United States Bureau of the Census, (2) subject-matter areas for which the Bureau of the Census collects and compiles statistical information, (3) nature and scope of the major statistical programs maintained by other federal government agencies, (4) techniques and scope of the periodic censuses and statistical surveys, and statistical compilations undertaken by the Bureau of the Census, and (5) relation of censuses to other statistical data collected and analyzed by U.S. agencies.

(b) Seminars laboratory exercises and observation of work in the Census Bureau and other agencies with specific applicability to the participant such as (1) development of census and survey questionnaires, (2) methods of field and mail enumeration, (3) procedures for editing and coding statistical forms, (4) use of office machines, electromechanical tabulation equipment, and automatic data processing systems for mass processing of statistical data, (5) definitions and scope of the subject matters involved in the censuses and statistical programs of the Bureau of the Census, (6) classification of industrial and business establishments, (7) classification of imports and exports, (8) techniques of making intercensal estimates of population, (9) sampling techniques and quality control procedures, (10) analyses and publication of data, and development of certain indexes; and (11) other topics, particularly in the development of new statistical programs and techniques.

(c) Formal courses at a college or university to supplement the seminars, conference-courses, and individual statistical projects developed, presented, or assigned by the Bureau; or enrolled on a full-time basis in a college or university to obtain the appropriate academic background for further work in the field of statistics in accordance with needs of participants and/or the program requirements of their countries.

(d) Observation trips to various academic institutions with recognized statistical activities, to private marketing and research agencies, to regional field offices of the Bureau, to the government statistical agencies of Canada, and to such activities that will supplement or illustrate the application and end use of statistical data.

(e) Case study workshops on selected census and statistical activities presented at the Bureau, in other locations in the United States, or outside the continental limits of the United States.

(f) Such field training, special research, or university program as appears advisable to the Director of the Bureau of the Census in accordance with the technical needs of the participants.

§ 40.2 Qualifications.

(a) To be eligible for a training grant at the Bureau of the Census the applicant must be:

(1) A bona-fide citizen of a country with whom the United States has proper diplomatic arrangements for such training programs.

(2) Able to speak, read, write, and understand the English language.

(3) Sponsored by his government either directly with the United States or through a public international agency.

(4) Physically able to undertake the activities incident to the course of training and free from communicable diseases.

(b) [Reserved]

§ 40.3 Cooperation with bilateral technical assistance programs of the United States.

In compliance with the provisions contained in the Memorandum of Agreement executed between the Department of Commerce and the Foreign Operations Administration (now AID) on June 10, 1954, the Bureau of the Census is authorized within its areas of competence and available resources to continue its training of foreign nationals under the general guidance of the Department of Commerce and in cooperation with the bilateral technical assistance programs of the United States Government.

§ 40.4 Administrative provisions on selection of participants and funding of costs.

(a) Within the framework of the aforementioned Memorandum of Agreement, the Bureau of the Census will arrange at the request and expense of the Agency for International Development, a program for technical training of foreign participants in censuses and statistics. The Bureau of the Census will be furnished biographic materials, information about the training objecttives including, where appropriate, each participant's education and experience, type of training desired, present and future positions with descriptions of duties, and the terms of the training project for each participant or group as far in advance of his arrival in the United States as possible.

(b) The Bureau reserves the right to accept, based on biographical information to be furnished in advance, only those participants whom it finds qualified to make satisfactory use of its training facilities and resources. The Bureau would prefer to develop programs for foreign participants with substantive experience in the statistical activities of their home country.

(c) Arrangements for security clearances, insurance, orientation, international travel, housing, and other administrative responsibilities will be the responsibility of AID under the provisions of the Memorandum of Agreement (Reference: Appendix II, Training of Foreign Nationals).

§ 40.5 Other cooperative arrangements.

The Bureau of the Census also undertakes the training of foreign nationals proposed through the Department of State under the International Exchange Service (IES) or under the sponsorship of public international agencies.

PART 50—SPECIAL SERVICES AND STUDIES BY THE BUREAU OF THE CENSUS

AUTHORITY: 15 U.S.C. 1525–1527 and 13 U.S.C. 3 and 8.

§ 50.1 General.

(a) Fee structure for age search and citizenship service, special population censuses, and for foreign trade and shipping statistics.

(b) In accordance with the provisions of the acts authorizing the Department of Commerce to make special statistical surveys and studies, and to perform other specified services upon the payment of the cost thereof, the following fee structure is hereby established. No transcript of any record will be furnished under authority of these acts which would violate existing or future acts requiring that information furnished be held confidential.

(c) Requests for age search and citizenship service should be addressed to the Personal Census Search Unit, Data Preparation Division, Bureau of the Census, P.O. Box 1545, Jeffersonville, Indiana 47131. Application forms may be obtained at Department of Commerce field offices or Social Security offices or by writing to the Jeffersonville, Indiana office.

(d) If a search is unsuccessful and additional information for a further search is requested by the Census Bureau, such information must be received within 90 days of the request or the case will be considered closed. Additional information received after 90 days must be accompanied by a new fee and will be considered a new request.

(15 U.S.C. 1526 and 13 U.S.C. 8)

[36 FR 905, Jan. 20, 1971, as amended at 49 FR 3980, Feb. 1, 1984; 56 FR 35815, July 29, 1991; 68 FR 42586, July 18, 2003]

§ 50.5 Fee structure for age search and citizenship information.

Type of service	Fee
Searches of one census for one person and one transcript	$65.00
Each additional copy of census transcript	2.00
[1] Each full schedule requested	10.00

[1] The $10.00 for each full schedule requested is in addition to the $65.00 transcript fee.

NOTE: An additional charge of $20.00 per case is charged for expedited requests requiring search results within one day.

[69 FR 45580, July 30, 2004]

§ 50.10 Fee structure for special population censuses.

The Bureau of the Census is authorized to conduct special population censuses at the request of and at the expense of the community concerned. To obtain a special population census, an authorized official of the community should write a letter to the Associate Director for Demographic Fields, Bureau of the Census, Washington, D.C. 20233, requesting detailed information and stating the approximate present population. The Associate Director will reply giving an estimate of the cost and other pertinent information. Title 13, United State Code, section 196, Special Censuses, requires payment to the Bureau of the actual or estimated cost of each such special census.

[47 FR 18, Jan. 4, 1982]

§ 50.30 Fee structure for foreign trade and shipping statistics.

(a) The Bureau of the Census is willing to furnish on a cost basis foreign trade and shipping statistics provided there is no serious interruption of the Bureau's regular work program.

(b) In instances where information requested is not shown separately or not summarized in the form desired, it is necessary to conduct a prelimary investigation at the requestor's expense to determine whether the information can be compiled from the basic records and what the total cost will be. The preliminary investigation normally costs $250 but may be more depending on the circumstances. The total cost of the final report generally ranges from $500 to several thousand dollars for data covering a 12-month period.

(c) Upon receipt of a request, information will be furnished as to whether the statistics are available and if so, the cost; or that a preliminary investigation must be conducted. When an investigation is completed, information will be furnished as to the cost of preparing the material, or as to the reason if the statistics cannot be compiled from our basic records.

(15 U.S.C. 1526 and 13 U.S.C. 8)

[28 FR 120, Jan. 4, 1963, as amended at 49 FR 3980, Feb. 1, 1984]

§ 50.40 Fee structure for statistics for city blocks in the 1980 Census of Population and Housing.

(a) As part of the regular program of the 1980 census, the Census Bureau will publish printed reports containing certain summary population and housing statistics for each city block, drawn from the subjects which are being covered on a 100-percent basis. For these subjects, a substantial amount of additional data by block will be available on computer tape.

(b) The 1980 block data under the regular program will be prepared for:

(1) Each urbanized area in the United States. An urbanized area is delineated by the Census Bureau in each standard metropolitan statistical area and generally consists of a city or group of contiguous cities with a 1970 population of 50,000 or more, together with adjacent densely populated land (*i.e.*, land having a population density of at least 1,000 persons per square mile).

(2) And, outside urbanized areas, for each incorporated place (such as a city or village) that was reported as having 10,000 or more inhabitants in:

(i) The 1970 census, or

(ii) The 1973, 1975, or 1976 official population estimates published by the Bureau, or

(iii) A special census conducted by the Bureau on or before December 31, 1977.

(c) Outside the above-mentioned urbanized areas and places, State and local government authorities will be able to contract with the Bureau of the Census to produce block data for their areas. In undertaking this contract, the requesting authority will be required to pay a fee, supply certain maps, and meet certain time deadlines as follows:

(1) *Fee:* (i) Population size:

	Fee per area
Under 2,500	$500
2,500 to 4,999	600
5,000 to 9,999	700

(ii) The final fee will be based upon the 1980 census population counts. A refund or additional charge will be made if the contracting area is in a different population size group as a result of the census.

(iii) The cost for an area with a population of 10,000 or more will be determined on an individual basis.

(iv) Multiple area contracts may be negotiated at a savings.

(v) The fee is based on estimated 1980 costs. If the 1980 cost exceeds the estimated cost, an additional fee may be requested from the contracting area. If actual costs are less than the estimated cost, a refund may be made.

(vi) Any incorporated place which contracts for block statistics and which reaches a population of 10,000 or more in the 1980 census will have the fee completely refunded, as the place will then be considered to be part of the regular block statistics program.

(vii) If the area submits maps which are not adequate for the Bureau's purposes (see Maps, below) and therefore have to be redrafted by the Bureau, a surcharge of $300 per map sheet requiring revision will be applied to the fee for the particular area.

(2) *Maps:* (i) In order for the Bureau to provide data on a block-by-block basis, it must have a map which clearly delineates each block. The contracting government authority must supply such maps. A copy of the specifications for preparing the block maps will be provided upon request and, in any event, will accompany the copy of the contract which is sent to the government authority for signature.

(ii) The maps must be furnished to the Census Bureau within 30 calendar days after the government authority signs the contract.

(iii) The Bureau will review the maps and, if revision is necessary, return them within 30 calendar days to the government authority.

(iv) Within 30 calendar days thereafter, the revised maps must be transmitted to the Bureau and, if they are still inadequate and must therefore be redrafted by the Bureau, the abovementioned surcharge of $300 per map sheet requiring revision will be imposed.

(3) *Timing:* (i) The contract must be signed, and a downpayment of $250 per area made, by April 1, 1978. A check or money order should be made payable to "Commerce—Census."

(ii) If an area decides to withdraw after signing a contract and making a downpayment, the cost of work performed to date will be deducted from the refund.

(iii) The balance of the fee must be mailed to the Bureau by January 1, 1980.

(d) In consideration of the fees paid and maps supplied, the Bureau will:

(1) Identify the individual blocks in its records and tabulations.

(2) Make available the block data for the particular area in the same manner as for areas in the regular block statistics program (*i.e.*, both in terms of printed reports and computer summary tapes). Two copies of the printed report (including the printed maps) which contain the block statistics for the particular area will be furnished to the contracting government authority.

(e) Requests for participation in the contract block statistics program or for further information should be addressed to the Director, Bureau of the Census, Washington, DC 20233.

[43 FR 3903, Jan. 30, 1978; 43 FR 59835, Dec. 22, 1978]

§ 50.50 Request for certification.

(a) Upon request, the Census Bureau certifies certain statistical materials (such as the population and housing unit counts of government entities, published tabulations, maps, and other documents). The Census Bureau charges customers a preset fee for this service according to the kind of certification requested (either an impressed document or an attestation) and the level of difficulty involved in compiling it (easy, moderate, or difficult, determined according to the resources expended) as well as the set cost of the data product (e.g., report or map) to be certified. Certification prices are shown in the following table:

PRICE BY TYPE OF CERTIFICATION

Product	Estimated price	Estimated time to complete (in hours)
Impress-easy	$70.00	1.5
Impress-medium	110.00	3
Impress-difficult	150.00	4.5
Attestation-easy	160.00	3
Attestation-medium	200.00	4.5
Attestation-difficult	240.00	6

(b) There are two forms of certification available: Impressed Documents and Attestation.

(1) *Impressed documents.* An impressed document is one that is certified by impressing the Census Bureau seal on the document itself. The Census Bureau act, Title 13, United States Code, Section 3, provides that the seal of the Census Bureau shall be affixed to all documents authenticated by the Census Bureau and that judicial notice shall be taken of the seal. This process attests that the document on which the seal is impressed is a true and accurate copy of a Census Bureau record.

(2) *Attestation.* Attestation is a more formal process of certification. It consists of a signed statement by a Census Bureau official that the document is authentic and produced or published by the agency, followed by a signed statement of another Census Bureau official witnessing the authority of the first.

(c) Requests for certification should be submitted on Form BC 1868(EF), Request for Official Certification, to the Census Bureau by fax, (301) 457–4714 or by e-mail, *webmaster@census.gov.* Form BC–1868(EF) is available on the Census Bureau's Web site at: *http://www.census.gov/mso/www/certification/.* A letter request—without Form BC–1868(EF)—will be accepted only if it contains the information necessary to complete a Form BC–1868(EF). No certification request will be processed without payment of the required fee.

[67 FR 54951, Aug. 27, 2002]

§ 50.60 Request for certification.

(a) *Certification process.* Upon request, the Census Bureau certifies population and housing counts of standard governmental units to reflect boundary updates, including new incorporations, annexations, mergers, and so forth. The Census Bureau will produce a certificate, that is, a signed statement by a Census Bureau official attesting to the authenticity of the certified Census 2000 population and housing counts to reflect updates to the legal boundaries of governmental units after those in effect for Census 2000. This service will be a permanent process, but one that will be temporarily suspended during future decennial censuses. Typically, the Census Bureau will suspend this service, and direct its resources to the decennial census, for a total of five years—the two years preceding the decennial census, the decennial census year, and the two years following it. The Census Bureau will issue notices in the FEDERAL REGISTER announcing when it suspends and, in turn, resumes, the service.

(1) The Census Bureau charges customers a preset fee for this service according to the amount of work involved in compiling the population and housing counts, as determined by the resources expended to meet customer requirements and the set cost of the product (one certificate). Certification fees may increase somewhat if the customer requests additional original certificates. Each additional certificate costs $35.00. Certification prices are shown in the following table:

DESCRIPTION AND ESTIMATED FEE

Standard governmental units	Estimated fee
Annual Certification	$693 to $1,799.
Expedited Certification	1,530 to 9,075.

(2) [Reserved]

(b) *Description of certification types.* The Census Bureau will process requests for population certificates for standard governmental units, in accordance with the Census Bureau's annual certification schedule or under an expedited certification arrangement. The boundaries for standard governmental units are regularly and customarily updated between decennial censuses by the Census Bureau's geographic support system. These governmental units include a variety of legally defined general- and special-purpose governmental units, including counties and statistically equivalent entities, minor civil divisions, incorporated places, consolidated cities, federally recognized American Indian reservations, and school districts. A complete list of entities is defined in paragraph (c) of this section.

(1) *Annual certification.* Annual population and housing certification is available around October 1 of each calendar year to new or existing governmental units that report legal boundary updates in the Census Bureau's annual Boundary and Annexation Survey. In accordance with reporting requirements of this survey, the legally effective dates of the boundary updates may not be later than January 1 of the calendar year. These certifications are available through September of the following year.

(i) The annual certification service also is available to standard governmental units that are not in the Boundary and Annexation Survey of that year. Governmental units electing participation in this service must draft the legal boundary updates upon Census Bureau-supplied maps. The legally effective dates of the boundaries may not be later than January 1 of the calendar year. The Census Bureau must receive the census maps annotated with the legally certified boundaries and associated address ranges by April 1 of the same calendar year. The Census Bureau will determine that the legal boundary updates are acceptable by verifying that the information is complete, legible, and usable, and that the legal boundaries on the maps have been attested by the governmental unit as submitted in accordance with state law or tribal authority.

(ii) [Reserved]

(2) *Expedited certification.* (i) Expedited certification will be available where the customer requests any of the following:

(A) Certification of boundary updates legally effective after January 1 of the current calendar year; or

(B) Certification of boundary updates reported to the Census Bureau after April 1 of the current calendar year; or

(C) Certification of boundary updates by the Census Bureau before October 1 of the current calendar year.

(ii) Governmental units electing participation in this service must draft the legal boundary updates upon Census Bureau-supplied maps. To allow sufficient processing time, the Census Bureau must receive acceptable census maps annotated with the legally certified boundaries and associated address ranges no later than three months before the date requested by the customer to receive the population certificate. The Census Bureau will determine that the legal boundary updates are acceptable by verifying that the information is complete, legible, and usable and that the legal boundaries on the maps have been attested as submitted in accordance with state law or tribal authority.

(c) *List of standard governmental units.* The following is a list of the standard governmental units eligible for the Geographically Updated Population Certification Program:

(1) Federally recognized American Indian reservations and off-reservation trust land entities [tribal government]; this includes a reservation designated as a colony, community, Indian community, Indian village, pueblo, rancheria, reservation, reserve, and village.

(2) Counties and statistically equivalent entities, including the following: counties in 48 states; boroughs, municipalities, and census areas in Alaska [state official]; parishes in Louisiana; and municipios in Puerto Rico.

(3) Minor civil divisions as recognized in Census 2000 in the following 28 states: Arkansas, Connecticut, Illinois, Indiana, Iowa, Kansas, Louisiana, Maine, Maryland, Massachusetts, Michigan, Minnesota, Mississippi, Missouri, Nebraska, New Hampshire, New Jersey, New York, North Carolina, North Dakota, Ohio, Pennsylvania, Rhode Island, South Dakota, Vermont, Virginia, West Virginia, and Wisconsin.

(4) Incorporated places, including the following: boroughs in Connecticut, New Jersey, and Pennsylvania; cities in 49 states and the District of Columbia; cities, boroughs, and municipalities in Alaska; towns in 30 states (excluding towns in New England, New York, and Wisconsin, which are minor civil divisions); and villages in 20 states.

(5) Consolidated cities.

(6) School districts.

(d) *Non-standard certifications.* Certifications for population and housing counts of non-standard geographic areas or of individual census blocks are not currently available under this program but will be announced under a separate notice at a later date.

(e) *Submitting certification requests.* Submit requests for certifications on Form BC–1869(EF), Request for Geographically Updated Official Population Certification, to the Census Bureau by fax, (301) 457–4714, or by e-mail, *MSO.certify@census.gov.* Form BC–1869(EF) will be available on the Census Bureau's Web site at: *http://www.census.gov/mso/www/certification/.* A letter or e-mail communication requesting the service without Form BC–1869(EF) will be accepted only if it contains the information necessary to complete a Form BC–1869(EF).

[67 FR 72096, Dec. 4, 2002]

PART 60—PUBLIC INFORMATION

AUTHORITY: 5 U.S.C. 301, 552, 553, Reorganization Plan No. 5 of 1950; 31 U.S.C. 3717.

§ 60.1 Public information.

The rules and procedures regarding public access to the records of the Bureau of the Census are found at 15 CFR part 4.

[57 FR 40841, Sept. 8, 1992]

PART 70—CUTOFF DATES FOR RECOGNITION OF BOUNDARY CHANGES FOR THE 2010 CENSUS

Sec.

AUTHORITY: 13 U.S.C. 4 and Department of Commerce Organization Order 35–2A (40 FR 42765).

SOURCE: 51 FR 24653, July 8, 1986, unless otherwise noted.

EDITORIAL NOTE: Nomenclature changes to part 70 appear at 63 FR 10303, Mar. 3, 1998, and at 73 FR 46553, Aug. 11, 2008.

§ 70.1 Cutoff dates and effect on enumeration and data tabulation.

For the tabulation and publication of data from the 2010 Census of Population and Housing, the Bureau of the Census will recognize only those boundaries legally in effect on January 1, 2010 that have been reported officially to the Bureau of the Census no later than March 1, 2010. The Bureau of the Census enumerates respondents on the date of the decennial census as residing within the legal limits of municipalities, county subdivisions, counties, States, and equivalent areas as those limits exist on January 1, 2010.

§ 70.2 "Municipality" and "county subdivision" defined for census purposes.

For the purposes of this part, the Bureau of the Census defines "municipalities" and "county subdivisions" to include the areas identified as incorporated places (such as cities and villages) and minor civil divisions (such as townships and magisterial districts). A more complete description appears on pages A–12 and A–13 of Appendix A, Census 2000 Geographic Terms and Concepts.

[51 FR 24653, July 8, 1986, as amended at 63 FR 10303, Mar. 3, 1998; 73 FR 46553, Aug. 11, 2008]

§ 70.3 Effect of boundary changes occurring or reported after the cutoff dates.

The Bureau of the Census will not recognize changes in boundaries that become effective after January 1, 2010 in taking the 2010 Decennial Census; the Bureau of the Census will enumerate the residents of any area that are transferred to another jurisdiction after that date and report them for the 2010 Census as residents of the area in which they resided on January 1, 2010. The Bureau of the Census will not recognize in the data tabulations prepared for the 2010 census changes occurring on or before January 1, 2010, but not submitted officially to the Bureau of the Census until after March 1, 2010 except as necessary to conduct decennial census operations.

PART 80—FURNISHING PERSONAL CENSUS DATA FROM CENSUS OF POPULATION SCHEDULES

AUTHORITY: Sec. 1, Pub. L. 83–1158, 68 Stat. 1013 (13 U.S.C. 8).

§ 80.1 General requirements.

(a) Data from records of decennial census of population questionnaires pertaining to an individual will be released only in accordance with these rules.

(b) Census information contains only the responses recorded by the Census enumerator; no changes of any of these entries have been or can be made.

(c) Requests for information from decennial census of population records (herein "Census Information") should be made available on Form BC–600, which is available from offices at the Census Bureau in Suitland, Maryland 20233, and Jeffersonville, Indiana 47131; all county courthouses; Social Security Administration field offices; post offices; and Immigration and Naturalization Service offices. A letter request—without Form BC–600—will be accepted only if it contains the information necessary to complete a Form BC–600. No application will be processed without payment of the required fee as set forth in 15 CFR 50.5.

(d) The Bureau may require verification of the identity of the applicant requesting Census information and it may require the applicant to submit the following notarized statement:

I, ________________ (Printed name), do hereby certify that I am the individual to whom the requested record pertains or that I am within the class of persons authorized to act on his behalf in accordance with 15 CFR, Part 80.

(Signature) ____________________

(Date)________________

In the County of ____________________

State of __________________________________

On this _____ day of _______, 19___, __________________ (Name of individual) who is personally known to me, did appear before me and sign the above certificate.

(Signature) ____________________

(Date)________________

(S) My commission expires ______________

(e) Except as otherwise provided, Census information will be provided only to the individual to whom the record pertains. It will include the names of the subject and the head of the household, the relationship of the subject to the head of the household, and the subject's age and birthplace.

(f) Similar Census information pertaining to other members of a household will be furnished only upon written authorization of the individual whose record is requested, except as provided in § 80.3.

(g) Census information will not be furnished to another person unless the person to whom the information relates authorizes such release in the space provided on the Form BC–600.

(Approved by the Office of Management and Budget under control number 0607–0117)

[40 FR 53232, Nov. 17, 1975, as amended at 48 FR 56744, Dec. 23, 1983; 68 FR 42586, July 18, 2003]

§ 80.2 Rules pertaining to records of the living.

(a) An individual who has attained age 18 may request his or her own Census information.

(b) A parent may request Census information for and in behalf of a child who has not reached age 18. The request must be signed by one of the parents.

(c) A legal guardian may obtain Census information relating to a ward by submitting a certified copy of the order of guardianship appointment.

(Approved by the Office of Management and Budget under control number 0607–0117)

[40 FR 53232, Nov. 17, 1975, as amended at 48 FR 56744, Dec. 23, 1983]

§ 80.3 Rules applicable to deceased persons and estates.

(a) Census information relating to a deceased person may be released only to a parent, child, grandchild, brother, sister, spouse, insurance beneficiary, or the executor or administrator of a deceased person's estate. The request must be signed by a person entitled to receive the information as provided herein, state the relationship of the applicant to the deceased, and include a certified copy of the death certificate or other adequate proof of death. The request of an executor or administrator must be accompanied by a certified copy of the court order of appointment.

(b) Except for a spouse, a person related to the deceased person through marriage, such as an in-law relationship, is not eligible to request Census information on the deceased, whether or not the applicant was a member of the household of the deceased.

(Approved by the Office of Management and Budget under control number 0607–0117)

[40 FR 53232, Nov. 17, 1975, as amended at 48 FR 56744, Dec. 23, 1983]

§ 80.4 Signature of persons unable to sign their name.

A person requesting Census information who is unable to sign his or her name shall make an "X" mark where signature is required, and the mark must be witnessed by two persons who know the applicant. They must also sign the application certifying the applicant's identity. In the case of such persons who are unable to make an "X" mark, Census information can be released upon receipt of a physician's sworn statement verifying the disability and the written request of a parent, brother, sister, child or a spouse.

(Approved by the Office of Management and Budget under control number 0607–0117)

[40 FR 53232, Nov. 17, 1975, as amended at 48 FR 56744, Dec. 23, 1983]

§ 80.5 Detrimental use of information.

Section 8 of Title 13, United States Code requires that,

In no case shall information furnished under the authority of this section be used to the detriment of the persons to whom such information relates.

[40 FR 53232, Nov. 17, 1975]

§ 80.6 False statements.

Any false statement or forgery on the application or supporting papers required to obtain Census information is punishable by a fine and/or imprisonment pursuant to section 1001 of Title 18 of the United States Code.

(Approved by the Office of Management and Budget under control number 0607–0117)

[40 FR 53232, Nov. 17, 1975, as amended at 48 FR 56744, Dec. 23, 1983]

PART 90—PROCEDURE FOR CHALLENGING POPULATION ESTIMATES

Sec.

AUTHORITY: 13 U.S.C. 4 and 181.

SOURCE: 78 FR 259, Jan. 3, 2013, unless otherwise noted.

§ 90.1 Scope and applicability.

Between decennial censuses, the Census Bureau annually prepares statistical estimates of the number of people residing in states and their governmental units. In general, these estimates are developed by updating the population counts produced in the most recent decennial census with demographic components of change data and/or other indicators of population change. These rules prescribe the administrative procedure available to governmental units to request a challenge to the most current of these estimates.

§ 90.2 Policy of the Census Bureau.

It is the policy of the Census Bureau to provide the most accurate population estimates possible given the constraints of time, money, and available statistical techniques. It is also the policy of the Census Bureau to provide governmental units the opportunity to seek a review and provide additional data to these estimates and to present evidence relating to the accuracy of the estimates.

§ 90.3 Definitions.

As used in this part (except where the context clearly indicates otherwise) the following definitions shall apply:

(a) *Census Bureau* means the U.S. Census Bureau, Department of Commerce.

(b) *Population Estimates Challenge* means, in accordance with this part, the process a governmental unit may use to provide additional input data for the Census Bureau's population estimate and the submission of substantive documentation in support thereof.

(c) *Director* means Director of the Census Bureau, or an individual designated by the Director to perform under this part.

(d) *Population estimate* means a statistically developed calculation of the number of people living in a governmental unit to update the preceding census or earlier estimate.

(e) A *governmental unit* means the government of a county, municipality, township, incorporated place, or other minor civil division, which is a unit of general-purpose government below the State.

(f) A *non-functioning county or statistical equivalent* means a sub-state entity that does not function as an active general-purpose governmental unit. This situation exists in Connecticut, Rhode Island, for selected counties in Massachusetts, and for the Census Areas in Alaska.

(g) For the purposes of this program, an *eligible governmental unit* also includes the District of Columbia and non-functioning counties or statistical equivalents represented by a FSCPE member agency.

§ 90.4 General.

This part provides a procedure for a governmental unit to request a challenge of a population estimate of the Census Bureau. The Census Bureau, upon receipt of the appropriate documentation, will attempt to resolve the estimate with the governmental unit.

§ 90.5 Who may file a challenge.

A request for a challenge of a population estimate generated by the Census Bureau may be filed only by the chief executive officer or highest elected official of a governmental unit. In those instances where the FSCPE member agency represents a non-functioning county or statistical equivalent, the governor will serve as the chief executive officer or highest elected official.

§ 90.6 When a challenge may be filed.

(a) A request for a challenge to a population estimate may be filed any time up to 90 days after the release of the estimate by the Census Bureau. Publication by the Census Bureau on its Web site (*www.census.gov*) shall constitute release. Documentation requesting a challenge of any estimate may also be filed any time up to 90 days after the date the Census Bureau, on its own initiative, revises that estimate.

(b) If, however, a governmental unit has a sufficiently meritorious reason for not filing in a timely manner, the Census Bureau has the discretion to accept the late request.

§ 90.7 Where to file a challenge.

A request for a population estimate challenge must be prepared in writing by the governmental unit and filed with the Chief, Population Division, Census Bureau, Room 5H174, Mail Stop 8800, Washington, DC 20233. The governmental unit must designate a contact person who can be reached by telephone during normal business hours should questions arise with regard to the submitted materials.

§ 90.8 Evidence required.

(a) The governmental unit shall provide whatever evidence it has relevant to the request at the time of filing. The Census Bureau may request further evidence when necessary. The evidence submitted must be consistent with the criteria, standards, and regular processes the Census Bureau employs to generate the population estimate. The Census Bureau has revised the challenge process to no longer accept estimates developed from methods different from those used by the Census Bureau. In the revised challenge process, the Census Bureau will only accept a challenge when the evidence provided identifies the use of incorrect data, processes, or calculations in the estimates.

(b) For counties and statistical equivalents, the Census Bureau uses a cohort-component of change method to produce population estimates. Each year, the components of change are updated. These components include births, deaths, migration, and change in the group quarters population. The Census Bureau will consider a challenge based on additional information on one or more of the components of change or about the group quarters population in a locality.

(c) For minor civil divisions and incorporated places, the Census Bureau uses a housing unit method to distribute the county population. The components in this method include housing units, occupancy rates, and persons per household plus an estimate of the population in group quarters. The Census Bureau will consider a challenge based on data related to changes in an area's housing stock, such as data on demolitions, condemned units, uninhabitable units, building permits, or mobile home placements or other comparable housing inventory based data. The Census Bureau will also consider a challenge based on additional information about the group quarters population in a locality.

(d) The Census Bureau will also provide a guide on its Web site as a reference for governmental units to use in developing their data as evidence to support a challenge to the population estimate. In addition, a governmental unit may address any additional questions by contacting the Census Bureau at the address provided in § 90.7.

§ 90.9 Review of challenge.

The Chief, Population Division, Census Bureau, or the Chief's designee shall review the evidence provided with the request for the population estimate challenge, shall work with the governmental unit to verify the data provided by the governmental unit, and evaluate the data to resolve the issues raised by the governmental unit. Thereafter, the

Census Bureau shall respond in writing with a decision to accept or deny the challenge. In the event that the Census Bureau finds that the population estimate should be updated, it will also post the revised estimate on the Census Bureau's Web site (*www.census.gov*).

PART 100—SEAL

AUTHORITY: R.S. 161, as amended, sec. 3, 68 Stat. 1012, as amended (5 U.S.C. 301, 13 U.S.C. 3).

SOURCE: 25 FR 2163, Mar. 16, 1960, unless otherwise noted. Redesignated at 50 FR 23947, June 7, 1985.

§ 100.1 Authority.

Pursuant to section 3 of Title 13, United States Code, the Bureau of the Census official seal and design thereof, which accompanies and is made a part of this document, is hereby approved.

§ 100.2 Description.

Seal: On a shield an open book beneath which is a lamp of knowledge emitting rays above in base two crossed quills. Around the whole a wreath of single leaves, surrounded by an outer band bearing between two stars the words "U.S. Department of Commerce" in the upper portion and "Bureau of the Census" in the lower portion, the lettering concentric with an inner beaded rim and an outer dentilated rim.

§ 100.3 Custody.

The seal shall remain in the custody of the Director, Bureau of the Census or such officer or employee of the Bureau as he designates and shall be affixed to all certificates and attestations that may be required from the Bureau.

PART 101—RELEASE OF DECENNIAL CENSUS POPULATION INFORMATION

AUTHORITY: 5 U.S.C. 301; 13 U.S.C. 4, 141, 195; 15 U.S.C. 1512.

§ 101.1 Report of tabulations of population to states and localities pursuant to 13 U.S.C. 141(c).

(a)(1) The Secretary of Commerce shall make the final determination regarding the methodology to be used in calculating the tabulations of population reported to States and localities pursuant to 13 U.S.C. 141(c). The determination of the Secretary will be published in the FEDERAL REGISTER.

(2) The Secretary shall not make the determination specified in paragraph (a)(1) of this section until after he or she receives the recommendation of the Director of the Census, together with the report of the Executive Steering Committee for A.C.E. Policy, in accordance with paragraph (b)(1) of this section.

(b)(1) The Executive Steering Committee for A.C.E. Policy shall prepare a written report to the Director of the Census analyzing the methodologies that may be used in making the tabulations of population reported to States and localities pursuant to 13 U.S.C. 141(c), and the factors relevant to the possible choices of methodology. The Director of the Census will forward the Executive Steering Committee for

A.C.E. Policy report and his or her recommendation on methodology, if any, to the Secretary of Commerce.

(2) The recommendation of the Director of the Census, together with report of the Executive Steering Committee for A.C.E. Policy described in paragraph (b)(1) of this section, shall be released to the public at the same time it is delivered to the Secretary. This release to the public shall include, but is not limited to, posting of the report on the Bureau of the Census website and publication of the report in the FEDERAL REGISTER.

(3) The Executive Steering Committee for A.C.E. Policy is composed of the following employees of the Bureau of the Census:

(i) Deputy Director and Chief Operating Officer;

(ii) Principal Associate Director and Chief Financial Officer;

(iii) Principal Associate Director for Programs;

(iv) Associate Director for Decennial Census (Chair);

(v) Assistant Director for Decennial Census;

(vi) Associate Director for Demographic Programs;

(vii) Associate Director for Methodology and Standards;

(viii) Chief; Planning, Research, and Evaluation Division;

(ix) Chief; Decennial Management Division;

(x) Chief; Decennial Statistical Studies Division;

(xi) Chief; Population Division; and

(xii) Senior Mathematical Statistician.

[66 FR 11232, Feb. 23, 2001]

PARTS 102–199 [RESERVED]

CHAPTER II—NATIONAL INSTITUTE OF STANDARDS AND TECHNOLOGY, DEPARTMENT OF COMMERCE

SUBCHAPTER A—MEASUREMENT SERVICES

PART 200—POLICIES, SERVICES, PROCEDURES, AND FEES

AUTHORITY: Sec. 9, 31 Stat. 1450, as amended; 15 U.S.C. 277. Interprets or applies sec. 7, 31 Stat. 1450, 15 U.S.C. 275a.

SOURCE: 45 FR 55166, Aug. 19, 1980, unless otherwise noted.

§ 200.100 Statutory functions.

(a) The National Institute of Standards & Technology (NIST) has been assigned the following functions (15 U.S.C. 271 *et seq.*):

(1) The custody, maintenance, and development of the national standards of measurement, and the provision of means and methods for making measurements consistent with those standards, including the comparison of standards used in scientific investigations, engineering, manufacturing, commerce, and educational institutions with the standards adopted or recognized by the Government.

(2) The determination of physical constants and properties of materials when such data are of great importance to scientific or manufacturing interests and are not to be obtained with sufficient accuracy elsewhere.

(3) The development of methods for testing materials, mechanisms, and structures, and the testing of materials, supplies, and equipment, including items purchased for use of Government departments and independent establishments.

(4) Cooperation with other governmental agencies and with private organizations in the establishment of standard practices, incorporated in codes and specifications.

(5) Advisory service to Government agencies on scientific and technical problems.

(6) Invention and development of devices to serve special needs of the Government.

(b) The calibration and testing activities of NIST stem from the functions in paragraphs (a) (1) and (3) of this section. NIST provides the central basis within the United States for a complete and consistent system of measurement; coordinates that system, and the measurement systems of other nations; and furnishes essential services leading to accurate and uniform physical measurements throughout this Nation's scientific community, industry, and commerce.

(c) The provision of standard reference materials for sale to the public is assigned to the Office of Standard Reference Materials of the National Measurement Laboratory, NIST. That Office evaluates the requirements of science and industry for carefully characterized reference materials, stimulates efforts of NIST to develop methods for production of needed reference materials and directs their production and distribution. For further information on standard reference materials see Subchapter B, Chapter II, Part 230, of this title.

§ 200.101 Measurement research.

(a) The NIST staff continually reviews the advances in science and the trends in technology, examines the measurement potentialities of newly discovered physical phenomena, and uses these to devise and improve standards, measuring devices, and measurement techniques. As new requirements appear, there are continual shifts of program emphasis to meet the most urgent needs for the measurement of additional quantities, extended ranges, or improved accuracies.

(b) The basic research and development activities of NIST are primarily funded by direct appropriations, and are aimed at meeting broad general needs. NIST may also undertake investigations or developments to meet some specialized physical measurement problem of another Government agency, industrial group, or manufacturing firm, using funds supplied by the requesting organization.

§ 200.102 Types of calibration and test services.

(a) NIST has developed instrumentation and techniques for realizing standards for the seven base units of the International System of Units, as agreed upon by the General Conference of Weights and Measures. Reference standards have been established not only for these seven base units, but also for many derived quantities and their multiples and submultiples. Such reference standards, or equivalent working standards, are used to calibrate laboratory and plant standards for other organizations. Accuracy is maintained by stability checks, by comparison with the standards of other national and international laboratories, and by the exploration of alternative techniques as a means of reducing possible systematic error.

(b) Calibrations for many types of instruments and ranges of physical quantities are described in the NIST Special Publication 250 (SP 250). (See § 200.115 for details relating to the description of service items and listing of fees.)

(c) In recent years NIST has offered to the public new measurement services called measurement assurance programs. These programs are designed for laboratories whose measurement process involves the calibration of other standards. A measurement assurance program is a measurement quality control process. By use of carefully designed redundant measurements and measurements made on NIST transport standards a total uncertainty of the laboratories measurement process can be determined by NIST. The results of these tests are then reported to the customer as uncertainties of the customer's measurements relative to national standards.

(d) Special measurements not listed in SP 250 may be made upon request. These might involve unusual physical quantities, upper or lower extremes of range, higher levels of accuracy, fast response speeds, short durations, broader ranges of associated parameters, or special environmental conditions. Such inquiries should describe clearly the measurement desired. Indication of the scientific or economic basis for the requirements to be satisfied will be helpful in determining future NIST programs. Fees for work accepted will be based upon actual costs incurred.

(e) The principal emphasis of NIST is on those calibrations and other tests requiring such accuracy as can be obtained only by direct comparison with its standards.

(f) Other services which may be obtained include:

(1) Tests of measuring instruments to determine compliance with specifications or claims, when the evaluation is critical in national scientific or technical operations, and when suitable facilities are not available elsewhere; and

(2) Referee tests in important cases when clients are unable to agree upon the method of measurement, the results of tests, or the interpretation of these results, but have agreed in advance in writing to accept and abide by the findings of NIST.

(g) NIST reserves the right to decline any request for services if the work would interfere with other activities deemed by the Director to be of greater importance. In general, measurement services are not provided when available from commercial laboratories.

(h) Suggestions will be offered on measurement techniques and on other sources of assistance on calibration or measurement problems when the equipment and personnel of NIST are unable to undertake the work. The National Conference of Standards Laboratories issues a Directory of Standards Laboratories in the United States which perform calibration work (obtainable from NCSL Secretariat, c/o National Institute of Standards & Technology, Boulder, CO 80303). Those laboratories which perform testing are listed in the ASTM Directory of Testing Laboratories, Commercial and Institutional. (Directory available from the

Amercian Society for Testing and Materials, 1916 Race Street, Philadelphia, PA 19103.) Similar listings appear in buyer's guides for commercial products and in technical journals concerned with physical measurement.

§200.103 Consulting and advisory services.

(a) In areas of its special competence, NIST offers consulting and advisory services on various problems related to measurement, e.g., details of design and construction, operational aspects, unusual or extreme conditions, methods of statistical control of the measurement process, automated acquisition of laboratory data, and data reduction and analysis by computer. Brief consultation may be obtained at no charge; the fee for extended effort will be based upon actual costs incurred. The services outlined in this paragraph do not include services in connection with legal proceedings not involving the United States as a named party, nor to testimony or the production of data, information, or records in such legal proceedings which is governed by the policies and procedures set forth in Subchapter H, Chapter II, Part 275, of this title.

(b) To enhance the competence of standards laboratory personnel, NIST conducts at irregular intervals several group seminars on the precision measurement of specific types of physical quantities, offering the opportunity of laboratory observation and informal discussion. A brochure describing the current series of seminars can be obtained by writing the Office of Measurement Services, National Institute of Standards & Technology, Washington, DC 20234.

§200.104 Standard reference materials.

Often the performance of a device or structure can be evaluated at the user's laboratory by comparing its response to unknown materials with its response to a stable, homogeneous reference specimen which has been well-characterized with regard to the physical or chemical property being measured. For information regarding carefully characterized materials see Subchapter B, Chapter II, Part 230, of this title. The Office of Standard Reference Materials in the NIST National Measurement Laboratory administers a program to provide many types of well-characterized materials that are needed to calibrate a measurement system or to produce scientific data that can be readily referred to a common base. NIST SP 260 is a catalog of Standard Reference Materials available from NIST.

§200.105 Standard reference data.

Data on the physical and chemical properties of the large variety of substances used in science and technology need to be compiled and evaluated for application in research, development, engineering design, and commerce. The Office of Standard Reference Data (OSRD) in the NIST National Measurement Laboratory provides coordination of and access to a number of governmental and nongovernmental data centers throughout this country and the world which are responsive to user needs for data. The OSRD's present program is assembled under a series of tasks which include data for application in energy, environment and health, industrial process design, materials durability, and resource recovery. The subject data are disseminated as hard-copy information in the Journal of Physical and Chemical Reference Data, published jointly with the American Chemical Society and the American Institute of Physics, in the National Standard Reference Data System reports as the NSRDS-NIST series, and as NIST special reports. Magnetic tapes of data on selected topics are also issued through the OSRD and the National Technical Information Service. A newsletter, "Reference Data Report," is issued bimonthly describing current activities. Information concerning the above is available upon request from the OSRD.

§200.106 Publications.

Publications provide the primary means of communicating the results of the NIST programs and services to its varied technical audiences, as well as to the general public. NIST issues some fifteen categories of publications including three periodicals, ten non-periodicals series, interagency reports, and papers in the journals and books of professional organizations, technological associations, and commercial publications. The calibration services, standard reference materials and related measurement services along with changes and fees are published in two Special Publications (SP's) and their supplements. These are SP 250 "Calibration and Related Measurement Services of the National Institute of Standards & Technology"[1] and SP 260 "NIST Standard Reference Materials Catalog."[1] A complete catalog of all publications by NIST authors is issued annually as a supplement to SP 305 "Publications of the National Institute of Standards & Technology." Announcements and listings of recent NIST publications and services are published in each issue of the bimonthly "NIST Journal of Research"[2] and the NIST monthly magazine, "Dimensions/NIST"[2]. Complete citations to NIST publications, along with information on availability are published bimonthly in the "NIST Publications Newsletter", available free from the Technical Information and Publications Division, National Institute of Standards & Technology, Washington, DC 20234. NIST publications are also announced (with abstracts) in "Government Reports Announcements and Index" published every two weeks by the National Technical Information Service (NTIS), Springfield, Virginia 22161[3]. NTIS also sells microfiche copies of all NIST GPO-published documents, as well as paper copy and microfiche versions of NIST Interagency Reports.

[1] Single copies available free from the National Institute of Standards & Technology, Washington, DC 20234.

[2] For sale by the Superintendent of Documents, U.S. Government Printing Office, Washington, DC 20402, for a subscription price. The annual subscription price for the NIST Journal of Research on the date of the publication of these regulations is $13.00 and for Dimensions/NIST it is $11.00. Prices, however, for these publications are subject to change without notice.

[3] The annual subscription rate at the date of the publication of these regulations for this service is $275.00, North American Continent, $375.00 all others.

§ 200.107 WWV-WWVH-WWVB broadcasts.

(a) *Technical services.* The NIST radio stations WWV at Fort Collins, Colorado, and WWVH on the island of Kauai, Hawaii, broadcast a number of technical services continuously night and day. These services are:

(1) Standard radio frequencies, 2.5, 5, 10, 15, and 20, MHz (WWV) and 2.5, 5, 10, and 15 MHz (WWVH); (2) standard time signals; (3) time intervals; (4) UTI corrections; (5) standard audio frequencies; (6) standard musical pitch; (7) a slow time code; (8) Omega Navigation System status reports; (9) geophysical alerts; and (10) marine storm warnings. NIST also broadcasts time and frequency signals from its low frequency station, WWVB, also located at Fort Collins, Colorado.

(2) [Reserved]

(b) *Time announcements.* Once per minute voice announcements are made from WWV and WWVH. The two stations are distinguished by a female voice from WWVH and a male voice from WWV. The WWVH announcement occurs first, at 15 seconds before the minute, while the WWV announcement occurs at 7½ seconds before the minute. Coordinated Universal Time (UTC) is used in these announcements.

(c) *Time corrections.* The UTC time scale operates on atomic frequency, but by means of step adjustments is made to approximate the astronomical UTI scale. It may disagree from UTI by as much as 0.9 second before step adjustments of exactly 1 second are made. These adjustments, or leap seconds are required about once per year and will usually be made on December 31 or June 30. For those who need astronomical time more accurately than 0.9 second, a correction to UTC is encoded by the use of double ticks after the start of each minute. The first through the eighth seconds ticks will indicate a "plus" correction, and from the ninth through the 16th a "minus" correction. The correction is determined by counting the number of double ticks. For example, if the first, second, and third ticks are doubled, the correction is "plus" 0.3 second. If the ninth, 10th, 11th, and 12th ticks are doubled, the correction is "minus" 0.4 second.

(d) *Standard time intervals.* An audio pulse (5 cycles of 1000 Hz on WWV and 6 cycles of 1200 Hz on WWVH), resembling the ticking of a clock, occurs each second of the minute except on the 29th and 59th seconds. Each of these 5-millisecond second pulses occur within a 40-millisecond period, wherein all other modulation (voice or tone) is removed from the carrier. These pulses begin 10 milliseconds after the modulation interruption. A long pulse (0.8 second) marks the beginning of each minute.

(e) *Standard frequencies.* All carrier and audio frequencies occur at their nominal values according to the International System of Units (SI). For periods of 45-second duration, either 500-Hz or 600-Hz audio tones are broadcast in alternate minutes during most of each hour. A 440-Hz tone, the musical pitch A above middle C, is broadcast once per hour near the beginning of the hour.

(f) *Accuracy and stability.* The time and frequency broadcasts are controlled by the NIST atomic frequency standards, which realize the internationally defined cesium resonance frequency with an accuracy of 1 part in 10^{13}. The frequencies transmitted by WWV and WWVH are held stable to better than ±2 parts in 10^{11} at all times. Deviations at WWV are normally less than 1 part in 10^{12} from day to day. Incremental frequency adjustments not exceeding 1 part in 10^{12} are made at WWV and WWVH as necessary. Changes in the propagation medium (causing Doppler effect, diurnal shifts, etc.) result in fluctuations in the carrier frequencies as received which may be very much greater than the uncertainties described above.

(g) *Slow time code.* A modified IRIG H time code occurs continuously on a 100-Hz subcarrier. The format is 1 pulse per second with a 1-minute time frame. It gives day of the year, hours, and minutes in binary coded decimal form.

(h) *Omega announcements.* Omega Navigation System status reports are broadcast in voice from WWV at 16 minutes after the hour and from WWVH at 47 minutes after the hour. The international Omega Navigation System is a very low frequency (VLF) radio navigation aid operating in the 10 to 14 kHz frequency band. Eight stations are in operation around the world. Omega, like other radio navigation systems, is subject to signal degradation caused by ionospheric disturbances at high latitudes. The Omega announcements on WWV and WWVH are given to provide users with immediate notification of such events and other information on the status of the Omega system.

(i) *Geophysical alerts.* These occur in voice at the 18th minute of each hour from WWV. They point out outstanding events which are in process, followed by a summary of selected solar and geophysical events in the past 24 hours and a forecast for the next 24 hours. They are provided by the Space Environment Laboratory, National Oceanic and Atmospheric Administration, Boulder, CO 80303.

(j) *Marine storm information.* Weather information about major storms in the Atlantic and eastern North Pacific are broadcast in voice from WWV at 8, 9, and 10 minutes after each hour. Similar storm warnings covering the eastern and central North Pacific are given from WWVH at 48, 49, and 50 minutes after each hour. An additional segment (at 11 minutes after the hour on WWV and at 51 minutes on WWVH) may be used when there are unusually widespread storm conditions. The brief messages are designed to tell mariners of storm threats in their areas. If there are no warnings in the designated areas, the broadcasts will so indicate. The ocean areas involved are those for which the U.S. has warning responsibility under international agreement. The regular times of issue by the National Weather Service are 0500, 1100, 1700, and 2300 UTC for WWV and 0000, 0600, 1200, and 1800 UTC for WWVH. These broadcasts are updated effective with the next scheduled announcement following the time of issue.

(k) *"Silent" periods.* These are periods with no tone modulation during which the carrier, seconds ticks, minute time announcements, and 100 Hz modified IRIG H time code continue. They occur during the 16th through the 20th minute on WWVH and the 46th through the 51st minute on WWV.

(l) *WWVB.* This station (antenna coordinates 40°40′28.3″ N., 105°02′39.5″ W.; radiated power 12 kw.) broadcasts on 60 kHz. Its time scale is the same as for WWV and WWVH, and its frequency accuracy and stability are the same. Its entire format consists of a 1 pulse per second special binary time code giving minutes, hours, days, and the correction between its UTC time scale and UTI astronomical time. Identification of WWVB is made by its unique time code and a 45° carrier phase shift which occurs for the period between 10 minutes and 15 minutes after each hour. The useful coverage area of WWVB is within the continental United States. Propagation fluctuations are much less with WWVB than with high-frequency reception, permitting frequency comparisons to be made to a few parts in 10^{11} per day.

(m) *Special Publication 432.* This publication describes in detail the standard frequency and time service of NIST. Single copies may be obtained at no charge upon request from the National Institute of Standards & Technology, Time & Frequency Services Group, 524.06, Boulder, CO 80303. Quantities may be obtained from the Superintendent of Documents, U.S. Government Printing Office, Washington, DC 20402, at a nominal charge per copy.

§ 200.108 Request procedure.

(a) A formal purchase order for the calibration or test should be sent before or at the time the instrument or standard is shipped. The purchase order should provide clear identification of the apparatus being submitted, and give separate instructions for return shipment, mailing of report, and billing. If a customer wishes to minimize the time during which the equipment is out of service, the customer can usually arrange to be notified of the scheduled test date to allow timely shipment. (See § 200.110.) Requests from Federal agencies, or from State agencies, for calibrations or tests on material to be used on private or Federal contract work should be accompanied either by purchase order or by letter or document authorizing the cost of the work to be billed to the agency.

(b) The submission of a purchase order for measurement services under this subchapter shall be understood as constituting an agreement on the part of the customer to be bound by the restrictions on the use of results as set forth in § 200.113 of this part. Acceptance of purchase orders does not imply acceptance of any provisions set forth in the order contrary to the policy, practice, or regulations of NIST or the U.S. Government. (A statement to the effect that NIST is an agency of the U.S. Government should satisfy other Government agencies with regard to compliance with Government regulations and Executive orders.)

(c) A test number will be assigned by NIST to each instrument or group of similar instruments or standards when the order is accepted. This test number should be referred to in all subsequent communications. Also, each instrument in a group must be uniquely identified, usually by the manufacturer's name and instrument serial number. When the serial number is lacking, an alternative identifying mark should be provided. If none is found, NIST will mark the piece with an NIST identification number. If the apparatus submitted has been previously calibrated by NIST, the serial number or identifying mark should be given on the new order, so that a continuing record of stability history can be established.

(d) Inquiries for measurement services should be directed to the NIST address listed in the various sections of the Appendix to SP 250.

§ 200.109 Shipping, insurance, and risk of loss.

(a) Shipment of apparatus to NIST for calibration or other test should be made only after the customer has accepted the estimate of cost and the tentative scheduling. Repairs and adjustments on apparatus submitted should be attended to by the owner, since NIST will not undertake them except by special arrangement. Apparatus not in good condition will not be calibrated. If defects are found after calibration has begun, the effort may be terminated, a report issued summarizing such information as has been found, and a fee charged in accordance with the amount of work done.

(b) The customer should pack apparatus sent to NIST so as to minimize the likelihood of damage in shipment and handling. Suggestions on packing and shipping are made in some sections of SP 250. In every case, the sender should consider the nature of the apparatus, pack it accordingly, and clearly label shipments containing fragile instruments or materials, such as glass and the like.

(c) To minimize damage during shipment resulting from inadequate packing, the use of strong reusable containers is recommended. As an aid in preventing loss of such containers, the customer's name should be legibly and permanently marked on the outside. In order to prolong the container's use the notation "REUSABLE CONTAINER, DO NOT DESTROY" should be marked on the outside.

(d) Shipping and insurance coverage instructions should be clearly and legibly shown on the purchase order for the calibration or test. The customer must pay shipping charges to and from NIST; shipments from NIST will be made collect. The method of return transportation should be stated, and it is recommeded that return shipments be insured, since NIST will not assume liability for their loss or damage. For long-distance shipping it is found that air express and air freight provide an advantage in reduction of time in transit. If return shipment by parcel post is requested or is a suitable mode of transportation, shipments will be prepaid by NIST, but without covering insurance. When no shipping or insurance instructions are furnished, return shipment will be made by common carrier collect, but uninsured.

(e) NIST will not be responsible for the risk of loss or damage to any item during shipment to or from NIST. Any arrangements for insurance covering this risk must be made by the customer. Return shipment will be made by NIST as indicated in paragraph (d) of this section. The purchase order should always show the value of the equipment, and if transit insurance is carried by the customer, this fact should be stated.

(f) The risk of loss or damage in handling or testing of any item by NIST must be assumed by the customer, except when it is determined by NIST that such loss or damage was occasioned solely by the negligence of NIST personnel.

(g) When a test number has been assigned prior to shipment to NIST, this number should be clearly marked on the shipping container. When a test number has not been assigned, an invoice, copy of the purchase order, or letter should be enclosed in the shipment to insure proper identification. The original purchase order should be forwarded as appropriate to:

Office of Measurement Services, National Institute of Standards & Technology, Washington, DC 20234; or to Measurement Services Clerk, National Institute of Standards & Technology, Boulder, CO 80303.

(h) The calibrations listed in SP 250 are performed at Boulder, Colorado and Gaithersburg, Maryland.

§200.110 Priorities and time of completion.

Schedule work assignments for calibrations and other tests will generally be made in the order in which confirmed requests are received. However, Government work may be given priority. On the regular services, the workload is usually such that the turnaround interval, between the date a customer's apparatus is received and the date it is prepared for return shipment, will be not more than 45 days. Some types of instruments may require considerably longer, particularly if their abnormal behavior requires reruns to check reliability. The customer who can spare the instrument for only a short time can usually arrange by letter or telephone call for shipping it to NIST just as the assigned starting date approaches. A notice will be sent acknowledging receipt of the customer's standard and/or purchase order. If both a confirmed purchase order (or equivalent) and the apparatus have been received, estimates of the completion date and the calibration fee will be sent upon request.

§200.111 Witnessing of operations.

NIST welcomes scientists and engineers who may wish to visit its laboratories and discuss its methods. Ordinarily visitors will not be permitted to witness the actual carrying out of highly precise measurements because their presence introduces distraction that may lead to errors or delays. This policy may be waived in those cases where NIST determines that the visitor can be of service in setting up apparatus of a new or unusual nature, in the case of referee tests, or in other cases in which the legal validity of the result may require the presence of duly authorized witnesses.

§ 200.112 Reports.

(a) Results of calibrations and other tests are issued to the customer as formal reports entitled, "National Institute of Standards & Technology Report of Calibration," "National Institute of Standards & Technology Report of Test," or "National Institute of Standards & Technology Report of Analysis," as appropriate. Copies are not supplied to other parties except under applicable Federal law. Whenever formal certification is required by law, or to meet special conditions adjudged by NIST to warrant it, a letter will be provided certifying that the particular item was received and calibrated or tested, and identifying the report containing the results.

(b) NIST reports of calibration generally include in sentence form a statement of the uncertainty attached to the numerical values reported. Limits of uncertainty usually comprise an estimate of systematic error plus a value of imprecision. Details on how these estimates are arrived at are in many cases included in the calibration report. Additional information may be found in SP 250.

(c) The NIST practice is to express data given in calibration or test reports in the SI or International System of Units. The International System of Units (SI) was defined and given official status by the 11th General Conference of Weights and Measures, 1960. A complete listing of SI units is presented in detail in NIST SP 330. The NIST will express data in SI units unless this makes communication excessively complicated. For example, commercial gage designations, commonly used items identified by nominal dimensions, or other commercial nomenclatures or devices (such as drill sizes, or commercial standards for weights and measures) expressed in customary units are an exception from this practice. However, even in such instances, when practical and meaningful, SI and customary units may be given in parallel. Users of NIST calibration services may specify the units to be used in the calibration, especially for commercial devices and standards using customary units or units having some legal definition.

§ 200.113 Use of results or reports.

(a) As the national standards laboratory of the United States, NIST maintains and establishes the primary standards from which measurements in science and industry ultimately derive. It is therefore sometimes desirable for manufacturers or users of measurement standards to make appropriate reference to the relationship of their calibrations to NIST calibrations. The following considerations must be borne in mind, and shall be understood as constituting an agreement on the part of the NIST customer to be bound thereby in making reference to NIST calibration and test reports.

(b) The results of calibrations and tests performed by NIST are intended solely for the use of the organization requesting them, and apply only to a particular device or specimen at the time of its test. The results shall not be used to indicate or imply that they are applicable to other similar items. In addition, such results must not be used to indicate or imply that NIST approves, recommends, or endorses the manufacturer, the supplier, or the user of such devices or specimens, or that NIST in any way "guarantees" the later performance of items after calibration or test.

(c) NIST declares it to be in the national interest that it maintain an impartial position with respect to any commercial product. Advertising the findings on a single instrument could be misinterpreted as an indication of performance of other instruments of identical or similar type. There will be no objection, however, to a statement that the manufacturer's primary standards have been periodically calibrated by NIST, if this is actually the case, or that the customer might arrange to have NIST calibrate the item purchased from the manufacturer.

(d) NIST does not approve, recommend, or endorse any proprietary product or proprietary material. No reference shall be made to NIST, or to reports or results furnished by NIST in any advertising or sales promotion which would indicate or imply that NIST approves, recommends, or endorses any proprietary product or proprietary material, or which has as its purpose an intent to cause directly or indirectly the advertised product to be used or purchased because of NIST test reports or results.

In its own activities as a scientific institution, NIST uses many different materials, products, types of equipment, and services. This use does not imply that NIST has given them a preferential position or a formal endorsement. Therefore, NIST discourages references, either in advertising or in the scientific literature, which identify it as a user of any proprietary product, material, or service. Occasionally, effective communication of results by NIST to the scientific community requires that a proprietary instrument, product, or material be identified in an NIST publication. Reference in an NIST publication, report, or other document to a proprietary item does not constitute endorsement or approval of that item and such reference should not be used in any way apart from the context of the NIST publication, report, or document without the advance express written consent of NIST.

§200.114 Fees and bills.

(a) In accordance with 15 U.S.C. 271 *et seq.*, fees are charged for all measurement services performed by NIST, unless waived by the Director, or the Director's designee, when deemed to be in the interest of the Government. The above-mentioned statutes authorize the issuance from time to time of appropriate regulations regarding the payment of fees, the limits of tolerance on standards submitted for verification, and related matters.

(b) The minimum fee for any service request accepted by NIST is $10, unless otherwise indicated in SP 250. If apparatus is returned without testing, a minimum charge of $10 may be made to cover handling. Charges commensurate with the work performed will be assessed for calibrations which cannot be completed because of faulty operation of the customer's device. Fees for calibrations or tests include the cost of preparation of an NIST report. Remittances should be made payable to the National Institute of Standards & Technology.

§200.115 Description of services and list of fees, incorporation by reference.

(a) NIST Special Publication 250, "Calibration and Related Measurement Services of the National Institute of Standards & Technology" is hereby incorporated by reference, pursuant to 5 U.S.C. 552(a)(1) and 1 CFR Part 51. SP 250 states the authority under which NIST performs various types of measurement services including calibrations and tests and charges fees therefor, states the general conditions under which the public may secure such services, decribes these services in considerable detail, and lists the fees to be charged, and sets out the instructions for requesting them in an appendix which is reviewed, revised and reissued semi-annually (December and June). The Director, Office of the Federal Register, approved the incorporation by reference on December 28, 1967.

(b) SP 250 is available at the following places:

(1) Superintendent of Documents, Government Printing Office, Washington, DC 20402.

(2) Technical Information and Publications Division, National Institute of Standards & Technology, Washington, DC 20234.

(3) District Offices of the U.S. Department of Commerce.

(4) Federal Depository Libraries.

(c) Revisions of SP 250 will be issued from time to time by the National Institute of Standards & Technology, Washington, DC 20234.

(d) Further information concerning policies, procedures, services, and fees may be obtained by writing the Office of Measurement Services, National Institute of Standards & Technology, Washington, DC 20234.

SUBCHAPTER B—STANDARD REFERENCE MATERIALS

PART 230—STANDARD REFERENCE MATERIALS

Subpart A—General Information

Subpart B—Purchase Procedure

Subpart C—Description of Services and List of Fees

AUTHORITY: Sec. 9, 31 Stat. 1450, as amended; 15 U.S.C. 277. Interprets and applies sec. 7, 70 Stat. 959; 15 U.S.C. 275a.

SOURCE: 41 FR 8472, Feb. 27, 1976, unless otherwise noted.

Subpart A—General Information

§ 230.1 Introduction.

This part states the procedure for ordering Standard Reference Materials (SRM's) issued by the National Institute of Standards & Technology. SRM's are used to calibrate measurement systems, evaluate measurement methods, or produce scientific data that can be referred to a common base. NIST Special Publication 260, "Catalog of NIST Standard Reference Materials," lists and describes the SRM's issued by NIST. SP 260 is periodically revised to include new SRM's and eliminate those that have been discontinued. Between editions of SP 260, supplements are issued that list new or renewal SRM's not listed in SP 260. In addition, these supplements list the fees charged for available SRM's.

[41 FR 8472, Feb. 27, 1976, as amended at 55 FR 38315, Sept. 18, 1990]

§ 230.2 Identification of Standard Reference Materials.

The SRM's are listed by category in SP 260 and by sequential number in the supplements. The number uniquely identifies a particular SRM. Renewals are indicated by the addition of a letter to the original number. Thus, 11a is the first, 11b the second, and 11c the third renewal of SRM 11, Basic Open-Hearth Steel, 0.2 percent carbon. In this way, a particular number or number and letter always represent a material of fixed or approximately fixed composition.

§ 230.3 New Standard Reference Materials.

When new SRM's or renewals of old ones are issued, announcements are made in SP 260, its supplement, and in scientific and trade journals.

Subpart B—Purchase Procedure

§ 230.4 Ordering.

Orders should be addressed to the Office of Standard Reference Materials, National Institute of Standards & Technology, Washington, DC 20234. Orders should give the amount (number of units), catalog number and name of the standard requested. *For example:* 1 each, SRM 11h, Basic Open-Hearth Steel, 0.2 percent C. These materials are distributed only in the units listed.

[41 FR 8472, Feb. 27, 1976, as amended at 55 FR 38315, Sept. 18, 1990]

§ 230.5 Terms and shipping.

(a) Prices are given in the SP 260 supplement. These prices are subject to revision and orders will be billed for prices in effect at the time of shipment. No discounts are given on purchases of SRM's.

(b) Payment need not accompany a purchase order. Payment is due within 30 days of receipt of an invoice.

(c) SRM's are shipped in the most expeditious manner that complies with transportation and postal laws and regulations.

§230.6 Standard Reference Materials out of stock.

Orders for out-of-stock SRM's will be returned with information as to future availability.

Subpart C—Description of Services and List of Fees

§230.7 Description of services and list of fees, incorporation by reference.

(a) The text of NIST Special Publication 260, "Catalog of NIST Standard Reference Materials," and its supplement are hereby incorporated by reference pursuant to 5 U.S.C. 552(a)(1) and 1 CFR Part 51.

(b) SP 260 describes the SRM's that are available and states the procedure for ordering the materials. SP 260 is available at the following places:

Superintendent of Documents, Government Printing Office, Washington, DC 20402.

Office of Standard Reference Materials, National Institute of Standards & Technology, Washington, DC 20234.

(c) Supplements are issued when needed to reflect additions, deletions, and corrections to SP 260, and to list fees charged for the SRM's. Supplements are available from the Office of Standard Reference Materials, National Institute of Standards & Technology, Washington, DC 20234.

[41 FR 8472, Feb. 27, 1976, as amended at 55 FR 38315, Sept. 11, 1990]

SUBCHAPTER C—TRANSCRIPT SERVICES [RESERVED]

SUBCHAPTER D—STANDARDS FOR BARRELS

PART 240—BARRELS AND OTHER CONTAINERS FOR LIME

AUTHORITY: Sec. 4, 39 Stat. 531; 15 U.S.C. 240.

SOURCE: 13 FR 8372, Dec. 28, 1948, unless otherwise noted.

§ 240.1 Title of act.

The act, "Pub. L. 228, 64th Congress," approved August 23, 1916 (39 Stat. 530; 15 U.S.C. 237–242), entitled "An Act to standardize lime barrels," shall be known and referred to as the "Standard Lime-Barrel Act."

§ 240.2 Application.

The rules and regulations in this part are to be understood and construed to apply to lime in barrels, or other containers packed, sold, or offered for sale for shipment from any State or Territory or the District of Columbia to any other State or Territory or the District of Columbia; and to lime in containers of less capacity than the standard small barrel sold in interstate or foreign commerce; and to lime imported in barrels from a foreign country and sold or offered for sale; also to lime not in barrels or containers of less capacity than the standard small barrel, sold, charged for, or purported to be delivered as a large or small barrel or a fractional part of said small barrel of lime, from any State or Territory or the District of Columbia to any other State or Territory or the District of Columbia.

§ 240.3 Permissible sizes.

Lime in barrels shall be packed only in barrels containing 280 pounds or 180 pounds, net weight. For the purposes of this section the word "barrel" is defined as a cylindrical or approximately cylindrical vessel, cask or drum.

(Sec. 2, 39 Stat. 530; 15 U.S.C. 238)

§ 240.4 Definitions.

(a) The term *container of less capacity than the standard small barrel*, as mentioned in section 3 of the law and as used in the rules and regulations in this part, is defined as any container not in barrel form containing therein a net weight of lime of less than 180 pounds.

(b) The term *label* as used in the rules and regulations in this part is defined as any printed, pictorial, or other matter upon the surface of a barrel or other container of lime subject to the provisions of this act, or upon cloth or paper or the like which is permanently affixed to it by pasting or in a similar manner.

(c) The term *tag* is defined as a tough and strong strip of cloth or paper or the like, bearing any printed, pictorial, or other matter, which is loose at one end and which is secured to a container of lime subject to the provisions of the act.

(Sec. 3, 39 Stat. 530; 15 U.S.C. 239)

§ 240.5 Required marking.

(a) The lettering required upon barrels of lime by section 2 of the law shall be as follows: The statement of net weight shall be in boldface capital letters and figures at least 1 inch in height and not expanded or condensed; it shall be clear, legible, and permanent, and so placed with reference to the other lettering that it is conspicuous. The name of the manufacturer of the lime and where manufactured, and, if imported, the name of the country from which it is imported, shall be in boldface letters at least one-half inch in height and not expanded or condensed, and shall be clear, legible, conspicuous, and permanent. None of these letters and figures shall be superimposed upon each other, nor shall any other characters be superimposed upon the required lettering or otherwise obscure it. All the above statements shall form parts of the principal label.

(b) The information required upon containers of lime of less capacity than the standard small barrel by section 3 of the law shall be included in a label:

Provided, however, That in order to allow the utilization of second-hand or returnable bags made of cloth, burlap, or the like, such information may be upon a tag firmly attached to the container in a prominent and conspicuous position. In case a tag is used to give the required information there must not be any label or another tag upon the container which bears any statement having reference to lime, or any statement of weight whatever, which is not identical with the information upon the tag mentioned above; if a container is to be utilized which bears any such inaccurate information upon a label, such container shall be turned inside out or such information shall be obliterated in so far as it is inaccurate by blotting out the letters or figures; or if such inaccurate information is upon a tag, by removing such tag.

(c) If the required lettering is upon a label, the statement of net weight shall be in bold-face capital letters and figures at least three-fourths inch in height and not expanded or condensed; it shall be clear, legible, and permanent, and so placed with reference to the other lettering that it is conspicuous. The word "net" shall form part of the statement of weight. The name of the manufacturer of the lime and the name of the brand, if any, under which it is sold, and, if imported, the name of the country from which it is imported, shall be in bold face letters at least one-half inch in height and not expanded or condensed, and shall be clear, legible, conspicuous, and permanent. None of these letters and figures shall be superimposed upon each other, nor shall any other characters be superimposed upon the required lettering or otherwise obscure it. All the above statements shall form parts of the principal label.

(d) If the required lettering is upon a tag, the statement of net weight shall be in bold-face capital letters and figures not less than one-half the height of the largest letters or figures used upon such tag: *Provided, however,* That in every case they shall be not less than one-eighth inch in height (12–point capitals), and not expanded or condensed. The word "net" shall form part of the statement of weight. The statement shall be clear, legible, and permanent, and so placed with reference to the other lettering that it is conspicuous. The name of the manufacturer of the lime, and the name of the brand, if any, under which it sold, and, if imported, the name of the country from which it is imported, shall be in bold-face letters and figures not less than one-eighth inch in height (12–point capitals), and not expanded or condensed, and shall be clear, legible, conspicuous, and permanent. None of these letters and figures shall be superimposed upon each other nor shall any other characters be superimposed upon the required lettering or otherwise obscure it. All the above statements shall be included upon the same side of the tag.

(e) In case the lime is actually packed in barrels or in containers of less capacity than the standard small barrel by some person other than the manufacturer of the lime, the information mentioned above must be given in the manner there described, and in addition there must be a statement to this effect: "Packed by ________________" (giving the name and address of the packer). This statement shall be in letters not smaller than is specified for the general statement required in the case of barrels and containers of less capacity than the standard small barrel, respectively (see paragraphs (a) and (b) of this section); it shall not be obscured and shall form part of the principal label or be upon the same side of the tag as in those cases provided.

(f) In the case of all lime sold in barrels, the actual place of manufacture of the lime shall be stated on the barrel. In general, this will be the name of the post office nearest or most accessible to the plant. However, when the actual place of manufacture of the lime and the offices of the company are separated but are within the boundaries of the same county of a State, or when, though not within the boundaries of the same county they are so close together that the post-office address of the offices represents substantially and to all intents and purposes the actual place of manufacture of the lime, then the post-office address of the offices of the company will be sufficient: *Provided, however,* That the address given shall always correctly show the State in which the lime is actually manufactured.

(g) More than one place of manufacture of a manufacturer shall not be shown on the same barrel unless the one at which the particular lime in question is manufactured is pointed out.

(h) If the location of the home offices is stated and this is not the place of manufacture within the meaning of the above definition, an additional statement must be included to this effect: "Manufactured at ______" (giving the location of the plant).

(Secs. 2, 3, 39 Stat. 530; 15 U.S.C. 238, 239)

§ 240.6 Tolerances.

(a) When lime is packed in barrels the tolerance to be allowed on the large barrel or the small barrel of lime shall be 5 pounds in excess or in deficiency on any individual barrel: *Provided, however,* That the average error on 10 barrels of the same nominal weight and packed by the same manufacturer shall in no case be greater than 2 pounds in excess or in deficiency. In case all the barrels available are not weighed, those which are weighed shall be selected at random.

(b) When lime is packed in containers of less capacity than the standard small barrel, the tolerance to be allowed in excess or in deficiency on individual containers of various weights, shall be the values given in the column headed "Tolerance on individual package," of the following table: *Provided, however,* That the average error on 10 containers of the same nominal weight and packed by the same manufacturer shall in no case be greater than the values given in the column headed "Tolerance on average weight," of the following table. In case all the containers available are not weighed, those which are weighed shall be selected at random.

Weight of packaged	Tolerance on individual package (pounds)	Tolerance on average weight (pounds)
Not greater than 50 lbs	1½	⅝
More than 50 lb. and not greater than 100 lbs	2	¾
More than 100 lb. and not greater than 150 lb	3	1¼
More than 150 lb. and less than 180 lb	4	1½

(c) When lime in bulk is sold, charged for, or purported to be delivered as a definite number of large or small barrels, the tolerance to be allowed in excess or in deficiency on such amounts of lime shall be 15 pounds per 1,800 pounds (10 small barrels), or 25 pounds per 2,800 pounds (10 large barrels).

PART 241—BARRELS FOR FRUITS, VEGETABLES AND OTHER DRY COMMODITIES, AND FOR CRANBERRIES

Sec.

AUTHORITY: Sec. 3, 38 Stat. 1187; 15 U.S.C. 236.

SOURCE: 13 FR 8373, Dec. 28, 1948, unless otherwise noted.

NOTE: The rules and regulations in this part refer entirely to individual barrels, and no separate tolerance has been placed on the average content of a number of barrels taken at random from a shipment. It is not believed that barrels can be so made as to take advantage of the tolerances, and, of course, no attempt should be made to do this. It is, therefore, expected that as many barrels will be above as below the standard capacity.

§ 241.1 Capacities.

(a) The capacities of the standard barrel for fruits, vegetables, and other dry commodities, other than cranberries, and its subdivisions, are as follows:

Size	Cubic inches	Bushels [1]	Quarts [1]
Barrel	7,056	3.281	105
¾ barrel	5,292	2.46	78¾
½ barrel	3,528	1.641	52½
⅓ barrel	2,352	1.094	35

[1] Struck measure.

(b) The capacities of the standard cranberry barrel and its subdivisions are as follows:

Size	Cubic inches	Bushels [1]	Quarts [1]
Cranberry barrel	5,826	2.709	86 45/64
¾ cranberry barrel	4,369.5	2.032	65 1/64
½ cranberry barrel	2,913	1.355	43 11/32
⅓ cranberry barrel	1,942	.903	28 29/32

[1] Struck measure.

(Sec. 1, 38 Stat. 1186; 15 U.S.C. 234)

§241.2 Legal standard barrels.

(a) Any barrel having the dimensions specified for a standard barrel for fruits, vegetables, and other dry commodities, other than cranberries, in section 1 of the standard-barrel law, or any barrel or a subdivision thereof having the contents specified in section 1 of the standard-barrel law and in §241.1(a) regardless of its form or dimensions, is a legal standard barrel for fruits, vegetables, or other dry commodities other than cranberries, or a legal subdivision thereof. No other barrel or subdivision in barrel form is a legal container for fruits, vegetables, or other dry commodities other than cranberries.

(b) Any barrel having the dimensions specified for a standard barrel for cranberries in section 1 of the standard-barrel law, or any subdivision thereof having the contents specified in §241.1(b), regardless of its form or dimensions, is a legal standard barrel for cranberries or a legal subdivision thereof. No other barrel or subdivision in barrel form is a legal container for cranberries.

(Sec. 1, 38 Stat. 1186; 15 U.S.C. 234)

§241.3 Application of tolerance for "distance between heads."

The tolerance established in this part for the dimension specified as "distance between heads" shall be applied as follows on the various types of barrels in use:

(a) When a barrel or subdivision thereof has two heads, the tolerance shall be applied to the distance between the inside surfaces of the heads and perpendicular to them.

(b) When a barrel or subdivision thereof has but one head and a croze ring or other means for the insertion of a head, such as an inside hoop, etc., at the opposite end, the tolerance shall be applied to the distance from the inside surface of the bottom head and perpendicular to it to the inside edge of the croze ring, or to a point where the inside surface of a head would come were such head inserted in the barrel.

(c) When a barrel or subdivision thereof has but one head and no croze ring or other means for the insertion of a head, such as an inside hoop, etc., at the opposite end, the tolerance shall be applied to the distance from the inside surface of the bottom head and perpendicular to it to a point 1⅛ inches from the opposite end of the staves in the case of a barrel or a ¾ barrel, and to a point 1 inch or ⅞ inch from the opposite end of the staves in the case of the ½ barrel and ⅓ barrel, respectively. When a barrel or subdivision thereof has been manufactured with but one head and no croze ring or other means for the insertion of a head at the opposite end, and it is desired to insert a second head, the croze ring shall be so cut that the inside edge shall not be more than 1⅛ inches from the end of the staves in the case of a barrel or ¾ barrel or not more than 1 inch or ⅞ inch from the end of the staves in the case of the ½ barrel and ⅓ barrel, respectively, or the other means shall be so adjusted that the inside surface of the head when inserted shall not exceed these distances from the end of the staves.

§241.4 Application of tolerance for "diameter of head."

(a) The tolerance established in this part for the dimension specified as "diameter of head" shall be applied to the diameter of the head over all, including the part which fits into the croze ring of the completed barrel.

(b) The tolerance established in this part for the dimension specified as "effective diameter of head" shall be applied as follows on the various types of barrels and subdivisions in use;

(1) When a barrel or subdivision thereof has two heads, the tolerance shall be applied to the mean of the average diameters from inside to inside of staves at the inner edges of the heads.

(2) When a barrel or subdivision thereof has but one head and a croze

ring or other means for the insertion of a head at the opposite end, the tolerance shall be applied to the mean of the average diameters, one taken from inside to inside of staves at the inner edge of the head, the other from inside to inside of staves at the inner edge of the croze ring, or from inside to inside of staves at a point where the inside surface of a head would come were such head inserted in the barrel.

(3) When a barrel or subdivision thereof has but one head and no croze ring or other means for the insertion of a head at the opposite end, the tolerance shall be applied to the mean of the average diameters, one taken from inside to inside of staves at the inner edge of the head, the other taken from inside to inside of staves at a point 1⅛ inches from the end of the staves in the case of a barrel or ¾ barrel, or at a point 1 inch or ⅞ inch from the end of the staves in the case of a ½ barrel or ⅓ barrel, respectively.

(c) The standard allowance for depth of croze ring shall be 3⁄16 inch. Therefore, the standard "effective diameter of head" in the case of the standard barrel is 16¾ inches and in the case of the standard cranberry barrel is 15⅞ inches.

§241.5 Standard dimensions.

Whenever in the rules and regulations in this part the error on a dimension is mentioned, this error shall be determined by taking the difference between the actual measured dimension and the standard dimension. The error is an error in excess and is to be preceded by a plus sign when the measured dimension is greater than the standard dimension. The error is an error in deficiency and is to be preceded by a minus sign when the measured dimension is less than the standard dimension.

(a) The standard dimensions of a barrel for fruits, vegetables, and other dry commodities other than cranberries, and of a barrel for cranberries, with which the actual measured dimensions are to be compared, are as follows:

Dimensions	Barrel for fruits, vegetables, and other dry commodities other than cranberries (inches)	Barrel for cranberries (inches)
Diameter of head	17⅛	16¼
Effective diameter of head (see §241.4)	16¾	15⅞
Distance between heads	26	25¼
Circumference of bulge, outside measurement	64	58½
Length of stave	28½	28½

(b) In the case of all subdivisions of the barrel for fruits, vegetables, and other dry commodities other than cranberries, and all subdivisions of the barrel for cranberries, the following dimensions are hereby standardized for the purpose of the application of tolerances, and the actual measured dimensions are to be compared with these:

SUBDIVISIONS OF BARREL FOR FRUITS, VEGETABLES, AND OTHER DRY COMMODITIES OTHER THAN CRANBERRIES

Dimensions	¾ barrel (inches)	½ barrel (inches)	⅓ barrel (inches)
Effective diameter of head (see §241.4)	15¼	13⅜	11⅝
Distance between heads	23½	20½	18
Circumference of bulge, outside measurement	58½	51½	45¼
SUBDIVISIONS OF BARREL FOR CRANBERRIES			
Effective diameter of head (see §241.4)	14⅜	12⅝	11
Distance between heads	23	20	17½
Circumference of bulge, outside measurement	53⅜	47	41⅜

(Sec. 1, 38 Stat. 1186; 15 U.S.C. 234)

§241.6 Classes of barrels for tolerance application.

For the purpose of the application of tolerances, barrels for fruits, vegetables, and other dry commodities other than cranberries, are hereby divided into two classes as follows:

(a) Class 1 shall include (1) all barrels no dimension of which is in error by more than the following amounts, and (2) all barrels one or more of the dimensions of which are in error by more than the following amounts, and which in addition have no dimension in error in the opposite direction:

	Error, inches
Effective diameter of head	¼
Distance between heads	¼

	Error, inches
Circumference of bulge, outside measurement ..	1½

(b) Class 2 shall include all barrels at least one dimension of which is in error by more than the amounts given above, but which in addition have at least one dimension in error in the opposite direction. (This class includes all barrels mentioned in section 1 of the law in the proviso reading: "*Provided,* That any barrel of a different form having a capacity of seven thousand and fifty-six cubic inches shall be a standard barrel.")

(Sec. 1, 38 Stat. 1186; 15 U.S.C. 234)

§241.7 Tolerances to be allowed.

(a) The tolerances to be allowed in excess or in deficiency on the dimensions of all barrels of Class 1 shall be as follows:

	Tolerance inches
Diameter of head	¼
Effective diameter of head	¼
Distance between heads	¼
Circumference of bulge, outside measurement ..	1½
Length of stave	½

(1) If no dimension of a barrel of Class 1 is in error by more than the tolerance given above, then the barrel is within the tolerance allowed.

(2) If one or more of the dimensions of a barrel of Class 1 is in error by more than the tolerance given above, then the barrel is not within the tolerance allowed.

(b) The tolerance to be allowed in excess or in deficiency on all barrels of Class 2 shall be 1½ inches (1.5) inches, and this tolerance is to be applied to the result obtained by the application of the following rule:

(1) Having determined the errors of each dimension and given to each its proper sign (see §241.4), add the errors on the effective diameter of head and the distance between heads algebraically and multiply the result by 1.67 (or 5⁄3). Then add this result to the error on the circumference of bulge algebraically. If the result obtained is not greater than the tolerance given above, then the barrel is within the tolerance allowed; if the result is greater than this tolerance, then the barrel is not within the tolerance allowed.

NOTE: To find the algebraic sum of a number of quantities having different signs, first add all those having one sign; then add all those having the opposite sign; then subtract the smaller sum from the larger, giving this result the sign of the larger quantity.

(2) [Reserved]

(c) The tolerance to be allowed in excess or in deficiency on the dimensions of all barrels for cranberries shall be as follows:

	Tolerance, inches
Diameter of head	¼
Effective diameter of head	¼
Distance between heads	¼
Circumference of bulge, outside measurement ..	1⅜
Length of stave	½

(1) If no dimension of a barrel for cranberries is in error by more than the tolerance given above, then the barrel is within the tolerance allowed.

(2) If one or more of the dimensions of a barrel for cranberries is in error by more than the tolerance given above, then the barrel is not within the tolerance allowed.

(d) The tolerances to be allowed in excess or in deficiency on all subdivisions of the standard barrel for fruits, vegetables, and other dry commodities other than cranberries, and on all subdivisions of the standard barrel for cranberries, shall be the values given in the following table, and these tolerances are to be applied to the result obtained by the application of the following rule:

(1) Having determined the errors on each dimension and given to each its proper sign (see §241.5), add the errors on the effective diameter of head and the distance between heads algebraically and multiply the result by 1.67 (or 5⁄3). Then add this result to the error on the circumference of bulge algebraically. If the result obtained is not greater than the tolerance given in the following table for the proper subdivision, then the barrel is within the tolerance allowed; if the result is greater than this tolerance, then the barrel is not within the tolerance allowed.

Size of subdivision	Tolerance	
	For fruits, vegetables, and other dry commodities (inches)	For cranberries (inches)
¾ barrel	1⅜ (1.375)	1¼ (1.25)
½ barrel	1¼ (1.25)	1⅛ (1.125)
⅓ barrel	1⅛ (1.125)	1 (1.00)

SUBCHAPTER E—FELLOWSHIPS AND RESEARCH ASSOCIATES

PART 255—FELLOWSHIPS IN LABORATORY STANDARDIZATION AND TESTING FOR QUALIFIED CITIZENS OF OTHER AMERICAN REPUBLICS

AUTHORITY: R.S. 161; sec. 1, 53 Stat. 1290; 22 U.S.C. 501.

SOURCE: 13 FR 8374, Dec. 28, 1948, unless otherwise noted.

§ 255.1 Type of fellowships.

Fellowships shall be of the combined intern-training and training-in-research type, and may include any or all of the following courses:

(a) Orientation courses consisting of lectures and conferences at the National Institute of Standards & Technology pertaining to laboratory standardization and testing.

(b) Practical laboratory training in various branches of physics, chemistry, and engineering research, under the direction of the National Institute of Standards & Technology, which will include the usual subdivisions of physics (weights and measures, heat, optics, mechanics, atomic physics, electrical measurements and radio) and also technologic applications in research and testing on metals, rubber, leather, paper, textiles, plastics, and clay and silicate products.

(c) Observation and study in such other laboratories within the continental United States as may be selected by the Director of the National Institute of Standards & Technology.

(d) Courses of instruction or research assignments supplementing the practical laboratory training, in universities or colleges selected by the Director of the National Institute of Standards & Technology.

[13 FR 8374, Dec. 28, 1948, as amended at 55 FR 38315, Sept. 18, 1990]

§ 255.2 Qualifications.

Each applicant selected for a fellowship shall be:

(a) A citizen of an American republic other than the United States;

(b) In possession of a certificate of medical examination issued by a licensed physician within 60 days of the date of application, describing the applicant's physical condition and stating that he is free from any communicable disease, physical deformity or disability that would interfere with the proper pursuit of training, research, or any other activity or work incident to the fellowship;

(c) Able to speak, read, write and understand the English language;

(d) Of good moral character and possessing intellectual ability and suitable personal qualities; and

(e) In possession of acceptable evidence that he has successfully completed the equivalent of a four-year university course in a recognized university, college or other institution of learning, with some training or experience in the field of activity which he desires to pursue. Equivalent experience may be substituted for the university training in the case of candidates who are otherwise specially well qualified.

§ 255.3 Award of fellowships.

Fellowships shall be awarded by the Director of the National Institute of Standards & Technology, with the approval of the Secretary of Commerce and the Secretary of State, or the duly authorized representative of the Secretary of State. Applications shall be transmitted to the Secretary of State by the government of the American republic of which the applicant is a citizen through the American diplomatic mission accredited to that government.

[13 FR 8374, Dec. 28, 1948, as amended at 55 FR 38315, Sept. 18, 1990]

§ 255.4 Allowances and expenses.

Allowances and expenses shall be as provided in State Department regulations given in 22 CFR Part 61, and as provided in Department of Commerce Administrative Order No. 202–3.[1]

§ 255.5 Progress reports.

Applicants awarded fellowships under the regulations in this part shall submit written reports of progress in training and research at such intervals as the Director of the National Institute of Standards & Technology may determine.

[13 FR 8374, Dec. 28, 1948, as amended at 55 FR 38316, Sept. 18, 1990]

§ 255.6 Duration of fellowships.

Fellowships may be awarded for periods of varying length, not exceeding one 12–month period of actual training and research and may be extended for not exceeding the same periods in the manner prescribed under § 255.3 and subject to the availability of appropriations. Fellowships may be cancelled for cause by the Director of the National Institute of Standards & Technology, with the approval of the Secretary of Commerce and the Secretary of State, or the duly authorized representative of the Secretary of State.

[13 FR 8374, Dec. 28, 1948, as amended at 55 FR 38316, Sept. 18, 1990]

§ 255.7 Official notification.

Each applicant selected by the Director of the National Institute of Standards & Technology and approved by the Secretary of Commerce and the Secretary of State, or the duly authorized representative of the Secretary of State, shall be notified of his award through diplomatic channels. The notification shall state the duration and type of fellowship, outline the program of training and research, and state the allowances authorized: *Provided, however*, That the Director of the National Institute of Standards & Technology may subsequently amend the program and duration of the fellowship if in his opinion such action would be in the interest of obtaining training and research better suited to the needs and capabilities of the fellow than those prescribed in the notification. The amount originally authorized for monthly allowances and other expenses may also be amended, if necessary, with the approval of the Secretary of Commerce and the Secretary of State, or the duly authorized representative of the Secretary of State.

[13 FR 8374, Dec. 28, 1948, as amended at 55 FR 38316, Sept. 18, 1990]

PART 256—RESEARCH ASSOCIATE PROGRAM

Sec.

AUTHORITY: 27 Stat. 395, 31 Stat. 1039; 20 U.S.C. 91.

SOURCE: 32 FR 10252, July 12, 1967, unless otherwise noted.

§ 256.1 Introduction.

This part states policies and procedures concerning the Research Associate Program at the National Institute of Standards & Technology. In the exercise of its functions as a major scientific agency of the Federal Government, the National Institute of Standards & Technology may make its facilities available to persons other than Bureau employees to work with scientists and engineers in collaborative research aimed at furthering the Nation's scientific, industrial, and economic growth. Such cooperative programs may be sponsored by professional, technical, or industrial organizations or associations. Such participants, when so sponsored, are designated "Research Associates".

§ 256.2 The Research Associate Program.

The Bureau provides its facilities, scientific competence, and technical supervision for defined scientific or technical research by a Research Associate when such research is complementary to and compatible with scientific or technical research being performed or to be undertaken by NIST under its statutory mission and authority. The Sponsors pay the salaries

[1] Not filed with the Office of the Federal Register.

of their Research Associates and Sponsor-furnished technical assistants and secretaries of the Research Associates, if any, their travel costs, and other related expenses. Additionally, Sponsors reimburse NIST for the cost of research equipment, services, or materials obtained for the Research Associate.

[32 FR 10252, July 12, 1967, as amended at 40 FR 50707, Oct. 31, 1975]

§256.3 Procedure.

Arrangements for collaborative research by NIST with a Research Associate generally begin through discussions or correspondence between NIST scientists and representatives of potential sponsoring companies, trade associations or professional organizations. These preliminary steps are followed by the consummation of a Memorandum of Agreement which is signed by NIST, the sponsoring organization and the Research Associate. The agreement sets out the respective responsibilities and obligations of all parties.

§256.4 Qualifications.

Each candidate selected to serve as a Research Associate must be determined to be scientifically qualified by the Sponsor and by the NIST, and found by NIST to be of good moral character and to possess suitable personal qualities.

§256.5 Duration of projects.

The work of a Research Associate is generally conducted on a full-time basis. Typically, Research Associates are in residence at NIST for 6 to 18 months; longer-term programs may be carried on by a succession of Research Associates. Agreements provide for cancellation by any of the parties.

§256.6 Information concerning the Research Associate Program.

Information concerning the Research Associate Program may be obtained from the Industrial Liaison Officer, National Institute of Standards & Technology, Washington, DC 20234.

[40 FR 50707, Oct. 31, 1975]

SUBCHAPTER F—REGULATIONS GOVERNING TRAFFIC AND CONDUCT

PART 265—REGULATIONS GOVERNING TRAFFIC AND CONDUCT ON THE GROUNDS OF THE NATIONAL INSTITUTE OF STANDARDS & TECHNOLOGY, GAITHERSBURG, MARYLAND, AND BOULDER AND FORT COLLINS, COLORADO

Subpart A—General

Subpart B—Traffic and Vehicular Regulations

Subpart C—Buildings and Grounds

Subpart D—Penalties

AUTHORITY: Sec. 9, 31 Stat. 1450, as amended (15 U.S.C. 277). Applies sec. 1, 72 Stat 1711, as amended, (15 U.S.C. 278e(b)).

SOURCE: 39 FR 41170, Nov. 25, 1974, unless otherwise noted.

Subpart A—General

§ 265.1 Definitions.

As used in this part:

(a) *Site* means those grounds and facilities of the National Institute of Standards & Technology, Department of Commerce located in Montgomery County, Maryland, and in Boulder and Larimer Counties, Colorado, over which the Federal Government has acquired concurrent jurisdiction in accordance with appropriate authority.

(b) *Uniformed guard* means a designated employee appointed by the Director for purposes of carrying out the authority of a U.S. Special Policeman, as provided by 40 U.S.C. 318.

(c) *Director* means the Director of the National Institute of Standards & Technology.

[39 FR 41170, Nov. 25, 1974, as amended at 41 FR 51787, Nov. 24, 1976; 55 FR 38316, Sept. 18, 1990]

§ 265.2 Applicability.

The regulations in this part establish rules with respect to the parking and operation of motor vehicles and other activities and conduct on the site. These regulations are intended to supplement the rules and regulations regarding conduct in Part O of Subtitle A of this title and in other officially issued orders and regulations of the Department of Commerce and the National Institute of Standards & Technology

[39 FR 41170, Nov. 25, 1974, as amended at 55 FR 38316, Sept. 18, 1990]

§ 265.3 Compliance with directions.

No person shall fail or refuse to comply with any lawful order or direction of a uniformed guard in connection with the control or regulation of traffic and parking or other conduct on the site.

§265.4 Making or giving of false reports.

No person shall knowingly give any false or fictitious report or information to any authorized person investigating an accident or apparent violation of law or these regulations. Nothing in this section shall affect the applicability of 18 U.S.C. 1001 regarding false, fictitious or fraudulent statements or entries.

§265.5 Laws of Maryland and Colorado applicable.

Unless otherwise specifically provided herein, the laws of the State of Maryland and of the State of Colorado shall be applicable to the site located within those respective States. The applicability of State laws shall not, however, affect or abrogate any other Federal law or regulation applicable under the circumstances.

Subpart B—Traffic and Vehicular Regulations

§265.11 Inspection of license and registration.

No person may operate any motor vehicle on the site unless he holds a current operator's license, nor may he, if operating a motor vehicle on the site, refuse to exhibit for inspection, upon request of a uniformed guard, his operator's license or proof of registration of the vehicle under his control at time of operation.

§265.12 Speeding or reckless driving.

(a) No person shall drive a motor vehicle on the site at a speed greater than or in a manner other than is reasonable and prudent for the particular location, given the conditions of traffic, weather, and road surface and having regard to the actual and potential hazards existing.

(b) Except when a special hazard exists that requires lower speed for compliance with paragraph (a) of this section, the speed limit on the site is 25 m.p.h., unless another speed limit has been duly posted, and no person shall drive a motor vehicle on the site in excess of the speed limit.

§265.13 Emergency vehicles.

No person shall fail or refuse to yield the right-of-way to an emergency vehicle when operating with siren or flashing lights.

§265.14 Signs.

Every driver shall comply with all posted traffic and parking signs.

§265.15 Right-of-way in crosswalks.

No person shall fail or refuse to yield the right-of-way to a pedestrian or bicyclist crossing a street in a marked crosswalk.

§265.16 Parking.

No person, unless otherwise authorized by a posted traffic sign or directed by a uniformed guard, shall stand or park a motor vehicle:

(a) On a sidewalk;

(b) Within an intersection or within a crosswalk;

(c) Within 15 feet of a fire hydrant, 5 feet of a driveway or 30 feet of a stop sign or traffic control device;

(d) At any place which would result in the vehicle being double parked;

(e) At curbs painted yellow;

(f) In a direction facing on-coming traffic;

(g) In a manner which would obstruct traffic;

(h) In a parking space marked as not intended for his use;

(i) Where directed not to do so by a uniformed guard;

(j) Except in an area specifically designated for parking or standing;

(k) Except within a single space marked for such purposes, when parking or standing in an area with marked spaces;

(l) At any place in violation of any posted sign; or

(m) In excess of 24 hours, unless permission has been granted by the Physical Security office.

§265.17 Parking permits.

No person, except visitors, shall park a motor vehicle on the site without having a valid parking permit displayed on such motor vehicle in compliance with instructions of the issuing authority. Such permits may be revoked by the issuing authority for violation of any of the provisions of this part.

§ 265.18 Prohibited servicing of vehicles.

No person shall make nonemergency repairs on privately owned vehicles on the site.

§ 265.19 Unattended vehicles.

No person shall leave a motor vehicle unattended on the site with the engine running or a key in the ignition switch or the vehicle not effectively braked.

§ 265.20 Towing of improperly parked vehicles.

Any motor vehicle that is parked in violation of these regulations may be towed away or otherwise moved if a determination is made by a uniformed guard that it is a nuisance or hazard. A reasonable amount for the moving service and for the storage of the vehicle, if any, may be charged, and the vehicle is subject to a lien for that charge.

§ 265.21 Improper use of roads as thoroughfares.

Except as otherwise provided herein, no person shall drive a motor vehicle or bicycle onto the site for the sole purpose of using the roads of the site as a thoroughfare between roads bordering the site. This section shall not apply to bicyclists using officially approved bike paths on the site.

§ 265.22 Bicycle traffic.

No person shall ride a bicycle other than in a manner exercising due caution for pedestrian and other traffic. No person shall ride a bicycle on sidewalks or inside any building, nor shall any person park a bicycle on sidewalks or inside any building nor in a roadway or parking lot, provided, however, that these parking restrictions shall not apply to bicycles parked at bicycle racks located in these areas.

Subpart C—Buildings and Grounds

§ 265.31 Closing the site.

As determined by the Director (Director, NIST Boulder Laboratories, for sites in Colorado), the site may be closed to the public in emergency situations and at such other times as may be necessary for the orderly conduct of the Government's business. At such times no person shall enter the site except authorized individuals, who may be required to sign a register and display identification when requested by a uniformed guard.

[39 FR 41170, Nov. 25, 1974, as amended at 56 FR 66969, Dec. 27, 1991]

§ 265.32 Trespassing.

No person shall come onto the site other than in pursuance of official government business or other properly authorized activities.

§ 265.33 Preservation of property.

No person shall, without authorization, willfully destroy, damage, or deface any building, sign, equipment, marker, or structure, tree, flower, lawn, or other public property on the site.

§ 265.34 Conformity with posted signs.

No person shall fail or refuse to comply with officially posted signs of a prohibitory nature or with directions of a uniformed guard.

§ 265.35 Nuisances.

(a) No person shall willfully disrupt the conduct of official business on the site, or engage in disorderly conduct; nor shall any person unreasonably obstruct the usual use of entrances, foyers, lobbies, corridors, offices, elevators, stairways, parking lots, sidewalks, or roads.

(b) No person shall litter or dispose of rubbish except in a receptacle provided for that purpose; nor shall any person throw articles of any kind from a building or from a motor vehicle or bicycle.

§ 265.36 Intoxicating beverages.

Except as expressly authorized by the Director, the consumption or use on the site of intoxicating beverages is prohibited.

§ 265.37 Narcotics and other drugs.

The possession, sale, consumption, or use on the site of narcotic or other drugs illegal under the laws of the State in which the particular site is situated is prohibited. The provisions of this section are not intended to preclude the applicability of any State or local laws and regulations with respect to the possession, sale, consumption, or use of narcotic or other drugs.

§265.38 Intoxication or other impairment of function.

No person shall enter or remain on the site while noticeably impaired by the use of intoxicating beverages or narcotics or other drugs, and any such person found on the site in such a state of impairment may be removed from the site.

§265.39 Weapons and explosives.

Except in connection with the conduct of official business on the site, no person other than uniformed guards specifically authorized, or other Federal, State, or local law enforcement officials so authorized, shall carry, transport, or otherwise possess on the site, firearms whether loaded or not, other dangerous or deadly weapons or materials, or explosives, either openly or concealed, without the written permission of the Director or his designee.

§265.40 Nondiscrimination.

No person shall discriminate against any other person because of race, creed, color, sex, or national origin, in furnishing, or by refusing to furnish to such person the use of any facility of a public nature, including all services, privileges, accommodations, and activities provided thereby on the site.

§265.41 Gambling.

No person shall participate on the site in games for money or other property, or in the operation of gambling devices, the conduct of lotteries or pools, or in the selling or purchasing of numbers tickets, or the taking or placing of bets.

§265.42 Photography for advertising or commercial purposes; advertising and soliciting.

(a) Except as otherwise provided herein or where security regulations would preclude, photographs may be taken in entrances, lobbies, foyers, corridors, and auditoriums without prior approval. Photography for advertising and commercial purposes may be conducted only with the written permission of the Chief, Public Affairs Division of the National Institute of Standards and Technology (Public Affairs Officer for Boulder for sites in Colorado,) provided, however, that this shall not apply to photography for purposes of civic promotion.

(b) Commercial advertisements and other material which are not directly pertinent or applicable to NIST employees but which nevertheless may be of interest or benefit to them may, with the approval of the Director of Administration (Executive Office, Boulder, for sites in Colorado), be placed in an appropriate location and made available to employees who visit that area. Except with approval as provided herein, no person shall distribute commercial advertising literature or engage in commercial soliciting on the site.

[39 FR 41170, Nov. 25, 1974, as amended at 55 FR 38316, Sept. 18, 1990; 56 FR 66969, Dec. 27, 1991]

§265.43 Pets and other animals.

Except in connection with the conduct of official business on the site or with the approval of the Associate Director for Administration (Executive Officer, IBS/Boulder, for sites in Colorado), no person shall bring upon the site any cat, dog, or other animal, provided, however, that blind persons may have the use of seeing eye dogs.

Subpart D—Penalties

§265.51 Penalties—other laws.

Except with respect to the laws of the State of Maryland and the State of Colorado assimilated by §265.5 or otherwise, whoever shall be found guilty of violating these regulations is subject to a fine of not more than $50 or imprisonment of not more than 30 days, or both (40 U.S.C. 318c). Except as expressly provided in this part, nothing contained in these regulations shall be construed to abrogate any other Federal laws or regulations, or any State and local laws and regulations applicable to the area in which the site is situated.

SUBCHAPTER G—NATIONAL CONSTRUCTION SAFETY TEAMS

PART 270—NATIONAL CONSTRUCTION SAFETY TEAMS

AUTHORITY: Pub. L. 107–231, 116 Stat. 1471 (15 U.S.C. 7301 *et seq.*).

SOURCE: 68 FR 4694, Jan. 30, 2003, unless otherwise noted.

Subpart A—General

§ 270.1 Description of rule; purpose; applicability.

(a) The National Construction Safety Team Act (the Act) (Pub. L. 107–231) provides for the establishment of investigative teams to assess building performance and emergency response and evacuation procedures in the wake of any building failure that has resulted in substantial loss of life or that posed significant potential of substantial loss of life.

(b)(1) The purpose of the Act is to provide for the establishment of investigative teams to assess building performance and emergency response and evacuation procedures in the wake of any building failure that has resulted in substantial loss of life or that posed significant potential of substantial loss of life. The role of NIST in implementing the Act is to understand the factors contributing to the building failure and to develop recommendations for improving national building and fire model codes, standards, and practices. To do this, the Teams produce technical reports containing data, findings, and recommendations for consideration by private sector bodies responsible for the affected national building and fire model code, standard, or practice. While NIST is an active participant in many of these organizations, NIST's recommendations are one of many factors considered by these bodies. NIST is not now and will not become a participant in the processes and adoption of practices, standards, or codes by state or local regulatory authorities.

(2) It is not NIST's role to determine whether a failed building resulted from a criminal act, violated any applicable federal requirements or state or local code or regulatory requirements, or to determine any culpability associated therewith. These are matters for other federal, state, or local authorities, who enforce their regulations.

(c) This part is applicable to the establishment and deployment of Teams and the conduct of investigations under the Act.

[68 FR 4694, Jan. 30, 2003, as amended at 68 FR 66704, Nov. 28, 2003; 69 FR 33571, June 16, 2004]

§270.2 Definitions used in this part.

The following definitions are applicable to this part:

Act. The National Construction Safety Team Act (Pub. L. 107–231, 116 Stat. 1471).

Advisory Committee. The National Construction Safety Team Advisory Committee.

Credentials. Credentials issued by the Director, identifying a person as a member of a National Construction Safety Team, including photo identification and other materials, including badges, deemed appropriate by the Director.

Director. The Director of the National Institute of Standards and Technology.

Evidence. Any document, record, book, artifact, building component, material, witness testimony, or physical evidence collected pursuant to an investigation.

General Counsel. The General Counsel of the U.S. Department of Commerce.

Investigation participant. Any person participating in an investigation under the Act, including all Team members, other NIST employees participating in the investigation, private sector experts, university experts, representatives of professional organizations, employees of other Federal, state, or local government entities, and other contractors.

Lead Investigator. A Team member who is a NIST employee and is designated by the Director to lead a Team.

NIST. The National Institute of Standards and Technology.

Team. A team established by the Director and deployed to conduct an investigation under the Act.

[68 FR 4694, Jan. 30, 2003, as amended at 68 FR 66704, Nov. 28, 2003]

Subpart B—Establishment and Deployment of Teams

SOURCE: 68 FR 66704, Nov. 28, 2003, unless otherwise noted.

§270.100 General.

(a) Based on prior NIST experience, NIST expects that the Director will establish and deploy a Team to conduct an investigation at a frequency of approximately once per year or less.

(b) For purposes of this part, a building failure may involve one or more of the following: structural system, fire protection (active or passive) system, air-handling system, and building control system. Teams established under the Act and this part will investigate these technical causes of building failures and will also investigate the technical aspects of evacuation and emergency response procedures, including multiple-occupant behavior or evacuation (egress or access) system, emergency response system, and emergency communication system.

(c) For purposes of this part, the number of fatalities considered to be "substantial" will depend on the nature of the event, its impact, its unusual or unforeseen character, historical norms, and other pertinent factors.

[68 FR 66704, Nov. 28, 2003, as amended at 69 FR 33571, June 16, 2004]

§ 270.101 Preliminary reconnaissance.

(a) To the extent the Director deems it appropriate, the Director may conduct a preliminary reconnaissance at the site of a building failure. The Director may establish and deploy a Team to conduct the preliminary reconnaissance, as described in § 270.102 of this subpart, or may have information gathered at the site of a building failure without establishing a Team.

(b) If the Director establishes and deploys a Team to conduct the preliminary reconnaissance, the Team shall perform all duties pursuant to section 2(b)(2) of the Act, and may perform all activities that Teams are authorized to perform under the Act and these procedures, including gathering and preserving evidence. At the completion of the preliminary reconnaissance, the Team will report its findings to the Director in a timely manner. The Director may either determine that the Team should conduct further investigation, or may direct the Team to prepare its public report immediately.

(c) If the preliminary reconnaissance is conducted without the establishment of a Team, the leader of the initial assessment will report his/her findings to the Director in a timely manner. The Director will decide whether to establish a Team and conduct an investigation using the criteria established in § 270.102 of this subpart.

§ 270.102 Conditions for establishment and deployment of a Team.

(a) The Director may establish a Team for deployment after an event that caused the failure of a building or buildings that resulted in substantial loss of life or posed significant potential for substantial loss of life. The Director will determine the following prior to deploying a Team:

(1) The event was any of the following:

(i) A major failure of one or more buildings or types of buildings due to an extreme natural event (earthquake, hurricane, tornado, flood, etc.);

(ii) A fire that resulted in a building failure of the building of origin and/or spread beyond the building of origin.

(iii) A major building failure at significantly less than its design basis, during construction, or while in active use; or

(iv) An act of terrorism or other event resulting in a Presidential declaration of disaster and activation of the National Response Plan; and

(2) A fact-finding investigation of the building performance and emergency response and evacuation procedures will likely result in significant and new knowledge or building code revision recommendations needed to reduce or mitigate public risk and economic losses from future building failures.

(b) In making the determinations pursuant to paragraph (a) of this section, the Director will consider the following:

(1) Whether sufficient financial and personnel resources are available to conduct an investigation; and

(2) Whether an investigation of the building failure warrants the advanced capabilities and experiences of a Team; and

(3) If the technical cause of the failure is readily apparent, whether an investigation is likely to result in relevant knowledge other than reaffirmation of the technical cause; and

(4) Whether deployment of a Team will substantially duplicate local or state resources equal in investigatory and analytical capability and quality to a Team; and

(5) Recommendations resulting from a preliminary reconnaissance of the site of the building failure.

(c) To the maximum extent practicable, the Director will establish and deploy a Team within 48 hours after such an event.

[68 FR 66704, Nov. 28, 2003, as amended at 69 FR 33571, June 16, 2004]

§ 270.103 Publication in the Federal Register.

The Director will promptly publish in the FEDERAL REGISTER notice of the establishment of each Team.

§270.104 Size and composition of a Team.

(a) *Size of a Team.* The size of a Team will depend upon the likely scope and complexity of the investigation. A Team may consist of five or less members if the investigation is narrowly focused, or a Team may consist of twenty or more members divided into groups if the breadth of the investigation spans a number of technical issues. In addition, Teams may be supported by others at NIST, in other federal agencies, and in the private sector, who may conduct supporting experiments, analysis, interviews witnesses, and/or examine the response of first responders, occupants, etc.

(b) *Composition of a Team.* (1) A Team will be composed of individuals selected by the Director and led by a Lead Investigator designated by the Director.

(2) The Lead Investigator will be a NIST employee, selected based on his/her technical qualifications, ability to mobilize and lead a multi-disciplinary investigative team, and ability to deal with sensitive issues and the media.

(3) Team members will include at least one employee of NIST and will include experts who are not employees of NIST, who may include private sector experts, university experts, representatives of professional organizations with appropriate expertise, and appropriate Federal, State, or local officials.

(4) Team members who are not Federal employees will be Federal Government contractors.

(5) Teams may include members who are experts in one or more of the following disciplines: civil, structural, mechanical, electrical, fire, forensic, safety, architectural, and materials engineering, and specialists in emergency response, human behavior, and evacuation.

(c) *Duration of a Team.* A Team's term will end 3 months after the Team's final public report is published, but the term may be extended or terminated earlier by the Director.

[68 FR 66704, Nov. 28, 2003, as amended at 69 FR 33571, June 16, 2004]

§270.105 Duties of a Team.

(a) A Team's Lead Investigator will organize, conduct, and control all technical aspects of the investigation, up to and including the completion of the final investigation public report and any subsequent actions that may be required. The Lead Investigator has the responsibility and authority to supervise and coordinate all resources and activities of NIST personnel involved in the investigation. The Lead Investigator may be the Contracting Officer's Technical Representative (COTR) on any contract for service on the Team or in support of the Team; while the COTR remains the technical representative of the Contracting Officer for purposes of contract administration, the Lead Investigator will oversee all NIST personnel acting as COTRs for contracts for service on the Team or in support of the Team. The Lead Investigator's duties will terminate upon termination of the Team. The Lead Investigator will keep the Director and the NCST Advisory Committee informed about the status of investigations.

(b) A Team will:

(1) Establish the likely technical cause or causes of the building failure;

(2) Evaluate the technical aspects of evacuation and emergency response procedures;

(3) Recommend, as necessary, specific improvements to building standards, codes, and practices based on the findings made pursuant to paragraphs (b)(1) and (b)(2) of this section;

(4) Recommend any research and other appropriate actions needed to improve the structural safety of buildings, and improve evacuation and emergency response procedures, based on the findings of the investigation; and

(5) Not later than 90 days after completing an investigation, issue a public report in accordance with §270.205 of this subpart.

(c) In performing these duties, a Team will:

(1) Not interfere unnecessarily with services provided by the owner or operator of the buildings, building components, materials, artifacts, property, records, or facility;

(2) Preserve evidence related to the building failure consistent with the ongoing needs of the investigation;

(3) Preserve evidence related to a criminal act that may have caused the building failure;

(4) Not impede and coordinate its investigation with any search and rescue efforts being undertaken at the site of the building failure;

(5) Coordinate its investigation with qualified researchers who are conducting engineering or scientific research (including social science) relating to the building failure;

(6) Cooperate with State and local authorities carrying out any activities related to a Team's investigation;

(d) In performing these duties, in a manner consistent with the procedures set forth in this part, a Team may:

(1) Enter property where a building failure being investigated has occurred and take necessary, appropriate, and reasonable action to carry out the duties described in paragraph (b) of this section;

(2) Inspect any record, process, or facility related to the investigation during reasonable hours;

(3) Inspect and test any building components, materials, and artifacts related to the building failure; and

(4) Move records, components, materials, and artifacts related to the building failure.

§ 270.106 Conflicts of interest related to service on a Team.

(a) Team members who are not Federal employees will be Federal Government contractors.

(b) Contracts between NIST and Team members will include appropriate provisions to ensure that potential conflicts of interest that arise prior to award or during the contract are identified and resolved.

Subpart C—Investigations

SOURCE: 68 FR 66704, Nov. 28, 2003, unless otherwise noted.

§ 270.200 Technical conduct of investigation.

(a) *Preliminary reconnaissance.* (1) An initial assessment of the event, including an initial site reconnaissance, if deemed appropriate by the Director, will be conducted. This assessment will be done within a few hours of the event, if possible. The Director may establish and deploy a Team to conduct the preliminary reconnaissance, using the criteria established in § 270.102 of this part, or may have information gathered at the site of a building failure without establishing a Team.

(2) If the Director establishes and deploys a Team to conduct the preliminary reconnaissance, the Team shall perform all duties pursuant to section 2(b)(2) of the Act, and may perform all activities that Teams are authorized to perform under the Act and these procedures, with a focus on gathering and preserving evidence, inspecting the site of the building failure, and interviewing of eyewitnesses, survivors, and first responders. Collections of evidence by a Team established for preliminary reconnaissance are investigatory in nature and will not be considered research for any purpose. At the completion of the preliminary reconnaissance, the Team will report its findings to the Director in a timely manner. The Director may either determine that the Team should conduct further investigation, or may direct the Team to immediately prepare the public report as required by section 8 of the Act.

(3) If the preliminary reconnaissance is conducted without the establishment of a Team, the leader of the initial assessment will report his/her findings to the Director in a timely manner. The Director will decide whether to establish a team and conduct an investigation using the criteria established in § 270.102 of this part.

(b) *Investigation plan.* (1) If the Director establishes a Team without ordering preliminary reconnaissance, establishes a Team after preliminary reconnaissance, or establishes a Team to conduct preliminary reconnaissance and subsequently determines that further investigation is necessary prior to preparing the public report required by section 8 of the Act, the Director, or his/her designee, will formulate a plan that includes:

(i) A brief description of the building failure;

(ii) The criteria upon which the decision to conduct the investigation was based;

(iii) Supporting effort(s) by other organizations either in place or expected in the future;

(iv) Identification of the Lead Investigator and Team members;

(v) The technical investigation plan;

(vi) Site, community, and local, state, and Federal agency liaison status; and

(vii) Estimated duration and cost.

(2) To the extent practicable, the Director will include the most appropriate expertise on each Team from within NIST, other government agencies, and the private sector. The NCST Advisory Committee may be convened as soon as feasible following the launch of an investigation to provide the Director the benefit of its advice on investigation Team activities.

(c) *Investigation.* (1) The duration of an investigation that proceeds beyond preliminary reconnaissance will be as little as a few months to as long as a few years depending on the complexity of the event.

(2) Tasks that may be completed during investigations that proceed beyond preliminary reconnaissance include:

(i) Consult with experts in building design and construction, fire protection engineering, emergency evacuation, and members of other investigation teams involved in the event to identify technical issues and major hypotheses requiring investigation.

(ii) Collect data from the building(s) owner and occupants, local authorities, and contractors and suppliers. Such data will include relevant building and fire protection documents, records, video and photographic data, field data, and data from interviews and other oral and written accounts from building occupants, emergency responders, and other witnesses.

(iii) Collect and analyze physical evidence, including material samples and other forensic evidence, to the extent they are available.

(iv) Determine the conditions in the building(s) prior to the event, which may include the materials of construction and contents; the location, size, and condition of all openings that may have affected egress, entry, and fire conditions (if applicable); the installed security and/or fire protection systems (if applicable); the number of occupants and their approximate locations at the time of the event.

(v) Reconstruct the event within the building(s) using computer models to identify the most probable technical cause (or causes) of the failure and the uncertainty(ies) associated with it (them). Such models may include initial damage, blast effects, pre-existing deficiencies and phenomena such as fire spread, smoke movement, tenability, occupant behavior and response, evacuation issues, cooperation of security and fire protection systems, and building collapse.

(vi) Conduct small and full-scale experiments to provide additional data and verify the computer models being used.

(vii) Examine the impact of alternate building/system/equipment design and use on the survivability of the building and its occupants.

(viii) Analyze emergency evacuation and occupant responses to better understand the actions of the first responders and the impediments to safe egress encountered by the occupants.

(ix) Analyze the relevant building practices, including code adoption and enforcement practices, to determine the extent to which the circumstances that led to this building failure have regional or national implications.

(x) Identify specific areas in building and fire codes, standards, and building practices that may warrant revisions based on investigation findings.

(xi) Identify research and other appropriate actions required to help prevent future building failures.

(d) If a disaster site contains multiple building failures, the Director will narrow the scope of the investigation plan taking into account available financial and personnel resources, and giving priority to failures offering the most opportunity to advance the safety of building codes. The Director may consider the capabilities of NIST in establishing priorities.

[68 FR 66704, Nov. 28, 2003, as amended at 69 FR 33571, June 16, 2004]

§ 270.201 Priority of investigation.

(a) *General.* Except as provided in this section, a Team investigation will have priority over any other investigation of any other Federal agency.

(b) *Criminal acts.* (1) If the Attorney General, in consultation with the Director, determines, and notifies the Director that circumstances reasonably indicate that the building failure being investigated by a Team may have been caused by a criminal act, the Team will relinquish investigative priority to the appropriate law enforcement agency.

(2) If a criminal investigation of the building failure being investigated by a Team is initiated at the state or local level, the Team will relinquish investigative priority to the appropriate law enforcement agency.

(3) The relinquishment of investigative priority by the Team will not otherwise affect the authority of the Team to continue its investigation under the Act.

(c) *National Transportation Safety Board.* If the National Transportation Safety Board is conducting an investigation related to an investigation of a Team, the National Transportation Safety Board investigation will have priority over the Team investigation. Such priority will not otherwise affect the authority of the Team to continue its investigation under the Act.

(d) Although NIST will share any evidence of criminal activity that it obtains in the course of an investigation under the Act with the appropriate law enforcement agency, NIST will not participate in the investigation of any potential criminal activity.

§ 270.202 Coordination with search and rescue efforts.

NIST will coordinate its investigation with any search and rescue or search and recovery efforts being undertaken at the site of the building failure, including FEMA urban search and rescue teams, local emergency management agencies, and local emergency response groups. Upon arrival at a disaster site, the Lead Investigator will identify the lead of the search and rescue operations and will work closely with that person to ensure coordination of efforts.

[68 FR 66704, Nov. 28, 2003, as amended at 69 FR 33571, June 16, 2004]

§ 270.203 Coordination with Federal, State, and local entities.

NIST will enter into Memoranda of Understanding with Federal, State, and local entities, as appropriate, to ensure the coordination of investigations.

§ 270.204 Provision of additional resources and services needed by a Team.

The Director will determine the appropriate resources that a Team will require to carry out its investigation and will ensure that those resources are available to the Team.

§ 270.205 Reports.

(a) Not later than 90 days after completing an investigation, a Team shall issue a public report which includes:

(1) An analysis of the likely technical cause or causes of the building failure investigated;

(2) Any technical recommendations for changes to or the establishment of evacuation or emergency response procedures;

(3) Any recommended specific improvements to building standards, codes, and practices; and

(4) Recommendations for research and other appropriate actions needed to help prevent future building failures.

(b) A Team that is directed to prepare its public report immediately after conducting a preliminary reconnaissance will issue a public report not later than 90 days after completion of the preliminary reconnaissance. The public report will be in accordance with paragraph (a) of this section, but will be summary in nature.

(c) A Team that continues to conduct an investigation after conducting a preliminary reconnaissance will issue a public report not later than 90 days after completing the investigation in accordance with paragraph (a) of this section.

§270.206 Public briefings and requests for information.

(a) NIST will establish methods to provide updates to the public on its planning and progress of an investigation. Methods may include:

(1) A public Web site;

(2) Mailing lists, to include an emphasis on e-mail;

(3) Semi-annual written progress reports;

(4) Media briefings; and

(5) Public meetings.

(b) Requests for information on the plans and conduct of an investigation should be submitted to the NIST Public and Business Affairs Division.

Subpart D—Collection and Preservation of Evidence; Information Created Pursuant to an Investigation; and Protection of Information

§270.300 Scope.

During the course of an investigation conducted pursuant to the Act, evidence will be collected, and information will be created by the Team, NIST, and other investigation participants. This subpart sets forth the policy and procedures for the collection, preservation, and protection of evidence obtained and information created pursuant to an investigation.

§270.301 Policy.

Evidence collected and information created by Team members and all other investigation participants will be collected, preserved, and protected in accordance with the procedures set forth in this subpart.

COLLECTION OF EVIDENCE

§270.310 Evidence collected by investigation participants who are not NIST employees.

Upon receipt of evidence pursuant to an investigation under the Act, each investigation participant who is not a NIST employee shall:

(a) As soon as practicable, transfer the original evidence to NIST, and retain a copy of the evidence only if necessary to carry out their duties under the investigation; and

(b) For any evidence that cannot reasonably be duplicated, retain the evidence in accordance with NIST procedures for preserving evidence as described in §270.330 of this subpart, and upon completion of the duties for which retention of the evidence is necessary, transfer the evidence to NIST.

[68 FR 4694, Jan. 30, 2003, as amended at 68 FR 24345, May 7, 2003]

§270.311 Collection of evidence.

(a) In the course of an investigation, evidence normally will be collected following the procedures described in §§270.312 through 270.315 of this subpart.

(b) Upon a written showing by the Lead Investigator of urgent and compelling reasons to believe that evidence may be destroyed, or that a witness may become unavailable, were the procedures described in §§270.312 through 270.314 of this subpart followed, the Director, with the concurrence of the General Counsel, may immediately issue a subpoena for such evidence or testimony, pursuant to §270.315 of this subpart.

§270.312 Voluntary submission of evidence.

After the Director establishes and deploys a Team, members of the public are encouraged to voluntarily submit to the Team non-privileged evidence that is relevant to the subject matter of the pending investigation.

[68 FR 4694, Jan. 30, 2003, as amended at 68 FR 24345, May 7, 2003]

§270.313 Requests for evidence.

(a) After the Director establishes and deploys a Team, the Lead Investigator, or their designee, may request the testimony of any person by deposition, upon oral examination or written questions, and may request documents or other physical evidence without seeking prior approval of the Director.

(b) Requests for responses to written questions will be made in writing and shall include:

(1) A statement that the request is made to gather evidence necessary to an investigation being conducted under the Act;

(2) Identification of the person whose responses are sought;

(3) Contact information for the person to whom the responses should be submitted;

(4) The date and time by which the responses are requested;

(5) A statement that the questions for which responses are sought are attached; and

(6) Contact information for the person to whom questions or problems regarding the request should be addressed.

(c) Requests for documents or other physical evidence will be made in writing and shall include:

(1) A statement that the request is made to gather evidence necessary to an investigation being conducted under the Act;

(2) A description of the documents or other physical evidence sought;

(3) Identification of the person or persons to whom the request is made;

(4) A request that each person to whom the request is directed produce and permit inspection and copying of the documents and physical evidence in the possession, custody, or control of that person at a specific time and place; and

(5) Contact information for the person to whom questions or problems regarding the request should be addressed.

(d) Requests for witness testimony will be made in writing and shall include:

(1) The name of the person whose testimony is requested;

(2) The date, time, and place of the deposition;

(3) A statement that the person whose testimony is requested may be accompanied by an attorney; and

(4) Contact information for the person to whom questions or problems regarding the request should be addressed.

(e) Collections of evidence under paragraphs (b), (c), and (d) of this section are investigatory in nature and will not be considered research for any purpose.

[68 FR 4694, Jan. 30, 2003, as amended at 68 FR 66707, Nov. 28, 2003]

§ 270.314 Negotiations.

The Lead Investigator may enter into discussions with appropriate parties to address problems identified with the submission of evidence requested pursuant to § 270.313 of this subpart. Should negotiations fail to result in the submission of such evidence, a subpoena may be issued pursuant to § 270.315.

[68 FR 4694, Jan. 30, 2003, as amended at 68 FR 24345, May 7, 2003]

§ 270.315 Subpoenas.

(a) *General.* Subpoenas requiring the attendance of witnesses or the production of documentary or physical evidence for the purpose of taking depositions or at a hearing may be issued only under the signature of the Director with the concurrence of the General Counsel, but may be served by any person designated by the Counsel for NIST on behalf of the Director.

(b) *Determination whether to issue a subpoena.* In determining whether to issue a subpoena, the Director will consider the following factors:

(1) Whether the testimony, documentary, or physical evidence is required for an investigation being conducted pursuant to the Act;

(2) Whether the evidence sought is relevant to the purpose of the investigation;

(3) Whether NIST already has the evidence in its possession; and

(4) Whether the evidence required is described with specificity.

(c) *Contents of a subpoena.* A subpoena issued by the Director will contain the following:

(1) A statement that the subpoena is issued by the Director pursuant to section 5 of the Act;

(2) A description of the documents or physical evidence or the subject matter of the testimony required by the subpoena;

(3) A command that each person to whom it is directed attend and give testimony or produce and permit inspection and copying of designated books, documents or physical evidence in the possession, custody or control of that person at a time and place specified in the subpoena;

(4) A statement that any person whose testimony is required by the subpoena may be accompanied by an attorney; and

(5) The signature of the Director.

(d) *Service of a subpoena.* Service of a subpoena will be effected:

(1) By personal service upon the person or agent of the person whose testimony is required or who is in charge of the documentary or physical evidence required; or

(2) By certified mail, return receipt requested, or delivery to the last known residence or business address of such person or agent; or

(3) Where personal service, mailing, or delivery has been unsuccessful, service may also be effected by publication in the FEDERAL REGISTER.

(e) *Witness fees.* Witnesses will be entitled to the same fees and mileage as are paid to witnesses in the courts of the United States.

(f) *Failure to obey a subpoena.* If a person disobeys a subpoena issued by the Director under the Act, the Attorney General, acting on behalf of the Director, may bring civil action in a district court of the United States to enforce the subpoena. The court may punish a failure to obey an order of the court to comply with the subpoena as a contempt of court.

[68 FR 4694, Jan. 30, 2003, as amended at 68 FR 24345, May 7, 2003; 68 FR 66707, Nov. 28, 2003]

§270.316 Public hearings.

(a) During the course of an investigation by a Team, if the Director considers it to be in the public interest, NIST may hold a public hearing for the purposes of gathering testimony from witnesses and informing the public on the progress of the investigation.

(b) Should NIST plan to hold a public hearing, NIST will publish a notice in the FEDERAL REGISTER, setting forth the date, time, and place of the hearing, and procedures for members of the public wishing to speak at the hearing. In addition, witnesses may be subpoenaed to provide testimony at a public hearing, in accordance with §270.315 of this subpart.

(c) The Director, or his designee, will preside over any public hearing held pursuant to this section.

ENTRY AND INSPECTION

§270.320 Entry and inspection of site where a building failure has occurred.

When the Director establishes and deploys a Team, the Team members will be issued notices of inspection authority to enter and inspect the site where the building failure has occurred.

§270.321 Entry and inspection of property where building components, materials, artifacts, and records with respect to a building failure are located.

(a) In the course of an investigation, entry and inspection of property where building components, materials, artifacts and records with respect to a building failure are located normally will be conducted following the procedures described in §§270.322 through 270.325 of this subpart.

(b) Upon a written showing by the Lead Investigator of urgent and compelling reasons to believe that building components, materials, artifacts or records located on a particular property may be destroyed were the procedures described in §§270.322 through 270.324 of this subpart followed, the Director, with the concurrence of the General Counsel may immediately issue a notice of inspection authority for such property, pursuant to §270.325 of this subpart.

§270.322 Voluntary permission to enter and inspect property where building components, materials, artifacts, and records with respect to a building failure are located.

After the Director establishes and deploys a Team, members of the public are encouraged to voluntarily permit Team members to enter property where building components, materials, artifacts, and records with respect to the building failure are located, and take action necessary, appropriate, and reasonable in light of the nature of the property to be inspected and to carry out the duties of the Team.

§ 270.323 Requests for permission to enter and inspect property where building components, materials, artifacts, and records with respect to a building failure are located.

(a) After the Director establishes and deploys a Team, the Lead Investigator or their designee may request permission to enter and inspect property where building components, materials, artifacts, and records with respect to a building failure are located, and take action necessary, appropriate, and reasonable in light of the nature of the property to be inspected and to carry out the duties of the Team.

(b) Requests for permission to enter and inspect such property will be made in writing and shall include:

(1) The name and title of the building owner, operator, or agent in charge of the building;

(2) If appropriate, the name of the building to be inspected;

(3) The address of the building to be inspected;

(4) The date and time of the inspection;

(5) If appropriate, a description of particular items to be inspected; and

(6) Contact information for the person to whom questions or problems regarding the request should be addressed.

§ 270.324 Negotiations.

The Lead Investigator may enter into discussions with appropriate parties to address problems identified with the goal of obtaining the permission requested pursuant to § 270.323 of this subpart.

§ 270.325 Notice of authority to enter and inspect property where building components, materials, artifacts, and records with respect to a building failure are located.

(a) *General.* In investigating a building failure pursuant to the Act, any member of a Team, or any other person authorized by the Director to support a Team, on display of written notice of inspection authority provided by the Director with concurrence of the General Counsel and appropriate credentials, may

(1) Enter property where a building failure being investigated has occurred, or where building components, materials, and artifacts with respect to the building failure are located, and take action necessary, appropriate, and reasonable in light of the nature of the property to be inspected and to carry out the duties of the Team;

(2) During reasonable hours, inspect any record (including any design, construction, or maintenance record), process, or facility related to the investigation;

(3) Inspect and test any building components, materials, and artifacts related to the building failure; and

(4) Move any record, component, material and artifact as provided by this part.

(b) *Conduct of inspection, test, or other action.* An inspection, test, or other action taken by a Team pursuant to section 4 of the Act will be conducted in a way that does not interfere unnecessarily with services provided by the owner or operator of the building components, materials, or artifacts, property, records, process, or facility, and to the maximum extent feasible, preserves evidence related to the building failure, consistent with the ongoing needs of the investigation.

(c) *Determination whether to issue a notice of inspection authority.* In determining whether to issue a notice of inspection authority, the Director will consider whether the specific entry and inspection is reasonable and necessary for the Team to carry out its duties under the Act.

(d) *Notice of inspection authority.* Notice of inspection authority will be made in writing and shall include:

(1) A statement that the notice of inspection authority is issued pursuant to section 4 of the Act;

(2) The name and title of the building owner, operator, or agent in charge of the building;

(3) If appropriate, the name of the building to be inspected;

(4) The address of the building to be inspected;

(5) The date and time of the inspection;

(6) If appropriate, a description of particular items to be inspected; and

(7) The signature of the Director.

(e) *Refusal of entry on to property.* If upon being presented with a notice of inspection by any member of a Team, or any other person authorized by the Director, the owner, operator, or agent in charge of the building or property being inspected refuses to allow entry or inspection, the Director may seek the assistance of the Department of Justice to obtain a warrant or other authorized judicial order enabling entry on to the property.

PRESERVATION OF EVIDENCE

§270.330 Moving and preserving evidence.

(a) A Team and NIST will take all necessary steps in moving and preserving evidence obtained during the course of an investigation under the Act to ensure that such evidence is preserved.

(b) In collecting and preserving evidence in the course of an investigation under the Act, a Team and NIST will:

(1) Maintain records to ensure that each piece of evidence is identified as to its source;

(2) Maintain and document an appropriate chain of custody for each piece of evidence;

(3) Use appropriate means to preserve each piece of evidence; and

(4) Ensure that each piece of evidence is kept in a suitably secure facility.

(c) If a Federal law enforcement agency suspects and notifies the Director that a building failure being investigated by a Team under the Act may have been caused by a criminal act, the Team, in consultation with the Federal law enforcement agency, will take necessary actions to ensure that evidence of the criminal act is preserved and that the original evidence or copies, as appropriate, are turned over to the appropriate law enforcement authorities.

INFORMATION CREATED PURSUANT TO AN INVESTIGATION

§270.340 Information created by investigation participants who are not NIST employees.

Unless requested sooner by the Lead Investigator, at the conclusion of an investigation, each investigation participant who is not a NIST employee shall transfer any original information they created pursuant to the investigation to NIST. An investigation participant may retain a copy of the information for their records but may not use the information for purposes other than the investigation, nor may they release, reproduce, distribute, or publish any information first developed pursuant to the investigation, nor authorize others to do so, without the written permission of the Director or their designee. Pursuant to 15 U.S.C. 281a, no such information may be admitted or used as evidence in any suit or action for damages arising out of any matter related to the investigation.

PROTECTION OF INFORMATION

§270.350 Freedom of Information Act.

As permitted by section 7(b) of the Act, the following information will not be released:

(a) Information described by section 552(b) of Title 5, United States Code, or protected from disclosure by any other law of the United States; and

(b) Copies of evidence collected, information created, or other investigation documents submitted or received by NIST, a Team, or any other investigation participant, until the final investigation report is issued.

§270.351 Protection of voluntarily submitted information.

Notwithstanding any other provision of law, a Team, NIST, any investigation participant, and any agency receiving information from a Team, NIST, or any other investigation participant, will not disclose voluntarily provided safety-related information if that information is not directly related to the building failure being investigated and the Director finds that the disclosure of the information would inhibit the voluntary provision of that type of information.

§270.352 Public safety information.

A Team, NIST, and any other investigation participant will not publicly release any information it receives in the course of an investigation under the Act if the Director finds that the disclosure might jeopardize public safety.

SUBCHAPTER H—MAKING OF TOY, LOOK-ALIKE, AND IMITATION FIREARMS

PART 272—MARKING OF TOY, LOOK-ALIKE AND IMITATION FIREARMS

AUTHORITY: Section 4 of the Federal Energy Management Improvement Act of 1988, 15 U.S.C. 5001.

SOURCE: 54 FR 19358, May 5, 1989, unless otherwise noted. Redesignated at 78 FR 4765, Jan. 23, 2013.

§ 272.1 Applicability.

This part applies to toy, look-alike, and imitation firearms ("devices") having the appearance, shape, and/or configuration of a firearm and produced or manufactured and entered into commerce on or after May 5, 1989, including devices modelled on real firearms manufactured, designed, and produced since 1898. This part does not apply to:

(a) Non-firing collector replica antique firearms, which look authentic and may be a scale model but are not intended as toys modelled on real firearms designed, manufactured, and produced prior to 1898;

(b) Traditional B–B, paint-ball, or pellet-firing air guns that expel a projectile through the force of compressed air, compressed gas or mechanical spring action, or any combination thereof, as described in American Society for Testing and Materials standard F 589–85, Standard Consumer Safety Specification for Non-Powder Guns, June 28, 1985. This incorporation by reference was approved by the Director of the Federal Register in accordance with 5 U.S.C. 552(a) and 1 CFR part 51. Copies may be obtained from the IHS Inc., 15 Inverness Way East, Englewood, CO 80112, *www.global.ihs.com*, Phone: 800.854.7179 or 303.397.7956, Fax: 303.397.2740, Email: *global@ihs.com*. A copy is available for inspection in the Office of the Chief Counsel for NIST, National Institute of Standards and Technology, Telephone: (301) 975–2803, or at the National Archives and Records Administration (NARA). For information on the availability of this material at NARA, call 202–741–6030, or go to: *http://www.archives.gov/federal_register/code_of_federal_regulations/ibr_locations.html*.

(c) Decorative, ornamental, and miniature objects having the appearance, shape and/or configuration of a firearm, including those intended to be displayed on a desk or worn on bracelets, necklaces, key chains, and so on, provided that the objects measure no more than thirty-eight (38) millimeters in height by seventy (70) millimeters in length, the length measurement excluding any gun stock length measurement.

[57 FR 48453, Oct. 26, 1992, as amended at 69 FR 18803, Apr. 9, 2004. Redesignated and amended at 78 FR 4765, Jan. 23, 2013]

§ 272.2 Prohibitions.

No person shall manufacture, enter into commerce, ship, transport, or receive any toy, look-alike, or imitation firearm ("device") covered by this part as set forth in § 272.1 unless such device contains, or has affixed to it, one of the markings set forth in § 272.3, or unless this prohibition has been waived by § 272.4.

[78 FR 4765, Jan. 23, 2013]

§ 272.3 Approved markings.

The following markings are approved by the Secretary of Commerce:

(a) A blaze orange (Fed-Std-595B 12199) or orange color brighter than that specified by the federal standard color number, solid plug permanently affixed to the muzzle end of the barrel as an integral part of the entire device and recessed no more than 6 millimeters from the muzzle end of the barrel.

(b) A blaze orange (Fed-Std-595B 12199) or orange color brighter than that specified by the Federal Standard color number, marking permanently affixed to the exterior surface of the barrel, covering the circumference of the barrel from the muzzle end for a depth of at least 6 millimeters.

(c) Construction of the device entirely of transparent or translucent materials which permits unmistakable observation of the device's complete contents.

(d) Coloration of the entire exterior surface of the device in white, bright red, bright orange, bright yellow, bright green, bright blue, bright pink, or bright purple, either singly or as the predominant color in combination with other colors in any pattern.

(e) This incorporation by reference was approved by the Director of the Federal Register in accordance with 5 U.S.C. 552(a) and 1 CFR part 51. Copies of Federal Standard 595B, December 1989, color number 12199 (Fed-Std-595B 12199), may be obtained from the General Services Administration at General Services Administration, Federal Acquisition Service, FAS Office of General Supplies and Services, Engineering and Cataloging Division (QSDEC) Arlington, VA 22202 or at the General Services Administration Web site at: *http://apps.fas.gsa.gov/pub/fedspecs/*. A copy may be inspected in the Office of the Chief Counsel for NIST, National Institute of Standards and Technology, Telephone: (301) 975–2803 or at the National Archives and Records Administration (NARA). For information on the availability of this material at NARA, call 202 741–6030, or go to: *http://www.archives.gov/federal_register/code_of_federal_regulations/ibr_locations.html.*

[54 FR 19358, May 5, 1989, as amended at 57 FR 48454, Oct. 26, 1992; 69 FR 18803, Apr. 9, 2004. Redesignated and amended at 78 FR 4765, Jan. 23, 2013]

§272.4 Waiver.

The prohibitions set forth in §272.2 may be waived for any toy, look-alike or imitation firearm that will be used only in the theatrical, movie or television industry. A request for such a waiver should be made, in writing, to the Chief Counsel for NIST, National Institute of Standards and Technology, 100 Bureau Drive, Mail Stop 1052, Gaithersburg, Maryland 20899–1052. The request must include a sworn affidavit which states that the toy, look-alike, or imitation firearm will be used only in the theatrical, movie or television industry. A sample of the item must be included with the request.

[78 FR 4765, Jan. 23, 2013]

§272.5 Preemption.

In accordance with section 4(g) of the Federal Energy Management Improvement Act of 1988 (15 U.S.C. 5001(g)), the provisions of section 4(a) of that Act and the provisions of this part supersede any provision of State or local laws or ordinances which provides for markings or identification inconsistent with the provisions of section 4 of that Act or the provisions of this part.

[54 FR 19358, May 5, 1989. Redesignated at 78 FR 4765, Jan. 23, 2013]

SUBCHAPTER I—METRIC CONVERSION POLICY FOR FEDERAL AGENCIES

PART 273—METRIC CONVERSION POLICY FOR FEDERAL AGENCIES

AUTHORITY: 15 U.S.C. 1512 and 3710, 15 U.S.C. 205a, DOO 30–2A.

SOURCE: 56 FR 160, Jan. 2, 1991, unless otherwise noted. Redesignated at 56 FR 41283, Aug. 20, 1991, and further redesignated at 78 FR 4766, Jan. 23, 2013.

§ 273.1 Purpose.

To provide policy direction for Federal agencies in their transition to use of the metric system of measurement.

§ 273.2 Definition.

Metric system means the International System of Units (SI) established by the General Conference of Weights and Measures in 1960, as interpreted or modified from time to time for the United States by the Secretary of Commerce under the authority of the Metric Conversion Act of 1975 and the Metric Education Act of 1978.

Other business-related activities means measurement sensitive commerical or business directed transactions or programs, *i.e.*, standard or specification development, publications, or agency statements of general applicability and future effect designed to implement, interpret, or prescribe law or policy or describing the procedure or practice requirements of an agency. "Measurement sensitive" means the choice of measurement unit is a critical component of the activity, *i.e.*, an agency rule/regulation to collect samples or measure something at specific distances or to specific depths, specifications requiring intake or discharge of a product to certain volumes or flow rates, guidelines for clearances between objects for safety, security or environmental purposes, etc.

§ 273.3 General policy.

The Omnibus Trade and Competitiveness Act of 1988 (Pub. L. 100–418, section 5164) amended the Metric Conversion Act of 1975 to, among other things, require that each Federal agency, by a date certain and to the extent economically feasible by the end of the fiscal year 1992, use the metric system of measurement in its procurements, grants, and other business-related activities, except to the extent that such use is impractical or is likely to cause significant inefficiencies or loss of markets to United States firms, such as when foreign competitors are producting competing products in non-metric units.

(a) The Director of the National Institute of Standards and Technology will assist in coordinating the efforts of Federal agencies in meeting their obligations under the Metric Conversion Act, as amended.

(b) Federal agencies shall coordinate and plan for the use of the metric system in their procurements, grants and other business-related activities consistent with the requirements of the Metric Conversion Act, as amended. Federal agencies shall encourage and support an environment which will facilitate the transition process. When taking initiatives, they shall give due consideration to known effects of their actions on State and local governments and the private sector, paying particular attention to effects on small business.

(c) Each Federal agency shall be responsible for developing plans, establishing necessary organizational structure, and allocating appropriate resources to carry out this policy.

[56 FR 160, Jan. 2, 1991. Redesignated at 56 FR 41283, Aug. 20, 1991, and further redesignated and amended at 78 FR 4766, Jan. 23, 2013]

§ 273.4 Guidelines.

Each agency shall:

(a) Establish plans and dates for use of the metric system in procurements, grants and other business-related activities;

(b) Coordinate metric transition plans with other Federal agencies, State and local governments and the private sector;

(c) Require maximum practical use of metric in areas where Federal procurement and activity represents a predominant influence on industry standards (e.g.: weapon systems or space exploration). Strongly encourage metrication in industry standards where Federal procurement and activity is not the predominant influence, consistent with the legal status of the metric system as *the preferred system of weights and measures for United States trade and commerce*;

(d) Assist in resolving metric-related problems brought to the attention of the agency that are associated with agency actions, activities or programs undertaken in compliance with these guidelines or other laws or regulations;

(e) Identify measurement-sensitive agency policies and procedures and ensure that regulations, standards, specifications, procurement policies and appropriate legislative proposals are updated to remove barriers to transition to the metric system;

(f) Consider cost effects of metric use in setting agency policies, programs and actions and determine criteria for the assessment of their economic feasibility. Such criteria should appropriately weigh both agency costs and national economic benefits related to changing to the use of metric;

(g) Provide for full public involvement and timely information about significant metrication policies, programs and actions;

(h) Seek out ways to increase understanding of the metric system of measurement through educational information and guidance and in agency publications;

(i) Consider, particularly, the effects of agency metric policies and practices on small business; and

(j) Consistent with the Federal Acquisition Regulation System (48 CFR), accept, without prejudice, products and services dimensioned in metric when they are offered at competitive prices and meet the needs of the Government, and ensure that acquisition planning considers metric requirements.

§ 273.5 Recommendations for agency organization.

Each agency shall:

(a) Participate, as appropriate, in the Interagency Council on Metric Policy (ICMP), and/or its working committee, the Metrication Operating Committee (MOC), in coordinating and providing policy guidance for the U.S. Government's transtion to use of the metric system.

(b) Designate a senior policy official to be responsible for agency metric policy and to represent the agency on the ICMP.

(c) Designate an appropriate official to represent the agency on the Metrication Operating Committee (MOC), an interagency committee reporting to the ICMP.

(d) Maintain liaison with private sector groups (such as the American National Metric Council and the U.S Metric Association) that are involved in planning for or coordinating National transition to the metric system.

(e) Provide for internal guidelines, training and documentation to assure employee awareness and understanding of agency metric policies and programs.

§ 273.6 Reporting requirement.

Each Federal agency shall, as part of its annual budget submission each fiscal year, report to the Congress on the metric implementation actions it has taken during the previous fiscal year. The report will include the agency's implementation plans, with a current timetable for the agency's transition to the metric system, as well as actions planned for the budget year involved to implement fully the metric system, in accordance with this policy. Reporting shall cease for an agency in the fiscal year after it has fully implemented metric usage, as prescribed by the Metric Conversion Act (15 U.S.C. 205b(2).)

§§ 273.7–273.199 [Reserved]

SUBCHAPTER J—ACCREDITATION AND ASSESSMENT PROGRAMS

PART 280—FASTENER QUALITY

Subpart A—General

AUTHORITY: 15 U.S.C. 5401 *et seq.;* Pub. L. 101–592, 104 Stat. 2943, as amended by Pub. L. 104–113, 110 Stat. 775; Pub. L. 105-234, 112 Stat. 1536; and Pub. L. 106–34, 113 Stat. 118.

SOURCE: 61 FR 50558, Sept. 26, 1996, unless otherwise noted.

Subpart A—General

§ 280.1 Description of rule/Delegation of authority.

(a) Description of rule. The Fastener Quality Act (the Act) (15 U.S.C. 5401 *et seq.*, as amended by Public Law 104–113, Public Law 105–234, and Public Law 106–34):

(1) Protects against the sale of mismarked, misrepresented, and counterfeit fasteners; and

(2) Eliminates unnecessary requirements.

(b) Delegations of authority. The Director, National Institute of Standards and Technology has authority to promulgate regulations in this part regarding certification and accreditation. The Secretary of Commerce has delegated concurrent authority to amend the regulations regarding enforcement of the Act, as contained in subpart C of this part, to the Under Secretary for Export Administration. The Secretary of Commerce has also delegated concurrent authority to amend the regulations regarding record of insignia, as contained in subpart D of this part, to the Under Secretary for Intellectual Property and Director of the United States Patent and Trademark Office.

[65 FR 39801, June 28, 2000]

§280.2 Definitions used in this subpart.

In addition to the definitions provided in 15 U.S.C. 5402, the following definitions are applicable to this part:

Abandonment of the Application. The application for registration of a trademark on the Principal Register is no longer pending at the United States Patent and Trademark Office.

Act. The Fastener Quality Act (15 U.S.C. 5401 *et seq.*, as amended by Pub. L. 104–113, Pub. L. 105–234, and Public Law 106–34).

Administrative law judge (ALJ). The person authorized to conduct hearings in administrative enforcement proceedings brought under the Act.

Assistant Secretary. The Assistant Secretary for Export Enforcement, Bureau of Export Administration.

Department. The United States Department of Commerce, specifically, the Bureau of Export Administration, NIST and the Patent and Trademark Office.

Director, NIST. The Director of the National Institute of Standards and Technology.

Director, USPTO. The Under Secretary for Intellectual Property and Director of the United States Patent and Trademark Office.

Fastener Insignia Register. The register of recorded fastener insignias maintained by the Director.

Final decision. A decision or order assessing a civil penalty or otherwise disposing of or dismissing a case, which is not subject to further review under this part, but which is subject to collection proceedings or judicial review in an appropriate Federal district court as authorized by law.

Initial decision. A decision of the administrative law judge which is subject to review by the Under Secretary for Export Administration, but which becomes the final decision of the Department in the absence of such an appeal.

Party. The Department and any person named as a respondent under this part.

Principal Register. The register of trademarks established under 15 U.S.C. 1051.

Respondent. Any person named as the subject of a charging letter, proposed charging letter, or other order proposed or issued under this part.

Revisions includes changes made to existing ISO/IEC Guides or other documents, and redesignations of those Guides or documents.

Under Secretary. The Under Secretary for Export Administration, United States Department of Commerce.

[61 FR 50558, Sept. 26, 1996. Redesignated and amended at 65 FR 39801, June 28, 2000]

Subpart B—Petitions, Affirmations, and Laboratory Accreditation

SOURCE: 65 FR 39801, June 28, 2000, unless otherwise noted.

§280.101 Petitions for approval of documents.

(a) *Certification.* (1) A person publishing a document setting forth guidance or requirements for the certification of manufacturing systems as fastener quality assurance systems by an accredited third party may petition the Director, NIST, to approve such document for use as described in section 3(7)(B)(iii)(I) of the Act (15 U.S.C. 5402(7)(B)(iii)(I)).

(2) Petitions should be submitted to: FQA Document Certification, NIST, 100 Bureau Drive, Gaithersburg, MD 20899.

(3) The Director, NIST, shall approve such petition if the document provides equal or greater rigor and reliability as compared to ISO/IEC Guide 62, including revisions from time to time. A petition shall contain sufficient information to allow the Director, NIST, to make this determination.

(b) *Accreditation.* (1) A person publishing a document setting forth guidance or requirements for the approval of accreditation bodies to accredit third parties described in paragraph (a) of this section may petition the Director, NIST, to approve such document for use as described in section 3(7)(B)(iii)(I) of the Act (15 U.S.C. 5402(7)(B)(iii)(I)).

(2) Petitions should be submitted to: FQA Document Certifications, NIST, 100 Bureau Drive, Gaithersburg, MD 20899.

(3) The Director, NIST, shall approve such petition if the document provides equal or greater rigor and reliability as

compared to ISO/IEC Guide 61, including revisions from time to time. A petition shall contain sufficient information to allow the Director, NIST, to make this determination.

(c) *Laboratory accreditation.* (1) A person publishing a document setting forth guidance or requirements for the accreditation of laboratories may petition the Director, NIST, to approve such document for use as described in section 3(1)(A) of the Act (15 U.S.C. 5402(1)(A)).

(2) Petitions should be submitted to: FQA Document Certifications, NIST, 100 Bureau Drive, Gaithersburg, MD 20899.

(3) The Director, NIST, shall approve such petition if the document provides equal or greater rigor and reliability as compared to ISO/IEC Guide 25, including revisions from time to time. A petition shall contain sufficient information to allow the Director, NIST, to make this determination.

(d) *Approval of accreditation bodies.* (1) A person publishing a document setting forth guidance or requirements for the approval of accreditation bodies to accredit laboratories may petition the Director, NIST, to approve such document for use as described in section 3(1)(B) of the Act (15 U.S.C. 5402(1)(B)).

(2) Petitions should be submitted to: FQA Document Certifications, NIST, 100 Bureau Drive, Gaithersburg, MD 20899.

(3) The Director, NIST, shall approve such petition if the document provides equal or greater rigor and reliability as compared to ISO/IEC Guide 58, including revisions from time to time. A petition shall contain sufficient information to allow the Director, NIST, to make this determination.

(e) Electronic copies of ISO/IEC Guides may be purchased through the American National Standards Institute (ANSI), Internet: *http://www.ansi.org*. Copies of the relevant ISO/IEC Guides are available for inspection in the U.S. Department of Commerce Reading Room, 14th Street and Constitution Avenue, NW, Washington, DC 20230, Room B–399.

§ 280.102 Affirmations.

(a)(1) An accreditation body accrediting third parties who certify manufacturing systems as fastener quality assurance systems as described in section 3(7)(B)(iii)(I) of the Act (15 U.S.C. 5402(7)(B)(iii)(I)) shall affirm to the Director, NIST, that it meets the requirements of ISO/IEC Guide 61 (or another document approved by the Director, NIST, under section 10(b) of the Act (15 U.S.C. 5411a(b)) and § 280.101(a) of this part), including revisions from time to time.

(2) An accreditation body accrediting laboratories as described in section 3(1)(B) of the Act (15 U.S.C. 5402(1)(B)) shall affirm to the Director, NIST, that it meets the requirements of ISO/IEC Guide 58 (or another document approved by the Director, NIST, under section 10(d) of the Act (15 U.S.C. 5411a(d)) and § 280.101(d) of this part), including revisions from time to time.

(b) An affirmation required under paragraph (a)(1) or (a)(2) of this section shall take the form of a self-declaration that the accreditation body meets the requirements of the applicable Guide, signed by an authorized representative of the accreditation body. No supporting documentation is required.

(c) Affirmations should be submitted to: FQA Document Certifications, NIST, 100 Bureau Drive, Gaithersburg, MD 20899.

(d) Any affirmation submitted in accordance with this section shall be considered to be a continuous affirmation that the accreditation body meets the requirements of the applicable Guide, unless and until the affirmation is withdrawn by the accreditation body.

§ 280.103 Laboratory accreditation.

A laboratory may be accredited by any laboratory accreditation program that may be established by any entity or entities, which have affirmed to the Director, NIST, under § 280.102 of this subpart, or by the National Voluntary Laboratory Accreditation Program for fasteners, established by the Director, NIST, under part 285 of this chapter.

Subpart C—Enforcement

SOURCE: 61 FR 50558, Sept. 26, 1996, unless otherwise noted. Redesignated at 65 FR 39802, June 28, 2000.

§280.200 Scope.

Section 280.201 of this part specifies that failure to take any action required by or taking any action prohibited by this part constitutes a violation of this part. Section 280.202 describes the penalties that may be imposed for violations of this part. Sections 280.204 through 280.222 establish the procedures for imposing administrative penalties for violations of this part.

[65 FR 39802, June 28, 2000]

§280.201 Violations.

(a) *Engaging in prohibited conduct.* No person may engage in any conduct prohibited by or contrary to, or refrain from engaging in any action required by the Act, this part, or any order issued thereunder.

(b) *Sale of fasteners.* It shall be unlawful for a manufacturer or distributor, in conjunction with the sale or offer for sale of fasteners from a single lot, to knowingly misrepresent or falsify—

(1) The record of conformance for the lot of fasteners;

(2) The identification, characteristics, properties, mechanical or performance marks, chemistry, or strength of the lot of fasteners; or

(3) The manufacturers' insignia.

(c) Manufacturers' insignia. Unless the specifications provide otherwise, fasteners that are required by the applicable consensus standard or standards to bear an insignia identifying their manufacturer shall not be offered for sale or sold in commerce unless

(1) The fasteners bear such insignia; and

(2) The manufacturer has complied with the insignia recordation requirements established under 15 U.S.C. 5407(b).

[61 FR 50558, Sept. 26, 1996, as amended at 63 FR 18275, Apr. 14, 1998; 63 FR 34965, June 26, 1998; 63 FR 51526, Sept. 28, 1998. Redesignated and amended at 65 FR 39802, June 28, 2000]

§280.202 Penalties, remedies, and sanctions.

(a) *Civil remedies.* The Attorney General may bring an action in an appropriate United States district court for declaratory and injunctive relief against any person who violates the Act or any regulation issued thereunder. Such action may not be brought more than 10 years after the cause of action accrues.

(b) *Civil penalties.* Any person who is determined, after notice and opportunity for a hearing, to have violated the Act or any regulation issued thereunder shall be liable to the United States for a civil penalty of not more than $25,000 for each violation.

(c) *Criminal penalties.* (1) Whoever knowingly certifies, marks, offers for sale, or sells a fastener in violation of the Act or a regulation issued thereunder shall be fined under title 18, United States Code, or imprisoned not more than 5 years, or both.

(2) Whoever intentionally fails to maintain records relating to a fastener in violation of the Act or a regulation issued thereunder shall be fined under title 18, United States Code, or imprisoned not more than five years or both.

(3) Whoever negligently fails to maintain records relating to a fastener in violation of the Act or a regulation issued thereunder shall be fined under title 18, United States Code, or imprisoned not more than two years or both.

§280.203 Administrative enforcement proceedings.

Sections 280.204 through 280.222 set forth the procedures for imposing administrative penalties for violations of the Act and this part.

[65 FR 39802, June 28, 2000]

§280.204 Institution of administrative enforcement proceedings.

(a) *Charging letters.* The Director of the Office of Export Enforcement (OEE) may begin administrative enforcement proceedings under this part by issuing a charging letter. The charging letter shall constitute the formal complaint and will state that there is reason to believe that a violation of this part has occurred. It will set forth the essential facts about each alleged violation, refer to the specific regulatory or other provisions involved, and give notice of the sanctions available under the Act and this part. The charging letter will inform the respondent that failure to answer the charges as provided in §280.207 of this part will be treated as a default under

§ 280.208 of this part, that the respondent is entitled to a hearing if a written demand for one is requested with the answer, and that the respondent may be represented by counsel, or by other authorized representative. A copy of the charging letter shall be filed with the administrative law judge, which filing shall toll the running of the applicable statute of limitations. Charging letters may be amended or supplemented at any time before an answer is filed, or, with permission of the administrative law judge, afterwards. The Department may unilaterally withdraw charging letters at any time, by notifying the respondent and the administrative law judge.

(b) *Notice of issuance of charging letter instituting administrative enforcement proceeding.* A respondent shall be notified of the issuance of a charging letter, or any amendment or supplement thereto:

(1) By mailing a copy by registered or certified mail addressed to the respondent at the respondent's last known address;

(2) By leaving a copy with the respondent or with an officer, a managing or general agent, or any other agent authorized by appointment or by law to receive service of process for the respondent; or

(3) By leaving a copy with a person of suitable age and discretion who resides at the respondent's last known dwelling.

(4) Delivery of a copy of the charging letter, if made in the manner described in paragraph (b)(2) or (3) of this section, shall be evidenced by a certificate of service signed by the person making such service, stating the method of service and the identity of the person with whom the charging letter was left. The certificate of service shall be filed with the administrative law judge.

(c) *Date.* The date of service of notice of the issuance of a charging letter instituting an administrative enforcement proceeding, or service of notice of the issuance of a supplement or amendment to a charging letter, is the date of its delivery, or of its attempted delivery if delivery is refused.

[61 FR 50558, Sept. 26, 1996. Redesignated and amended at 65 FR 39802, June 28, 2000]

§ 280.205 Representation.

A respondent individual may appear and participate in person, a corporation by a duly authorized officer or employee, and a partnership by a partner. If a respondent is represented by counsel, counsel shall be a member in good standing of the bar of any State, Commonwealth or Territory of the United States, or of the District of Columbia, or be licensed to practice law in the country in which counsel resides if not the United States. A respondent personally, or through counsel or other representative who has the power of attorney to represent the respondent, shall file a notice of appearance with the administrative law judge. The Department will be represented by the Office of Chief Counsel for Export Administration, U.S. Department of Commerce.

§ 280.206 Filing and service of papers other than charging letter.

(a) *Filing.* All papers to be filed shall be addressed to "FQA Administrative Enforcement Proceedings," at the address set forth in the charging letter, or such other place as the administrative law judge may designate. Filing by United States mail, first class postage prepaid, by express or equivalent parcel delivery service, or by hand delivery, is acceptable. Filing by mail from a foreign country shall be by airmail. In addition, the administrative law judge may authorize filing of papers by facsimile or other electronic means, provided that a hard copy of any such paper is subsequently filed. A copy of each paper filed shall be simultaneously served on each party.

(b) *Service.* Service shall be made by personal delivery or by mailing one copy of each paper to each party in the proceeding. Service by delivery service or facsimile, in the manner set forth in paragraph (a) of this section, is acceptable. Service on the Department shall be addressed to the Chief Counsel for Export Administration, Room H–3839, U.S. Department of Commerce, 14th Street and Constitution Avenue, NW., Washington, DC 20230. Service on a respondent shall be to the address to which the charging letter was sent or to such other address as respondent may provide. When a party has appeared by counsel or other representative, service on counsel or other representative shall constitute service on that party.

(c) *Date.* The date of filing or service is the day when the papers are deposited in the mail or are delivered in person, by delivery service, or by facsimile.

(d) *Certificate of service.* A certificate of service signed by the party making service, stating the date and manner of service, shall accompany every paper, other than the charging letter, filed and served on parties.

(e) *Computing period of time.* In computing any period of time prescribed or allowed by this part or by order of the administrative law judge or the Under Secretary, the day of the act, event, or default from which the designated period of time begins to run is not to be included. The last day of the period so computed is to be included unless it is a Saturday, a Sunday, or a legal holiday (as defined in Rule 6(a) of the Federal Rules of Civil Procedure), in which case the period runs until the end of the next day which is neither a Saturday, a Sunday, nor a legal holiday. Intermediate Saturdays, Sundays, and legal holidays are excluded from the computation when the period of time prescribed or allowed is seven days or less.

§280.207 Answer and demand for hearing.

(a) *When to answer.* The respondent must answer the charging letter within 30 days after being served with notice of the issuance of a charging letter instituting an administrative enforcement proceeding, or within 30 days of notice of any supplement or amendment to a charging letter, unless time is extended under §280.217 of this part.

(b) *Contents of answer.* The answer must be responsive to the charging letter and must fully set forth the nature of the respondent's defense or defenses. The answer must admit or deny specifically each separate allegation of the charging letter; if the respondent is without knowledge, the answer must so state and will operate as a denial. Failure to deny or controvert a particular allegation will be deemed an admission of that allegation. The answer must also set forth any additional or new matter the respondent believes supports a defense or claim of mitigation. Any defense or partial defense not specifically set forth in the answer shall be deemed waived, and evidence thereon may be refused, except for good cause shown.

(c) *Demand for hearing.* If the respondent desires a hearing, a written demand for one must be submitted with the answer. Any demand by the Department for a hearing must be filed with the administrative law judge within 30 days after service of the answer. Failure to make a timely written demand for a hearing shall be deemed a waiver of the party's right to a hearing, except for good cause shown. If no party demands a hearing, the matter will go forward in accordance with the procedures set forth in §280.216 of this part.

(d) *English language required.* The answer, all other papers, and all documentary evidence must be submitted in English, or translations into English must be filed and served at the same time.

[61 FR 50558, Sept. 26, 1996. Redesignated and amended at 65 FR 39802, June 28, 2000]

§280.208 Default.

(a) *General.* Failure of the respondent to file an answer within the time provided constitutes a waiver of the respondent's right to appear and contest the allegations in the charging letter. In such event, the administrative law judge, on the Department's motion and without further notice to the respondent, shall find the facts to be as alleged in the charging letter and render an initial decision containing findings of fact and appropriate conclusions of law and issue an initial decision and order imposing appropriate sanctions. The decision and order may be appealed to the Under Secretary in accordance with the applicable procedures set forth in §280.222 of this part.

(b) *Petition to set aside default*—(1) *Procedure.* Upon petition filed by a respondent against whom a default order has been issued, which petition is accompanied by an answer meeting the requirements of 280.207(b) of this part, the Under Secretary may, after giving all parties an opportunity to comment, and for good cause shown, set aside the default and vacate the order entered thereon and remand the matter to the administrative law judge for further proceedings.

(2) *Time limits.* A petition under this section must be made within one year of the date of entry of the order which the petition seeks to have vacated.

[61 FR 50558, Sept. 26, 1996. Redesignated and amended at 65 FR 39802, 39803, June 28, 2000]

§ 280.209 Summary decision.

At any time after a proceeding has been initiated, a party may move for a summary decision disposing of some or all of the issues. The administrative law judge may render an initial decision and issue an order if the entire record shows, as to the issue(s) under consideration:

(a) That there is no genuine issue as to any material fact; and

(b) That the moving party is entitled to a summary decision as a matter of law.

§ 280.210 Discovery.

(a) *General.* The parties are encouraged to engage in voluntary discovery regarding any matter, not privileged, which is relevant to the subject matter of the pending proceeding. The provisions of the Federal Rules of Civil Procedure relating to discovery apply to the extent consistent with this part and except as otherwise provided by the administrative law judge or by waiver or agreement of the parties. The administrative law judge may make any order which justice requires to protect a party or person from annoyance, embarrassment, oppression, or undue burden or expense. These orders may include limitations on the scope, method, time and place of discovery, and provisions for protecting the confidentiality of classified or otherwise sensitive information.

(b) *Interrogatories and requests for admission or production of documents.* A party may serve on any party interrogatories, requests for admission, or requests for production of documents for inspection and copying, and a party concerned may apply to the administrative law judge for such enforcement or protective order as that party deems warranted with respect to such discovery. The service of a discovery request shall be made at least 20 days before the scheduled date of the hearing unless the administrative law judge specifies a shorter time period. Copies of interrogatories, requests for admission and requests for production of documents and responses thereto shall be served on all parties, and a copy of the certificate of service shall be filed with the administrative law judge. Matters of fact or law of which admission is requested shall be deemed admitted unless, within a period designated in the request (at least 10 days after service, or within such additional time as the administrative law judge may allow), the party to whom the request is directed serves upon the requesting party a sworn statement either denying specifically the matters of which admission is requested or setting forth in detail the reasons why the party to whom the request is directed cannot truthfully either admit or deny such matters.

(c) *Depositions.* Upon application of a party and for good cause shown, the administrative law judge may order the taking of the testimony of any person by deposition and the production of specified documents or materials by the person at the deposition. The application shall state the purpose of the deposition and set forth the facts sought to be established through the deposition.

(d) *Enforcement.* The administrative law judge may order a party to answer designated questions, to produce specified documents or things or to take any other action in response to a proper discovery request. If a party does not comply with such an order, the administrative law judge may make a determination or enter any order in the proceeding as the ALJ deems reasonable and appropriate. The ALJ may strike related charges or defenses in whole or in part or may take particular facts relating to the discovery request to which the party failed or refused to respond as being established for purposes of the proceeding in accordance with the contentions of the party seeking discovery. In addition, enforcement by a district court of the United States may be sought under 15 U.S.C. 5408(b)(6).

[61 FR 50558, Sept. 26, 1996. Redesignated and amended at 65 FR 39802, June 28, 2000]

§280.211 Subpoenas.

(a) *Issuance.* Upon the application of any party, supported by a satisfactory showing that there is substantial reason to believe that the evidence would not otherwise be available, the administrative law judge may issue subpoenas requiring the attendance and testimony of witnesses and the production of such books, records or other documentary or physical evidence for the purpose of the hearing, as the ALJ deems relevant and material to the proceedings, and reasonable in scope. Witnesses summoned shall be paid the same fees and mileage that are paid to witnesses in the courts of the United States. In case of contempt or refusal to obey a subpoena served upon any person pursuant to this paragraph, the district court of the United States for any district in which such person is found, resides, or transacts business, upon application by the United States and after notice to such person, shall have jurisdiction to issue an order requiring such person to appear and give testimony before the administrative law judge or to appear and produce documents before the administrative law judge, or both, and any failure to obey such order of the court may be punished by such court as contempt thereof.

(b) *Service.* Subpoenas issued by the administrative law judge may be served in any of the methods set forth in §280.206(b) of this part.

(c) *Timing.* Applications for subpoenas must be submitted at least 10 days before the scheduled hearing or deposition, unless the administrative law judge determines, for good cause shown, that extraordinary circumstances warrant a shorter time.

[61 FR 50558, Sept. 26, 1996. Redesignated and amended at 65 FR 39802, June 28, 2000]

§280.212 Matter protected against disclosure.

(a) *Protective measures.* The administrative law judge may limit discovery or introduction of evidence or issue such protective or other orders as in the ALJ's judgment may be needed to prevent undue disclosure of classified or sensitive documents or information. Where the administrative law judge determines that documents containing the classified or sensitive matter need to be made available to a party to avoid prejudice, the ALJ may direct that an unclassified and/or nonsensitive summary or extract of the documents be prepared. The administrative law judge may compare the extract or summary with the original to ensure that it is supported by the source document and that it omits only so much as must remain undisclosed. The summary or extract may be admitted as evidence in the record.

(b) *Arrangements for access.* If the administrative law judge determines that this procedure is unsatisfactory and that classified or otherwise sensitive matter must form part of the record in order to avoid prejudice to a party, the administrative law judge may provide the parties an opportunity to make arrangements that permit a party or a representative to have access to such matter without compromising sensitive information. Such arrangements may include obtaining security clearances or giving counsel for a party access to sensitive information and documents subject to assurances against further disclosure, including a protective order, if necessary.

§280.213 Prehearing conference.

(a) The administrative law judge, on his or her own motion or on request of a party, may direct the parties to participate in a prehearing conference, either in person or by telephone, to consider:

(1) Simplification of issues;

(2) The necessity or desirability of amendments to pleadings;

(3) Obtaining stipulations of fact and of documents to avoid unnecessary proof; or

(4) Such other matters as may expedite the disposition of the proceedings.

(b) The administrative law judge may order the conference proceedings to be recorded electronically or taken by a reporter, transcribed and filed with the ALJ.

(c) If a prehearing conference is impracticable, the administrative law judge may direct the parties to correspond with the ALJ to achieve the purposes of such a conference.

(d) The administrative law judge will prepare a summary of any actions agreed on or taken pursuant to this section. The summary will include any written stipulations or agreements made by the parties.

§ 280.214 Hearings.

(a) *Scheduling.* The administrative law judge, by agreement with the parties or upon notice to all parties of not less than 30 days, will schedule a hearing. All hearings will be held in Washington, DC., unless the administrative law judge determines, for good cause shown, that another location would better serve the interests of justice.

(b) *Hearing procedure.* Hearings will be conducted in a fair and impartial manner by the administrative law judge, who may limit attendance at any hearing or portion thereof to the parties, their representatives and witnesses if the administrative law judge deems this necessary or advisable in order to protect sensitive matter (see § 280.212 of this part) from improper disclosure. The rules of evidence prevailing in courts of law do not apply, and all evidentiary material deemed by the administrative law judge to be relevant and material to the proceeding and not unduly repetitious will be received and given appropriate weight.

(c) *Testimony and record.* Witnesses will testify under oath or affirmation. A verbatim record of the hearing and of any other oral proceedings will be taken by reporter or by electronic recording, transcribed and filed with the administrative law judge. A respondent may examine the transcript and may obtain a copy by paying any applicable costs. Upon such terms as the administrative law judge deems just, the ALJ may direct that the testimony of any person be taken by deposition and may admit an affidavit or declaration as evidence, provided that any affidavits or declarations have been filed and served on the parties sufficiently in advance of the hearing to permit a party to file and serve an objection thereto on the grounds that it is necessary that the affiant or declarant testify at the hearing and be subject to cross-examination.

(d) *Failure to appear.* If a party fails to appear in person or by counsel at a scheduled hearing, the hearing may nevertheless proceed, and that party's failure to appear will not affect the validity of the hearing or any proceedings or action taken thereafter.

[61 FR 50558, Sept. 26, 1996. Redesignated and amended at 65 FR 39802, June 28, 2000]

§ 280.215 Interlocutory review of rulings.

(a) At the request of a party, or on the administrative law judge's own initiative, the administrative law judge may certify to the Under Secretary for review a ruling that does not finally dispose of a proceeding, if the administrative law judge determines that immediate review may hasten or facilitate the final disposition of the matter.

(b) Upon certification to the Under Secretary of the interlocutory ruling for review, the parties will have 10 days to file and serve briefs stating their positions, and five days to file and serve replies, following which the Under Secretary will decide the matter promptly.

§ 280.216 Proceeding without a hearing.

If the parties have waived a hearing, the case will be decided on the record by the administrative law judge. Proceeding without a hearing does not relieve the parties from the necessity of proving the facts supporting their charges or defenses. Affidavits or declarations, depositions, admissions, answers to interrogatories and stipulations may supplement other documentary evidence in the record. The administrative law judge will give each party reasonable opportunity to file rebuttal evidence.

§ 280.217 Procedural stipulations; extension of time.

(a) *Procedural stipulations.* Unless otherwise ordered, a written stipulation agreed to by all parties and filed with the administrative law judge will modify any procedures established by this part.

(b) *Extension of time.* (1) The parties may extend any applicable time limitation, by stipulation filed with the administrative law judge before the time limitation expires.

(2) The administrative law judge may, on the judge's own initiative or upon application by any party, either before or after the expiration of any applicable time limitation, extend the time within which to file and serve an answer to a charging letter or do any other act required by this part.

§ 280.218 Decision of the administrative law judge.

(a) *Predecisional matters.* Except for default proceedings under § 280.208 of this part, the administrative law judge will give the parties reasonable opportunity to submit the following, which will be made a part of the record:

(1) Exceptions to any ruling by the judge or to the admissibility of evidence proffered at the hearing;

(2) Proposed findings of fact and conclusions of law;

(3) Supporting legal arguments for the exceptions and proposed findings and conclusions submitted; and

(4) A proposed order.

(b) *Decision and order.* After considering the entire record in the proceeding, the administrative law judge will issue a written initial decision. The decision will include findings of fact, conclusions of law, and findings as to whether there has been a violation of the Act, this part, or any order issued thereunder. If the administrative law judge finds that the evidence of record is insufficient to sustain a finding that a violation has occurred with respect to one or more charges, the ALJ shall order dismissal of the charges in whole or in part, as appropriate. If the administrative law judge finds that one or more violations have been committed, the ALJ may issue an order imposing administrative sanctions, as provided in this part. The decision and order shall be served on each party, and shall become effective as the final decision of the Department 30 days after service, unless an appeal is filed in accordance with § 280.222 of this part. In determining the amount of any civil penalty the ALJ shall consider the nature, circumstances and gravity of the violation and, with respect to the person found to have committed the violation, the degree of culpability, any history of prior violations, the effect on ability to continue to do business, any good faith attempt to achieve compliance, ability to pay the penalty, and such other matters as justice may require.

(c) *Suspension of sanctions.* Any order imposing administrative sanctions may provide for the suspension of the sanction imposed, in whole or in part and on such terms of probation or other conditions as the administrative law judge or the Under Secretary may specify. Any suspension order may be modified or revoked by the signing official upon application by the Department showing a violation of the probationary terms or other conditions, after service on the respondent of notice of the application in accordance with the service provisions of § 280.206 of this part, and with such opportunity for response as the responsible signing official in his/her discretion may allow. A copy of any order modifying or revoking the suspension shall also be served on the respondent in accordance with the provisions of § 280.607 of this part.

[61 FR 50558, Sept. 26, 1996. Redesignated and amended at 65 FR 39802, 39803, June 28, 2000]

§ 280.219 Settlement.

(a) *Cases may be settled before service of a charging letter.* In cases in which settlement is reached before service of a charging letter, a proposed charging letter will be prepared, and a settlement proposal consisting of a settlement agreement and order will be submitted to the Assistant Secretary for approval and signature. If the Assistant Secretary does not approve the proposal, he/she will notify the parties and the case will proceed as though no settlement proposal had been made. If the Assistant Secretary approves the proposal, he/she will issue an appropriate order, and no action will be required by the administrative law judge.

(b) *Cases may also be settled after service of a charging letter.* (1) If the case is pending before the administrative law judge, the ALJ shall stay the proceedings for a reasonable period of time, usually not to exceed 30 days, upon notification by the parties that they have entered into good faith settlement negotiations. The administrative law judge may, in his/her discretion, grant additional stays. If settlement is reached, a proposal will be submitted to the Assistant Secretary for approval and signature. If the Assistant Secretary approves the proposal, he/she will issue an appropriate order, and notify the administrative law judge that the case is withdrawn from adjudication. If the Assistant Secretary does not approve the proposal, he/she will notify the parties and the case will proceed to adjudication by the administrative law judge as though no settlement proposal had been made.

(2) If the case is pending before the Under Secretary under § 280.222 of this part, the parties may submit a settlement proposal to the Under Secretary for approval and signature. If the Under Secretary approves the proposal, he/she will issue an appropriate order. If the Under Secretary does not approve the proposal, the case will proceed to final decision in accordance with Section 280.623 of this part, as appropriate.

(c) Any order disposing of a case by settlement may suspend the administrative sanction imposed, in whole or in part, on such terms of probation or other conditions as the signing official may specify. Any such suspension may be modified or revoked by the signing official, in accordance with the procedures set forth in § 280.218(c) of this part.

(d) Any respondent who agrees to an order imposing any administrative sanction does so solely for the purpose of resolving the claims in the administrative enforcement proceeding brought under this part. This reflects the fact that the Department has neither the authority nor the responsibility for instituting, conducting, settling, or otherwise disposing of criminal proceedings. That authority and responsibility is vested in the Attorney General and the Department of Justice.

(e) Cases that are settled may not be reopened or appealed.

[61 FR 50558, Sept. 26, 1996. Redesignated and amended at 65 FR 39802, 39803, June 28, 2000]

§ 280.220 Reopening.

The respondent may petition the administrative law judge within one year of the date of the final decision, except where the decision arises from a default judgment or from a settlement, to reopen an administrative enforcement proceeding to receive any relevant and material evidence which was unknown or unobtainable at the time the proceeding was held. The petition must include a summary of such evidence, the reasons why it is deemed relevant and material, and the reasons why it could not have been presented at the time the proceedings were held. The administrative law judge will grant or deny the petition after providing other parties reasonable opportunity to comment. If the proceeding is reopened, the administrative law judge may make such arrangements as the ALJ deems appropriate for receiving the new evidence and completing the record. The administrative law judge will then issue a new initial decision and order, and the case will proceed to final decision and order in accordance with § 280.222 of this part.

[61 FR 50558, Sept. 26, 1996. Redesignated and amended at 65 FR 39802, 39803, June 28, 2000]

§ 280.221 Record for decision and availability of documents.

(a) *General.* The transcript of hearings, exhibits, rulings, orders, all papers and requests filed in the proceedings and, for purposes of any appeal under § 280.222 of this part, the decision of the administrative law judge and such submissions as are provided for by § 280.623 of this part, will constitute the record and the exclusive basis for decision. When a case is settled after the service of a charging letter, the record will consist of any and all of the foregoing, as well as the settlement agreement and the order. When a case is settled before service of a charging letter, the record will consist of the proposed charging letter, the settlement agreement and the order.

(b) *Restricted access.* On the administrative law judge's own motion, or on the motion of any party, the administrative law judge may direct that there be a restricted access portion of the record for any material in the record to which public access is restricted by law or by the terms of a protective order entered in the proceedings. A party seeking to restrict access to any portion of the record is responsible for submitting, at the time specified in paragraph (c)(2) of this section, a version of the document proposed for public availability that reflects the requested deletion. The restricted access portion of the record will be placed in a separate file and the file will be clearly marked to avoid improper disclosure and to identify it as a portion of the official record in the proceedings. The administrative law judge may act at any time to permit material that becomes declassified or unrestricted through passage of time to be transferred to the unrestricted access portion of the record.

(c) *Availability of documents*—(1) *Scope*. All charging letters, answers, initial decisions, and orders disposing of a case will be made available for public inspection in the BXA Freedom of Information Records Inspection Facility, U.S. Department of Commerce, Room H–6624, 14th Street and Pennsylvania Avenue, NW, Washington, DC 20230. The complete record for decision, as defined in paragraphs (a) and (b) of this section will be made available on request.

(2) *Timing*. Documents are available immediately upon filing, except for any portion of the record for which a request for segregation is made. Parties that seek to restrict access to any portion of the record under paragraph (b) of this section must make such a request, together with the reasons supporting the claim of confidentiality, simultaneously with the submission of material for the record.

[61 FR 50558, Sept. 26, 1996. Redesignated and amended at 65 FR 39802, 39803, June 28, 2000]

§280.222 Appeals.

(a) *Grounds*. A party may appeal to the Under Secretary from an order disposing of a proceeding or an order denying a petition to set aside a default or a petition for reopening, on the grounds:

(1) That a necessary finding of fact is omitted, erroneous or unsupported by substantial evidence of record;

(2) That a necessary legal conclusion or finding is contrary to law;

(3) That prejudicial procedural error occurred; or

(4) That the decision or the extent of sanctions is arbitrary, capricious or an abuse of discretion. The appeal must specify the grounds on which the appeal is based and the provisions of the order from which the appeal is taken.

(b) *Filing of appeal*. An appeal from an order must be filed with the Office of the Under Secretary for Export Administration, Bureau of Export Administration, U.S. Department of Commerce, Room H–3898, 14th Street and Constitution Avenue, NW., Washington, DC 20230, within 30 days after service of the order appealed from. If the Under Secretary cannot act on an appeal for any reason, the Under Secretary will designate another Department of Commerce official to receive and act on the appeal.

(c) *Effect of appeal*. The filing of an appeal shall not stay the operation of any order, unless the order by its express terms so provides or unless the Under Secretary, upon application by a party and with opportunity for response, grants a stay.

(d) *Appeal procedure*. The Under Secretary normally will not hold hearings or entertain oral argument on appeals. A full written statement in support of the appeal must be filed with the appeal and be simultaneously served on all parties, who shall have 30 days from service to file a reply. At his/her discretion, the Under Secretary may accept new submissions, but will not ordinarily accept those submissions filed more than 30 days after the filing of the reply to the appellant's first submission.

(e) *Decisions*. The decision will be in writing and will be accompanied by an order signed by the Under Secretary giving effect to the decision. The order may either dispose of the case by affirming, modifying or reversing the order of the administrative law judge or may refer the case back to the administrative law judge for further proceedings.

(f) *Delivery*. The final decision and implementing order shall be served on the parties and will be publicly available in accordance with § 280.221 of this part.

(g) *Judicial review.* The charged party may appeal the Under Secretary's written order within 30 days to the appropriate United States District Court pursuant to section 9(b)(3) of the Act (15 U.S.C. 5408(b)(3)) by filing a notice of appeal in such court within 30 days from the date of such order and by simultaneously sending a copy of such notice by certified mail to the Chief Counsel for Export Administration, Room H–3839, U.S. Department of Commerce, 14th Street and Constitution Avenue, NW., Washington, DC 20230. The findings and order of the Under Secretary shall be set aside by such court if they are found to be unsupported by substantial evidence, as provided in section 706(2) of title 5 United States Code.

[61 FR 50558, Sept. 26, 1996. Redesignated and amended at 65 FR 39802, June 28, 2000]

Subpart D—Recordal of Insignia

§ 280.300 Recorded insignia required prior to offer for sale.

Unless the specifications provide otherwise, if a fastener is required by the applicable consensus standard(s) to bear an insignia identifying its manufacturer, the manufacturer must:

(a) Record the insignia with the U.S. Patent and Trademark Office prior to any sale or offer for sale of the fastener; and

(b) Apply the insignia to any fastener that is sold or offered for sale. The insignia must be readable, and must be applied using the method for applying a permanent insignia that is provided for in the applicable consensus standard(s), or, if the applicable consensus standard(s) do(es) not specify a method for applying a permanent insignia, through any means of imprinting a permanent impression.

[65 FR 39803, June 28, 2000]

THE WRITTEN APPLICATION

§ 280.310 Application for insignia.

(a) Each manufacturer must submit a written application for recordal of an insignia on the Fastener Insignia Register along with the prescribed fee. The application must be in a form prescribed by the Director, USPTO.

(b) The written application must be in the English language and must include the following:

(1) The name of the manufacturer;

(2) The address of the manufacturer;

(3) The entity, domicile, and state of incorporation, if applicable, of the manufacturer;

(4) Either:

(i) A request for recordal and issuance of a unique alphanumeric designation by the Director, USPTO, or

(ii) A request for recordal of a trademark, which is the subject of either a duly filed application or a registration for fasteners in the name of the manufacturer in the U.S. Patent and Trademark Office on the Principal Register, indicating the application serial number or registration number and accompanied by a copy of the drawing that was included with the application for trademark registration, or a copy of the registration;

(5) A statement that the manufacturer will comply with the applicable provisions of the Fastener Quality Act;

(6) A statement that the applicant for recordal is a "manufacturer" as that term is defined in 15 U.S.C. 5402;

(7) A statement that the person signing the application on behalf of the manufacturer has personal knowledge of the facts relevant to the application and that the person possesses the authority to act on behalf of the manufacturer;

(8) A verification stating that the person signing declares under penalty of perjury under the laws of the United States of America that the information and statements included in the application are true and correct; and

(9) The application fee.

(c) A manufacturer may designate only one trademark for recordal on the Fastener Insignia Register in a single application. The trademark application or registration that forms the basis for the fastener recordal must be in active status, that is, a pending application or a registration which is not expired, or canceled, at the time of the application for recordal.

(d) Applications and other documents should be addressed to: Director,

United States Patent and Trademark Office, ATTN: FQA, 600 Dulany Street, MDE–10A71, Alexandria, VA 22314–5793.

[61 FR 50558, Sept. 26, 1996. Redesignated and amended at 65 FR 39803, June 28, 2000; 70 FR 50181, Aug. 26, 2005; 72 FR 30704, June 4, 2007]

§ 280.311 Review of the application.

The Director, USPTO, will review the application for compliance with § 280.310. If the application does not contain one or more of the elements required by § 280.310, the Director, USPTO, will not issue a certificate of recordal, and will return the papers and fees. The Director, USPTO, will notify the applicant for recordal of any defect in the application. Applications for recordal of an insignia may be resubmitted to the Director, USPTO, at any time.

[65 FR 39803, June 28, 2000]

§ 280.312 Certificate of recordal.

(a) If the application complies with the requirements of § 280.310, the Director, USPTO, shall accept the application and issue a certificate of recordal. Such certificate shall be issued in the name of the United States of America, under the seal of the United States Patent and Trademark Office, and a record shall be kept in the United States Patent and Trademark Office. The certificate of recordal shall display the recorded insignia of the manufacturer, and state the name, address, legal entity and domicile of the manufacturer, as well as the date of issuance of such certificate.

(b) Certificates that were issued prior to June 8, 1999, shall remain in active status and may be maintained in accordance with the provisions of § 280.320 of this subpart, but only if:

(1) The certificate is held by a manufacturer, and

(2) The fasteners associated with the certificate are fasteners that must bear an insignia pursuant to 15 U.S.C. 5407.

[65 FR 39803, June 28, 2000]

§ 280.313 Recordal of additional insignia.

(a) A manufacturer to whom the Director, USPTO, has issued an alphanumeric designation may apply for recordal of its trademark for fasteners if the trademark is the subject of a duly filed application or is registered in the United States Patent and Trademark Office on the Principal Register. Upon recordal, either the alphanumeric designation or the trademark, or both, may be used as recorded insignias.

(b) A manufacturer for whom the Director, USPTO, has recorded a trademark as its fastener insignia may apply for issuance and recordal of an alphanumeric designation as a fastener insignia. Upon recordal, either the alphanumeric designation or the trademark, or both, may be used as recorded insignias.

[61 FR 50558, Sept. 26, 1996. Redesignated and amended at 65 FR 39803, June 28, 2000]

POST-RECORDAL MAINTENANCE

§ 280.320 Maintenance of the certificate of recordal.

(a) Certificates of recordal remain in an active status for five years and may be maintained in an active status for subsequent five-year periods running consecutively from the date of issuance of the certificate of recordal upon compliance with the requirements of paragraph (c) of this section.

(b) Maintenance applications shall be required only if the holder of the certificate of recordal is a manufacturer at the time the maintenance application is required.

(c) Certificates of recordal will be designated as inactive unless, within six months prior to the expiration of each five-year period running consecutively from the date of issuance, the certificate holder files the prescribed maintenance fee and the maintenance application. The maintenance application must be in the English language and must include the following:

(1) The name of the manufacturer;

(2) The address of the manufacturer;

(3) The entity, domicile, and state of incorporation, if applicable, of the manufacturer;

(4) A copy of manufacturer's certificate of recordal;

(5) A statement that the manufacturer will comply with the applicable provisions of the Fastener Quality Act;

(6) A statement that the applicant for recordal is a "manufacturer" as that term is defined in 15 U.S.C. 5402;

(7) A statement that the person signing the application on behalf of the manufacturer has knowledge of the facts relevant to the application and that the person possesses the authority to act on behalf of the manufacturer;

(8) A verification stating that the person signing declares under penalty of perjury under the laws of the United States of America that the information and statements included in the application are true and correct; and

(9) The maintenance application fee.

(d) Where no maintenance application is timely filed, a certificate of recordal will be designated inactive. However, such certificate may be designated active if the certificate holder files the prescribed maintenance fee and application and the additional surcharge within six months following the expiration of the certificate of recordal.

(e) After the six-month period following the expiration of the certificate of recordal, the certificate of recordal shall be deemed active only if the certificate holder files a new application for recordal with the prescribed fee for obtaining a fastener insignia and attaches a copy of the expired certificate of recordal.

(f) A separate maintenance application and fee must be filed and paid for each recorded insignia.

[61 FR 50558, Sept. 26, 1996. Redesignated and amended at 65 FR 39803, 39804, June 28, 2000]

§ 280.321 Notification of changes of address.

The applicant for recordal or the holder of a certificate of recordal shall notify the Director, USPTO, of any change of address or change of name no later than six months after the change. The holder must do so whether the certificate of recordal is in an active or inactive status.

[61 FR 50558, Sept. 26, 1996. Redesignated and amended at 65 FR 39803, 39804, June 28, 2000]

§ 280.322 Transfer or amendment of the certificate of recordal.

(a) The certificate of recordal cannot be transferred or assigned.

(b) The certificate of recordal may be amended only to show a change of name or change of address.

[61 FR 50558, Sept. 26, 1996. Redesignated at 65 FR 39803, June 28, 2000]

§ 280.323 Transfer or assignment of the trademark registration or recorded insignia.

(a) A trademark application or registration which forms the basis of a fastener recordal may be transferred or assigned. Any transfer or assignment of such an application or registration must be recorded in the United States Patent and Trademark Office within three months of the transfer or assignment. A copy of such transfer or assignment must also be sent to: Director, United States Patent and Trademark Office, ATTN: FQA, 600 Dulany Street, MDE–10A71, Alexandria, VA 22314–5793.

(b) Upon transfer or assignment of a trademark application or registration which forms the basis of a certificate of recordal, the Director, USPTO, shall designate the certificate of recordal as inactive. The certificate of recordal shall be deemed inactive as of the effective date of the transfer or assignment. Certificates of recordal designated inactive due to transfer or assignment of a trademark application or registration cannot be reactivated.

(c) An assigned trademark application or registration may form the basis for a new application for recordal of a fastener insignia.

(d) A fastener insignia consisting of an alphanumeric designation issued by the Director, USPTO, can be transferred or assigned.

(e) Upon transfer or assignment of an alphanumeric designation, the Director, USPTO, shall designate such alphanumeric designation as inactive. The alphanumeric designation shall be deemed inactive as of the effective date of the transfer or assignment. Alphanumeric designations which are designated inactive due to transfer or assignment may be reactivated upon application by the assignee of such alphanumeric designation. Such application must meet all the requirements of § 280.310 and must include a copy of the pertinent portions of the document assigning rights in the alphanumeric designation. Such application must be filed within six months of the date of assignment.

(f) An alphanumeric designation that is reactivated after it has been transferred or assigned shall remain in active status until the expiration of the five year period that began upon the issuance of the alphanumeric designation to its original owner.

[61 FR 50558, Sept. 26, 1996. Redesignated and amended at 65 FR 39803, 39804, June 28, 2000; 72 FR 30704, June 4, 2007]

§280.324 Change in status of trademark registration or amendment of the trademark.

(a) The Director, USPTO, shall designate the certificate of recordal as inactive, upon:

(1) Issuance of a final decision on appeal which refuses registration of the application which formed the basis for the certificate of recordal;

(2) Abandonment of the application which formed the basis for the certificate of recordal;

(3) Cancellation or expiration of the trademark registration which formed the basis of the certificate of recordal; or

(4) An amendment of the mark in a trademark application or registration that forms the basis for a certificate of recordal. The certificate of recordal shall become inactive as of the date the amendment is filed. A new application for recordal of the amended trademark application or registration may be submitted to the Commissioner at any time.

(b) Certificates of recordal designated inactive due to cancellation, expiration, or amendment of the trademark registration, or abandonment or amendment of the trademark application, cannot be reactivated.

[61 FR 50558, Sept. 26, 1996. Redesignated and amended at 65 FR 39803, 39804, June 28, 2000]

§280.325 Cumulative listing of recordal information.

The Director, USPTO, shall maintain a record of the names, current addresses, and legal entities of all recorded manufacturers and their recorded insignia.

[65 FR 39804, June 28, 2000]

§280.326 Records and files of the United States Patent and Trademark Office.

The records relating to fastener insignia shall be open to public inspection. Copies of any such records may be obtained upon request and payment of the fee set by the Director, USPTO.

[61 FR 50558, Sept. 26, 1996. Redesignated and amended at 65 FR 39803, 39804, June 28, 2000]

PART 285—NATIONAL VOLUNTARY LABORATORY ACCREDITATION PROGRAM

Sec.

AUTHORITY: 15 U.S.C. 272 *et seq.*

SOURCE: 66 FR 29221, May 30, 2001, unless otherwise noted.

§285.1 Purpose.

The purpose of part 285 is to set out procedures and general requirements under which the National Voluntary Laboratory Accreditation Program (NVLAP) operates as an unbiased third party to accredit both testing and calibration laboratories. Supplementary technical and administrative requirements are provided in supporting handbooks and documents as needed, depending on the criteria established for specific Laboratory Accreditation Programs (LAPs)

§ 285.2 Confidentiality.

To the extent permitted by applicable laws, NVLAP will protect the confidentiality of all information obtained relating to the application, on-site assessment, proficiency testing, evaluation, and accreditation of laboratories.

§ 285.3 Referencing NVLAP accreditation.

The term *NVLAP* (represented by the NVLAP logo) is a federally registered certification mark of the National Institute of Standards and Technology and the federal government, who retain exclusive rights to control the use thereof. Permission to use the term and/or logo is granted to NVLAP-accredited laboratories for the limited purposes of announcing their accredited status, and for use on reports that describe only testing and calibration within the scope of accreditation. NIST reserves the right to control the quality of the use of the term *NVLAP* and of the logo itself.

§ 285.4 Establishment of laboratory accreditation programs (LAPs) within NVLAP.

NVLAP establishes LAPs in response to legislative actions or to requests from private sector entities and government agencies. For legislatively mandated LAPs, NVLAP shall establish the LAP. For requests from private sector entities and government agencies, the Chief of NVLAP shall analyze each request, and, after consultation with interested parties through public workshops or other means to ensure open participation, shall establish the requested LAP, if the Chief of NVLAP determines there is need for the requested LAP.

[66 FR 29221, May 30, 2001, as amended at 76 FR 78815, Dec. 20, 2011]

§ 285.5 Termination of a LAP.

(a) The Chief of NVLAP may terminate a LAP when he/she determines that a need no longer exists to accredit laboratories for the services covered under the scope of the LAP. In the event that the Chief of NVLAP proposes to terminate a LAP, a notice will be published in the FEDERAL REGISTER setting forth the basis for that determination.

(b) When a LAP is terminated, NVLAP will no longer grant or renew accreditations following the effective date of termination. Accreditations previously granted shall remain effective until their expiration date unless terminated voluntarily by the laboratory or revoked by NVLAP. Technical expertise will be maintained by NVLAP while any accreditation remains effective.

§ 285.6 Application for accreditation.

A laboratory may apply for accreditation in any of the established LAPs. The applicant laboratory shall provide a completed application to NVLAP, pay all required fees and agree to certain conditions as set forth in the NVLAP Application for Accreditation, and provide a quality manual to NVLAP (or a designated NVLAP assessor) prior to the assessment process.

§ 285.7 Assessment.

(a) *Frequency and scheduling.* Before initial accreditation, during the first renewal year, and every two years thereafter, an on-site assessment of each laboratory is conducted to determine compliance with the NVLAP criteria.

(b) *Assessors.* NVLAP shall select qualified assessors to evaluate all information collected from an applicant laboratory pursuant to § 285.6 of this part and to conduct the assessment on its behalf at the laboratory and any other sites where activities to be covered by the accreditation are performed.

(c) *Conduct of assessment.* (1) Assessors use checklists provided by NVLAP so that each laboratory receives an assessment comparable to that received by others.

(2) During the assessment, the assessor meets with management and laboratory personnel, examines the quality system, reviews staff information, examines equipment and facilities, observes demonstrations of testing or calibrations, and examines tests or calibration reports.

(3) The assessor reviews laboratory records including resumes, job descriptions of key personnel, training, and

competency evaluations for all staff members who routinely perform, or affect the quality of the testing or calibration for which accreditation is sought. The assessor need not be given information which violates individual privacy, such as salary, medical information, or performance reviews outside the scope of the accreditation program. The staff information may be kept in the laboratory's official personnel folders or separate folders that contain only the information that the NVLAP assessor needs to review.

(4) At the conclusion of the assessment, the assessor conducts an exit briefing to discuss observations and any deficiencies with the authorized representative who signed the NVLAP application and other responsible laboratory staff.

(d) *Assessment report.* At the exit briefing, the assessor submits a written report on the compliance of the laboratory with the accreditation requirements, together with the completed checklists, where appropriate.

(e) *Deficiency notification and resolution.* (1) Laboratories are informed of deficiencies during the on-site assessment, and deficiencies are documented in the assessment report (see paragraph (d) of this section).

(2) A laboratory shall, within thirty days of the date of the assessment report, provide documentation that the specified deficiencies have either been corrected and/or a plan of corrective actions as described in the NVLAP handbooks.

(3) If substantial deficiencies have been cited, NVLAP may require an additional on-site assessment, at additional cost to the laboratory, prior to granting accreditation. All deficiencies and resolutions will be subject to thorough review and evaluation prior to an accreditation decision.

(4) After the assessor submits their final report, NVLAP reviews the report and the laboratory's response to determine if the laboratory has met all of the on-site assessment requirements.

§285.8 Proficiency testing.

(a) NVLAP proficiency testing is consistent with the provisions contained in ISO/IEC Guide 43 (Parts 1 and 2), Proficiency testing by interlaboratory comparisons, where applicable, including revisions from time to time. Proficiency testing may be organized by NVLAP itself or a NVLAP-approved provider of services. Laboratories must participate in proficiency testing as specified for each LAP in the NVLAP program handbooks.

(b) *Analysis and reporting.* Proficiency testing data are analyzed by NVLAP and reports of the results are made known to the participants. Summary results are available upon request to other interested parties; e.g., professional societies and standards writing bodies. The identity and performance of individual laboratories are kept confidential.

(c) *Proficiency testing deficiencies.* (1) Unsatisfactory participation in any NVLAP proficiency testing program is a technical deficiency which must be resolved in order to obtain initial accreditation or maintain accreditation.

(2) Proficiency testing deficiencies are defined as, but not limited to, one or more of the following:

(i) Failure to meet specified proficiency testing performance requirements prescribed by NVLAP;

(ii) Failure to participate in a regularly scheduled "round" of proficiency testing for which the laboratory has received instructions and/or materials;

(iii) Failure to submit laboratory control data as required; and

(iv) Failure to produce acceptable test or calibration results when using NIST Standard Reference Materials or special artifacts whose properties are well-characterized and known to NIST/NVLAP.

(3) NVLAP will notify the laboratory of proficiency testing deficiencies and actions to be taken to resolve the deficiencies. Denial or suspension of accreditation will result from failure to resolve deficiencies.

§285.9 Granting accreditation.

(a) The Chief of NVLAP is responsible for all NVLAP accreditation actions, including granting, denying, renewing, suspending, and revoking any NVLAP accreditation.

(b) Initial accreditation is granted when a laboratory has met all NVLAP requirements. One of four accreditation renewal dates (January 1, April 1, July

1, or October 1) is assigned to the laboratory and is usually retained as long as the laboratory remains in the program. Initial accreditation is granted for a period of one year; accreditation expires and is renewable on the assigned date.

(c) Renewal dates may be reassigned to provide benefits to the laboratory and/or NVLAP. If a renewal date is changed, the laboratory will be notified in writing of the change and any related adjustment in fees.

(d) When accreditation is granted, NVLAP shall provide to the laboratory a Certificate of Accreditation and a Scope of Accreditation,

§ 285.10 Renewal of accreditation.

(a) An accredited laboratory must submit both its application for renewal and fees to NVLAP prior to expiration of the laboratory's current accreditation to avoid a lapse in accreditation.

(b) On-site assessments of currently accredited laboratories are performed in accordance with the procedures in § 285.7. If deficiencies are found during the assessment of an accredited laboratory, the laboratory must follow the procedures set forth in § 285.7(e)(2) or face possible suspension or revocation of accreditation.

§ 285.11 Changes to scope of accreditation.

A laboratory may request in writing changes to its Scope of Accreditation. If the laboratory requests additions to its Scope, it must meet all NVLAP criteria for the additional tests or calibrations, types of tests or calibrations, or standards. The need for an additional on-site assessment and/or proficiency testing will be determined on a case-by-case basis.

§ 285.12 Monitoring visits.

(a) In addition to regularly scheduled assessments, monitoring visits may be conducted by NVLAP at any time during the accreditation period. They may occur for cause or an a random selection basis. While most monitoring visits will be scheduled in advance with the laboratory, NVLAP may conduct unannounced monitoring visits.

(b) The scope of a monitoring visit may range from checking a few designated items to a complete review. The assessors may review deficiency resolutions, verify reported changes in the laboratory's personnel, facilities, or operations, or administer proficiency testing, when appropriate.

§ 285.13 Denial, suspension, revocation, or termination of accreditation.

(a) A laboratory may at any time voluntarily terminate its participation and responsibilities as an accredited laboratory by advising NVLAP in writing of its desire to do so.

(b) If NVLAP finds that an accredited laboratory does not meet all NVLAP requirements, has violated the terms of its accreditation, or does not continue to comply with the provisions of these procedures, NVLAP may suspend the laboratory's accreditation, or advise of NVLAP's intent to revoke accreditation.

(1) If a laboratory's accreditation is suspended, NVLAP shall notify the laboratory of that action stating the reasons for and conditions of the suspension and specifying the action(s) the laboratory must take to have its accreditation reinstated. Conditions of suspension will include prohibiting the laboratory from using the NVLAP logo on its test or calibration reports, correspondence, or advertising during the suspension period in the area(s) affected by the suspension.

(2) NVLAP will not require a suspended laboratory to return its Certificate and Scope of Accreditation, but the laboratory must refrain from using the NVLAP logo in the area(s) affected until such time as the problem(s) leading to the suspension has been resolved. When accreditation is reinstated, NVLAP will authorize the laboratory to resume testing or calibration activities in the previously suspended area(s) as an accredited laboratory.

(c) If NVLAP proposes to deny or revoke accreditation of a laboratory, NVLAP shall inform the laboratory of the reasons for the proposed denial or revocation and the procedure for appealing such a decision.

(1) The laboratory will have thirty days from the date of receipt of the proposed denial or revocation letter to

appeal the decision to the Director of NIST. If the laboratory appeals the decision to the Director of NIST, the proposed denial or revocation will be stayed pending the outcome of the appeal. The proposed denial or revocation will become final through the issuance of a written decision to the laboratory in the event that the laboratory does not appeal the proposed denial or revocation within the thirty-day period.

(2) If accreditation is revoked, the laboratory may be given the option of voluntarily terminating the accreditation.

(3) A laboratory whose accreditation has been revoked must cease use of the NVLAP logo on any of its reports, correspondence, or advertising related to the area(s) affected by the revocation. If the revocation is total, NVLAP will instruct the laboratory to return its Certificate and Scope of Accreditation and to remove the NVLAP logo from all test or calibration reports, correspondence, or advertising. If the revocation affects only some, but not all of the items listed on a laboratory's Scope of Accreditation, NVLAP will issue a revised Scope that excludes the revoked area(s) in order that the laboratory might continue operations in accredited areas.

(d) A laboratory whose accreditation has been voluntarily terminated, denied or revoked, may reapply and be accredited if the laboratory:

(1) Completes the assessment and evaluation process; and

(2) Meets the NVLAP conditions and criteria for accreditation.

§285.14 Criteria for accreditation.

The requirements for laboratories to be recognized by the National Voluntary Laboratory Accreditation Program as competent to carry out tests and/or calibrations are contained in clauses 4 and 5 of ISO/IEC 17025, *General requirements for the competence of testing and calibration laboratories*, including revisions from time to time.

§285.15 Obtaining documents.

(a) Application forms, NVLAP handbooks, and other NVLAP documents and information may be obtained by contacting the NVLAP, National Institute of Standards and Technology, 100 Bureau Drive, Mail Stop 2140, Gaithersburg, Maryland 20899–2140; phone: 301–975–4016; fax: 301–926–2884; e-mail: *nvlap@nist.gov*.

(b) Copies of all ISO/IEC documents are available for purchase from the American National Standards Institute's eStandards Store at *http://webstore.ansi.org*. You may inspect copies of all applicable ISO/IEC documents at the National Voluntary Laboratory Accreditation Program, National Institute of Standards and Technology, 100 Bureau Drive, Room B115, Gaithersburg, MD. For access to the NIST campus, please contact NVLAP by phone at 301–975–4016 or by e-mail at *NVLAP@nist.gov* to obtain instructions for visitor registration.

[66 FR 29221, May 30, 2001, as amended at 72 FR 36347, July 3, 2007]

PART 286—NATIONAL VOLUNTARY CONFORMITY ASSESSMENT SYSTEM EVALUATION (NVCASE) PROGRAM

AUTHORITY: 15 U.S.C. 272 *et seq.*

SOURCE: 59 FR 19131, Apr. 22, 1994, unless otherwise noted.

§286.1 Purpose.

The purpose of this program is to enable U.S. industry to satisfy mandated foreign technical requirements using the results of U.S.-based conformity assessment programs that perform technical evaluations comparable in their rigor to practices in the receiving country. Under this program, the Department of Commerce, acting through the National Institute of Standards and Technology, evaluates U.S.-based conformity assessment bodies in order to be able to give assurances to a foreign government that qualifying bodies meet that government's requirements and can provide results that are acceptable to that government. The program is intended to provide a technically-based U.S. approval process for U.S. industry to gain foreign market access; the acceptability of conformity assessment results to the relevant foreign government will be a matter for agreement between the two governments.

§ 286.2 Scope.

(a) For purposes of this program, conformity assessment consists of product sample testing, product certification, and quality system registration. Associated activities can be classified by level:

(1) *Conformity level:* This level encompasses comparing a product, process, service, or system with a standard or specification. As appropriate, the evaluating body can be a testing laboratory, product certifier or certification body, or quality system registrar.

(2) *Accreditation level:* This level encompasses the evaluation of a testing laboratory, a certification body, or a quality system registrar by an independent body—an accreditation body—based on requirements for the acceptance of these bodies, and the granting of accreditation to those which meet the established requirements.

(3) *Recognition level:* This level encompasses the evaluation of an accreditation body based on requirements for its acceptance, and the recognition by the evaluating body of the accreditation body which satisfies the established requirements.

(b) NIST operates the NVCASE program as follows:

(1) *Conformity level:* Under this program NIST accepts requests for evaluations of U.S. bodies involved in activities related to conformity assessment. NIST does not perform conformity assessments as part of the program and therefore does not accept requests for such evaluations.

(2) *Accreditation level:* NIST accepts requests for accreditation of conformity assessment bodies only when (i) directed by U.S. law; (ii) requested by another U.S. government agency; or (iii) requested to respond to a specific U.S. industrial or technical need, relative to a mandatory foreign technical requirement, if it has been determined after public consultation that (A) there is no satisfactory accreditation alternative available and the private sector has declined to make acceptable accreditation available, and (B) there is evidence that significant public disadvantage would result from the absence of any alternative.

(3) *Recognition level:* NIST accepts requests for recognition of bodies that accredit testing laboratories, certification bodies, and quality system registrars when (i) directed by U.S. law; (ii) requested by another U.S. government agency; or (iii) requested to respond to a specific U.S. industrial or technical need relative to a mandatory foreign technical requirement if it has been determined after public consultation that (A) there is no suitable alternative available and (B) there is evidence that significant public disadvantage would result from the absence of any alternative.

§ 286.3 Objective.

The objective of the program is to identify the activities of requesting U.S.-based conformity assessment bodies that have been evaluated as meeting requirements established for their acceptance by foreign governments. The evaluations may be provided by NIST or by bodies recognized by NIST for this purpose under the scope of this program.

§ 286.4 Implementation.

The program is operated on a cost reimbursable basis. It is open for voluntary participation by any U.S.-based body that conducts activities related to conformity assessment falling within the program's scope. A common procedural approach is followed in responding to a request to participate. (See § 286.7 Evaluation process.) All evaluation activities rely on the use of generic program requirements based on standards and guides for the operation and acceptance of activities related to conformity assessment. Specific criteria for use in each evaluation are derived from the program requirements, as appropriate, for the mandated foreign technical requirements specified in the request to participate. A request involving a foreign technical requirement not previously addressed by NVCASE will result in an announcement of NIST's intent to develop evaluation criteria specific to the relevant requirements. NIST will contact all cognizant and interested federal agencies to coordinate appropriate actions and procedures.

§ 286.5 Program requirements.

NIST provides and maintains documented generic requirements to be applied in evaluations related to accreditation and recognition within the scope of the program. Available documentation is provided on request to prospective program participants and other interested parties. Generic requirements are developed with public input and are based on guides for the acceptance of conformity assessment activities issued by such international organizations as the International Organization for Standardization and the International Electrotechnical Commission. NIST also provides and maintains documented criteria provided in response to requests for evaluations specific to mandated foreign technical requirements. Criteria are developed with public input derived from the application and interpretation of generic program requirements in relation to specified mandated requirements. Both documented generic requirements and specific criteria are developed and maintained with input from the public.

§ 286.6 Public consultation.

NIST relies on substantial advice and technical assistance from all parties interested in program requirements and related specific criteria. Interested U.S. government agencies are routinely to be informed of prospective NVCASE actions, and advice is sought from those agencies on any actions of mutual interest. In preparing program documentation, input is also sought from workshops announced in the FEDERAL REGISTER and open tothe general public and other public means to identify appropriate standards and guides and to develop and maintain generic requirements, based on the identified standards and guides. Where relevant Federal advisory committees are available, their advice may also be sought. Similar procedures will be followed with respect to each request for evaluation which necessitates the development of criteria, derived from the generic requirements, specific to mandated foreign technical requirements.

§ 286.7 Evaluation process.

(a) Each applicant requesting to be evaluated under NVCASE is expected to initiate the process and assume designated responsibilities as NIST proceeds with its evaluation:

(1) *Application.* The applicant completes and submit a request to be evaluated.

(2) *Fee.* The applicant submits a partial payment with the application and agrees to submit the remaining balance based on evaluation costs as a condition for satisfactory completion of the process.

(3) *Documentation.* The applicant operates a system and procedures that meet the applicable generic requirements and specific criteria. Relevant documentation submitted with the application is reviewed by NIST.

(4) *On-site assessment.* The applicant and NIST cooperate in the scheduling and conduct of all necessary on-site evaluations, including the resolution of any deficiencies cited.

(5) *Final review.* The applicant provides any supplementary materials requested by NIST, then NIST completes the review and decides on appropriate action.

(b) NIST may take one of the following actions with regard to an applicant:

(1) *Certificate.* If an applicant fully demonstrates conformity with all program requirements and specific criteria, NIST issues a certificate documenting this finding. Each certificate is accompanied by a document describing the specific scope of the accreditation or recognition.

(2) *Denial.* If an applicant cannot demonstrate conformity with all program requirements and specific criteria, NIST may deny award of the certificate. An applicant who has failed to complete the evaluation satisfactorily may reapply when prepared to demonstrate full conformance with program requirements.

§ 286.8 Confidentiality of information.

All information collected relative to an applicant during an evaluation is maintained as confidential. Information is released only as required under the terms of the Freedom of Information Act or other legal requirement, subject to the rules of the Department of Commerce for such disclosure as found in 15 CFR part 4.

§ 286.9 Maintaining recognized status.

Each program participant remaining in the program shall continuously meet all program requirements and cooperate with NIST in the conduct of all surveillance and reassessment activities. Participants shall reimburse NIST for expenses incurred for these purposes.

§ 286.10 Appeal.

Any applicant or other affected party may appeal to the NIST Director any action taken under the program. When appropriate, the Director may seek an independent review by the Deputy Chief Counsel.

§ 286.11 Listings.

(a) NIST maintains lists of all bodies holding current NIST program certificates, together with the assessment areas for which they are issued.

(b) NIST also maintains lists of those qualified conformity assessment bodies that are currently accredited by bodies recognized by NIST, along with the activities of the assessment bodies within the scope of the NIST recognition program.

(c) The lists are made available to the public through various media, e.g., printed directories, electronic bulletin boards, or other means to ensure accessibility by all potential users.

(d) With respect to the lists specified in paragraph (a) and (b) of this section, NIST may delist any body if it determines the action to be in the public interest.

§ 286.12 Terminations.

(a) *Voluntary termination.* Any participant may voluntarily terminate participation at any time by written notification to NIST.

(b) *Involuntary termination.* If a participant does not continue to meet all program requirements, or if NIST determines it to be necessary in the public interest, NIST may withdraw that participant's certificate. A body that has had its status as a certificate holder terminated may reapply when prepared to demonstrate full conformance with program requirements.

PART 287—GUIDANCE ON FEDERAL CONFORMITY ASSESSMENT

Sec.

AUTHORITY: Sec. 12, Pub. L. 104–113, 110 Stat. 782 (15 U.S.C. 272).

SOURCE: 65 FR 48900, Aug. 10, 2000, unless otherwise noted.

§ 287.1 Purpose and scope of this guidance.

(a) This part provides guidance for each Federal agency to use in evaluating the efficacy and efficiency of its conformity assessment activities. Each agency should coordinate its conformity assessment activities with those of other appropriate government agencies and with those of the private sector to reduce unnecessary duplication. This guidance is intended to help Federal agencies improve the management and coordination of their own conformity assessment activities with respect to other government entities and the private sector. This will help ensure more productive use of the increasingly limited Federal resources available to conduct conformity assessment activities. This will also support the role of the U.S. Government in pursuing international trade and other related negotiations and agreements with foreign countries and U.S. industry in pursuing agreements with foreign national and international private sector organizations.

(b) This guidance applies to all agencies, which set policy for, manage, operate, or use conformity assessment activities and results, both domestic and international, except for activities carried out pursuant to treaties.

(c) This guidance does not preempt the agencies' authority and responsibility to make regulatory or procurement decisions authorized by statute or required to meet programmatic objectives and requirements. These decision-making activities include: determining the level of acceptable regulatory or procurement risk; setting the level of protection; balancing risk, cost and availability of technology (where statutes permit) in establishing regulatory and procurement objectives; and determining or implementing procurement or regulatory requirements necessary to meet programmatic or regulatory objectives. Each agency retains broad discretion in its selection and use of regulatory and procurement conformity assessment practices and may elect not to use or recognize alternative conformity assessment practices if the agency deems them to be inappropriate, inadequate, or inconsistent with statutory criteria or programmatic objectives and requirements. Nothing contained herein shall give any party any claim or cause of action against the Federal government or any agency thereof. Each agency remains responsible for representation of the agency's views on conformity assessment in matters under its jurisdiction. Each agency also remains the primary point of contact for information on the agency's regulatory and procurement conformity assessment actions.

§287.2 Definitions.[1]

Accreditation means a procedure used to provide formal notice that a body or person is competent to carry out specific tasks. These tasks include: sampling and testing; inspection; certification; and registration.[2]

Agency means any Executive Branch Department, independent commission, board, bureau, office, agency, government-owned or controlled corporation, or other establishment of the Federal government. It also includes any regulatory commission or board, except for independent regulatory commission subject to separate statutory requirements regarding policy setting, management, operation, and use of conformity assessment activities. It does not include the legislative or judicial branches of the Federal government.

Agency Standards Executive means an official designated by an agency as its representative on the Interagency Committee for Standards Policy (ICSP) and delegated the responsibility for agency implementation of OMB Circular A–119 and the guidance in this part.

Certification means a procedure used to provide written assurance that a product, process, service, or person's qualifications conforms to specified requirements.

Conformity assessment means any activity concerned with determining directly or indirectly that requirements are fulfilled. Requirements for products, services, systems, and organizations are those defined by law or regulation or by an agency in a procurement action. Conformity assessment includes: sampling and testing; inspection; supplier's declaration of conformity; certification; and quality and environmental management system assessment and registration. It also includes accreditation and recognition. Conformity assessment does not include mandatory administrative procedures (such as registration notification) for granting permission for a good or service to be produced, marketed, or used for a stated purpose or under stated conditions. Conformity assessment activities may be conducted by the supplier (first party) or by the buyer

[1] Definitions of accreditation, certification, conformity assessment, inspection, supplier's declaration of conformity, registration and testing are based on the International Organization for Standardization (ISO)/International Electrotechnical Commission (IEC), Guide 2 (1996). In certain industrial sectors, it is recognized that organizations other than ISO or IEC may issue definitions relevant to conformity assessment, such as the Codex Alimentarius Commission with respect to the food industry sector.

[2] For some agencies, accreditation may mean that a body or person meets requirements defined in a specific section(s) of the CFR. The referenced section(s) may include only limited requirements for demonstration of technical competency.

(second party) either directly or by another party on the supplier's or buyer's behalf, or by a body not under the control or influence of either the buyer or the seller (third party).

Inspection is defines ad the evaluation by observation and judgment accompanied as appropriate by measurement, testing or gauging of the conformity of a product, process or service to specified requirements.

NIST means the National Institute of Standards and Technology, an agency within the United States Department of Commerce.

Recognition means a procedure used to provide formal notice that an accreditation body is competent to carry out specific tasks. These tasks include: the accreditation of testing laboratories and inspection, certification, and registration bodies. A governmental recognition system is a set of one or more procedures used by a Federal agency to provide recognition.

Registration means a procedure used to give written assurance that a system conforms to specified requirements. Such systems include those established for the management of product, process or service quality and environmental performance.

Sampling means the selection of one or more specimens of a product, process, or service for the purpose of evaluating the conformity of the product, process or service to specified requirements.

Supplier's declaration of conformity means a procedure by which a supplier gives written assurance that a product, process, service or organization conforms to specified requirements.

Testing means the action of carrying out one or more technical operations (tests) that determine one or more characteristics or performance of a given product, material, equipment, organism, person's qualifications, physical phenomenon, process, or service according to a specified technical procedure (test method).

§ 287.3 Responsibilities of the National Institute of Standards and Technology.

(a) Work with agencies through the Interagency Committee on Standards Policy (ICSP) to coordinate Federal, state and local conformity assessment activities with private sector conformity assessment activities. NIST chairs the ICSP; assists the ICSP in developing and publishing policies and guidance on conformity assessment related issues; collects and disseminates information on Federal, state and private sector conformity assessment activities; and increases public awareness of the importance of conformity assessment and nature and extent of national and international conformity assessment activities.

(b) Encourage participation in the ICSP by all affected agencies and ensure that all agency views on conformity assessment are considered.

(c) To the extent that resources are available, develop information on state conformity assessment practices; and, upon request by a state government agency, work with that state agency to reduce duplication and complexity in state conformity assessment activities.

(d) Review within three years from August 10, 2000, the effectiveness of the final guidance and recommend modifications to the Secretary as needed.

§ 287.4 Responsibilities of Federal agencies.

Each agency should:

(a) Implement the policies contained in the guidance in this part.

(b) Provide a rationale for its use of specified conformity assessment procedures and processes in rulemaking and procurement actions to the extent feasible. Further, when notice and comment rulemaking is otherwise required, each agency should provide the opportunity for public comment on the rationale for the agency's conformity assessment decision.

(c) Use the results of other governmental agency and private sector organization conformity assessment activities to enhance the safety and efficacy of proposed new conformity assessment requirements and measures. An example of this would be to collect and review information on similar activities conducted by other Federal, state and international organizations and agencies and private sector organizations to determine if the results of these activities can be used to improve the effectiveness of a proposed Federal agency conformity assessment activity.

(d) Use relevant guides or standards for conformity assessment practices published by domestic and international standardizing bodies as appropriate in meeting regulatory and procurement objectives. Guides and standards for sampling, testing, inspection, certification, quality and environmental management systems, management system registration and accreditation are issued by organizations which include, but are not limited to, the American National Standards Institute, the International Organization for Standardization (ISO), the International Electrotechnical Commission (IEC), the International Telecommunications Union (ITU) and the Organization for Economic Cooperation and Development (OECD), the World Health Organization (WHO), and the Codex Alimentarius Commission. Each agency retains responsibility for determining which, if any, of these documents are relevant to its needs.

(e) Identify appropriate private sector conformity assessment practices and programs and consider the results of such practices and/or programs as appropriate in existing regulatory and procurement actions. Responsibility for the determination of appropriateness rests with each agency. Examples: an agency could use the results of private sector or other governmental conformity assessment activities to schedule procurement type audits more effectively. This could allow agencies to reduce the number and extent of audits conducted at companies which are performing in accordance with contract specifications and which are under review by a third party or another agency and to concentrate agency audit efforts on companies which have shown problems in conforming to contract specifications. Another example is the Federal Communications Commission's (FCC) Telecommunication Certification Body (TCB) program, which allows designated private entities to issue telecommunications equipment approvals for specified regulatory requirements. In addition, under Part 15, FCC premarketing approval requirements for certain types of equipment have been replaced with suppliers declaration of conformity to the regulations, provided test results supporting the declaration are obtained from an accredited testing lab.

(f) Consider using the results of other agencies' conformity assessment procedures. Example: An agency could use the results of another agency's inspection/audit of a supplier to eliminate or reduce the scope of its own inspection/audit of that supplier.

(g) Participate in efforts designed to improve coordination among governmental and private sector conformity assessment activities. These efforts include, but are not limited to, the National Cooperation for Laboratory Accreditation (NACLA) organization, the National Environmental Laboratory Accreditation (NELAC), the International Organizations for Standardization's (ISO) Committee on Conformity Assessment (CASCO), conformity assessment related activities of the American National Standards Institute (ANSI), and ICSP working groups dealing with conformity assessment issues.

(h) Work with other agencies to avoid unnecessary duplication and complexity in Federal conformity assessment activities. Examples: An agency can participate in another agency's conformity assessment activities by conducting joint procurement audits/inspections of suppliers that sell to both agencies. An agency can share conformity assessment information with other agencies. An agency can use conformity assessment information provided by other agencies to the extent appropriate to improve the effectiveness and efficiency in its own conformity assessment activities. Conformity assessment information may include: Conformity assessment procedures and results, technical data on the operation of conformity assessment programs, processing methods and requirements for applications, fees, facility site data, complaint review procedures, and confidentiality procedures.

(i) Encourage domestic and international recognition of U.S. conformity assessment results by supporting the work of the U.S. Government in international trade and related negotiations with foreign countries and U.S. industry in pursuing agreements with foreign national and international private sector organizations and any resulting activities/requirements resulting from those negotiations/agreements.

(j) Participate in the development of private sector conformity assessment standards to ensure that Federal viewpoints are represented.

(k) Work with other agencies to harmonize Federal requirements for quality and environmental management systems for use in procurement and regulation, including provisions which will allow the use of one quality or environmental management system per supplier facility in the Federal procurement process and the sharing and usage of audit results and related information as appropriate.

(l) Work with other ICSP members, NIST, and the private sector to develop national infrastructures for coordinating and harmonizing U.S. conformity assessment needs, practices and requirements in support of the efforts of the U.S. Government and U.S. industry to increase international market access for U.S. products.

(m) Work with other ICSP members, NIST, and the private sector as necessary and appropriate to establish criteria for the development and implementation of governmental recognition systems to meet government recognition requirements imposed by other nations and regional groups to support the efforts of the U.S. Government to facilitate international market access for U.S. products.

(n) Assign an Agency Standard Executive responsibility for coordinating the agency-wide implementation of the guidance in this part.

§ 287.5 Responsibilities of an Agency Standards Executive.

In addition to carrying out the duties described in OMB Circular A–119 related to standards activities, an Agency Standards Executive should:

(a) Promote the following goals:

(1) Effective use of agency conformity assessment related resources and participation in conformity assessment related activities of agency interest.

(2) Development and dissemination of agency technical and policy positions.

(3) Development of agency positions on conformity assessment related issues that are in the public interest.

(b) Ensure that agency participation in conformity assessment related activities is consistent with agency missions, authorities, priorities, and budget.

(c) Cooperate with NIST in carrying out agency responsibilities under the guidance in this part.

(d) Consult with NIST, as necessary, in the development and issuance of internal agency procedures and guidance implementing the policies in this part.

(e) Establish an ongoing process for reviewing his/her agency's existing conformity assessment activities and identifying areas where efficiencies can be achieved through coordination with other agency and private sector conformity assessment activities.

(f) Work with other parts of his/her agency to develop and implement improvements in agency conformity assessment related activities.

(g) Report to NIST, on a voluntary basis, on agency conformity assessment activities for inclusion in the annual report to the Office of Management and Budget (OMB) on the agency's implementation of OMB Circular A–119.

SUBCHAPTER K—NIST EXTRAMURAL PROGRAMS

PART 290—REGIONAL CENTERS FOR THE TRANSFER OF MANUFACTURING TECHNOLOGY

AUTHORITY: 15 U.S.C. 278k.

SOURCE: 55 FR 38275, Sept. 17, 1990, unless otherwise noted.

§ 290.1 Purpose.

This rule provides policy for a program to establish Regional Centers for the Transfer of Manufacturing Technology as well as the prescribed policies and procedures to insure the fair, equitable and uniform treatment of proposals for assistance. In addition, the rule provides general guidelines for the management of the program by the National Institute of Standards and Technology, as well as criteria for the evaluation of the Centers, throughout the lifecycle of financial assistance to the Centers by the National Institute of Standards and Technology.

§ 290.2 Definitions.

(a) The phrase *advanced manufacturing technology* refers to new technologies which have recently been developed, or are currently under development, for use in product or part design, fabrication, assembly, quality control, or improving production efficiency.

(b) The term *Center* or *Regional Center* means a NIST-established Regional Center for the Transfer of Manufacturing Technology described under these procedures.

(c) The term *operating award* means a cooperative agreement which provides funding and technical assistance to a Center for purposes set forth in § 290.3 of these procedures.

(d) The term *Director* means the Director of the National Institute of Standards and Technology.

(e) The term *NIST* means the National Institute of Standards and Technology, U.S. Department of Commerce.

(f) The term *Program* or *Centers Program* means the NIST program for establishment of, support for, and cooperative interaction with Regional Centers for the Transfer of Manufacturing Technology.

(g) The term *qualified proposal* means a proposal submitted by a nonprofit organization which meets the basic requirements set forth in § 290.5 of these procedures.

(h) The term *Secretary* means the Secretary of Commerce.

(i) The term *target firm* means those firms best able to absorb advanced manufacturing technologies and techniques, especially those developed at NIST, and which are already well prepared in an operational, management and financial sensse to improve the levels of technology they employ.

§ 290.3 Program description.

(a) The Secretary, acting through the Director, shall provide technical and financial assistance for the creation and support of Regional Centers for the Transfer of Manufacturing Technology. Each Center shall be affiliated with a U.S.-based nonprofit institution or organization which has submitted a qualified proposal for a Center Operating Award under these procedures. Support may be provided for a period not to exceed six years. The Centers work with industry, universities, nonprofit economic development organizations and state governments to transfer advanced manufacturing technologies, processes, and methods as defined in § 290.2 to small and medium sized firms. These technology transfer efforts focus on the continuous and incremental improvement of the target firms. The advanced manufacturing technology which is the focus of the Centers is the subject of research in NIST's Automated Manufacturing Research Facility (AMRF). The core of AMRF research has principally been applied in discrete part manufacturing, including electronics, composites, plastics, and metal parts fabrication and assembly. Centers will be afforded the opportunity for interaction with the AMRF and will be given access to reasearch projects and results to strengthen their technology transfer. Where elements of a solution are available from an existing source, they should be employed. Where private-sector consultants who can meet the needs of a small- or medium-sized manufacturer are available, they should handle the task. Each Center should bring to bear the technology expertise described in § 290.3(d) to assist small- and medium-sized manufacturing firms in adopting advanced manufacturing technology.

(b) *Program objective.* The objective of the NIST Manufacturing Technology Centers is to enhance productivity and technological performance in United States manufacturing. This will be accomplished through:

(1) The transfer of manufacturing technology and techniques developed at NIST to Centers and, through them, to manufacturing companies throughout the United States;

(2) The participation of individuals from industry, universities, State governments, other Federal agencies, and, when appropriate, NIST in cooperative technology transfer activities;

(3) Efforts to make new manufacturing technology and processes usable by United States-based small- and medium-sized companies;

(4) The active dissemination of scientific, engineering, technical, and management information about manufacturing to industrial firms, including small- and medium-sized manufacturing companies; and

(5) The utilization, when appropriate, of the expertise and capability that exists in Federal laboratories other than NIST.

(c) *Center activities.* The activities of the Centers shall include:

(1) The establishment of automated manufacturing systems and other advanced production technologies based on research by NIST and other Federal laboratories for the purpose of demonstrations and technology transfer;

(2) The active transfer and dissemination of research findings and Center expertise to a wide range of companies and enterprises, particularly small- and medium-sized manufacturers; and

(3) Loans, on a selective, short-term basis, of items of advanced manufacturing equipment to small manufacturing firms with less than 100 employees.

(d) *Center organization and operation.* Each Center will be organized to transfer advanced manufacturing technology to small and medium sized manufacturers located in its service region. Regional Centers will be established and operated via cooperative agreements between NIST and the award-receiving organizations. Individual awards shall be decided on the basis of merit review, geographical diversity, and the availability of funding.

(e) *Leverage.* The Centers program must concentrate on approaches which can be applied to other companies, in other regions, or by other organizations. The lessons learned in assisting a particular target firm should be documented in order to facilitate the use of those lessons by other target firms. A Center should build on unique solutions developed for a single company to develop techniques of broad applicability. It should seek wide implementation with well-developed mechanisms for distribution of results. Leverage is the principle of developing less resource-intensive methods of delivering technologies (as when a Center staff person has the same impact on ten firms as was formerly obtained with the resources used for one, or when a project once done by the Center can be carried out for dozens of companies by the private sector or a state or local organization.) Leverage does not imply a larger non-federal funding match (that is, greater expenditure of non-federal dollars for each federal dollar) but rather a greater impact per dollar.

(f) *Regional impact.* A new Center should not begin by spreading its resources too thinly over too large a geographic area. It should concentrate first on establishing its structure, operating style, and client base within a manageable service area.

§290.4 Terms and schedule of financial assistance.

(a) NIST may provide financial support to any Center for a period not to exceed six years, subject to the availability of funding and continued satisfactory performance. Awards under this program shall be subject to all Federal and Departmental regulations, policies, and procedures applicable to Federal assistance awards. NIST may not provide more than 50 percent of the capital and annual operating and maintenance required to create and maintain such Center. Allowable capital costs may be treated as an expense in the year expended or obligated.

(b) *NIST contribution*. The funds provided by NIST may be used for capital and operating and maintenance expenses. Each Center will operate on one-year, annually renewable cooperative agreements, contingent upon successful completion of informal annual reviews. Funding can not be provided after the sixth year of support. A formal review of each Center will be conducted during its third year of operation by an independent Merit Review Panel in accordance with §290.8 of these procedures. Centers will be required to demonstrate that they will be self-sufficient by the end of six years of operation. The amount of NIST investment in each Center will depend upon the particular requirements, plans, and performance of the Center, as well as the availability of NIST funds. NIST may support the budget of each Center on a matching-funds basis not to exceed the Schedule of Financial Assistance outlined in Table 1. The remaining portion of the Center's funding shall be provided by the host organization.

TABLE 1—SCHEDULE OF NIST MATCHING FUNDS

Year of center operation	Maximum NIST share
1–3	½
4	⅖
5–6	⅓

(c) *Host contribution*. The host organization may count as part of its share:

(1) Dollar contributions from state, county, city, industrial, or other sources;

(2) Revenue from licensing and royalties;

(3) Fees for services performed,

(4) In-kind contributions of full-time personnel,

(5) In-kind contribution of part-time personnel, equipment, software, rental value of centrally located space (office and laboratory) and other related contributions up to a maximum of one-half of the host's annual share. Allowable capital expenditures may be applied in the award year expended or in subsequent award years.

[55 FR 38275, Sept. 17, 1990, as amended at 59 FR 22505, May 2, 1994]

§290.5 Basic proposal qualifications.

(a) NIST shall designate each proposal which satisfies the qualifications criteria below as "qualified proposal" and subject the qualified proposals to a merit review. Applications which do not meet the requirements of this section will not receive further consideration.

(1) *Qualified organizations*. Any nonprofit institution, or group thereof, or consortium of nonprofit institutions, including entities which already exist or may be incorporated specifically to manage the Center.

(2) *Proposal format*. Proposals for Center Operating Awards shall:

(i) Be submitted with a Standard Form 424 to the above address;

(ii) *Not exceed 25 typewritten pages in length for the basic proposal document* (which must include the information requirements of paragraph (a)(3) of this section); it may be accompanied by additional appendices of relevant supplementary attachments and tabular material. Basic proposal documents which exceed 25 pages in length will not be qualified for further review.

(3) *Proposal requirements*. In order to be considered for a Center Operating Award, proposals must contain:

(i) A plan for the allocation of intellectual property rights associated with any invention or copyright which may result from the involvement in the Center's technology transfer or research activities consistent with the conditions of §290.9;

(ii) A statement which provides adequate assurances that the host organization will contribute 50 percent or more of the proposed Center's capital and annual operating and maintenance costs for the first three years and an increasing share for each of the following three additional years. Applicants should provide evidence that the proposed Center will be self-supporting after six years.

(iii) A statement describing linkages to industry, government, and educational organizations within its service region.

(iv) A statement defining the initial service region including a statement of the constituency to be served and the level of service to be provided, as well as outyear plans.

(v) A statement agreeing to focus the mission of the Center on technology transfer activities and not to exclude companies based on state boundaries.

(vi) A proposed plan for the annual evaluation of the success of the Center by the Program, including appropriate criteria for consideration, and weighting of those criteria.

(vii) A plan to focus the Center's technology emphasis on areas consistent with NIST technology research programs and organizational expertise.

(viii) A description of the planned Center sufficient to permit NIST to evaluate the proposal in accordance with § 290.6 of these procedures.

(b) [Reserved]

§ 290.6 Proposal evaluation and selection criteria.

(a) In making a decision whether to provide financial support, NIST shall review and evaluate all qualified proposals in accordance with the following criteria, assigning equal weight to each of the four categories.

(1) *Identification of target firms in proposed region.* Does the proposal define an appropriate service region with a large enough population of target firms of small- and medium-sized manufacturers which the applicant understands and can serve, and which is not presently served by an existing Center?

(i) *Market analysis.* Demonstrated understanding of the service region's manufacturing base, including business size, industry types, product mix, and technology requirements.

(ii) *Geographical location.* Physical size, concentration of industry, and economic significance of the service region's manufacturing base. Geographical diversity of Centers will be a factor in evaluation of proposals; a proposal for a Center located near an existing Center may be considered only if the proposal is unusually strong and the population of manufacturers and the technology to be addressed justify it.

(2) *Technology resources.* Does the proposal assure strength in technical personnel and programmatic resources, full-time staff, facilities, equipment, and linkages to external sources of technology to develop and transfer technologies related to NIST research results and expertise in the technical areas noted in these procedures?

(3) *Technology delivery mechanisms.* Does the proposal clearly and sharply define an effective methodology for delivering advanced manufacturing technology to small- and medium-sized manufacturers?

(i) *Linkages.* Development of effective partnerships or linkages to third parties such as industry, universities, nonprofit economic organizations, and state governments who will amplify the Center's technology delivery to reach a large number of clients in its service region.

(ii) *Program leverage.* Provision of an effective strategy to amplify the Center's technology delivery approaches to achieve the proposed objectives as described in § 290.3(e).

(4) *Management and financial plan.* Does the proposal define a management structure and assure management personnel to carry out development and operation of an effective Center?

(i) *Organizational structure.* Completeness and appropriateness of the organizational structure, and its focus on the mission of the Center. Assurance of full-time top management of the Center.

(ii) *Program management.* Effectiveness of the planned methodology of program management.

(iii) *Internal evaluation.* Effectiveness of the planned continuous internal evaluation of program activities.

(iv) *Plans for financial matching.* Demonstrated stability and duration of the applicant's funding commitments as well as the percentage of operating and capital costs guaranteed by the applicant. Identification of matching fund sources and the general terms of the funding commitments. Evidence of the applicant's ability to become self-sustaining in six years.

(v) *Budget.* Suitability and focus of the applicant's detailed one-year budget and six-year budget outline.

§290.7 Proposal selection process.

Upon the availability of funding to establish Regional Centers, the Director shall publish a notice in the FEDERAL REGISTER requesting submission of proposals from interested organizations. Appliclants will be given an established time frame, not less than 60 days from the publication date of the notice, to prepare and submit a proposal. The proposal evaluation and selection process will consist of four principal phases: Proposal qualification; Proposal review and selection of finalists; Finalist site visits; and, Award determination. Further descriptions of these phases are provided in the following:

(a) *Proposal qualification.* All proposals will be reviewed by NIST to assure compliance with §290.5 of these procedures. Proposals which satisfy these requirements will be designated qualified proposals; all others will be disqualified at this phase of the evaluation and selection process.

(b) *Proposal review and selection of finalists.* The Director of NIST will appoint an evaluation panel to review and evaluate all qualified proposals in accordance with the criteria set forth in section 290.6 of these procedures, assigning equal weight to each of the four categories. From the qualified proposals, a group of finalists will be selected based on this review.

(c) *Finalist site visits.* NIST representatives will visit each finalist organization. Finalists will be reviewed and assigned numeric scores using the criteria set forth in §290.6 of these procedures assigning equal weight to each of the four categories. NIST may enter into negotiations with the finalists concerning any aspect of their proposal.

(d) *Award determination.* The Director of NIST or his designee shall select awardees for Center Operating Awards based upon the rank order of applicants, the need to assure appropriate regional distribution, and the availability of funds. Upon the final award decision, a notification will be made to each of the proposing organizations.

§290.8 Reviews of centers.

(a) *Overview.* Each Center will be reviewed at least annually, and at the end of its third year of operation according to the procedures and criteria set out below. There will be regular management interaction with NIST and the other Centers for the purpose of evaluation and program shaping. Centers are encouraged to try new approaches, must evaluate their effectiveness, and abandon or adjust those which do not have the desired impact.

(b) *Annual reviews of centers.* Centers will be reviewed annually as part of the funding renewal process using the criteria set out in §290.8(d). The funding level at which a Center is renewed is contingent upon a positive program evaluation and will depend upon the availability of federal funds and on the Center's ability to obtain suitable match, as well as on the budgetary requirements of its proposed program. Centers must continue to demonstrate that they will be self-supporting after six years.

(c) *Third year review of centers.* Each host receiving a Center Operating Award under these procedures shall be evaluated during its third year of operation by a Merit Review Panel appointed by the Secretary of Commerce. Each such Merit Review Panel shall be composed of private experts, none of whom shall be connected with the involved Center, and Federal officials. An official of NIST shall chair the panel. Each Merit Review Panel shall measure the involved Center's performance against the criteria set out in §290.8(d). The Secretary shall not provide funding for the fourth through the sixth years of such Center's operation unless the evaluation is positive on all grounds. As a condition of receiving continuing funding, the Center must show evidence at the third year review that they are making substantial progress toward self-sufficiency. If the evaluation is positive and funds are available, the Secretary of Commerce may provide continued funding through the sixth year at declining levels, which are designed to insure that the Center no longer needs financial support from NIST by the seventh year. In no event shall funding for a Center be provided by the NIST Manufacturing Technology Centers Program after the sixth year of support.

(d) *Criteria for annual and third year reviews.* Centers will be evaluated under the following criteria in each of the annual reviews, as well as the third year review:

(1) The program objectives specified in § 290.3(b) of these procedures;

(2) Funds-matching performance;

(3) The extent to which the target firms have successfully implemented recently developed or currently developed advanced manufacturing technology and techniques transferred by the Center;

(4) The extent to which successes are properly documented and there has been further leveraging or use of a particular advanced manufacturing technology or process;

(5) The degree to which there is successful operation of a network, or technology delivery mechanism, involving the sharing or dissemination of information related to manufacturing technologies among industry, universities, nonprofit economic development organizations and state governments.

(6) The extent to which the Center can increasingly develop continuing resources—both technological and financial—such that the Centers are finally financially self-sufficient.

§ 290.9 Intellectual property rights.

(a) Awards under the Program will follow the policies and procedures on ownership to inventions made under grants and cooperative agreements that are set out in Public Law 96–517 (35 U.S.C. chapter 18), the Presidential Memorandum on Government Patent Policy to the Heads of Executive Departments and Agencies Dated February 18, 1983, and part 401 of title 37 of the Code of Federal Regulations, as appropriate. These policies and procedures generally require the Government to grant to Centers selected for funding the right to elect to obtain title to any invention made in the course of the conduct of research under an award, subject to the reservation of a Government license.

(b) Except as otherwise specifically provided for in an Award, Centers selected for funding under the Program may establish claim to copyright subsisting in any data first produced in the performance of the award. When claim is made to copyright, the funding recipient shall affix the applicable copyright notice of 17 U.S.C. 401 or 402 and acknowledgment of Government sponsorship to the data when and if the data are delivered to the Government, are published, or are deposited for registration as a published work in the U.S. Copyright Office. For data other than computer software, the funding recipient shall grant to the Government, and others acting on its behalf, a paid up, nonexclusive, irrevocable, worldwide license for all such data to reproduce, prepare derivative works, distribute copies to the public, and perform publicly and display publicly, by or on behalf of the Government. For computer software, the funding recipient shall grant to the Government, and others acting on its behalf, a paid up, nonexclusive, irrevocable, worldwide license for all such computer software to reproduce, prepare derivative works, distribute copies to the public, and perform publicly and display publicly, by or on behalf of the Government.

PART 291—MANUFACTURING EXTENSION PARTNERSHIP; ENVIRONMENTAL PROJECTS

AUTHORITY: 15 U.S.C. § 272(b)(1) and (c)(3) and § 2781.

SOURCE: 60 FR 4082, Jan. 20, 1995, unless otherwise noted.

§ 291.1 Program description.

(a) In accordance with the provisions of the National Institute of Standards and Technology Act (15 U.S.C. § 272(b)(1) and (c)(3) and § 2781), as amended, NIST will provide financial assistance to integrate environmentally-related services and resources into the national manufacturing extension system. This assistance will be provided by NIST often in cooperation with the EPA. Under the NIST Manufacturing Extension Partnership (MEP), NIST will periodically make merit-based awards to existing MEP manufacturing extension affiliates for integration of environmental services into extension centers and to non-profit organizations for development of environmentally-related tools and techniques. In addition, NIST will initiate pilot centers providing environmental information for specific industrial sectors to be specified in solicitations. MEP assumes a broad definition of manufacturing, and recognizes a wide range of technology and concepts, including durable goods production; chemical, biotechnology, and other materials processing; electronic component and system fabrication; and engineering services associated with manufacturing, as lying within the definition of manufacturing.

(b) *Announcements of solicitations.* Announcements of solicitations will be made in the Commerce Business Daily. Specific information on the level of funding available and the deadline for proposals will be contained in that announcement. In addition, any specific industry sectors or types of tools and techniques to be focused on will be specified in the announcement.

(c) *Proposal workshops.* Prior to an announcement of solicitation, NIST may announce opportunities for potential applicants to learn about these projects through workshops. The time and place of the workshop(s) will be contained in a Commerce Business Daily announcement.

(d) *Indirect costs.* The total dollar amount of the indirect costs proposed in an application under this program must not exceed the indirect cost rate negotiated and approved by a cognizant Federal agency prior to the proposed effective date of the award or 100 percent of the total proposed direct costs dollar amount in the application, whichever is less.

(e) *Proposal format.* The Proposal must not exceed 20 typewritten pages in length for integration proposals. Proposals for tools and techniques projects and national information centers must not exceed 30 pages in length. The proposal must contain both technical and cost information. The Proposal page count shall include every page, including pages that contain words, table of contents, executive summary, management information and qualifications, resumes, figures, tables, and pictures. All proposals shall be printed such that pages are single-sided, with no more than fifty-five (55) lines per page. Use 21.6 × 27.9 cm (8½″ × 11″) paper or A4 metric paper. Use an easy-to-read font of not more than about 5 characters per cm (fixed pitch font of 12 or fewer characters per inch or proportional font of point size 10 or larger). Smaller type may be used in figures and tables, but must be clearly legible. Margins on all sides (top, bottom, left and right) must be at least 2.5 cm. (1″). The applicant may submit a separately bound document of appendices, containing letters of support for the Basic Proposal. The basic proposal should be self-contained and not rely on the appendices for meeting criteria. Excess pages in the Proposal will not be considered in the evaluation. Applicants must submit one signed original plus six copies of the proposal along with Standard Form 424, 424A (Rev 4/92) and Form CD–511.

(f) *Content of basic proposal.* The Basic Proposal must, at a minimum, include the following:

(1) An executive summary summarizing the planned project consistent with the Evaluation Criteria stated in this notice.

(2) A description of the planned project sufficient to permit evaluation of the proposal in accordance with the proposal Evaluation Criteria stated in this notice.

(3) A budget for the project which identifies all sources of funds and which breaks out planned expenditures by both activity and object class (e.g., personnel, travel, etc.).

(4) A description of the qualifications of key personnel who will be assigned to work on the proposed project.

(5) A statement of work that discusses the specific tasks to be carried out, including a schedule of measurable events and milestones.

(6) A Standard Form 424, 424A (Rev 4–92) prescribed by the applicable OMB circular and Form CD–511, Certification Regarding Debarment, Suspension and Other Responsibility Matters; Drug-Free Workplace Requirements and Lobbying. SF–424, 424A (Rev 4–92) and Form CD–511 will not be considered part of the page count of the Basic Proposal.

(7) The application requirements and the standard form requirements have been approved by OMB (OMB Control Number 0693–0010, 0348–0043 and 0348–0044).

(g) *Applicable federal and departmental guidance.* This includes: Administrative Requirements, Cost Principles, and Audits. [Dependent upon type of Recipient organization: nonprofit, for-profit, state/local government, or educational institution]

(1) *Nonprofit organizations.*

(i) OMB Circular A–110—Uniform Administrative Requirements of Grants and Agreements with Institutions of Higher Education, Hospitals, and Other Nonprofit Organizations.

(ii) OMB Circular A–122—Cost Principles for Nonprofit Organizations.

(iii) 15 CFR part 29b—Audit Requirements for Institutions of Higher Education and Other Nonprofit Organizations [implements OMB Circular A–133—Audits for Institutions of Higher Education and Other Nonprofit Organizations].

(2) *State/local governments.*

(i) 15 CFR part 24—Uniform Administrative Requirements for Grants and Cooperative Agreements to State and Local Governments.

(ii) OMB Circular A–87—Cost Principles for State and Local Governments.

(iii) 15 CFR part 29a—Audit Requirements for State and Local Governments [implements OMB Circular A–128—Audit of State and Local Governments].

(3) *Educational institutions.*

(i) OMB Circular A–110—Administrative Requirements for Grants and Agreements with Institutions of Higher Education, Hospitals, and Other Nonprofit Organizations.

(ii) OMB Circular A–21—Cost Principles for Educational Institutions.

(iii) 15 CFR part 29b—Audit Requirements for Institutions of Higher Education and Other Nonprofit Organizations [implements OMB Circular A–133—Audits for Institutions of Higher Education and Other Nonprofit Organizations].

§291.2 Environmental integration projects.

(a) *Eligibility criteria.* Eligible applicants for these projects are manufacturing extension centers or state technology extension programs which at the time of solicitation have grants, cooperative agreements or contracts with the NIST Manufacturing Extension Partnership. Only one proposal per organization per solicitation is permitted in this category.

(b) *Project objective.* The purpose of these projects is to support the integration of environmentally-focused technical assistance, and especially pollution prevention assistance, for smaller manufacturers into the broader services provided by existing MEP manufacturing extension centers. Proposers are free to structure their project in whatever way will be most effective and efficient in increasing the ability of the center to deliver high quality environmental and pollution prevention technical assistance (either directly or in partnership with other organizations). Following are some examples of purposes for which these funds could be used. This list is by no means meant to be all inclusive. A center might propose a set of actions encompassing several of these examples as well as others.

(1) *Environmental needs assessment.* Detailed assessment of the environmentally-related technical assistance needs of manufacturers within the state or region of the manufacturing extension center. This would be done as part of a broader plan to incorporate environmentally related services into

the services of the manufacturing extension center. The center might propose to document its process and findings so that other centers may learn from its work.

(2) *Partnership with another organization.* The center might propose to partner with an existing organization which is providing environmentally-focused technical assistance to manufacturers. The partnership would lead to greater integration of service delivery through joint technical assistance projects and joint training.

(3) *Accessing private-sector environmental resources.* The center might propose to increase it's ability to access environmental technical services for smaller manufacturers from environmental consultants or environmental firms.

(4) *Training of field engineers/agents in environmental topics.* Funding for training which empowers the field engineer/agent with the knowledge needed to recognize potential environmental, and especially pollution prevention, problems and opportunities. In addition, training might be funded which empowers the field engineer/agent with the knowledge needed to make appropriate recommendations for solutions or appropriate referrals to other sources of information or expertise. The over-arching goal is for the field engineer/agent to enable the manufacturer to be both environmentally clean and competitive.

(5) *Access to environmentally related information or expertise.* A center might propose to fund access to databases or other sources of environmentally-related information or expertise which might be necessary to augment the environmentally focused activities of the manufacturing extension center.

(6) *Addition of environmentally focused staff.* It may be necessary for manufacturing extension centers to have an environmental program manager or lead field engineer/agent with environmental training and experience. Funds could be requested to hire this person. However, the proposer would have to demonstrate a clear and reasonable plan for providing for the support of this person after the funds provided under this project are exhausted since no commitment is being made to ongoing funding.

(c) *Award period.* Projects initiated under this category may be carried out over multiple years. The proposer should include optional second and third years in their proposal. Proposals selected for award may receive one, two or three years of funding from currently available funds at the discretion of DOC. If an application is selected for funding, DOC has no obligation to provide any additional future funding in connection with that award. A separate cooperative agreement will be written with winning applicants. Renewal of an award to increase funding or extend the period of performance is at the total discretion of DOC. It is anticipated that successful projects will be given the opportunity to roll the funding for these efforts into the base funding for the extension center. Such a roll-over will be based on a performance review and the availability of funds.

(d) *Matching requirements.* No matching funds are required for these proposals. However, the presence of matching funds (cash and in-kind) will be considered in the evaluation under the Financial Plan criteria.

(e) *Environmental integration projects evaluation criteria.* In most solicitations, preference will be given to projects which are focused on a single industry sector. This is desired to build on the expertise and resources which are being built in tools and resources projects in these industry sectors. Industry focus will be specified in the solicitation announcement. However, actual services need not be limited exclusively to this sector. In addition preference may be given to extension centers which do not have extensive environmentally-related services already in place. In addition to these preferences, the criteria for selection of awards will be as follows in descending order of importance:

(1) *Demonstrated commitment to incorporating environmentally related services.* The extension center must demonstrate its commitment to incorporate environmentally-related technical services into its overall manufacturing extension services even after funding for this project is exhausted. It

is not the objective of this effort to establish completely autonomous environmentally focused extension centers. Rather, the goal is to ensure that such services are integrated directly with general manufacturing extension services focused on competitiveness. The center must demonstrate that such integration will take place. Factors that may be considered include: The amount of matching funds devoted to the efforts proposed as demonstration of the center's commitment to the activity; indication that environmental services are a significant aspect of the organization's long range planning; strength of commitment and plans for continuing service beyond funding which might be awarded through this project; the degree to which environmental services will become an integral part of each field engineers' portfolio of services; the level of current or planned education and training of staff on relevant environmental issues; and the extent of environmentally related information and expert resources which will be easily accessible by field engineers.

(2) *Demonstrated understanding of the environmentally related technical assistance needs of manufacturers in the target population.* Target population must be clearly defined. The manufacturing center must demonstrate that it understands the populations environmentally related needs or include a coherent methodology for identifying those needs. The proposal should show that the efforts being proposed will enable the center to better meet those needs. Factors that may be considered include: A clear definition of the target population, its size and demographic characteristics; demonstrated understanding of the target population's environmental technical assistance needs or a plan to develop this understanding; and appropriateness of the size of the target population and the anticipated impact for the proposed expenditure.

(3) *Coordination with other relevant organizations.* Wherever possible the project should be coordinated with and leverage other organizations which are providing high quality environmentally-related services to manufacturers in the same target population or which have relevant resources which can be of assistance in the proposed effort. If no such organizations exist, the proposal should build the case that there are no such organizations. Applicants will need to describe how they will coordinate to allow for increased economies of scale and to avoid duplication of services in providing assistance to small and medium-sized manufacturers. Factors that may be considered include: Demonstrated understanding of existing organizations and resources relevant for providing technology assistance related services to the target population; adequate linkages and partnerships with existing organizations and clear definition of those organizations' roles in the proposed activities; and that the proposed activity does not duplicate existing services or resources.

(4) *Program evaluation:* The applicant should specify plans for evaluation of the effectiveness of the proposed program and for ensuring continuous improvement of program activities. Factors that may be considered include: Thoroughness of evaluation plans, including internal evaluation for management control, external evaluation for assessing outcomes of the activity, and "customer satisfaction" measures of performance.

(5) *Management experience and plans.* Applicants should specify plans for proper organization, staffing, and management of the implementation process. Factors that may be considered include: Appropriateness and authority of the governing or managing organization to conduct the proposed activities; qualifications of the project team and its leadership to conduct the proposed activity; soundness of any staffing plans, including recruitment, selection, training, and continuing professional development; appropriateness of the organizational approach for carrying out the proposed activity; evidence of involvement and support by private industry.

(6) *Financial plan:* Applicants should show the relevance and cost effectiveness of the financial plan for meeting the objectives of the project; the firmness and level of the applicant's total financial support for the project; and a plan to maintain the program after the cooperative agreement has expired.

Factors that may be considered include: Reasonableness of the budget both in income and expenses; strength of commitment and amount of the proposer's cost share, if any; effectiveness of management plans for control of budget; appropriateness of matching contributions; and plans for maintaining the program after the cooperative agreement has expired.

§ 291.3 Environmental tools and techniques projects.

(a) *Eligibility criteria.* Eligible applicants for these projects include all nonprofit organizations including universities, community colleges, state governments, state technology programs and independent nonprofit organizations. Organizations may submit multiple proposals under this category in each solicitation for unique projects.

(b) *Project objective.* The purpose of these projects is to support the initial development and implementation of tools or techniques which will aide manufacturing extension organizations in providing environmentally-related services to smaller manufacturers and which may also be of direct use by the smaller manufacturers themselves. Specific industry sectors to be addressed and sub-categories of tools and techniques may be specified in solicitations. These sectors or sub-categories will be specified in the solicitation announcement. Examples of tools and techniques include, but are not limited to, manufacturing assessment tools, environmental benchmarking tools, training delivery programs, electronically accessible environmental information resources, environmental demonstration facilities, software tools, etc. Projects must be completed within the scope of the effort proposed and should not require on-going federal support.

(c) *Award period.* Projects initiated under this category may be carried out over up to three years. Proposals selected for award will receive all funding from currently available funds. If an application is selected for funding, DOC has no obligation to provide any additional future funding in connection with that award. Renewal of an award to increase funding or extend the period of performance is at the total discretion of DOC.

(d) *Matching requirements.* No matching funds are required for these proposals. However, the presence of matching funds (cash and in-kind) will be considered in the evaluation under the Financial Plan criteria.

(e) *Environmental tools and techniques projects evaluation criteria.* Proposals from applicants will be evaluated and rated on the basis of the following criteria listed in descending order of importance:

(1) *Demonstrated understanding of the environmentally-related technical assistance needs of manufacturers and technical assistance providers in the target population.* Target population must be clearly defined. The proposal must demonstrate that it understands the population's environmentally related tool or technique needs. The proposal should show that the efforts being proposed meet the needs identified. Factors that may be considered include: A clear definition of the target population, size and demographic distribution; demonstrated understanding of the target population's environmental tools or techniques needs; and appropriateness of the size of the target population and the anticipated impact for the proposed expenditure.

(2) *Technology and information sources.* The proposal must delineate the sources of technology and/or information which will be used to create the tool or resource. Sources may include those internal to the center (including staff expertise) or from other organizations. Factors that may be considered include: Strength of core competency in the proposed area of activity; and demonstrated access to relevant technical or information sources external to the organization.

(3) *Degree of integration with the manufacturing extension partnership.* The proposal must demonstrate that the tool or resource will be integrated into and will be of service to the NIST Manufacturing Extension Centers. Factors that may be considered include: Ability to access the tool or resource especially for MEP extension centers; methodology for disseminating or promoting use of the tool or technique especially within the MEP system; and

demonstrated interest in using the tool or technique especially by MEP extension centers.

(4) *Coordination with other relevant organizations.* Wherever possible the project should be coordinated with and leverage other organizations which are developing or have expertise on similar tools or techniques. If no such organizations exist, the proposal should show that this the case. Applicants will need to describe how they will coordinate to allow for increased economies of scale and to avoid duplication. Factors that may be considered include: Demonstrated understanding of existing organizations and resources relevant to the proposed project; Adequate linkages and partnerships with existing organizations and clear definition of those organizations' roles in the proposed activities; and that the proposed activity does not duplicate existing services or resources.

(5) *Program evaluation.* The applicant should specify plans for evaluation of the effectiveness of the proposed tool or technique and for ensuring continuous improvement of the tool. Factors that may be considered include: Thoroughness of evaluation plans, including internal evaluation for management control, external evaluation for assessing outcomes of the activity, and "customer satisfaction" measures of performance.

(6) *Management experience and plans.* Applicants should specify plans for proper organization, staffing, and management of the implementation process. Factors that may be considered include: Appropriateness and authority of the governing or managing organization to conduct the proposed activities; qualifications of the project team and its leadership to conduct the proposed activity; soundness of any staffing plans, including recruitment, selection, training, and continuing professional development; and appropriateness of the organizational approach for carrying out the proposed activity.

(7) *Financial plan:* Applicants should show the relevance and cost effectiveness of the financial plan for meeting the objectives of the project; the firmness and level of the applicant's total financial support for the project; and a plan to maintain the program after the cooperative agreement has expired. Factors that may be considerable include: Reasonableness of the budget, both in income and expenses; strength of commitment and amount of the proposers's cost share, if any; effectiveness of management plans for control of budget appropriateness of matching contributions; and plan for maintaining the program after the cooperative agreement has expired.

§ 291.4 National industry-specific pollution prevention and environmental compliance resource centers.

(a) *Eligibility criteria.* Eligible applicants for these projects include all nonprofit organizations including universities, community colleges, state governments, state technology programs and independent nonprofit organizations. Only one proposal per organization is permitted in this category.

(b) *Project objective.* These centers will provide easy access to relevant, current, reliable and comprehensive information on pollution prevention opportunities, regulatory compliance and technologies and techniques for reducing pollution in the most competitive manner for a specific industry sector or industrial process. The sector or industrial process to be addressed will be specified in the solicitation. The center will enhance the ability of small businesses to implement risk based pollution prevention alternatives to increase competitiveness and reduce adverse environmental impacts. The center should use existing resources, information and expertise and will avoid duplication of existing efforts. The information provided by the center will create links between relevant EPA Pollution Prevention programs, EPA and other technical information, NIST manufacturing extension efforts, EPA regulation and guidance, and state requirements. The center will emphasize pollution prevention methods as the principal means to both comply with government regulations and enhance competitiveness.

(c) *Project goal.* To improve the environmental and competitive performance of smaller manufacturers by:

(1) Enhancing the national capability to provide pollution prevention and

regulatory requirements information (federal, state and local) to specific industries.

(2) Providing easy access to relevant and reliable information and tools on pollution prevention technologies and techniques that achieve manufacturing efficiency and enhanced competitiveness with reduced environmental impact.

(3) Providing easy access to relevant and reliable information and tools to enable specific industries to achieve the continued environmental improvement to meet or exceed compliance requirements.

(d) *Project customers.* (1) The customers for this center will be the businesses in the industrial sector or businesses which use the industrial process specified as the focus for the solicitation. In addition, consultants providing services to those businesses, the NIST Manufacturing Extension Centers, and federal state and local programs providing technical, pollution prevention and compliance assistance.

(2) The center should assist the customer in choosing the most cost- effective, environmentally sound options or practices that enhance the company's competitiveness. Assistance must be accessible to all interested customers. The center, wherever feasible, shall use existing materials and information to enhance and develop the services to its customers. The centers should rarely, if ever, perform research, but should find and assimilate data and information produced by other sources. The center should not duplicate any existing distribution system. The center should distribute and provide information, but should not directly provide on-site assistance to customers. Rather, referrals to local technical assistance organizations should be given when appropriate. Information would likely be available through multiple avenues such as phone, fax, electronically accessible data bases, printed material, networks of technical experts, etc.

(e) *Award period.* The pilot initiated under this category may be carried out over multiple years. The proposers should include optional second and third years in their proposal. Proposals selected for award may receive one, two or three years of funding from currently available finds at the discretion of DOC. If an application is selected for funding, DOC has no obligation to provide any additional future funding in connection with that award. Renewal of an award to increase funding or extend the period of performance is at the total discretion of DOC. Successful centers may be given an opportunity to receive continuing funding as a NIST manufacturing center after the expiration of their initial cooperative agreement. Such a roll-over will be based upon the performance of the center and availability of funding.

(f) *Matching requirements.* A matching contribution from each applicant will be required. NIST may provide financial support up to 50% of the total budget for the project. The applicant's share of the budget may include dollar contributions from state, county, industrial or other non-federal sources and non-federal in-kind contributions necessary and reasonable for proper accomplishment of project objectives.

(g) *Resource center evaluation criteria.* Proposals from applicants will be evaluated and rated on the basis of the following criteria listed in descending order of importance:

(1) *Demonstrated understanding of the environmentally-related information needs of manufacturers and technical assistance providers in the target population.* Understanding the environmentally-related needs of the target population (*i.e.*, customers) is absolutely critical to the success of such a resource center. Factors that may be considered include: A clear definition of the target population, size and demographic distribution; demonstrated understanding of the target population's environmentally-related information needs or a clear plan for identifying those customer needs; and methodologies for continually improving the understanding of the target population's environmentally-related information needs.

(2) *Delivery mechanisms.* The proposal must set forth clearly defined, effective mechanisms for delivery of services to target population. Factors that may be considered include: Potential effectiveness and efficiency of proposed delivery systems; and demonstrated capacity to

form the effective linkages and partnerships necessary for success of the proposed activity.

(3) *Technology and information sources.* The proposal must delineate the sources of information which will be used to create the informational foundation of the resource center. Sources may include those internal to the Center (including staff expertise), but it is expected that many sources will be external. Factors that may be considered include: Strength of core competency in the proposed area of activity; demonstrated access to relevant technical or information sources external to the organization.

(4) *Degree of integration with the manufacturing extension partnership and other technical assistance providers.* The proposal must demonstrate that the source center will be integrated into the system of services provided by the NIST Manufacturing Extension Partnership and other technical assistance providers. Factors that may be considered include: Ability of the target population including MEP Extension Centers to access the resource center; and methodology for disseminating or promoting use of the resource center especially within the MEP system.

(5) *Coordination with other relevant organizations.* Wherever possible the project should be coordinated with and leverage other organizations which are developing or have expertise on similar tools or techniques. If no such organizations exist, the proposal should show that this is the case. Applicants will need to describe how they will coordinate to allow for increased economies of scale and to avoid duplication. Factors that may be considered include: Demonstrated understanding of existing organizations and resources relevant to the proposed project; and adequate linkages and partnerships with existing organizations and clear definition of those organizations' roles in the proposed activities.

(6) *Program evaluation.* The applicant should specify plans for evaluation of the effectiveness of the proposed resource center and for ensuring continuous improvement. Factors that may be considered include: Thoroughness of evaluation plans, including internal evaluation for management control, external evaluation for assessing outcomes of the activity, and "customer satisfaction" measures of performance; and the proposer's plan must include documentation, analysis of the results, and must show how the results can be used in improving the resource center.

(7) *Management experience and Plans.* Applicants should specify Plans for proper organization, staffing, and management of the implementation process. Factors that may be considered include: Appropriateness and authority of the governing or managing organization to conduct the proposed activities; qualifications and experience of the project team and its leadership to conduct the proposed activity; soundness of any staffing plans, including recruitment, selection, training, and continuing professional development; and appropriateness of the organizational approach for carrying out the proposed activity.

(8) *Financial plan.* Applicants should show the relevance and cost effectiveness of the financial plan for meeting the objectives of the project; the firmness and level of the applicant's total financial support for the project; and a plan to maintain the program after the cooperative agreement has expired. Factors that may be considered include: Reasonableness of the budget, both in income and expenses; strength of commitment and amount of the proposer's *cost share;* effectiveness of management plans for control of the budget; and appropriateness of matching contributions.

§ 291.5 Proposal selection process.

The proposal evaluation and selection process will consist of three principal phases: Proposal qualification; proposal review and selection of finalists; and award determination.

(a) *Proposal qualification.* All proposals will be reviewed by NIST to assure compliance with the proposal content and other basic provisions of this notice. Proposals which satisfy these requirements will be designated qualified proposals; all others will be disqualified at this phase of the evaluation and selection process.

(b) *Proposal review and selection of finalists.* NIST will appoint an evaluation panel composed of NIST and in some cases other federal employees to review and evaluate all qualified proposals in accordance with the evaluation criteria and values set forth in this notice. A site visit may be required to make full evaluation of a proposal. From the qualified proposals, a group of finalists will be numerically ranked and recommended for award based on this review.

(c) *Award determination.* The Director of the NIST, or her/his designee, shall select awardees based on total evaluation scores, geographic distribution, and the availability of funds. All three factors will be considered in making an award. Upon the final award decision, a notification will be made to each of the proposing organizations.

§ 291.6 Additional requirements; Federal policies and procedures.

Recipients and subrecipients are subject to all Federal laws and Federal and Department of Commerce policies, regulations, and procedures applicable to Federal financial assistance awards.

PART 292—MANUFACTURING EXTENSION PARTNERSHIP; INFRASTRUCTURE DEVELOPMENT PROJECTS

Sec.

AUTHORITY: 15 U.S.C. 272 (b)(1) and (c)(3) and 2781.

SOURCE: 60 FR 44751, Aug. 29, 1995, unless otherwise noted.

§ 292.1 Program description.

(a) *Purpose.* In accordance with the provisions of the National Institute of Standards and Technology Act (15 U.S.C. 272 (b)(1) and (c)(3) and 2781), as amended, NIST will provide financial assistance to develop the infrastructure of the national manufacturing extension system. Under the NIST Manufacturing Extension Partnership (MEP), NIST will periodically make merit-based awards to develop and deploy training capability and technical tools, techniques, practices, and analyses. In addition, NIST will develop and implement information infrastructure services and pilots. MEP assumes a broad definition of manufacturing, and recognizes a wide range of technology and concepts, including durable goods production; chemical, biotechnology, and other materials processing; electronic component and system fabrication; and engineering services associated with manufacturing, as lying within the definition of manufacturing.

(b) *Announcements of solicitations.* Announcements of solicitations will be made in the Commerce Business Daily. Specific information on the level of funding available and the deadline for proposals will be contained in that announcement. In addition, any specific industry sectors or types of tools and techniques to be focused on will be specified in the announcement, as well as any further definition of the selection criteria.

(c) *Proposal workshops.* Prior to an announcement of solicitation, NIST may announce opportunities for potential applicants to learn about these projects through workshops. The time and place of the workshop(s) will be contained in a Commerce Business Daily announcement.

(d) *Indirect costs.* The total dollar amount of the indirect costs proposed in an application under this program must not exceed the indirect cost rate negotiated and approved by a cognizant Federal agency prior to the proposed effective date of the award or 100 percent of the total proposed direct costs dollar amount in the application, whichever is less.

(e) *Proposal format.* The proposal must contain both technical and cost information. The proposal page count shall include every page, including pages that contain words, table of contents, executive summary, management information and qualifications, resumes, figures, tables, and pictures. All proposals shall be printed such that pages are single-sided, with no more than fifty-five (55) lines per page. Use 21.6 × 27.9 cm (8½″ × 11″) paper or A4 metric paper. Use an easy-to-read font of not more than about 5 characters per cm (fixed pitch font of 12 or fewer characters per inch or proportional font of point size 10 or larger). Smaller type may be used in figures and tables, but must be clearly legible. Margins on all sides (top, bottom, left and right) must be at lease 2.5 cm. (1″). Length limitations for proposals will be specified in solicitations. The applicant may submit a separately bound document of appendices, containing letters of support for the proposal. The proposal should be self-contained and not rely on the appendices for meeting criteria. Excess pages in the proposal will not be considered in the evaluation. Applicants must submit one signed original plus six copies of the proposal and Standard Form 424, 424A, and 424B (Rev 4/92), Standard Form LLL, and Form CD–511. Applicants for whom the submission of six copies presents financial hardship may submit one original and two copies of the application.

(f) *Content of proposal.* (1) The proposal must, at a minimum, include the following:

(i) An executive summary summarizing the planned project consistent with the Evaluation Criteria stated in this part.

(ii) A description of the planned project sufficient to permit evaluation of the proposal in accordance with the proposal Evaluation Criteria stated in this part.

(iii) A budget for the project which identifies all sources of funds and which breaks out planned expenditures by both activity and object class (e.g., personnel, travel, etc.).

(iv) A description of the qualifications of key personnel who will be assigned to work on the proposed project.

(v) A statement of work that discusses the specific tasks to be carried out, including a schedule of measurable events and milestones.

(vi) A completed Standard Form 424, 424A, and 424B (Rev 4–92) prescribed by the applicable OMB circular, Standard Form LLL, and Form CD–511, Certification Regarding Debarment, Suspension and Other Responsibility Matters; Drug-Free Workplace Requirements and Lobbying. SF–424, 424A, 424B (Rev 4–92), SF-LLL, and Form CD–511 will not be considered part of the page count of the proposal.

(2) The application requirements and the standard form requirements have been approved by OMB (OMB Control Number 0693–0005, 0348–0043 and 0348–0044).

(g) *Applicable federal and departmental guidance.* The Administrative Requirements, Cost Principles, and Audits are dependent upon type of Recipient organization as follows:

(1) *Nonprofit organizations.* (i) OMB Circular A–110—Uniform Administrative Requirements for Grants and Agreements with Institutions of Higher Education, Hospitals, and Other Nonprofit Organizations.

(ii) OMB Circular A–122—Cost Principles for Nonprofit Organizations.

(iii) 15 CFR Part 29b—Audit Requirements for Institutions of Higher Education and Other Nonprofit Organizations (implements OMB Circular A–133—Audits for Institutions of Higher Education and Other Nonprofit Organizations).

(2) *State/local governments.* (i) 15 CFR Part 24—Uniform Administrative Requirements for Grants and Cooperative Agreements to State and Local Governments.

(ii) OMB Circular A–87—Cost Principles for State and Local Governments.

(iii) 15 CFR Part 29a—Audit Requirements for State and Local Governments (implements OMB Circular A–128—Audit of State and Local Governments).

(3) *Educational institutions.* (i) OMB Circular A–110—Administrative Requirements for Grants and Agreements with Institutions of Higher Education, Hospitals, and Other Nonprofit Organizations.

(ii) OMB Circular A–21—Cost Principles for Educational Institutions.

(iii) 15 CFR Part 29b—Audit Requirements for Institutions of Higher Education and Other Nonprofit Organizations (implements OMB Circular A–133—Audits for Institutions of Higher Education and Other Nonprofit Organizations).

(4) *For-profit organizations.* (i) OMB Circular A–110—Administrative Requirements for Grants and Agreements with Institutions of Higher Education, Hospitals, and Other Nonprofit Organizations.

(ii) 48 CFR Part 31—Federal Acquisition Regulation, Contract Cost Principles and Procedures.

(iii) 15 CFR Part 29b—Audit Requirements for Institutions of Higher Education and Other Nonprofit Organizations (implements OMB Circular A–133).

(h) *Availability of forms and circulars.* (1) Copies of forms referenced in this part may be obtained from the Manufacturing Extension Partnership, National Institute of Standards and Technology, Room C121, Building 301, Gaithersburg, MD 20899.

(2) Copies of OMB Circulars may be obtained from the Office of Administration, Publications Office, 725 17th St., NW, Room 2200, New Executive Office Building, Washington, DC 20503.

§292.2 Training development and deployment projects.

(a) *Eligibility criteria.* In general, eligible applicants for these projects include all for-profit and nonprofit organizations including universities, community colleges, state governments, state technology programs and independent nonprofit organizations. However, specific limitations on eligibility may be specified in solicitations. Organizations may submit multiple proposals under this category in each solicitation for unique projects.

(b) *Project objective.* The purpose of these projects is to support the development and deployment of training programs which will aid manufacturing extension organizations in providing services to smaller manufacturers. While primarily directed toward the field agents/engineers of the extension organizations, the training may also be of direct use by the smaller manufacturers themselves. Specific industry sectors to be addressed and sub-categories of training may be specified in solicitations. Examples of training topic areas include, but are not limited to, manufacturing assessment functions, business systems management, quality assurance assistance, and financial management activities. Examples of training program deployment include, but are not limited to, organization and conduct of training courses, development and conduct of train-the-trainer courses, preparations and delivery of distance learning activities, and preparation of self-learning and technical-guideline materials. Projects must be completed within the scope of the effort proposed and should not require on-going federal support.

(c) *Award period.* Projects initiated under this category may be carried out over a period of up to three years. If an application is selected for funding, DOC has no obligation to provide any additional future funding in connection with that award. Renewal of an award to increase funding or extend the period of performance is at the total discretion of DOC.

(d) *Matching requirements.* Matching fund requirements for these proposals will be specified in solicitations including the breakdown of cash and in-kind requirements. For those projects not requiring matching funds, the presence of match will be considered in the evaluation under the Financial Plan criteria.

(e) *Training development and deployment projects evaluation criteria.* Proposals will be evaluated and rated on the basis of the following criteria listed in descending order of importance:

(1) *Demonstration that the proposed project will meet the training needs of technical assistance providers and manufacturers in the target population.* The target population must be clearly defined and the proposal must demonstrate that it understands the population's training needs within the proposed project area. The proposal should show that the efforts being proposed meet the needs identified. Factors that may be considered include: A clear definition of the target population, size and demographic distribution; demonstrated understanding of the target population's training needs; and appropriateness of the size of the target population and the anticipated impact for the proposed expenditure.

(2) *Development/deployment methodology and use of appropriate technology and information sources.* The proposal must describe the technical plan for the development or deployment of the training, including the project activities to be used in the training development/deployment and the sources of technology and/or information which will be used to create or deploy the

training activity. Sources may include those internal to the proposer or from other organizations. Factors that may be considered include: Adequacy of the proposed technical plan; strength of core competency in the proposed area of activity; and demonstrated access to relevant technical or information sources external to the organization.

(3) *Delivery and implementation mechanisms.* The proposal must set forth clearly defined, effective mechanisms for delivery and/or implementation of proposed services to the target population. The proposal also must demonstrate that training activities will be integrated into and will be of service to the NIST Manufacturing Extension Centers. Factors that may be considered include: Ease of access to the training activity especially for MEP extension centers; methodology for disseminating or promoting involvement in the training especially within the MEP system; and demonstrated interest in the training activity especially by MEP extension centers.

(4) *Coordination with other relevant organizations.* Wherever possible the project should be coordinated with and leverage other organizations which are developing or have expertise with similar training. If no such organizations exist, the proposal should show that this is the case. Applicants will need to describe how they will coordinate to allow for increased economies of scale and to avoid duplication. Factors that may be considered include: Demonstrated understanding of existing organizations and resources relevant to the proposed project; adequate linkages and partnerships with existing organizations and clear definition of those organizations' roles in the proposed activities; and that the proposed activity does not duplicate existing services or resources.

(5) *Program evaluation.* The applicant should specify plans for evaluation of the effectiveness of the proposed training activity and for ensuring continuous improvement of the training. Factors that may be considered include: Thoroughness of evaluation plans, including internal evaluation for management control, external evaluation for assessing outcomes of the activity, and "customer satisfaction" measures of performance.

(6) *Management and organizational experience and plans.* Applicants should specify plans for proper organization, staffing, and management of the implementation process. Factors that may be considered include: Appropriateness and authority of the governing or managing organization to conduct the proposed activities; qualifications of the project team and its leadership to conduct the proposed activity; soundness of any staffing plans, including recruitment, selection, training, and continuing professional development; and appropriateness of the organizational approach for carrying out the proposed activity.

(7) *Financial plan.* Applicants should show the relevance and cost effectiveness of the financial plan for meeting the objectives of the project; the firmness and level of the applicant's total financial support for the project; and a plan to maintain the program after the cooperative agreement has expired. Factors that may be considered include: Reasonableness of the budget, both in income and expenses; strength of commitment and amount of the proposer's cost share, if any; effectiveness of management plans for control of budget; appropriateness of matching contributions; and plan for maintaining the program after the cooperative agreement has expired.

§ 292.3 Technical tools, techniques, practices, and analyses projects.

(a) *Eligibility criteria.* In general, eligible applicants for these projects include all for profit and nonprofit organizations including universities, community colleges, state governments, state technology programs and independent nonprofit organizations. However, specific limitations on eligibility may be specified in solicitations. Organizations may submit multiple proposals under this category in each solicitation for unique projects.

(b) *Project objective.* The purpose of these projects is to support the initial development, implementation, and analysis of tools, techniques, and practices which will aid manufacturing extension organizations in providing services to smaller manufacturers and which may also be of direct use by the smaller manufacturers themselves. Specific industry sectors to be addressed and sub-categories of tools, techniques, practices, and analyses may be specified in solicitations. Examples of tools, techniques, and practices include, but are not limited to, manufacturing assessment tools, benchmarking tools, business systems management tools, quality assurance assistance tools, financial management tools, software tools, practices for partnering, techniques for urban or rural firms, and comparative analysis of assessment methods. Projects must be completed within the scope of the effort proposed and should not require on-going federal support.

(c) *Award period.* Projects initiated under this category may be carried out over a period of up to three years. If an application is selected for funding, DOC has no obligation to provide any additional future funding in connection with that award. Renewal of an award to increase funding or extend the period of performance is at the total discretion of DOC.

(d) *Matching requirements.* Matching fund requirements for these proposals will be specified in solicitations including the breakdown of cash and in-kind requirements. For those projects not requiring matching funds, the presence of match will be considered in the evaluation under the Financial Plan criteria.

(e) *Tools, techniques, practices, and analyses projects evaluation criteria.* Proposals from applicants will be evaluated and rated on the basis of the following criteria listed in descending order of importance:

(1) *Demonstration that the proposed project will meet the technical assistance needs of technical assistance providers and manufacturers in the target population.* Target population must be clearly defined. The proposal must demonstrate that it understands the population's tool or technique needs within the proposed project area. The proposal should show that the efforts being proposed meet the needs identified. Factors that may be considered include: A clear definition of the target population, size and demographic distribution; demonstrated understanding of the target population's tools or technique needs; and appropriateness of the size of the target population and the anticipated impact for the proposed expenditure.

(2) *Development methodology and use of appropriate technology and information sources.* The proposal must describe the technical plan for the development of the tool or resource, including the project activities to be used in the tool/resource development and the sources of technology and/or information which will be used to create the tool or resource. Sources may include those internal to the proposer or from other organizations. Factors that may be considered include: Adequacy of the proposed technical plan; strength of core competency in the proposed area of activity; and demonstrated access to relevant technical or information sources external to the organization.

(3) *Degree of integration with the manufacturing extension partnership.* The proposal must demonstrate that the tool or resource will be integrated into and will be of service to the NIST Manufacturing Extension Centers. Factors that may be considered include: Ability to access the tool or resource especially for MEP extension centers; methodology for disseminating or promoting use of the tool or technique especially within the MEP system; and demonstrated interest in using the tool or technique especially by MEP extension centers.

(4) *Coordination with other relevant organizations.* Wherever possible the project should be coordinated with and leverage other organizations which are developing or have expertise on similar tools, techniques, practices, or analyses. If no such organizations exist, the proposal should show that this is the case. Applicants will need to describe how they will coordinate to allow for increased economies of scale and to avoid duplication. Factors that may be considered include: Demonstrated understanding of existing organizations and resources relevant to the proposed project; adequate linkages and partnerships with existing organizations and clear definition of those organizations' roles in the proposed activities; and that the proposed activity does not duplicate existing services or resources.

(5) *Program evaluation.* The applicant should specify plans for evaluation of the effectiveness of the proposed tool or technique and for ensuring continuous improvement of the tool. Factors that may be considered include: Thoroughness of evaluation plans, including internal evaluation for management control, external evaluation for assessing outcomes of the activity, and "customer satisfaction" measures of performance.

(6) *Management experience and plans.* Applicants should specify plans for proper organization, staffing, and management of the implementation process. Factors that may be considered include: Appropriateness and authority of the governing or managing organization to conduct the proposed activities; qualifications of the project team and its leadership to conduct the proposed activity; soundness of any staffing plans, including recruitment, selection, training, and continuing professional development; and appropriateness of the organizational approach for carrying out the proposed activity.

(7) *Financial plan.* Applicants should show the relevance and cost effectiveness of the financial plan for meeting the objectives of the project; the firmness and level of the applicant's total financial support for the project; and a plan to maintain the program after the cooperative agreement has expired. Factors that may be considered include: Reasonableness of the budget, both in income and expenses; strength of commitment and amount of the proposer's cost share, if any; effectiveness of management plans for control of budget; appropriateness of matching contributions; and plan for maintaining the program after the cooperative agreement has expired.

§ 292.4 Information infrastructure projects.

(a) *Eligibility criteria.* In general, eligible applicants for these projects include all for profit and nonprofit organizations including universities, community colleges, state governments, state technology programs and independent nonprofit organizations. However, specific limitations on eligibility may be specified in solicitations. Organizations may submit multiple proposals under this category in each solicitation for unique projects.

(b) *Project objective.* The purpose of these projects is to support and act as a catalyst for the development and implementation of information infrastructure services and pilots. These projects will aid manufacturing extension organizations and smaller manufacturers in accessing the technical information they need or will accelerate the rate of adoption of electronic commerce. Specific industry sectors to be addressed or subcategories of information infrastructure projects include, but are not limited to, pilot demonstration of electronic data interchange in a supplier chain, implementation of an electronic information service for field engineers at MEP extension centers, and industry specific electronic information services for MEP centers and smaller manufacturers.

(c) *Award period.* Projects initiated under this category may be carried out over a period of up to three years. If an application is selected for funding, DOC has no obligation to provide any additional future funding in connection with that award. Renewal of an award to increase funding or extend the period of performance is at the total discretion of DOC.

(d) *Matching requirements.* Matching fund requirements for these proposals will be specified in solicitations including the breakdown of cash and in-kind requirements. For those projects not requiring matching funds, the presence of match will be considered in the evaluation under the Financial Plan criteria.

(e) *Information infrastructure projects evaluation criteria.* Proposals from applicants will be evaluated and rated on the basis of the following criteria listed in descending order of importance:

(1) *Demonstration that the proposed project will meet the need of the target customer base.* The target customer base must be clearly defined and, in general, will be technical assistance providers and/or smaller manufacturers. The proposal should demonstrate a clear understanding of the customer base's needs within the proposed project area. The proposal should also show that the efforts being proposed meet the needs

identified. Factors that may be considered include: A clear definition of the customer base, size and demographic distribution; demonstrated understanding of the customer base's needs within the project area; and appropriateness of the size of the customer base and the anticipated impact for the proposed expenditure.

(2) *Development plans and delivery/implementation mechanisms.* The proposal must set forth clearly defined, effective plans for the development, delivery and/or implementation of proposed services to the customer base. The proposal must delineate the sources of information which will be used to implement the project. Sources may include those internal to the center (including staff expertise) or from other organizations. Factors that may be considered include: Adequacy of plans; potential effectiveness and efficiency of proposed delivery and implementation systems; demonstrated capacity to form effective linkages; partnerships necessary for success of the proposed activity; strength of core competency in the proposed area of activity; and demonstrated access to relevant technical or information sources external to the organization.

(3) *Coordination with other relevant organizations.* Wherever possible the project should be coordinated with and leverage other organizations which are developing or have expertise within the project area. In addition, the project should demonstrate that it does not duplicate efforts which already are being performed by the private sector without government support. Applicants will need to describe how they will coordinate to allow for increased economies of scale and to avoid duplication. If the proposer will not be partnering with any other organizations, then the proposal should clearly explain why the project will be more successful if implemented as proposed. A proposal which makes a credible case for why there are no, or very limited, partnerships will not be penalized in evaluation. Factors that may be considered include: Demonstrated understanding of existing organizations and resources relevant to the proposed project; Adequate linkages and partnerships with relevant existing organizations; clear definition of the roles of partnering organizations in the proposed activities; and that the proposed activity does not duplicate existing services or resources.

(4) *Management and organizational experience and plans.* Applicants should specify plans for proper organization, staffing, and management of the project. Factors that may be considered include: Appropriateness and authority of the governing or managing organization to conduct the proposed activities; qualifications of the project team and its leadership to conduct the proposed activity; soundness of any staffing plans, including recruitment, selection, training, and continuing professional development; and appropriateness of the organizational approach for carrying out the proposed activity.

(5) *Financial plan.* Applicants should show the relevance and cost effectiveness of the financial plan for meeting the objectives of the project; the firmness and level of the applicant's total financial support for the project; and the ability of the project to continue after the cooperative agreement has expired without federal support. While projects that appear to require ongoing public support will be considered, in general, they will be evaluated lower than those which show a strong ability to become self-sufficient. Factors that may be considered include: Reasonableness of the budget, both in income and expenses; strength of commitment and amount of the proposer's cost share, if any; effectiveness of management plans for control of budget; appropriateness of matching contributions; and plan for maintaining the program after the cooperative agreement has expired.

(6) *Evaluation.* The applicant should specify plans for evaluation of the effectiveness of the proposed project and for ensuring continuous improvement. Factors that may be considered include: Thoroughness of evaluation plans, including internal evaluation for management control, external evaluation for assessing outcomes of the activity, and "customer satisfaction" measures of performance.

§ 292.5 Proposal selection process.

The proposal evaluation and selection process will consist of three principal phases: Proposal qualifications; proposal review and selection of finalists; and award determination as follows:

(a) *Proposal qualification.* All proposals will be reviewed by NIST to assure compliance with the proposal content and other basic provisions of this part. Proposals which satisfy these requirements will be designated qualified proposals; all others will be disqualified at this phase of the evaluation and selection process.

(b) *Proposal review and selection of finalists.* NIST will appoint an evaluation panel to review and evaluate all qualified proposals in accordance with the evaluation criteria and values set forth in this part. Evaluation panels will consist of NIST employees and in some cases other federal employees or non-federal experts who sign non-disclosure agreements. A site visit may be required to make full evaluation of a proposal. From the qualified proposals, a group of finalists will be numerically ranked and recommended for award based on this review.

(c) *Award determination.* The Director of the NIST, or her/his designee, shall select awardees based on total evaluation scores, geographic distribution, and the availability of funds. All three factors will be considered in making an award. Upon the final award decision, a notification will be made to each of the proposing organizations.

§ 292.6 Additional requirements.

Federal policies and procedures. Recipients and subrecipients are subject to all Federal laws and Federal and Department of Commerce policies, regulations, and procedures applicable to Federal financial assistance awards.

PART 295—ADVANCED TECHNOLOGY PROGRAM

Subpart A—General

Sec.

Subpart B—Assistance to United States Industry-Led Joint Research and Development Ventures

Subpart C—Assistance to Single-Proposer U.S. Businesses

AUTHORITY: 15 U.S.C. 278n.

SOURCE: 55 FR 30145, July 24, 1990, unless otherwise noted.

Subpart A—General

§ 295.1 Purpose.

(a) The purpose of the Advanced Technology Program (ATP) is to assisted United States businesses to carry out research and development on high risk, high pay-off, emerging and enabling technologies. These technologies are:

(1) High risk, because the technical challenges make success uncertain;

(2) High pay-off, because when applied they offer significant benefits to the U.S. economy; and

(3) Emerging and enabling, because they offer wide breadth of potential application and form an important technical basis for future commercial applications.

(b) The rules in this part prescribe policies and procedures for the award of cooperative agreements under the Advanced Technology Program in order to ensure the fair treatment of all proposals. While the Advanced Technology Program is authorized to enter into grants, cooperative agreements, and contracts to carry out its mission, the rules in this part address only the award of cooperative agreements. The Program employs cooperative agreements rather than grants because such agreements allow ATP to exercise appropriate management oversight of projects and also to link ATP-funded projects to ongoing R&D at the National Institute of Standards and Technology wherever such linkage would increase the likelihood of success of the project.

(c) In carrying out the rules in this part, the Program endeavors to put more emphasis on joint ventures and consortia with a broad range of participants, including large companies, and less emphasis on support of individual large companies.

[62 FR 64684, Dec. 9, 1997]

§ 295.2 Definitions.

(a) For the purposes of the ATP, the term *award* means Federal financial assistance made under a grant or cooperative agreement.

(b) The term *company* means a for-profit organization, including sole proprietors, partnerships, limited liability companies (LLCs), or corporations.

(c) The term *cooperative agreement* refers to a Federal assistance instrument used whenever the principal purpose of the relationship between the Federal Government and the recipient is the transfer of money, property, or services, or anything of value to the recipient to accomplish a public purpose of support or stimulation authorized by Federal statute, rather than acquisition by purchase, lease, or barter, of property or services for the direct benefit or use of the Federal Government; and substantial involvement is anticipated between the executive agency, acting for the Federal Government, and the recipient during performance of the contemplated activity.

(d) The term *direct costs* means costs that can be identified readily with activities carried out in support of a particular final objective. A cost may not be allocated to an award as a direct cost if any other cost incurred for the same purpose in like circumstances has been assigned to an award as an indirect cost. Because of the diverse characteristics and accounting practices of different organizations, it is not possible to specify the types of costs which may be classified as direct costs in all situations. However, typical direct costs could include salaries of personnel working on the ATP project and associated reasonable fringe benefits such as medical insurance. Direct costs might also include supplies and materials, special equipment required specifically for the ATP project, and travel associated with the ATP project. ATP shall determine the allowability of direct costs in accordance with applicable Federal cost principles.

(e) The term *foreign-owned company* means a company other than a United States-owned company as defined in § 295.2(q).

(f) The term *grant* means a Federal assistance instrument used whenever the principal purpose of the relationship between the Federal Government and the recipient is the transfer of money, property, services, or anything of value to the recipient in order to accomplish a public purpose of support or stimulation authorized by Federal statute, rather than acquisition by purchase, lease, or barter, of property or services for the direct benefit or use of the Federal Government; and no substantial involvement is anticipated between the executive agency, acting for the Federal Government, and the recipient during performance of the contemplated activity.

(g) The term *independent research organization* (IRO) means a nonprofit research and development corporation or association organized under the laws of any state for the purpose of carrying out research and development on behalf of other organizations.

(h) The term *indirect costs* means those costs incurred for common or joint objectives that cannot be readily identified with activities carried out in support of a particular final objective. A cost may not be allocated to an award as an indirect cost if any other cost incurred for the same purpose in like circumstances has been assigned to an award as a direct cost. Because of diverse characteristics and accounting practices it is not possible to specify the types of costs which may be classified as indirect costs in all situations. However, typical examples of indirect costs include general administration expenses, such as the salaries and expenses of executive officers, personnel administration, maintenance, library expenses, and accounting. ATP shall determine the allowability of indirect costs in accordance with applicable Federal cost principles.

(i) The term *industry-led joint research and development venture* or *joint venture* means a business arrangement that consists of two or more separately-owned, for-profit companies that perform research and development in the project; control the joint venture's membership, research directions, and funding priorities; and share total project costs with the Federal government. The joint venture may include additional companies, independent research organizations, universities, and/or governmental laboratories (other than NIST) which may or may not contribute funds (other than Federal funds) to the project and perform research and development. A for-profit company or an independent research organization may serve as an Administrator and perform administrative tasks on behalf of a joint venture, such as handling receipts and disbursements of funds and making antitrust filings. The following activities are not permissible for ATP funded joint ventures:

(1) Exchanging information among competitors relating to costs, sales, profitability, prices, marketing, or distribution of any product, process, or service that is not reasonably required to conduct the research and development that is the purpose of such venture;

(2) Entering into any agreement or engaging in any other conduct restricting, requiring, or otherwise involving the production or marketing by any person who is a party to such joint venture of any product, process, or service, other than the production or marketing of proprietary information developed through such venture, such as patents and trade secrets; and

(3) Entering into any agreement or engaging in any other conduct:

(i) To restrict or require the sale, licensing, or sharing of inventions or developments not developed through such venture, or

(ii) To restrict or require participation by such party in other research and development activities, that is not reasonably required to prevent misappropriation of proprietary information contributed by any person who is a party to such venture or of the results of such venture.

(j) The term *intellectual property* means an invention patentable under title 35, United States Code, or any patent on such an invention.

(k) The term *large business* for a particular ATP competition means any business, including any parent company plus related subsidiaries, having annual revenues in excess of the amount published by ATP in the relevant annual notice of availability of funds required by § 295.7(a). In establishing this amount, ATP may consider the dollar value of the total revenues of the 500th company in Fortune Magazine's Fortune 500 listing.

(l) The term *matching funds or cost sharing* means that portion of project costs not borne by the Federal government. Sources of revenue to satisfy the required cost share include cash and in-kind contributions. Cash contributions can be from recipient, state, county, city, or other non-federal sources. In-kind contributions can be made by recipients or non-federal third parties (except subcontractors working on an ATP project) and include but are not limited to equipment, research tools, software, and supplies. Except as specified at § 295.25, the value of in-kind contributions shall be determined in accordance with OMB Circular A–110, Subpart C, Section 23. The value of in-kind contributions will be prorated according to the share of total use dedicated to the ATP program. ATP restricts the total value of in-kind contributions that can be used to satisfy the cost share by requiring that such contributions not exceed 30 percent of the non-federal share of the total project costs. ATP shall determine the allowability of matching share costs in accordance with applicable federal cost principles.

(m) The term *person* shall be deemed to include corporations and associations existing under or authorized by the laws of either the United States, the laws of any of the Territories, the laws of any State, or the laws of any foreign country.

(n) The term *Program* means the Advanced Technology Program.

(o) The term *Secretary* means the Secretary of Commerce or the Secretary's designee.

(p) The term *small business* means a business that is independently owned and operated, is organized for profit, and is not dominant in the field of operation in which it is proposing, and meets the other requirements found in 13 CFR part 121.

(q) The term *United States-owned company* means a for-profit organization, including sole proprietors, partnerships, or corporations, that has a majority ownership or control by individuals who are citizens of the United States.

[55 FR 30145, July 24, 1990, as amended at 59 FR 666, 667, Jan. 6, 1994; 62 FR 64684, 64685, Dec. 9, 1997; 63 FR 64413, Nov. 20, 1998]

§ 295.3 Eligibility of United States- and foreign-owned businesses.

(a) A company shall be eligible to receive an award from the Program only if:

(1) The Program finds that the company's participation in the Program would be in the economic interest of the United States, as evidenced by investments in the United States in research, development, and manufacturing (including, for example, the manufacture of major components or subassemblies in the United States); significant contributions to employment in the United States; and agreement with respect to any technology arising from assistance provided by the Program to promote the manufacture within the United States of products resulting from that technology (taking into account the goals of promoting the competitiveness of United States industry), and to procure parts and materials from competitive suppliers; and

(2) Either the company is a United States-owned company, or the Program finds that the company is incorporated in the United States and has a parent company which is incorporated in a country which affords to United States-owned companies opportunities, comparable to those afforded to any other company, to participate in any joint venture similar to those authorized under the Program; affords the United States-owned companies local investment opportunities comparable to those afforded to any other company; and affords adequate and effective protection for the intellectual property rights of United States-owned companies.

(b) The Program may, within 30 days after notice to Congress, suspend a company or joint venture from continued assistance under the Program if the Program determines that the company, the country of incorporation of the company or a parent company, or the joint venture has failed to satisfy any of the criteria contained in paragraph (a) of this section, and that it is in the national interest of the United States to do so.

(c) Companies owned by legal residents (green card holders) may apply to the Program, but before an award can be given, the owner(s) must either become a citizen or ownership must be transferred to a U.S. citizen(s).

[59 FR 667, Jan. 6, 1994, as amended at 62 FR 64685, Dec. 9, 1997]

§ 295.4 The selection process.

(a) The selection process for awards is a multi-step process based on the criteria listed in § 295.6. Source evaluation boards (SEB) are established to ensure that all proposals receive careful consideration. In the first step, called "preliminary screening," proposals may be eliminated by the SEB that do not meet the requirements of this Part of the annual FEDERAL REGISTER Program announcement. Typical but not exclusive of the reasons for eliminating a proposal at this stage are that the proposal: is deemed to have serious deficiencies in either the technical or business plan; involves product development rather than high-risk R&D; is not industry-led; is significantly overpriced or underpriced given the scope of the work; does not meet the requirements set out in the notice of availability of funds issued pursuant to

§ 295.7; or does not meet the cost-sharing requirement. NIST will also examine proposals that have been submitted to a previous competition to determine whether substantive revisions have been made to the earlier proposal, and, if not, may reject the proposal.

(b) In the second step, referred to as the "technical and business review," proposals are evaluated under the criteria found in § 295.6. Proposals judged by the SEB after considering the technical and business evaluations to have the highest merit based on the selection criteria receive further consideration and are referred to as "semifinalists."

(c) In the third step, referred to as "selection of finalists," the SEB prepares a final ranking of semifinalist proposals by a majority vote, based on the evaluation criteria in § 295.6. During this step, the semifinalist proposers will be invited to an oral review of their proposals with NIST, and in some cases site visits may be required. Subject to the provisions of § 295.6, a list of ranked finalists is submitted to the Selecting Official.

(d) In the final step, referred to as "selection of recipients," the Selecting Official selects funding recipients from among the finalists, based upon: the SEB rank order of the proposals on the basis of all selection criteria (§ 295.6); assuring an appropriate distribution of funds among technologies and their applications; the availability of funds; and adherence to the Program selection criteria. The Program reserves the right to deny awards in any case where information is uncovered which raises a reasonable doubt as to the responsibility of the proposer. The decision of the Selecting Official is final.

(e) NIST reserves the right to negotiate the cost and scope of the proposed work with the proposers that have been selected to receive awards. For example, NIST may request that the proposer delete from the scope of work a particular task that is deemed by NIST to be product development or otherwise inappropriate for ATP support.

[63 FR 64413, Nov. 20, 1998]

§ 295.5 Use of pre-proposals in the selection process.

To reduce proposal preparation costs incurred by proposers and to make the selection process more efficient, NIST may use mandatory or optional preliminary qualification processes based on pre-proposals. In such cases, announcements requesting pre-proposals will be published as indicated in § 295.7, and will seek abbreviated proposals (pre-proposals) that address both of the selection criteria, but in considerably less detail than full proposals. The Program will review the pre-proposals in accordance with the selection criteria and provide written feedback to the proposers to determine whether the proposed projects appear sufficiently promising to warrant further development into full proposals. Proposals are neither "accepted" or "rejected" at the pre-proposal stage. When the full proposals are received in response to the notice of availability of funds described in § 295.7, the review and selection process will occur as described in § 295.4.

[63 FR 64414, Nov. 20, 1998]

§ 295.6 Criteria for selection.

The evaluation criteria to be used in selecting any proposal for funding under this program, and their respective weights, are listed in this section. No proposal will be funded unless the Program determines that it has scientific and technological merit and that the proposed technology has strong potential for broad-based economic benefits to the nation. Additionally, no proposal will be funded that does not require Federal support, that is product development rather than high risk R&D, that does not display an appropriate level of commitment from the proposer, or does not have an adequate technical and commercialization plan.

(a) *Scientific and technological merit (50%).* The proposed technology must be highly innovative. The research must be challenging, with high technical risk. It must be aimed at overcoming an important problem(s) or exploiting a promising opportunity. The technical leverage of the technology must be adequately explained. The research must have a strong potential for advancing the state of the art and contributing significantly to the U.S. scientific and technical knowledge base. The technical plan must be clear and concise, and must clearly identify the core innovation, the technical approach, major technical hurdles, the attendant risks, and clearly establish feasibility through adequately detailed plans linked to major technical barriers. The plan must address the questions of "what, how, where, when, why, and by whom" in substantial detail. The Program will assess the proposing team's relevant experience for pursuing the technical plan. The team carrying out the work must demonstrate a high level of scientific/technical expertise to conduct the R&D and have access to the necessary research facilities.

(b) *Potential for broad-based economic benefits (50%).* The proposed technology must have a strong potential to generate substantial benefits to the nation that extend significantly beyond the direct returns to the proposing organization(s). The proposal must explain why ATP support is needed and what difference ATP funding is expected to make in terms of what will be accomplished with the ATP funding versus without it. The pathways to economic benefit must be described, including the proposer's plan for getting the technology into commercial use, as well as additional routes that might be taken to achieve broader diffusion of the technology. The proposal should identify the expected returns that the proposer expects to gain, as well as returns that are expected to accrue to others, *i.e.*, spillover effects. The Program will assess the proposer's relevant experience and level of commitment to the project and project's organizational structure and management plan, including the extent to which participation by small businesses is encouraged and is a key component in a joint venture proposal, and for large company single proposers, the extent to which subcontractor/subrecipient teaming arrangements are featured and are a key component of the proposal.

[63 FR 64414, Nov. 20, 1998]

§295.7 Notice of availability of funds.

The Program shall publish at least annually a FEDERAL REGISTER notice inviting interested parties to submit proposals, and may more frequently publish invitations for proposals in the Commerce Business Daily, based upon the annual notice. Proposals must be submitted in accordance with the guidelines in the ATP Proposal Preparation Kit as identified in the published notice. Proposals will only be considered for funding when submitted in response to an invitation published in the FEDERAL REGISTER, or a related announcement in the Commerce Business Daily.

[63 FR 64414, Nov. 20, 1998]

§295.8 Intellectual property rights; publication of research results.

(a)(1) *Patent rights.* Title to inventions arising from assistance provided by the Program must vest in a company or companies incorporated in the United States. Joint ventures shall provide to NIST a copy of their written agreement which defines the disposition of ownership rights among the members of the joint venture, and their contractors and subcontractors as appropriate, that complies with the first sentence of this paragraph. The United States will reserve a nonexclusive, nontransferable, irrevocable, paid-up license to practice or have practiced for or on behalf of the United States any such intellectual property, but shall not, in the exercise of such license, publicly disclose proprietary information related to the license. Title to any such intellectual property shall not be transferred or passed, except to a company incorporated in the United States, until the expiration of the first patent obtained in connection with such intellectual property. Nothing in this paragraph shall be construed to prohibit the licensing to any company of intellectual property rights arising from assistance provided under this section.

(2) *Patent procedures.* Each award by the Program shall include provisions assuring the retention of a governmental use license in each disclosed invention, and the government's retention of march-in rights. In addition, each award by the Program will contain procedures regarding reporting of subject inventions by the funding Recipient to the Program, including the

subject inventions of members of the joint venture (if applicable) in which the funding Recipient is a participant, contractors and subcontractors of the funding Recipient. The funding Recipient shall disclose such subject inventions to the Program within two months after the inventor discloses it in writing to the Recipient's designated representative responsible for patent matters. The disclosure shall consist of a detailed, written report which provides the Program with the following: the title of the present invention; the names of all inventors; the name and address of the assignee (if any); an acknowledgment that the United States has rights in the subject invention; the filing date of the present invention, or, in the alternative, a statement identifying that the Recipient determined that filing was not feasible; an abstract of the disclosure; a description or summary of the present invention; the background of the present invention or the prior art; a description of the preferred embodiments; and what matter is claimed. Upon issuance of the patent, the funding Recipient or Recipients must notify the Program accordingly, providing it with the Serial Number of the patent as issued, the date of issuance, a copy of the disclosure as issued, and if appropriate, the name, address, and telephone number(s) of an assignee.

(b) *Copyrights:* Except as otherwise specifically provided for in an Award, funding recipients under the Program may establish claim to copyright subsisting in any data first produced in the performance of the award. When claim is made to copyright, the funding recipient shall affix the applicable copyright notice of 17 U.S.C. 401 or 402 and acknowledgment of Government sponsorship to the data when and if the data are delivered to the Government, are published, or are deposited for registration as a published work in the U.S. Copyright Office. The funding recipient shall grant to the Government, and others acting on its behalf, a paid up, nonexclusive, irrevocable, worldwide license for all such data to reproduce, prepare derivative works, perform publicly and display publicly, and for data other than computer software to distribute to the public by or on behalf of the Government.

(c) *Publication of research results:* The decision on whether or not to publish research results will be made by the funding recipient(s). Unpublished intellectual property owned and developed by any business or joint research and development venture receiving funding or by any member of such a joint venture may not be disclosed by any officer or employee of the Federal Government except in accordance with a written agreement between the owner or developer and the Program. The licenses granted to the Government under § 295.8(b) shall not be considered a waiver of this requirement.

[55 FR 30145, July 24, 1990. Redesignated and amended at 59 FR 667, 669, Jan. 6, 1994; 63 FR 64414, Nov. 20, 1998]

§ 295.9 Protection of confidential information.

As required by section 278n(d)(5) of title 15 of the United States Code, the following information obtained by the Secretary on a confidential basis in connection with the activities of any business or joint research and development venture receiving funding under the program shall be exempt from disclosure under the Freedom of Information Act—

(1) Information on the business operation of any member of the business or joint venture;

(2) Trade secrets possessed by any business or any member of the joint venture.

[55 FR 30145, July 24, 1990. Redesignated at 59 FR 667, Jan. 6, 1994]

§ 295.10 Special reporting and auditing requirements.

Each award by the Program shall contain procedures regarding technical, business, and financial reporting and auditing requirements to ensure that awards are being used in accordance with the Program's objectives and applicable Federal cost principles. The purpose of the technical reporting is to monitor "best effort" progress toward overall project goals. The purpose of the business reporting system is to monitor project performance against the Program's mission as required by the Government Performance and Results Act (GPRA) mandate for program evaluation. The audit standards to be applied to ATP awards are the "Government Auditing Standards" (GAS) issued by the Comptroller General of the United States (also known as yellow book standards) and the ATP program-specified audit guidelines. The ATP program-specific audit guidelines include guidance on the number of audits required under an award. In the interest of efficiency, the recipients are encouraged to retain their own independent CPA firm to perform these audits. The Department of Commerce's Office of Inspector General (OIG) reserves the right to conduct audits as deemed necessary and appropriate.

[62 FR 64686, Dec. 9, 1997. Redesignated at 63 FR 64415, Nov. 20, 1998]

§295.11 Technical and educational services for ATP recipients.

(a) Under the Federal Technology Transfer Act of 1986, the National Institute of Standards and Technology of the Technology Administration has the authority to enter into cooperative research and development agreements with non-Federal parties to provide personnel, services, facilities, equipment, or other resources except funds toward the conduct of specified research or development efforts which are consistent with the missions of the laboratory. In turn, the National Institute of Standards and Technology has the authority to accept funds, personnel, services, facilities, equipment and other resources from the non-Federal party or parties for the joint research effort. Cooperative research and development agreements do not include procurement contracts or cooperative agreements as those terms are used in sections 6303, 6304, and 6305 of title 31, United States Code.

(b) In no event will the National Institute of Standards and Technology enter into a cooperative research and development agreement with a recipient of awards under the Program which provides for the payment of Program funds from the award recipient to the National Institute of Standards and Technology.

(c) From time to time, ATP may conduct public workshops and undertake other educational activities to foster the collaboration of funding Recipients with other funding resources for purposes of further development and commercialization of ATP-related technologies. In no event will ATP provide recommendations, endorsements, or approvals of any ATP funding Recipients to any outside party.

[55 FR 30145, July 24, 1990. Redesignated at 59 FR 667, Jan. 6, 1994. Redesignated and amended at 63 FR 64415, Nov. 20, 1998]

Subpart B—Assistance to United States Industry-Led Joint Research and Development Ventures

§295.20 Types of assistance available.

This subpart describes the types of assistance that may be provided under the authority of 15 U.S.C. 278n(b)(1). Such assistance includes but is not limited to:

(a) Partial start-up funding for joint research and development ventures.

(b) A minority share of the cost of joint research and development ventures for up to five years.

(c) Equipment, facilities and personnel for joint research and development ventures.

§295.21 Qualifications of proposers.

Subject to the limitations set out in §295.3, assistance under this subpart is available only to industry-led joint research and development ventures. These ventures may include universities, independent research organizations, and governmental entities. Proposals for funding under this Subpart may be submitted on behalf of a joint venture by a for-profit company or an independent research organization that is a member of the joint venture. Proposals should include letters of commitment or excerpts of such letters from all proposed members of the joint venture, verifying the availability of cost-sharing funds, and authorizing the party submitting the proposal to act on behalf of the venture with the Program on all matters pertaining to the proposal. No costs shall be incurred under an ATP project by the joint venture members until such time as a joint venture agreement has been executed by all of the joint venture members and approved by NIST. NIST will withhold approval until it determines that a sufficient number of members have signed the joint venture agreement. Costs will only be allowed after the execution of the joint venture agreement and approval by NIST.

[63 FR 64415, Nov. 20, 1998]

§ 295.22 Limitations on assistance.

(a) An award will be made under this subpart only if the award will facilitate the formation of a joint venture or the initiation of a new research and development project by an existing joint venture.

(b) The total value of any in-kind contributions used to satisfy the cost sharing requirement may not exceed 30 percent of the non-federal share of the total project costs.

[62 FR 64687, Dec. 9, 1997]

§ 295.23 Dissolution of joint research and development ventures.

Upon dissolution of any joint research and development venture receiving funds under these procedures or at a time otherwise agreed upon, the Federal Government shall be entitled to a share of the residual assets of the joint venture proportional to the Federal share of the costs of the joint venture as determined by independent audit.

§ 295.24 Registration.

Joint ventures selected for funding under the Program must notify the Department of Justice and the Federal Trade Commission under the National Cooperative Research Act of 1984. No funds will be released prior to receipt by the Program of copies of such notification.

[63 FR 64415, Nov. 20, 1998]

§ 295.25 Special rule for the valuation of transfers between separately-owned joint venture members.

(a) *Applicability*. This section applies to transfers of goods, including computer software, and services provided by the transferor related to the maintenance of those goods, when those goods or services are transferred from one joint venture member to other separately-owned joint venture members.

(b) *Rule*. The greater amount of the actual cost of the transferred goods and services as determined in accordance with applicable Federal cost principles, or 75 percent of the best customer price of the transferred goods and services, shall be deemed to be allowable costs; provided, however, that in no event shall the aggregate of these allowable costs exceed 30 percent of the non-Federal share of the total cost of the joint research and development program.

(c) *Definition*. The term "best customer price" shall mean the GSA schedule price, or if such price is unavailable, the lowest price at which a sale was made during the last twelve months prior to the transfer of the particular good or service.

[62 FR 64687, Dec. 9, 1997]

Subpart C—Assistance to Single-Proposer U.S. Businesses

§ 295.30 Types of assistance available.

This subpart describes the types of assistance that may be provided under the authority of 15 U.S.C. 278n(b)(2). Such assistance includes but is not limited to entering into cooperative agreements with United States businesses, especially small businesses.

[59 FR 670, Jan. 6, 1994]

§ 295.31 Qualification of proposers.

Awards under this subpart will be available to all businesses, subject to the limitations set out in §§ 295.3 and 295.32.

[62 FR 64687, Dec. 9, 1997]

§ 295.32 Limitations on assistance.

(a) The Program will not directly provide funding under this subpart to any governmental entity, academic institution or independent research organization.

(b) For proposals submitted to ATP after December 31, 1997, awards to large businesses made under this subpart shall not exceed 40 percent of the total project costs of those awards in any year of the award.

(c) Awards under this subpart may not exceed $2,000,000, or be for more than three years, unless the Secretary provides a written explanation to the authorizing committees of both Houses of Congress and then, only after thirty days during which both Houses of Congress are in session. No funding for indirect costs, profits, or management fees shall be available for awards made under this subpart.

(d) The total value of any in-kind contributions used to satisfy a cost sharing requirement may not exceed 30 percent of the non-federal share of the total project costs.

[62 FR 64687, Dec. 9, 1997]

PART 296—TECHNOLOGY INNOVATION PROGRAM

Subpart A—General

AUTHORITY: 15 U.S.C. 278n (Pub. L. 110–69 section 3012)

SOURCE: 73 FR 35915, June 25, 2008, unless otherwise noted.

Subpart A—General

§296.1 Purpose.

(a) The purpose of the Technology Innovation Program (TIP) is to assist United States businesses and institutions of higher education or other organizations, such as national laboratories and nonprofit research institutes, to support, promote, and accelerate innovation in the United States through high-risk, high-reward research in areas of critical national need within NIST's areas of technical competence.

(b) The rules in this part prescribe policies and procedures for the award and administration of financial assistance (grants and/or cooperative agreements) under the TIP. While the TIP is authorized to enter into grants, cooperative agreements, and contracts to carry out the TIP mission, the rules in this part address only the award of grants and/or cooperative agreements.

§296.2 Definitions.

Award means Federal financial assistance made under a grant or cooperative agreement.

Business or company means a for-profit organization, including sole proprietors, partnerships, limited liability companies (LLCs), and corporations.

Contract means a procurement contract under an award or subaward, and a procurement subcontract under a recipient's or subrecipient's contract.

Contractor means the legal entity to which a contract is made and which is accountable to the recipient, subrecipient, or contractor making the contract for the use of the funds provided.

Cooperative agreement refers to a Federal assistance instrument used whenever the principal purpose of the relationship between the Federal government and the recipient is to transfer something of value, such as money, property, or services to the recipient to accomplish a public purpose of support or stimulation authorized by Federal statute instead of acquiring (by purchase, lease, or barter) property or services for the direct benefit or use of the Federal government; and substantial involvement is anticipated between the Federal government and the recipient during performance of the contemplated activity.

Critical national need means an area that justifies government attention because the magnitude of the problem is large and the societal challenges that need to be overcome are not being addressed, but could be addressed through high-risk, high-reward research.

Direct costs means costs that can be identified readily with activities carried out in support of a particular final objective. A cost may not be allocated to an award as a direct cost if any other cost incurred for the same purpose in like circumstances has been assigned to an award as an indirect cost. Because of the diverse characteristics and accounting practices of different organizations, it is not possible to specify the types of costs which may be classified as direct costs in all situations. However, typical direct costs could include salaries of personnel working on the TIP project, travel, equipment, materials and supplies, subcontracts, and other costs not categorized in the preceding examples. NIST shall determine the allowability of direct costs in accordance with applicable Federal cost principles.

Director means the Director of the National Institute of Standards and Technology (NIST).

Eligible company means a small-sized or medium-sized business or company that satisfies the ownership and other requirements stated in this part.

Grant means a Federal assistance instrument used whenever the principal purpose of the relationship between the Federal government and the recipient is to transfer something of value, such as money, property, or services to the recipient to accomplish a public purpose of support or stimulation authorized by Federal statute instead of acquiring (by purchase, lease, or barter) property or services for the direct benefit or use of the Federal government; and no substantial involvement is anticipated between the Federal government and the recipient during performance of the contemplated activity.

High-risk, high-reward research means research that:

(1) Has the potential for yielding transformational results with far-ranging or wide-ranging implications;

(2) Addresses areas of critical national need that support, promote, and accelerate innovation in the United States and is within NIST's areas of technical competence; and

(3) Is too novel or spans too diverse a range of disciplines to fare well in the traditional peer-review process.

Indirect costs means those costs incurred for common or joint objectives that cannot be readily identified with activities carried out in support of a particular final objective. A cost may not be allocated to an award as an indirect cost if any other cost incurred for the same purpose in like circumstances has been assigned to an award as a direct cost. Because of diverse characteristics and accounting practices it is not possible to specify the types of costs which may be classified as indirect costs in all situations. However, typical examples of indirect costs include general administration expenses, such as the salaries and expenses of executive officers, personnel administration, maintenance, library expenses, and accounting. NIST shall determine the allowability of indirect costs in accordance with applicable Federal cost principles.

Institution of higher education means an educational institution in any State that—

(1) Admits as regular students only persons having a certificate of graduation from a school providing secondary education, or the recognized equivalent of such a certificate;

(2) Is legally authorized within such State to provide a program of education beyond secondary education;

(3) Provides an educational program for which the institution awards a bachelor's degree or provides not less than a 2-year program that is acceptable for full credit toward such a degree;

(4) Is a public or other nonprofit institution; and

(5) Is accredited by a nationally recognized accrediting agency or association, or if not so accredited, is an institution that has been granted preaccreditation status by such an agency or association that has been recognized by the Secretary of Education for the granting of

preaccreditation status, and the Secretary of Education has determined that there is satisfactory assurance that the institution will meet the accreditation standards of such an agency or association within a reasonable time (20 U.S.C. 1001). For the purpose of this paragraph (1) only, the term *State* includes, in addition to the several States of the United States, the Commonwealth of Puerto Rico, the District of Columbia, Guam, American Samoa, the United States Virgin Islands, the Commonwealth of the Northern Mariana Islands, and the Freely Associated States. The term *Freely Associated States* means the Republic of the Marshall Islands, the Federated States of Micronesia, and the Republic of Palau.

Intellectual property means an invention patentable under title 35, United States Code, or any patent on such an invention, or any work for which copyright protection is available under title 17, United States Code.

Joint venture means a business arrangement that:

(1) Includes either:

(i) At least two separately owned companies that are both substantially involved in the project and both of which are contributing to the cost-sharing required under the TIP statute, with the lead company of the joint venture being an eligible company; or

(ii) At least one eligible company and one institution of higher education or other organization, such as a national laboratory, governmental laboratory (not including NIST), or nonprofit research institute, that are both substantially involved in the project and both of which are contributing to the cost-sharing required under the TIP statute, with the lead entity of the joint venture being either the eligible company or the institution of higher education; and

(2) May include additional for-profit companies, institutions of higher education, and other organizations, such as national laboratories and nonprofit research institutes, that may or may not contribute non-Federal funds to the project.

Large-sized business means any business, including any parent company plus related subsidiaries, having annual revenues in excess of the amount published by the Program in the relevant FEDERAL REGISTER notice of availability of funds in accordance with § 296.20. In establishing this amount, the Program may consider the dollar value of the total revenues of the 1000th company in Fortune magazine's Fortune 1000 listing.

Matching funds or *cost sharing* means that portion of project costs not borne by the Federal government. Sources of revenue to satisfy the required cost share include cash and third party in-kind contributions. Cash may be contributed by any non-Federal source, including but not limited to recipients, state and local governments, companies, and nonprofits (except contractors working on a TIP project). Third party in-kind contributions include but are not limited to equipment, research tools, software, supplies, and/or services. The value of in-kind contributions shall be determined in accordance with § 14.23 of this title and will be prorated according to the share of total use dedicated to the TIP project. NIST shall determine the allowability of matching share costs in accordance with applicable Federal cost principles.

Medium-sized business means any business that does not qualify as a *small-sized business* or a *large-sized business* under the definitions in this section.

Member means any entity that is identified as a joint venture member in the award and is a signatory on the joint venture agreement required by § 296.8.

Nonprofit research institute means a nonprofit research and development entity or association organized under the laws of any state for the purpose of carrying out research and development.

Participant means any entity that is identified as a recipient, subrecipient, or contractor on an award to a joint venture under the Program.

Person will be deemed to include corporations and associations existing under or authorized by the laws of the United States, the laws of any of the Territories, the laws of any State, or the laws of any foreign country.

Program or *TIP* means the Technology Innovation Program.

Recipient means an organization receiving an award directly from NIST under the Program.

Small-sized business means a business that is independently owned and operated, is organized for profit, has fewer than 500 employees, and meets the other requirements found in 13 CFR part 121.

Societal challenge means a problem or issue confronted by society that when not addressed could negatively affect the overall function and quality of life of the Nation, and as such justifies government attention.

State, except for the limited purpose described in paragraph (l) of this section, means any of the several States of the United States, the District of Columbia, the Commonwealth of Puerto Rico, and any territory or possession of the United States, or any agency or instrumentality of a State exclusive of local governments. The term does not include any public and Indian housing agency under the United States Housing Act of 1937.

Subaward means an award of financial assistance made under an award by a recipient to an eligible subrecipient or by a subrecipient to a lower tier subrecipient. The term includes financial assistance when provided by any legal agreement, even if the legal agreement is called a contract, but does not include procurement of goods and services.

Subrecipient means the legal entity to which a subaward is made and which is accountable to the recipient for the use of the funds provided.

Transformational results means potential project outcomes that enable disruptive changes over and above current methods and strategies. Transformational results have the potential to radically improve our understanding of systems and technologies, challenging the status quo of research approaches and applications.

United States owned company means a for-profit organization, including sole proprietors, partnerships, limited liability companies (LLCs), and corporations, that has a majority ownership by individuals who are citizens of the United States.

§ 296.3 Types of assistance available.

Subject to the limitations of this section and § 296.4, assistance under this part is available to eligible companies or joint ventures that request either of the following:

(a) *Single company awards*: No award given to a single company shall exceed a total of $3,000,000 over a total of 3 years.

(b) *Joint venture awards*: No award given to a joint venture shall exceed a total of $9,000,000 over a total of 5 years.

§ 296.4 Limitations on assistance.

(a) The Federal share of a project funded under the Program shall not be more than 50 percent of total project costs.

(b) Federal funds awarded under this Program may be used only for direct costs and not for indirect costs, profits, or management fees.

(c) No large-sized business may receive funding as a recipient or subrecipient of an award under the Program. When procured in accordance with procedures established under the Procurement Standards required by part 14 of Subtitle A of this title, recipients may procure supplies and other expendable property, equipment, real property and other services from any party, including large-sized businesses.

(d) If a project ends before the completion of the period for which an award has been made, after all allowable costs have been paid and appropriate audits conducted, the unspent balance of the Federal funds shall be returned by the recipient to the Program.

§ 296.5 Eligibility requirements for companies and joint ventures.

Companies and joint ventures must be eligible in order to receive funding under the Program and must remain eligible throughout the life of their awards.

(a) A company shall be eligible to receive an award from the Program only if:

(1) The company is a small-sized or medium-sized business that is incorporated in the United States and does a

majority of its business in the United States; and

(2) Either

(i) The company is a United States owned company; or

(ii) The company is owned by a parent company incorporated in another country and the Program finds that:

(A) The company's participation in TIP would be in the economic interest of the United States, as evidenced by investments in the United States in research, development, and manufacturing (including, for example, the manufacture of major components or subassemblies in the United States); significant contributions to employment in the United States; and agreement with respect to any technology arising from assistance provided by the Program to promote the manufacture within the United States of products resulting from that technology, and to procure parts and materials from competitive United States suppliers; and

(B) That the parent company is incorporated in a country which affords to United States-owned companies opportunities, comparable to those afforded to any other company, to participate in any joint venture similar to those authorized to receive funding under the Program; affords to United States-owned companies local investment opportunities comparable to those afforded to any other company; and affords adequate and effective protection for the intellectual property rights of United States-owned companies.

(b) NIST may suspend a company or joint venture from continued assistance if it determines that the company, the country of incorporation of the company or a parent company, or any member of the joint venture has failed to satisfy any of the criteria contained in paragraph (a) of this section, and that it is in the national interest of the United States to do so.

(c) Members of joint ventures that are companies must be incorporated in the United States and do a majority of their business in the United States and must comply with the requirements of paragraph (a)(2) of this section. For a joint venture to be eligible for assistance, it must be comprised as defined in § 296.2.

§ 296.6 Valuation of transfers.

(a) This section applies to transfers of goods, including computer software, and services provided by the transferor related to the maintenance of those goods, when those goods or services are transferred from one joint venture member to another separately-owned joint venture member.

(b) The greater amount of the actual cost of the transferred goods and services as determined in accordance with applicable Federal cost principles, or 75 percent of the best customer price of the transferred goods and services, shall be deemed to be allowable costs. Best customer price means the GSA schedule price, or if such price is unavailable, the lowest price at which a sale was made during the last twelve months prior to the transfer of the particular good or service.

§ 296.7 Joint venture registration.

Joint ventures selected for assistance under the Program must notify the Department of Justice and the Federal Trade Commission under section 6 of the National Cooperative Research Act of 1984, as amended (15 U.S.C. 4305). No funds will be released prior to receipt by the Program of copies of such notification.

§ 296.8 Joint venture agreement.

NIST shall not issue a TIP award to a joint venture and no costs shall be incurred under a TIP project by the joint venture members until such time as a joint venture agreement has been executed by all of the joint venture members and approved by NIST.

§ 296.9 Activities not permitted for joint ventures.

The following activities are not permissible for TIP-funded joint ventures:

(a) Exchanging information among competitors relating to costs, sales, profitability, prices, marketing, or distribution of any product, process, or service that is not reasonably required to conduct the research and development that is the purpose of such venture;

(b) Entering into any agreement or engaging in any other conduct restricting, requiring, or otherwise involving the marketing, distribution, or provision by any person who is a party to such joint venture of any product, process, or service, other than the distribution among the parties to such venture, in accordance with such venture, of a product, process, or service produced by such venture, the marketing of proprietary information, such as patents and trade secrets, developed through such venture, or the licensing, conveying, or transferring of intellectual property, such as patents and trade secrets, developed through such venture; and

(c) Entering into any agreement or engaging in any other conduct:

(1) To restrict or require the sale, licensing, or sharing of inventions or developments not developed through such venture; or

(2) To restrict or require participation by such party in other research and development activities, that is not reasonably required to prevent misappropriation of proprietary information contributed by any person who is a party to such venture or of the results of such venture.

§ 296.10 Third party in-kind contribution of research services.

NIST shall not issue a TIP award to a single recipient or joint venture whose proposed budget includes the use of third party in-kind contribution of research as cost share, and no costs shall be incurred under such a TIP project, until such time as an agreement between the recipient and the third party contributor of in-kind research has been executed by both parties and approved by NIST.

§ 296.11 Intellectual property rights and procedures.

(a) *Rights in data.* Except as otherwise specifically provided for in an award, authors may copyright any work that is subject to copyright and was developed under an award. When claim is made to copyright, the applicable copyright notice of 17 U.S.C. 401 or 402 and acknowledgment of Federal government sponsorship shall be affixed to the work when and if the work is delivered to the Federal government, is published, or is deposited for registration as a published work in the U.S. Copyright Office. The copyright owner shall grant to the Federal government, and others acting on its behalf, a paid up, nonexclusive, irrevocable, worldwide license for all such works to reproduce, publish, or otherwise use the work for Federal purposes.

(b) *Invention rights.* (1) Ownership of inventions developed from assistance provided by the Program under § 296.3(a) shall be governed by the requirements of chapter 18 of title 35 of the United States Code.

(2) Ownership of inventions developed from assistance provided by the Program under § 296.3(b) may vest in any participant in the joint venture, as agreed by the members of the joint venture, notwithstanding section 202(a) and (b) of title 35, United States Code. Title to any such invention shall not be transferred or passed, except to a participant in the joint venture, until the expiration of the first patent obtained in connection with such invention. In accordance with § 296.8, joint ventures will provide to NIST a copy of their written agreement that defines the disposition of ownership rights among the participants of the joint venture, including the principles governing the disposition of intellectual property developed by contractors and subcontractors, as appropriate, and that complies with these regulations.

(3) The United States reserves a nonexclusive, nontransferable, irrevocable paid-up license, to practice or have practiced for or on behalf of the United States any inventions developed using assistance under this section, but shall not in the exercise of such license publicly disclose proprietary information related to the license. Nothing in this subsection shall be construed to prohibit the licensing to any company of intellectual property rights arising from assistance provided under this section.

(4) Should the last existing participant in a joint venture cease to exist prior to the expiration of the first patent obtained in connection with any invention developed from assistance provided under the Program, title to such patent must be transferred or passed to a United States entity that can commercialize the technology in a timely fashion.

(c) *Patent procedures.* Each award by the Program will include provisions assuring the retention of a governmental use license in each disclosed invention, and the government's retention of march-in rights. In addition, each award by the Program will contain procedures regarding reporting of subject inventions by the recipient through the Interagency Edison extramural invention reporting system (iEdison), including the subject inventions of recipients, including members of the joint venture (if applicable), subrecipients, and contractors of the recipient or joint venture members.

§296.12 Reporting and auditing requirements.

Each award by the Program shall contain procedures regarding technical, business, and financial reporting and auditing requirements to ensure that awards are being used in accordance with the Program's objectives and applicable Federal cost principles. The purpose of the technical reporting is to monitor "best effort" progress toward overall project goals. The purpose of the business reporting is to monitor project performance against the Program's mission as required by the Government Performance and Results Act (GPRA) mandate for program evaluation. The purpose of the financial reporting is to monitor the status of project funds. The audit standards to be applied to TIP awards are the "Government Auditing Standards" (GAS) issued by the Comptroller General of the United States and any Program-specific audit guidelines or requirements prescribed in the award terms and conditions. To implement paragraph (f) of §14.25 of this title, audit standards and award terms may stipulate that "total Federal and non-Federal funds authorized by the Grants Officer" means the total Federal and non-Federal funds authorized by the Grants Officer annually.

Subpart B—The Competition Process

§296.20 The selection process.

(a) To begin a competition, the Program will solicit proposals through an announcement in the FEDERAL REGISTER, which will contain information regarding that competition, including the areas of critical national need that proposals must address. An Evaluation Panel(s) will be established to evaluate proposals and ensure that all proposals receive careful consideration.

(b)(1) A preliminary review will be conducted to determine whether the proposal:

(i) Is in accordance with §296.3;

(ii) Complies with either paragraph (a) or paragraph (c) of §296.5;

(iii) Addresses the award criteria of paragraphs (a) through (c) of §296.22;

(iv) Was submitted to a previous TIP competition and if so, has been substantially revised; and

(v) Is complete.

(2) Complete proposals that meet the preliminary review requirements described in paragraphs (b)(1)(i) through (v) of this section will be considered further. Proposals that are incomplete or do not meet any one of these preliminary review requirements will normally be eliminated.

(c) The Evaluation Panel(s) will then conduct a multi-disciplinary peer review of the remaining proposals based on the evaluation criteria listed in §296.21 and the award criteria listed in §296.22. In some cases NIST may conduct oral reviews and/or site visits. The Evaluation Panel(s) will present funding recommendations to the Selecting Official in rank order for further consideration. The Evaluation Panel(s) will not recommend for further consideration any proposal determined not to meet all of the eligibility and award requirements of this part and the FEDERAL REGISTER notice announcing the availability of funds.

(d) In making final selections, the Selecting Official will select funding recipients based upon the Evaluation Panel's rank order of the proposals and the following selection factors: assuring an appropriate distribution of funds among technologies and their applications, availability of funds, and/or Program priorities. The selection of proposals by the Selecting Official is final.

(e) NIST reserves the right to negotiate the cost and scope of the proposed work with the proposers that have been selected to receive awards. This may include requesting that the proposer delete from the scope of work a particular task that is deemed by NIST to be inappropriate for support against the evaluation criteria. NIST also reserves the right to reject a proposal where information is uncovered that raises a reasonable doubt as to the responsibility of the proposer. The final approval of selected proposals and award of assistance will be made by the NIST Grants Officer as described in the FEDERAL REGISTER notice announcing the competition. The award decision of the NIST Grants Officer is final.

§ 296.21 Evaluation criteria.

A proposal must be determined to be competitive against the Evaluation Criteria set forth in this section to receive funding under the Program. Additionally, no proposal will be funded unless the Program determines that it has scientific and technical merit and that the proposed research has strong potential for meeting identified areas of critical national need.

(a)(1) The proposer(s) adequately addresses the scientific and technical merit and how the research may result in intellectual property vesting in a United States entity including evidence that:

(i) The proposed research is novel;

(ii) The proposed research is high-risk, high-reward;

(iii) The proposer(s) demonstrates a high level of relevant scientific/technical expertise for key personnel, including contractors and/or informal collaborators, and have access to the necessary resources, for example research facilities, equipment, materials, and data, to conduct the research as proposed;

(iv) The research result(s) has the potential to address the technical needs associated with a major societal challenge not currently being addressed; and

(v) The proposed research plan is scientifically sound with tasks, milestones, timeline, decision points and alternate strategies.

(2) Total weight of (a)(1)(i) through (v) is 50%.

(b)(1) The proposer(s) adequately establishes that the proposed research has strong potential for advancing the state-of-the-art and contributing significantly to the United States science and technology knowledge base and to address areas of critical national need through transforming the Nation's capacity to deal with a major societal challenge(s) that is not currently being addressed, and generate substantial benefits to the Nation that extend significantly beyond the direct return to the proposer including an explanation in the proposal:

(i) Of the potential magnitude of transformational results upon the Nation's capabilities in an area;

(ii) Of how and when the ensuing transformational results will be useful to the Nation; and

(iii) Of the capacity and commitment of each award participant to enable or advance the transformation to the proposed research results (technology).

(2) Total weight of (b)(1)(i) through (iii) is 50%.

§ 296.22 Award criteria.

NIST must determine that a proposal successfully meets all of the Award Criteria set forth in this section for the proposal to receive funding under the Program. The Award Criteria are:

(a) The proposal explains why TIP support is necessary, including evidence that the research will not be conducted within a reasonable time period in the absence of financial assistance from TIP;

(b) The proposal demonstrates that reasonable and thorough efforts have been made to secure funding from alternative funding sources and no other alternative funding sources are reasonably available to support the proposal;

(c) The proposal explains the novelty of the research (technology) and demonstrates that other entities have not already developed, commercialized, marketed, distributed, or sold similar research results (technologies);

(d) The proposal has scientific and technical merit and may result in intellectual property vesting in a United States entity that can commercialize the technology in a timely manner;

(e) The proposal establishes that the research has strong potential for advancing the state-of-the-art and contributing significantly to the United States science and technology knowledge base; and

(f) The proposal establishes that the proposed transformational research (technology) has strong potential to address areas of critical national need through transforming the Nation's capacity to deal with major societal challenges that are not currently being addressed, and generate substantial benefits to the Nation that extend significantly beyond the direct return to the proposer.

Subpart C—Dissemination of Program Results

§ 296.30 Monitoring and evaluation.

The Program will provide monitoring and evaluation of areas of critical national need and its investments through periodic analyses. It will develop methods and metrics for assessing impact at all stages. These analyses will contribute to the establishment and adoption of best practices.

§ 296.31 Dissemination of results.

Results stemming from the analyses required by § 296.30 will be disseminated in periodic working papers, fact sheets, and meetings, which will address the progress that the Program has made from both a project and a portfolio perspective. Such disseminated results will serve to educate both external constituencies as well as internal audiences on research results, best practices, and recommended changes to existing operations based on solid analysis.

§ 296.32 Technical and educational services.

(a) Under the Federal Technology Transfer Act of 1986, NIST has the authority to enter into cooperative research and development agreements with non-Federal parties to provide personnel, services, facilities, equipment, or other resources except funds toward the conduct of specified research or development efforts which are consistent with the missions of the laboratory. In turn, NIST has the authority to accept funds, personnel, services, facilities, equipment and other resources from the non-Federal party or parties for the joint research effort. Cooperative research and development agreements do not include procurement contracts or cooperative agreements as those terms are used in sections 6303, 6304, and 6305 of title 31, United States Code.

(b) In no event will NIST enter into a cooperative research and development agreement with a recipient of an award under the Program which provides for the payment of Program funds from the award recipient to NIST.

(c) From time to time, TIP may conduct public workshops and undertake other educational activities to foster the collaboration of funding Recipients with other funding resources for purposes of further development and diffusion of TIP-related technologies. In no event will TIP provide recommendations, endorsements, or approvals of any TIP funding Recipients to any outside party.

§ 296.33 Annual report.

The Director shall submit annually to the Committee on Commerce, Science, and Transportation of the Senate and the Committee on Science and Technology of the House of Representatives a report describing the Technology Innovation Program's activities, including a description of the metrics upon which award funding decisions were made in the previous fiscal year, any proposed changes to those metrics, metrics for evaluating the success of ongoing and completed awards, and an evaluation of ongoing and completed awards. The first annual report shall include best practices for management of programs to stimulate high-risk, high-reward research.

PARTS 297–299 [RESERVED]

FINDING AIDS

A list of CFR titles, subtitles, chapters, subchapters and parts and an alphabetical list of agencies publishing in the CFR are included in the CFR Index and Finding Aids volume to the Code of Federal Regulations which is published separately and revised annually.

Table of CFR Titles and Chapters
Alphabetical List of Agencies Appearing in the CFR
List of CFR Sections Affected

Table of CFR Titles and Chapters

(Revised as January 1, 2014)

Title 1—General Provisions

I Administrative Committee of the Federal Register (Parts 1—49)

II Office of the Federal Register (Parts 50—299)

III Administrative Conference of the United States (Parts 300—399)

IV Miscellaneous Agencies (Parts 400—500)

Title 2—Grants and Agreements

SUBTITLE A—OFFICE OF MANAGEMENT AND BUDGET GUIDANCE FOR GRANTS AND AGREEMENTS

I Office of Management and Budget Governmentwide Guidance for Grants and Agreements (Parts 2—199)

II Office of Management and Budget Guidance (Parts 200—299)

SUBTITLE B—FEDERAL AGENCY REGULATIONS FOR GRANTS AND AGREEMENTS

III Department of Health and Human Services (Parts 300— 399)

IV Department of Agriculture (Parts 400—499)

VI Department of State (Parts 600—699)

VII Agency for International Development (Parts 700—799)

VIII Department of Veterans Affairs (Parts 800—899)

IX Department of Energy (Parts 900—999)

XI Department of Defense (Parts 1100—1199)

XII Department of Transportation (Parts 1200—1299)

XIII Department of Commerce (Parts 1300—1399)

XIV Department of the Interior (Parts 1400—1499)

XV Environmental Protection Agency (Parts 1500—1599)

XVIII National Aeronautics and Space Administration (Parts 1800—1899)

XX United States Nuclear Regulatory Commission (Parts 2000—2099)

XXII Corporation for National and Community Service (Parts 2200—2299)

XXIII Social Security Administration (Parts 2300—2399)

XXIV Housing and Urban Development (Parts 2400—2499)

XXV National Science Foundation (Parts 2500—2599)

XXVI National Archives and Records Administration (Parts 2600—2699)

XXVII Small Business Administration (Parts 2700—2799)

XXVIII Department of Justice (Parts 2800—2899)

Title 2—Grants and Agreements—Continued

Title 3—The President

Title 4—Accounts

Title 5—Administrative Personnel

Chap.	
XXXIII	Overseas Private Investment Corporation (Parts 4300—4399)
XXXIV	Securities and Exchange Commission (Parts 4400—4499)
XXXV	Office of Personnel Management (Parts 4500—4599)
XXXVII	Federal Election Commission (Parts 4700—4799)
XL	Interstate Commerce Commission (Parts 5000—5099)
XLI	Commodity Futures Trading Commission (Parts 5100—5199)
XLII	Department of Labor (Parts 5200—5299)
XLIII	National Science Foundation (Parts 5300—5399)
XLV	Department of Health and Human Services (Parts 5500—5599)
XLVI	Postal Rate Commission (Parts 5600—5699)
XLVII	Federal Trade Commission (Parts 5700—5799)
XLVIII	Nuclear Regulatory Commission (Parts 5800—5899)
XLIX	Federal Labor Relations Authority (Parts 5900—5999)
L	Department of Transportation (Parts 6000—6099)
LII	Export-Import Bank of the United States (Parts 6200—6299)
LIII	Department of Education (Parts 6300—6399)
LIV	Environmental Protection Agency (Parts 6400—6499)
LV	National Endowment for the Arts (Parts 6500—6599)
LVI	National Endowment for the Humanities (Parts 6600—6699)
LVII	General Services Administration (Parts 6700—6799)
LVIII	Board of Governors of the Federal Reserve System (Parts 6800—6899)
LIX	National Aeronautics and Space Administration (Parts 6900—6999)
LX	United States Postal Service (Parts 7000—7099)
LXI	National Labor Relations Board (Parts 7100—7199)
LXII	Equal Employment Opportunity Commission (Parts 7200—7299)
LXIII	Inter-American Foundation (Parts 7300—7399)
LXIV	Merit Systems Protection Board (Parts 7400—7499)
LXV	Department of Housing and Urban Development (Parts 7500—7599)
LXVI	National Archives and Records Administration (Parts 7600—7699)
LXVII	Institute of Museum and Library Services (Parts 7700—7799)
LXVIII	Commission on Civil Rights (Parts 7800—7899)
LXIX	Tennessee Valley Authority (Parts 7900—7999)
LXX	Court Services and Offender Supervision Agency for the District of Columbia (Parts 8000—8099)
LXXI	Consumer Product Safety Commission (Parts 8100—8199)
LXXIII	Department of Agriculture (Parts 8300—8399)
LXXIV	Federal Mine Safety and Health Review Commission (Parts 8400—8499)
LXXVI	Federal Retirement Thrift Investment Board (Parts 8600—8699)
LXXVII	Office of Management and Budget (Parts 8700—8799)
LXXX	Federal Housing Finance Agency (Parts 9000—9099)
LXXXIII	Special Inspector General for Afghanistan Reconstruction (Parts 9300—9399)

Title 5—Administrative Personnel—Continued

Chap.

LXXXIV Bureau of Consumer Financial Protection (Parts 9400—9499)

LXXXVI National Credit Union Administration (Parts 9600—9699)

XCVII Department of Homeland Security Human Resources Management System (Department of Homeland Security—Office of Personnel Management) (Parts 9700—9799)

XCVII Council of the Inspectors General on Integrity and Efficiency (Parts 9800—9899)

Title 6—Domestic Security

I Department of Homeland Security, Office of the Secretary (Parts 1—99)

X Privacy and Civil Liberties Oversight Board (Parts 1000—1099)

Title 7—Agriculture

SUBTITLE A—OFFICE OF THE SECRETARY OF AGRICULTURE (PARTS 0—26)

SUBTITLE B—REGULATIONS OF THE DEPARTMENT OF AGRICULTURE

I Agricultural Marketing Service (Standards, Inspections, Marketing Practices), Department of Agriculture (Parts 27—209)

II Food and Nutrition Service, Department of Agriculture (Parts 210—299)

III Animal and Plant Health Inspection Service, Department of Agriculture (Parts 300—399)

IV Federal Crop Insurance Corporation, Department of Agriculture (Parts 400—499)

V Agricultural Research Service, Department of Agriculture (Parts 500—599)

VI Natural Resources Conservation Service, Department of Agriculture (Parts 600—699)

VII Farm Service Agency, Department of Agriculture (Parts 700—799)

VIII Grain Inspection, Packers and Stockyards Administration (Federal Grain Inspection Service), Department of Agriculture (Parts 800—899)

IX Agricultural Marketing Service (Marketing Agreements and Orders; Fruits, Vegetables, Nuts), Department of Agriculture (Parts 900—999)

X Agricultural Marketing Service (Marketing Agreements and Orders; Milk), Department of Agriculture (Parts 1000—1199)

XI Agricultural Marketing Service (Marketing Agreements and Orders; Miscellaneous Commodities), Department of Agriculture (Parts 1200—1299)

XIV Commodity Credit Corporation, Department of Agriculture (Parts 1400—1499)

XV Foreign Agricultural Service, Department of Agriculture (Parts 1500—1599)

XVI Rural Telephone Bank, Department of Agriculture (Parts 1600—1699)

Chap.	
XVII	Rural Utilities Service, Department of Agriculture (Parts 1700—1799)
XVIII	Rural Housing Service, Rural Business-Cooperative Service, Rural Utilities Service, and Farm Service Agency, Department of Agriculture (Parts 1800—2099)
XX	Local Television Loan Guarantee Board (Parts 2200—2299)
XXV	Office of Advocacy and Outreach, Department of Agriculture (Parts 2500—2599)
XXVI	Office of Inspector General, Department of Agriculture (Parts 2600—2699)
XXVII	Office of Information Resources Management, Department of Agriculture (Parts 2700—2799)
XXVIII	Office of Operations, Department of Agriculture (Parts 2800—2899)
XXIX	Office of Energy Policy and New Uses, Department of Agriculture (Parts 2900—2999)
XXX	Office of the Chief Financial Officer, Department of Agriculture (Parts 3000—3099)
XXXI	Office of Environmental Quality, Department of Agriculture (Parts 3100—3199)
XXXII	Office of Procurement and Property Management, Department of Agriculture (Parts 3200—3299)
XXXIII	Office of Transportation, Department of Agriculture (Parts 3300—3399)
XXXIV	National Institute of Food and Agriculture (Parts 3400—3499)
XXXV	Rural Housing Service, Department of Agriculture (Parts 3500—3599)
XXXVI	National Agricultural Statistics Service, Department of Agriculture (Parts 3600—3699)
XXXVII	Economic Research Service, Department of Agriculture (Parts 3700—3799)
XXXVIII	World Agricultural Outlook Board, Department of Agriculture (Parts 3800—3899)
XLI	[Reserved]
XLII	Rural Business-Cooperative Service and Rural Utilities Service, Department of Agriculture (Parts 4200—4299)

Title 8—Aliens and Nationality

I	Department of Homeland Security (Immigration and Naturalization) (Parts 1—499)
V	Executive Office for Immigration Review, Department of Justice (Parts 1000—1399)

Title 9—Animals and Animal Products

I	Animal and Plant Health Inspection Service, Department of Agriculture (Parts 1—199)

Title 9—Animals and Animal Products—Continued

Chap.

Chap.	
II	Grain Inspection, Packers and Stockyards Administration (Packers and Stockyards Programs), Department of Agriculture (Parts 200—299)
III	Food Safety and Inspection Service, Department of Agriculture (Parts 300—599)

Title 10—Energy

I	Nuclear Regulatory Commission (Parts 0—199)
II	Department of Energy (Parts 200—699)
III	Department of Energy (Parts 700—999)
X	Department of Energy (General Provisions) (Parts 1000—1099)
XIII	Nuclear Waste Technical Review Board (Parts 1300—1399)
XVII	Defense Nuclear Facilities Safety Board (Parts 1700—1799)
XVIII	Northeast Interstate Low-Level Radioactive Waste Commission (Parts 1800—1899)

Title 11—Federal Elections

I	Federal Election Commission (Parts 1—9099)
II	Election Assistance Commission (Parts 9400—9499)

Title 12—Banks and Banking

I	Comptroller of the Currency, Department of the Treasury (Parts 1—199)
II	Federal Reserve System (Parts 200—299)
III	Federal Deposit Insurance Corporation (Parts 300—399)
IV	Export-Import Bank of the United States (Parts 400—499)
V	Office of Thrift Supervision, Department of the Treasury (Parts 500—599)
VI	Farm Credit Administration (Parts 600—699)
VII	National Credit Union Administration (Parts 700—799)
VIII	Federal Financing Bank (Parts 800—899)
IX	Federal Housing Finance Board (Parts 900—999)
X	Bureau of Consumer Financial Protection (Parts 1000—1099)
XI	Federal Financial Institutions Examination Council (Parts 1100—1199)
XII	Federal Housing Finance Agency (Parts 1200—1299)
XIII	Financial Stability Oversight Council (Parts 1300—1399)
XIV	Farm Credit System Insurance Corporation (Parts 1400—1499)
XV	Department of the Treasury (Parts 1500—1599)
XVI	Office of Financial Research (Parts 1600—1699)
XVII	Office of Federal Housing Enterprise Oversight, Department of Housing and Urban Development (Parts 1700—1799)
XVIII	Community Development Financial Institutions Fund, Department of the Treasury (Parts 1800—1899)

Title 13—Business Credit and Assistance

Chap.	
I	Small Business Administration (Parts 1—199)
III	Economic Development Administration, Department of Commerce (Parts 300—399)
IV	Emergency Steel Guarantee Loan Board (Parts 400—499)
V	Emergency Oil and Gas Guaranteed Loan Board (Parts 500—599)

Title 14—Aeronautics and Space

I	Federal Aviation Administration, Department of Transportation (Parts 1—199)
II	Office of the Secretary, Department of Transportation (Aviation Proceedings) (Parts 200—399)
III	Commercial Space Transportation, Federal Aviation Administration, Department of Transportation (Parts 400—1199)
V	National Aeronautics and Space Administration (Parts 1200—1299)
VI	Air Transportation System Stabilization (Parts 1300—1399)

Title 15—Commerce and Foreign Trade

	SUBTITLE A—OFFICE OF THE SECRETARY OF COMMERCE (PARTS 0—20)
	SUBTITLE B—REGULATIONS RELATING TO COMMERCE AND FOREIGN TRADE
I	Bureau of the Census, Department of Commerce (Parts 30—199)
II	National Institute of Standards and Technology, Department of Commerce (Parts 200—299)
III	International Trade Administration, Department of Commerce (Parts 300—399)
IV	Foreign-Trade Zones Board, Department of Commerce (Parts 400—499)
VII	Bureau of Industry and Security, Department of Commerce (Parts 700—799)
VIII	Bureau of Economic Analysis, Department of Commerce (Parts 800—899)
IX	National Oceanic and Atmospheric Administration, Department of Commerce (Parts 900—999)
XI	Technology Administration, Department of Commerce (Parts 1100—1199)
XIII	East-West Foreign Trade Board (Parts 1300—1399)
XIV	Minority Business Development Agency (Parts 1400—1499)
	SUBTITLE C—REGULATIONS RELATING TO FOREIGN TRADE AGREEMENTS
XX	Office of the United States Trade Representative (Parts 2000—2099)
	SUBTITLE D—REGULATIONS RELATING TO TELECOMMUNICATIONS AND INFORMATION
XXIII	National Telecommunications and Information Administration, Department of Commerce (Parts 2300—2399)

Title 16—Commercial Practices

Chap.

I Federal Trade Commission (Parts 0—999)

II Consumer Product Safety Commission (Parts 1000—1799)

Title 17—Commodity and Securities Exchanges

I Commodity Futures Trading Commission (Parts 1—199)

II Securities and Exchange Commission (Parts 200—399)

IV Department of the Treasury (Parts 400—499)

Title 18—Conservation of Power and Water Resources

I Federal Energy Regulatory Commission, Department of Energy (Parts 1—399)

III Delaware River Basin Commission (Parts 400—499)

VI Water Resources Council (Parts 700—799)

VIII Susquehanna River Basin Commission (Parts 800—899)

XIII Tennessee Valley Authority (Parts 1300—1399)

Title 19—Customs Duties

I U.S. Customs and Border Protection, Department of Homeland Security; Department of the Treasury (Parts 0—199)

II United States International Trade Commission (Parts 200—299)

III International Trade Administration, Department of Commerce (Parts 300—399)

IV U.S. Immigration and Customs Enforcement, Department of Homeland Security (Parts 400—599)

Title 20—Employees' Benefits

I Office of Workers' Compensation Programs, Department of Labor (Parts 1—199)

II Railroad Retirement Board (Parts 200—399)

III Social Security Administration (Parts 400—499)

IV Employees' Compensation Appeals Board, Department of Labor (Parts 500—599)

V Employment and Training Administration, Department of Labor (Parts 600—699)

VI Office of Workers' Compensation Programs, Department of Labor (Parts 700—799)

VII Benefits Review Board, Department of Labor (Parts 800—899)

VIII Joint Board for the Enrollment of Actuaries (Parts 900—999)

IX Office of the Assistant Secretary for Veterans' Employment and Training Service, Department of Labor (Parts 1000—1099)

Title 21—Food and Drugs

Chap.

I Food and Drug Administration, Department of Health and Human Services (Parts 1—1299)

II Drug Enforcement Administration, Department of Justice (Parts 1300—1399)

III Office of National Drug Control Policy (Parts 1400—1499)

Title 22—Foreign Relations

I Department of State (Parts 1—199)

II Agency for International Development (Parts 200—299)

III Peace Corps (Parts 300—399)

IV International Joint Commission, United States and Canada (Parts 400—499)

V Broadcasting Board of Governors (Parts 500—599)

VII Overseas Private Investment Corporation (Parts 700—799)

IX Foreign Service Grievance Board (Parts 900—999)

X Inter-American Foundation (Parts 1000—1099)

XI International Boundary and Water Commission, United States and Mexico, United States Section (Parts 1100—1199)

XII United States International Development Cooperation Agency (Parts 1200—1299)

XIII Millennium Challenge Corporation (Parts 1300—1399)

XIV Foreign Service Labor Relations Board; Federal Labor Relations Authority; General Counsel of the Federal Labor Relations Authority; and the Foreign Service Impasse Disputes Panel (Parts 1400—1499)

XV African Development Foundation (Parts 1500—1599)

XVI Japan-United States Friendship Commission (Parts 1600—1699)

XVII United States Institute of Peace (Parts 1700—1799)

Title 23—Highways

I Federal Highway Administration, Department of Transportation (Parts 1—999)

II National Highway Traffic Safety Administration and Federal Highway Administration, Department of Transportation (Parts 1200—1299)

III National Highway Traffic Safety Administration, Department of Transportation (Parts 1300—1399)

Title 24—Housing and Urban Development

SUBTITLE A—OFFICE OF THE SECRETARY, DEPARTMENT OF HOUSING AND URBAN DEVELOPMENT (PARTS 0—99)

SUBTITLE B—REGULATIONS RELATING TO HOUSING AND URBAN DEVELOPMENT

I Office of Assistant Secretary for Equal Opportunity, Department of Housing and Urban Development (Parts 100—199)

Chap.	
II	Office of Assistant Secretary for Housing-Federal Housing Commissioner, Department of Housing and Urban Development (Parts 200—299)
III	Government National Mortgage Association, Department of Housing and Urban Development (Parts 300—399)
IV	Office of Housing and Office of Multifamily Housing Assistance Restructuring, Department of Housing and Urban Development (Parts 400—499)
V	Office of Assistant Secretary for Community Planning and Development, Department of Housing and Urban Development (Parts 500—599)
VI	Office of Assistant Secretary for Community Planning and Development, Department of Housing and Urban Development (Parts 600—699) [Reserved]
VII	Office of the Secretary, Department of Housing and Urban Development (Housing Assistance Programs and Public and Indian Housing Programs) (Parts 700—799)
VIII	Office of the Assistant Secretary for Housing—Federal Housing Commissioner, Department of Housing and Urban Development (Section 8 Housing Assistance Programs, Section 202 Direct Loan Program, Section 202 Supportive Housing for the Elderly Program and Section 811 Supportive Housing for Persons With Disabilities Program) (Parts 800—899)
IX	Office of Assistant Secretary for Public and Indian Housing, Department of Housing and Urban Development (Parts 900—1699)
X	Office of Assistant Secretary for Housing—Federal Housing Commissioner, Department of Housing and Urban Development (Interstate Land Sales Registration Program) (Parts 1700—1799)
XII	Office of Inspector General, Department of Housing and Urban Development (Parts 2000—2099)
XV	Emergency Mortgage Insurance and Loan Programs, Department of Housing and Urban Development (Parts 2700—2799)
XX	Office of Assistant Secretary for Housing—Federal Housing Commissioner, Department of Housing and Urban Development (Parts 3200—3899)
XXIV	Board of Directors of the HOPE for Homeowners Program (Parts 4000—4099)
XXV	Neighborhood Reinvestment Corporation (Parts 4100—4199)

Title 25—Indians

I	Bureau of Indian Affairs, Department of the Interior (Parts 1—299)
II	Indian Arts and Crafts Board, Department of the Interior (Parts 300—399)
III	National Indian Gaming Commission, Department of the Interior (Parts 500—599)
IV	Office of Navajo and Hopi Indian Relocation (Parts 700—799)
V	Bureau of Indian Affairs, Department of the Interior, and Indian Health Service, Department of Health and Human Services (Part 900)

Title 25—Indians—Continued

Chap.

VI Office of the Assistant Secretary-Indian Affairs, Department of the Interior (Parts 1000—1199)

VII Office of the Special Trustee for American Indians, Department of the Interior (Parts 1200—1299)

Title 26—Internal Revenue

I Internal Revenue Service, Department of the Treasury (Parts 1—End)

Title 27—Alcohol, Tobacco Products and Firearms

I Alcohol and Tobacco Tax and Trade Bureau, Department of the Treasury (Parts 1—399)

II Bureau of Alcohol, Tobacco, Firearms, and Explosives, Department of Justice (Parts 400—699)

Title 28—Judicial Administration

I Department of Justice (Parts 0—299)

III Federal Prison Industries, Inc., Department of Justice (Parts 300—399)

V Bureau of Prisons, Department of Justice (Parts 500—599)

VI Offices of Independent Counsel, Department of Justice (Parts 600—699)

VII Office of Independent Counsel (Parts 700—799)

VIII Court Services and Offender Supervision Agency for the District of Columbia (Parts 800—899)

IX National Crime Prevention and Privacy Compact Council (Parts 900—999)

XI Department of Justice and Department of State (Parts 1100—1199)

Title 29—Labor

SUBTITLE A—OFFICE OF THE SECRETARY OF LABOR (PARTS 0—99)

SUBTITLE B—REGULATIONS RELATING TO LABOR

I National Labor Relations Board (Parts 100—199)

II Office of Labor-Management Standards, Department of Labor (Parts 200—299)

III National Railroad Adjustment Board (Parts 300—399)

IV Office of Labor-Management Standards, Department of Labor (Parts 400—499)

V Wage and Hour Division, Department of Labor (Parts 500—899)

IX Construction Industry Collective Bargaining Commission (Parts 900—999)

X National Mediation Board (Parts 1200—1299)

XII Federal Mediation and Conciliation Service (Parts 1400—1499)

XIV Equal Employment Opportunity Commission (Parts 1600—1699)

Chap.

XVII Occupational Safety and Health Administration, Department of Labor (Parts 1900—1999)

XX Occupational Safety and Health Review Commission (Parts 2200—2499)

XXV Employee Benefits Security Administration, Department of Labor (Parts 2500—2599)

XXVII Federal Mine Safety and Health Review Commission (Parts 2700—2799)

XL Pension Benefit Guaranty Corporation (Parts 4000—4999)

Title 30—Mineral Resources

I Mine Safety and Health Administration, Department of Labor (Parts 1—199)

II Bureau of Safety and Environmental Enforcement, Department of the Interior (Parts 200—299)

IV Geological Survey, Department of the Interior (Parts 400—499)

V Bureau of Ocean Energy Management, Department of the Interior (Parts 500—599)

VII Office of Surface Mining Reclamation and Enforcement, Department of the Interior (Parts 700—999)

XII Office of Natural Resources Revenue, Department of the Interior (Parts 1200—1299)

Title 31—Money and Finance: Treasury

SUBTITLE A—OFFICE OF THE SECRETARY OF THE TREASURY (PARTS 0—50)

SUBTITLE B—REGULATIONS RELATING TO MONEY AND FINANCE

I Monetary Offices, Department of the Treasury (Parts 51—199)

II Fiscal Service, Department of the Treasury (Parts 200—399)

IV Secret Service, Department of the Treasury (Parts 400—499)

V Office of Foreign Assets Control, Department of the Treasury (Parts 500—599)

VI Bureau of Engraving and Printing, Department of the Treasury (Parts 600—699)

VII Federal Law Enforcement Training Center, Department of the Treasury (Parts 700—799)

VIII Office of International Investment, Department of the Treasury (Parts 800—899)

IX Federal Claims Collection Standards (Department of the Treasury—Department of Justice) (Parts 900—999)

X Financial Crimes Enforcement Network, Department of the Treasury (Parts 1000—1099)

Title 32—National Defense

SUBTITLE A—DEPARTMENT OF DEFENSE

I Office of the Secretary of Defense (Parts 1—399)

Title 32—National Defense—Continued

Chap.	
V	Department of the Army (Parts 400—699)
VI	Department of the Navy (Parts 700—799)
VII	Department of the Air Force (Parts 800—1099)
	SUBTITLE B—OTHER REGULATIONS RELATING TO NATIONAL DEFENSE
XII	Defense Logistics Agency (Parts 1200—1299)
XVI	Selective Service System (Parts 1600—1699)
XVII	Office of the Director of National Intelligence (Parts 1700—1799)
XVIII	National Counterintelligence Center (Parts 1800—1899)
XIX	Central Intelligence Agency (Parts 1900—1999)
XX	Information Security Oversight Office, National Archives and Records Administration (Parts 2000—2099)
XXI	National Security Council (Parts 2100—2199)
XXIV	Office of Science and Technology Policy (Parts 2400—2499)
XXVII	Office for Micronesian Status Negotiations (Parts 2700—2799)
XXVIII	Office of the Vice President of the United States (Parts 2800—2899)

Title 33—Navigation and Navigable Waters

I	Coast Guard, Department of Homeland Security (Parts 1—199)
II	Corps of Engineers, Department of the Army (Parts 200—399)
IV	Saint Lawrence Seaway Development Corporation, Department of Transportation (Parts 400—499)

Title 34—Education

	SUBTITLE A—OFFICE OF THE SECRETARY, DEPARTMENT OF EDUCATION (PARTS 1—99)
	SUBTITLE B—REGULATIONS OF THE OFFICES OF THE DEPARTMENT OF EDUCATION
I	Office for Civil Rights, Department of Education (Parts 100—199)
II	Office of Elementary and Secondary Education, Department of Education (Parts 200—299)
III	Office of Special Education and Rehabilitative Services, Department of Education (Parts 300—399)
IV	Office of Vocational and Adult Education, Department of Education (Parts 400—499)
V	Office of Bilingual Education and Minority Languages Affairs, Department of Education (Parts 500—599)
VI	Office of Postsecondary Education, Department of Education (Parts 600—699)
VII	Office of Educational Research and Improvement, Department of Education (Parts 700—799) [Reserved]
	SUBTITLE C—REGULATIONS RELATING TO EDUCATION
XI	National Institute for Literacy (Parts 1100—1199)
XII	National Council on Disability (Parts 1200—1299)

Title 35 [Reserved]

Chap.

Title 36—Parks, Forests, and Public Property

I National Park Service, Department of the Interior (Parts 1—199)

II Forest Service, Department of Agriculture (Parts 200—299)

III Corps of Engineers, Department of the Army (Parts 300—399)

IV American Battle Monuments Commission (Parts 400—499)

V Smithsonian Institution (Parts 500—599)

VI [Reserved]

VII Library of Congress (Parts 700—799)

VIII Advisory Council on Historic Preservation (Parts 800—899)

IX Pennsylvania Avenue Development Corporation (Parts 900—999)

X Presidio Trust (Parts 1000—1099)

XI Architectural and Transportation Barriers Compliance Board (Parts 1100—1199)

XII National Archives and Records Administration (Parts 1200—1299)

XV Oklahoma City National Memorial Trust (Parts 1500—1599)

XVI Morris K. Udall Scholarship and Excellence in National Environmental Policy Foundation (Parts 1600—1699)

Title 37—Patents, Trademarks, and Copyrights

I United States Patent and Trademark Office, Department of Commerce (Parts 1—199)

II U.S. Copyright Office, Library of Congress (Parts 200—299)

III Copyright Royalty Board, Library of Congress (Parts 300—399)

IV Assistant Secretary for Technology Policy, Department of Commerce (Parts 400—599)

Title 38—Pensions, Bonuses, and Veterans' Relief

I Department of Veterans Affairs (Parts 0—199)

II Armed Forces Retirement Home (Parts 200—299)

Title 39—Postal Service

I United States Postal Service (Parts 1—999)

III Postal Regulatory Commission (Parts 3000—3099)

Title 40—Protection of Environment

I Environmental Protection Agency (Parts 1—1099)

IV Environmental Protection Agency and Department of Justice (Parts 1400—1499)

V Council on Environmental Quality (Parts 1500—1599)

VI Chemical Safety and Hazard Investigation Board (Parts 1600—1699)

Chap.

VII Environmental Protection Agency and Department of Defense; Uniform National Discharge Standards for Vessels of the Armed Forces (Parts 1700—1799)

Title 41—Public Contracts and Property Management

SUBTITLE A—FEDERAL PROCUREMENT REGULATIONS SYSTEM [NOTE]

SUBTITLE B—OTHER PROVISIONS RELATING TO PUBLIC CONTRACTS

50 Public Contracts, Department of Labor (Parts 50–1—50–999)

51 Committee for Purchase From People Who Are Blind or Severely Disabled (Parts 51–1—51–99)

60 Office of Federal Contract Compliance Programs, Equal Employment Opportunity, Department of Labor (Parts 60–1—60–999)

61 Office of the Assistant Secretary for Veterans' Employment and Training Service, Department of Labor (Parts 61–1—61–999)

62—100 [Reserved]

SUBTITLE C—FEDERAL PROPERTY MANAGEMENT REGULATIONS SYSTEM

101 Federal Property Management Regulations (Parts 101–1—101–99)

102 Federal Management Regulation (Parts 102–1—102–299)

103—104 [Reserved]

105 General Services Administration (Parts 105–1—105–999)

109 Department of Energy Property Management Regulations (Parts 109–1—109–99)

114 Department of the Interior (Parts 114–1—114–99)

115 Environmental Protection Agency (Parts 115–1—115–99)

128 Department of Justice (Parts 128–1—128–99)

129—200 [Reserved]

SUBTITLE D—OTHER PROVISIONS RELATING TO PROPERTY MANAGEMENT [RESERVED]

SUBTITLE E—FEDERAL INFORMATION RESOURCES MANAGEMENT REGULATIONS SYSTEM [RESERVED]

SUBTITLE F—FEDERAL TRAVEL REGULATION SYSTEM

300 General (Parts 300–1—300–99)

301 Temporary Duty (TDY) Travel Allowances (Parts 301–1—301–99)

302 Relocation Allowances (Parts 302–1—302–99)

303 Payment of Expenses Connected with the Death of Certain Employees (Part 303–1—303–99)

304 Payment of Travel Expenses from a Non-Federal Source (Parts 304–1—304–99)

Title 42—Public Health

I Public Health Service, Department of Health and Human Services (Parts 1—199)

IV Centers for Medicare & Medicaid Services, Department of Health and Human Services (Parts 400—599)

Chap.

V Office of Inspector General-Health Care, Department of Health and Human Services (Parts 1000—1999)

Title 43—Public Lands: Interior

SUBTITLE A—OFFICE OF THE SECRETARY OF THE INTERIOR (PARTS 1—199)

SUBTITLE B—REGULATIONS RELATING TO PUBLIC LANDS

I Bureau of Reclamation, Department of the Interior (Parts 400—999)

II Bureau of Land Management, Department of the Interior (Parts 1000—9999)

III Utah Reclamation Mitigation and Conservation Commission (Parts 10000—10099)

Title 44—Emergency Management and Assistance

I Federal Emergency Management Agency, Department of Homeland Security (Parts 0—399)

IV Department of Commerce and Department of Transportation (Parts 400—499)

Title 45—Public Welfare

SUBTITLE A—DEPARTMENT OF HEALTH AND HUMAN SERVICES (PARTS 1—199)

SUBTITLE B—REGULATIONS RELATING TO PUBLIC WELFARE

II Office of Family Assistance (Assistance Programs), Administration for Children and Families, Department of Health and Human Services (Parts 200—299)

III Office of Child Support Enforcement (Child Support Enforcement Program), Administration for Children and Families, Department of Health and Human Services (Parts 300—399)

IV Office of Refugee Resettlement, Administration for Children and Families, Department of Health and Human Services (Parts 400—499)

V Foreign Claims Settlement Commission of the United States, Department of Justice (Parts 500—599)

VI National Science Foundation (Parts 600—699)

VII Commission on Civil Rights (Parts 700—799)

VIII Office of Personnel Management (Parts 800—899)

X Office of Community Services, Administration for Children and Families, Department of Health and Human Services (Parts 1000—1099)

XI National Foundation on the Arts and the Humanities (Parts 1100—1199)

XII Corporation for National and Community Service (Parts 1200—1299)

XIII Office of Human Development Services, Department of Health and Human Services (Parts 1300—1399)

Title 45—Public Welfare—Continued

Chap.	
XVI	Legal Services Corporation (Parts 1600—1699)
XVII	National Commission on Libraries and Information Science (Parts 1700—1799)
XVIII	Harry S. Truman Scholarship Foundation (Parts 1800—1899)
XXI	Commission on Fine Arts (Parts 2100—2199)
XXIII	Arctic Research Commission (Part 2301)
XXIV	James Madison Memorial Fellowship Foundation (Parts 2400—2499)
XXV	Corporation for National and Community Service (Parts 2500—2599)

Title 46—Shipping

I	Coast Guard, Department of Homeland Security (Parts 1—199)
II	Maritime Administration, Department of Transportation (Parts 200—399)
III	Coast Guard (Great Lakes Pilotage), Department of Homeland Security (Parts 400—499)
IV	Federal Maritime Commission (Parts 500—599)

Title 47—Telecommunication

I	Federal Communications Commission (Parts 0—199)
II	Office of Science and Technology Policy and National Security Council (Parts 200—299)
III	National Telecommunications and Information Administration, Department of Commerce (Parts 300—399)
IV	National Telecommunications and Information Administration, Department of Commerce, and National Highway Traffic Safety Administration, Department of Transportation (Parts 400—499)

Title 48—Federal Acquisition Regulations System

1	Federal Acquisition Regulation (Parts 1—99)
2	Defense Acquisition Regulations System, Department of Defense (Parts 200—299)
3	Health and Human Services (Parts 300—399)
4	Department of Agriculture (Parts 400—499)
5	General Services Administration (Parts 500—599)
6	Department of State (Parts 600—699)
7	Agency for International Development (Parts 700—799)
8	Department of Veterans Affairs (Parts 800—899)
9	Department of Energy (Parts 900—999)
10	Department of the Treasury (Parts 1000—1099)
12	Department of Transportation (Parts 1200—1299)
13	Department of Commerce (Parts 1300—1399)
14	Department of the Interior (Parts 1400—1499)

Chap.

15 Environmental Protection Agency (Parts 1500—1599)

16 Office of Personnel Management, Federal Employees Health Benefits Acquisition Regulation (Parts 1600—1699)

17 Office of Personnel Management (Parts 1700—1799)

18 National Aeronautics and Space Administration (Parts 1800—1899)

19 Broadcasting Board of Governors (Parts 1900—1999)

20 Nuclear Regulatory Commission (Parts 2000—2099)

21 Office of Personnel Management, Federal Employees Group Life Insurance Federal Acquisition Regulation (Parts 2100—2199)

23 Social Security Administration (Parts 2300—2399)

24 Department of Housing and Urban Development (Parts 2400—2499)

25 National Science Foundation (Parts 2500—2599)

28 Department of Justice (Parts 2800—2899)

29 Department of Labor (Parts 2900—2999)

30 Department of Homeland Security, Homeland Security Acquisition Regulation (HSAR) (Parts 3000—3099)

34 Department of Education Acquisition Regulation (Parts 3400—3499)

51 Department of the Army Acquisition Regulations (Parts 5100—5199)

52 Department of the Navy Acquisition Regulations (Parts 5200—5299)

53 Department of the Air Force Federal Acquisition Regulation Supplement (Parts 5300—5399) [Reserved]

54 Defense Logistics Agency, Department of Defense (Parts 5400—5499)

57 African Development Foundation (Parts 5700—5799)

61 Civilian Board of Contract Appeals, General Services Administration (Parts 6100—6199)

63 Department of Transportation Board of Contract Appeals (Parts 6300—6399)

99 Cost Accounting Standards Board, Office of Federal Procurement Policy, Office of Management and Budget (Parts 9900—9999)

Title 49—Transportation

SUBTITLE A—OFFICE OF THE SECRETARY OF TRANSPORTATION (PARTS 1—99)

SUBTITLE B—OTHER REGULATIONS RELATING TO TRANSPORTATION

I Pipeline and Hazardous Materials Safety Administration, Department of Transportation (Parts 100—199)

II Federal Railroad Administration, Department of Transportation (Parts 200—299)

III Federal Motor Carrier Safety Administration, Department of Transportation (Parts 300—399)

IV Coast Guard, Department of Homeland Security (Parts 400—499)

Title 49—Transportation—Continued

Chap.

V National Highway Traffic Safety Administration, Department of Transportation (Parts 500—599)

VI Federal Transit Administration, Department of Transportation (Parts 600—699)

VII National Railroad Passenger Corporation (AMTRAK) (Parts 700—799)

VIII National Transportation Safety Board (Parts 800—999)

X Surface Transportation Board, Department of Transportation (Parts 1000—1399)

XI Research and Innovative Technology Administration, Department of Transportation (Parts 1400—1499) [Reserved]

XII Transportation Security Administration, Department of Homeland Security (Parts 1500—1699)

Title 50—Wildlife and Fisheries

I United States Fish and Wildlife Service, Department of the Interior (Parts 1—199)

II National Marine Fisheries Service, National Oceanic and Atmospheric Administration, Department of Commerce (Parts 200—299)

III International Fishing and Related Activities (Parts 300—399)

IV Joint Regulations (United States Fish and Wildlife Service, Department of the Interior and National Marine Fisheries Service, National Oceanic and Atmospheric Administration, Department of Commerce); Endangered Species Committee Regulations (Parts 400—499)

V Marine Mammal Commission (Parts 500—599)

VI Fishery Conservation and Management, National Oceanic and Atmospheric Administration, Department of Commerce (Parts 600—699)

Alphabetical List of Agencies Appearing in the CFR

(Revised as of January 1, 2014)

Agency	CFR Title, Subtitle or Chapter
Administrative Committee of the Federal Register	1, I
Administrative Conference of the United States	1, III
Advisory Council on Historic Preservation	36, VIII
Advocacy and Outreach, Office of	7, XXV
Afghanistan Reconstruction, Special Inspector General for	22, LXXXIII
African Development Foundation	22, XV
Federal Acquisition Regulation	48, 57
Agency for International Development	2, VII; 22, II
Federal Acquisition Regulation	48, 7
Agricultural Marketing Service	7, I, IX, X, XI
Agricultural Research Service	7, V
Agriculture Department	2, IV; 5, LXXIII
Advocacy and Outreach, Office of	7, XXV
Agricultural Marketing Service	7, I, IX, X, XI
Agricultural Research Service	7, V
Animal and Plant Health Inspection Service	7, III; 9, I
Chief Financial Officer, Office of	7, XXX
Commodity Credit Corporation	7, XIV
Economic Research Service	7, XXXVII
Energy Policy and New Uses, Office of	2, IX; 7, XXIX
Environmental Quality, Office of	7, XXXI
Farm Service Agency	7, VII, XVIII
Federal Acquisition Regulation	48, 4
Federal Crop Insurance Corporation	7, IV
Food and Nutrition Service	7, II
Food Safety and Inspection Service	9, III
Foreign Agricultural Service	7, XV
Forest Service	36, II
Grain Inspection, Packers and Stockyards Administration	7, VIII; 9, II
Information Resources Management, Office of	7, XXVII
Inspector General, Office of	7, XXVI
National Agricultural Library	7, XLI
National Agricultural Statistics Service	7, XXXVI
National Institute of Food and Agriculture	7, XXXIV
Natural Resources Conservation Service	7, VI
Operations, Office of	7, XXVIII
Procurement and Property Management, Office of	7, XXXII
Rural Business-Cooperative Service	7, XVIII, XLII, L
Rural Development Administration	7, XLII
Rural Housing Service	7, XVIII, XXXV, L
Rural Telephone Bank	7, XVI
Rural Utilities Service	7, XVII, XVIII, XLII, L
Secretary of Agriculture, Office of	7, Subtitle A
Transportation, Office of	7, XXXIII
World Agricultural Outlook Board	7, XXXVIII
Air Force Department	32, VII
Federal Acquisition Regulation Supplement	48, 53
Air Transportation Stabilization Board	14, VI
Alcohol and Tobacco Tax and Trade Bureau	27, I
Alcohol, Tobacco, Firearms, and Explosives, Bureau of	27, II
AMTRAK	49, VII
American Battle Monuments Commission	36, IV
American Indians, Office of the Special Trustee	25, VII

Agency	CFR Title, Subtitle or Chapter
Animal and Plant Health Inspection Service	7, III; 9, I
Appalachian Regional Commission	5, IX
Architectural and Transportation Barriers Compliance Board	36, XI
Arctic Research Commission	45, XXIII
Armed Forces Retirement Home	5, XI
Army Department	32, V
Engineers, Corps of	33, II; 36, III
Federal Acquisition Regulation	48, 51
Bilingual Education and Minority Languages Affairs, Office of	34, V
Blind or Severely Disabled, Committee for Purchase from People Who Are	41, 51
Broadcasting Board of Governors	22, V
Federal Acquisition Regulation	48, 19
Bureau of Ocean Energy Management, Regulation, and Enforcement	30, II
Census Bureau	15, I
Centers for Medicare & Medicaid Services	42, IV
Central Intelligence Agency	32, XIX
Chemical Safety and Hazardous Investigation Board	40, VI
Chief Financial Officer, Office of	7, XXX
Child Support Enforcement, Office of	45, III
Children and Families, Administration for	45, II, III, IV, X
Civil Rights, Commission on	5, LXVIII; 45, VII
Civil Rights, Office for	34, I
Council of the Inspectors General on Integrity and Efficiency	5, XCVIII
Court Services and Offender Supervision Agency for the District of Columbia	5, LXX
Coast Guard	33, I; 46, I; 49, IV
Coast Guard (Great Lakes Pilotage)	46, III
Commerce Department	2, XIII; 44, IV; 50, VI
Census Bureau	15, I
Economic Analysis, Bureau of	15, VIII
Economic Development Administration	13, III
Emergency Management and Assistance	44, IV
Federal Acquisition Regulation	48, 13
Foreign-Trade Zones Board	15, IV
Industry and Security, Bureau of	15, VII
International Trade Administration	15, III; 19, III
National Institute of Standards and Technology	15, II
National Marine Fisheries Service	50, II, IV
National Oceanic and Atmospheric Administration	15, IX; 50, II, III, IV, VI
National Telecommunications and Information Administration	15, XXIII; 47, III, IV
National Weather Service	15, IX
Patent and Trademark Office, United States	37, I
Productivity, Technology and Innovation, Assistant Secretary for	37, IV
Secretary of Commerce, Office of	15, Subtitle A
Technology Administration	15, XI
Technology Policy, Assistant Secretary for	37, IV
Commercial Space Transportation	14, III
Commodity Credit Corporation	7, XIV
Commodity Futures Trading Commission	5, XLI; 17, I
Community Planning and Development, Office of Assistant Secretary for	24, V, VI
Community Services, Office of	45, X
Comptroller of the Currency	12, I
Construction Industry Collective Bargaining Commission	29, IX
Consumer Financial Protection Bureau	5, LXXXIV; 12, X
Consumer Product Safety Commission	5, LXXI; 16, II
Copyright Royalty Board	37, III
Corporation for National and Community Service	2, XXII; 45, XII, XXV
Cost Accounting Standards Board	48, 99
Council on Environmental Quality	40, V
Court Services and Offender Supervision Agency for the District of Columbia	5, LXX; 28, VIII
Customs and Border Protection	19, I

Agency	CFR Title, Subtitle or Chapter
Defense Contract Audit Agency	32, I
Defense Department	2, XI; 5, XXVI; 32, Subtitle A; 40, VII
Advanced Research Projects Agency	32, I
Air Force Department	32, VII
Army Department	32, V; 33, II; 36, III, 48, 51
Defense Acquisition Regulations System	48, 2
Defense Intelligence Agency	32, I
Defense Logistics Agency	32, I, XII; 48, 54
Engineers, Corps of	33, II; 36, III
National Imagery and Mapping Agency	32, I
Navy Department	32, VI; 48, 52
Secretary of Defense, Office of	2, XI; 32, I
Defense Contract Audit Agency	32, I
Defense Intelligence Agency	32, I
Defense Logistics Agency	32, XII; 48, 54
Defense Nuclear Facilities Safety Board	10, XVII
Delaware River Basin Commission	18, III
District of Columbia, Court Services and Offender Supervision Agency for the	5, LXX; 28, VIII
Drug Enforcement Administration	21, II
East-West Foreign Trade Board	15, XIII
Economic Analysis, Bureau of	15, VIII
Economic Development Administration	13, III
Economic Research Service	7, XXXVII
Education, Department of	2, XXXIV; 5, LIII
Bilingual Education and Minority Languages Affairs, Office of	34, V
Civil Rights, Office for	34, I
Educational Research and Improvement, Office of	34, VII
Elementary and Secondary Education, Office of	34, II
Federal Acquisition Regulation	48, 34
Postsecondary Education, Office of	34, VI
Secretary of Education, Office of	34, Subtitle A
Special Education and Rehabilitative Services, Office of	34, III
Vocational and Adult Education, Office of	34, IV
Educational Research and Improvement, Office of	34, VII
Election Assistance Commission	2, LVIII; 11, II
Elementary and Secondary Education, Office of	34, II
Emergency Oil and Gas Guaranteed Loan Board	13, V
Emergency Steel Guarantee Loan Board	13, IV
Employee Benefits Security Administration	29, XXV
Employees' Compensation Appeals Board	20, IV
Employees Loyalty Board	5, V
Employment and Training Administration	20, V
Employment Standards Administration	20, VI
Endangered Species Committee	50, IV
Energy, Department of	2, IX; 5, XXIII; 10, II, III, X
Federal Acquisition Regulation	48, 9
Federal Energy Regulatory Commission	5, XXIV; 18, I
Property Management Regulations	41, 109
Energy, Office of	7, XXIX
Engineers, Corps of	33, II; 36, III
Engraving and Printing, Bureau of	31, VI
Environmental Protection Agency	2, XV; 5, LIV; 40, I, IV, VII
Federal Acquisition Regulation	48, 15
Property Management Regulations	41, 115
Environmental Quality, Office of	7, XXXI
Equal Employment Opportunity Commission	5, LXII; 29, XIV
Equal Opportunity, Office of Assistant Secretary for	24, I
Executive Office of the President	3, I
Administration, Office of	5, XV
Environmental Quality, Council on	40, V
Management and Budget, Office of	2, Subtitle A; 5, III, LXXVII; 14, VI; 48, 99

Agency	CFR Title, Subtitle or Chapter
National Drug Control Policy, Office of	21, III
National Security Council	32, XXI; 47, 2
Presidential Documents	3
Science and Technology Policy, Office of	32, XXIV; 47, II
Trade Representative, Office of the United States	15, XX
Export-Import Bank of the United States	2, XXXV; 5, LII; 12, IV
Family Assistance, Office of	45, II
Farm Credit Administration	5, XXXI; 12, VI
Farm Credit System Insurance Corporation	5, XXX; 12, XIV
Farm Service Agency	7, VII, XVIII
Federal Acquisition Regulation	48, 1
Federal Aviation Administration	14, I
Commercial Space Transportation	14, III
Federal Claims Collection Standards	31, IX
Federal Communications Commission	5, XXIX; 47, I
Federal Contract Compliance Programs, Office of	41, 60
Federal Crop Insurance Corporation	7, IV
Federal Deposit Insurance Corporation	5, XXII; 12, III
Federal Election Commission	5, XXXVII; 11, I
Federal Emergency Management Agency	44, I
Federal Employees Group Life Insurance Federal Acquisition Regulation	48, 21
Federal Employees Health Benefits Acquisition Regulation	48, 16
Federal Energy Regulatory Commission	5, XXIV; 18, I
Federal Financial Institutions Examination Council	12, XI
Federal Financing Bank	12, VIII
Federal Highway Administration	23, I, II
Federal Home Loan Mortgage Corporation	1, IV
Federal Housing Enterprise Oversight Office	12, XVII
Federal Housing Finance Agency	5, LXXX; 12, XII
Federal Housing Finance Board	12, IX
Federal Labor Relations Authority	5, XIV, XLIX; 22, XIV
Federal Law Enforcement Training Center	31, VII
Federal Management Regulation	41, 102
Federal Maritime Commission	46, IV
Federal Mediation and Conciliation Service	29, XII
Federal Mine Safety and Health Review Commission	5, LXXIV; 29, XXVII
Federal Motor Carrier Safety Administration	49, III
Federal Prison Industries, Inc.	28, III
Federal Procurement Policy Office	48, 99
Federal Property Management Regulations	41, 101
Federal Railroad Administration	49, II
Federal Register, Administrative Committee of	1, I
Federal Register, Office of	1, II
Federal Reserve System	12, II
Board of Governors	5, LVIII
Federal Retirement Thrift Investment Board	5, VI, LXXVI
Federal Service Impasses Panel	5, XIV
Federal Trade Commission	5, XLVII; 16, I
Federal Transit Administration	49, VI
Federal Travel Regulation System	41, Subtitle F
Financial Crimes Enforcement Network	31, X
Financial Research Office	12, XVI
Financial Stability Oversight Council	12, XIII
Fine Arts, Commission on	45, XXI
Fiscal Service	31, II
Fish and Wildlife Service, United States	50, I, IV
Food and Drug Administration	21, I
Food and Nutrition Service	7, II
Food Safety and Inspection Service	9, III
Foreign Agricultural Service	7, XV
Foreign Assets Control, Office of	31, V
Foreign Claims Settlement Commission of the United States	45, V
Foreign Service Grievance Board	22, IX
Foreign Service Impasse Disputes Panel	22, XIV
Foreign Service Labor Relations Board	22, XIV
Foreign-Trade Zones Board	15, IV

Agency	CFR Title, Subtitle or Chapter
Forest Service	36, II
General Services Administration	5, LVII; 41, 105
Contract Appeals, Board of	48, 61
Federal Acquisition Regulation	48, 5
Federal Management Regulation	41, 102
Federal Property Management Regulations	41, 101
Federal Travel Regulation System	41, Subtitle F
General	41, 300
Payment From a Non-Federal Source for Travel Expenses	41, 304
Payment of Expenses Connected With the Death of Certain Employees	41, 303
Relocation Allowances	41, 302
Temporary Duty (TDY) Travel Allowances	41, 301
Geological Survey	30, IV
Government Accountability Office	4, I
Government Ethics, Office of	5, XVI
Government National Mortgage Association	24, III
Grain Inspection, Packers and Stockyards Administration	7, VIII; 9, II
Harry S. Truman Scholarship Foundation	45, XVIII
Health and Human Services, Department of	2, III; 5, XLV; 45, Subtitle A,
Centers for Medicare & Medicaid Services	42, IV
Child Support Enforcement, Office of	45, III
Children and Families, Administration for	45, II, III, IV, X
Community Services, Office of	45, X
Family Assistance, Office of	45, II
Federal Acquisition Regulation	48, 3
Food and Drug Administration	21, I
Human Development Services, Office of	45, XIII
Indian Health Service	25, V
Inspector General (Health Care), Office of	42, V
Public Health Service	42, I
Refugee Resettlement, Office of	45, IV
Homeland Security, Department of	2, XXX; 6, I; 8, I
Coast Guard	33, I; 46, I; 49, IV
Coast Guard (Great Lakes Pilotage)	46, III
Customs and Border Protection	19, I
Federal Emergency Management Agency	44, I
Human Resources Management and Labor Relations Systems	5, XCVII
Immigration and Customs Enforcement Bureau	19, IV
Transportation Security Administration	49, XII
HOPE for Homeowners Program, Board of Directors of	24, XXIV
Housing and Urban Development, Department of	2, XXIV; 5, LXV; 24, Subtitle B
Community Planning and Development, Office of Assistant Secretary for	24, V, VI
Equal Opportunity, Office of Assistant Secretary for	24, I
Federal Acquisition Regulation	48, 24
Federal Housing Enterprise Oversight, Office of	12, XVII
Government National Mortgage Association	24, III
Housing—Federal Housing Commissioner, Office of Assistant Secretary for	24, II, VIII, X, XX
Housing, Office of, and Multifamily Housing Assistance Restructuring, Office of	24, IV
Inspector General, Office of	24, XII
Public and Indian Housing, Office of Assistant Secretary for	24, IX
Secretary, Office of	24, Subtitle A, VII
Housing—Federal Housing Commissioner, Office of Assistant Secretary for	24, II, VIII, X, XX
Housing, Office of, and Multifamily Housing Assistance Restructuring, Office of	24, IV
Human Development Services, Office of	45, XIII
Immigration and Customs Enforcement Bureau	19, IV
Immigration Review, Executive Office for	8, V
Independent Counsel, Office of	28, VII
Indian Affairs, Bureau of	25, I, V

Agency	CFR Title, Subtitle or Chapter
Indian Affairs, Office of the Assistant Secretary	25, VI
Indian Arts and Crafts Board	25, II
Indian Health Service	25, V
Industry and Security, Bureau of	15, VII
Information Resources Management, Office of	7, XXVII
Information Security Oversight Office, National Archives and Records Administration	32, XX
Inspector General	
Agriculture Department	7, XXVI
Health and Human Services Department	42, V
Housing and Urban Development Department	24, XII, XV
Institute of Peace, United States	22, XVII
Inter-American Foundation	5, LXIII; 22, X
Interior Department	2, XIV
American Indians, Office of the Special Trustee	25, VII
Bureau of Ocean Energy Management, Regulation, and Enforcement	30, II
Endangered Species Committee	50, IV
Federal Acquisition Regulation	48, 14
Federal Property Management Regulations System	41, 114
Fish and Wildlife Service, United States	50, I, IV
Geological Survey	30, IV
Indian Affairs, Bureau of	25, I, V
Indian Affairs, Office of the Assistant Secretary	25, VI
Indian Arts and Crafts Board	25, II
Land Management, Bureau of	43, II
National Indian Gaming Commission	25, III
National Park Service	36, I
Natural Resource Revenue, Office of	30, XII
Ocean Energy Management, Bureau of	30, V
Reclamation, Bureau of	43, I
Secretary of the Interior, Office of	2, XIV; 43, Subtitle A
Surface Mining Reclamation and Enforcement, Office of	30, VII
Internal Revenue Service	26, I
International Boundary and Water Commission, United States and Mexico, United States Section	22, XI
International Development, United States Agency for	22, II
Federal Acquisition Regulation	48, 7
International Development Cooperation Agency, United States	22, XII
International Joint Commission, United States and Canada	22, IV
International Organizations Employees Loyalty Board	5, V
International Trade Administration	15, III; 19, III
International Trade Commission, United States	19, II
Interstate Commerce Commission	5, XL
Investment Security, Office of	31, VIII
Iraq Reconstruction, Special Inspector General for	5, LXXXVII
James Madison Memorial Fellowship Foundation	45, XXIV
Japan–United States Friendship Commission	22, XVI
Joint Board for the Enrollment of Actuaries	20, VIII
Justice Department	2, XXVIII; 5, XXVIII; 28, I, XI; 40, IV
Alcohol, Tobacco, Firearms, and Explosives, Bureau of	27, II
Drug Enforcement Administration	21, II
Federal Acquisition Regulation	48, 28
Federal Claims Collection Standards	31, IX
Federal Prison Industries, Inc.	28, III
Foreign Claims Settlement Commission of the United States	45, V
Immigration Review, Executive Office for	8, V
Offices of Independent Counsel	28, VI
Prisons, Bureau of	28, V
Property Management Regulations	41, 128
Labor Department	5, XLII
Employee Benefits Security Administration	29, XXV
Employees' Compensation Appeals Board	20, IV
Employment and Training Administration	20, V

Agency	CFR Title, Subtitle or Chapter
Employment Standards Administration	20, VI
Federal Acquisition Regulation	48, 29
Federal Contract Compliance Programs, Office of	41, 60
Federal Procurement Regulations System	41, 50
Labor-Management Standards, Office of	29, II, IV
Mine Safety and Health Administration	30, I
Occupational Safety and Health Administration	29, XVII
Office of Workers' Compensation Programs	20, VII
Public Contracts	41, 50
Secretary of Labor, Office of	29, Subtitle A
Veterans' Employment and Training Service, Office of the Assistant Secretary for	41, 61; 20, IX
Wage and Hour Division	29, V
Workers' Compensation Programs, Office of	20, I
Labor-Management Standards, Office of	29, II, IV
Land Management, Bureau of	43, II
Legal Services Corporation	45, XVI
Library of Congress	36, VII
Copyright Royalty Board	37, III
U.S. Copyright Office	37, II
Local Television Loan Guarantee Board	7, XX
Management and Budget, Office of	5, III, LXXVII; 14, VI; 48, 99
Marine Mammal Commission	50, V
Maritime Administration	46, II
Merit Systems Protection Board	5, II, LXIV
Micronesian Status Negotiations, Office for	32, XXVII
Millennium Challenge Corporation	22, XIII
Mine Safety and Health Administration	30, I
Minority Business Development Agency	15, XIV
Miscellaneous Agencies	1, IV
Monetary Offices	31, I
Morris K. Udall Scholarship and Excellence in National Environmental Policy Foundation	36, XVI
Museum and Library Services, Institute of	2, XXXI
National Aeronautics and Space Administration	2, XVIII; 5, LIX; 14, V
Federal Acquisition Regulation	48, 18
National Agricultural Library	7, XLI
National Agricultural Statistics Service	7, XXXVI
National and Community Service, Corporation for	2, XXII; 45, XII, XXV
National Archives and Records Administration	2, XXVI; 5, LXVI; 36, XII
Information Security Oversight Office	32, XX
National Capital Planning Commission	1, IV
National Commission for Employment Policy	1, IV
National Commission on Libraries and Information Science	45, XVII
National Council on Disability	34, XII
National Counterintelligence Center	32, XVIII
National Credit Union Administration	5, LXXXVI; 12, VII
National Crime Prevention and Privacy Compact Council	28, IX
National Drug Control Policy, Office of	21, III
National Endowment for the Arts	2, XXXII
National Endowment for the Humanities	2, XXXIII
National Foundation on the Arts and the Humanities	45, XI
National Highway Traffic Safety Administration	23, II, III; 47, VI; 49, V
National Imagery and Mapping Agency	32, I
National Indian Gaming Commission	25, III
National Institute for Literacy	34, XI
National Institute of Food and Agriculture	7, XXXIV
National Institute of Standards and Technology	15, II
National Intelligence, Office of Director of	32, XVII
National Labor Relations Board	5, LXI; 29, I
National Marine Fisheries Service	50, II, IV
National Mediation Board	29, X
National Oceanic and Atmospheric Administration	15, IX; 50, II, III, IV, VI
National Park Service	36, I
National Railroad Adjustment Board	29, III

Agency	CFR Title, Subtitle or Chapter
National Railroad Passenger Corporation (AMTRAK)	49, VII
National Science Foundation	2, XXV; 5, XLIII; 45, VI
Federal Acquisition Regulation	48, 25
National Security Council	32, XXI
National Security Council and Office of Science and Technology Policy	47, II
National Telecommunications and Information Administration	15, XXIII; 47, III, IV
National Transportation Safety Board	49, VIII
Natural Resources Conservation Service	7, VI
Natural Resource Revenue, Office of	30, XII
Navajo and Hopi Indian Relocation, Office of	25, IV
Navy Department	32, VI
Federal Acquisition Regulation	48, 52
Neighborhood Reinvestment Corporation	24, XXV
Northeast Interstate Low-Level Radioactive Waste Commission	10, XVIII
Nuclear Regulatory Commission	2, XX; 5, XLVIII; 10, I
Federal Acquisition Regulation	48, 20
Occupational Safety and Health Administration	29, XVII
Occupational Safety and Health Review Commission	29, XX
Ocean Energy Management, Bureau of	30, V
Offices of Independent Counsel	28, VI
Office of Workers' Compensation Programs	20, VII
Oklahoma City National Memorial Trust	36, XV
Operations Office	7, XXVIII
Overseas Private Investment Corporation	5, XXXIII; 22, VII
Patent and Trademark Office, United States	37, I
Payment From a Non-Federal Source for Travel Expenses	41, 304
Payment of Expenses Connected With the Death of Certain Employees	41, 303
Peace Corps	2, XXXVII; 22, III
Pennsylvania Avenue Development Corporation	36, IX
Pension Benefit Guaranty Corporation	29, XL
Personnel Management, Office of	5, I, XXXV; 45, VIII
Human Resources Management and Labor Relations Systems, Department of Homeland Security	5, XCVII
Federal Acquisition Regulation	48, 17
Federal Employees Group Life Insurance Federal Acquisition Regulation	48, 21
Federal Employees Health Benefits Acquisition Regulation	48, 16
Pipeline and Hazardous Materials Safety Administration	49, I
Postal Regulatory Commission	5, XLVI; 39, III
Postal Service, United States	5, LX; 39, I
Postsecondary Education, Office of	34, VI
President's Commission on White House Fellowships	1, IV
Presidential Documents	3
Presidio Trust	36, X
Prisons, Bureau of	28, V
Privacy and Civil Liberties Oversight Board	6, X
Procurement and Property Management, Office of	7, XXXII
Productivity, Technology and Innovation, Assistant Secretary	37, IV
Public Contracts, Department of Labor	41, 50
Public and Indian Housing, Office of Assistant Secretary for	24, IX
Public Health Service	42, I
Railroad Retirement Board	20, II
Reclamation, Bureau of	43, I
Recovery Accountability and Transparency Board	4, II
Refugee Resettlement, Office of	45, IV
Relocation Allowances	41, 302
Research and Innovative Technology Administration	49, XI
Rural Business-Cooperative Service	7, XVIII, XLII, L
Rural Development Administration	7, XLII
Rural Housing Service	7, XVIII, XXXV, L
Rural Telephone Bank	7, XVI
Rural Utilities Service	7, XVII, XVIII, XLII, L

Agency	CFR Title, Subtitle or Chapter
U.S. Copyright Office	37, II
Utah Reclamation Mitigation and Conservation Commission	43, III
Veterans Affairs Department	2, VIII; 38, I
Federal Acquisition Regulation	48, 8
Veterans' Employment and Training Service, Office of the Assistant Secretary for	41, 61; 20, IX
Vice President of the United States, Office of	32, XXVIII
Vocational and Adult Education, Office of	34, IV
Wage and Hour Division	29, V
Water Resources Council	18, VI
Workers' Compensation Programs, Office of	20, I
World Agricultural Outlook Board	7, XXXVIII

List of CFR Sections Affected

All changes in this volume of the Code of Federal Regulations (CFR) that were made by documents published in the FEDERAL REGISTER since January 1, 2009 are enumerated in the following list. Entries indicate the nature of the changes effected. Page numbers refer to FEDERAL REGISTER pages. The user should consult the entries for chapters, parts and subparts as well as sections for revisions.

For changes to this volume of the CFR prior to this listing, consult the annual edition of the monthly List of CFR Sections Affected (LSA). The LSA is available at *www.fdsys.gov*. For changes to this volume of the CFR prior to 2001, see the ''List of CFR Sections Affected, 1949–1963, 1964–1972, 1973–1985, and 1986–2000'' published in 11 separate volumes. The ''List of CFR Sections Affected 1986–2000'' is available at *www.fdsys.gov*.

2009

15 CFR

74 FR Page

Chapter I

30.1 (c) amended; interim 38916

30.3 (a), (e)(1)(ii) and (2)(vi) revised; interim 38916

30.6 (a)(1)(iii) and (b)(1)(i) revised; interim 38916

2010

15 CFR

75 FR Page

Chapter I

30.1 Regulation at 74 FR 38916 confirmed 7548

30.3 Regulation at 74 FR 38916 confirmed 7548

30.6 Regulation at 74 FR 38916 confirmed 7548

90 Stayed indefinitely 46

2011

15 CFR

76 FR Page

Subtitle A

4 Appendix B amended 39769

Chapter II

285.4 Amended 78815

2012

15 CFR

77 FR Page

Chapter I

6.4 Revised 72916

6.5 Revised 72917

2013

15 CFR

78 FR Page

Chapter I

30.1 Amended; eff. 1–8–14..............16373

Regulation at 78 FR 16373 eff. date delayed to 4–5–14 67927

30.2 (a)(1)(iv)(E), (2), (b)(3), (d) introductory text, (2) and (4) revised; (a)(1)(iv)(H), note and (d)(5) added; eff. 1–8–14 16375

Regulation at 78 FR 16375 eff. date delayed to 4–5–14 67927

30.3 (b)(2) introductory text, (iii) and (c)(2)(ii) revised; (b)(4) and (c)(3) added; eff. 1–8–14 16375

Regulation at 78 FR 16375 eff. date delayed to 4–5–14 67927

30.4 (a)(9), (10) and (b)(3) redesignated as (a)(10), (11) and (b)(4); (a)(9), new (b)(3) and (5) added; (a)(6), (8), (b)(1), (2) introductory text, new (b)(4) and (c) revised; eff. 1–8–14..............16376

Regulation at 78 FR 16376 eff. date delayed to 4–5–14 67927

15 CFR—Continued

15 CFR—Continued

15 CFR—Continued

78 FR Page

Chapter I—Continued

Regulation at 78 FR 16383 eff. date delayed to 4–5–14 67927

Appendix D revised; eff. 1–8–14 16384

Regulation at 78 FR 16384 eff. date delayed to 4–5–14 67927

Appendix E revised; eff. 1–8–14.......16384

Regulation at 78 FR 16384 eff. date delayed to 4–5–14 67927

Appendix F revised; eff. 1–8–14.......16388

Regulation at 78 FR 16384 eff. date delayed to 4–5–14 67927

90 Stay at 75 FR 46 lifted; revised...259

15 CFR—Continued

78 FR Page

Chapter II

272 (Subchapter H) Heading added 4765

272 Redesignated from Part 1150 4765

272.1 (b) revised 4765

272.2 Revised.................................4765

272.3 (a) and (b) revised; (e) added 4765

272.4 Revised.................................4765

273 (Subchapter I) Heading added 4765

273 Redesignated from Part 1170 4766

273.3 (a) revised 4766

○